HIGHWAY LAW

AUSTRALIA AND NEW ZEALAND
The Law Book Company Ltd.
Sydney : Melbourne : Perth

CANADA AND U.S.A.
The Carswell Company Ltd.
Agincourt, Ontario

INDIA
N.M. Tripathi Private Ltd.
Bombay
and
Eastern Law House Private Ltd.
Calcutta and Delhi
M.P.P. House
Bangalore

ISRAEL
Steimatzky's Agency Ltd.
Jerusalem : Tel Aviv : Haifa

MALAYSIA : SINGAPORE : BRUNEI
Malayan Law Journal (Pte.) Ltd.
Singapore and Kuala Lumpur

¡ **WARNING !**
OUT OF DATE
PUBLICATION
Use at own Risk!

HIGHWAY LAW

by

Stephen J. Sauvain, M.A., LL.B.
of Lincoln's Inn and the
Northern Circuit, Barrister

LONDON
SWEET & MAXWELL
1989

Published in 1989 by
Sweet & Maxwell Limited of
11 New Fetter Lane, London
Computerset by Promenade Graphics Limited, Cheltenham
Printed and bound in Great Britain by
Butler & Tanner Ltd, Frome and London

British Library Cataloguing in Publication Data
Sauvain, Stephen
    Highway law.—(The local government
    library).
    1. England. Highways. Law
    I. Title   II. Series
    344.103'942
    ISBN 0–421–31190–8

To Christine,
Nicholas, David and Alan

PREFACE

The object of this book is to provide the practitioner with a working knowledge of the principles of highway law and a useful reference work on the powers and duties of highway authorities, the rights of users of the highway and the rights and responsibilities of owners of land adjoining highways. Modern highway law is a mixture of statutory provisions—principally contained in the Highways Act 1980—and several centuries of development of the common law. The Highways Act 1980 is derived from the massive consolidation of statutory provisions which was achieved in the Highways Act 1959. Such a consolidation inevitably lacks the ordered form of a newly created statutory code. The legislation is by no means comprehensive, and builds upon common law principles; nowhere in the legislation, for example, is there a comprehensive definition of what is a "highway".

This work, therefore, seeks to set out highway law as a coherent subject by putting the statutory provisions and common law principles into their mutual context. Consideration has been given to the history and development of the law where it has been felt that this is necessary in order to obtain a proper understanding of the modern law. The aim has been to provide a sufficiently detailed work to be of use to the practitioner whilst staying within the confines of a text seeking to emphasise principle and provide explanation.

I have attempted to devote the greatest detail and exposition to those areas where experience suggests that the most frequent problems arise, for example, Chapter 9 on the stopping up and diversion of highways. I have not attempted to cover areas of law which incidentally affect highways but which justify textbooks of their own. Thus, the principles of compulsory purchase and compensation are left to other works and Chapter 14 only purports to set out those provisions specifically relating to highways.

Only highways over land are considered. The rules of navigable waterways must be found elsewhere. The distinction is drawn between the law relating to the fabric of the highway and passage over it, and the laws and regulations governing traffic. The latter are not covered, save where they are unavoidably intertwined with highway law.

A number of people deserve thanks and recognition. I am greatly indebted to Vincent Fraser, barrister, who lent his expertise and eye for detail to the task of writing Chapter 13. The staff of Sweet and Maxwell deserve especial credit and mention for their patience in coaxing a manuscript from an elusive author. I am grateful to Elisabeth Ingham for compiling the index. Above all others, I am indebted to my colleague Charles Cross for encouragement, suggestions, criticism and faith.

Manchester   Stephen J. Sauvain
September 1988

CONTENTS

CHAPTER 11: BRIDGES

CHAPTER 12: FOOTPATHS AND BRIDLEWAYS

CHAPTER 13: THE PUBLIC UTILITIES STREET WORKS ACT 1950

CONTENTS

TABLE OF CASES

TABLE OF STATUTES

lv

TABLE OF STATUTORY INSTRUMENTS

CHAPTER 1

HIGHWAYS AND HIGHWAY AUTHORITIES

CHARACTERISTICS OF A HIGHWAY

Introduction

A highway is essentially a public right of way over a defined route. **1–01**
This description contains within it four elements.

(a) The way must be open to the public at large.
(b) The public use must be as of right.
(c) The public right must be for passage.
(d) The public right of passage must follow a defined route.

Some of these elements are more obvious and easy to ascertain than are others. Whilst this work is concerned with highways over land, a highway may also exist over water and rights of navigation over water have great similarities to the public rights of passage over land.[1] A ferry is also a right in the nature of a highway.[2] A railway, however, is not a highway, since the right of a member of the public to use the railway depends upon a contract to travel in the train which uses the railway company's track. There is no general right in the public to use a towpath along a canal or river[3] although public rights may be dedicated expressly or by implication over a towpath.[4]

Open to the public

Unless the public at large—rather than a defined section of the pub- **1–02**
lic—have the right to use it, the way will carry a *private* right of way rather than a highway. A road serving the occupiers of adjoining land, together with their invitees, but otherwise not open to the public, is not a highway.[5] Churchways and other roads over which only the parishioners of a particular parish or manor have, through immemorial

---

[1] See *Miles* v. *Rose* (1814) 5 Taunt. 705; *Iveagh (Earl)* v. *Martin* [1961] 1 Q.B. 232 (tidal waters); *R.* v. *Montague* (1825) 4 B. & C. 598; *Orr Ewing* v. *Colquhoun* (1877) 2 App. Cas. 839; *Williams* v. *Wilcox* (1838) 8 Ad. & El. 314; *Original Hartlepool Collieries* v. *Gibb* (1877) 5 Ch.D. 713.
[2] *Hilton* v. *Scarborough (Lord)* (1714) 2 Eq. Cas. Abr. 171.
[3] *Monmouthshire Canal & Ry. Co.* v. *Hill* (1859) 4 H. & N. 421.
[4] *Ball* v. *Herbert* (1789) 3 T.R. 253; *Winch* v. *Thames Conservators* (1872) L.R. 7 C.P. 458; *Grand Junction Canal Co.* v. *Petty* (1888) 21 Q.B.D. 273; *cf. Thames Conservators* v. *Kent* [1918] 2 K.B. 272. See also Highways Act 1980, s.329(2).
[5] See *Selby* v. *Crystal Palace Gas Co.* (1862) 4 De G.F. & J. 246.

custom, obtained the right to pass, are not highways.[6] However, roads which begin as private rights of way may, over a period of time, become public highways through the usual principles of dedication and acceptance.[7]

Use as of right

1–03   Creation of a highway involves a permanent[8] surrender by the landowner, over whose land the highway lies, of a part of his dominium. A highway is created by grant—express or implied. Once created, the public right cannot be lost save by operation of law (by means of an extinguishment order) or, possibly, by the physical destruction of the land on which it lies.[9] This principle is often expressed in the maxim "once a highway always a highway."[10] The distinction is, therefore, between permissive use of a way and use as of right against the landowner.[11] Where a road or a path is physically identifiable three distinct possibilities arise. There may be a purely private road or path open only to the landowner and his invitees; any other person entering the road will be a trespasser. The road may be open to the public in the sense that the public have access to it in fact but only by virtue of the landowner's continuing acquiescence—which he may withdraw at any time. This category of road may be a "road to which the public have access" for the purposes of the road traffic legislation and certain legal consequences will follow with regard to the traffic which may use such roads.[12] However, such a road is not a highway. The third situation is where the landowner no longer has the right to exclude members of the public using the road. This type of road is a highway.

Legal nature of the public right

1–04   From time to time, judicial consideration has been given to the exact legal nature of the public right to use a highway and as to how this right can be fitted into the general scheme of property concepts. It has generally been described as a form of easement.[13] The extent of the easement was considered by the Court of Appeal in *Harrison* v. *Rutland (Duke)*,[14] where Lopes L.J. said:

---

[6] See *Farquhar* v. *Newbury R.D.C.* [1909] 1 Ch. 12; *Brocklebank* v. *Thompson* [1903] 2 Ch. 344; *Poole* v. *Huskinson* (1843) 11 M. & W. 827; *Shury* v. *Piggot* (1626) 3 Bulst. 339.

[7] See *Farquhar* v. *Newbury R.D.C.*, n. 6 above and, generally, Chap. 2.

[8] See *Dawes* v. *Hawkins* (1860) 29 L.J. C.P. 343.

[9] See para. 9–03, below.

[10] *St. Ives Corpn.* v. *Wadsworth* (1908) 72 J.P. 73.

[11] See *Att.-Gen.* v. *Mallock* (1931) 30 L.G.R. 141; *Att.-Gen.* v. *Antrobus* [1905] 2 Ch. 188.

[12] See *Harrison* v. *Hill* (1932) J.C. 13; *R.* v. *Shaw* [1974] R.T.R. 255, C.A.; *Cox* v. *White* [1976] R.T.R. 248; *Deacon* v. *A.T. (A Minor)* [1976] R.T.R. 244.

[13] See *Dovaston* v. *Payne* (1795) 2 Hy.Bl. 527, *per* Heath J. at 531.

[14] [1893] 1 Q.B. 142 at 154.

"The easement acquired by the public is a right to pass and re-pass at their pleasure for the purpose of legitimate travel, and the use of the soil for any other purpose, whether lawful or unlawful, is an infringement of the rights of the owner of the soil, who has, subject to this easement, precisely the same estate in the soil as he had previously to any easement being acquired by the public."

The idea of a highway as a type of public easement does not fit in happily with the usually understood meaning of the term "easement" since there is no dominant tenement to which the easement can attach. The dictum of Heath J., quoted above, has been subjected to much criticism on this account. In *Rangeley* v. *Midland Railway Company*,[15] Lord Cairns L.J. expressed the view that[16]:

"In truth, a public road or highway is not an easement; it is a dedication to the public of the occupation of the surface of the land for the purpose of passing and re-passing. . . . It is quite clear that that is a very different thing from an ordinary easement where the occupation remains in the owner of the servient tenement subject to the easement."

It has been suggested that the dominant tenement in the case of a highway is the whole of the kingdom[17] but this seems both an artificial and unsatisfactory attempt to squeeze a unique public right into an existing and different legal category. The approach of Lord Cairns is itself unsatisfactory. Although there may be said to be physical control of the "top two spits" of the highway when the highway vests in a highway authority,[18] it is difficult to see how the public right could be said to "occupy" the surface of the highway in any legal sense.

Where the highway becomes maintainable by the highway authority, **1–05** there becomes vested in that authority a determinable fee simple in the "top two spits" which will give the authority a right to possession of the highway surface.[19] This interest must be distinguished from the rights of the public at large to pass over the highway—which rights exist whether or not the highway has become vested in the highway authority. Very probably the public right of passage and the consequent public interest in the surface of the land over which the highway passes can be regarded as a right *sui generis*. In practice the extent of the public right is relatively well established.

[15] (1868) 3 Ch.App. 306.

[16] See also *Hawkins* v. *Rutter* [1892] 1 Q.B. 668.

[17] *per* Lord Gifford in *Sutherland* v. *Thomson* (1876) 3 R. (Ct. of Sess.) 489; *Orr Ewing* v. *Colquhoun* (1877) 2 App.Cas. 839.

[18] See *Rolls* v. *St. George the Martyr, Southwark, Vestry* (1880) 14 Ch.D. 785; *Tithe Redemption Commission* v. *Runcorn U.D.C.* [1954] 1 Ch. 383.

[19] See *Wiltshire C.C.* v. *Frazer* (1984) 82 L.G.R. 313.

A public right of passage

1–06　　The public have the right to pass and re-pass along the highway and to do those things which are reasonably incidental to that right of passage. In *Goodtitle d. Chester* v. *Alker & Elmes*,[20] Lord Mansfield, adapting the description found in *Rolle's Abridgement*,[21] stated the law to be that[22]:

> "The King has nothing but the passage for himself and his people, but the freehold and all profits belong to the owner of the soil."

If, therefore, the person using the highway goes beyond his right to pass and re-pass, he may commit a trespass to the subsoil which is actionable by the owner of that subsoil.[23] In *Harrison* v. *Rutland (Duke)*,[24] the defendant was the owner of a moor, across which ran a highway. During a shooting party held by the defendant in the adjoining land, the plaintiff, for the express purpose of annoying the defendant, went onto the highway and tried to divert grouse which were being driven towards the highway in the direction of the butts. The defendant's keepers, having asked the plaintiff to cease his activities, eventually took hold of him and led him off the highway. This led to an action for assault and false imprisonment. The Court of Appeal held that the plaintiff was a trespasser as against the defendant. His actions had gone far beyond what was reasonable in the exercise of the public right. However, the court did not regard the public right as being too restrictively defined. Lord Esher M.R. said[25]:

> "I do not think that the law is that the public must always be passing and doing nothing else on a highway. There are many things often done and usually done on a highway by the public, and if a person does not transgress any such usual and reasonable mode of using a highway, I do not think he is a trespasser."

It appears from that case and from other authority[26] that it is not necessary for the activity on the highway itself to be unlawful in order to constitute the trespass but only that the use of the highway should be something in excess of the exercise of the public right. In *Hickman* v. *Maisey*,[27] the defendant, who was walking up and down a highway observing and noting the performance of the plaintiff's racehorses in

---

[20] (1757) 1 Burr. 133.

[21] 1 *Rolle's Abridgement* 392 B.pl.1,2.

[22] See also *Anon.* (1468) Y.B.8 Edw.4,Fo.9,pl.7; *Anon.* (1626) 3 Salk. 183.

[23] But not by other highway users. See *Cox* v. *Burbidge* (1863) 32 L.J. C.P. 89; *Hadwell* v. *Righton* [1907] 2 K.B. 345; *Higgins* v. *Searle* (1909) 73 J.P. 185; *Hubbard* v. *Pitt* [1976] Q.B. 142.

[24] [1893] 1 Q.B. 142.

[25] *Ibid.* at 146. See also *Hickman* v. *Maisey* [1900] 1 Q.B. 752; *Randall* v. *Tarrant* [1955] 1 W.L.R. 255; *Rodgers* v. *Ministry of Transport* [1952] W.N. 136.

[26] See also *R.* v. *Pratt* (1855) 4 E. & B. 860; *Mayhew* v. *Wardley* (1863) 14 C.B.(N.S.) 550; *Dovaston* v. *Payne*, n. 13 above; *Stevens* v. *Whistler* (1809) 11 East 51; *Hickman* v. *Maisey* [1900] 1 Q.B. 752; *Coventry (Earl)* v. *Willes* (1863) 9 L.T.(N.S.) 384.

[27] [1900] 1 Q.B. 752.

training, was admittedly passing and re-passing over a 15 yard length of highway. He was held, however, liable in trespass. It was said[28]:

> "Although in modern times a reasonable extension has been given to the use of the highway as such, the authorities show that the primary purpose of the dedication must always be kept in view. The right of the public to pass and repass on a highway is subject to all those reasonable extensions which may from time to time be recognised as necessary to its existence in accordance with the enlarged notions of people in a country becoming more populous and highly civilised, but they must be such as are not inconsistent with the maintenance of the paramount idea that the right of the public is that of passage."

Thus, it seems that parking a car for a reasonable length of time on the highway will not constitute a trespass, nor will pausing to rest or stopping to draw a sketch.[29] The test must be whether the actions in question are reasonably incidental to the exercise of the right of passage or whether they go further and require the assertion of an independent right.[30] It seems that every act of being present on the highway which is capable of constituting an obstruction of the highway[31] will also be capable of being a trespass to the subsoil.

Where the highway surface has vested in the highway authority, that **1–07** authority may be able to mount an action based upon trespass. This view is supported by the decision in *Wiltshire County Council* v. *Frazer*,[32] where it was held that a highway authority could maintain proceedings, under Order 113 of the Rules of the Supreme Court, seeking a summary order of possession against squatters who had pitched their caravans on the highway.[33]

Where land over which there is an alleged highway is subjected to **1–08** other uses, a careful analysis of the public's right to enter on that land must be made. Where an established user of the land is inconsistent with the co-existence of a highway then this may be evidence that there is no highway. Later user of an established highway for inconsistent purposes will constitute a public nuisance.[34] Thus, there is no right to hold meetings on a highway since these would, by their nature, obstruct free pas-

---

[28] *Hickman* v. *Maisey* [1900] 1 Q.B. 752, *per* Collins J. at 757–758.
[29] *Randall* v. *Tarrant* [1955] 1 W.L.R. 255. See also *Hadwell* v. *Righton* [1907] 2 K.B. 345; *Hickman* v. *Maisey* [1900] 1 Q.B. at 756; *cf. Fielden* v. *Cox* (1906) 22 T.L.R. 411; *Iveagh (Earl)* v. *Martin* [1961] 1 Q.B. 232.
[30] See, further, Chap. 7.
[31] *Sowerby* v. *Wadsworth* (1863) 3 F. & F. 734; *Coventry (Earl)* v. *Willes* (1863) 9 L.T.(N.S.) 384; *Mayhew* v. *Wardley* (1863) 14 C.B.(N.S.) 550.
[32] (1984) 82 L.G.R. 313, C.A.
[33] *cf. Hubbard* v. *Pitt* [1976] Q.B. 142.
[34] See *Coventry (Earl)* v. *Willes* (1863) 9 L.T.(N.S.) 384; *Sowerby* v. *Wadsworth* (1863) 3 F. & F. 734; *Ex p. Lewis* (1888) 21 Q.B.D. 191.

sage.[35] In *Sandgate Urban District Council* v. *Kent County Council*,[36] the use of an esplanade, over which a highway was alleged to have been established, for purposes of amusement, was held not to be inconsistent with the esplanade being part of a public highway. One area of potential conflict between the highway use and other, possibly inconsistent, uses is in the market place. The right to hold a market can necessarily involve the creation of obstructions and the gathering of crowds in an area which may well be part of the highway.[37] Highways are occasionally dedicated subject to market rights and where market rights are created by statute or charter they may co-exist alongside the highway rights.[38] It seems that, although market rights cannot usually be lost by disuse, the lack of such user over the statutory period[39] may create a presumption in favour of more extensive highway rights to the extinction of the market.[40]

1–09   The existence of a public right of passage across land implies some reason for the public to exercise the right of way. Traditionally, highways have been links between towns or villages. Thus, the need for a public terminus at either end (a *terminus a quo* and a *terminus ad quem*) has been considered in the past as a necessary characteristic of a highway.[41] This must, however, be considered with some caution. Certainly it has been held that if access to a highway is cut off at both ends, as a result of stopping up orders, the remaining section, to which the public could only have access by trespassing over private land, ceases to be a highway.[42] However, it has long been accepted that roads leading to a river,[43] to the sea,[44] or to a public beauty spot,[45] may be highways. Essentially, the existence of a public terminus is an important question of evidence to prove a highway: "It is always a strong observation to a jury that the way leads nowhere."[46] However, there is no rule of law that a cul-de-sac may not be a highway, whether it be in a town[47] or in

---

[35] *Ex p. Lewis*, n. 34 above; *R.* v. *Cunninghame Graham & Burns* (1888) 4 T.L.R. 212; *Shirebrook Colliery Co.* v. *Burke* (1898) 42 S.J. 764; see also Chap. 7.

[36] (1898) 79 L.T. 425.

[37] See *McIntosh* v. *Romford Local Board* (1889) 61 L.T. 185.

[38] *Elwood* v. *Bullock* (1844) 6 Q.B. 383; *Att.-Gen.* v. *Horner* (1885) 11 App.Cas. 66; *Stepney Corpn.* v. *Gingell, Son & Foskett* [1909] A.C. 245; *cf. R.* v. *Smith* (1802) 4 Esp. 111.

[39] See Highways Act 1980, s.31, paras. 2–32 *et seq.*, below.

[40] See *Gloucestershire C.C.* v. *Farrow* [1985] 1 W.L.R. 741.

[41] *Campbell* v. *Lang* (1853) 1 Eq.Rep. 98; *Young* v. *Cuthbertson* (1854) 1 Macq. 455.

[42] *Bailey* v. *Jamieson* (1876) 1 C.P.D. 329.

[43] *The Medmenham Case* cited at 81 L.T. 179; *Campbell* v. *Lang* (1853) 1 Eq.Rep. 98; *R.* v. *St. Issey (Inhabitants)* (1849) 14 L.T.(o.s.) 176.

[44] *Williams Ellis* v. *Cobb* [1935] 1 K.B. 310.

[45] *Moser* v. *Ambleside U.D.C.* (1925) 89 J.P. 118.

[46] *per* Crompton J. in *Bateman* v. *Bluck* (1852) 18 Q.B. 870. See also *Att.-Gen.* v. *Sewell* (1918) 88 L.J.K.B. 425.

[47] *Rugby Charity Trustees* v. *Merryweather* (1790) 11 East 375n.; *R.* v. *Lloyd* (1808) 1 Camp. 260; *Bateman* v. *Bluck*, n.46 above; *Souch* v. *East London Rail Co.* (1873) L.R. 16 Eq. 108; *Vernon* v. *St. James, Westminster, Vestry* (1880) 16 Ch.D. 449; *Josselsohn* v. *Weiler* (1911) 75 J.P. 513.

the country.[48] In the latter case, however, a practical evidential problem may arise in establishing some reason for the growth of the public right of way. In *Moser* v. *Ambleside Urban District Council*,[49] Atkin L.J., in considering the application of the principles of establishing a highway in a country cul-de-sac said[50]:

> "One of the first questions that one always has to enquire into in such a case as this is from whence does the highway come and whither does it lead? It has been suggested that you cannot have a highway except in so far as it connects two other highways. That seems to me to be too large a proposition. I think you can have a highway leading to a place of popular resort even though when you have got to the place of popular resort which you wish to see you have to return on your tracks by the same highway."

In *Eyre* v. *New Forest Highway Board*,[51] Wills J. said:

> "what would be the meaning in a country place like that of a highway which ends in a *cul de sac,* and ends at a gate on to a common . . . where one of the public, if there were any public who wanted to use it at all, would drive up to that gate for the purpose of driving back again."

Where no obvious reason for public use of a cul-de-sac appears, then other evidence (for example, of repair) will assume greater importance in establishing that the road is a highway.[52] Where an admitted highway has been stopped up or enclosed at one end, so as to make it a cul-de-sac, there is no alteration in its status.[53]

A public right to pass along a defined route

It is of the essence of a highway that the public right of passage follows a known, defined line. The common law did not recognise any public right to wander across countryside (*jus spatiendi*).[54] Thus, where there has been regular use of woodlands through which the public had wandered at will, it was held that this use was not sufficient to infer dedi-   **1–10**

---

[48] *Roberts* v. *Webster* (1967) 66 L.G.R. 298; *Eyre* v. *New Forest Highway Board* (1892) 56 J.P. 517; *Moser* v. *Ambleside U.D.C.* (1925) 89 J.P. 118.

[49] (1925) 89 J.P. 118.

[50] *Ibid.* at 120.

[51] (1892) 56 J.P. 517 at 518.

[52] See *Vernon* v. *St. James, Westminster, Vestry* (1880) 16 Ch.D. 449; *cf. Vine* v. *Wenham* (1915) 84 L.J. Ch. 913; *Kingston-upon-Hull Corpn.* v. *North Eastern Ry. Co.* (1916) 1 Ch. 31; *Att.-Gen. & London Property Investment Trust Ltd.* v. *Richmond Corpn. & Gosling & Sons* (1903) 89 L.T. 700.

[53] *R.* v. *Downshire* (1836) 4 A. & E. 698; *Gwyn* v. *Hardwicke* (1856) 25 L.J.(M.C.) 97; *Esher and Dittons U.C.* v. *Marks* (1902) 71 L.J.(K.B.) 309; *cf.* where the road is closed at both ends: *Bailey* v. *Jamieson* (1876) 1 C.P.D. 329.

[54] *Eyre* v. *New Forest Highway Board* (1892) 56 J.P. 517; *Wimbledon & Putney Commons Conservators* v. *Dixon* (1875) 1 Ch.D. 362; *Robinson* v. *Cowpen Local Board* (1893) 63 L.J.Q.B. 235; *Att.-Gen.* v. *Antrobus* [1905] 2 Ch. 188; *cf. Re Ellenborough Park, Re Davies, decd., Powell and Others* v. *Maddison* [1956] Ch. 131.

cation to the public of the woodland tracks as public paths.[55] Rights over public open space,[56] commons and village greens may, therefore, have to be distinguished from highway rights.[57] In the absence of dedication of a defined path there is no public right of way across the foreshore.[58]

CLASSES OF PUBLIC RIGHTS OF WAY

1–11 Although a public highway must be open to all members of the public, the extent of the public right may be limited to a certain kind of user. Three classes of highway were known generally to the common law[59]:

> "At common law highways are of three kinds according to the degree of restriction of the public rights of passage over them. A full highway or "cartway" is one over which the public have right of way (1) on foot, (2) riding on or accompanied by a beast of burden and (3) with vehicles and cattle. A "bridleway" is a highway over which the rights of passage are cut down by the exclusion of the right of passage with vehicles and sometimes, though not invariably, the exclusion of the right of driftway, i.e. driving cattle, while a footpath is one over which the only public right of passage is on foot."

The greater right will generally encompass the lesser right[60] but, since a highway is created by dedication, this is subject to exceptions dependent on the terms of the dedication (express or implied).[61]

Carriageway highways

1–12　　The full public right over a highway is a vehicular right. At common law the rights of pedestrians, horsemen, and carriages usually extended to the full width of the highway.[62] Statute has since placed some limitations on the extent of public user within carriageways. The pavement or path running along the side of the road is a "footway," defined in section 329(1) of the Highways Act 1980 as "a way comprised in a highway

---

[55] *Chapman* v. *Cripps* (1862) 2 F. & F. 864; *Schwinge* v. *Dowell* (1862) 2 F. & F. 845.

[56] See *Att.-Gen.* v. *Manchester Corpn.* (1930) 28 L.G.R. 634.

[57] Rights of commons and over village greens will usually be of a different nature of user in that they are open only to a defined section of the public and are for purposes other than passage; *Fitch* v. *Rawling* (1795) 2 H.Bl. 393.

[58] See *Blundell* v. *Catterall* (1821) 5 B. & Ald. 268; *Llandudno U.C.* v. *Woods* [1899] 2 Ch. 705; *Brinckman* v. *Matley* [1904] 2 Ch. 313; *Maddock* v. *Wallasey Local Board* (1886) 55 L.J.Q.B. 267; *cf. Seaton* v. *Slama* (1932) 31 L.G.R. 41.

[59] *per* Lord Diplock in *Suffolk C.C.* v. *Mason* [1979] A.C. 705, at 709; see also Co. Lit. 56a.

[60] *R.* v. *Hatfield (Inhabitants)* (1736) Lee Temp. Hard. 315; *Davies* v. *Stephens* (1836) 7 C. & P. 570, N.P.; *Wells* v. *London, Tilbury and Southend Ry. Co.* (1877) 5 Ch.D. 126.

[61] *R.* v. *Severn & Wye Ry. Co.* (1819) 2 B. & Ald. 646; *Ballard* v. *Dyson* (1808) 1 Taunt. 279; *Fisher* v. *Prowse* (1862) 2 B. & S. 770.

[62] *Hutton* v. *Hamboro* (1860) 2 F. & F. 218 N.P.; *Nicol* v. *Beaumont* (1883) 53 L.J. 853; *Att.-Gen.* v. *Esher Linoleum Co. Ltd.* [1901] 2 Ch. 647; *Boss* v. *Litton* (1832) 5 C. & P. 407.

which also comprises a carriageway, being a way over which the public have a right of way on foot only." Thus, a footway, being only part of a carriageway highway, must be distinguished from a *footpath* which is an independent highway in its own right.[63] Secondly, once a pavement or path is identified as a statutory "footway," there is an immediate limitation on the rights of vehicles to use the full width of the highway (since the right over the footway is "on foot only")[64] but there is no corresponding limitation on the pedestrian who strays onto the main carriageway. The definition of "carriageway"[65] is

> "a way constituting or comprised in a highway, being a way (other than a cycle track) over which the public have a right of way for the passage of vehicles."

This would not appear to limit the pedestrian right of way to the footway.[66] Thus, whilst the holding of a public meeting on the carriageway will be an obstruction to the highway,[67] the march of a procession over the carriageway may not be an obstruction.[68] A footway is created by a highway authority exercising its powers under section 66 of the Highways Act 1980. Indeed, section 66 imposes a duty on a highway authority to make provision for footways at the side of all highways maintainable at the public expense, whenever the authority considers it necessary or desirable for the safety or accommodation of pedestrians.

A carriageway highway will presumptively encompass a right to drive **1–13** cattle along it (the right of driftway) but this presumption can be displaced.[69] The fact that the width of a highway is insufficient to allow for the passage of all types of carriages does not prevent the way being a carriageway.[70] However, all other things being equal, the width of the way will be important evidence, in the event of a dispute as to the extent of the public right over it, of the kind of past public user. Statute has now placed restrictions on the public user of certain kinds of carriageways—and these restrictions relate to types and weights of vehicles allowed to use the way and to the purposes of such user.[71] Within the carriageway class of highways there are further categories defined by statute. Whilst these categories do not all affect the kind of user to which they may be put, it is useful to consider them all at this stage.

---

[63] See *Derby C.C.* v. *Matlock Bath & Scarthin Nick U.D.C.* [1896] A.C. 315. As to whether the footway includes the grass verge, see *Bishop* v. *Green* (1971) 69 L.G.R. 579.

[64] It may constitute an offence under the Towns Police Clauses Act 1847, s.28.

[65] Highways Act 1980, s.329(1).

[66] This was certainly the case at common law; see *Boss* v. *Litton* (1832) 5 C. & P. 407.

[67] *R.* v. *Cunninghame Graham & Burns* (1888) 4 T.L.R. 212.

[68] *Burden* v. *Rigler* [1911] 1 K.B. 337; *Tynan* v. *Balmer* [1967] 1 Q.B. 91. See also Chap. 7.

[69] *Ballard* v. *Dyson* (1808) 1 Taunt. 279.

[70] *R.* v. *Lyon* (1825) 5 Dow & Ry. K.B. 497.

[71] Road Traffic Regulation Act 1984, ss.17–22; Highways Act 1980, s.16(3) and Sched. 4; Special Roads (Classes of Traffic) Order 1971 (S.I. 1971 No. 1156).

Special roads

1–14   Special roads are highways (necessarily carriageway highways) provided pursuant to a scheme under the Highways Act 1980, section 16,[72]
or its predecessors.[73] A special road may be created by means of the
construction of a new road along the route prescribed by the scheme, by
the appropriation of an existing highway lying in the route proposed by
the scheme,[74] or by the transfer of an existing road to the special road
authority.[75] The special road authority is the highway authority authorised by the scheme to provide a special road.[76] Once a special road has
been created, then different rules will apply as to the laying of statutory
undertakers' apparatus therein, as to the traffic which may use them,
and as to the powers available for diversion and extinguishment.[77]

Trunk roads

1–15   A trunk road is simply a carriageway highway forming part of the
national system of routes for through traffic and for which the Minister
is the highway authority.[78] The Minister is under a duty to keep the
national system of roads for through traffic under review and to create
new trunk roads or de-trunk existing routes where he is satisfied, after
taking into consideration the requirements of local and national planning, including the requirements of agriculture, that it is expedient for
the purpose of extending, improving or re-organising that national system.[79] Again, the trunk road status will affect the various statutory
powers which exist in respect of diversion and extinguishment orders,
the apparatus of statutory undertakers and the responsibilities for maintenance and improvement.[80]

Classified roads

1–16   The designation "classified road" has little practical significance
today. Until April 1, 1975, the designation of a road as classified was
important for grant purposes. The Ministry of Transport Act 1919[81] had
given the Minister the power of classification of roads for the purpose of
making advances for the construction, improvement and maintenance
of roads. Roads so classified by the Minister as Class I or II (or declared

---

[72] Highways Act 1980, s.329(1).

[73] *i.e.* Special Roads Act 1949, s.1 and Sched. 1, and Highways Act 1959, s.11.

[74] So long as the highway authority for that highway is the same body as the special road
authority; Highways Act 1980, s.16(5)(*b*).

[75] *Ibid.* s.16(5)(*c*).

[76] Or, if two or more authorities jointly submit a scheme to the Minister, the special road
authority will be one of those authorities as the scheme may designate; Highways Act
1980, s.16(10).

[77] See *ibid.* ss.16–21; see also Chaps. 9 and 13.

[78] See Trunk Roads Act 1936, s.1 (now repealed); Highways Act 1980, s.10.

[79] *Ibid.* s.10(2) and Sched. 1. See also *Walters* v. *Secretary of State for Wales* (1978) 77
L.G.R. 529.

[80] See Chaps. 4 and 6.

[81] s.17(2), now repealed.

by him to be not inferior to those classes)[82] were treated for the purposes of subsequent legislation as being "classified roads." A third classification was introduced in 1946.[83] The Local Government Act 1966[84] altered the basis by which highways were to be financed and introduced a new category of "principal roads." By the Local Government Act 1974,[85] highways were no longer to be classified for grant purposes, although the term has been retained for other purposes and those roads classified prior to 1974 remain as classified roads. The Minister has power to classify further roads for the purposes of the highway legislation after he has consulted with local highway authorities.[86] A few statutory provisions continue to refer to classified roads.[87]

Principal roads

The designation "principal road" was introduced for grant purposes **1–17** by the Local Government Act 1966.[88] By the Local Government Act 1974,[89] the classification for grant purposes of roads as principal roads ceased to have effect, although (as with classified roads) this designation was still to remain for other purposes. By the Highways Act 1980,[90] principal roads continue to retain their designation. Effectively, principal roads include Class I roads and are treated for the purposes of the present legislation as being classified roads.[91] By section 13 of the 1980 Act, the Minister is given power to change the designation of principal roads by statutory instrument. A principal road is described as being[92] one which was an essential route for traffic and which had a sufficiently important place in the national highway network to justify central government interest in its planning, and Exchequer assistance in its improvement.

County roads and main roads

Both of these classifications are now obsolete. Main roads included **1–18** many erstwhile turnpike roads together with roads declared to be main roads by Quarter Sessions or by county councils and roads constructed by county councils with the financial assistance of the Ministry of

---

[82] See Local Government Act 1929, s.134; Trunk Roads Act 1936, s.13(1).
[83] See Ministry of Transport Circular 595.
[84] s.27(2).
[85] ss.40 and 42(2), Sched. 8. See also Highways Act 1980, s.12(1), (2).
[86] *Ibid.* s.27(3).
[87] *e.g.* Highways Act 1980, ss.14, 116, 125(2)(*b*) and Sched. 12; Town and Country Planning Act 1971, s.24; Local Government Act 1972, s.182, Sched. 16, para. 17(*a*) and the General Development Order 1977 (S.I. 1977 No. 289).
[88] s.27(2), (3).
[89] s.40.
[90] s.12(1).
[91] *Ibid.* s.12(4).
[92] See Circular No. Roads 9/66.

Transport.[93] The significance of the designation "main road" was that, initially, the burden of repair fell partly on the county and partly on the highway authority. The Local Government Act 1888[94] put the whole of the maintenance responsibility onto the county councils for this class of roads and by the Local Government Act 1929,[95] they became simply "county roads." County roads also included all those other roads in areas where the county was, by virtue of the 1929 Act, to become the highway authority, *i.e.* within all rural districts.[96] Thereafter, roads constructed by or transferred to the county council also became county roads.[97] Since the passing of the Local Government Act 1972[98] and the rationalisation of highway authorities, the term "county road" has had no significance.

Metropolitan roads

1–19   The London Government Act 1963[99] prescribed that certain specified roads in the Greater London area were to be known as metropolitan roads and were to be the responsibility of the Greater London Council as highway authority. The Local Government Act 1985, in abolishing the Greater London Council, also removed the status of metropolitan road. Most metropolitan roads thereafter became trunk roads.[1] All other public highways in London are now the responsibility of the London boroughs and of the Common Council of the City of London.

Footpaths and bridleways

1–20   Non-carriageway highways broadly fall into two categories—footpaths and bridleways. However, a number of other terms are associated with these kinds of highways which it may be helpful to consider together with footpaths and bridleways.

Bridleways

1–21   A "bridleway" is defined in the Highways Act 1980, section 329(1),[2] as being:

> "a highway over which the public have the following, but no other, rights of way, that is to say, a right of way on foot and a right of way on horseback or leading a horse, with or without a right to drive animals of any description along the highway."

---

[93] Highways and Locomotives (Amendment) Act 1878, ss.13, 15, 16, 38; Local Government Act 1888, ss.3(viii), 109; Development and Road Improvement Funds Act 1909, s.10(2).

[94] s.11.

[95] s.29(1).

[96] *Ibid.* s.30.

[97] Development and Road Improvement Funds Act 1909, s.10(2); Special Roads Act 1949, ss.1, 3; Highways Act 1959, s.21.

[98] s.187.

[99] s.17 and Sched. 7.

[1] See the Metropolitan Roads Trunking Order 1986 (S.I. 1986 No. 153).

[2] See also Wildlife and Countryside Act 1981, s.66(1).

Since 1968[3] cyclists have had the right to ride bicycles which are not motor vehicles on bridleways but are required to give way to pedestrians and persons on horseback. "Motor vehicle" is defined in the Road Traffic Act 1972[4] as meaning "a mechanically propelled vehicle intended or adapted for use on roads." Motor cycles and "mopeds" will be excluded. The right to cycle on bridleways may itself be subject to any by-laws or orders made by the local authority and does not impose any greater obligation of maintenance on the highway authority than already exists in relation to bridleways. A distinction between bridleways and highways open to all types of user was recognised and maintained from quite an early stage.[5] Bridleways are in many cases derived from those old packhorse routes which were never extended by user to become cartways or carriageways when, during the seventeenth and eighteenth centuries, wheeled traffic began to replace the packhorse as the principal means of transporting goods by road.[6]

Footpaths

Footpaths are highways which carry only a public right of way on foot **1–22** and which are not footways.[7] As with bridleways, with which they are linked in almost all the statutory provisions, footpaths are subject to the same general rules relating to creation, maintenance, improvement and protection as are all other highways.[8]

Public paths

The expression "public path" is not defined in the Highways Act **1–23** 1980, although that Act has provisions dealing with public path creation orders and agreements.[9] "Public path" is defined in the Wildlife and Countryside Act 1981 as meaning a highway being either a footpath or a bridleway.[10]

Roads used as public paths

This is a classification which had relevance for the demarcation of cer- **1–24** tain kinds of paths on the definitive map prepared under the National Parks and Access to the Countryside Act 1949 and the Countryside Act 1968. The Wildlife and Countryside Act 1981 now requires the reclassification of these roads used as public paths (RUPPS) as byways open to all traffic, bridleways or footpaths. However, they may still appear on definitive maps pending such reclassification. The 1949 Act defined

---

[3] See Countryside Act 1968, s.30.
[4] s.190(1).
[5] See *R.* v. *Saintiff* (1704) 6 Mod.Rep. 255; *R.* v. *Aldborough* (1853) 17 J.P. 648.
[6] See generally, Sidney and Beatrice Webb, *The Story of the Kings Highway* (2nd ed., 1963).
[7] Highways Act 1980, s.329(1); Wildlife and Countryside Act 1981, s.66(1); as to footways, see para. 1–12 above.
[8] See Chap. 12.
[9] Highways Act 1980, ss.25 and 26.
[10] Wildlife and Countryside Act 1981, s.66(1).

RUPPS as highways other than public paths used by the public mainly for the purposes for which footpaths and bridleways are so used.[11] Such paths, whilst they are recorded as RUPPS on the definitive map, are deemed to carry footpath and bridleway rights but without prejudice as to whether they in fact carry vehicular rights as well.[12]

Byways open to all traffic

1–25　　This is a class of highway which is also relevant for the purposes of the definitive map and is defined as being a highway over which the public have a right of way for vehicular and all other kinds of traffic, but which is used by the public mainly for the purposes for which footpaths and bridleways are so used.[13] While so recorded on the definitive map, such a path is deemed to carry vehicular and all other public rights of way.[14]

Cycle tracks

1–26　　A cycle track is a way constituting or comprised in a highway being a way over which the public have a right of way on pedal cycles (other than pedal cycles which are motor vehicles within the meaning of the Road Traffic Act 1972) with or without a right of way on foot and over which there are no other rights of way.[15] There is specific power in highway authorities to construct cycle tracks in or by the side of carriageway highways, and the cycle track then becomes part of that highway.[16] The Cycle Tracks Act 1984 empowers a highway authority to convert footpaths into cycle tracks.[17] Thus, as is implied in the definition of a cycle way, a cycle track may be a statutory highway in its own right. Cycle tracks will always be maintainable at the public expense.[18]

Walkways

1–27　　A walkway is a peculiar kind of highway. It is a footpath over, through, or under a building. Most commonly it will be found in the indoor shopping centres that now proliferate in our cities. The walkway, being attached to the building rather than to land as such, has a number of characteristics which set it apart from the common law highway. Many of the statutory provisions and principles of common law which apply to highways will not apply to walkways. A walkway can only be created by an agreement made under section 35 of the Highway Act 1980. Whilst all highways may be dedicated subject to restrictions, the walkway may be governed by provisions in the agreement which run contrary to the principles usually applying to highway law. In particular,

---

[11] National Parks and Access to the Countryside Act 1949, s.27(6), now repealed.
[12] See Chap. 12.
[13] Wildlife and Countryside Act 1981, s.66(1).
[14] *Ibid.* s.56(1).
[15] Highways Act 1980, s.329(1).
[16] *Ibid.* s.65(1).
[17] See also the Cycle Tracks Regulations 1984 (S.I. 1984 No. 1431).
[18] Highways Act 1980, s.65(1); Cycle Tracks Act 1984, s.3.

a walkway agreement may be terminated as may be provided for in that agreement. The walkway will regularly be closed to the public and the rights of the building owner and his successors in title are preserved by the statute and by the regulations made under it.[19] A number of the statutory provisions applying to highways do not apply to walkways, including the powers in Part VII of the 1980 Act to stop up and divert highways, the provisions relating to new and private streets, and some of the powers of compulsory acquisition.[20] A number of other statutory provisions, empowering authorities to carry out works in relation to, place objects on, or to take action with respect to, highways may only be done with the consent of the owner of the building unless the walkway agreement otherwise provides.[21] By-laws may be made which govern the conduct of persons using the walkway, the times at which it may be closed to the public and the placing of structures in, on, or over the walkway.[22] The agreement may provide for the responsibility for maintenance, cleansing, drainage, lighting and support of the walkway and for payments to be made to the owner of the building.[23] A walkway is therefore a highway which lasts only for so long as may be agreed in the walkway agreement, which may be maintained by someone other than the highway authority and which may be closed to the public or restricted to particular users by the building owner. To understand fully the rights and responsibilities of the owner and the relevant local authority, it will be necessary to look at the agreement itself, the regulations mentioned above and any by-laws that may have been made with respect to the walkway.

Other pedestrian ways

Pedestrianised areas are frequently to be found in the centres of **1–28** modern cities. In many cases, these will simply be footpaths or bridleways which have been created by the extinguishment of vehicular rights of way under the provisions of section 212 of the Town and Country Planning Act 1971.[24] In other cases, these ways may be walkways as described above. There may also be local Act powers which have permitted the highway authority to create "local Act walkways." Generally these will be subject to the same provisions as walkways created under the Highways Act 1980; however, it will always be important to consider the specific provisions of the local Act in order to establish the extent of the public rights of way over such ways.[25]

---

[19] See the Walkways Regulations 1973 (S.I. 1973 No. 686) as amended by the Walkways (Amendment) Regulations 1974 (S.I. 1974 No. 735).
[20] For a full list see Highways Act 1980, Sched. 1.
[21] Walkways Regulations 1973 (S.I. 1973 No. 686), reg. 3.
[22] Highways Act 1980, s.35(6).
[23] *Ibid.* s.35(3). See also para. 2–11, below.
[24] See para. 9–65, below.
[25] See also Part VIIA of the Highways Act 1980 which does distinguish these walkways: Chap. 11, below.

HIGHWAY AUTHORITIES

1–29   Highway authorities fall into two categories: the Minister and local highway authorities.

The Minister

1–30   The Secretary of State for Transport is "the Minister" for the purposes of the highway legislation in England. In Wales, the Secretary of
State for Wales will be "the Minister".[26] The Minister is the highway
authority for any trunk road, for roads constructed by him (except
where under statute the local highway authority is made the highway
authority)[27] and for any roads which are designated by statutory order
as being roads for which he will be the highway authority.[28]

Local highway authorities

1–31   Outside of London, local highway authorities are the county councils
or metropolitan district councils.[29] Within London, the London
borough councils and the Common Council of the City of London are
the local highway authorities for all highways within their areas, save for
those for which the Minister is the highway authority.

1–32   Non-metropolitan district councils are not local highway authorities
but they do have certain highway functions. Under section 42 and Part I
of Schedule 7 to the 1980 Act, these councils, on giving notice to the
county council, may undertake the maintenance of certain highways
within their district which are maintainable at the public expense. The
highways covered by this power are footpaths, bridleways, and "urban
roads" which are neither trunk roads nor classified roads and which
either carry speed restrictions or which are streets within an urban
area.[30] The procedure to be adopted by non-metropolitan district councils which exercise these powers is set out in Part I of Schedule 7 to the
1980 Act.[31]

1–33   Councils of non-metropolitan districts, parishes or communities may
undertake the maintenance of footpaths or bridleways within their area
which are not otherwise maintainable by anyone or which are privately
maintainable. District councils are again governed by Part I of Schedule
7 to the 1980 Act. Councils of parishes and communities may also
undertake the maintenance of footpaths and bridleways, within their
parish or community, which are highways at the public expense.[32]

---

[26] Highways Act 1980, s. 329(1); Transfer of Functions (Transport) Order 1981 (S.I. 1981
No. 235).
[27] *e.g.* by an order made under the Highways Act 1980, s.14(1)(*b*).
[28] *e.g.* an order made under the Town and Country Planning Act 1971, s.209(2)(*b*).
[29] Highways Act 1980, s.1(2) as amended by the Local Government Act 1985, s.8 and
Sched. 4.
[30] Highways Act 1980, s.42(2); Road Traffic Regulation Act 1984, ss.81 and 84.
[31] See Chap. 4.
[32] Highways Act 1980, s.43.

Several powers contained within the Highways Act 1980 are given to   **1–34**
"councils" which are defined[33] as meaning a county council or a local
highway authority. A "local authority" is defined[34] as the council of a
district or London borough or the Common Council.

Delegation, agreements between authorities and agency agreements

Various powers are given to highway authorities to enter into agree-   **1–35**
ments with other authorities for the exercise of certain of their functions. In some cases the nature of these agreements is that the other
authority effectively becomes the highway authority, but in the majority
of instances the highway authority will itself remain liable under its
duties of maintenance.

Agreements between the Minister and local highway authorities

The Minister and a local highway authority may enter into an agree-   **1–36**
ment for providing that the Minister shall exercise specified powers of
improvement in relation to a named highway maintainable by the local
highway authority. Such an agreement may only relate to highways
which cross or enter the route of a trunk road or which will otherwise be
affected by the construction or improvement of a trunk road. The agreement may be subject to conditions.[35] Where such an agreement is
entered into, the Minister thereafter has the same powers, including
land acquisition powers, as the local highway authority for the purpose
of exercising the improvement functions which were the subject of the
agreement, and will be subject to the same liabilities.[36] Where such an
agreement contemplates the construction of a highway, every highway
authority in whose area the proposed highway will be situated must be a
party to the agreement, and provision must be made within the agreement for a local highway authority to become the highway authority for
the road on its completion.

The Minister may agree with a local highway authority that it should   **1–37**
undertake the maintenance and improvement of a highway (other than
a trunk road) which he proposes to construct or has constructed. The
local highway authority which enters into such an agreement, at a date
specified in the agreement, thereafter becomes the highway authority
for that highway.[37]

The Minister may also delegate to a local highway authority, by   **1–38**
agreement, all or any of his functions with respect to the maintenance or
improvement of, and other dealings with, any trunk road or any land

---

[33] Highways Act 1980, s.329(1).
[34] *Ibid.*
[35] Including conditions relating to payments to be made by the Minister to the local highway authority or vice versa in respect of incurred liabilities: Highways Act 1980, s.4(4).
[36] *e.g.* there may be a liability to pay compensation; See Chap. 14.
[37] Highways Act 1980, s.5.

acquired[38] in connection with a trunk road.[39] The agreement may include land or a trunk road which is outside the area of the local a highway authority, but this may only be done with the consent of the local highway authority in whose area the road or land lies.[40] Thereafter, the local highway authority will act as the Minister's agent. The agreement may contain conditions preserving the Minister's control over certain aspects of the works to be carried out.[41] If at any time the Minister is satisfied that a trunk road or land to which a delegation agreement applies is not in proper repair and condition, he may give notice to the council requiring it to put it into proper repair and condition within such time as may be specified in the notice. The Minister may then himself do the work in default.[42] It follows, therefore, that the ultimate responsibility for the maintenance of the trunk road remains with the Minister. Agreements may be determined by the Minister or relinquished by the local highway authority by giving at least six months' notice expiring on April 1.

1-39   Similiar agreements may be entered into between the Minister and a local highway authority for the construction of a trunk road or for the carrying out by the local highway authority of any work of improvement of, or any dealing with, any trunk road or land acquired in connection with a trunk road. These are distinguished from delegation agreements but are otherwise subject to similar conditions.[43]

1-40   Where the Minister has delegated powers to or has entered into an agreement with a county council, that council may itself enter into arrangements with district councils for the carrying out of the functions which were the subject of the delegation or agreement.[44] Such arrangements may relate to roads or land outside the area of the district council but only with the consent of the metropolitan or non-metropolitan district concerned.[45]

Agreements between local highway authorities for doing works

1-41   Local highway authorities may enter into agreements with each other in relation to the construction, reconstruction, alteration, improvement or maintenance of their highways. Such agreements may provide that the functions of one highway authority should be exercised by another.[46] The agreement may be subject to terms and conditions. Where an authority is acting under the terms of such an agreement, it

---

[38] *i.e.* under Highways Act 1980, s.239(1) or (4).
[39] *Ibid.* s.6.
[40] *Ibid.* s.6(1A).
[41] A series of departmental circulars and Trunk Road Management and Maintenance Notices prescribe general conditions relative to these agreements. See the Encyclopedia of Highway Law, Vol. 3 (Sweet & Maxwell).
[42] Highways Act 1980, s.6(3).
[43] *Ibid.* s.6(5).
[44] *Ibid.* s.6(6).
[45] *Ibid.* s.6(6A).
[46] *Ibid.* s.8(2).

will have all the powers and be subject to the same liabilities as the local highway authority for that highway. Agreements of this sort are only permissible between adjoining authorities in the case of county councils. Metropolitan district councils may enter into such agreements with adjoining county councils or with other metropolitan districts within the same or the adjoining county.[47]

Agency agreements under the Local Government Act 1972, section 101

Any local authority may arrange for the discharge of its functions by **1–42** another authority by virtue of an agency agreement under the Local Government Act 1972. Agreements of this sort are commonly entered into between the county council and the district council with respect to highways within the area of the district. When an authority exercises these agency powers it is acting in the name of the local highway authority, which authority remains liable for the maintenance of the highway and is subject to the same liabilities as before in respect of that highway.

---

[47] Highways Act 1980, s.8(4) (as amended by the Local Government Act 1985, s.8 and Sched. 4).

CHAPTER 2

CREATION OF HIGHWAYS

INTRODUCTION

2–01   At common law there have always been two essential elements to the creation of a highway—dedication by the owner of the soil and acceptance by the public of the way thereby dedicated. Prior to the passing of the Highway Act 1835, liability for the repair of almost all highways fell upon the inhabitants of the parish in which the highway was situated. Such liability, however, arose only where the utility of the way to the public had been accepted. Thus, the mere act of dedication was not sufficient to impose the burden of repair upon the local inhabitants.

2–02   Although statute has now established other ways by which a highway may be created—mainly by allowing a particular form of dedication to be sufficient of itself[1]—the basic common law rules are still of considerable importance. Whilst express dedication will today usually follow one or other of the statutory procedures, the common law principles are still of relevance in establishing the status of disputed ways which are alleged to have been dedicated in the past. Statutory intervention in the rules for ascertaining whether dedication may be presumed after a number of years' proven public use[2] has been intended to clarify the common law position rather than to alter it in substance.

CREATION UNDER STATUTE

Creation by construction

2–03   The present rules for creation of highways by statute are now found in Part III of the Highways Act 1980. By section 24 of that Act both the Minister and local highway authorities are given power to construct highways. This can, of course, be achieved by the dedication of the land as a highway by the landowner and by the subsequent construction of a road over it. However, the invariable practice is for the land to be acquired under compulsory powers[3] for highway purposes and, after completion and on being opened to the public, the way will immediately become a public highway.

2–04   The powers of the Minister to construct highways are not confined to special and trunk roads. In theory, he may construct any kind of highway, including footpaths and bridleways. Where he proposes to con-

---

[1] *e.g.* the various Inclosure Acts, the Turnpike Acts and Highways Act 1980, ss.24, 25, 30, 35 and 38.
[2] See Highways Act 1980, s.31.
[3] See Highways Act 1980, Part XII; Acquisition of Land Act 1981, Chap. 14.

struct any kind of highway other than a trunk road, special road, a road entering or crossing a trunk road,[4] or a highway constructed pursuant to an agreement with a local highway authority under section 4 of the 1980 Act, he must give notice to and consider representations made by every council[5] through whose area the highway will pass.[6] A local highway authority has power to construct highways, subject, where the proposed highway connects with a road for which the Minister is the highway authority,[7] to his approval.

In the case of special roads and trunk roads, the construction will be   **2–05** part of and subject to a scheme (under section 16) or orders (under sections 10 and 18). Equally, where the highway being constructed crosses or joins a trunk or a classified road, then the construction will be subject to the provisions of section 14 of the 1980 Act. A number of other statutory provisions permit the construction of highways incidental to other major schemes.[8]

Once constructed under statutory provisions, a road or way becomes   **2–06** a highway of the class intended by the constructing authority. There is no room in relation to these kinds of highways for the argument, open to the private dedicator of land, that the highway is dedicated in its existing condition subject to any existing obstructions or declared limitations. In *Baxter* v. *Stockton-on-Tees Corporation*[9] a highway authority was sued for negligence under the Fatal Accidents Acts in respect of the siting and condition of a traffic island. The authority sought to argue that, since the highway had been dedicated to the public with the island in situ, the public must have taken the highway subject to this obstruction. This argument was rejected by the Court of Appeal.

Where a highway is created by statutory provisions there is, there-   **2–07** fore, no need for any demonstrated acts of acceptance on behalf of the public. The statutory provisions themselves have set out the only preconditions for the creation of the highway.[10] Where the authorising provisions have not been fully complied with, it may be necessary for the status of the constructed road as a highway to be established by evidence of public user.[11]

Creation by agreement

A local highway authority may agree under section 38 of the High-   **2–08** ways Act 1980 to adopt a private carriageway or occupation way which is either already in existence, or is to be constructed. The highway

---

[4] Under Highways Act 1980, ss.14 or 18.
[5] The term "council" here embraces district councils (and the Common Council) as well as local highway authorities; see Highways Act 1980, s.329(1).
[6] See Highways Act 1980, s.24(1).
[7] *Ibid.* s.24(2).
[8] *e.g.* Civil Aviation Act 1982, s.48; New Towns Act 1981, ss.19–25.
[9] [1959] 1 Q.B. 441.
[10] See *R.* v. *Lyon* (1825) 5 Dow. & Ry. K.B. 497; *R.* v. *French* (1879) 4 Q.B.D. 507.
[11] See *Cubitt* v. *Maxse* (1873) L.R. 8 C.P. 704; *R.* v. *Lordsmere* (*Inhabitants*) (1850) 15 Q.B. 689.

thereby created is maintainable at the public expense. The agreement must be made between the authority and a person having the necessary capacity to dedicate the land as a highway.[12] This is by far the most common method whereby a newly created road becomes a highway. The road may be constructed by the developer or by the highway authority on his behalf. In the former case, the road must be constructed to the required standard and to the satisfaction of the highway authority. The agreement may prescribe the date on which the road is to become a highway maintainable at the public expense. Until that date arrives, the road will not become a highway of any sort, unless the common law principles as to dedication and acceptance are fulfilled.[13]

2–09   Footpaths and bridleways may also be created by agreement between the landowner and any local authority.[14] In entering into such an agreement the authority must have due regard to the needs of agriculture and forestry.[15] Dedication may be conditional or subject to limitations defined in the agreement. Once such an agreement has been made, the local authority is under a duty to take all the necessary steps to ensure that dedication in accordance with the agreement takes place.[16] The public are to be given notice of the dedication.[17] Whenever the agreement is made with an authority which is not the highway authority, the way must be surveyed and certified by the highway authority as being fit for use by the public.[18] Agreements made under section 25 are called "public path creation agreements."

2–10   Parish and community councils have power to enter into these agreements where such dedication would, in the opinion of the council, be beneficial to the inhabitants of the parish or community concerned.[19] Thereafter, that council will have power to carry out works of maintenance and improvement (or contribute to the expense thereof) consequential upon and incidental to the making of that agreement.[20] A highway dedicated under an agreement made under this section will not become a highway maintainable at the public expense.

2–11   An unusual kind of highway may be created by an agreement under section 35 of the 1980 Act. A "walkway" is a footpath "in, through or under" a building. A "walkway" can, in fact, *only* be created by agreement and is a creature of statute. As such, it does not conform to all the rules usually understood to apply to a highway. A walkway may regularly be closed to the public. It may be terminated by agreement. A

---

[12] Highways Act 1980, s.38(3). As to capacity to dedicate, see para. 2–17, below.
[13] See *Cubitt* v. *Maxse* (1873) L.R. 8 C.P. 704; *R.* v. *Lordsmere* (*Inhabitants*) (1850) 15 Q.B. 689.
[14] The term "local authority" is defined as including district councils, joint planning boards, London Borough Councils, the Common Council and the Greater London Council.
[15] Highways Act 1980, s.29.
[16] *Ibid.* s.25(5).
[17] *Ibid.* s.25(6).
[18] *Ibid.* s.27.
[19] "or any part thereof." Highways Act 1980, s.30(1).
[20] *Ibid.* s.30.

walkway agreement must be made between the council of the district or the local highway authority,[21] and the person who has the necessary power to provide and dedicate as footpaths, ways over, through, or under parts of a building or any structure attached to a building. Such a person may have a more limited interest in land than is usually required for the dedication of a highway, since the lifetime of the walkway is necessarily limited to that of the building and, in any event, might be given a limited duration by the agreement. Any covenants entered into by the building owner will run with the land and will be enforceable against successors in title.[22] Dedication may be subject to limitations and conditions and the agreement may reserve the rights of the land-owner or his successors in title. Such limitations may override the normal statutory provisions affecting highways.[23] Provision may be made for the maintenance, cleansing, drainage, lighting and support of the walkway. In many respects, therefore, the walkway agreement will provide its own code of regulation of the responsibilities relating to the highway, separate from, and taking the place of, the statutory code normally affecting highways in general.[24]

Creation by declaration

By section 34 of the Highways Act 1980, a street which is not a high-way, and land treated as being a private street under section 232 of that Act, may become a highway by virtue of a declaration made by a county council, a metropolitan district council, a London borough council or the Common Council[25] under the provisions of Part XI of the Act.[26] This provision is unique, in that it involves the possibility of land being made into a public highway by court order, against the wishes of a relevant owner,[27] without the possibility of compensation, and possibly after the landowner has already been compelled to contribute to the expense of the street works under the street works code. The effect of such a declaration is that the street thereafter becomes a highway maintainable at the public expense which, of course, is in many respects to the advantage of the owners of the street.

Creation by order

Footpaths and bridleways may be created by orders made under section 26 of the Highway Act 1980. Such orders are called "public path creation orders." District and county councils, joint planning boards, London borough councils and the Common Council all have power to

---

[21] Each in consultation with the other.
[22] Highways Act 1980, s.35(4).
[23] See the Walkways Regulations 1973 (S.I. 1973 No. 686), reg. 2.
[24] See para. 1–27, above.
[25] *i.e.* the street works authority, see Chap. 10.
[26] As to the circumstances in which this may occur, see para. 10–56, below.
[27] As to the acquiring of highway rights against a landowner over a period of time, see para. 2–32, below.

make these orders. The criteria for the making of an order are that it must appear to the local authority that there is a need for the creation of a path over land within its area, and the authority, after having regard to a number of matters specified in the section, must be satisfied that it is expedient that the path should be created. These matters are:

(a) the extent to which the path or way would add to the convenience or enjoyment of a substantial section of the public, or to the convenience of persons resident in the area, and

(b) the effect which the creation of the way would have on the rights of persons interested in the land, bearing in mind the compensation provisions contained in section 28.

2–14 Where a public path creation order is opposed, it must be submitted to the Secretary of State for confirmation. Otherwise it may be confirmed by the order-making authority as an unopposed order. The authority has a duty to consult with the other authorities in whose area the land lies. The Secretary of State has similiar powers to make these orders after due consultation with the authorities in whose area the land lies. The procedure to be followed in making an order is set out in Schedule 6 to the 1980 Act and follows a similar form to that required for a public path extinguishment or diversion order.[28] The form of the order is prescribed by regulations.[29]

2–15 New paths may also be created on the diversion of existing paths. There are provisions in the Highways Act 1980 and in a number of other statutes which empower the creation of new paths and roads, either in substitution for or as part of the diversion of existing ways.[30]

CREATION AT COMMON LAW

Need for both dedication and acceptance

2–16 At common law the two necessary preconditions to the creation of a highway are dedication by the landowner of a public right of way across his land, and acceptance by the public of that right of way. Dedication may be by the express act or declaration of the landowner or, in the absence of clear evidence of his express intention, it may be implied from evidence of user by the public and of acquiescence in that user by the landowner. The acceptance of the way as a highway is invariably to be implied from evidence of public use of the way. Evidence of acceptance is necessary whether the dedication is express[31] or implied. Where dedication is implied, the need for evidence of public user of the way is also important to establish that the user has been as of right.

---

[28] See Chap. 9.
[29] Public Path Orders and Extinguishment of Public Right of Way Orders Regulations 1983 (S.I. 1983 No. 23). See also Highways Act 1980, s.26(5).
[30] See Chap. 9.
[31] See *R.* v. *Mellor* (1828) 1 Lewin 158; *Cubitt* v. *Maxse* (1873) L.R. 8 C.P. 704; *Mackett* v. *Herne Bay Commissioners* (1876) 35 L.T. 202.

Dedication in perpetuity and capacity to dedicate

Dedication has to be capable of creating in perpetuity a way open to 2–17
the public at large. It follows, therefore, that only an owner with the
capacity to bind the land in perpetuity has the power to dedicate a highway to the public. Lessees and other limited owners are not capable,
therefore, of dedicating a way without the concurrence of the freehold
owner.[32]

Lessees

Whilst a lessee cannot dedicate a highway so as to bind the owner of 2–18
the freehold reversion, it is not entirely clear whether or not a purported
dedication will be totally devoid of legal effect. In *Dawes* v. *Hawkins*,
Byles J. said[33]: "It is clear that there can be no dedication of a way to the
public for a limited time, certain or uncertain. If dedicated at all, it must
be dedicated in perpetuity." However, in *Corsellis* v. *London County
Council*,[34] the Court of Appeal expressed the view that rights based on
estoppel or contract might have been created where a lessee had ineffec-
tively purported to dedicate land as a highway. In *Attorney-General* v.
Biphosphated Guano Company,[35] the Court of Appeal had left open the
question as to whether there could, in law, be a dedication to the public
limited to the period of the lease. There are difficulties with both views.
The concept of a highway limited in duration is contrary to the tra-
ditional thinking of the common law. Further, it is unsupported by any
clear authority, and would require a considerable interference with the
structure of highway law, to deal with the problem which is unlikely to
arise with any great frequency. Whilst there may not be any conceptual
problem in treating the purported dedication by a lessee as being an
agreement which is enforceable by the highway authority, interesting
questions arise as to what rights can be said to have been created by the
agreement. There may well also be practical problems of enforcement.
Where the agreement is made with the highway authority for consideration, or where specific performance of the obligation is otherwise available, then these problems may be overcome.[36] However, the
uncertainties of the powers of a highway authority to deal with the
limited right of way thereby created would be likely to discourage
reliance on such an agreement.

The concurrence of the freehold reversioner in the dedication may be 2–19
implied by long public user just as it may in the case of a single absolute

---

[32] See *Wood* v. *Veal* (1822) 5 B. & Ald. 454; *Davies* v. *Stephens* (1836) 7 Car. & P. 570; *R.*
v. *East Mark (Inhabitants)* (1848) 11 Q.B. 877; *Corsellis* v. *L.C.C.* [1907] 1 Ch. 704,
affirmed by the Court of Appeal at [1908] 1 Ch. 13; but see *Att.-Gen.* v. *Biphosphated
Guano Co.* (1879) 11 Ch.D. 327, *per* Fry J.

[33] (1860) 8 C.B.(N.S.) 848 at 857.

[34] [1907] 1 Ch. 704.

[35] (1879) 11 Ch.D. 327.

[36] See Lawrance J.'s approach in *Hoare & Co. Ltd.* v. *Lewisham Corpn.* (1901) 85 L.T.
281.

owner. At common law such concurrence is difficult to establish.[37] Evidence of the acts and knowledge of the freeholder prior to the grant and after expiry of the lease are important.[38] Proof of continued public user over successive leases may also be significant.[39] Where land has been let on a building lease, the consent (express or implied) of the reversioner to the laying out of streets does not necessarily indicate his intention that those streets are to become public highways.[40]

2–20   The statutory presumption in section 31 of the Highways Act 1980[41] envisages the situation where public rights are being sought to be established by long user over the land of a limited owner. Subsection (4) gives to the owner of the reversion a right (as against the tenant but not so as to injure the tenant's business or occupation) to use the procedures to avoid the presumption arising. From a practical point of view, it is the lessee in possession whose sufferance of the public use of the way will give rise to the operation of the statutory presumption in the first place. Section 31 creates only a rebuttable presumption subject to sufficient evidence to the contrary, and evidence both as to knowledge and as to the reaction in the light of such knowledge of both the lessee and the reversioner will no doubt be of significance.

Settled land

2–21   Under the Settled Land Act 1925, section 56(2), the tenant for life is given the same power to dedicate land for public purposes as an absolute owner. The tenant for life with the power of sale is treated as the owner for the purposes of section 31 of the Highways Act 1980. However, the person entitled to the remainder or reversion immediately expectant upon the determination of a tenancy for life is also given like remedies, by action for trespass or an injunction, to prevent the acquisition by the public of a right of way over the land, in the same way as if he were in possession of it.[42]

Public bodies

2–22   A statutory body has powers limited by the statute which created it. The statute may, therefore, empower or restrict the creation of public rights of way by the body concerned. Generally, however, the power to dedicate will be considered incidental to and ancillary to any powers which the body might have to own and alienate land. Problems have arisen in relation to the powers of public bodies to enter into long-term

---

[37] See *Davies* v. *Stephens* (1836) 7 Car. & P. 570; *Corsellis* v. *L.C.C.* [1907] 1 Ch. 704.
[38] See *Winterbottom* v. *Derby* (*Lord*) (1867) L.R. 2 Exch. 316; *Shearburn* v. *Chertsey R.D.C.* (1914) 78 J.P. 289; *Rugby Charity Trustees* v. *Merryweather* (1790) 11 East 375 n.; *Att.-Gen.* v. *Chandos Land and Building Society* (1910) 74 J.P. 401.
[39] See *R.* v. *Barr* (1814) 4 Camp 16, N.P.; *Davies* v. *Stephens* (1836) 7 Car. & P. 570.
[40] See *Espley* v. *Wilkes* (1872) L.R. 7 Exch. 298; *cf. Pryor* v. *Pryor* (1872) 26 L.T.(N.S.) 758.
[41] See para. 2–32, below.
[42] Highways Act 1980, s.33.

binding commitments which might be considered to fetter unlawfully the future exercise of their executive discretions.[43] Whilst the creation of long-term rights and obligations by a public body is not *ultra vires* simply because the creation of those rights and obligations necessarily restricts that body in the future exercise of other statutory powers,[44] the creation of rights and obligations which will be incompatible with the purposes for which the public body was created will be *ultra vires*.[45] The question of incompatibility is one of fact to be determined in the light of the circumstances known at the time the way is questioned, after consideration of the purposes of the public body, and in the light of the probable requirements of that body in fulfilling its statutory purposes.[46] The test is whether or not the dedication might reasonably be supposed to be incompatible.[47] Section 31 of the 1980 Act is also restricted in its operation to bodies with limited jurisdiction by subsection (8). The prohibition on the fettering of the exercise of future discretions will apply to any agreement to dedicate land as a highway in the future, as it will to a present or past dedication.[48]

The creation of public rights of way over accommodation bridges running over and under railway lines has been held not to be incompatible with the objects of a railway company unless it would preclude the widening of the rails at the point where the bridge crossed.[49] Similarly, an accommodation carriage bridge constructed pursuant to statutory powers by a canal company, which bridge also carried an existing public bridleway, has been held to have become a public carriageway after proof of sufficient public user by carriages. Dedication generally to the public was inferred because public use with carriages was to be expected, and the company would have had to put itself to great expense to prevent indiscriminate use by the public.[50]   **2–23**

Railway crossings may become subject to a public right of way unless   **2–24** such dedication might endanger the user of the line or of the public who use the railway.[51] Public rights over embankments and along towing paths have also been held capable of being established in appropriate

---

[43] See *Ayr Harbour Trustees* v. *Oswald* (1883) 8 App.Cas. 623.
[44] See *Dowty Boulton Paul* v. *Wolverhampton Corpn.* [1971] 1 W.L.R. 204; *Stourcliffe Estates Co. Ltd.* v. *Bournemouth Corpn.* [1910] 2 Ch. 12.
[45] *British Transport Commission* v. *Westmorland C.C.* [1958] A.C. 126; *R.* v. *Leake (Inhabitants)* (1833) 5 B. & Ad. 469; *Paterson* v. *St. Andrews Provost* (1881) 6 App. Cas. 833; *Blake* v. *Hendon Corpn.* [1962] 1 Q.B. 283.
[46] cf. *British Railways Board* v. *Glass* [1965] Ch. 538.
[47] *British Transport Commissioners* v. *Westmorland C.C.* (n. 45 above) at 144 and 160.
[48] *Tunbridge Wells Improvement Commissioners* v. *Southborough Local Board* (1888) 60 L.T. 172.
[49] See *Taff Vale Ry.* v. *Pontypridd U.D.C.* (1905) 93 L.T. 126; *British Transport Commission* v. *Westmorland C.C.* [1958] A.C. 126.
[50] See *Grand Surrey Canal Co.* v. *Hall* (1840) 1 Man. & G. 392.
[51] *Att.-Gen.* v. *London and South Western Ry. Co.* (1905) 69 J.P. 110; *South Eastern Ry. Co.* v. *Warr* (1923) 21 L.G.R. 669.

cases.[52] Evidence that public user may be destructive of the embankment, or may lead to greatly increased expenditure on the part of the public body in keeping the embankment in repair, has resulted in dedication being held to be incompatible with the purposes of a canal company.[53] In every case the purposes for which the public body was created will have to be considered and these purposes measured against the likely demands of the public highway.[54] Where the purposes or powers of a public body may fairly be construed as including the power to dedicate land as a highway, the courts will not interfere with the exercise of any such discretionary powers.[55]

The Crown

2–25   The Crown may dedicate a highway over lands within its ownership and the common law principles of dedication and acceptance apply in the same way as with a private person.[56]

Intention to dedicate to the public at large

2–26   In deciding whether a highway has been created, it is necessary to consider the intention of the landowner at the time of creation and whether the object of that intention is capable of being a highway. The throwing open of a way only to persons of a particular class will not, therefore, create a public highway.[57] In theory, all that is required to ascertain that intention is evidence of the circumstances of the creation of the way, and the interpretation, perhaps by the construction of documents,[58] of that evidence. In practice, however, the facts surrounding the creation of the vast majority of highways are obscure, either because they are lost in the mists of time or because the public way has grown up over land through the years rather than by express creation. In the latter situation, the law is prepared to imply and, in certain circumstances presume, that the landowner's acquiescence in the habitual crossing of his land by the public is evidence of an intention to dedicate the land irrevocably to the public. In proving the existence of any highway, therefore, evidence of the degree and quality of public user will be required. In

---

[52] See *Grand Junction Canal Co.* v. *Petty* (1888) 21 Q.B.D. 273; *Lancashire & Yorkshire Ry. Co.* v. *Davenport* (1906) 70 J.P. 129; *Greenwich Board of Works* v. *Maudslay* (1870) L.R. 5 Q.B. 397; *R.* v. *Leake (Inhabitants)* (1833) 5 B. & Ad. 469; *Hunwick* v *Essex Rivers Catchment Board* [1952] 1 All E.R. 765.
[53] *Great Western Ry. Co.* v. *Solihull R.D.C.* (1902) 86 L.T. 852.
[54] See *Paterson* v. *St Andrews Provost* (1881) 6 App.Cas. 833; *Coats* v. *Hereford C.C.* [1909] 2 Ch. 579, affirmed [1909] 2 Ch. 601; *Att.-Gen.* v. *Blackpool Corporation* (1907) 71 J.P. 478; *Sandgate U.D.C.* v. *Kent C.C.* (1898) 79 L.T. 425.
[55] *Att.-Gen.* v. *Bradford Corpn.* (1911) 75 J.P. 553.
[56] *R.* v. *East Mark (Inhabitants)* (1848) 11 Q.B. 877; *Turner* v. *Walsh* (1881) 6 App.Cas. 636; *Harper* v. *Charlesworth* (1825) 4 B. & C. 574.
[57] See *Leckhampton Quarries Co. Ltd.* v. *Ballinger and Cheltenham R.D.C.* (1904) 68 J.P. 464.
[58] See *e.g. Austerberry* v. *Oldham Corpn.* (1855) 29 Ch.D. 750.

cases involving implied dedication, the evidence called to establish public acceptance will often be indistinguishable from the evidence relied upon to show an implied or presumed intention to dedicate.

A highway may be dedicated by the unequivocal act of the landowner **2–27** in throwing his land open to the public for highway use.[59] However, it has also been held that actions of a landowner which induce the supposition in members of the public that the way is dedicated do not necessarily lead to dedication.[60] The courts have distinguished a tolerance of public use from an intention to dedicate to the public. Heath J., in *Steel* v. *Houghton*, said[61]: "It is the wise policy of the law, not to construe acts of charity, though continued and repeated for never so many years, in such a manner as to make them the foundation of legal obligation." But the expressed intention has also to be seen in the light of evidence of subsequent public user, which might be taken to establish a change in that intention and which might give rise to an implication or presumption of subsequent dedication.[62]

The laying out of an estate road for the use of the inhabitants of that **2–28** estate will not, without more, be an act of dedication to the public.[63] However, many highways began as occupation ways, and the question usually before a court is whether the public user thereafter has been sufficient to establish a public right. Where the landowner's actions are consistent with the grant of a mere permission to cross his land, no highway will have been created[64]; instead, the public will have only a licence. In *Holloway* v. *Egham Urban District Council*,[65] Neville J. sounded a warning about the implication of dedication in respect of estate and occupation roads. There will inevitably be a certain amount of user by persons other than the owners or occupiers of the property within the estate. Tradesmen, social visitors, the police and local authority officials passing over the road to visit or service property, or acting in the course of their official duties may all be treated as a special section of the public, falling within one or other of the categories of invitees or licensees, and whose user cannot be ascribed to any assertion of a public right.[66] Where a road is shown to have been first laid out as an occupation road, the courts will, at least, look closely at the type of user which is claimed to have changed the character of the way.[67] A similiar

---

[59] See *Woodyer* v. *Hadden* (1813) 5 Taunt. 125; *R.* v. *Lloyd* (1808) 1 Camp. 260.
[60] See *Simpson* v. *Att.Gen.* [1904] A.C. 476, *per* Lord Macnaghten, at 493–499.
[61] (1788) 1 Hy.Bl. 51 at 60.
[62] See *Barraclough* v. *Johnson* (1838) 8 A. & E. 99.
[63] *Selby* v. *Crystal Palace Gas Co.* (1862) 4 De G. F. & J. 246.
[64] See *Barraclough* v. *Johnson*, n. 62 above; *Thornhill* v. *Weeks* (*No. 3*) [1915] 1 Ch.106; *Fenwick* v. *Huntingdon R.D.C.* (1928) 92 J.P. 41.
[65] (1908) 72 J.P. 433 at 434.
[66] *Kreft* v. *Rawcliffe*, *The Times*, May 12, 1984.
[67] *R.* v. *Bradfield* (*Inhabitants*) (1874) L.R. 9 Q.B. 552; *R.* v. *St. Benedict, Cambridge* (*Inhabitants*) (1821) 4 B. & Ald. 447; *Fuller* v. *Chippenham R.D.C.* (1914) 79 J.P. 4.

approach has also been followed by the courts in the interpretation of the words "road open to the public" in the Road Traffic Acts.[68]

2–29   The purposes of the users of the way may be relevant if those purposes throw light on the quality of the right of passage claimed in respect of the way. Evidence that the users of the way were solely visiting particular properties is consistent with an implied permission.[69] Similarly, evidence that workers on their way to a particular factory regularly crossed the land of their employer in order to reach their place of employment is unlikely to be in itself sufficient to establish a public right of way. But the situation may be different if the workers had to pass over the land of a number of landowners—although this could also be consistent with licences granted to their employer. Paths leading to churches or to old flour mills are more likely to be established as highways at least where they cross the land of more than one person.[70] Where the public user of the way is established by other evidence, the motive of that user is itself irrelevant.[71]

2–30   Proof of actual knowledge, in a resident landowner, of the public use is of great significance.[72] However, the length of user and other circumstances may be sufficient to imply such knowledge.[73] Lord Blackburn in *Mann* v. *Brodie* said[74]:

> "Where there has been evidence of a user by the public so long and in such a manner that the owner of the fee, whoever he was, must have been aware that the public were acting under the belief that the way had been dedicated and has taken no steps to disabuse them of that belief, it is not conclusive evidence, but evidence on which those who have to find the fact may find that there was a dedication by the owner whoever he was."

It has always, of course, been possible for a landowner to take steps to prevent a right of way growing up across his land. Any proved act of interruption of the way by the landowner will be regarded as being of significance. Parke B. said, in *Poole* v. *Huskinson*,[75] " . . . a single act of interruption by the owner is of much more weight, upon a question of intention, than many acts of enjoyment." The presence of a gate across a path or road may be evidence of such an attempt on behalf of that landowner but on the other hand it may also be consistent with the dedi-

---

[68] See *Harrison* v. *Hill* 1932 S.C.(J.C.) 13; *Deacon* v. *A.T.* (*A Minor*) [1976] R.T.R. 244; *Cox* v. *White* [1976] R.T.R. 248; *Adams* v. *Commissioner of Police* [1980] R.T.R. 289.

[69] See, *per* Neville J., in *Holloway* v. *Egham U.D.C.* (1908) 72 J.P. 433 at 434.

[70] But see *Att.-Gen.* v. *Mallock* (1931) 30 L.G.R. 141.

[71] *Hue* v. *Whiteley* [1929] 1 Ch. 440.

[72] See *Chinnock* v. *Hartley Wintney R.D.C.* (1899) 63 J.P. 327.

[73] See *Folkestone Corpn.* v. *Brockman* [1914] A.C. 338; *Att.-Gen.* v. *Tasker* (1928) 92 J.P. 157; *Williams Ellis* v. *Cobb* [1935] 1 K.B. 310.

[74] (1885) 10 App.Cas. 378 at 386.

[75] (1843) 11 M. & W. 827 at 830; see also *Chinnock* v. *Hartley Wintney R.D.C.* (1899) 63 J.P. 327.

cation of the way, subject to existing obstacles.[76] The erection of a gate, or any other evidence of interruption, cannot have any great significance if it occurs after the public right of way has already been established.[77] Nor can too much reliance be put on acts done or obstructions created which in fact were not done with any intention to exclude the public.[78] The acquiescence of the landowner in the throwing down of a gate by persons asserting the public right may itself be evidence of his recognition of a previous dedication.[79] However, the courts are understandably reluctant to give much weight to acts of the public in overcoming obstacles which were placed by the landowner with the obvious intention of preventing the acquisition of a public right.[80] Closure of the way for one or more days a year has been regarded as a clear indication of lack of any intention to dedicate.[81] Other matters which have been regarded as sufficient to prevent the development of a public right of way include the erection of notices,[82] and a demand for payment by the landowner.[83] Acts of the owner which are referable to his ownership of the soil, rather than to the exclusion of the public, may confirm his continued acquiescence in the user of the surface by the public.[84] Acquiescence by an adjoining landowner in a deviation from the highway onto his land has generally been found to be insufficient to establish a new right of way over that land, at least where he himself has not obstructed the highway.[85]

The degree of user which is necessary at common law to establish or **2–31** prove a dedication to the public has never been defined. Every case must depend upon its own facts. Dedication may be inferred almost immediately in an appropriate case where the acts of the landowner are sufficiently clear and where the public acceptance has occurred contemporaneously.[86] Otherwise, evidence of the amount of public user will have to be considered in the light of the overall circumstances. The degree of user that may be sufficient to establish a highway in a remote

[76] See *Barraclough* v. *Johnson* (1838) 8 A. & E. 99; *Davies* v. *Stephens* (1836) 7 C. & P. 570.
[77] See Lord Cranworth in *Young* v. *Cuthbertson* (1854) 1 Macq. 455; *Openshaw* v. *Pickering* (1912) 77 J.P. 27; *South Eastern Ry.* v. *Warr* (1923) 21 L.G.R. 669.
[78] *Att.-Gen.* v. *Hemingway* (1916) 81 J.P. 112.
[79] *Roberts* v. *Karr* (1808) 1 Camp. 262 n.; *cf. Lethbridge* v. *Winter* (1808) 1 Camp. 263 n.
[80] See *R.* v. *Secretary of State for the Environment, ex p. William Greaves Blake* [1984] J.P.L. 101; *Stone* v. *Jackson* (1855) 16 C.B. 199.
[81] See *Rugby Charity Trustees* v. *Merryweather* (1790) 11 East 375 n.; *British Museum Trustees* v. *Finnis* (1833) 5 C. & P. 460.
[82] *Moser* v. *Ambleside U.D.C.* (1925) 89 J.P. 59; *Poole* v. *Huskinson* (1843) 11 M. & W. 827; *Att.-Gen.* v. *Mallock* (1931) 30 L.G.R. 141.
[83] *Folkestone Corpn.* v. *Brockman* [1914] A.C. 338.
[84] *Coats* v. *Herefordshire C.C.* [1909] 2 Ch. 579.
[85] *Dawes* v. *Hawkins* (1860) 8 C.B.(N.S.) 848; *British Museum Trustees* v. *Finnis* (1833) 5 C. & P. 460.
[86] See *Woodyer* v. *Hadden* (1813) 5 Taunt. 125; *North London Rail Co.* v. *St. Mary Islington, Vestry* (1872) 27 L.T. 672; *Rowley* v. *Tottenham U.D.C.* [1914] A.C. 95.

rural area will not necessarily be sufficient in urban surroundings.[87] Where there is other evidence of dedication, then user by a few persons without interruption will be enough for acceptance by the public, and may be evidence of implied dedication.[88]

Presumption of dedication

2–32   The Rights of Way Act 1932 introduced a 20 year period of public use giving rise to a presumption that the way had been dedicated as a highway. The presumption, which is rebuttable, is now contained in the Highways Act 1980, section 31. At common law, length of user has always been a material factor and a sufficiently lengthy period, in effect, gives rise to an inference of dedication.[89] But this is not a presumption of law.[90] The present section is worded:

> "(1) Where a way over any land, other than a way of such a character that use of it by the public could not give rise at common law to a presumption of dedication, has actually been enjoyed by the public as of right and without interruption for a full period of 20 years, the way is to be deemed to have been dedicated as a highway unless there is sufficient evidence that there was no intention during that period to dedicate it."

Where the 20 year period is established, the burden of proof is on the landowner to show that a way is *not* a highway.[91] The onus is also on the landowner to take steps to challenge the existence of the highway since the 20 year period is calculated from the time when he brings existence of the public right into question.[92]

2–33   Section 31 does not allow the presumption to operate where, at common law, no presumption of dedication could arise—although it is not easy to understand what type of ways were of "such a character" that public use of them could not give rise to a presumption of dedication at common law. Owners of land who were not able to dedicate at common law are dealt with in subsections (4) and (8). Subsection (9) specifically makes it clear that the operation of the presumption is not to be regarded as the exclusive means by which dedication may be implied. Where at common law a highway might be presumed by user for a period less than 20 years, this proof will still be sufficient to establish the way.[93] In short, therefore, section 31 creates a rebuttable presumption

---

[87] See *Macpherson* v. *Scottish Rights of Way and Recreation Society* (1888) 13 App.Cas. 744.

[88] *R.* v. *South Eastern Ry. Co.* (1850) 16 L.T. (o.s.) 124.

[89] *R.* v. *Hudson* (1732) 2 Stra. 909; *Young* v. *Cuthbertson* (1854) 1 Macq. 455; *Rugby Charity Trustees* v. *Merryweather* (1790) 11 East 375n.; *Openshaw* v. *Pickering* (1912) 77 J.P. 27.

[90] See *Folkestone Corpn.* v. *Brockman* [1914] A.C. 356; *Turner* v. *Walsh* (1881) 6 App. Cas. 636.

[91] See *Fairey* v. *Southampton C.C.* [1956] 2 Q.B. 439.

[92] Highways Act 1980, s.31(2).

[93] *Ibid.* s.31(9).

of dedication upon proof of 20 years' user, but a lesser period may still be relied on to prove a highway where the evidence is sufficient without the need to rely on any presumption of law.

Bringing into question the existence of the way

The 20 year period required by section 31 is calculated retrospectively 2–34 from the date when the right of the public to use the way is brought into question.[94] No starting point, therefore, is prescribed. The period may both have begun and ended before the coming into force of the Rights of Way Act 1932.[95] There may be more than one occasion when existence of the way is brought into question, but the critical factor is whether there has been 20 years' user for an uninterrupted period, ending at the date of any of those occasions.[96] There must have been some positive act on the part of the landowner, challenging the public right to use the way, in order to have the way "brought into question" so as to define the date at which the operation of the presumption is to be decided. The turning back of the occasional stranger will not be a sufficiently positive act—at least where the way continues to be used by locals.[97] The Act prescribes certain methods by which the way may formally be brought into question.[98] It would seem reasonable to suppose that any act of "interruption" of the way[99] would also bring existence of the way into question. In one case, however, ploughing up a path has been held not to be such an act[1]—apparently on the ground that, although a technical offence under the relevant Highways Act, such an act was a common occurrence in the country and did not imply the necessary intent on the part of the farmer.

In order to establish the presumption, it must be shown that the way 2–35 has actually been enjoyed by the public *as of right*. The public must be openly asserting their right to use the way, rather than acting under any licence or permission. This means that the way must have been used "*nec vi, nec clam, nec precario*,"[2] *i.e.* without compulsion, secrecy or licence. The belief of the users of the way that they are acting by virtue of a public right rather than by licence is of importance.[3] Enjoyment has been defined as meaning "having had the amenity or advantage of using."[4]

---

[94] Highways Act 1980, s.31(2); *Fairey* v. *Southampton C.C.* [1956] 2 Q.B. 439.

[95] See *Att.-Gen.* v. *Dyer* [1946] 2 All E.R. 252; *Fairey* v. *Southampton C.C.*, n. 94 above.

[96] *Rothschild* v. *Buckinghamshire C.C.* (1957) 55 L.G.R. 595.

[97] See *Fairey* v. *Southamptson C.C.* [1956] 2 Q.B. 439.

[98] Highways Act 1980, s.31(3), (6); see also para. 2–39, below.

[99] See para. 2–36, below.

[1] See *Owen* v. *Buckinghamshire C.C.* (1957) 55 L.G.R. 373.

[2] See *Merstham Manor Ltd.* v. *Coulsdon U.D.C.* [1937] 2 K.B. 77; *Jones* v. *Bates* [1938] 2 All E.R. 237.

[3] See *Jones* v. *Bates*, n. 2 above; *Lewis* v. *Thomas* [1950] 1 K.B. 438; *Hue* v. *Whiteley* [1929] 1 Ch. 440.

[4] *per* Hilbery J., in *Merstham Manor Ltd.* v. *Coulsdon U.D.C.* [1937] 2 K.B. 77.

Without interruption

2-36   Not only must the way have been used as of right, but the public right
must have been exercised without interruption. Interruption appears to
require some positive and physical act preventing the exercise of the
alleged right of way. In *Merstham Manor Ltd.* v. *Coulsdon Urban District Council*, Hilbery J.[5] considered the alternatives:

> "As it is actual enjoyment which must be without interruption, one
> would suppose that the interruption contemplated must be actual.
> One can scarcely interrupt acts except by some physical act which
> stops them. I therefore think that the word "interruption" in the
> expression in the Act "without interruption" is properly to be con-
> strued as meaning actual and physical stopping of the enjoyment,
> and not that the enjoyment has been free of any acts which merely
> challenged the public right to that enjoyment."

A distinction may also be drawn between interruption of the period and
interruption of the right itself, since public use of a way is often intermit-
tent.[6] Whether or not a sufficient interruption has taken place is a question of fact and does not depend on the intention of the landowner.[7]
Intention is, however, important in determining whether existence of
the way has been "brought into question."

Significance of the landowner's intentions

2-37   It is important to approach the operation of section 31 of the Highways Act 1980 in stages, otherwise confusion may arise as to the part
played by the landowner's intention, express or presumed, to dedicate
or not to dedicate his land as a highway. Whether or not the way has
been used as of right and without interruption for the necessary period is
a question of fact which gives rise to the operation of the presumption.
To this extent it resembles a special form of prescription. In *Fairey* v.
Southampton County Council,[8] Denning L.J. said: "It creates a new
statutory right to a highway by prescription and addition to the old right
by dedication. It reverses the burden of proof . . . " All members of the
Court of Appeal in that case noted the similarity between section 31 and
the Prescription Act 1832.

2-38   Section 31 avoids the artificiality of the judicial decisions prior to the
passing of the Rights of Way Act 1932, where, faced with a dearth of
evidence and the request to deem an intention where none could readily
be found, the courts developed confusing and conflicting principles on
which an implied dedication could be based. However, the intention of
the landowner is still relevant to the issue of whether or not the public

---

[5] [1937] 2 K.B. 77 at 85.
[6] *Jones* v. *Bates* [1938] 2 All E.R. 237 at 246; but *cf. Rothschild* v. *Buckinghamshire C.C.*
(1957) 55 L.G.R. 595.
[7] *Lewis* v. *Thomas* [1950] 1 K.B. 438.
[8] [1956] 2 Q.B. 439 at 458.

right has been brought into question and, in many cases, to the question whether user has been as of right and without interruption. Evidence of intent is again required to rebut the presumption. The landowner must show that during the period over which the presumption has arisen there was in fact no intention to dedicate the land as a highway. Evidence of overt acts on the part of the landowner, sufficient to show the public at large (*i.e.* those that used the highway) that he had no intention to dedicate, will be required.[9]

Section 31 provides specific means whereby a landowner may bring **2–39** the existence of a public right of way into question, thereby indicating a contrary intention for the purposes of subsection (1).[10] A notice, erected in such a manner as to be visible to persons using the way, inconsistent with the dedication of the way and maintained thereafter is, in the absence of any further contrary intention, sufficient to rebut the presumption. In the cases of leases, the owner of the freehold reversion has the right to place such a notice, so long as no injury is thereby done to the business of the tenant. Strangely, the right to erect the statutory notices under section 31 appears to be placed solely in the reversioner rather than the tenant.[11] Where any notice is torn down or defaced, the landowner is not obliged to continue to maintain further notices, provided he gives notice to the appropriate council that there is no public right of way. In any event the landowner may deposit with the council[12] a map of his land,[13] together with a statement indicating what ways have been dedicated over that land as highways. This statement must be augmented by statutory declarations (at not less than six-year intervals) that no additional rights of way have been dedicated or, if there have been such, identifying any new rights of way. This action will be sufficient to negative the presumption in the absence of evidence of a contrary intention.

Enlargement of highway rights by use of the presumption

Section 31 can be used to establish an unrestricted dedication to the **2–40** public where previously only a restricted right had existed,[14] and to establish a right to a bridleway where previously only a footpath had existed.[15] The operation of the section may override franchise market rights.[16]

---

[9] *Fairey* v. *Southampton C.C.* [1956] 2 Q.B. 439.
[10] Highways Act 1980, s.31(3)–(6).
[11] See the definition of "owner" in subs. (7).
[12] *i.e.* the County Council, London Borough Council or the Common Council.
[13] At a scale of not less than 6 inches to 1 mile.
[14] *Gloucester C.C.* v. *Farrow* [1985] 1 W.L.R. 741.
[15] See *R.* v. *Secretary of State for the Environment, ex p. Blake* [1984] J.P.L. 101; although in this case the claim was not successful.
[16] See *Brandon* v. *Barnes* [1966] 1 W.L.R. 1505; *Gloucester C.C.* v. *Farrow*, n. 14 above.

Limited dedication

2–41   A landowner may dedicate to the public a right of way across his land subject to some reservation of his own rights or subject to some physical restriction or obstruction. In *Fisher* v. *Prowse*; *Cooper* v. *Walker*,[17] Blackburn J. gave this explanation:

> "It is, of course, not obligatory on the owner of the land to dedicate the use of it as a highway to the public. It is equally clear that it is not compulsory on the public to accept use of a way when offered to them. If the use of the soil as a way is offered by the owner to the public under given conditions and subject to certain reservations, and the public accept the use under such circumstances, there can be no injustice in holding them to the terms on which the benefit was conferred. On the other hand, great injustice and hardship would often arise if, when a public right of way has been acquired under a given state of circumstances, the owner of the soil should be held bound to alter that state of circumstances to his own disadvantage and loss, and to be bound to make further concessions to the public altogether beyond the scope of his original intention."

This approach has been applied to a number of different types of obstacles and excavations which would otherwise have constituted a nuisance.[18]

2–42   The principle of limited dedication extends beyond physical obstructions in the highway. Dedication subject to the reservation by the landowner of the right to carry on activities which would otherwise be a nuisance to highway users is also permissible. If a highway may be dedicated subject to the existence of the canal or excavation by its side, clearly it can be dedicated subject to the rights of the landowner to carry on in relation to that excavation or canal those of his accustomed activities which would be otherwise lawful. Thus, a way may be dedicated subject to the right of adjoining occupiers to deposit goods in the highway.[19] In rural areas the dedication by a farmer of a way across his land may be subject to the reservation of the right to plough the land from time to time,[20] or to the future erection of obstructions in the interests of good husbandry.[21] A highway may also be dedicated subject to existing

---

[17] (1862) 2 B. & S. 770.

[18] *Cornwell* v. *Metropolitan Commissioners of Sewers* (1855) 10 Ex. 771 (ditches); *Bateman* v. *Burge* (1834) 6 C. & P. 391; *Att.-Gen.* v. *Meyrick & Jones* (1915) 79 J.P. 515 (gates and stiles); *Warner* v. *Wandsworth District Board of Works* (1889) 53 J.P. 471 (low bridge); *Stillwell* v. *New Windsor Corpn.* [1932] 2 Ch. 155 (trees).

[19] *Morant* v. *Chamberlin* (1861) 6 H. & N. 541; *Le Neve* v. *Mile End Old Town Vestry* (1858) 8 E. & B. 1054; *Hitchman* v. *Watt* (1894) 58 J.P. 720; *cf. Spice* v. *Peacock* (1875) 39 J.P. 581.

[20] *Mercer* v. *Woodgate* (1869) L.R. 5 Q.B. 26; *Arnold* v. *Blaker* (1871) L.R. 6 Q.B. 433; *cf. Brackenborough* v. *Thorsby* (1869) 19 L.T. 692; *Harrison* v. *Danby* (1870) 34 J.P. 759.

[21] See *Davies* v. *Stephens* (1836) 7 C. & P. 570; *Nicol* v. *Beaumont* (1883) 53 L.J. Ch. 853.

market rights.[22] Where there is an existing private road, dedication of that road as a highway may be subject to that private right.[23] This may have two consequences. Where the private right and the highway rights are of the same nature, the main consequence will be that if the highway should become extinguished the private right will remain unaffected.[24] Where the private right is greater than the public right, then potentially inconsistent rights may exist over the same way. In any case, the person entitled to the private right may enforce his private remedies which are not affected by the existence of the public right of way.[25]

The reservation of private rights and the dedication of highways sub- **2–43** ject to restrictions has always to be judged against the requirement that the rights created should be capable of being in the nature of a public highway. Where an alleged reservation is such that one of those essential attributes of a highway is removed, then the courts have to assess whether the dominant intention was to create a highway, so that the reservation, to the extent that it is inconsistent, is ineffective, or whether the reservation itself belies the existence of any intention to dedicate at all. The former approach is more likely to arise in the cases of implied or presumed dedication.[26] Examples of the latter approach are found in a number of cases.[27] Where the evidence indicates clearly both the existence of a highway and the reservation by the landowner of private rights, the courts may construe the extent of those private rights in such a way as not to conflict with normal highway use. Thus in *Nicol v. Beaumont*,[28] the right claimed by the landowner to cut grips and trenches in the verge of a country road was held to be restricted to a right to make only such grips and trenches as were necessary for the drainage of the road and which did not constitute a danger to the users of the way.

Physical extent of dedication

Unless an express dedication has taken place which, in terms, defines **2–44** the width of the way in question, it may be difficult to establish precisely what is its full physical extent. Generally, this will be a question of fact to be proved by evidence of the extent of public user.[29] Where the way is defined on the ground by a well-worn track, and where no other

---

[22] *Lawrence* v. *Hitch* (1868) L.R. 3 Q.B. 521; *Att.-Gen.* v. *Horner* (1885) 11 App.Cas. 66; *Stepney Corpn.* v. *Gingell, Son & Foskett Ltd.* [1909] A.C. 245; *Gloucestershire C.C.* v. *Farrow* [1985] 1 W.L.R. 741.
[23] *Brownlow* v. *Tomlinson* (1840) 1 Man. & G. 484; *Duncan* v. *Louch* (1845) 6 Q.B. 904.
[24] See *Walsh* v. *Oates* [1953] 1 Q.B. 578; *Wells* v. *Tilbury & Southend Ry. Co.* (1877) 5 Ch.D. 126.
[25] *Allen* v. *Ormond* (1806) 8 East 4; *Brownlow* v. *Tomlinson*, n. 23 above.
[26] See *R.* v. *Charlesworth* (1851) 16 Q.B. 1012.
[27] See *R.* v. *Chorley* (1848) 12 Q.B. 515; *Austerberry* v. *Oldham Corpn.* (1885) 29 Ch.D. 750; *Midland Ry. Co.* v. *Watton* (1886) 17 Q.B.D. 30.
[28] (1883) 53 L.J. Ch. 853 (a private right of way).
[29] *R.* v. *Johnson* (1859) 1 F. & F. 657; *Easton* v. *Richmond Highway Board* (1871) L.R. 7 Q.B. 69.

boundaries are apparent, it will be presumed that the track defines the extent of the way.[30] Where a metalled road has been laid out, this may be taken to indicate the width of the public right, despite the existence of fences beyond the limits of the metalled area.[31] More commonly it has been accepted that a road may often consist of both a metalled portion and a part that is left unmetalled, for example, a verge which is nonetheless part of the highway.[32]

Significance of hedges and ditches

2–45   Unless the fence or hedge is shown to have been established by reference to some factor other than the existence of the highway, it will be presumed that all the enclosed area between the fences or hedges was intended to form part of the highway.[33] The assumption is that the fence was constructed or the hedge grown in order to separate the adjoining land from the highway.[34] Some of the cases suggest that it is sufficient simply to prove the fact of the existence of the hedges in order to raise the presumption.[35] However, the circumstances may dictate against the presumption arising.[36]

2–46   Once the presumption is raised, it may be rebutted by other evidence showing that the fences or hedges were constructed or grown for reasons unconnected with the highway,[37] or by evidence of acts of ownership by the landowner.[38] Acts of the landowner inconsistent with the dedication of the roadside strips must date from sufficiently early a time to have prevented the extension of the way up to the physical limits created by the fence or hedge.[39] Proof that roadside strips were entered in the rolls of the manor as being part of the waste of that manor has been regarded as a relevant factor in rebutting the presumption.[40] Other relevant factors may include the nature of the district in which the highway is situated (for example the existence commonly of private strips alongside

---

[30] *Evans* v. *Oakley & Phillips* (1843) 1 Car. & Kirk. 125; *Easton* v. *Richmond Highway Board*, n. 29 above.

[31] *Belmore (Countess)* v. *Kent C.C.* [1901] 1 Ch. 873; *cf. Rowley* v. *Tottenham U.D.C.* [1914] A.C. 95.

[32] See *Easton* v. *Richmond Highway Board*, n. 29 above.

[33] *Loveridge* v. *Hodsoll* (1831) 2 B. & Ad. 602; *R.* v. *United Kingdom Electric Telegraph Co. Ltd.* (1862) 3 F. & F. 73; *Locke-King* v. *Woking U.D.C.* (1897) 77 L.T. 790; *Harvey* v. *Truro R.C.* [1903] 2 Ch. 638; *Att.-Gen.* v. *Beynon* [1970] 1 Ch. 1.

[34] See, *per* Vaughan Williams L.J., in *Neeld* v. *Hendon U.D.C.* (1889) 81 L.T. 405.

[35] See *R.* v. *United Kingdom Electric Telegraph Co. Ltd.*, n. 33 above; *Locke-King* v. *Woking U.D.C.*, n. 33 above; *Att.-Gen. & Croydon R.D.C.* v. *Moorsom Roberts* (1908) 72 J.P. 123; but see *Offin* v. *Rochford R.C.* [1906] 1 Ch. 342.

[36] *Hinds & Diplock* v. *Breconshire C.C.* [1938] 4 All E.R. 24.

[37] *Att.-Gen. & Croydon R.D.C.* v. *Moorsom Roberts*, n. 33 above.

[38] See *Neeld* v. *Hendon U.D.C.* (1899) 81 L.T. 405; *Belmore (Countess)* v. *Kent C.C.* [1901] 1 Ch. 873.

[39] *Harvey* v. *Truro R.C.* [1903] 2 Ch. 638; *Offin* v. *Rochford R.C.* [1906] 1 Ch. 342; *Coats* v. *Hertfordshire C.C.* [1909] 2 Ch. 579; *East* v. *Berkshire C.C.* (1912) 106 L.T. 65; *Att.-Gen.* v. *Beynon* [1970] 1 Ch. 1.

[40] *Friern Barnet U.D.C.* v. *Richardson* (1898) 62 J.P. 547; *cf. Locke-King* v. *Woking U.D.C.* (1897) 77 L.T. 790.

highways within the area), the nature of the surrounding ground, the regularity of the fences and the width and regularity of the margins.[41] The fact that the roadside strips have at all times been impassable may be sufficient to rebut the presumption,[42] but not the fact that the strips have simply fallen into disuse and have become overgrown.[43] The acts of a highway authority in making up the roadside waste will be of significance, both as a recognition of the extent of the highway and because of the acquiescence of the landowner in the highway authority's acts. The presumption may apply even where the highway is bounded only on one side by the fence,[44] but not where a public right of way less than a carriageway exists over a private occupation road.[45]

Ditches, on the other hand, give rise to an entirely different presump- **2–47** tion. A ditch is not part of an area over which the public can pass and repass. Rather it is an obstacle to passage. The initial presumption is, therefore, that a ditch is not part of the highway but rather that it belongs to the adjoining landowner whose land it no doubt drains.[46] This presumption may be rebutted by evidence that the ditch was constructed to drain the highway or was incorporated within the original dedication.[47]

Evidence and proof of dedication

Generally, the burden of proof is on the person who asserts the exis- **2–48** tence of a highway.[48] Even where the presumption in section 31 of the Highways Act 1980 applies, there is an initial burden of proof involved in satisfying a court that the way in question has been used by the public for the required period. As can be seen from the earlier discussion, during the course of a case the burden of proof may shift to the landowner—either where the presumption applies or where the width of a highway bounded by fences is in issue.[49]

One of the problems facing the practitioner lies in discovering what **2–49** documentary evidence there may be as to the existence of a particular highway, the extent to which that evidence is admissible and the weight likely to be given to it by a court. The courts have, in fact, adopted a flexible approach as to the nature of the evidence which is admissible to

---

[41] See *Belmore (Countess)* v. *Kent C.C.*, n. 38 above; *Harvey* v. *Truro R.C.* [1903] 1 Ch. 638; *Att.-Gen.* v. *Beynon* [1970] 1 Ch. 1.

[42] *Evans* v. *Oakley & Phillips* (1843) 1 Car. & Kir. 125.

[43] *Turner* v. *Ringwood Highway Board* (1870) L.R. 9 Eq. 418.

[44] See *Evelyn* v. *Mirrielees* (1900) 17 T.L.R. 152.

[45] *Ford* v. *Harrow U.D.C.* (1903) 88 L.T. 394.

[46] See *Simcox* v. *Yardley R.D.C.* (1905) 69 J.P. 66; *Chippendale* v. *Pontefract R.D.C.* (1907) 71 J.P. 231; *Chorley Corpn.* v. *Nightingale* [1907] 2 K.B. 637; *Hanscombe* v. *Bedfordshire C.C.* [1938] 1 Ch. 544.

[47] See *Chorley Corpn.* v. *Nightingale*, n. 46 above.

[48] See *Folkestone Corpn.* v. *Brockman* [1914] A.C. 338; *contra* the burden of proving that an admitted highway is not maintainable at the public expense, see Chap. 4.

[49] As to the practical problems raised by the shifting of the burden of proof by reliance upon a presumption, see *Folkestone Corpn.* v. *Brockman* [1914] A.C. 338 at 354–5, *per* Lord Kinnear.

prove a right of way. Section 32 of the Highways Act 1980 requires that any court or other tribunal:

> "before determining whether a way has or has not been dedicated, or the date on which such dedication, if any, took place, shall take into consideration any map, plan or history of the locality or other relevant document which is tendered in evidence . . . "

This section, which was first contained in section 3 of the Rights of Way Act 1932, is, in any event, declaratory of the common law.[50] The weight to be given to any of these kinds of documents is also touched on by section 32, which continues:

> "and shall give such weight thereto as the court or other tribunal considers justified by the circumstances, including the antiquity of the tendered document, the status of the person by whom and the purpose for which it was made or compiled, and the custody in which it has been kept and from which it is produced."

The various types of document referred to in the section require separate consideration.

2–50 There are a number of sources of maps which may be of assistance to the practitioner in preparing evidence as to the existence of a highway at a particular time. It should be noted, however, that the majority of these sources will only provide evidence as to the existence on the ground of a road or path as a physical feature, and will not be evidence of the status of that road or path. Some kinds of map may purport to deal with status.

The definitive map

2–51 County councils are required by the provisions of the Wildlife and Countryside Act 1981 to maintain and keep under review maps recording the existence of all public paths within their area. These maps, which record the paths as falling into one of three categories (by-ways open to all traffic, bridleways, or footpaths) will be conclusive evidence of the existence of specified minimum highway rights over a given line. They are not, however, conclusive as to the full extent of any such highway rights.[51]

Inclosure plans

2–52 These plans, when read together with the relevant Inclosure Act and the awards made thereunder,[52] may record roads set out by the Inclosure Commissioners which were to be maintained as public highways.

---

[50] See *Webb* v. *Eastleigh B.C.* (1957) 56 L.G.R. 124.
[51] See Wildlife and Countryside Act 1981, s.56, overruling the effect of the decision of the House of Lords in *Suffolk* v. *Mason* [1979] A.C. 7005. See Chap. 12.
[52] See *R.* v. *Cottingham* (*Inhabitants*) (1794) 6 Term Rep. 20; *R.* v. *Wright* (1832) 2 B. & Ad. 681.

This will not be conclusive as to the status of the road, and must be seen in the light of evidence showing both that a road was in fact laid out in accordance with the award and that the road was subsequently accepted by the public.[53] The plans may also show other roads already in existence.[54]

Ordnance survey maps

It is well established that these maps are not evidence of the status of **2–53** a road but only of what the surveyor found on the ground.[55] They are, nonetheless, very useful in showing the existence of a road at a particular date and perhaps even more useful in showing the non-existence of a road at that date. Ordnance Survey maps became very much more accurate after the passing of the Ordnance Survey Act 1841, under which, the appointed surveyors were granted important powers to enter onto private property.[56] The series of one inch ordnance maps published soon after the passing of the Act is often of importance when the existence of an ancient highway is in dispute—since this series is often the first detailed map available at such a scale, and may show established roads in existence shortly after the passing of the Highway Act 1835.

Tithe maps

Tithe maps have been held to be admissible in evidence to prove the **2–54** existence of a road, but again they are not evidence as to the status of the road thereby recorded.[57] Roads were not tithable and since tithe maps were prepared under the authority of Act of Parliament by Commissioners who had the power to take evidence on oath, the inclusion of a road on, or the omission of a road from, the map was a material matter to a landowner over whose land a road might pass. The assertion by the landowner of the existence of a road—which would have exempted the part of his land from tithe—would be strong evidence of his acceptance of the existence of a defined way across his land. Equally, his failure to assert the existence of any road might be regarded as significant evidence at least that he did not recognise the existence of a highway over his land at that time.

---

[53] See *R.* v. *Wright*, n. 52 above.
[54] See *R.* v. *Berger* [1894] 1 Q.B. 823.
[55] See *Att.-Gen.* v. *Antrobus* [1905] 2 Ch. 188; *Moser* v. *Ambleside U.D.C.* (1925) 89 J.P. 118; *Att.-Gen.* v. *Meyrick and Jones* (1915) 79 J.P. 515; *Att.-Gen. and Croydon D.C.* v. *Moorsom Roberts* (1908) 72 J.P. 123.
[56] See J.B. Harley and C.W. Phillips, *The Historian's Guide to Ordnance Survey Maps* (1964), reprinted from *The Amateur Historian*, published for the Standing Conference for Local History by the National Council of Social Service; and J.B. Harley, *Ordnance Survey Maps: A Descriptive Manual* (1975).
[57] *Att.-Gen.* v. *Antrobus* [1905] 2 Ch. 188; *Copestake* v. *West Sussex C.C.* (1911) 2 Ch. 331; *Stoney* v. *Eastbourne R.D.C.* [1927] 1 Ch. 367; *Att.-Gen.* v. *Stokesley R.D.C.* (1928) 26 L.G.R. 440; *Att.-Gen.* v. *Beynon* [1970] 1 Ch. 1.

Other map makers

2–55　　There are a number of county maps, prepared by private surveyors for publication, which may be useful evidence as to whether a road or path existed at a given date. It is often on these map makers that reliance must be placed in order to show that, prior to 1836, a particular road had been created, so as to be an ancient highway. Again, these maps are not evidence of status and they are of vastly differing reliability. It is not the place of this work to analyse the accuracy of the many and varied county map makers.[58] The county archivist may be able to assist as to the relative reliability of particular map makers for a particular county. So far as other local maps are concerned the court will have regard to the custody from which the map is produced, the position and status of the map maker and the purpose for which the map was made.[59] Subject, therefore, to these provisos, the deeds of private property,[60] railway maps,[61] coal mining maps and manorial maps[62] may all deserve investigation.

2–56　　Other relevant evidence may depend upon evidence from persons expert in the local history of the area. It will often be of considerable importance to ascertain why a highway should have become established in a given location at a particular time. Evidence relating to the existence of a church, hamlet, mill, mine, or other industrial enterprise may establish reasons for public user at a particular period.[63] Topographical features may also be relevant. However, it is now established that the fact that a highway does not lead anywhere (*i.e.* a cul-de-sac) is not conclusive as to the non-existence of a highway at that location—even in the countryside—although it may still be relevant evidence.[64] The user of the immediately contiguous land and the ownership on each side over the length of the claimed highway may also be of significance.[65] Evidence of local residents as to the past user of a way and as to its reputation may also be admissible.[66] Specifically, the report and estimate of a deceased surveyor made in the course of his duty has been held to be

[58] At any trial of such an issue, expert evidence as to the significance of any map may be required. Useful guides to the subject include R.V. Tooley, *Maps and Map-Makers*, J.B. Harley, *Maps for the Local Historian* (1972), reprinted from *The Local Historian*, published for the Standing Conference for Local History by the National Council of Social Service.

[59] *Pollard* v. *Scott* (1790) Peake 26, N.P.; *R.* v. *Chorley* (1848) 12 Q.B. 515; *Pipe* v. *Fulcher* (1858) 1 E. & E. 111; *Vyner* v. *Wirral R.D.C.* (1909) 73 J.P. 242; *R.* v. *Norfolk C.C.* (1910) 26 T.L.R. 269; *Att.-Gen.* v. *Horner* (*No. 2*) [1913] 2 Ch. 140.

[60] See *R.* v. *Chorley*, n. 59 above; *Mildred* v. *Weaver* (1862) 3 F. & F. 30.

[61] *Att.-Gen.* v. *Antrobus* [1905] 2 Ch. 188.

[62] See *Pipe* v. *Fulcher*, n. 59 above.

[63] See *Att.-Gen.* v. *Antrobus*, n. 61 above; *Macpherson* v. *Scottish Rights of Way & Recreation Society* (1888) 13 App.Cas. 744.

[64] *Att.-Gen.* v. *Antrobus*, n. 61 above; *Williams Ellis* v. *Cobb* [1935] 1 K.B. 310; *Roberts* v. *Webster* (1967) 66 L.G.R. 298.

[65] *Coats* v. *Hertfordshire C.C.* [1909] 2 Ch. 579.

[66] *Crease* v. *Barrett* (1835) 1 Cr. M. & R. 919.

admissible.[67] Evidence of the indictment of a township for non-repair of a highway and of a person for obstruction of a highway have been held to be admissible.[68] In the High Court and county court, the admissibility of documentary evidence to prove the existence or non-existence of a highway will be affected by the Civil Evidence Act 1968, sections 4, 5, 9 and 11.

Proceedings to establish whether a highway does or does not exist **2–57** may be commenced by an action for a declaration in the High Court. A declaration may also be obtained from the county court, either in its own right as being in relation to land, or as ancillary to other proceedings within the jurisdiction of that court.[69] The issue may, therefore, arise as part of proceedings for trespass, public nuisance or even negligence. Where the issue is whether a highway is an ancient highway, or is otherwise repairable at the public expense, the issue may be determined by the magistrates (with an appeal to the Crown Court) when it arises in the context of the street works code, or by the Crown Court by means of an application under section 56 of the Highways Act 1980.[70]

[67] *North Staffordshire Ry. Co.* v. *Hanley Corpn.* (1909) 73 J.P. 477.
[68] *R.* v. *Brightside Bierlow* (*Inhabitants*) (1849) 13 Q.B. 933; *Petrie* v. *Nuttall* (1856) 11 Exch. 569.
[69] See *The County Court Practice* (1988).
[70] See Chap. 4.

CHAPTER 3

RIGHTS OF THE HIGHWAY AUTHORITY AND OF
ADJOINING LANDOWNERS IN, UNDER AND OVER THE
HIGHWAY

INTRODUCTION

The various interests which may be involved

3–01   When land is dedicated to the public as a highway, the public acquire
only the right of passage along the highway. There has been discussion
in Chapter 1 as to the nature of this public right. Whether or not the
public right is properly to be regarded as an easement, it is a right *over*
the land rather than a right *in* the land. Where the highway is not maintainable at the public expense, the landowner retains his interest in the
land which he then holds subject to the rights of the public to pass over
it. His right to deal with the land as he would wish is restricted only by
his duty not to interfere with the passage of the public over the land. He
may not obstruct the highway. He may be restricted in his activities on
adjacent land.[1] Furthermore, once the land has been dedicated as a
highway, it will remain as such until the highway is extinguished by legal
process. It cannot be extinguished by agreement, by abandonment, or
by estoppel. The dedication of a highway, therefore, imposes a substantial burden on the land which carries the highway.

3–02   Many highways are maintainable at the public expense by the highway authority.[2] When a highway becomes maintainable at the public
expense, a part of the land then becomes vested in the highway authority. The highway authority's interest in the land in this case is a limited
interest for specific purposes—the protection and the maintenance of
the highway. It is limited in duration and in extent. The landowner will
retain an interest in the subsoil and he will be entitled to resume his full
interest in the land when the highway ceases to exist.[3] In some
instances, however, land is acquired, either compulsorily or by agreement, for the construction or improvement of the highway. In such a
case the highway authority will, subject to the terms of the agreement or
compulsory purchase order, acquire the full legal interest in the land
carrying the highway.

3–03   A consideration of the different interests of the highway authority and
of the landowner adjoining the highway is sometimes necessary in order
to establish whether the highway authority is acting within its powers or

---

[1] These matters are dealt with in Chaps. 7 and 8.
[2] The circumstances in which highways become maintainable at the public expense are
dealt with in Chap. 4.
[3] *i.e* by legal extinguishment: see Chap. 9.

whether the adjoining landowner is entitled to take action affecting the highway. To some extent, the relationship between the different interests is regulated by the powers of the highway authority relating to public nuisances and other kinds of interference with the highway.[4] In two respects the courts have recently had to consider the extent to which highway authorities can have rights in relation to, and be under obligations in respect of, their ownership of and control over the surface of the highway. Highway authorities have been held liable for nuisances caused by the incursion of tree roots[5] onto adjoining property and have been held entitled to apply for and to obtain summary orders for possession of the highway against squatters.[6]

Even where the highway has become vested in the highway authority,   **3–04** and during the continued existence of the highway, the adjoining landowners will have certain rights in relation to the highway. They will have the right of access onto the highway from any part of their land, although this right is now circumscribed very largely by planning control. They will have the right to connect their private services to the public services in the street, and, subject to statutory control, to break open the street in order to make and to maintain those connections.

Legal Interest of the Highway Authority

At common law

All highways which were in existence prior to the passing of the High-   **3–05** way Act 1835 were maintainable by some body or person. Prima facie the parish would be responsible for repair unless they could prove that some other person or body had repaired the road by reason of tenure of land, by prescription, or by virtue of enclosure of land.[7] However, while the common law enforced the duty of the parish to repair, the question as to whether any legal interest in the highway had passed to the parish did not arise. The obligation to repair fell upon the inhabitants at large of the parish and such an unincorporated body of persons could not hold any interest in land. However, in their consideration of the extent of the rights of the landowner, as against the rights of the public to travel over the land, the courts appear to have taken the view that the landowner's ownership remained intact subject only to the right of passage of the public. Thus, in *Goodtitle d. Chester* v. *Alker*,[8] Foster J. was able to say[9]:

> "The owner of the soil has a right to all above and under ground, except only the right of passage, for the King and his people."

[4] These powers are considered in Chaps. 7 and 8.
[5] *Russell* v. *Barnet L.B.C.* (1985) 83 L.G.R. 152.
[6] *Wiltshire C.C.* v. *Frazer* (1984) 82 L.G.R. 313.
[7] See Chap. 4.
[8] (1757) 1 Burr. 133.
[9] *Ibid.* at 146.

It was left to statute, therefore, to create an interest in land which was to be held by the body on whom the duty to repair had fallen.

3–06   The Highway Act 1835[10] stated that the scrapings of the highways should be vested in the surveyor of highways. There was no definition of the word "scrapings" but it may perhaps be assumed that it was intended to refer to the materials comprising the surface of the highway and which the parish had, pursuant to its duty of repair, from time to time laid on the highway. The Public Health Act 1848[11] was the first statute to provide for the vesting in urban authorities of all streets "being or which at any time become highways repairable by the inhabitants at large within any urban district." Subsequently, all highways maintainable at the public expense became vested in the highway authority responsible for their maintenance.[12]

Under the Highways Act 1980

3–07   By section 263(1) of the Highways Act 1980 it is provided that:

> "every highway maintainable at the public expense, together with the materials and scrapings thereof, vests in the authority who are for the time being the highway authority for the highway."

There is, however, no further statutory definition of the extent of the highway authority's interest, nor even of the highway itself.[13] It is to judicial decisions that we must look in order to understand the precise extent and the legal nature of the highway authority's interest.

Physical extent of the interest

3–08   When the courts were first called upon to analyse the nature of the interest vested by statute in the highway authority, they found themselves dealing with an unusual species of property right. The interest was created by statute and appeared to take away, without compensation, part of the interest of the landowner which had previously been regarded as being intact—subject only to highway rights over it. The courts were likely, therefore, to take a narrow view of the extent of the highway authority's acquired interest. In *Coverdale* v. *Charlton*,[14] the court had to consider the physical extent of the highway authority's interest. The issue in the case was whether the highway authority had the right to let out the pasturage on a highway which fell within the defi-

---

[10] s.41.
[11] s.68.
[12] See also Metropolis Management Act 1855, s.312; Public Health Act 1875, ss.6, 144 and 149; Local Government Act 1888, s.34; Development and Road Improvement Funds Act 1909, s.9; Local Government Act 1929, ss.29(2), 32(1) and 34; Trunk Roads Act 1936, s.7.
[13] Highways Act 1980, s.328 does provide a partial definition of the word "highway" but this is not helpful in this context.
[14] (1878) 4 Q.B.D. 104.

nition of "street" within the Public Health Act 1875. Bramwell L.J.[15] said:

" 'street' comprehends what we may call the surface, that is to say, not a surface bit of no reasonable thickness, but a surface of such a thickness as the local board may require for the purpose of doing to the street that which is necessary for it as a street, and also of doing those things which commonly are done in or under the streets; and to that extent they had property in it."

The court went on to relate the depth of the interest to the nature of the powers of the urban authority with regard to the highway.

The exact depth to which the interest of the highway authority **3–09** extends remains necessarily imprecise. Maintenance needs may differ according to the changes in traffic and improvements of engineering design. The nature of the supporting land for the highway may also affect the depth to which the highway authority's responsibilities extend. Eve J., in *Schweder* v. *Worthing Gas Light and Coke Company* (*No. 2*),[16] commented:

"How much of the subsoil is necessarily dedicated for this purpose is a matter of evidence in each case. It may be that the subsoil is of such a nature that only a very shallow stratum is required for the maintenance of the surface as a road; on the other hand it may be that the character of the subsoil renders a much thicker stratum necessary."

In *Tithe Redemption Commissioners* v. *Runcorn Urban District Council*,[17] Lord Denning M.R. said[18]: "The statute of 1929 vested in the local authority the top spit, or perhaps, I should say the top two spits, of the road. . . . "

Whether the depth of the interest extended to that required for the laying of sewers was doubted in *Tunbridge Wells Corporation* v. *Baird*.[19] The depth of two feet at which an electric lighting company had laid its pipes and wires was held to go beyond the interest of the highway authority in *Battersea Vestry* v. *County of London & Brush Provincial Electric Lighting Company*.[20]

Mineral rights under the highway

The right of the adjoining landowner to minerals under the highway is **3–10** not affected by the vesting of the highway in the authority. After the decision in *Coverdale* v. *Charlton*,[21] this was expressly recognised in the

---

[15] *Coverdale* v. *Charlton* (1878) 4 Q.B.D. 104 at 118.
[16] [1913] 1 Ch. 118.
[17] [1954] 1 Ch. 383.
[18] At 407; see also Local Government Act 1929, s.29.
[19] [1896] A.C. 434.
[20] [1899] 1 Ch. 474.
[21] (1878) 4 Q.B.D. 104.

Highways and Locomotives (Amendment) Act 1878,[22] but it may be the case that statutory undertakers have the right to support for their apparatus laid under the highway pursuant to statutory powers, thereby imposing a limitation on the landowner's ability to deal with his interest in his land.[23] Removal of support for the highway, causing damage to the highway, will also be actionable by the highway authority.[24]

Sewers, pipes and cables

3–11   The highway authority does not itself have power to authorise the laying of pipes or cables in the sub-soil by other bodies[25]; the authorities and statutory undertakers who have these powers are given express power to lay their apparatus in the highway.[26] The highway authority may, however, need to lay drains in the highway or to culvert streams under a highway. The extent of the highway authority's interest will be sufficient for these purposes because they are necessary for the functions of maintaining and protecting the highway. The authority may, however, have a limited power at common law to authorise and licence the opening of a highway[27] where the interference with the highway surface is confined to that part of the highway within its ownership and where the interference is such that no nuisance is caused.[28] In the case of bridges it appears that a distinction may have to be drawn in some cases between the soil and pavement of the highway crossing the bridge and the structure of the bridge itself. It has been held that water pipes could not be suspended under a bridge pursuant to powers contained in the Waterworks Clauses Act 1847.[29]

Subways, public conveniences and structures under the highway

3–12   Express power is given by the Highways Act 1980[30] to highway authorities to construct subways under highways. The consent of the adjoining landowner will not be required for the exercise of this power. However, the power will be construed narrowly and may not be used to construct an underground public convenience with approaches from either side of the street.[31] Local authorities also have power under the

---

[22] The inclusion of this provision perhaps indicates the uncertainty then felt about the extent of the highway authority's interest following that decision. See now Highways Act 1980, s.302.

[23] *Normanton Gas Co.* v. *Pope & Pearson Ltd.* (1883) 52 L.J. Q.B. 629.

[24] *Benfieldside Local Board* v. *Consett Iron Co.* (1877) 3 Ex. D. 54.

[25] *Salt Union Ltd. and Droitwich Salt Co. Ltd.* v. *Harvey & Co.* (1897) 13 T.L.R. 297.

[26] See *e.g.* Public Health Act 1936, s.15; *Schweder* v. *Worthing Gas Light and Coke Co. (No. 2)* [1913] 1 Ch. 118; *Porter* v. *Ipswich Corpn.* [1932] 2 K.B. 145.

[27] *Edgeware Highway Board* v. *Harrow Gas Co.* (1874) L.R. 10 Q.B. 92; *cf. Att.-Gen.* v. *Barker* (1900) 83 L.T. 245; *Preston Corpn.* v. *Fullwood Local Board* (1885) 53 L.T. 718.

[28] For statutory powers in relation to the breaking open of highways, see Chap. 13.

[29] *Glasgow (Lord Provost)* v. *Glasgow and South Western Ry. Co.* [1895] A.C. 376. See also Chap. 11.

[30] s.69.

[31] *London and North Western Ry. Co.* v. *Westminster Corpn.* [1902] 1 Ch. 269.

Public Health Act 1936, section 87(1) to construct public conveniences "in proper and convenient situations," and the reference in subsection (2) to the necessity of obtaining the consent of the highway authority before providing any such convenience in or under a highway implies that the power extends to the provision of such conveniences under highways. However, in *Tunbridge Wells Corporation* v. *Baird*,[32] it was held that the highway authority's interest does extend sufficiently deep to enable the construction of public lavatories without the consent of the owner of the sub-soil. It appears, therefore, that it would be necessary to exercise compulsory purchase powers to acquire the sub-soil for this purpose.[33] The highway authority has no right to restrain the construction of a tunnel under a highway, so long as the tunnel is in the sub-soil and does not undermine the highway.[34]

Trees growing in the highway

The ownership of trees and herbage growing in the highway has raised **3–13** many problems. Trees may have been sown prior to the vesting of the highway in the authority, or subsequent to that vesting. They may have been planted by the highway authority itself, by the landowner, or they may be self-sown. The consequences of ownership have been somewhat reduced, in relation to the law of nuisance, by recent decisions by the courts on the question of who has control of the tree. Trees are dealt with separately later in this chapter.[35]

The air above the highway

The same basic rule applies to the air above a highway as it does to the **3–14** sub-soil beneath the highway. The interest of the highway authority is limited to that area which is required by it for the exercise of its powers and the performance of its statutory duties.[36]

Rights and responsibilities which flow from the ownership of the highway authority

Rights

At common law, the owner of the land subject to the highway would **3–15** have a remedy in trespass against anyone causing damage to the land (including the surface of the highway) and could maintain an action for ejectment.[37] When the surface of the highway is vested in the highway authority there seems to be no reason why similiar remedies should not

---

[32] [1896] A.C. 434.
[33] See *e.g.* Public Health Act 1936, s.306.
[34] *Poplar Corpn.* v. *Millwall Dock Co.* (1904) 68 J.P. 339.
[35] See paras. 3–35 *et seq.*, below.
[36] *Wandsworth Board of Works* v. *United Telephone Co.* (1884) 13 Q.B.D. 904; *Finchley Electric Lighting Co.* v. *Finchley Urban Council* [1903] 1 Ch. 437; *Bradford* v. *Eastbourne Corpn.* [1896] 2 Q.B. 205; *Kelly* v. *Barrett* [1924] 2 Ch. 379.
[37] *Goodtitle d. Chester* v. *Alker* (1757) 1 Burr. 133.

be available to that authority, although an action in public nuisance where obstruction or damage occurs would be the more appropriate remedy. It has recently been confirmed that the highway authority is entitled to possessory remedies in respect of the highway surface. In *Wiltshire County Council* v. *Frazer*,[38] it was held that the highway authority was entitled to possession of the surface of the highway so as to entitle it to obtain an order for possession under the summary procedure provided by Order 113 of the Rules of the Supreme Court. The highway authority has a sufficient interest in the surface of the highway to maintain an action in respect of any damage which is caused to the highway.[39] Provided that a public nuisance is not caused, and subject to statutory powers governing the breaking open of highways, the highway authority may be entitled to licence the breaking open of the highway surface.[40]

Responsibilities arising out of the authority's interest in the highway and its powers of control over the highway

3–16   It is now established that a highway authority may be liable for a private nuisance occurring to property adjoining a highway due to the presence of a tree growing within the highway boundary.[41] However, it would appear to follow that the highway authority has a sufficient interest and sufficient control over the surface of the highway and over the other furniture provided by the authority within the highway to be liable in nuisance for damage caused in other ways to adjoining occupiers. One example of this might be the escape of water from the highway or from highway drains.[42]

RIGHTS OF THE ADJOINING LANDOWNER

The presumption of ownership

3–17   The landowner who dedicates a highway over his land gives to the public only a right of passage over that land and retains all the other rights of ownership over that land which are not inconsistent with that right of passage. It was always accepted at common law that highways did not destroy the ownership of the landowner,[43] and this proposition continued to be applied to certain kinds of highways created under statutory powers.[44] Statutory powers of purchase were, however, given

---

[38] (1984) 82 L.G.R. 313.
[39] *Benfieldside Local Board* v. *Consett Iron Co.* (1877) 3 Ex.D. 54.
[40] See cases cited at n. 27 above.
[41] See paras. 3–35 *et seq.*, below.
[42] See *Milward* v. *Redditch Local Board of Health* (1873) 21 W.R. 429.
[43] *Goodtitle d. Chester* v. *Alker* (1757) 1 Burr. 133.
[44] *Davison* v. *Gill* (1800) 1 East 64 at 70; *Salisbury* v. *Great Northern Rail Co.* (1858) 5 C.B. (N.S.) 174.

to trustees under the Turnpike Acts and in some cases these trustees would acquire the whole interest of the land underlying the highway.[45]

The owners of land adjoining a highway are presumed in law to own **3–18** the subsoil of the highway up to the middle point of the road—*usque ad medium filum viae*. This is a rebuttable presumption of law, which may be displaced by actual evidence of ownership of the soil. The adjoining landowners are each presumed to have contributed a portion of their land to the formation of the highway but in a number of cases the presumption has been applied also to situations where this assumption could not really apply—for example, where a stream or a lake separated the adjoining land from the highway.[46] The presumption may perhaps be said to be a rule of convenience arising from the difficulties in establishing the ownership of the subsoil.[47] Many highways will have been created so far in the past that actual knowledge of the ownership of the subsoil will no longer exist. Where highways have arisen more recently, however, the presumption is nonetheless quite difficult to displace.

The presumption of ownership applies whether the land adjoining an **3–19** existing highway is enclosed or unenclosed.[48] The presumption generally applies to former Turnpike Roads as well as to highways established at common law,[49] although to some extent this depends upon the powers exercised by the turnpike commissioners. It has been doubted whether the presumption applies to grants from the Crown,[50] and there is some authority that it will not be applicable where the highway was set out under an inclosure award.[51] The reason for this latter exception is twofold. First, the presumption rests upon the supposition that the highway grew up across private land and that, where it ran along the boundaries of land in different ownerships, each owner contributed half of the land over which the right of way extended. This supposition could not apply where the highway was created for the first time by the inclosure award and where the land on either side of the new highway was specifically allotted to the new beneficiaries under the award. Secondly, the courts have held that in the absence of compensation granted to the lord of the manor for the loss of his rights in the soil, the ownership of the sub-soil will remain, by default, in him.[52] However, where the inclosure award expressly allotted land to the lord of the manor to compensate him for his rights of soil, it was held that the soil of roads set out under the award vested in the adjoining landowners.[53]

---

[45] *Northam Bridge and Roads Co.* v. *South Stoneham R.D.C.* (1907) 71 J.P. 345; *Conservators of River Lea Navigation* v. *Button* (1881) 6 App. Cas. 685.
[46] See *e.g. Frost* v. *Richardson* (1910) 103 L.T. 22.
[47] See, *per* Cockburn C.J., in *Holmes* v. *Bellingham* (1859) 7 C.B. (N.S.) 329 at 336.
[48] *Cooke* v. *Green* (1823) 11 Price 736; *Doe d. Pring* v. *Pearsey* (1827) 7 B. & C. 304.
[49] *Hodges* v. *Lawrance* (1854) 18 J.P. 347.
[50] *Mappin Bros.* v. *Liberty & Co. Ltd.* [1903] 1 Ch. 118.
[51] *R.* v. *Hatfield (Inhabitants)* (1835) 4 A. & E. 156; *R.* v. *Edmonton (Inhabitants)* (1831) 1 Moo. & R. 24.
[52] *Poole* v. *Huskinson* (1843) 11 M. & W. 827.
[53] *Neaverson* v. *Peterborough R.C.* [1901] 1 Ch. 22; *cf. Haigh* v. *West* [1893] 2 Q.B. 29.

Private occupation roads

3–20   There seems to be a similiar presumption in relation to private occupation roads.[54] In *Holmes* v. *Bellingham*,[55] it was pointed out that the same principles which led to the reliance on the presumption in the case of public roads applied also in the case of private roads. The presumption is rebuttable by acts of ownership and, therefore, evidence of user in the exercise of a claim of ownership may displace the presumption.[56]

Roadside waste

3–21   A strip of land between the highway and the enclosed land adjoining it will usually also belong to the owner of that land.[57] However, if that strip communicates with open commons or larger portions of land, the presumption may be rebutted or considerably reduced in its weight.[58] Evidence of acts of ownership over other similarly placed portions of waste within the same manor may also rebut the presumption.[59]

The rule applied to the conveyance of property

3–22   Conveyances of property adjoining the highway will usually be presumed to carry with them half of the highway. The expression "abutting on a highway" will not be construed as defining the land ownership as ending at the highway, but rather will be interpreted as including the right to the soil *usque ad medium filum viae*.[60] Even where the conveyance describes land as bounded by a way or river and where the land is described by reference to a plan and to land area, the presumption will not be rebutted.[61] This applies even where the measurements of the plan would exclude the road.[62]

Rebutting the presumption

3–23   The tenure of the surrounding land has not been regarded as significant in rebutting the presumption.[63] The presumption may apply to leaseholds.[64] The existence of a ditch at the side of the road or of land

---

[54] *Holmes* v. *Bellingham* (1859) 7 C.B. (N.S.) 329; *Smith* v. *Howden* (1863) 14 C.B. (N.S.) 398; see also *Russell* v. *Barnet L.B.C.* (1985) 83 L.G.R. 152, at 161; *cf. Leigh* v. *Jack* (1879) 5 Ex. D. 264.

[55] (1859) 7 C.B. (N.S.) 329.

[56] As to the position where the road is set out under an inclosure award, see the cases cited at n. 51 above.

[57] *Steel* v. *Prickett* (1819) 2 Stark. 463; *Doe d. Pring* v. *Pearsey* (1827) 7 B. & C. 304; *Scoones* v. *Morrell* (1839) 1 Beav. 251.

[58] *Grose* v. *West* (1816) 7 Taunt. 39; *Plumbley* v. *Lock* (1902) 67 J.P. 237; *cf. Dendy* v. *Simpson* (1861) 7 Jur. (N.S.) 1058.

[59] *Grose* v. *West* (1816) 7 Taunt. 39; *Doe d. Harrison* v. *Hampson* (1847) 4 C.B. 267; *Doe d. Barrett* v. *Kemp* (1831) 7 Bing. 332; (1835) 2 Bing. N.C. 102.

[60] *R.* v. *Strand Board of Works* (1864) 4 B. & S. 551; *London City Land Tax Commissioners* v. *Central London Ry. Co.* [1913] A.C. 364.

[61] *Micklethwait* v. *Newlay Bridge Co.* (1886) 33 Ch.D. 133.

[62] *Berridge* v. *Ward* (1861) 10 C.B. (N.S.) 400.

[63] *Doe d. Pring* v. *Pearsey* (1827) 7 B. & C. 304; *Steel* v. *Prickett* (1819) 2 Stark. 463; *Tilbury* v. *Silva* (1890) 45 Ch.D. 98.

[64] *Haynes* v. *King* [1893] 3 Ch. 439; *cf. Noye* v. *Reed* (1827) 1 Man. & Ry. K.B. 63.

covered in water has not of itself been regarded as sufficient rebuttal evidence.[65] Where the road was shown with a separate parcel number on the Ordnance Survey map and there was evidence that trees shown on the road were not included in the valuation of the property, this was held to be sufficient to rebut the presumption.[66]

Actual evidence of ownership will rebut the presumption, but owner- **3–24** ship often has to be proved from a series of inferences and not all of these are sufficiently strong in themselves to displace the presumption. Evidence of unequivocal acts of ownership may be sufficient. Where evidence suggests that the vendor of land owned more or less than half of the width of the highway, then the interest of the vendor in the subsoil as far as it was in fact vested in him will be presumed to pass.[67]

Application of the presumption in towns

Whether the presumption of ownership continues to have any rel- **3–25** evance in streets laid out in towns has from time to time been doubted.[68] The value of the presumption in the reality of the urban environment is questionable, and has been judicially described as "a wholly unrealistic fiction."[69] The decision which is usually cited as indicating judicial doubt over the extent of the presumption in towns is *Beckett* v. *Leeds Corporation.*[70] In that case the question arose whether the presumption applied to houses fronting Briggate in Leeds—described as a very wide street in which markets and fairs had formerly been held. James L.J. felt that this evidence suggested that this was not the usual case of houses built at the side of an ordinary highway[71]:

> "It appears to me that in such a case to presume that where the lord of the borough had allowed his dependent burgesses to have what is called a toft fronting towards the market-place and fair-place, which was also used as a road, and then by a grant enlarged the tenure of that toft into a fee simple tenure in borough English, the lord intended to grant, or that the tenant intended to take, half of the vacant space between the one row of tofts and the other row of tofts, would be to make a presumption inconsistent with common sense and inconsistent with the meaning which the common usage of mankind would apply to such a grant."

It appears that the width of the street and its usage for markets and fairs

---

[65] *Frost* v. *Richardson* (1910) 103 L.T. 22.
[66] *Pryor* v. *Petre* [1894] 2 Ch. 11; *Salisbury* v. *Great Northern Rail Co.* (1858) 5 C.B. (N.S.) 174.
[67] *Re Whites's Charities, Charity Commissioners* v. *Mayor of London* [1898] 1 Ch. 659.
[68] See *Beckett* v. *Leeds Corpn.* (1872) 7 Ch. App. 421; *Solloway* v. *Hants C.C.* (1980) (unrep.), *per* Stocker J.; *cf. Bridges* v. *Harrow L.B.C.* (1981) 260 E.G. 284; *Russell* v *Barnet L.B.C.* (1985) 83 L.G.R. 152.
[69] *Solloway* v. *Hants C.C.* (1980) (first instance) (unrep.), *per* Stocker J., quoted in *Russell* v. *Barnet L.B.C.* (1985) 83 L.G.R. 152 at 162.
[70] (1872) 7 Ch. App. 421.
[71] *Ibid.* at 425.

from which the lord had retained the profits were regarded as strong evidence rebutting the operation of the presumption. The existence of land, on which the fairs had been held, between the original road and the adjoining properties also seems to have been important. There was also other evidence of acts of ownership by the lord. On balance, therefore, it seems that *Beckett* can be seen as a particular example where the presumption was rebutted, rather than real indication that the presumption cannot apply within towns or cities.

3-26   The second decision which has sometimes been quoted as throwing doubt on the operation of the presumption in towns is *Leigh* v. *Jack*.[72] This case involved land adjoining an area of land laid out as an intended street, but which had not been dedicated to the public. Again the decision demonstrates only that on the evidence the presumption did not apply to the particular circumstances before the court. However, one factor influencing the court was that the owner of the land must have intended to retain ownership of the street if he intended to dedicate it to the public in the future, for otherwise he would, by conveying the street along with the adjoining land, be taking it out of his power to effect that dedication. This proposition, whilst having a logicial attraction, would seem to strike at the presumption in very many cases where estates are constructed and properties sold before there has been any formal dedication to the public of the street by the landowner. The operation of the presumption in relation to building estates or schemes has also been doubted in *Mappin Brothers* v. *Liberty & Company Ltd.*[73]

3-27   In *Re White's Charities, Charity Commissioners* v. *Mayor of London*,[74] Romer J. pointed out that if the rule were said not to apply to streets in towns, it was difficult to see where the exceptions to the rule would end:

> "Would a country town be excepted? Would a small town? Would a village? Would a hamlet? Where are you to stop? It seems to me that unless there are special circumstances connected with a particular town, the rule applies to streets in towns as it does to highways in the country."

In *Russell* v. *Barnet London Borough Council*,[75] Tudor Evans J. said of the presumption:

> "If I may say so, I agree that in many urban conditions, ownership of the sub-soil to the middle line is, in practical terms, of little or no value, at least in relation to highway authorities. Although theoretically the owners' rights are unaffected, in reality it is very difficult to conceive of circumstances in which rights in relation to a

[72] (1879) 5 Ex. D. 264.
[73] [1903] 1 Ch. 118.
[74] [1898] 1 Ch. 659; see also *Landrock* v. *Metropolitan District Ry. Co.* (1886) 3 T.L.R. 162.
[75] (1985) 83 L.G.R. 152.

tree growing in the highway and arising from the presumption of law can be exercised. It is really nothing more than ownership without rights. But I have not been referred to any authority which supports the observation of Stocker, J. that it has been doubted that the presumption is a valid proposition in urban surroundings. Mr O'Brien suggested that *Leigh* v. *Jack* (*supra*) is such an authority but that is not how I understand the case."

It would appear, therefore, that the balance of authority suggests that the presumption of ownership in half the highway applies in towns in the same way as elsewhere. However, the presumption is always rebuttable by actual evidence of ownership, and evidence of the actual intention of the developer may be more readily available where the road is laid out as part of an estate.

Rights arising out of the ownership of the soil

Rights in relation to the sub-soil

The landowner is entitled to deal with the subsoil of the highway as he **3–28** chooses, so long as he does not interfere with the public right of way along the highway. The balance of the rights of the landowner with the highway user were described in *St Mary, Newington, Vestry* v. *Jacobs*[76] in the following way:

"The owner, who dedicates to public use as a highway a portion of his land, parts with no other right than a right of passage to the public over the land so dedicated, and may exercise all other rights of ownership, not inconsistent therewith. . . . We do not deny that the owner cannot derogate from the grant of roadway made by him to the public, and cannot do anything which would really and substantially interfere with the right of passage by the public."

Thus, he may tunnel under a highway and extract minerals therefrom, provided that by so doing he does not remove support for the highway and does not interfere with apparatus lawfully laid in the highway by statutory undertakers.[77] However, in many instances his rights are now curtailed by statute. Cellars and vaults may not be constructed under, nor bridges, buildings, rails and beams constructed over, a highway without the consent of the highway authority.[78]

The adjoining landowner will be able to maintain an action in trespass **3–29** arising from, and may have the right to restrain, any interference with his rights to the sub-soil, even where, in practice, he cannot exercise

---

[76] (1871) L.R. Q.B. 47 at 53.

[77] *Cunliffe* v. *Whalley* (1851) 13 Beav. 411; *Normanton Gas Co.* v. *Pope & Pearson Ltd.* (1883) 52 L.J.Q.B. 629; *Walker U.D.C.* v. *Wigham, Richardson & Co. Ltd.* (1901) 85 L.T. 579; *Poplar Corpn.* v. *Millwall Dock Co.* (1904) 68 J.P. 339.

[78] Highways Act 1980, ss.176–9.

those rights himself.[79] Thus, in *Goodson* v. *Richardson*[80] an injunction was granted to a landowner to restrain the laying without statutory authority of water pipes under a highway, notwithstanding that his interest in the sub-soil was of little or no value.

The right to restrain acts going beyond the ordinary user of the highway

3–30   Since dedication of the highway is for the purposes of public passage, it is an interesting question whether use of the highway which goes beyond passage and re-passage constitutes a trespass to the ownership of the sub-soil owner. It seems that this could only be true where the surface of the highway has not become vested in the highway authority. In such cases the abuse of the public right of passage could only be a wrong against the person or body in control of the highway surface. In *Harrison* v. *Rutland (Duke)*[81] and *Hickman* v. *Maisey*,[82] acts which exceeded the ordinary and reasonable user of the highway were found to be trespasses to the owner of the sub-soil.[83]

3–31   It also appears that the owner of the sub-soil may be entitled to remove from the surface of the highway anything which is not justified by the public right of way, even if it is not a nuisance to the way.[84] However, the extent of this right is uncertain, and where a remedy is available in the courts in order to test the lawfulness of certain actions or activities, it is obviously wiser to pursue these remedies rather than self-help.

Rights of access to and from the highway

3–32   The right of the owner of land adjoining the highway to have access from any part of his land onto that highway was recognised at common law as a distinct private right separate from the general right of the public to use the highway.[85] This right is independent of the ownership of the sub-soil, and may be claimed by any adjoining landowner whether or not he is the presumptive owner of the sub-soil.[86] The right is not simply limited to the right of passage to and from the highway, but may include access from the highway to the walls of buildings adjoining the highway, for the purpose of repair or the placing of advertisements upon them.[87] Whilst this right of access is an independent private right, it appears that the right to unload goods from the highway across the pub-

---

[79] *Lade* v. *Shepherd* (1735) 2 Stra. 1004.
[80] (1874) 9 Ch. App. 221; see also *Salt Union Ltd.* v. *Harvey & Co.* (1897) 13 T.L.R. 297; *Marriott* v. *East Grinstread Gas & Water Co.* [1909] 1 Ch. 70.
[81] [1893] 1 Q.B. 142.
[82] [1900] 1 Q.B. 752; see also *R.* v. *Pratt* (1855) 4 E. & B. 860; *Mayhew* v. *Wardley* (1863) 14 C.B.N.S. 550; *cf. Randall* v. *Tarrant* [1955] 1 W.L.R. 225.
[83] See para. 1–06, above.
[84] *R.* v. *Mathias* (1861) 2 F. & F. 570.
[85] *Lyon* v. *Fishmongers' Co.* (1876) 1 App. Cas. 662; *Berridge* v. *Ward* (1860) 2 F. & F. 208, N.P.; *Att.-Gen.* v. *Thames Conservators* (1862) 1 Hem. & M. 1; *Marshall* v. *Ulleswater Steam Navigation Co.* (1871) L.R. 7 Q.B. 166.
[86] *Ramuz* v. *Southend Local Board* (1892) 67 L.T. 169.
[87] *Cobb* v. *Saxby* [1914] 3 K.B. 822.

lic pavement is part of the public right of user of the highway,[88] and must, therefore, be subject to the test of overall reasonableness in terms of duration and extent, in order to be lawful.[89]

The right of access to and from the highway may be exercised in a **3–33** manner which is required for the reasonable enjoyment of the land in question. In *St Mary, Newington, Vestry* v. *Jacobs*[90] it was held that a landowner had a defence to a prosecution brought against him, under the Metropolis Local Management Act, for causing damage to the pavement of a highway by crossing the pavement onto his land with heavy vehicles and machinery. The court found that the use of the crossing for this purpose was necessary for the reasonable enjoyment of the adjoining land, and that the landowner's rights of ownership could be exercised jointly with the general welfare, so that his rights prevailed over the statutory prohibition contained in the Act.[91] On the other hand there are a number of decisions which indicate that a highway authority exercising its powers of improvement of the highway may interfere with the right of access of a landowner from every part of his land, so long as the power is not exercised unreasonably.[92]

Where the right of access to and from the highway is obstructed by an **3–34** unreasonable use of the highway, the landowner may recover damages.[93] In some cases, where the access is obstructed by an authority exercising statutory powers, there may be a right to compensation under the provisions of the Public Health Act 1936, section 278.[94]

Highway trees

Introduction

Trees growing in highways or in highway land may have pre-dated the **3–35** dedication or the adoption of the highway. In the former case, the highway may have to be treated as being dedicated subject to the existing obstruction of the tree. In such a case it would appear logical that the highway authority, whilst having certain statutory powers to deal with the tree, could not require its removal as a common law obstruction to the highway. In the case where the tree has grown up in the highway after dedication but before adoption, it would seem that it constitutes a potential obstruction to the highway and may be removed as such. Trees, however, are often regarded as amenity features and highway authorities have had powers to plant trees in highways since 1890.[95] In

---

[88] *Chaplin (W.H.) & Co. Ltd.* v. *Westminster Corpn.* [1901] 2 Ch. 329.
[89] *Harper* v. *Haden & Sons Ltd.* [1933] 1 Ch. 298.
[90] (1871) L.R. Q.B. 47.
[91] See also *Rowley* v. *Tottenham U.D.C.* [1914] A.C. 95; *Marshall* v. *Blackpool Corpn.* [1935] A.C. 16.
[92] See para. 6–05, below.
[93] *Fritz* v. *Hobson* (1880) 14 Ch.D. 542.
[94] See *Pearsall* v. *Brierley Hill Local Board* (1883) 11 Q.B.D. 735; *Nutter* v. *Accrington Local Board of Health* (1874) 4 Q.B.D. 375; see also the cases cited at para. 7–42, below.
[95] See Public Health Acts Amendment Act 1890, s.43, now repealed.

some cases they may be planted in highway land but not within the highway itself. Trees may, however, present particular problems. The branches may cause an obstruction and a potential danger to the highway and its users. In recent years, the potential danger to the structure of houses from the incursion of roots undermining their foundations has been better appreciated. The particular problems involving highway trees have arisen from the division of responsibility between the highway authority and the adjoining landowner in respect of such trees. The tree may be in the ownership of the adjoining landowner—perhaps the same landowner whose house has suffered damage. However, the highway authority may have wide powers of control over the tree, whereas the rights of the adjoining landowner to enter onto the highway in order to take preventative or remedial action are not entirely clear.

The ownership of trees growing in the highway

3-36   At common law there was no real difficulty; trees and herbage in the highway belonged to the owner of the sub-soil.[96] Indeed, there was no other body in whom they could have vested. The owner of the sub-soil was entitled to the timber and fruits of the tree as he was entitled to other profits, over and under the land, which did not conflict with the right of the public to pass over the highway. However, the vesting of the surface of the highway and its materials in the highway authority gave rise to the question as to whether trees, or any part of a tree, growing through that surface, were carried with the highway when it vested in the authority. The courts have never satisfactorily settled the question of ownership in this case. They have been faced with the difficult problem of a tree with its roots in the sub-soil passing through and into the area which is clearly within the ownership of the highway authority, but extending to a height where it might well be argued that the landowner's interest revived. The courts have, therefore, tended to look at questions of control over the tree—including the question of who has the right to remove the tree.

3-37   In *Turner* v. *Ringwood Highway Board*,[97] the issue before the court was whether a highway board were entitled to cut down and remove for sale trees which had grown up in land allotted (but not in fact used) for highway purposes by commissioners under an Inclosure Act. The court held that the public were entitled to the whole width of the highway and not just to the *via trita*. The fact that trees had grown up did not extinguish the rights of the public over the full width of the road as awarded under the Inclosure Act. The public, through the Highway Board, were, therefore, entitled to remove the trees as a nuisance. The court found that the plaintiff had not in fact established his title to the

[96] 1 Rolle's Abridgement 392; *Goodtitle d. Chester* v. *Alker* (1757) 1 Burr. 133; *Turner* v. *Ringwood Highway Board* (1870) L.R. 9 Eq. 418; *Nicol* v. *Beaumont* (1884) 53 L.J. Ch. 853.
[97] (1870) L.R. 9 Eq. 418.

soil in which the trees were growing, and had not, in any event, sought to restrain the removal of the trees for sale. The issue of ownership of the trees was not, as a consequence directly attacked, although it appears that the court would have listened carefully to an argument that the landowner was entitled to restrain the sale of the trees.[98] This case, therefore, does not consider the position once the highway has vested in the highway authority or where the trees have predated the dedication of the highway.

In *Coverdale* v. *Charlton*,[99] the court was concerned with the right of **3–38** the Highway Board to let the pasturage on a public highway. It was held that the highway authority had the right and power, arising from their property in the surface of the highway created by the vesting clauses in the Public Health Acts 1848 and 1875, to let the pasturage. Brett L.J.,[1] after stating that the interest of the highway authority included the surface, "and so much of the depth as may be not unfairly used, as streets are used," concluded that:

> "If the enactment gives the local board that property in so much of the land, it gives them the absolute property in everything growing on the surface of the land. The legislature have, because the right of owners to the soil in a 'street' is of so little value, intentionally taken away that right and have given it to the extent I have mentioned to the local board."

Bramwell L.J. had been more cautious. After referring to the penalties imposed by statute for damage to the street, and to the trees within it, and to the right of the local board to compensation for damage to the street, he said[2]:

> "Does that mean that the local board have a property in the tree and in the soil? I doubt very much whether that ought to be the construction put upon that enactment, but if it is, it goes a long way to show that the local board had such a property as they claim in this herbage. Even if it does not, if it will not apply to the tree which although surrounded by the street could be said in one sense to be no part of it, for the public had no right to pass over where the tree stood; and if it does not apply to a tree now in existence, but only to the trees the local board may plant or become otherwise entitled to, why even then it would show that they must have some property in the soil and its produce . . . "

Bramwell L.J. also concluded that the interest of the authority in the surface of the highway was sufficient for the purposes of the issue before the court. It should perhaps be remembered that this decision related to

---

[98] *Turner* v. *Ringwood Highway Board* (1870) L.R. 9 Eq. 418 at 423.
[99] (1878) 4 Q.B.D. 104.
[1] *Ibid.* at 121.
[2] *Ibid.* at 117.

the right to pasturage, and that grass does not generally have deep roots. Nonetheless, *Coverdale* v. *Charlton* gives a wide meaning to the extent of the highway authority's interest, which interest has perhaps been regarded in subsequent cases as being rather more limited.

3–39   In *Stillwell* v. *New Windsor Corporation*,[3] the owner of land adjoining a highway sought an injunction to restrain the highway authority from removing trees growing between the footway and the carriageway of two highways. The highway authority had served notice on the plaintiff requiring her to remove the trees under the Highway Act 1835, section 64, alleging that the trees were a danger and an obstruction to the highway. Certain findings of fact were made. The trees were about 110 years old. They were found in some cases to be a serious hindrance to traffic using the highways, and in other cases to be an immediate or prospective source of danger to the public using the roads because of their diseased and decayed state. The highways in question had become repairable at the public expense in 1920. The trees were found to postdate the highway and to have been planted in ancient highways over which the public had the right of passage. The judge further assumed that the trees had been planted in the highway by the road authority with the consent of the owner of the soil, or alternatively by the owner with the leave or acquiescence of the highway authority. On these findings of fact the judge had no difficulty in concluding that the trees amounted prima facie to an obstruction of the highway and that the highway authority had not only the right but also the duty to remove them if they constituted a danger to users of the highway. However, the court was also asked to consider the question whether the plaintiff had any rights in the trees at all once the highway had been vested in the highway authority under the Public Health Act 1875. Clauson J. expressed a view on whether the highway authority had acquired rights in the trees themselves[4]:

> "In my view, for all the purposes of exercising the rights of the highway authority, these trees are to be treated as the highway authority's trees, and if they think it convenient to remove them it is proper that they should remove them. I am not called upon in this action to decide to whom the timber would belong when the trees were removed."

This statement is capable of more than one interpretation. On a narrow view it does no more than the judge had already achieved in determining that the authority had the right to remove the trees as obstructions. However, whilst this interpretation would suggest that the finding that the trees postdated the dedication of the highway no longer became crucial, and that the trees might have been removed in any event, such a conclusion is not inevitable. Trees planted before dedication might well

[3] [1932] 2 Ch. 155.
[4] *Ibid.* at 165.

have been excluded from the dedication and never become part of the street which vested in the highway authority in the first place. On a wider view, the judge appears to have decided that a right of property, rather than simply a right to take action to deal with obstructions arose in the highway authority, co-extensive with the right of property in the remainder of the street.[5]

3–40 Two approaches to the potential ownership of the highway authority in trees situated in the highway emerge from these cases. The one view is that the tree is a profit of the soil rather than a part of the street. Ownership will then be in the landowner or the highway authority, depending upon whether the interest of the highway authority is regarded as going sufficiently deep. The other view is that the tree vests with the remainder of the surface of the highway in the authority for so long as and to the extent that the authority exercises its powers in relation to the highway. In that sense it is part of the street but on severance should revert to the landowner. It may also follow that the ownership of the authority is not absolute and that it could not deal with the tree other than for highway purposes. The line between control and ownership becomes somewhat blurred when one looks at the approach of the courts towards highway trees, and for this reason it has been control which has figured more prominently in determining liability in respect of tree roots.

3–41 In *Russell* v. *Barnet London Borough Council*,[6] the issue was whether the highway authority might be liable in nuisance for the incursion of the roots of a highway tree onto adjoining land, causing subsidence. The trees in question were adjacent to the property which had suffered the damage, so that on the usual presumption of ownership *usque ad medium filum viae* it was argued that the highway authority had neither ownership nor control over the trees so as to render it liable in nuisance. The trees in question pre-dated the vesting of the street in the highway authority. Tudor Evans J. appreciated the differences in approach which might be needed to explain ownership in pre-dedication trees and post-dedication trees. The road had become dedicated by adoption in 1949, when the relevant statutory provision relating to the 'vesting' of the street was still section 149 of the Public Health Act 1875. Tudor Evans J. considered all the authorities and, after noting that *Stillwell* v. *New Windsor Corporation*[7] had been concerned with post-adoption trees,[8] he went on to consider the effect of the vesting provisions on pre-existing trees[9]:

---

[5] See, in particular, *Stillwell* v. *New Windsor Corpn.* [1932] 2 Ch. 155 at 165–166.
[6] (1985) 83 L.G.R. 152.
[7] [1932] 2 Ch. 155.
[8] By which he appears to have meant that the trees in that case had grown up in a pre-existing ancient highway rather than after the vesting of the highway under the Public Health Acts 1848 or 1875.
[9] At 167.

"The question whether pre-adoption trees fall within section 149 must turn upon the proper construction of the language of the section. There are two possible constructions: first, that what 'vests in' and is 'under the control' of the urban authority are the streets, all the other matters referred to in the first paragraph of the section "and other things provided for the purposes thereof" (that is, for the purposes of the street). . . . On this construction, following the decision in *Coverdale* v. *Charlton* (supra), unless the street can fairly be said to extend to the subsoil, any tree growing out of the subsoil would not be owned by the highway authority. . . . The second construction of section 149 is that Parliament provided that all trees in a street, once it was adopted, should be deemed to be part of the street and therefore owned by the highway authority: hence the penal and compensation clause, so worded that not even the presumed owner of the subsoil could exercise his right in relation to the tree without the permission of the highway authority. . . . "

Tudor Evans J. preferred the former interpretation and held that section 149 did not vest pre-adoption trees in the highway authority.[10] Such a construction was consistent with section 82 of the Highways Act 1959, which had, until its amendment by the Highways (Miscellaneous Provisions) Act 1961, limited control to trees planted by the highway authority. The judge pointed to the fact that the offence which earlier legislation had created, in relation to damage caused to a highway tree, was replaced in the Highways Act 1959 by a criminal offence limited by the words "without lawful authority or excuse." The use of these words implied a recognition of the rights of an owner in relation to a tree although the learned judge agreed that it was difficult in practice to envisage circumstances in which such a right could be exercised. His view of the ownership of the trees appears to have been intended to apply to pre-dedication and pre-adoption trees.

Powers of the highway authority in relation to trees

3–42   It appears from *Coverdale* v. *Charlton*[11] and *Stillwell* v. *New Windsor Corporation*,[12] that the rights which the highway authority has in relation to the highway give wide general powers of control over highway trees apart from ownership. These powers are, however, for the purpose of fulfilling their responsibilities as highway authority. Wherever a tree has become an obstruction to the highway, or a danger to highway users, it would appear that the highway authority would be entitled by virtue of its common law responsibilities to take steps to abate that nuisance by lopping the tree or by removing it. This would not necessarily be

[10] In *Solloway* v. *Hampshire C.C.* (1981) 79 L.G.R. 449. Stocker J., at first instance, (1980) (unrep.) appears to have taken the view that such trees did vest.
[11] (1878) 4 Q.B.D. 104.
[12] [1935] 2 Ch. 155.

the case where the tree pre-dated dedication and the highway was dedicated subject to the existing obstruction of the tree. Statute, however, has given highway authorities a number of specific powers in relation to trees.

Power to plant trees and shrubs in highways maintainable at the public expense is given to highway authorities in the Highways Act 1980, section 96(1). That section also gives power to: **3–43**

> "do anything expedient for the maintenance or protection of trees, shrubs and grass verges planted or laid out, whether or not by them, in such a highway."

Section 96(1) replaced the Highways Act 1959, section 82(1), which in turn had replaced the Public Health Acts Amendment Act 1907,[13] but that section had been amended by the Highways (Miscellaneous Provisions) Act 1961, adding the words "whether or not by them." It appears that until the 1961 Act was passed, the highway authority only had statutory power to take such steps in relation to trees planted by them under this section or its predecessors. By section 96(6) no tree, shrub, etc., may be planted under the section, or if planted under the section, be allowed to remain in such a situation as to hinder the reasonable use of the highway by any person entitled to use it, or so as to be a nuisance or injurious to the owner or occupier of premises adjacent to the highway. Where damage is caused to property of any person (other than that caused by his own negligence) through the exercise of powers under this section, compensation is payable. It appears from *Russell* v. *Barnet London Borough Council*[14] that subsection (6) applies, whether or not the trees were originally planted by the highway authority.

Where a hedge, tree or shrub overhangs a highway, or any other road or footpath to which the public have access, so as to endanger or obstruct the passage of vehicles or pedestrians, or obstructs or interferes with the view of drivers of vehicles or the light from a public lamp, a competent authority[15] may serve a notice on the owner of the tree or the occupier of the land on which it is growing requiring him within 14 days to lop or cut the tree so as to remove the danger, obstruction or interference. A similar notice may be served if the tree or shrub is dead, diseased, damaged or insecurely rooted and is likely to cause a danger by falling on the highway, road or footpath.[16] A more general power to deal with dangerous trees wherever they may be, is given to local authorities under the Local Government (Miscellaneous Provisions) Act 1976, section 23. **3–44**

---

[13] s.43; see also Roads Improvement Act 1925, s.1(1); Restriction of Ribbon Development Act 1935, s.13(4).
[14] (1985) 83 L.G.R. 152: see below.
[15] *i.e.* a highway authority or a district council.
[16] Highways Act 1980, s.154(2).

Liability for nuisance caused by highway trees

3–45   In *Russell* v. *Barnet London Borough Council*,[17] the question arose whether the powers of control of a highway authority were such as to give rise to liability for nuisance. The court held that the effect of the amendment of section 82 of the Highways Act 1959 by the Highways (Miscellaneous Provisions) Act 1961 was that highway authorities have the power to maintain all trees whether pre-adoption or post-adoption and are similarly prohibited from permitting them to become a nuisance. That power is sufficient to create the control over such trees which is necessary for the imposition of liability in nuisance. A similar view was taken at first instance in *Solloway* v. *Hampshire County Council*.[18] The fact that the tree might be owned by the landowner whose house had suffered damage did not alter the question of liability. It was unrealistic to consider that the owner of the tree could exercise any rights in relation to it even if he had lawful justification or excuse—which the judge doubted.

3–46   Liability for nuisance caused by the roots of highway trees will arise where the person responsible for the tree knew or ought to have known of the existence of the nuisance or danger caused by it. The duty of such a person is to take reasonable steps to prevent or minimise the known danger of damage occurring, bearing in mind the practicability of the steps required and their cost.[19] Liability will arise irrespective of whether the tree was planted or self-sown. Where a highway authority is aware of an appreciable risk of substantial damage to property, it is also likely that liability will arise in negligence.[20] What steps will be required to be taken, in order to prevent liability for nuisance arising, depends very much on the facts and circumstances before the court. It may be necessary and desirable to remove the tree, or it may be sufficient to lop or to provide some form of root barrier.[21] Present knowledge of the tendency of tree roots to cause damage to neighbouring property by reason of the incursion of tree roots is sufficiently widespread to mean that highway authorities will not be able, in the future, to plead ignorance of the problem, although lack of any reason to suspect that it might arise in a particular case is still an arguable defence.

3–47   Although the recent cases have tended to concentrate on the problems caused by tree roots, it is reasonable to suppose that similar principles will apply to dangers and nuisances caused by the branches of highway trees, or from the dangerous state of the whole tree itself. The liability for overhanging branches has been considered in a number of

---

[17] (1985) 83 L.G.R. 152.
[18] First instance (1980) unrep., but quoted in *Russell* v. *Barnet* (1985) 83 L.G.R. 152 at 169–170.
[19] *Solloway* v. *Hampshire C.C.* (1981) 79 L.G.R. 449, C.A.; *Leakey* v. *National Trust for Places of Historic Interest or Natural Beauty* [1980] Q.B. 485; *Russell* v. *Barnet* (1985) 83 L.G.R. 152.
[20] *Russell* v. *Barnet* (1985) 83 L.G.R. 152.
[21] See *e.g.* the approach of the court in *Bridges* v. *Harrow L.B.C.* (1981) 260 E.G. 284.

cases but more often in the context of trees overhanging the highway and causing a highway nuisance. In *British Road Services* v. *Slater*,[22] the issue before the court was whether the owner of the land adjoining the highway was liable for a nuisance caused to a highway user by overhanging branches. Although on the facts he was held not to be so liable, the court found that liability would arise where the occupier of the land containing the tree was aware of the nuisance and had failed to remedy it.[23] The court considered the question as to the potential liability of the occupier if in fact the tree was within the highway boundary, and concluded that in law the occupiers could be liable. It seems clear that the highway authority would now be regarded as having sufficient control over such a tree to be liable in nuisance.[24] However, the question as to whether the occupier of the land adjoining the highway might also be liable to users of the highway, or to the owners of other land affected by the tree from overhanging branches, is not quite so clear. The cases on roots have turned, to a greater or lesser extent, on the conclusion of the court that the owner of the tree would have no right to enter onto the highway and break it open in order to deal with the tree. However, the lopping of the branches of a tree would not require the breaking open of the highway, and the obstruction caused by the lopping operation would arguably be of such a brief duration as not to be an actionable obstruction in the first place.[25] It may be, therefore, that the occupier still has sufficient control over highway trees to be liable for some purposes. On balance, it would appear that the law must be the same for branches as it is for roots, and that the reasoning of the judges in the *Russell* and *Solloway* cases[26] applies equally to branches. It cannot be a desirable consequence that every landowner in a tree-lined street should have to enter onto the highway regularly to lop trees which he cannot remove, and whose retention he may not desire.

Summary

It cannot be said that the law on the ownership of trees in highways is **3–48** clear, although it now appears that the question of liability based upon control is established. The following propositions seem to be supported by the case law:

   (a) Where a tree, whether self-sown or planted by a body other than the highway authority, grows within the highway after its dedication, it will, prima facie, be an obstruction and may, as such, be removed by the highway authority.[27]

---

[22] [1964] 1 W.L.R. 498; *cf. Tregellas* v. *L.C.C.* (1897) 14 T.L.R. 55.
[23] This decision and other cases on highway nuisance caused by natural objects is discussed in Chap. 7.
[24] See *Hale* v. *Hants & Dorset Motor Services Ltd.* [1947] 2 All E.R. 628.
[25] See Chap. 7.
[26] n. 19 above.
[27] *Turner* v. *Ringwood Highway Board* (1870) L.R. 9 Eq. 418; *Stillwell* v. *New Windsor Corpn.* [1932] 2 Ch. 155.

(b) The highway authority may be regarded as the absolute owners of any herbage which grows entirely within that part of the highway which is vested by statute in the authority.[28]

(c) The vesting provisions of the Highways Act 1980 and its predecessors did not vest in the highway authority pre-adoption trees,[29] but the highway authority will have rights and powers, in relation to the tree, analogous to ownership.[30]

(d) The right to sell the timber of a tree (except perhaps one planted by the highway authority itself) remains in the owner of the subsoil whether the tree had been sown before or after the creation of the highway.[31]

(e) Effective control over trees planted within the highway has, since the amendment of section 82 of the Highways Act 1959 by the Highways (Miscellaneous Provisions) Act 1961, been exercisable by highway authorities in relation to both post-adoption and pre-adoption trees, to render them liable for nuisance caused by the tree.[32]

(f) Liability in nuisance will only arise where the highway authority knew or ought to have known of the existence of the nuisance and danger caused by the tree, and has failed to take reasonable steps to prevent or minimise the known danger of damage occurring—bearing in mind the practicability of those steps and their costs.[33]

---

[28] *Coverdale* v. *Charlton* (1878) 4 Q.B.D. 104.
[29] *Russell* v. *Barnet L.B.C.* (1985) 83 L.G.R. 152.
[30] *Stillwell* v. *New Windsor Corpn.* [1932] 2 Ch. 155.
[31] *Turner* v. *Ringwood Highway Board* (1870) L.R. 9 Eq. 418.
[32] *Russell* v. *Barnet L.B.C.* (1985) 83 L.G.R. 152.
[33] *Solloway* v. *Hampshire C.C.* (1981) 79 L.G.R. 449, C.A.; *Leakey* v. *National Trust for Places of Historic Interest or Natural Beauty* [1980] Q.B. 485; *Russell* v. *Barnet,* n. 32 above.

CHAPTER 4

THE MAINTENANCE OF HIGHWAYS

INTRODUCTION

At common law

Until the passing of the Highway Act 1835, all highways were **4–01**
regarded as maintainable by the inhabitants at large of the parish in
which they were situated, unless and until some other person was
proved to be liable by reason of tenure, enclosure or prescription.[1] In
certain exceptional cases, by immemorial custom, the liability could fall
on some smaller unit of the population instead of the parish, such as a
township, tithing, hamlet or vill.[2] In such cases the liability of the
smaller unit to repair was accompanied by a corresponding exemption
from liability to repair the remaining roads in the parish. However, the
general rule, of which judicial notice was taken, was that the parish as a
whole had the liability for repair, and the burden was on the persons
asserting the liability of another person or unit, or asserting the exemption of a part of the parish, to prove the exception.

The liability of the parish extended to all of the highways within its **4–02**
area, whenever constructed, and whether or not the parish had ever previously carried out acts of repair.[3] This liability fell onto all of the
inhabitants of the parish whether or not the road actually benefited
them or was in their part of the parish.[4] In order that liability should
arise, however, it had to be shown that the road or way in question was
indeed a public highway. This required evidence both of dedication and
of the acceptance of the road or way by the public. Past repair by the
parish could, therefore, be evidence that the road was a highway maintainable by the inhabitants at large, subject to the parish showing that
the repair had been undertaken under a mistaken apprehension as to
the status of the way.[5] Once established, the liability to repair remained
so long as the highway continued to exist, or until the liability was taken
away or transferred by statute. However, the courts were inclined to

[1] *R. v. Shoreditch (Inhabitants)* (1639) Mar.N.R. 26; *Anon.* 3 Salk. 182; *Austin's Case*
(1672) 1 Vent. 189; *R. v. Great Broughton (Inhabitants)* (1771) 5 Burr. 2700; *R. v. Sheffield (Inhabitants)* (1787) 2 T.R. 106; *R. v. Leake (Inhabitants)* (1833) 5 B. & Ad. 469.
[2] *R. v. Ecclesfield (Inhabitants)* (1818) 1 B. & Ald. 348; *R. v. Kingsmoor (Inhabitants)*
(1823) 2 B. & C. 190; *R. v. King's Newton (Inhabitants)* (1831) 1 B. & Ad. 826; *R. v.
Bishop Auckland (Inhabitants)* (1834) 1 Ad. & El. 744 *R. v. Barnoldswick (Inhabitants)*
(1843) 4 Q.B. 499; *R. v. Lordsmere (Inhabitants)* (1886) 54 L.T. 766.
[3] *R. v. Netherthong (Inhabitants)* (1818) 2 B. & A. 179; *R. v. Newbold (Inhabitants)*
(1869) 33 J.P. 115.
[4] *R. v. Clifton (Inhabitants)* (1794) 5 T.R. 498.
[5] See *R. v. Edmonton (Inhabitants)* (1831) 1 Moo. & R. 24.

interpret such statutory provisions restrictively and, in the absence of clear words to the contrary, the liability of the new person or body would be concurrent with the liability of the parish.[6] Thus, where turnpike roads or roads set out by the Inclosure Commissioners were created, the ultimate liability of the parish to repair generally remained.[7]

The Highway Act 1835

4–03 The purpose of section 23 of the Highway Act 1835 was to relieve the parish of its automatic liability to repair all highways within the parish. The section was not retrospective, however, and all highways existing prior to the passing of that Act remained repairable by the inhabitants at large. The section provided a procedure whereby the standard of construction of the proposed road could be inspected by the parish surveyor and by the local justices, and the utility of the road to the public could be assessed. Roads satisfying these tests would be recorded in the rolls of the quarter sessions.

4–04 Section 23 of the Highway Act 1835 applied both to highways to be constructed after the date the Act came into force, and to roads already constructed but not yet dedicated as highways. It did not apply to highways already dedicated at the time of the passing of the Act. It has, therefore, become important to know whether a particular road was or was not dedicated as a highway prior to the passing of the 1835 Act— whether it is an "ancient highway." If it was so dedicated, then the highway will be maintainable at the public expense unless it can be proved that someone else was liable to maintain it by reason of statute, prescription, tenure or inclosure. Roads dedicated after 1835 will be maintainable at the public expense only if the adoption procedure contained in the 1835 Act or its successors has been followed, or if statute expressly declares them so to be.[8] The 1835 Act applied to roads or occupation ways, and to those private driftways and horsepaths which had been set out by commissioners under an inclosure award. It did not apply to footpaths.[9]

4–05 Subsequent legislation created other procedures whereby roads could become maintainable by the public at large.[10] New adoption procedures were introduced by the Public Health Act 1875, the Public Health Acts Amendment Act 1890,[11] and the Private Street Works Act 1892. How-

---

[6] *R.* v. *St George, Hanover Square (Inhabitants)* (1812) 3 Camp. 222; *R.* v. *Preston (Inhabitants)* (1838) 2 Lew C.C. 193; *Little Bolton (Inhabitants)* v. *R.* (1843) 12 L.J. (M.C.) 104; *R.* v. *Sheffield Canal Co.* (1849) 13 Q.B. 913; *R.* v. *Brightside Bierlow (Inhabitants)* (1849) 13 Q.B. 933; *R.* v. *Poole Corporation* (1887) 19 Q.B.D. 602.

[7] *Bussey* v. *Storey* (1832) 4 B. & Ad. 98; *R.* v. *Netherthong (Inhabitants)* (1812) 2 B. & Ald. 179; *R.* v. *Nether Hallam (Inhabitants)* (1854) 6 Cox C.C. 435; *Att.-Gen. & Settle R.D.C.* v. *Lunesdale R.D.C.* (1902) 86 L.T. 822.

[8] But see *Leigh U.D.C.* v. *King* [1901] 1 Q.B. 747, where adoption was presumed.

[9] See para. 4–23, below.

[10] See Public Health Act 1875, s.146; Highways and Bridges Act 1891, s.3; Public Health Act 1875, s.154; Development and Road Improvement Funds Act 1909, ss.10, 11.

[11] s.41.

ever, the principle remained the same: unless one or other of the required statutory procedures had been followed, any road dedicated to the public after 1835 would not be maintainable by the inhabitants at large.

The Highways Act 1959

This Act abolished the liability of the inhabitants at large in respect of **4–06** the repair of highways and created the concept and status of "highways maintainable at the public expense."[12] These provisions of the Highways Act 1959 were consolidated and repeated in the Highways Act 1980.

HIGHWAYS CLASSED AS TO LIABILITY TO REPAIR

There are three classes of highway when it comes to a consideration of **4–07** the liability to repair:

(a) highways repairable by no-one;
(b) highways repairable by some person or body by virtue of statute, prescription, tenure or inclosure;
(c) highways repairable at the public expense.

Highways repairable by no-one

After August 31, 1835, any highway dedicated to the public and **4–08** accepted by public user but which had not complied with the statutory requirements of the Highway Act 1835 or its successors was not repairable by the inhabitants at large. Equally, however, there was no obligation on the person dedicating a way to repair it.[13] The carrying out by the dedicator of repairs on a voluntary basis did not create a continuing liability to repair. Statute in some instances abolished the duty of the inhabitants to repair certain highways and this may result in the highway being repairable by no-one.[14]

Highways repairable by reason of statute, prescription, tenure or inclosure

Prior to the passing of the Highway Act 1835, the parish had a **4–09** defence to an indictment for non-repair only if it could be proved that some other person or body was liable to repair the highway. The burden of proving that some other body or person was so liable fell firmly upon the parish.[15] Similarly, should any issue arise in modern times regarding

---

[12] Highways Act 1959, s.38.

[13] See *Roberts* v. *Hunt* (1850) 15 Q.B. 17; *Fawcett* v. *York and North Midland Rail Co.* (1851) 16 Q.B. 614n.; *R.* v. *Wilson* (1852) 18 Q.B. 348; *Mayor of Sunderland* v. *Herring* (1853) 17 J.P. 741; *Hunwick* v. *Essex Rivers Catchment Board* [1952] 1 All E.R. 765.

[14] See Highways Act 1980, s.47. See also earlier provisions, now repealed, *e.g.* Highways Act 1864, s.21; Highways Act 1878, s.24; National Parks and Access to the Countryside Act 1949, s.47(2).

[15] *R.* v. *Sheffield* (*Inhabitants*) (1787) 2 T.R. 106; *R.* v. *Penderryn* (*Inhabitants*) (1788) 2 T.R. 513; *R.* v. *Hatfield* (*Inhabitants*) (1820) 4 B. & A. 75.

the liability of some other person to repair a highway, the burden of proof will be on the highway authority which seeks to avoid liability for the repair of the way. Where liability of some person or body to repair is established, then that liability may be enforced under section 56 of the Highways Act 1980.[16]

By statute

4-10   The courts were reluctant to hold that a statute removed the liability of the parish for repair,[17] preferring to find that the effect of a statute imposing a duty of repair on some other person was to create a concurrent liability with that of the parish. However, where a statute did impose liability on a person other than the parish, then, so long as the conditions required by the statute had been complied with, that liability could be enforced by indictment.[18]

By prescription

4-11   A prescriptive liability must date from time immemorial. Many of the cases which discuss this form of liability arose over the claim by one parish that roads within its area had been repaired by another parish. It seems likely that any such liability, if it existed, would not now avail a local highway authority, since the duty to maintain arising from sections 36 and 41 of the 1980 Act applies to highways which, before the commencement of the Highways Act 1959, were maintainable by the inhabitants at large of *any* area.[19] Prescriptive liability was, in any event, relatively rare. The prescriptive liability of a corporation was easier to establish than was the liability of a private person.[20] The carrying out of acts repair, even over a substantial period of time, will not usually be sufficient to transfer liability from the public onto some other person or body. It seems that there must have been some original benefit to the repairer, in order to impose a prescriptive liability on a private person,[21] and possibly a continuing benefit.

By tenure

4-12   Whilst the existence of potential liability to repair by virtue of tenure is well recorded in judicial decisions and recognised by statute,[22] there are few decisions which depend upon such liability having been established.[23] Indeed, the judicial statements show differing and confusing justifications for the existence of the liability. On one view, liability to

---

[16] See para. 4–44, below.
[17] See the cases cited under n. 10 above.
[18] *R.* v. *Sheffield Canal Co.* (1849) 13 Q.B. 913; *R.* v. *Hatfield (Inhabitants)* (1835) 4 A. & E. 156; *R.* v. *Midville (Inhabitants)* (1843) 4 Q.B. 240.
[19] See Highways Act 1959, s.38(2)(*a*).
[20] 1 Hawk. c.76, s.8.
[21] *R.* v. *St. Giles, Cambridge (Inhabitants)* (1816) 5 M. & S. 260; *Lyme Regis Corpn.* v. *Henley* (1832) 3 B. & Ad. 77; *R.* v. *Ashby Folville (Inhabitants)* (1866) L.R. 1 Q.B. 213.
[22] See *e.g.* Highways Act 1980, ss.36(1), 41(3), 44, 49, 50, 52, 53, 54 and 56(1).
[23] See *Esher & Dittons U.D.C.* v. *Marks* (1902) 71 L.J.K.B. 309.

repair by reason of tenure is a species of prescriptive liability or, at least, is dependent upon repairs dating from time immemorial.[24] The liability to repair would seem to be based upon the grant of land in consideration for the promise to keep the highway in repair.[25] There are some statements to the effect that the grant has to date from time immemorial, or at least from a date prior to the passing of the statute *Quia Emptores* 1290, by which all tenure depended upon a grant from the Crown.[26] However, in *Esher and Dittons Urban Council* v. *Marks*,[27] Walton J. held that the grant of a licence from the King to stop up and inclose an existing highway for the benefit of himself and his heirs was capable of imposing a duty to repair *ratione tenurae* notwithstanding that the grant might have been subsequent to the reign of King Richard I. In this case the supposed licence could not be found, but the court was prepared to hold that there was a lost grant.

Whatever may be the correct derivation of the liability to repair **4–13** *ratione tenurae*, it will generally be proved by acts of repair carried out over a long period of time.[28] These acts of repair must, however, be substantial and go beyond the sorts of repairs that a landowner might be expected to carry out for his own benefit.[29] It has been held that evidence of reputation is not admissible, and that neither previous proceedings against a landowner, nor an award under a submission by a former tenant may be admitted as evidence.[30] It may be that where the evidence is unclear, the court may look at the utility of the way to the public in order to decide whether the acts of the adjoining landowner are sufficient to suggest acceptance of a liability to repair.[31]

It follows that if the liability to repair depends upon tenure, it can **4–14** only fall upon persons who are capable of owning land.[32] However, once the liability *ratione tenurae* is established, it appears that enforcement lies against the occupier of the land rather than the owner[33]; nonetheless, the occupier may be able to claim re-imbursement from the owner.[34] The liability operates as a charge on the land and runs with

---

[24] See *R.* v. *Kerrison* (1815) 1 M. & S. 526; *R.* v. *Hatfield* (*Inhabitants*) (1820) 4 B. & A. 75; *Ferrand* v. *Bingley U.D.C.* 1903 2 K.B. 445; *R.* v. *Blakemore* (1852) 2 Den. 410; *cf. R.* v. *Beeby* (1839) 8 L.J.M.C. 38; *R.* v. *Sheffield Canal Co.* (1849) 13 Q.B. 913.

[25] *Anon.* (1497) Y.B. 12 Hen. 7, fol. 15, pl.1; *Anon.* (1481) Y.B. 21 Edw. 4, fol. 38, pl.4.

[26] See *R.* v. *Hatfield* (*Inhabitants*) (1820) 4 B. & A. 75 and the discussion in Pratt and Mackenzie's *Law of Highways* (21st ed.) at 78–9.

[27] (1902) 71 L.J.K.B. 309.

[28] See *R.* v. *Skinner* (1805) 5 Esp. 219; *R.* v. *Hatfield* (*Inhabitants*) (1820) 4 B. & A. 75.

[29] See *R.* v. *Allanson* (1828) 1 Lew. C.C. 158; *Rundle* v. *Hearle* 1898 2 Q.B. 83; *Att.-Gen. & Public Trustee* v. *Woolwich Metropolitan B.C.* (1929) 93 J.P. 173; *cf. Hudson* v. *Tabor* (1877) 2 Q.B.D. 290 (sea wall).

[30] See *R.* v. *Cotton* (1813) 3 Camp. 444; *R.* v. *Franklyn* (1839) 3 J.P. 452; *R.* v. *Wavertree* (*Inhabitants*) (1841) 2 Mood. & R. 353; *cf.* Civil Evidence Act 1968, s.11.

[31] *R.* v. *Allanson* (1828) 1 Lew. C.C. 158.

[32] *R.* v. *Machynlleth and Pennegoes* (*Inhabitants*) (1823) 2 B. & C. 166; *R.* v. *Ecclesfield* (*Inhabitants*) (1818) 1 B. & Ald. 348.

[33] *R.* v. *Barker* (1890) 25 Q.B.D. 213; *Cuckfield R.D.C.* v. *Goring* [1898] 1 Q.B. 865; *Daventry R.D.C.* v. *Parker* [1900] 1 Q.B. 1.

[34] *Baker* v. *Greenhill* (1842) 3 Q.B. 148.

every part of that land.[35] It may be, therefore, that there are several persons who become concurrently liable for repair, some of whom no longer own land adjoining the highway.[36]

4-15   The liability to repair *ratione tenurae* continues whilst the highway subsists; if the highway is destroyed, then the liability to repair is also destroyed. This seemingly obvious statement gives rise to questions of interpretation as to when a highway does cease to exist.[37] Where the road was physically destroyed, then the liability disappeared with the road.[38] In deciding whether the highway could be said to have been destroyed it seems that the court would have regard to whether it could economically be repaired.[39] Equally, where the highway was totally altered in its course and character whilst the subject of a Turnpike Trust, it was held that on the expiry of the trust the liability to repair *ratione tenurae* did not revive.[40]

By inclosure

4-16   Where a highway crossed open land and the path of the highway had become foundrous and impassable, common law had recognised that a limited right of diversion onto adjoining land could be acquired by prescription.[41] When land on either side of the highway became inclosed, that right to deviate would, therefore, be lost. It was held from an early date that in such a case, the landowner who had had the benefit of the inclosure and whose acts had deprived the public of their right to deviate, fell under a duty to keep the highway in repair for as long as he maintained his inclosure.[42] The principle applied only where the highway had existed time out of mind; it could not apply to a known dedication, where the dedicating landowner also inclosed the land on either side of his grant.[43]

Highways repairable at the public expense

4-17   By the Highways Act 1959, the responsibility to repair highways maintainable at the public expense was placed on local highway authorities. The Minister, as a highway authority, also has a duty of repair in respect of those highways for which he is given statutory responsibility. By far the great majority of carriageway highways will now be maintainable at the public expense. In the case of carriageway highways, the test will be whether the highway was dedicated prior to the passing of the

---

[35] *R. v. Bucklugh* (*Duchess*) (1704) 1 Salk. 358.

[36] See *R. v. Bucklugh* (*Duchess*), above; *R. v. Oxfordshire* (*Inhabitants*) (1812) 16 East 223.

[37] See generally on this point, paras. 9–03 *et seq.*, below.

[38] *R. v. Hornsea* (*Inhabitants*) (1854) Dears. C.C. 291.

[39] *R. v. Bamber* (1843) 5 Q.B. 279; *R. v. Greenhow* (*Inhabitants*) (1876) 1 Q.B.D. 703.

[40] *R. v. Pickering Township* (1877) 41 J.P. 564; *R. v. Barker* (1890) 25 Q.B.D. 213; *Heath v. Weaverham Township Overseers* [1894] 2 Q.B. 108.

[41] *Absor* v. *French* (1678) 2 Show. 28; *Dawes* v. *Hawkins* (1860) 8 C.B.(N.S.) 848.

[42] *Henn's Case* (1632) W.Jo. 296; *Duncomb's Case* (1634) Cro. Car. 366.

[43] See *R. v. Flecknow* (*Inhabitants*) (1758) 1 Burr. 461; *R. v. Ramsden* (1858) E.B. & E. 949.

Highway Act 1835 or whether it was subsequently adopted in accordance with one or other of the statutory procedures contained in that and subsequent Acts of Parliament.[44] Lack of evidence that a highway was dedicated in accordance with one or other of the statutory procedures may not, in cases where there has been a history of repair by the highway authority, prove fatal to a claim that the highway authority is under the duty of repair. A doctrine similiar to that of "lost grant" has sometimes been applied by the courts in the absence of positive evidence of adoption but only where the highway authority has apparently acted under the belief that the way was repairable at the public expense. This is perhaps properly to be regarded as a question of evidence to establish compliance with the necessary formalities where records are inaccurate, rather than to suggest any exception to the general principle.

PUBLICLY MAINTAINABLE HIGHWAYS

Introduction

4–18   Section 36 of the Highways Act 1980 specifies which highways are to be regarded as being maintainable at the public expense. Subsection (1) indicates that all those highways which were highways maintainable at the public expense under the Highways Act 1959 are to continue to be so maintainable, unless an event has occurred[45] resulting in the particular highway ceasing to be so maintainable. Four specific situations are then set out where the highways concerned will be maintainable at the public expense. The 1980 Act[46] preserves the position of highways constructed under other statutory powers which may become maintainable at the public expense by virtue of those powers. Sections 37 to 40 then provide ways by which highways may become maintainable at the public expense by adoption. Additionally, there are other statutory provisions whereby highways may be created which will then become maintainable at the public expense. Most of these are discussed more fully in Chapter 2.

Highways maintainable by virtue of the Highways Act 1959

4–19   Section 38 of the Highways Act 1959 abolished the duty of the inhabitants at large to repair highways. Thereafter, those highways which were to be maintainable at the public expense were to be:

    (a) those which immediately before the passing of the 1959 Act were repairable either by the inhabitants at large or by a highway authority;

    (b) highways constructed after the passing of the 1959 Act by a highway authority otherwise than on behalf of some other person not being a highway authority;

---

[44] See paras. 4–24 *et seq.*, below.
[45] *e.g.* Highways Act 1980, ss.38(4), 47.
[46] As did the Highways Act 1959.

(c) highways constructed by borough or urban district councils within their own areas under the powers under Part V of the Housing Act 1957,[47] and highways constructed by the same authorities outside their areas in circumstances where, under Part V of that Act, liability to maintain was vested in the county, borough or district council in which the highway was situated;

(d) trunk roads and special roads[48];

(e) footpaths and bridleways created after the passing of the 1959 Act pursuant to public path creation or diversion orders and agreements.

The 1959 Act also contained provisions similiar to those in the 1980 Act whereby highways constructed after the passage of the 1959 Act could become highways maintainable at the public expense by agreement or by adoption.

Highways constructed by a highway authority

4-20   There are a number of powers under which a highway authority may construct highways. These powers, which are contained in Part II of the 1980 Act, have been discussed in Chapter 2. It is to be noted that highways constructed on behalf of some other person, which person is not itself a highway authority, will not, without more, become highways maintainable at the public expense.

Highways constructed under Part II of the Housing Act 1985

4-21   Part II of the 1985 Act provides powers for and imposes duties on housing authorities in respect of the provision of housing accommodation. Under section 13 the local authority may lay out and construct public streets or roads on land acquired or appropriated by itself for the purposes of Part V of the Act. By section 14(4), where a housing authority carries out housing operations outside its own area, the liability for public streets or roads constructed by it vests in the local highway authority in whose area the operations are carried out, unless that authority is not satisfied that the streets or roads have been properly constructed in accordance with the approved plans and specifications.

Trunk roads and special roads

4-22   Although trunk roads and special roads are maintainable at the public expense, the highway authority for these roads, with responsibility for their maintenance, will be the Minister rather than the local highway authority.[49]

---

[47] See now Part II of the Housing Act 1985.

[48] Excepting those parts of such roads, including bridges, which some other person is liable to maintain under charter, special enactment, tenure, prescription or inclosure.

[49] Although, in the case of trunk roads, the Minister may delegate his powers to local highway authorities under the Highways Act 1980, s.6.

Footpaths and bridleways

Section 23 of the Highway Act 1835 applied only to roads or occupa- **4–23**
tion ways, and to private horsepaths or driftways, set out in any award
by commissioners under an Inclosure Act. It did not apply to footpaths
and bridleways which did not fit within those descriptions. Since the rule
relating to maintenance of highways by the parish applied to all highways of whatever description, it followed that the inhabitants at large
remained under a duty to maintain footpaths and most bridleways. This
situation was remedied by the National Parks and Access to the Countryside Act 1949. Section 49 of that Act expressly applied the provisions
of section 23 of the Highway Act 1835 to all public paths dedicated after
the commencement of the 1949 Act.[50] Section 47 declared that otherwise the provisions of section 23 applied to public paths but indicated
that this was not to relieve persons liable to maintain such paths by
reason of tenure, prescription or enclosure. Such persons would, therefore, continue to be liable concurrently with the highway authority.[51]

Highways adopted in accordance with the Highways Act 1980, section 37

Any person wishing to dedicate a highway to the public, and who **4–24**
wishes that the highway thereby dedicated should be maintainable at the
public expense, may give notice[52] to the relevant local highway authority of his intention to dedicate. This notice must be given not less than
three months before the date of the proposed dedication and must describe the location and width of the proposed highway and the nature of
the proposed dedication.[53] Where the local highway authority consider
that the proposed way will not be of sufficient utility to justify its being
maintained at the public expense, it may then make a complaint to a
magistrates' court for an order to that effect. Alternatively, the local
highway authority may certify that the way has been dedicated in
accordance with the terms of the notice and that it has been made up in
a satisfactory manner. If such a certificate has been given, and so long as
the way is both used by the public for a period of twelve months from
the date of the certificate and is kept in repair by the dedicating landowner during that period, then the way will become a public highway
maintainable at the public expense at the expiry of the twelve month
period. If these conditions are not fulfilled, then the highway will be
repairable by no-one.[54] This section is relatively infrequently used by
landowners, the more common method being to enter into an agreement under section 38 of the Highway Act 1980.[55] The section bears a

---

[50] *i.e.* December 16, 1949.
[51] See now Highways Act 1980, ss.50, 57.
[52] As to the form and service of notices, see *ibid.* ss.320–322.
[53] *i.e.* whether the way is to be dedicated as a footpath, bridleway or carriageway. The
notice may also require any restrictions or reservations to the dedication to be stated.
[54] See *R. v. Wilson* (1852) 18 Q.B. 348.
[55] See para. 4–28, below.

certain similarity to section 23 of the Highway Act 1835, from which it was originally derived.

4–25   Section 37 does not place any restrictions on the actual dedication of highways. It is perfectly possible for highway to be effectively dedicated other than by following the procedure in this section; section 37 affects only the consequences of such a dedication. Dedication by this procedure, or by one or other of the other statutory procedures which are expressed to have the same effect, will ensure that the way becomes maintainable at the public expense. Dedication other than by way of one of these procedures will still create a highway, but one which is repairable by no-one.[56] Equally, to create a highway by dedication under section 37, the landowner must have the necessary capacity to dedicate.[57]

4–26   When faced with a notice under section 37, the local highway authority may make its own application[58] to the magistrates' court for an order that the way is not of sufficient public utility to justify its maintenance at the public expense. It appears from the concluding words of subsection (3) that the authority may be able to make such an application even though they have issued a certificate under subsection (3). The authority may, therefore, be able to wait and see what degree of public use is made of the way during part of the twelve month "trial" period. It is the existence of an order under subsection (2) which will prevent the way becoming maintainable at the public expense, and not the fact that the authority have made an application to the court. Where such an order is made, it appears that any change of mind in the highway authority will be precluded. Section 317 of the Highways Act 1980 gives a right of appeal to the Crown Court against orders of magistrates made under the 1980 Act, but only to a "person aggrieved."[59]

4–27   Where the authority refuses to issue a certificate under subsection (3), the landowner may himself appeal to the magistrates who may themselves issue such a certificate.[60] The order of the magistrates will contain a date from which the twelve month period under subsection (3) is to run. Again, the authority has the right of appeal to the Crown Court against the making of such an order.[61] Any certificate under subsection (3) or a copy of any order by the magistrates under subsection (4) must be deposited with the proper officer of the council and must be available for public inspection on payment of a reasonable charge.[62]

---

[56] See *Roberts* v. *Hunt* (1850) 15 Q.B. 17; *Fawcett* v. *York and North Midland Rail Co.* (1851) 16 Q.B. 614n.; *R.* v. *Wilson* (1852) 18 Q.B. 348; *Mayor of Sunderland* v. *Herring* (1853) 17 J.P. 741; *Hunwick* v. *Essex Rivers Catchment Board* 1952 1 All E.R. 765.
[57] See Chap. 2.
[58] By way of a complaint for an order: see Highways Act 1980, s.316.
[59] See paras. 15–34 *et seq.*, below.
[60] See Highways Act 1980, s.37(4). The notice of refusal must inform the landowner of his right of appeal; see s.315.
[61] See *ibid.* s.317.
[62] *Ibid.* s.37(5).

Highways adopted as a result of agreements under Highways Act 1980, section 38

Section 38 of the Highways Act 1980 deals with four distinct situations   **4–28**
in which a highway authority may become responsible for the maintenance of a highway by agreement. By subsection (1), an existing highway
which is maintainable by some other person may be taken over by the
highway authority. By subsection (3)(*a*), the authority may agree to
maintain an existing private carriage or occupation road which is to be
dedicated to the public. By subsection (3)(*b*), an agreement may be
entered into by which the authority agrees to maintain a road which *will*
be constructed. Lastly, by subsection (4), the highway authority may
take over the responsibility of repairing certain bridges or viaducts from
railway, canal or tramway undertakers.

Agreements under section 38 may contain provisions dealing with the   **4–29**
dedication of the way in question[63]—although this will only be appropriate in those agreements which deal with a road not already a highway.
They may include terms as to the bearing of the expenses of the construction, maintenance or improvement of the highway, road, viaduct or
bridge to which the agreement relates. There can be no doubt, therefore, that the agreement may require the landowner/developer to meet
the cost of bringing the highway, road, viaduct or bridge up to adoption
standard. Otherwise, the agreement may contain terms dealing with
"any other relevant matters as the authority making the agreement
think fit."[64] Although the section is phrased in wide terms and although
a local authority may have, in any event, wide power as to the content of
terms consensually agreed, an attempt by a highway authority to require
a landowner to enter into unreasonably onerous terms by way of an
agreement under this section might be subject to judicial review.

Highways which are privately maintainable by reason of tenure, inclo-   **4–30**
sure or prescription or by virtue of an Act of Parliament[65] may, by
agreement with the Minister (in the case of a trunk road) or with the
local highway authority (in all other cases), become maintainable at the
public expense from the date specified in the agreement. In such cases,
the liability of the body formerly liable to repair will become
extinguished. An agreement cannot be made under this part of section
38 in respect of privately maintainable bridges over which a highway
passes (which must be dealt with under section 94 of the Act) nor in
respect of any toll highway which may be transferred to the authority
under section 271.[66]

---

[63] See Highways Act 1980, s.38(6).
[64] *Ibid.*
[65] As to all of these, see paras. 4–09 *et seq.*, above.
[66] Hence the reference in this section to agreements under Parts V and XII of the Act. As
to the transfer of liability in these cases, see paras. 11–40 and 15–06, below. See also
Highways Act 1980, s.53.

4–31 Private carriageways or occupation ways which are already in existence may be taken over by the highway authority under subsection (3)(*a*). The landowner must have the capacity to dedicate the way as a highway.[67] He must also be willing to dedicate. The road will then become both a highway and will be maintainable at the public expense on the date specified in, and subject to such conditions as may be contained in, the agreement. Similarly, under subsection (3)(*b*), a landowner who has capacity to dedicate may agree in advance of constructing or completing a road that it should become a highway and be maintainable at the public expense at a date specified in the agreement. In both these cases, the failure of any of the conditions prescribed in the agreement will not only prevent the road becoming maintainable at the public expense, but may also prevent the dedication from being effective.[68]

4–32 The agreement may provide that the highway authority itself is to make up the road and, in such a case, will provide for the payment by the landowner of the authority's expenses. The usual practice where a road is to be constructed under this section is for the highway authority to require the developer to enter into a bond with a surety,[69] which will provide for the surety paying to the highway authority the cost of making up the road should the developer default.[70] In such a case the default of the developer would not necessarily prevent the way becoming a highway and being maintainable at the public expense.[71]

4–33 Agreements may also be made under section 38[72] by which a local highway authority may undertake to maintain as part of the highway maintainable at the public expense, a bridge or viaduct carrying a railway, canal, or tramway, *over* the highway. The agreement may relate to a bridge which is already in existence and which is privately maintainable, or to a bridge which is to be constructed by the relevant undertakers or by the highway authority on their behalf. The agreement will be between the local highway authority on the one part, and the railway, canal, or tramway, undertakers on the other part. A bridge crossing a highway will not be part of that highway.[73] Agreements under this section are not permitted where there is an alternative power under section 94. The agreement may contain provisions relating to the bearing of the expenses of constructing, maintaining or improving the bridge or via-

---

[67] See Chap. 2.

[68] *Cubitt* v. *Maxse* (1873) L.R. 8 C.P. 704; *R.* v. *Lordsmere* (*Inhabitants*) (1850) 15 Q.B. 689. See, generally, Chap. 2 on this point.

[69] As to the liability of the surety on the default of the builder, see *National Employers' Mutual General Insurance Association* v. *Herne Bay U.D.C.* (1972) 70 L.G.R. 542.

[70] Compare the alternative method of requiring the builder to make a deposit or give security under the provisions of the advance payments code; see Chap. 10.

[71] However, it is perhaps desirable for the agreement to deal expressly with this point.

[72] subs. (4).

[73] As to bridges carrying highways over railways, canals, etc., see s.94, below.

duct and any other relevant matters which the authority making the agreement thinks fit.[74]

Other powers of adoption of highways

Where the private street works code[75] is brought into operation, the **4–34** result will be that a road which was formerly not maintainable at the public expense—whether or not a highway—becomes a highway maintainable at the public expense. Under section 228(1) of the Highways Act 1980, where any street works have been carried out in a private street, the street works authority may initiate a procedure whereby the road becomes maintainable at the public expense. There is a procedure contained in the section for objections to be made by street owners and for reference of those objections to the magistrates' court where a majority in number of the street owners object.[76] Under section 228(7), where all street works have been carried out in a private street to the satisfaction of the street works authority, a majority of street owners (by rateable value) can themselves require the street works authority to declare the street to be maintainable at the public expense.

Highways which have ceased to be maintainable at the public expense **4–35** by virtue of an order under the Highways Act 1980, section 47[77] may become again so maintainable on an application being made to a magistrates' court under section 48. Notice of intention to make an application must be given to the relevant highway authority one month before it is made. Such an application may only be made by a person "interested in the maintenance of the highway." This expression would cover any person who had been concurrently liable to maintain the highway with the highway authority, or whose liability had become resurrected by the order under section 47. It may also be wide enough to cover any adjoining landowner and possibly any regular user of the way—both of which categories of person might claim to be so "interested," in that the highway may be deteriorating and interfering with their lawful use of it. However, the word "interest" would normally involve some form of other legal entitlement going beyond ordinary user of the highway.

Extent of the duty to maintain

The word "maintenance" implies keeping the highway in the con- **4–36** dition it was in when first created. However, traffic conditions change and, whilst the purpose of the highway may remain the same, the traffic

---

[74] Highways Act 1980, s.38(6).
[75] See Chap. 10.
[76] See the discussion of these powers at paras. 2–14—2–17, above.
[77] See para. 4–47, below.

which may in time come to use the highway may put greater strains on the fabric of the road than was originally contemplated. Although at one time a narrow approach was adopted towards the expected standard of repair,[78] it is now well established that the extent of the duty of a highway authority to maintain a highway is to keep the highway in such a state as to be safe and fit for the ordinary traffic which may reasonably be expected to use it.[79] As the needs of "ordinary" traffic may change with the passage of time, so the duty to repair must keep pace with these changes.[80] Conversely, it has not been accepted by the courts that the fact that a highway has been infrequently used should justify a lower standard of repair than had formerly been the case.[81]

4-37   By the time of the decision in *Sharpness New Docks and Gloucester and Birmingham Navigation Company* v. *Attorney-General,*[82] the law was sufficiently established for Lord Atkinson to say[83]:

> "In the argument of this appeal many authorities were cited to establish that it is the duty of road authorities to keep their public highways in a state fit to accommodate the ordinary traffic which passes or may be expected to pass along them. As the ordinary traffic expands or changes in character, so must the nature of the maintenance and repair of the highway alter to suit the change. No person really contests that principle."

The principle is also reflected in the matters which are to be proved in order to establish the statutory defence under the Highways Act 1980, section 58.[84] An increased load placed on a highway by a single landowner would not, however, be sufficient to increase the liability of the highway authority to repair. Indeed there is provision in the modern legislation for recovering the expenses of repairing a road damaged due to extraordinary traffic.[85]

4-38   The distinction between improvement of the highway and maintenance of the highway is demonstrated in a number of old cases which sought to determine what the surveyor of highways could be compelled to do in performance of his duties of repair. There is no duty to fence a

---

[78] See *R.* v. *Cluworth* (*Inhabitants*) (1704) 6 Mod. Rep. 163; *Manchester Corpn.* v. *Audenshaw U.C. & Denton U.C.* [1928] Ch. 763.

[79] *R.* v. *Henley* (*Inhabitants*) (1847) 2 Cox C.C. 334; *R.* v. *High Halden* (*Inhabitants*) (1859) 1 F. & F. 678; see also *Burgess* v. *Northwich Local Board* (1880) 6 Q.B.D. 264.

[80] *Att.-Gen.* v. *Scott* [1905] 2 K.B. 160; *Chichester Corpn.* v. *Foster* [1906] 1 K.B. 167; *cf. Weston-super-Mare U.D.C.* v. *Butt* (*Henry*) *& Co. Ltd.* [1922] 1 A.C. 340.

[81] See *R.* v. *Claxby* (*Inhabitants*) (1855) 24 L.J.Q.B. 223.

[82] [1915] A.C. 654.

[83] At 665. See also *R.* v. *Stretford* (*Inhabitants*) (1705) 2 Ld. Raym. 1169; *R.* v. *Devon* (*Inhabitants*) (1825) 4 B. & C. 670 at 677; *Burgess* v. *Northwich Local Board* (1883) 11 Q.B.D. 264; *Lodge Holes Colliery Co.* v. *Wednesbury Corpn.* [1908] A.C. 323.

[84] See paras. 5–27 *et seq.*, below.

[85] See *Weston-super-Mare U.D.C.* v. *Butt* (*Henry*) *& Co. Ltd.* [1922] 1 A.C. 340; Highways Act 1980, s.59 and the cases cited at paras. 4–55 *et seq.*, below.

previously unfenced highway, nor to maintain existing fences,[86] unless they have become part of the highway.[87]

That which must be maintained is, of course, the highway itself. Tra- **4–39** ditionally, the interest of the highway authority has been regarded as being in the "top two spits" of the surface of the land over which it crosses[88]—being the notional depth to which the authority might have to go in order to carry out its duties of repair.[89] However, the actual interest of the highway authority and the actual extent of the highway itself, for example where it crosses over a bridge or culvert, or where it is bounded by a retaining wall, may, in each case, be a difficult question to resolve.

Retaining walls

Whether a retaining wall is part of the highway is a question of fact.[90] **4–40** Evidence that the wall was constructed at the same time as the highway itself, or that it was constructed for the specific purpose of maintaining the highway, would normally be sufficient to establish that the wall was part of the highway.[91] Evidence that the wall presently supports the highway is not conclusive.[92] The wall may have been constructed in order to protect adjoining land and its supporting role for the highway may have postdated the establishment of the highway. It is possible for an easement of support to be obtained in such circumstances, but this will not necessarily impose any positive duty of repair upon the servient landowner.[93] It is then a difficult question as to whether the highway authority should be subjected to any duty of repair. It would appear that, even where the highway authority may not be liable to repair a retaining wall under its duty to maintain the highway, it may still be required to take action to protect highway users from danger, which action may itself involve repairing a road in danger of collapse.[94] It is probable that the courts will take a common sense view of such a situation on the basis that any structure which is essential for the continued existence of the highway should be regarded as maintainable as part of that highway. This approach was taken by Lord Halsbury in *Sandgate Urban District Council* v. *Kent County Council*[95] There, Lord Halsbury,

---

[86] See *R.* v. *Llandilo Roads Comms.* (1788) 2 Term Rep. 232; *Morgan* v. *Leach* (1842) 10 M. & W. 558; *Rotherham Corpn.* v. *Fullerton* (1884) 50 L.T. 364; *Caseley* v. *Bristol Corpn.* [1944] 1 All E.R. 14.
[87] See para. 4–41, below.
[88] See, *per* Denning L.J. in *Tithe Redemption Commissioners* v. *Runcorn U.D.C.* [1954] 1 Ch. 383.
[89] See para. 3–09, above.
[90] See *R.* v. *Lordsmere (Inhabitants)* (1886) 54 L.T. 766.
[91] See *e.g.* See *Reigate Corpn.* v. *Surrey C.C.* [1928] Ch. 359; *Att.-Gen.* v. *Staffordshire C.C.* [1905] 1 Ch. 336.
[92] *Sanitary Commissioners of Gibraltar* v. *Orfila* (1890) 15 App. Cas. 400.
[93] See *Stockport & Hyde Division of Macclesfield Hundred, Highway Board* v. *Grant* (1882) 51 L.J.Q.B. 357.
[94] See paras. 7–33 and 7–40, below.
[95] (1898) 79 L.T. 425.

dealing with the argument that a sea wall was not part of the highway, stated a more general proposition[96]:

> "Is it common sense to say that where the obligation is to maintain the road and keep it in repair, you can, by neglect, allow that duty to be so disregarded that in time the road may be washed away, so that your liability or obligation ceases? Such a proposition is, to my mind, absolutely monstrous. . . .
>
> I have no hesitation in saying that, assuming a thing to be necessary for the preservation of the road, and assuming that the local authority is under obligation to keep up the road, the law of England is that you shall keep up that road by whatever means are appropriate and necessary to do it."

The *Sandgate* decision was concerned with whether the repair of the sea wall constituted works of repair and maintenance for which the county council could be chargeable under the Local Government Act 1888. It was not, therefore, concerned with the specific question as to whether the authority would be acting under implicit common law powers in entering onto adjoining land to repair such a retaining wall. The power of entry now given by the Highways Act 1980, section 291, however, may not be sufficiently wide to deal with this situation since, strangely, it appears to exclude the right of entry to carry out works on a structure which is part of the highway and, further, omits retaining walls from the specific list of objects which can be included within the definition of "structure." That definition is not exhaustive, however, and the proper construction of the *Sandgate* case seems to be that the wall does not have to be part of the highway in order for its maintenance to be required by law. It also seems likely that the authority has a power at common law to enter and repair a wall which is necessary for the support of the highway.[97]

Other walls

4–41   A highway may be protected from falling rocks or debris by a wall or fence. Such walls and fences are unlikely to form part of the highway unless they were constructed at the same time as the highway and for the purpose of providing that protection, or unless they were constructed by the highway authority on highway land.[98] In those cases where the wall is not part of the highway, the highway authority will have no duty to repair but may have power to require the landowner to repair if the falling rocks and debris are likely to cause a danger—and therefore public nuisance—to highway users. Fence walls would not usually be part of the highway, unless the adjoining land is lower than the highway and the

---

[96] At 427.
[97] See *Bond* v. *Nottingham Corpn.* [1940] 1 Ch. 429.
[98] *Reigate Corpn.* v. *Surrey C.C.*, above; *cf. R.* v. *Whitney* (*Inhabitants*) (1835) 3 A. & E. 69.

difference in level is due to the making up or improvement of the carriageway.

Culverts and bridges

Historically, there was a separate liability to maintain bridges, falling **4–42** on bodies which were not necessarily under any duty to repair any highway.[99] However, some bridges over ditches, streams and small rivers were always regarded as being part of the highway itself. In each case it was a question of fact dependent upon the size of the bridge and the purpose of construction.[1] Culverts will almost invariably be regarded as part of the highway unless they can be shown to have been constructed purely for the purpose of draining adjoining land.

Cellar roofs, stiles and gates

In one case,[2] the issue arose whether the flagstones of a pavement, **4–43** which also formed the roof of a cellar under the highway, were repairable as part of the street[3] or by the landowner as part of the cellar itself. The evidence being that the wear on the flagstones had come from the highway traffic over them, it was held that the flagstones should be regarded as part of the pavement itself.[4] Whilst the decision is not at all surprising, it does raise, as a possible point of principle, that where doubt exists as to whether an object is or is not part of the highway, a court will be prepared to consider whether the need for maintenance stems from the highway or from private use and, therefore, to consider the importance of the object to the continued user of the highway. A similar approach seems to have been adopted in *Reigate Corporation* v. *Surrey County Council.*[5] There the court was concerned with the liability to maintain the walls and roof of a tunnel through which the highway passed. The point was in issue because the tunnel also went under another highway and had been constructed in order to take a private road. The original landowner might therefore have been liable to maintain the structure of the tunnel in such a way as to prevent the removal of support from the footpath. This was of importance in the context of the case. The court held that the walls and roof either formed part of the highway or were necessary for its maintenance. Stiles and gates may also be repairable as part of the highway if their existence and use is attributable to the use of the highway but not where they simply constitute obstructions reserved by the landowner in the terms of the dedication.

---

[99] See Chap. 11.

[1] See *R. v. Whitney (Inhabitants)* (1835) 3 A. & E. 69; *R. v. Lancaster County (Inhabitants)* (1868) 32 J.P. 711; *R. v. Southampton (Inhabitants)* (1852) 18 Q.B. 841.

[2] *Hamilton v. St George, Hanover Square* (1873) L.R. 9 Q.B. 42.

[3] Under Metropolis Management Act 1855.

[4] Normally a footway will be repairable as part of the road; see *Burslem Corpn. & Staffordshire C.C.* [1896] 1 Q.B. 24; *Derby C.C. v. Matlock Bath & Scarthin Nick U.D.C.* [1896] A.C. 315.

[5] [1928] Ch. 359.

Enforcement of the duty to repair

4-44   Where it is alleged that a way or a bridge is a highway maintainable at the public expense and that the highway is out of repair, a notice may be served on the highway authority, under the Highways Act 1980, section 56, requiring them to state whether they admit that the way or bridge is a highway and that they are liable to repair it. This procedure is appropriate both where the status of a particular highway is in dispute and where it is simply alleged that an admittedly adopted highway has not been properly repaired. It is also appropriate to be used against any person who or body which is liable to repair a highway by reason of statute, tenure, inclosure or prescription. Four issues can, therefore, be raised; whether the way or bridge is a highway, whether it is an adopted highway or an ancient highway, who is liable to repair it, and whether it is in fact out of repair.

4-45   The person served with the notice under section 56 may admit that the way or bridge is a highway maintainable by him or, in the case of a notice served on the highway authority, that it is repairable at the public expense. A period of one month is prescribed for the service on the complainant of this notice of admission. On receipt of the notice of admission, the complainant may, within the next six months, apply to a magistrates' court for an order requiring the repair of the highway. The magistrates will then have to decide whether the way or bridge is out of repair. If so, they have power to order that it is put into proper repair within such reasonable period as they may specify in the order.[6] At the expiry of the period defined in the order the magistrates' court, if satisfied that the highway has not been put in proper repair, may either extend the period for compliance, or authorise the complainant to carry out such works as may be necessary to put the highway in proper repair.[7] The complainant may then recover the expenses as a civil debt from the highway authority or other person against whom the order was made.[8]

4-46   Where no notice of admission is given by the highway authority or other person alleged to be liable to repair within one month of the original notice being served by the complainant, an application may be made by the complainant to the Crown Court for determination of the questions whether the way or bridge is a highway and whether the respondent to the notice is liable to repair it. Such an application must be by notice in writing to the appropriate officer of the Crown Court and must specify the situation of the way or bridge to which the application relates, the name of the respondent to the application, the part of the way or bridge which is alleged to be out of repair and the nature of the alleged disrepair. A copy of this notice must be served on the respon-

---

[6] Highways Act 1980, s.56(4).

[7] *Ibid.* s.56(6).

[8] *Ibid.* s.56(7). There may also be a right of recovery by the respondent to the order from any other person who is concurrently liable to maintain the highway.

dent.[9] If the court finds that it is a highway maintainable at the public expense and that it is out of repair, then an order will be made requiring the highway to be put into repair within such reasonable period as may be specified in the order. If the order is not complied with within the required period, then a magistrates' court may either extend the time for compliance or authorise the complainant to effect the repairs in the same way as may happen in relation to its own order for repair.[10]

Extinguishment of the liability to maintain a highway

The liability to maintain continues until the highway is extinguished,[11] **4-47** or until the liability is extinguished by an order of the court. Certain kinds of highway which are maintainable at the public expense but which are considered by the responsible highway authority to be unnecessary for public use may, by order of a magistrates' court, cease to be so maintained.[12] An application for such an order may only be made by the highway authority itself. The application cannot be made in respect of trunk or special roads, footpaths or bridleways. Notice of the application must be given to the district council and parish or community council[13] in which the highway is situated. If, within two months of the service of this notice on them, any of these bodies give notice that they refuse their consent then the application cannot be made.[14]

Following a preliminary view by two or more magistrates,[15] the jus- **4-48** tices first decide whether or not there are grounds for the making of the application. If they decide that there was no ground for the making of the application then no further proceedings may be taken on the application. If the justices find that there is ground for the making of the application, then their clerk must give the applicant highway authority six weeks' notice of a hearing date.[16] One month's notice of the hearing date must be given to the owners and occupiers of all land adjoining the highway to which the application relates.[17] These notices must indicate the purpose of the application to the court and the time and place at which the application is to be heard. Similarly, not less than four weeks immediately preceding the week in which the application is to be heard, the authority must publish in a local newspaper, circulating in the area in which the highway is situated, a notice stating that the application has been made, the purpose of the application, describing the highway and

---

[9] Highways Act 1980, s.56(3).
[10] See above. The expenses can be recovered as a civil debt and there is provision for contribution from any person under a concurrent liability; s.56(7), (8). See also s.57.
[11] See para. 4–15, above and Chap. 9.
[12] Highways Act 1980, s.47(1).
[13] Where there is no parish council, then the notice must be given to the chairman of the parish meeting; see s.47(4)(a).
[14] Highways Act 1980, s.47(3), (4).
[15] They must view together; see R. v. *Cambridgeshire J.J.* (1835) 4 Ad. & El. 111.
[16] Highways Act 1980, s.47(6).
[17] As to the meaning of "adjoining" see s.329(1) and the discussions at para. 10–28, below.

specifying the time and place at which the application is to be heard. A similiar notice must be fixed, at least fourteen days before the application is to be heard, to the principal doors of every church and chapel in the parish or community in which the highway is situated, or in some conspicuous position near the highway.[18] These requirements are mandatory and the magistrates must be satisfied as to their completion before they can begin to hear the application.[19] At the hearing itself, any objector to the application, who so wishes, must be heard. The magistrates may then either dismiss the application or make an order that the highway cease to be maintained at the public expense. Where the order is made, the highway immediately ceases to be maintainable at the public expense and the highway authority must give notice of the making of the order to any public utility undertakers having apparatus under, in, upon, over, along or across the highway to which the order relates.[20]

4–49   Extinguishment of the liability to maintain will mean that the way becomes repairable by no-one, unless there is a concurrent liability on some private person or body to maintain the highway by statute or by reason of tenure, inclosure or prescription. An order under section 47 is not final, since an application may subsequently be made to a magistrates' court for an order that the highway again become maintainable at the public expense on the grounds that there has been a change of circumstances since the original order under section 47 was made.[21] An application of this sort may be made by a person interested in the maintenance of the highway.[22] It would appear that "a person interested in the maintenance of the highway" includes a person who was liable to maintain the highway by statute or by reason of tenure, inclosure or prescription—whether his liability had always been concurrent with that of the highway authority or whether it had revived on the extinguishment of the public liability to maintain. Statutory undertakers whose apparatus was in danger of being damaged by the disrepair of the highway might fall within the meaning of the section. It is less obvious that the owner of the sub-soil, landowners served by the highway and ordinary highway users are covered by the wording in the section. The word "interest" is likely to be interpreted to mean something akin to a legal interest and since the relevant person must be interested[23] in "the maintenance" of the highway, the words are only sufficient to include those other persons who might also have some liability for the repair of the road.

---

[18] Highways Act 1980, s.47(7), (8).
[19] *Ibid.* s.47(7).
[20] *Ibid.* s.47(11).
[21] *Ibid.* s.48.
[22] One month's notice of intention to make the application must be given to the local highway authority: *ibid.* s.48(2).
[23] *cf.* the wide rights of audience given to objectors by s.47(9).

The liability of a person to maintain a highway by reason of tenure, **4-50** inclosure or prescription[24] may also be extinguished by order of a magistrates' court on the complaint of that person or of the highway authority[25]; in such a case the highway will then become a highway maintainable at the public expense. Where the complaint is made by the person liable to maintain the way, 21 days' notice must be given to the highway authority, and the authority then have the right to appear and be heard. On extinguishment, the person formerly liable to repair must pay to the highway authority a sum representing the value[26] to him of the extinguishment of his liability. Where a highway is diverted under the powers in section 116 of the Highways Act 1980, the new length of highway thereby created becomes maintainable at the public expense and a sum representing the value of the extinguishment again becomes payable to the highway authority.[27] It would also be open for a person liable to maintain a highway to apply for an order extinguishing the highway itself.[28] A number of provisions dealing with the extinguishment of the liability to maintain bridges are discussed in Chapter 11.

Powers available in order to perform the duty to maintain

When the parish surveyor had the duty cast upon him to repair the **4-51** highways within the parish, the source of labour and of materials was a constant problem to him, and, to some extent, conscripted part time labour was necessary. The need to obtain materials from locations as close as possible to the highway was of prime importance. Various statutes attempted to deal with the problem of obtaining materials.[29] Some of these powers can now be found in sections 45 and 46 of the Highways Act 1980. In the organised society in which we now live, the powers in section 45 are not of as great importance as they were in the days of the parish surveyor. Highway authorities will have general powers to contract to obtain materials and to employ labour under the Local Government Act 1972. By section 111 of that Act, a local authority has power to do anything (whether or not it involves the expenditure, borrowing, or lending of money, or the acquisition of or disposal of property or rights) which is calculated to facilitate, or is conducive or incidental to, the discharge of any of their functions. By section 112 of the 1972 Act, local authorities are given a wide discretion in the appointment of staff. Through these general powers, most of the functions of the highway authority in maintaining highways may be adequately performed.

Sections 45 and 46 of the Highways Act 1980 contain specific powers **4-52** for the obtaining of materials for the maintenance of publicly maintainable highways. By section 45(2), the highway authority is empowered to

---

[24] But not a liability imposed by statute.
[25] Highways Act 1980, s.53.
[26] To be agreed or determined by arbitration: *ibid.* s.53(3)–(5).
[27] *Ibid.* s.54.
[28] See Chap. 9.
[29] See *e.g.* Highways Act 1835, ss.45–55.

search for, dig, get and carry away gravel, sand, stone and other materials in and from any waste or common land. This power may be used to
obtain these materials from the bed of any river or brook flowing
through the waste or common land, subject to provisos prohibiting the
diversion or interruption of the course of the river or brook and the taking of any materials from any point within 50 yards above or below a
bridge, dam or weir.[30] There are further provisions governing the taking
of materials from sea beaches and from commons.[31] The highway authority may also gather and carry away stones lying on inclosed land in any
non-metropolitan county, metropolitan district or London Borough
within which the stones are to be used, with the consent of the landowner or under the authority of an order from a magistrates' court. Any
garden, yard, avenue to a house, lawn, park, paddock or inclosed plan-
tation, or inclosed wood not exceeding 100 acres in extent[32] is excluded
from the ambit of this power. There is further protection against the
excessive removal of stone from the seashore, causing an inundation or
danger of encroachment.[33] The magistrates should take into account the
particular needs of the occasion and the order cannot remain open indefinitely,[34] but will not necessarily be bad for failing either to specify the
precise period during which it is to be operative or the specific nature of
the repairs to be carried out.[35] Where the order does disclose the
repairs, it must not purport to operate for longer than is reasonably
necessary for the completion of those repairs.[36]

4–53   The highway authority may also take "rubbish or refuse stones" from
quarries within the non-metropolitan county or metropolitan district in
which the materials are to be used,[37] in order to maintain any bridge and
its approaches. Similarly, the authority may, with the owner's consent
or under the authority of an order from a magistrates' court, quarry
stone from such quarries provided that no court order may be made in
respect of any quarry which has not been worked within three years of
the making of the complaint for an order. Gardens and similiar areas are
also excluded.[38]

4–54   One month's notice of intention to make a complaint to the magistrates' court must be given to the owner and occupier of the land from
which the materials are to be taken.[39] Compensation is payable for the

---

[30] Highways Act 1980, s.45(2), (3)(*a*).
[31] *Ibid.* s.45(3)(*b*), (*c*); Commons Act 1876, s.20; see also *Hayes Common Conservators* v. *Bromley R.D.C.* [1897] 1 Q.B. 321.
[32] See hereon *R.* v. *Bradford* [1908] 1 K.B. 365.
[33] Highways Act 1980, s.45(4), (5)(*c*), (6).
[34] See *Manvers (Earl) and Browne* v. *Bartholomew* (1878) 4 Q.B.D. 5.
[35] *R.* v. *Adams, ex p. Pope* [1923] 1 K.B. 415; *cf. R.* v. *Manning* (1757) 2 Keny. 561.
[36] *R.* v. *Bradford* [1908] 1 K.B. 365.
[37] Or, within in Greater London, from any quarry within Greater London: Highways Act 1980, s.45(7).
[38] *Ibid.* s.45(8), (9).
[39] *Ibid.* s.45(11).

value of the materials taken from private land by virtue of a court order and also for any damage caused to *any* land by the carriage of the materials.[40] While excavating on land for materials, the highway authority must fence the excavation, fill in within three days where no materials are discovered and within 14 days after sufficient materials have been obtained, and make good and re-turf the ground. These requirements are backed up by a criminal penalty.[41] Damage or danger caused to any highway, occupation road, ford, dam, mine, building, works or apparatus during the exercise of the powers under section 45 similarly gives rise to a criminal penalty.[42] Any person taking away materials obtained for the purpose of repairing the highway also commits a criminal offence.[43]

Extraordinary traffic

Where a highway maintainable at the public expense is being   **4–55** damaged from use by vehicles of excessive weight passing along it or by other "extraordinary" traffic, the highway authority may, in certain circumstances, recover the excess expenses incurred in its repair from the person responsible for that traffic.[44] This power has to be seen in the context of the highway authority's responsibility to maintain its roads to the standard required for the changing needs of traffic.[45] The authority must act upon the certificate of its proper officer[46] to the effect that, having regard to the average expense of maintaining the highway or similar highways in the neighbourhood, extraordinary expenses have been or will be incurred by the authority in maintaining the highway and that such expenses have been caused by the extraordinary traffic passing along it. The certificate must be based upon fact rather than opinion[47] but clearly, where damage has not yet occurred, there will be an element of opinion in the assessment of likely damage. The comparison with the average expense of repairing roads in the neighbourhood is an aid to assessment and if these roads are in any event less expensive to maintain, this should be taken into account.[48] The certificate need not specify the details relating to comparative highways.[49] The certificate is

---

[40] Highways Act 1980, s.45(10).
[41] *Ibid.* s.46.
[42] *Ibid.* s.46(3).
[43] *Ibid.* s.46(4).
[44] *Ibid.* s.59.
[45] See para. 4–37, above; see also the discussion in *Weston-super-Mare U.D.C.* v. *Butt (Henry) & Co. Ltd.* [1922] 1 A.C. 340.
[46] Except where the authority is the Minister: Highways Act 1980, s.59(6).
[47] *Billericay R.D.C.* v. *Poplar Union and Keeling* [1911] 2 K.B. 801.
[48] *Aveland (Lord)* v. *Lucas* (1880) 5 C.P.D. 351; *Ledbury R.C.* v. *Colwall Park Granite Quarries Co. Ltd.* (1913) 108 L.T. 1002.
[49] *Epsom U.C.* v. *L.C.C.* [1900] 2 Q.B. 751; *Colchester Corpn.* v. *Gepp* [1912] 1 K.B. 477.

a condition precedent to the recovery of expenses.[50] A single certificate may be issued for several highways.[51]

Excess expenses

4–56   Excess expenses are recoverable through the county court (within the jurisdictional limits) or the High Court. Proceedings must be commenced within twelve months from the date on which the damage occurred or, where the damage is the result of a building contract[52] or of work extending over a long period of time, within six months from the completion of the contract[53] or work.[54] It will be a question of fact in each case when the contract or work, to which the damage is attributable, was completed.[55] The expenses recoverable are those which can be proved to the satisfaction of the court to have been, or to be likely to be incurred by the highway authority in maintaining the highway[56] by reason of the damage arising from the extraordinary traffic. Where reconstruction of the road is necessary, then these expenses may be claimed.[57] However, it may be necessary to make some allowance for betterment where the road is actually improved by the required works.[58] Damage to pipes or apparatus within the highway may be recoverable[59] but only, it would appear, where they may be said to be part of the highway. Where some of the expense of maintaining the road is attributable to other causes, then an allowance must be made for damage which would have been done to the road in any event due to these causes.[60] Where the authority seek to rely on the average expenditure on other highways, in calculating the excess expenditure claimed, they must give particulars of these other highways and the average expense of repairing them.[61]

4–57   There is specific provision for the agreement of expenses or their determination by arbitration where liability for prospective damage is admitted, and such agreement or determination then precludes the authority from commencing proceedings under the section for the recovery of any further expenses actually incurred.[62] The authority must

---

[50] *Pool Highway Board* v. *Gunning* (1882) 51 L.J.M.C. 49; *Bromley R.D.C.* v. *Chittenden* (1906) 70 J.P. 409.

[51] *Wirral Highway Board* v. *Newell* [1895] 1 Q.B. 287.

[52] See *Carlisle R.D.C.* v. *Carlisle Corpn.* [1909] 1 K.B. 471.

[53] See *Lancaster R.C.* v. *Fisher & Le Fanu* [1907] 2 K.B. 516; *Carlisle R.C.* v. *Carlisle Corpn.* [1909] 1 K.B. 471.

[54] *Kent C.C.* v. *Folkestone Corpn.* [1905] 1 K.B. 620.

[55] *Reigate R.D.C.* v. *Sutton District Water Co.* (1909) 78 L.J.K.B. 315; *Epsom U.C.* v. *L.C.C.* [1900] 2 Q.B. 751.

[56] Including expenses incurred in maintaining a cattle grid: Highways Act 1980, s.59(2).

[57] *Savin* v. *Oswestry Highway Board* (1880) 44 J.P. 766.

[58] *Colchester Corpn.* v. *Gepp* [1912] 1 K.B. 477.

[59] See *Chichester Corpn.* v. *Foster* [1906] 1 K.B. 167.

[60] *Cambridgeshire C.C.* v. *Pepper & Hollis* (1912) 76 J.P. 393; *Weston-super-Mare U.D.C.* v. *Butt (Henry) & Co. Ltd.* [1922] 1 A.C. 340.

[61] *Colchester Corpn.* v. *Gepp* [1912] 1 K.B. 477; *Morpeth R.C.* v. *Bullocks Hall Colliery Co. Ltd.* [1913] 2 K.B. 7; *cf. Bromley R.D.C.* v. *Chittenden* (1906) 70 J.P. 409.

[62] Highways Act 1980, s.59(3).

also be entitled to agree the amount of expenses where damage which has already occurred is admitted, although there is no express provision to this effect. The danger here would be that the time limits might run out before the money was actually recovered. However, there would seem to be no obstacle to an action based on a contractual agreement to pay those expenses supported by the authority's forbearance from bringing proceedings under the section. Such an agreement would not prevent later proceedings arising out of subsequent damage to the same highway.[63]

Person liable for excess expenses

4–58 The person from whom the expenses are recoverable is described as the "person ('the operator') by or in consequence of whose order the traffic has been conducted."[64] This strange form of wording was considered in the Court of Appeal by Lord Esher in *Kent County Council* v. *Gerard (Lord)*[65]:

> "It seems to me clear that the words of the section 'by whose order' cannot simply mean 'for whose advantage' and that the word 'order' cannot be confined to an order given to a servant who is bound to obey it. The explanation of the section must be sought within these two extremes. The best that I can give is that the expression may comprise a person by whose determination and direction the traffic has been taken along the road."

The employer of drivers who use the road in the course of their employment would, however, be covered by the wording. Where contractors are employed to deliver materials to a site, much will depend upon whether the route used was the only or inevitable route to be used by the contractors' vehicles, and the powers of direction over the manner of performance of the contract and over the routes to be taken which are retained by the employer.[66]

Excessive weight and extraordinary traffic

4–59 What constitutes excessive weight or extraordinary traffic can be difficult to determine. In *Hill* v. *Thomas*,[67] it was held that the expression "extraordinary traffic," as distinct from excessive weight, includes all such continuous or repeated user of the road by a person's vehicles as is out of the common order of traffic, and which may be calculated to damage the highway and increase the expenditure on its repair. *Per* Bowen L.J.[68]:

> " . . . extraordinary traffic is really a carriage of articles over the

---

[63] *High Wycombe R.D.C.* v. *Palmer* (1905) 69 J.P. 167.
[64] Highways Act 1980, s.59(1).
[65] [1897] A.C. 633.
[66] *Egham R.D.C.* v. *Gordon* [1902] 2 K.B. 120; *Bromley R.D.C.* v. *Croydon Corpn.* [1908] 1 K.B. 653; *Epsom U.C.* v. *L.C.C.* [1900] 2 Q.B. 751.
[67] [1893] 2 Q.B. 333.
[68] At 340–1.

road, at either one or more times, which is so exceptional in the quality or quantity or articles carried, or in the mode or time of user of the road, as substantially to alter and increase the burden imposed by ordinary traffic on the road, and to cause damage and expense thereby beyond what is common.''

Bowen L.J. cited, as an example of extraordinary traffic, the extra traffic generated by the building of a large house, factory or church, stressing that the provisions for recovery were not penal but remedial. The comparison which must be made is with the ordinary use of the road by all who use it rather than with the use made by other individual operators.

4-60   What is or is not extraordinary traffic is always a question of fact.[69] It is not possible to identify clear principles which will determine whether particular use of a highway is extraordinary. It is, however, possible to warn against the assumption that certain factors are conclusive and to point to factors which have been regarded as being relevant. Whilst it is proper to have regard to the nature of the goods carried by the traffic, the purpose for which they are carried and whether goods of this nature are commonly carried in the neighbourhood, none of these factors will be conclusive on the question of whether the traffic is extraordinary.[70] The nature and extent of the ordinary traffic on the road in question[71] must be determined before a sensible decision can be taken as to whether a particular use is extraordinary. Thus, the nature of the goods carried by the operator will rarely be an important factor of itself. The fact that the goods carried are the natural product of the land,[72] or are of the sort required by or produced in local factories,[73] or consist of stone from local quarries[74] will be relevant in determining the ordinary use of the road but will not prevent the traffic being regarded as extraordinary in appropriate circumstances. Mere increase in the amount of traffic of a kind commonly using the road will need to be sufficient in degree to be regarded as extraordinary.[75] On the other hand, the fact that the traffic generated is of unusual nature comparative to the traffic which generally

---

[69] See *e.g. Barnsley British Co-operative Society* v. *Worsborough U.D.C.* [1916] 1 A.C. 291.

[70] *Wallington* v. *Hoskins* (1880) 43 L.T. 597; *Geironydd R.D.C.* v. *Green* [1909] 2 K.B. 845; *Abingdon R.C.* v. *City of Oxford Electric Tramways Ltd.* [1917] 2 K.B. 318; *Weston-super-Mare U.D.C.* v. *Butt (Henry) & Co.* [1922] 1 A.C. 340.

[71] Rather than in the local area; *Etherley Grange Coal Co.* v. *Auckland District Highway Board* [1894] 1 Q.B. 37.

[72] *Williams* v. *Davies* (1880) 44 J.P. 347; *cf. Raglan Highway Board* v. *Monmouth Steam Co.* (1881) 46 J.P. 598.

[73] *Wycombe R.C.* v. *Smith* (1903) 67 J.P. 75.

[74] See *Tonbridge Highway Board* v. *Sevenoaks Highway Board* (1884) 49 J.P. 340; *cf. Ledbury R.C.* v. *Somerset* (1915) 113 L.T. 71.

[75] *R.* v. *Williamson* (1881) 45 J.P. 505; *Ledbury R.C.* v. *Somerset* (1915) 113 L.T. 71; *cf. Wolverhampton Corpn.* v. *Salop C.C.* (1895) 64 L.J.M.C. 179; *Abingdon R.C.* v. *City of Oxford Electric Tramways Ltd.* [1917] 2 K.B. 318.

uses the road becomes an important consideration.[76] It is not necessary to prove any negligence on the part of the operator.[77] Nor is it necessary to prove any unreasonable use of the highway—which would, in any event, be a nuisance.[78]

Excessive weight is determined not simply by having regard to the **4-61** aggregate weight but also to the conditions in which such weight is carried.[79] The fact that the pressure per square inch of the vehicles' wheels is less than that of the ordinary traffic or weight on the road in question, although material, is not conclusive that vehicles are not of excessive weight.[80] Traffic may be of excessive weight even though individual vehicles comply with the legal requirements as to axle weight.[81]

---

[76] *Whitebread* v. *Sevenoaks Highway Board* [1892] 1 Q.B. 8; *Norfolk C.C.* v. *Green* (1904) 90 L.T. 451; *Shepton Mallett R.D.C.* v. *Wainright (John) & Co.* (1908) 72 J.P. 459.
[77] *Chichester Corpn.* v. *Foster* [1906] 1 K.B. 167.
[78] See *Robinson* v. *London General Omnibus Co.* (1910) 74 J.P. 161.
[79] *Wallington* v. *Hoskins* (1880) 6 Q.B.D. 206.
[80] *Hemsworth R.D.C.* v. *Micklethwaite* (1904) 68 J.P. 345.
[81] *Aveland (Lord)* v. *Lucas* (1880) 5 C.P.D. 351.

CHAPTER 5

CIVIL LIABILITY FOR FAILURE TO MAINTAIN

INTRODUCTION

Position before 1961

5–01   The duty to maintain highways, which fell upon the inhabitants at large, was an absolute duty founded in nuisance and enforceable by indictment. The harshness of this rule was tempered, however, by another rule of the common law to the effect that a private individual who had suffered damage as a result of the highway being out of repair could not recover damages against the inhabitants at large if the lack of repair was due to the mere failure of the parish to maintain the highway (non-feasance) rather than to negligent acts of repair or other positive acts taken with respect to the highway (misfeasance).[1] When the duty on the inhabitants at large was replaced by a statutory duty on the relevant highway authority, the same distinction between non-feasance and misfeasance remained.[2] The exemption applied even where the highway was vested in the highway authority and where the road had been constructed by that authority.[3] It is not clear how far the exemption ever extended to persons liable to repair a highway by reason of tenure, prescription or inclosure.[4]

5–02   The line between non-feasance and misfeasance was sometimes a thin one. Where the highway authority had carried out some works and had left them incomplete or had not taken the works far enough, was this non-feasance in failing to do all the necessary works of repair or misfeasance in doing the works in a negligently incomplete way? To resolve this sort of question the courts often had to indulge in semantic exercises which reflected little credit on the common law.[5] The courts also attempted to confine the exemption within tight limits by holding that it

---

[1] *Russell* v. *Men of Devon* (1788) 2 Term Rep. 667; *Burton* v. *West Suffolk C.C.* [1960] 2 Q.B. 72.

[2] *Cowley* v. *Newmarket Local Board* [1892] A.C. 345; *Att.-Gen.* v. *Staffordshire C.C.* [1905] 1 Ch. 336; *Att.-Gen. & Ormerod Taylor & Son, Ltd.* v. *Todmorden B.C.* [1937] 4 All E.R. 588.

[3] *Gibson* v. *Preston Corpn.* (1870) L.R. 5 Q.B. 218; *Holloway* v. *Birmingham Corpn.* (1905) 69 J.P. 358; *Baxter* v. *Stockton-on-Tees Corpn.* [1959] 1 Q.B. 441.

[4] See *Russell* v. *Men of Devon* (1788) 2 Term Rep. 667; *Lyme Regis Corpn.* v. *Henley* (1832) 3 B. & Ad. 77; *McKinnon* v. *Penson* (1853) 8 Ex. 319; *Bathurst Borough* v. *Macpherson* (1879) 4 App.Cas. 256; *Rundle* v. *Hearle* [1898] 2 Q.B. 83.

[5] See *Burton* v. *West Suffolk C.C.* [1960] 2 Q.B. 72; *McClelland* v. *Manchester Corpn.* [1912] 1 K.B. 118; *Moul* v. *Tilling (Thomas) Ltd.* (1918) 88 L.J.K.B. 505; *Wilson* v. *Kingston-upon-Thames Corpn.* [1949] 1 All E.R. 679.

only applied to the highway authority acting in that capacity.[6]

Highways (Miscellaneous Provisions) Act 1961

The Highways (Miscellaneous Provisions) Act 1961, section 1, abro-   5–03
gated the rule of law exempting the inhabitants at large from civil liability for the non-repair of highways. The section came into force on
August 4, 1964 and was not retrospective. The Minister's immunity
from action was also removed. The effect of the 1961 Act was, therefore, that a highway authority, being under a statutory duty to maintain
the highway, under what is now the Highways Act 1980, section 41, was
exposed to the possibility of actions for breach of statutory duty for its
failure to maintain a highway. The Act expressly provided that the
reasonableness of the authority's actions in attempting to perform the
duty of maintenance could form a defence to the action. The burden of
proof was to be on the highway authority to establish that it had taken
such care as was in all the circumstances reasonably required to secure
that the part of the highway to which the action related was not dangerous for traffic. This statutory defence is now contained in the Highways
Act 1980, section 58.

Liability for a failure to maintain under the Highways Act 1980

The Highways Act 1980, section 41, imposes on a highway authority   5–04
the duty to maintain highways maintainable at the public expense. By
section 58, a statutory defence is provided where the highway authority
can establish that it has taken such care as is in all the circumstances
reasonably required to secure that the part of the highway to which the
action relates is not dangerous for traffic. The duty to maintain a highway extends to maintenance to the standard necessary to accommodate
the ordinary traffic which passes, or may reasonably be expected to
pass, along the highway.[7] This duty implies that the highway must be in
such a condition as to allow that passage of traffic free from danger.
Whether or not a cause of action now lies against the highway authority
depends upon whether the standard of repair is such that danger has
been caused to traffic. The wording of the statutory defence both
emphasises that there must be a causal link between a danger and the
accident and suggests the need for the reasonable anticipation of accident before any liability in civil proceedings results. A plaintiff must first
prove that the road was in such a condition as to be dangerous to traffic.[8] Foreseeability of danger must be established.[9] The dangerous condition must be shown to have been caused by the breach of duty to

---

[6] *Simon* v. *Islington B.C.* [1943] K.B. 188; *White* v. *Hindley Local Board* (1875) L.R. 10
Q.B. 219; *Blackmore* v. *Mile End Old Town Vestry* (1882) 9 Q.B.D. 451.
[7] See para. 4–36, above.
[8] *Burnside* v. *Emerson* [1968] 1 W.L.R. 1490.
[9] *Rider* v. *Rider* [1973] 1 Q.B. 505; *Burnside* v. *Emerson*, n. 8, above; *Bartlett* v. *Department of Transport* (1985) 83 L.G.R. 579.

maintain the highway. In some cases courts have drawn a distinction between permanent dangers and transient danger brought about by the elements. Thereafter, it is for the highway authority to establish the defence contained in the Highways Act 1980, section 58, in order to escape liability.

DANGEROUS CONDITION OF THE HIGHWAY

5–05 The fact that an accident has occurred owing to the condition of the highway might, at first glance, be thought to be good evidence that the highway was in a dangerous condition subject only to rebuttal evidence that the plaintiff brought the accident on himself or herself. However, the courts have, from an early stage, sought to prevent the highway authority from becoming the insurer of all highway users who suffer accidents from minor defects in the highway surface. The majority of disputed cases have involved tripping accidents on urban pavements.

5–06 In *Griffiths* v. *Liverpool Corporation*,[10] the Court of Appeal was faced with an accident which had occurred when a lady tripped on a flag-stone protruding half an inch above its fellows and which rocked when trodden upon. The county court judge had found as a fact that this paving stone constituted a danger to highway users and no appeal had been lodged against this finding. The Court of Appeal expressed reservations as to how far a relatively minor difference in the surface should be regarded as having created a danger giving rise to an action for breach of statutory duty. Sellers L.J. said[11]:

> "We are all of us accustomed to walk on uneven and irregular sur-faces and we can all of us trip on cobblestones, cat's eyes, studs marking pedestrian crossings, as well as other projections.
> If the finding that the half-inch projection of a solitary flagstone in a wide pavement has to be accepted as a danger because of the technicalities of this case, as my bretheren think, I have perhaps said enough to indicate that it is a standard which in my view should not become a precedent or guide in ordinary circumstances."

5–07 In *Meggs* v. *Liverpool Corporation*,[12] the plaintiff had fallen when walking on a pavement containing a group of uneven flagstones. One of these had a projecting point of a quarter of an inch. The evidence estab-lished that although local people knew of the condition of the pavement, they did not seek to avoid using it and no-one had reported its condition to the highway authority. It was held that the evidence was not sufficient to establish prima facie that the highway was dangerous to traffic so as to show a breach of the highway authority's obligation to repair. Dismiss-

---

[10] [1966] 1 Q.B. 374.
[11] *Ibid.* at 382.
[12] [1968] 1 W.L.R. 689.

ing the appeal against the judge's finding that the pavement was not dangerous, Lord Denning M.R. said[13]:

> "It seems to me, using ordinary knowledge of pavements, that everyone must take account of the fact that there may be unevenness here and there. There may be a ridge of half an inch or three quarters of an inch occasionally, but that is not the sort of thing which makes it dangerous or not reasonably safe."

Giving judgment for the highway authority in *Littler* v. *Liverpool* **5–08**
Corporation,[14–15] Cumming Bruce J. said:

> "The test in relation to a length of pavement is reasonable foreseeability of danger. A length of pavement is only dangerous if, in the ordinary course of human affairs, danger may reasonably be anticipated from its continued use by the public who usually pass over it. It is a mistake to isolate and emphasise a particular difference in levels between flagstones unless that difference is such that a reasonable person who noticed and considered it would regard it as presenting a real source of danger. Uneven surfaces and differences in level between flagstones of about an inch may cause a pedestrian temporarily off balance to trip and stumble, but such characteristics have to be accepted. A highway is not to be criticised by the standards of a bowling green."

Notwithstanding this warning, it has now become common for a difference in the surface of one inch to be used as an approximate guide to the point at which the potential liability in a highway authority, in tripping cases involving urban pavements, arises.

The cases on the extent of the liability of the highway authority to **5–09**
maintain road surfaces and footpaths outside of urban areas have been few. Clearly, a very different standard must apply to an unmetalled country footpath than to an urban pavement. Essentially, the test must be what the reasonable user of the highway may legitimately expect of the highway. The user of the country path will no doubt expect to find substantial depressions and differences in levels; problems presented by these paths are more likely to be in relation to the encroachment of undergrowth or of other obstacles into the path, thereby raising issues as to whether such encroachment is properly to be regarded as the result of a want of repair.[16]

A more difficult issue has been the extent to which the surface of the **5–10**
carriageway should be kept safe not only for vehicular traffic but also for

---

[13] [1968] 1 W.L.R. 689 at 692.
[14–15] [1968] 2 All E.R. 343 at 345; the "tripping point" in the pavement in this case was half an inch.
[16] See para. 5–16, below. See also *Whiting* v. *Hillingdon L.B.C.* (1970) 68 L.G.R. 437; *cf. Worcestershire C.C.* v. *Newman* [1974] 1 W.L.R. 938, D.C.; [1975] 1 W.L.R. 901, C.A.

the pedestrians who are entitled to use the full width of the highway.[17] In *Bird* v. *Tower Hamlets London Borough Council*,[18] a van driver stepped out of his vehicle and put his foot into a depression, variously described as being one and a half inches and three inches deep, injuring his ankle. It was argued that since this depression was in the carriageway rather than in the footway there had been no breach of duty, because the depression was not sufficiently great as to be a danger to vehicular traffic. Nield J. felt that he should not follow his personal inclination that such a depression was not in any event a danger and held that on the evidence before him it must be regarded as a danger to pedestrians. The judge rejected the argument that a different standard must be adopted for the carriageway than for the footway[19]:

> "The highway authority must foresee that pedestrians will cross the carrigeway, as they, indeed, are entitled to do, to pass and repass, and must, therefore, keep that part of the highway, as much as any other, safe for pedestrians."

On the other hand, in *Ford* v. *Liverpool Corporation*,[20] Watkins J. held that a metal grid in a roadway causing a depression of just over one inch in the road did not render the road of such dangerous condition that personal injury could reasonably have been anticipated to result from it. It had been argued that such a depression was more of a danger to the pedestrian who was seeking to cross the road than it would have been in the pavement. The judge rejected this argument on the basis that the general public must expect some obstructions to appear in the roadway, and quoted the examples given by Sellers L.J. in the *Griffiths* case.[21] It is difficult to reconcile these two decisions, and they can perhaps, only be explained on their different facts and on the different findings of the two judges as to the dangerous nature of the depressions in each case.

THE STATUTORY DUTY

An absolute duty

5–11   The issue has arisen in one series of cases as to whether the duty to maintain a highway is an absolute duty or whether a plaintiff is required to prove any element of fault in order to establish a prima facie case. Section 41 of the Highways Act 1980 states:

> "The authority who are for the time being the highway authority for a highway maintainable at the public expense are under a duty, . . . to maintain the highway."

Initially, the courts emphasised that the duty to maintain was histori-

---

[17] See para. 1–12, above.
[18] (1969) 67 L.G.R. 682.
[19] *Ibid.* at 685.
[20] (1972) 117 S.J. 167.
[21] See n. 10 above.

cally an absolute one and that the scheme of the 1961 Act had been to place the burden of establishing reasonable care on the highway authority.[22] However, in *Haydon* v. *Kent County Council*,[23] the extent of the duty to maintain the highway was considered in the context of the gritting and clearing of public paths. The highway authority did not plead the statutory defence and so the case turned on whether or not the plaintiff had made out the initial breach of duty. Whilst re-affirming that there was no duty on the plaintiff to negate the statutory defence, Goff L.J. said[24]:

> "In my judgment the plaintiff must prove . . . that the highway authority is at fault apart from merely failing to take steps to deal with the ice, or, which is the point in this case, that, having regard to the nature and importance of the way, sufficient time had elapsed to make it prima facie unreasonable for the authority to have failed to take remedial measures."

Shaw L.J. took a similiar view in finding that the plaintiff would have to show "a culpable breach of their duty to maintain." In *Bartlett* v. *Department of Transport*,[25] Boreham J., not without a measure of reluctance, felt constrained to follow the majority view in *Haydon*. This case involved the alleged failure of a highway authority to grit and clear ice and snow from the A34 in Oxfordshire, at a time when its employees were taking industrial action. Boreham J. held that the condition of the road had contributed to the accident which was the subject of the claim before him. He determined that the crucial question was whether the authority were "blameworthy." Holding that the highway authority, in declining to employ outside contractors to clear the roads, had acted prudently and out of concern for the danger of a spread of industrial action to other roads, which would have increased the danger to the public at large, rather than decreasing it, the judge determined that the authority was not in breach of its statutory duty.

Both the *Haydon* case and the *Bartlett* case concerned alleged **5–12** breaches by the highway authority to maintain its highway by failing to keep highways clear of snow and ice. Some doubt was expressed by the judges in both cases as to how far the action for damages based on the breach of the duty to maintain the highway could apply to cases such as these.[26] This qualification of the absolute nature of the duty to maintain the highway should, therefore, be seen in the context of those cases which concern aspects of maintenance going beyond repair of the physical structure of the highway and which arise from highway dangers caused by transient weather conditions. In these cases, liability may

---

[22] See *Griffiths* v. *Liverpool Corporation* [1967] 1 Q.B. 374.
[23] [1978] Q.B. 343.
[24] *Ibid.* at 363.
[25] (1985) 83 L.G.R. 579.
[26] See paras. 5–18 *et seq.*, below.

depend on proof of an element of negligence in the authority in not remedying the situation. Snow and ice may well be better regarded as obstructions in the highway than aspects of any failure to repair, and the importation of an element of fault into the standard of liability of the highway authority accords with the approach of the courts to obstructions which have been caused by natural events.[27] It is difficult, however, to resist the conclusion that the courts have been prepared to widen the scope of the duty of repair to include acts which go outside the ordinary ambit of section 41 only by placing restrictions on the absolute nature of the duty itself.

To whom is the duty owed?

5–13   The public are entitled to use a highway for the purposes of passage. It seems to be established that the duty to maintain the carriageway is owed both to pedestrians and to vehicular users.[28] In *Rider* v. *Rider*,[29] the Court of Appeal rejected an argument that the duty of care was owed only to the reasonably careful driver.[30] Sachs L.J. said[31]:

" . . . it is in my judgment clear that the corporation's statutory duty . . . is reasonably to maintain and repair the highway so that it is free of danger to all users who use that highway in the way normally to be expected of them—taking account, of course, of the traffic reasonably to be expected on the particular highway. . . . The highway authority must provide not merely for model drivers, but for the normal run of drivers to be found on their highways, and that includes those who make the mistakes which experience and common sense teaches are likely to occur. In these days, when the number and speed of vehicles on the roads is continually mounting and the potential results of accidents due to disrepair are increasingly serious, any other rule would become more and more contrary to the public interest."

Sachs L.J. expressly excluded drunken and reckless drivers from the normal run of drivers. Persons driving motor vehicles on bridleways and footpaths, and cyclists riding on footpaths might also qualify for exclusion from the ambit of the duty.

Maintenance and repair

5–14   The original liability of the inhabitants at large was a duty to keep their highways in repair. The liability of the inhabitants at large to repair highways was abolished in the Highways Act 1959. The expression

---

[27] See Chap. 7.
[28] *Bird* v. *Tower Hamlets L.B.C.* (1969) 67 L.G.R. 682; *cf. Ford* v. *Liverpool Corpn.* (1972) 117 S.J. 167.
[29] [1973] 1 Q.B. 505.
[30] Rejecting the obiter dictum of Lord Denning M.R. in *Bright* v. *Att.-Gen.* [1971] 2 Lloyd's Rep. 68.
[31] *Ibid.* at 514.

"repairable by the inhabitants at large" was replaced by the modern term "maintainable at the public expense." The word "maintenance," however, can be found in the statutory provisions at least as far back as the Highway Act 1835, where it was used to refer to the financial responsibility of the body responsible for the repair of the highway.[32] The responsibility imposed on the surveyor in that Act was a duty to "repair and keep in repair."[33] It was in the Highway Act 1862, section 17, that the expression "maintain in good repair" first appeared in the statement of the duties of the newly constituted highway boards.

"Maintenance" is defined in the Highways Act 1980, section 329(1) as   **5–15** including repair. A partial definition of this sort suggests a wider meaning beyond mere repair. Dealing with the word "street" in the Public Health Act 1875, Lord Selbourne said[34]:

> "An interpretation clause of this kind is not meant to prevent the word receiving its ordinary popular and natural sense, whenever that would be properly applicable; but to enable the word as used in the Act, when there is nothing in the context or subject matter to the contrary, to be applied to some things to which it ordinarily would not be applicable."

However, the highway authority has always had powers to take action to ensure that obstructions are removed, and may have had a duty to do so.[35] The authority was not liable to users of the highway for any damage or injury suffered by highway users through obstructions within the highway unless the same was caused by misfeasance. Again, the distinction between non-feasance and misfeasance was crucial. In *Tregellas* v. *London County Council*,[36] the plaintiff suffered personal injuries through the failure of the defendant council to lop the branches overhanging a highway. The court found that the authority was not liable because the injury was not the result of misfeasance.

The distinction between the duty to repair and the duty to keep a   **5–16** highway free from obstructions was demonstrated in *Worcestershire County Council* v. *Newman*.[37] In this case, the Court of Appeal had to consider whether certain highways (footpaths) were "out of repair" for the purposes of the Highways Act 1959, section 59.[38] The court held that where a highway was obstructed (in this case by a mixture of natural growth of hedges and man made obstructions, such as wire fences and the overflow from a cesspool) the question as to whether

---

[32] See Highway Act 1835, s.50.
[33] *Ibid.* s.6.
[34] *Robinson* v. *Barton-Eccles Local Board* (1883) 8 App.Cas. 798 at 801. See also *R.* v. *Kershaw* (1856) 26 L.J. (M.C.) 19; *Portsmouth Corpn.* v. *Smith* (1883) 13 Q.B.D. 184.
[35] *Bagshaw* v. *Buxton Local Board of Health* (1875) 1 Ch.D. 220.
[36] (1897) 14 T.L.R. 55. See, generally, *East Suffolk Rivers Catchment Board* v. *Kent* [1941] A.C. 74.
[37] [1975] 1 W.L.R. 901.
[38] See now Highways Act 1980, s.56.

it was "out of repair" for the purposes of the 1959 Act depended upon whether or not its surface was in some way defective or disturbed. Where a highway had become unusable because of an act of obstruction, it was not "out of repair" and the removal of the obstruction could not be viewed as being itself a repair. Cairns L.J. said[39]:

> "Not every defect in the surface would constitute being out of repair—*e.g.* an icy road would not in my view be out of repair. But if the surface is in a proper condition I do not think it can ever be said that the highway is out of repair."

A hawthorn hedge rooted in the path itself was sufficient to render the highway out of repair but the existence of fences or of branches which obstructed the way without affecting the surface could not render the way out of repair. The Divisional Court had already held that the flooding from a third party's cesspool was not sufficient to render the highway out of repair.

5–17   Section 1 of the Highways (Miscellaneous Provisions) Act 1961 sought only to abrogate the rule of law exempting "the inhabitants at large and any other persons as their successors from liability for non-repair of highways." The expression "maintainable at the public expense" had already been in existence since the passing of the 1959 Act.[40] On its face it would seem that the section did not purport to abrogate any other rule of law which drew a distinction between misfeasance and non-feasance, other than that related to repair. Liability for a failure to exercise statutory powers would now generally depend upon the application of the principles in *Anns* v. *Merton London Borough Council*.[41] Certainly, there is no indication that the section was aimed at dealing with the responsibility of the highway authority to take action to protect the highway by abating nuisances.

5–18   In *Haydon* v. *Kent County Council*,[42] the majority of the Court of Appeal adopted the reasoning in *Worcestershire County Council* v. *Newman*[43] and concluded that repair and maintenance were not synonymous; maintenance being wider than repair. Goff L.J. failed to see any real distinction between an obligation "to repair" and an obligation "to keep in repair." He decided, without giving detailed reasons, that the duty to maintain could include "clearing snow and ice or providing temporary protection by gritting." The plaintiff would, however, in the view of Goff L.J.,[44] have to prove an element of fault over and above failing to take steps to deal with the ice.[45]

---

[39] [1975] 1 W.L.R. 901 at 911.
[40] And had earlier been contained in the War Damage Act 1943.
[41] [1978] A.C. 728.
[42] [1978] Q.B. 343.
[43] [1974] 1 W.L.R. 938, D.C.; [1975] 1 W.L.R. 901, C.A.
[44] (1978) 76 L.G.R. 270 at 281.
[45] See also *McKenna* v. *Scottish Omnibuses and Northumberland C.C.* [1985] C.L. 2307.

Shaw L.J. gave greater explanation[46]:

> "Applying the primary canons of construction to what is an ordinary phrase, the ordinary meaning of 'to maintain' is to keep something in existence in a state which enables it to serve the purpose for which it exists. In the case of a highway that purpose is to provide a means of passage for pedestrians or vehicles or both (according to the character of the highway). To keep that purpose intact involves more than repairing or keeping in repair. Thus permitting the use of a highway for activities which would prevent or substantially impede movement to and fro, such as the setting up of a market, or the erection of barriers might be regarded as failures to maintain the highway in its function as a highway. . . . I feel, as does Goff L.J., that there may be extreme cases in special circumstances where a liability for failure to maintain not related to want of repair may arise. Such cases are not readily brought to mind although I would not wish to exclude them by confining the scope of maintenance to matters of repair and keeping in repair."

The court then rejected the plaintiff's claim, based on a failure to grit a footpath which had allegedly caused her to fall.

In *Bartlett* v. *Department of Transport*[47] Boreham J. felt constrained **5–19** to follow the reasoning of the majority in *Haydon* and found that the failure of the Department of Transport to clear the A34 of snow and ice was capable of giving rise to an action for damages based on a failure to maintain. The judge regarded the risk of danger to persons using the road as being foreseeable and that the situation which had caused the accident had existed for sufficiently long for the defendants to have appraised the situation and taken remedial measures. In the event, Boreham J. found that the duty of the highway authority had not been breached. In the course of his judgment, he pointed to the fact that the Highways (Miscellaneous Provisions) Act 1961 had abrogated the nonfeasance rule only in respect of non-repair. This, he felt, explained the Court of Appeal decision in *Haydon* as to why acts of maintenance would have to be related to repair in order to found an action based on breach of statutory duty.

The presence of water on a highway may be due either to the particu- **5–20** lar weather conditions, or to some defect either in the surface or in the drainage of the road. In *Burnside* v. *Emerson*[48] and *Tarrant* v. *Rowlands*[49] the flooding had lasted for sufficiently long for the court in each case to feel that there must be some defect in the drainage of the highway. The maintenance of the drainage system is as much an aspect of the maintenance of the highway as is the maintenance of the surface.

[46] [1978] Q.B. 343 at 364.
[47] (1985) 83 L.G.R. 579.
[48] [1968] 1 W.L.R. 1490.
[49] [1979] R.T.R. 144.

There is, therefore, little difficulty in fitting the *Burnside* and *Tarrant* decisions into a system which imposes a liability for failure to repair. However, the removal of snow and ice which have not themselves damaged the surface of the highway but which have rendered the way less easy to pass along is an extension of the concept of maintenance which has little support in the pre-1964 case law.[50]

Maintenance or improvement

5–21   A further distinction must be made between maintenance and improvement. There is no duty in the highway authority to improve highways.[51] Thus, there is no duty in the highway authority to widen an existing highway, even if an accident may be said to be attributable to the amount of traffic using a road which is too narrow. The authority has a power to improve and it may be that a negligent failure in an authority to exercise its powers would, in an extreme case, give rise to liability under the principles described in *Anns* v. *Merton London Borough Council.*[52] In *West* v. *Buckinghamshire*,[53] it was held that the decisions of a highway authority, in the exercise of its powers under the Road Traffic Regulation Act 1967,[54] as to the circumstances in which double white lines prohibiting overtaking should be placed in a stretch of highway, were policy decisions and not operational decisions within the principles set out in *Anns* v. *Merton London Borough Council.*[55] It seems likely that most decisions as to the criteria on which decisions to improve highways are taken will also fall within the policy rather than the operational sphere.[56] Liability will only arise in negligence; therefore, where the highway authority has arrived at its criteria in a negligent manner or where it has in practice negligently failed to apply those criteria to individual cases.

Highways to which the duty relates

5–22   A cause of action against a highway authority for breach of statutory duty can only arise in relation to those highways which are maintainable at the public expense and those which are maintainable by that highway authority. The questions which have to be asked and answered before an action for breach of statutory duty will succeed are: whether the place where the accident occurred is part of a highway; whether that highway is maintainable at the public expense; and which authority is the highway authority on whom that duty falls?

5–23   The first question has two elements to it. Clearly, the right of action will only arise if the accident happens on a piece of land which appears

[50] See, however, *Allison* v. *Corby D.C.* (1979) 78 L.G.R. 197.
[51] See Chaps. 4 and 6.
[52] [1978] A.C. 728.
[53] (1984) 83 L.G.R. 449; *cf. Bird* v. *Pearce* (1979) 77 L.G.R. 753.
[54] See now Road Traffic Regulation Act 1984.
[55] See n. 52 above.
[56] See *Just* v. *R. in Right of British Columbia* [1985] 5 W.W.R. 570.

to carry a public right of way. All highways, so long as they are maintainable at the public expense, are covered by the statutory duty. However, the duty to maintain footpaths[57] and bridleways in country areas may not be as extensive as the duty to maintain carriageway highways. Both the extent and the type of public user are relevant to this question. The circumstances in which highways become maintainable at the public expense differ, depending on whether the highway is a carriageway highway or a footpath or bridleway.[58] Local highway authorities will keep different records of carriageway highways and other highways.[59] Pedestrian ways in urban areas require to be treated with caution. Where they are attached to or go through buildings, they may be "walkways" created under the Highways Act 1980 or under local powers.[60] In other cases, they will be footpaths created by means of a public path creation order or agreement, or by the extinguishment of vehicular rights over a carriageway highway by means of an order under section 212 of the Town and Country Planning Act 1971.

The second question is whether or not the position of the accident is   **5–24** within the boundaries of the highway, and whether the accident has been caused by something in or on the highway which may properly be regarded as being part of that highway. Highways will include bridges but the duty of the highway authority to maintain a highway may not extend to the whole structure of a bridge.[61] The paths by the side of a carriageway highway will be footways forming part of that highway. The verges by the side of a country lane may or may not be part of the highway[62]; in any event, the duty to maintain these verges will not be high. Private forecourts by the side of roads must be distinguished from the highway and the duty to repair will be that of the private occupier under the Occupiers Liability Act 1957.[63] Although there are a number of statutory provisions rendering occupiers of premises adjoining a highway liable to a criminal penalty for dangers caused to highway users,[64] these provisions are unlikely to found an action for breach of statutory duty,[65] but there may be liability in nuisance where damage or injury is caused to a person actually on the highway.[66]

---

[57] "Footways" which are part of carriageway highways require a relatively high standard of repair.

[58] See para. 4–23, above, and Chap. 12.

[59] Most footpaths and bridleways will appear on the definitive map; see Chap. 12.

[60] See para. 1–28, above.

[61] See Chap. 11.

[62] See *Bishop* v. *Green* (1971) 69 L.G.R. 579. See, generally, Chap. 4.

[63] *Wood* v. *Morland & Co.* (1971) 115 S.J. 569. See also *Bromley* v. *Mercer* [1922] 2 K.B. 126; *Wilchick* v. *Marks & Silverstone* [1934] 2 K.B. 56; *Howard* v. *Walker* [1947] K.B. 860; *Jacobs* v. *London County Council* [1950] A.C. 361.

[64] See Highways Act 1980, ss.151–166.

[65] *Scott* v. *Green & Sons* [1969] 1 W.L.R. 301.

[66] *Tarry* v. *Ashton* (1876) 1 Q.B.D. 314; *Stewart* v. *Wright* (1893) 9 T.L.R. 480; see Chap. 8.

Highways maintainable at the public expense

5–25   The circumstances in which a highway may become maintainable at
the public expense are described in the preceding chapter.[67] In general
terms, the question is whether the highway is an ancient highway or
whether it has at some time been adopted by a highway authority under
one or other of the statutory procedures for adoption which have existed
since 1835. All local highway authorities are obliged to keep an up-
to-date list of the streets within their area which are maintainable at the
public expense.[68] Most authorities will, in fact, keep a register of all the
carriageway highways which they regard themselves as under a duty to
repair. So far as footpaths and bridleways are concerned, the definitive
map is a good guide to whether a path is maintainable at the public
expense. This map should include all paths which were in existence in
1949,[69] and all paths created since then by virtue of public path creation
orders and agreements. Most paths which are maintainable at the public
expense should, therefore, be on the map but it does not follow that all
paths on the map will, necessarily, be maintainable at the public
expense. The local highway authority should, therefore, be requested to
indicate whether a road or path is contained in its register of adopted
highways or is contained in any definitive map for the area. Where a
negative answer is received this is probably indicative of a lack of recent
maintenance or inspection by the authority and, whilst this is strongly
suggestive that the road or path is not maintainable at the public
expense, it is by no means conclusive.

5–26   Some roads are, of course, maintainable by the Minister[70] and it may
be necessary to make enquiries of the Department of Transport. Some
highways may, in fact, be maintainable by a non-metropolitan district
council exercising powers under the Highways Act 1980, section 42. In
these cases, the district council stands in the shoes of the highway authority and is liable for the failure to maintain. Local highway authorities
may enter into agreements with the Minister to maintain highways constructed by the Minister, and in these cases the local highway authority
becomes the highway authority for that road.[71] Otherwise, the fact that
a district council is exercising agency powers on behalf of the local highway authority[72] does not remove the ultimate liability of the highway
authority for the breach of statutory duty.[73] The same is true where the
Secretary of State delegates his maintenance responsibility to a county
council under the Highways Act 1980, section 6.[74]

---

[67] See paras. 4–18 *et seq.*, below.
[68] Highways Act 1980, s.36(6).
[69] And are therefore maintainable at the public expense; see Chap. 12.
[70] See Chap. 1.
[71] Highways Act 1980, s.5.
[72] *e.g.* under Local Government Act 1972, s.101.
[73] As to any liability for negligent works, see paras. 5–42 *et seq.*, below.
[74] See *e.g. Bartlett* v. *Department of Transport* (1985) 83 L.G.R. 579.

The Special Defence

General

Section 58 of the Highways Act 1980 provides a special defence for **5–27** highway authorities faced with an action for damages arising from a failure to maintain a highway maintainable at the public expense. The authority has a defence in such proceedings if it is able to prove that it had taken such care as in all the circumstances was reasonably required to secure that the part of the highway to which the action relates was not dangerous for traffic. The burden of proof is therefore on the authority to establish that it has taken such reasonable steps. "Traffic" includes pedestrians and animals.[75] Section 58 then goes on to specify a number of matters to which the court must have regard in deciding whether or not the authority has established its defence.[76] Although the court must have regard to these specified matters, it may also have regard to any other relevant matters which have a bearing on the questions of whether or not reasonable steps have been taken. In particular, it was pointed out in *Griffiths* v. *Liverpool Corporation*[77] that regard must be had to the particular circumstances of the highway authority concerned[78]:

> "The duty which the highway authority must prove that they have fulfilled is not a duty to secure a certain result but to 'take care' to do so and such a duty is fulfilled by the person upon whom it is imposed if he has done all that it is reasonably practicable for him to do to secure that result, even though, through circumstances which are beyond his control, he does not succeed in achieving it. This view as to the nature of the duty which the highway authority must prove that it has fulfilled is borne out by the provisions of paragraphs (*d*) and (*e*) of subs. (3), which in my view, clearly require that regard should be had to all the circumstances affecting the particular highway authority against which the action is brought."

With this in mind, a number of matters are commonly raised by highway authorities as part of their defence.

Availability of manpower

It is sometimes alleged that the manpower available to the authority **5–28** did not permit the detection of the danger, or its remedy prior to the accident. In *Griffiths* v. *Liverpool Corporation*,[79] Salmon L.J. accepted that whether a highway authority could reasonably have been expected to know of the condition of the highway, or to have carried out repairs, may depend on the labour force which it in fact had available or could

---

[75] Highways Act 1980, s.329(1).
[76] For an example of the judicial approach to each of these factors, see *Bramwell* v. *Shaw* [1971] R.T.R. 167.
[77] [1967] 1 Q.B. 374.
[78] *per* Diplock L.J. at 391–2.
[79] [1967] 1 Q.B. 374.

reasonably be expected to obtain.[80] This point has recently been put into perspective in *Bartlett* v. *Department of Transport*.[81] In that case, the Department of Transport had delegated its duty to maintain the A34 trunk road to the county council. The employees of the county council who were members of a particular union were involved with an industrial dispute and had refused to work on that trunk road. The result was that the A34 was not gritted or salted and snow was not cleared from it. The union had also indicated that if the county council were to employ private contractors in their place, they would withdraw their labour from other roads which were not at that time affected by the industrial action. Boreham J. held that the condition of the road was a contributing cause of the accident—although only to the extent of 20 per cent.— the main cause being the negligent driving of the deceased driver. However, he was mainly concerned with considering whether, in the circumstances of the industrial dispute, the highway authority, through its agents, the county council, were in breach of duty, and whether it had established the statutory defence. After finding that there had been no breach of duty, the judge went on to consider whether the statutory defence had been made out. The judge found that in placing warning notices and in seeking the assistance of motoring organisations and of the police in directing as much traffic as possible away from the A34, the authority had exercised all reasonable care to ensure that the road was not dangerous to traffic.

Regularity of inspection

5-29   The regularity of inspection was considered in *Pridham* v. *Hemel Hempstead Corporation*.[82] In this case, a pedestrian suffered an injury when she fell on a tarmacadam footpath. The highway authority produced evidence that it categorised its roads according to the degree of usage and that the footpath in question, in accordance with that system, had been inspected once every three months. At first instance, Mocatta J. found that the statutory defence had not been made out, since the path could in practice have been inspected more frequently than it was. The issue in the Court of Appeal was whether this was the correct approach. The Court of Appeal held that the authority needed only to show that it had exercised such care as was reasonably required and that, since the authority could show that it had adopted the quarterly inspection of these paths after careful consideration, and that additionally it had checked its complaints book, it had, in all the circumstances, made out the defence. Curiously, no evidence had been produced as to why these categories of inspection had been chosen, nor as to why the authority chose to examine roads such as the one in question at intervals of three months only. However, the Court of Appeal was apparently

[80] [1967] 1 Q.B. 374 at 394.
[81] (1985) 83 L.G.R. 579.
[82] [1971] 69 L.G.R. 523.

satisfied, from an examination of the authority's minutes, that sufficient consideration had been given to these questions.

Two notes of caution must be sounded with respect to the *Pridham*   **5–30** decision. First, there had been no expert evidence before the judge at first instance, nor the Court of Appeal, as to what regularity of inspection should have been required in respect of the path in question. Secondly, in the absence of such expert evidence, the Court of Appeal only felt able to deal with the issues on the grounds that the evidence before it suggested that the danger to footpath users was not from predictable wear and tear of the path but rather from unpredictable incidents, such as spillage of oil or acid, vehicles mounting the kerb or acts of deliberate damage. In those circumstances, in the words of Widgery L.J.[83]:

> "Accordingly, in deciding what is a reasonable interval between inspections, one cannot be guided by the expert opinion of an engineer, however highly qualified. One must instead determine what is reasonable by suitable compromise between conflicting considerations."

Otherwise, the regularity of inspection will depend on the susceptibility of the road or path in question to damage from ordinary wear and tear and will, therefore, require close consideration by a court of the specific factors set out in section 58(2).[84]

Character of the highway and the traffic reasonably expected to use it

The first matter to which the court is required to have regard is the   **5–31** character of the highway and the traffic reasonably expected to use it. Where a highway authority is aware that a footpath is regularly being used by other traffic (a user which would be illegal) it is under no duty to repair that footpath to a higher standard than is required for foot travellers. So long as the way is maintained to the footpath standard, the highway authority cannot be shown to have failed in its duty to maintain the way in the first place. Further, it must be doubtful whether a horserider or motorist, injured whilst riding or driving on a footpath, will be within the scope of the statutory duty. The location of the highway may also reflect upon its character. The standards required of country paths and of those forming part of an urban pedestrianised area may be very different.

In *Bramwell* v. *Shaw*,[85] the age of the road, the likelihood that it   **5–32** would break up and the heavy traffic which was to be expected to use the highway were all taken into account in deciding whether the

---

[83] [1971] 69 L.G.R. 523 at 531.
[84] See, however, *Whitaker* v. *West Yorkshire Metropolitan C.C. and Metropolitan Borough of Calderdale* [1982] C.L.Y. 1435, where the absence of any system of maintenance was not regarded as being conclusive of breach of statutory duty.
[85] [1971] R.T.R. 167.

highway authority had made out its statutory defence. Despite four-weekly inspections, the authority was held to be liable because the combination of the state of the road, and the traffic likely to use it, required an extremely good system of maintenance to be established and applied. In *Jacobs* v. *Hampshire County Council*,[86] the configuration of a road (tarmac adjoining cobbles), which led to a greater susceptibility to water penetration and consequent damage within a relatively short period, was found to be sufficient to establish a breach of duty notwithstanding six-monthly inspections.

Standard of maintenance appropriate for a highway of that character and used by such traffic

5–33   It has been well established that the extent of the duty to maintain a highway depends upon the traffic which passes or which may reasonably be expected to pass along it.[87] There will be differences in the standard of maintenance between roads carrying vehicular rights of way, depending on the amount of traffic which they carry and the purposes which particular roads serve. Highway authorities may class their carriageway highways and establish inspection and maintenance routines according to these factors. It seems that, where a highway authority can show that it has given careful consideration to these factors in establishing its system of inspection and maintenance, a court will, in the absence of expert evidence that such a system was inadequate, be prepared to find that the statutory defence has been established.[88]

State of repair in which a reasonable person would have expected to find the highway

5–34   This again follows on from the character of the highway and requires the court to compare the actual state of the highway with that which should reasonably be expected from a highway of such a kind. However, it may go further than this. The highway authority may have special knowledge of the highway and of the extent and the nature of the user of that highway, and may have adopted a low standard of maintenance based on that knowledge. A reasonable person not in possession of that knowledge might reasonably expect a highway of that type to be maintained to a higher standard. The Act does not indicate what knowledge the reasonable person must have of the character and actual user of the highway. However, it is likely that the presence or absence of any warning to travellers that the road might not be all that it seemed would be a relevant factor here.

---

[86] *The Times*, May 28, 1984.
[87] *Sharpness New Docks and Gloucester and Birmingham Navigation Co.* v. *Att.-Gen.* [1915] A.C. 654.
[88] *Pridham* v. *Hemel Hempstead Corpn.* [1971] 69 L.G.R. 523.

State of knowledge of the highway authority

The court is required to have regard to whether the highway authority **5–35** knew, or could reasonably have been expected to know, that the condition of the part of the highway to which the action relates was likely to cause danger to users of the highway. The knowledge, therefore, must relate both to the condition of the highway and to the likelihood of danger arising from that condition.

Warning notices

Once a highway authority is aware of the dangerous condition of one **5–36** of its highways, it necessarily comes under a duty to take action to repair it as quickly as possible. Where an accident occurs in the time between discovery of the danger and repair of the way, the authority will, in the more serious cases, be expected to place a warning notice near the place of the danger.[89]

Reliance upon independent contractors

Where statute has imposed an absolute duty on an individual or a **5–37** class of individuals, it is not open to the person or class of persons on whom the duty is placed to avoid the responsibility for the performance of that duty by seeking to rely on the employment of an independent contractor.[90] The concluding words of section 58(2) relate to this rule:

" . . . for the purposes of such a defence it is not relevant to prove that the highway authority had arranged for a competent person to carry out or supervise the maintenance of the part of the highway to which the action relates unless it is also proved that the authority had given him proper instructions with regard to the maintenance of the highway and that he had carried out the instructions."

If, therefore, the works carried out on behalf of the authority would be sufficient to satisfy the defence if carried out by the highway authority itself, then the fact that they have been carried out by an independent contractor will not put the authority in any worse a position. The rule which distinguishes casual or collateral acts of negligence by the contractor[91] would seem to apply to actions under the Highways Act 1980.

OTHER DEFENCES

Inevitable accident and Act of God

The defences of Act of God or inevitable accident remain available to **5–38** the highway authority, even where the existence of the danger on the highway is proved, and even where the failure to maintain the highway

---

[89] See *Bartlett* v. *Dept. of Transport* (1985) 83 L.G.R. 579.
[90] *Hardaker* v. *Idle D.C.* [1896] 1 Q.B. 335; *Smith* v. *Cammell Laird & Co. Ltd.* [1940] A.C. 242.
[91] See *Dalton* v. *Angus* (1881) 6 App.Cas. 740.

is established. These defences really go to the question of causation, and there is, therefore, no reason why they should not be available.[92] In *Griffiths* v. *Liverpool Corporation*,[93] Diplock L.J. agreed with the view taken by the county court judge, that the breach of duty did not require proof by the plaintiff that it was the lack of reasonable care which was the cause of the injury to him. However, this is not the same as saying that the plaintiff does not have to prove that it was the existence of the danger in the highway which was the cause of his accident.

Contributory negligence

5–39   It is now well established that the contributory negligence of the plaintiff, or of another highway user, may be relied upon by a highway authority which is found to have been in breach of its duty to maintain the highway. In *Bartlett* v. *Department of Transport*,[94] Boreham J. held that the highway authority was not in breach of its duty, but nonetheless considered the respective degrees of blame of the highway authority and the driver. He held that the condition of the highway was a contributing cause of the accident, although only to the extent of 20 per cent—the main cause being the negligent driving of the deceased driver. In *Burnside* v. *Emerson*,[95] the highway authority was held to be responsible for an accident to the extent of one-third whilst the first defendant driver was held to be liable to the remaining two-thirds' extent.[96]

Volenti non fit injuria

5–40   It seems that the defence of consent could apply to a failure to maintain a highway, but that the circumstances in which such a defence would be upheld are both extreme and rare. The limiting factor to the *volenti* principle is that knowledge does not necessarily imply consent. The fact, therefore, that a driver is aware that it is not appropriate to drive at high speeds, or to race, along country roads does not necessarily imply that he has consented to those roads being out of repair.[97]

ACCIDENTS OCCURRING AS A RESULT OF CODE REGULATED WORKS

5–41   Section 58(4) of the Highways Act 1980 expressly excludes from the application of the section any damage which results from code regulated works, where that damage results from an event which occurred either before the completion or making good of the relevant part of the street, in pursuance of the obligation imposed on the undertakers by section 7(2) of the Public Utilities Street Works Act 1950, or where the relevant

---

[92] *Griffiths* v. *Liverpool Corpn.* [1967] 1 Q.B. 374.
[93] *Ibid.*
[94] (1985) 83 L.G.R. 579.
[95] [1968] 1 W.L.R. 1490.
[96] See also *Tarrant* v. *Rowlands* [1979] R.T.R. 144.
[97] See generally *Dann* v. *Hamilton* [1939] 1 K.B. 509; *Owens* v. *Brimmell* [1977] Q.B. 859.

part of the street is the subject of an election[98] under Schedule 3 to that Act. The operation of the public utilities street works code is described fully in Chapter 13.

NEGLIGENCE

Prior to 1961, the immunity of the highway authority for the non-repair **5–42** of highways only related to nonfeasance and not to acts of misfeasance. There are numerous examples of what might be regarded as acts of misfeasance so as to give rise to liability in negligence.[99] Some of these decisions may now need to be read with care, since the desire of the courts to overcome the nonfeasance rule by artificially finding acts of misfeasance must be accounted for. Where an authority exercises powers and carries out works in such a way as to create a danger in the highway where previously there was no danger, then it will be liable in negligence. However, there are a number of authorities which indicate that where a danger already exists, the authority cannot be liable in negligence simply for failing to exercise its powers to remove that danger.[1] These cases now have to be considered in the light of the decision of the House of Lords in *Anns* v. *Merton London Borough Council.*[2]

The power of a highway authority to erect traffic signs warning motor- **5–43** ists of potential dangers has been considered in a number of cases. In *Bird* v. *Pearce,*[3] a highway authority had established a traffic system which gave priority to a major road, and had provided warnings along its length to users of all minor roads at junctions with the major road. After executing resurfacing works, the highway authority obliterated these signs at one particularly bad junction, and did not replace them with temporary warning notices. The authority was held liable in negligence in relation to an accident which occurred when a vehicle emerged from the minor road into collision with a vehicle on the major road. It had been argued that the fault of the authority, if any, had been in its failure to exercise its statutory powers to place the signs in the road. The Court of Appeal preferred to look at the events in a different way. The removal of the road markings in the first place had been undertaken in the exercise of statutory powers, and the highway authority then became under a duty to exercise reasonable care so as not to cause avoidable damage or injury to those whom it could reasonably foresee might be affected by such an exercise. The authority must refrain from

---

[98] *i.e.* limiting the obligation of undertakers to the execution of interim restoration during a specified period.

[99] See *Hill* v. *Tottenham U.D.C.* (1898) 79 L.T. 495; *Andrews* v. *Merton & Morden U.D.C.* (1921) 56 L.J. 466; *Meeling* v. *St. Mary, Newington, Vestry* (1893) 10 T.L.R. 54; *Smith (James) & Co.* v. *West Derby Local Board* (1878) 3 C.P.D. 423; *Pitman* v. *Southern Electricity Board* [1978] 3 All E.R. 901.

[1] *East Suffolk Rivers Catchment Board* v. *Kent* [1941] A.C. 74; *Sheppard* v. *Glossop Corpn.* [1921] 3 K.B. 132.

[2] [1978] A.C. 728.

[3] (1979) 77 L.G.R. 753.

creating a "trap" for road users.[4] The highway authority may also be liable if, by the placing of traffic signs in the highway, it creates an unnecessary risk to road users. In *Levine* v. *Morris*,[5] the highway authority, having had a choice of sites in which to place a road sign, was found to have placed the sign in such a position that it was foreseeably likely to give rise to an unnecessary and grave hazard to users of the carriageway. The authority was held to be liable in negligence.

5–44   The same principles apply to the negligent construction or improvement of the highway.[6] Highway authorities have, accordingly, been held liable where the route of a highway has been altered and a new way laid out and thrown open to the public which new way was unfenced adjacent to a dangerous embankment.[7]

5–45   In *Anns* v. *Merton London Borough Council*,[8] the House of Lords considered the circumstances in which public authorities could be held liable in negligence for failure to exercise their statutory powers and duties. Formerly, it had been considered that the failure of a highway authority to exercise statutory powers to remedy a dangerous situation on the highway was not actionable, unless the authority had caused the danger, or unless the authority had, itself, in some way created a trap for highway users which the exercise of its powers could have prevented.[9] The approach adopted by Lord Wilberforce[10] in *Anns* was rather to draw a distinction between the operational areas of a local authority's decision-making process, and the policy areas[11]:

> "Most, indeed probably all, statutes relating to public authorities or public bodies, contain in them a large area of policy. The courts call this 'discretion,' meaning that the decision is one for the authority or body to make, and not for the courts. Many statutes, also, prescribe or at least presuppose the practical execution of policy decisions: a convenient description of this is to say that in addition to the area of policy or discretion, there is an operational area. Although this distinction between the policy area and the operational area is convenient, and illuminating, it is probably a distinction of degree; many 'operational' powers or duties have in them some element of 'discretion.' It can safely be said that the more

---

[4] See also *Bright* v. *Minister of Transport* (1971) 69 L.G.R. 338.
[5] [1970] 1 W.L.R. 71.
[6] *Baxter* v. *Stockton-on-Tees Corpn.* [1959] 1 Q.B. 441; *Taylor* v. *St. Mary Abbotts, Kensington Vestry* (1886) 2 T.L.R. 668.
[7] *Evans* v. *Rhymney Local Board* (1887) 4 T.L.R. 72; *McClelland* v. *Manchester Corpn.* [1912] 1 K.B. 118.
[8] [1978] A.C. 728.
[9] *Sheppard* v. *Glossop Corpn.* [1921] 3 K.B. 132; *Fisher* v. *Ruislip-Northwood U.D.C.* [1945] K.B. 584; *Morrison* v. *Sheffield Corpn.* [1917] 2 K.B. 866; *McClelland* v. *Manchester Corpn.* [1912] 1 K.B. 118.
[10] With whom the majority agreed.
[11] [1978] A.C. 728 at 754.

'operational' a power or duty may be, the easier it is to superimpose on it a common duty of care."

Lord Wilberforce found it to be irrelevant to the creation of the duty of care whether the decision of the authority depends upon a power or a duty. It seems therefore, that where a local authority has a power to take action which will result in the removal of a known danger from the highway, then the failure to exercise that power may give rise to liability, unless the exercise of the power is classified as being outside the operational area. Whether or not liability will fall on the authority then requires a careful consideration as to whether the persons injured by the failure to exercise the power are persons to whom the duty of care is owed, and of the precise extent of the duty of care which is owed to them. The statutory purpose for the granting of the power, or the imposition of the duty, will substantially determine both these issues. Whilst it is difficult to make any general comments about a duty of care which depends upon a "sliding scale" between policy and action, it would seem that the greater the particularity that marks the discretionary decision, the more likely it is that the duty of care attaches. Thus, a decision not to take a certain type of action in respect of highways generally, on the grounds of manpower and finance, is unlikely to attract liability.[12] The decision not to take action in an individual case is more likely to do so. In *West* v. *Buckinghamshire County Council*,[13] Caulfield J. held that the decisions of a council, as to the circumstances in which double white lines, prohibiting overtaking, should be placed in a highway and as to the frequency of inspections, were policy decisions, which, having been exercised honestly and carefully, gave rise to no duty of care.

It is now well established that a highway authority cannot be held **5–46** liable under the provisions of the Occupiers Liability Acts 1957 and 1984,[14] apparently on the basis that an authority neither invites nor licences the public to use a footpath: rather they use it as of right, and the highway authority has no right to exclude them. The duty to maintain the footpath is not sufficient to establish the necessary control over the path to render the highway authority an occupier.[15]

---

[12] *Anns* v. *Merton L.B.C.* [1978] A.C. 728, and Lord Salmon at 762.

[13] (1984) 83 L.G.R. 449. See, generally, the approach now adopted by the courts in *Yuen Kun-Yeu* v. *Att.-Gen. of Hong Kong* [1987] 3 W.L.R. 776; *Jones* v. *Dept. of Employment* [1988] 2 W.L.R. 493.

[14] Liability under the 1984 Act is expressly excluded by section 1(7) of that Act.

[15] *Whiting* v. *Hillingdon L.B.C.* (1970) 68 L.G.R. 437; *Greenhalgh* v. *British Rys. Board* [1969] 2 Q.B. 286; *Holden* v. *White* [1982] Q.B. 679.

CHAPTER 6

IMPROVEMENT OF HIGHWAYS

INTRODUCTION

Background

6–01   The changing demands of traffic will, from time to time, require works of widening and improvement going beyond mere repair. The common law did not imply any power to widen.[1] While regular encroachment of traffic onto roadside waste might lead to the acquisition of highway rights over an extended width, in the majority of cases—particularly in towns—the width of the highway would be defined by the existence of houses, fences, hedges or ditches. An increase in width would involve, therefore, the acquisition of the land of adjoining owners. Awards under the Inclosure Acts often sought to ensure that highways should be of a stated and standard width. Powers to widen highways were eventually given to the parish surveyors in a number of general Acts of Parliament.[2] Where new streets and roads were to be laid out under statutory powers, minimum widths were also often required. Accompanying these powers to widen highways and to prescribe the width of streets, were powers preventing the construction of property close to the highway boundary and restricting the growth of trees or other vegetation which might subsequently encroach onto the highway.[3] Other powers of improvement arose from the need to provide highways of stronger construction and better alignment to take the heavier traffic which was being generated. Currently, highway authorities have wide powers to improve highways. These powers are contained in Part V of the Highways Act 1980.

Meaning of improvement

6–02   "Improvement," for the purposes of the Highways Act 1980, is defined[4] as the doing of any act under the powers contained in Part V of the Act, including "the erection, maintenance, alteration and removal of traffic signs, and the freeing of a highway or road ferry from tolls." Thus, improvement extends further than altering the physical structure of the highway. Section 62 of the Highways Act 1980 in fact lists nine specific kinds of improvement which *must* be carried out under specific powers, but gives a further general power to:

---

[1] See *R.* v. *Stretford* (*Inhabitants*) (1705) 2 Ld. Raym. 1169; *R.* v. *Devon* (*Inhabitants*) (1825) 4 B. & C. 670.
[2] *e.g.* see Highway Act 1773 and Highway Act 1835.
[3] See, *inter alia,* Highway Act 1773, ss.6, 7, 10; Highway Act 1835, ss.64, 65, 66, 80.
[4] At s.329(1).

116

"carry out, in relation to a highway maintainable at the public expense by them, any work (including the provision of equipment) for the improvement of the highway."

The definition in the 1980 Act is, therefore, somewhat circular and unhelpful. The Highways Act 1864 (now repealed) had provided a partial definition,[5] namely:

"The doing of any other work in respect of highways beyond ordinary repairs essential to placing a highway in a proper state of repair."

In *Rodgers* v. *Ministry of Transport*,[6] the construction of a lay-by from the highway verge and footway was held to be included in the powers to level or widen conferred by the Highways Act 1864. In *Hanscombe* v. *Bedfordshire County Council*,[7] the filling in of part of a ditch which was not part of the highway, for the purpose of laying pipes, was held not to fall within the general power of improvement in the Highways Act 1864. These cases do not assist very much in determining what may be the limits of any powers of improvement, because the construction of a lay-by obviously can be said to involve the widening of the highway, whilst entry onto the land of an adjoining landowner in order to to carry out works on that land necessarily requires clear statutory authority. If the works being carried out are similar in their nature to works contemplated by one of the specific powers contained in the Act, then they will be likely to be regarded as a lawful improvement. However, if the improvement is so similiar to one of the specific powers, it may be that it should be exercised through that power and in accordance with the requirements and restrictions governing the use of that power.[8] More generally, so long as the proposed improvement by the highway authority is related to a proper highway purpose, *i.e.* to facilitate the safe, unhindered passing and repassing by members of the public along the highway or to protect highway users, then it may be justified under the general power of section 62.

IMPROVEMENT POWERS UNDER THE HIGHWAYS ACT 1980

General power of improvement

The general power given by section 62(2) of the Highways Act 1980 is **6–03** subject to two limitations. First, the power is only available in relation to a highway maintainable at the public expense by the highway

---

[5] At s.8(5). See also Development and Road Improvement Funds Act 1909, s.8(5).
[6] [1952] 1 All E.R. 634.
[7] [1938] 1 Ch. 944.
[8] See Highways Act 1980, s.62(2).

authority itself. Secondly, the general power cannot be relied upon to carry out certain specified acts of improvement for which specific statutory power is granted later on in Part V of the 1980 Act.[9] These specific powers are:

(a) the division of carriageways, provision of roundabouts and variation of the relative widths of carriageways and footways;
(b) the construction of cycle tracks;
(c) the provision of subways, refuges, pillars, walls, barriers, rails, fences or posts for the use or protection of persons using a highway;
(d) the construction or reconstruction of bridges and alteration of the level of highways;
(e) the planting of trees, shrubs and other vegetation and laying out of grass verges;
(f) the provision, maintenance, alteration, improvement or other dealing with cattle grids, by-passes, gates and other works for use in connection with cattle grids;
(g) the execution of works for the purpose of draining a highway or of otherwise preventing surface water from flowing on to it;
(h) the provision of barriers or other works for the purpose of affording to a highway protection against hazards of nature.

Improvement of highways and compensation

6–04   Part V of the Highways Act 1980 makes no general provision for payment of compensation to persons who are affected by highway improvements, although there are provisions for compensation contained in individual sections. The Land Compensation Act 1973, does, however, give some rights of compensation to persons who have suffered a depreciation in the value of an interest in land caused by physical factors arising from the use of highways, and there are further provisions in Part II of that Act designed to mitigate the adverse effects of, *inter alia*, construction works and the use of improved highways.[10] Apart from these provisions, a landowner who has suffered loss by reason of improvement works to the highway will only have a right to compensation where the particular statutory power gives him such a right, or through an action for damages at common law.

6–05   The common law remedy may be available where the injury suffered is caused through the unreasonable exercise of the power, or where the injury is not an inevitable consequence of the exercise of the enabling

---

[9] Any works executed by the authority under its general power may be altered or removed: Highways Act 1980, s.62(4).
[10] As to the effect of these provisions, see Chap. 14.

power.[11] This will be so, even if the effect of the improvement is to interfere with the frontagers' rights of access.[12] Every power must be looked at carefully, in order to ascertain whether, on a true construction, the interference with private rights which is complained of is an inevitable consequence of the exercise of the power or, where an element of discretion is given to the authority as to the siting of its improvement works, whether the authority has acted reasonably.[13] The erection, for example, of a shelter in the highway, or the raising of the level of a highway, will inevitably affect the right of landowners to have access from the highway to every part of their land.[14] However, improvement works interfering with a landowner's only access, without the creation of accommodation works necessary to provide an equally convenient access, may well be an unreasonable exercise of the power. The lack of compensatory provisions in the enabling statute has been said to be an influencing factor in the construction of the statutory power. In *Metropolitan Asylum District* v. *Hill*,[15] Lord Blackburn said:

> "The legislature has very often interfered with the rights of private persons, but in modern times it has generally given compensation to those injured; and, if no compensation is given it affords a reason, though not a conclusive one, for thinking that the intention of the legislature was, not that the thing should be done at all events, but only that it should be done, if it could be done, without injury to others."

The general applicability of this as a principle of construction has, however, been doubted.[16] Negligence here has a wider meaning than in its normal tortious context[17]:

> " 'negligence' . . . being used in a special sense so as to require the undertaker, as a condition of obtaining immunity from action, to carry out the work and conduct the operation with all reasonable regard and care for the interests of other persons . . . "

The burden of proof is on the authority to show that the injury suffered by the plaintiff was an inevitable result of the use of the statutory

---

[11] See *Rochford* v. *Essex C.C.* (1916) 14 L.G.R. 33.

[12] *Sellors* v. *Matlock Bath Local Board* (1885) 14 Q.B.D. 928. See also *Goldberg & Son Ltd.* v. *Liverpool Corpn.* (1900) 82 L.T. 362; *Fremantle Corpn.* v. *Annois* [1902] A.C. 213; *Edgington* v. *Swindon Corpn.* [1939] 1 K.B. 86; *Ching Garage Limited* v. *Chingford Corpn.* [1961] 1 W.L.R. 470.

[13] See *Metropolitan Asylum District* v. *Hill* (1881) 6 App. Cas. 193.

[14] See paras. 6–16 *et seq.*, below.

[15] (1881) 6 App. Cas. 193 at 203; see also *Allen* v. *Gulf Oil Refining Ltd.* [1981] A.C. 1001.

[16] See *Edgington* v. *Swindon Corpn.* [1939] 1 K.B. 86; *London Brighton & South Coast Ry. Co.* v. *Truman* (1885) 11 App. Cas. 45; *Goldberg & Son Ltd.* v. *Liverpool Corpn.* (1900) 82 L.T. 362; *Fremantle Corpn.* v. *Annois* [1902] A.C. 213.

[17] *per* Lord Wilberforce in *Allen* v. *Gulf Oil Refining Ltd.* [1981] A.C. 1001 at 1011.

powers.[18] Where the authority is shown to have acted unreasonably, damages and possibly injunctive relief will flow as a result.[19]

Widening of highways

6–06   Section 72 of the Highways Act 1980 provides the power to widen highways. Section 72(1) specifically indicates one method by which this can be achieved—by entering into an agreement with an adjoining land-owner for the dedication of part of his land for highway purposes. This method widens the highway by a process similar to that of creation of a highway.[20] A highway authority may also acquire the right to use extra land as part of a highway by the means of acquiring the land itself, or by appropriating to highway purposes land which it already holds for other purposes. Under sections 238(1) and 239(3) of the Highways Act 1980, a highway authority is empowered to acquire (either compulsorily or by agreement) land required for the improvement of a highway, subject to certain distance limits where it seeks to acquire land compulsorily.[21] An authority also has powers under the Local Government Act 1972 to acquire land by agreement or compulsorily.[22] By section 122 of the Town and Country Planning Act 1971, a local authority may appropri-ate for highway purposes, land which it holds for other purposes.[23] Where the highway in question is a footpath or bridleway, the widening may be achieved by a public path creation agreement under section 25 of the Highways Act 1980.[24] A council of a parish or community may achieve a similar result by entering into an agreement for the dedication of the additional land under section 30 of the 1980 Act.

6–07   The power to widen the highway includes the power to construct a lay-by.[25] The acquisition of land for the purpose of road widening may include the acquisition of land which is not actually being used for the increased width of the road.[26] The highway authority has no duty to widen a highway,[27] nor to purchase land for that purpose.[28]

6–08   Highway authorities have two other means of securing that their high-ways are capable of being adequately widened to cope with the needs of traffic at some future time. Under section 73 of the 1980 Act, a highway

---

[18] *Manchester Corpn.* v. *Farnworth* [1930] A.C. 171.

[19] See *Milward* v. *Redditch Local Board of Health* (1873) 21 W.R. 429; *Howard-Flanders* v. *Maldon Corpn.* (1926) 135 L.T. 6.

[20] See Highways Act 1980, s.38, para. 2–10, above.

[21] *i.e.* 220 yards from the centre of the highway: see Highways Act 1980, s.249 and Sched. 18.

[22] Subject, in this case, to authorisation from the concerned Minister; see Local Govern-ment Act 1972, s.121(1).

[23] A similiar power is contained in Local Government Act 1972, s.122.

[24] See para. 2–11, above.

[25] See *Rodgers* v. *Ministry of Transport* [1952] 1 All E.R. 634.

[26] See Highways Act 1980, ss.240(2)(*a*) and 246(1); *Quinton* v. *Bristol Corpn.* (1874) L.R. 17 Eq. 524.

[27] *R.* v. *Stretford* (*Inhabitants*) (1705) 2 Ld. Raym. 1169.

[28] See *Perry* v. *Stanborough* (*Developments*) [1978] J.P.L. 36.

authority has the power to prescribe an improvement line, and by section 73 it has power to prescribe a building line.

Improvement lines

The power to prescribe an improvement line is found in section 73 of   **6–09** the Highways Act 1980. The power is only exercisable in a street[29] which is maintainable at the public expense. Preconditions to the exercise of the power are that the highway authority should be of the opinion either that the street is narrow or inconvenient, or is without any sufficiently regular boundary line, or that it should be widened. The highway authority may then prescribe an improvement line in relation to one or both sides of the street or, where only part of the street is to be included within the improvement line, at, or within a distance of, 15 yards from any corner of the street.

The effect of the improvement line is to prevent the erection of any   **6–10** new building or the creation of any permanent excavation at any point in advance of the line, without the consent of the authority which prescribed the line. The word "building" is specially defined for the purposes of this section[30] as including "any erection however, and with whatever material, it is constructed and any part of a building." "New building" is defined as including an addition to an existing building.[31] The rights of statutory undertakers to make excavations for the purpose of dealing with their apparatus are not affected by the making of an improvement line.[32] The consent of statutory undertakers, which must not be unreasonably withheld, may be required where their property is affected.[33]

An improvement line continues to exist until the authority is of the   **6–11** opinion that the line is no longer necessary or desirable. Contravention of the prohibitions imposed by an improvement line is punishable by a fine.[34] Consent for building or excavation between the improvement line and the street may be given by the highway authority; such consent may be for any period and may be subject to such conditions as the highway authority thinks expedient. A conditional consent will be registrable as a local land charge.[35] Such conditions then become binding upon the successors in title of the grantee and upon any occupier of the land to which it relates. Failure to comply with these conditions is also a criminal offence.[36]

---

[29] As to the meaning of street, see paras. 10–01 *et seq.*, below.
[30] At subs. (13).
[31] See *Sittingbourne U.D.C.* v. *Lipton* [1931] 1 K.B. 539.
[32] Highways Act 1980, s.73(3).
[33] *Ibid.* s.73(11); see also ss.338, 339 and Sched. 22.
[34] *Ibid.* s.73(6).
[35] In Part 4 of the register: Local Land Charges Act 1975, s.1; Local Land Charges Rules 1977 (S.I. 1977 No. 985).
[36] Highways Act 1980, s.73(6).

6–12   Before prescribing an improvement line, the highway authority must first consult with other councils within whose area the street is situated.[37] A plan showing the prescribed line and signed by the appropriate officer is placed on deposit and is open to inspection for a month. Notice of the proposal to prescribe the line must then be given to every owner, lessee, and occupier of the land affected.[38] Objections given within the next six weeks must be considered by the authority. If the authority decides to prescribe a line, it must prepare and authenticate a plan showing the line and give notice to the owners, lessees and occupiers of the land affected. Revocation of the line is achieved simply by the authority giving notice to the owners, etc., and to the council which keeps the local land charges register for the area of the affected street. Both the prescription of the line and its revocation by a local highway authority must be achieved by resolution.

6–13   Compensation for injurious affection is payable in relation to property affected by the prescription of an improvement line. This compensation is not available in respect of any building erected after the date on which a plan showing the building line was placed on deposit, except insofar as it relates to work done for the purpose of finishing a building which had already been started before that date or of carrying out a contract made before that date.[39] A similar result, prohibiting the erection of buildings within an area of a proposed road-widening scheme, can also be achieved by the exercise of planning powers. In *Westminster Bank* v. *Beverley Borough Council*,[40] it was held that a local authority was entitled to give the existence of a proposal for widening the highway as its reason for refusing planning permission for the development of land adjacent to a highway, even though its object was to avoid the payment of compensation for injurious affection which would have followed the prescription of an improvement line. The result of this decision has been that the improvement line procedure has become much less used.

Building lines

6–14   Prescription of a building line is governed by section 74 of the Highways Act 1980. The power relates to any highway maintainable at the public expense and can relate either to one or to both sides of the highway. It is described as being a "frontage line." The effect is to prohibit any new building, other than a boundary wall or fence, from being erected nearer to the centre line of the highway than the building line itself without the consent of the highway authority; it also prohibits permanent excavations within the same area. As with improvement lines,

[37] Highways Act 1980, Sched. 9, paras. 1 and 2.
[38] As to the contents of the notice, see *ibid.* para. 6.
[39] *Ibid.* s.73(10).
[40] [1971] A.C. 508.

the authority may grant any consent subject to conditions.[41] There are no preconditions to the exercise of the power. The building line continues in existence until revoked by the authority when it considers that the line or any part of it is no longer necessary or desirable. The procedure to be adopted in the prescription of a building line is similar to that concerning improvement lines and is contained in Schedule 9 to the 1980 Act. Prescription of a building line may be done by two or more authorities jointly by agreement (which may provide for the apportionment of expenses).

The rights of certain statutory undertakers to make excavations for   **6–15** the purpose of dealing with their apparatus are not affected by the prescription of building line.[42] The consent of statutory undertakers, which must not be unreasonably withheld, may be required where their property is affected.[43]

Levelling of highways

Highway authorities may execute works for levelling highways main-   **6–16** tainable at the public expense under the power granted by section 76. They may also raise or lower the levels of highways maintainable at the public expense under section 77. It is not clear to what extent these sections confer separate powers, since levelling of a highway might be presumed to involve some alteration in the levels of the highway. In *Rodgers* v. *Minister of Transport*,[44] it was held that the levelling of a grass verge in order to make a lay-by fell within similiar powers to level or widen a highway contained in the Highways Act 1864. Probably the power in section 76 is intended to mean "make level," in the sense of making the highway flatter or horizontal, whereas the power in section 77 involves an alteration of the height of the highway. Such a distinction is not supported by the *Rodgers* case and the reason for the wording of the two sections may be simply that they derive from separate repealed legislative codes.[45]

At common law there was no power to alter the levels of a highway   **6–17** except for the purposes of maintaining it in a fit state for ordinary traffic.[46] However, the highway surveyors were empowered to restore a highway to its former levels, after the passage of time and erosion by weather had lowered it.[47] Compensation is now payable under subsection (2) where damage is sustained by anyone through the exercise of

[41] Highways Act 1980, s.74(4), (5).
[42] *Ibid.* s.74(3); *cf.* s.73(3).
[43] *Ibid.* s.74(11); see also ss.338, 339 and Sched. 22.
[44] [1952] 1 All E.R. 634.
[45] Highways Act 1864, s.48 and Public Health Act 1875, s.149, respectively. As to the exercise by an urban authority of its powers under s.149 (now repealed), see *R.* v. *Brighton Corpn.*, *ex p. Shoosmith* (1907) 96 L.T. 762.
[46] See *Nutter* v. *Accrington Local Board* (1878) 4 Q.B.D. 375.
[47] See *Burgess* v. *Northwich Local Board* (1880) 6 Q.B.D. 264.

this power.[48] Otherwise, a landowner who has suffered damage through the exercise of powers to level highways may only bring legal proceedings if a power is exercised negligently, unreasonably, or in such a way as to cause unnecessary damage.[49] The power to alter the level of a highway does not empower the highway authority to encroach onto adjoining land, and damages for trespass may flow where this occurs.[50]

Corners

6–18   There are several powers available to a highway authority to deal with dangers at bends and corners. Two of these powers fall within that part of the Act dealing with improvements. A highway authority may execute works under section 78 of the Highways Act 1980 to cut off the corners of a highway maintainable by it at the public expense. An authority also has power under section 79 to take steps to prevent any obstruction to view at corners in relation to such a highway. The other powers which are available to deal with obstructions at corners are found in other parts of the Act. There is power to require that the angles of new buildings at corners of streets should be rounded off.[51] Highway authorities and district councils also have power to lop trees and vegetation overhanging highways,[52] and there is a restriction on the planting of trees in or within 15 feet from the centre of a made-up carriageway.[53]

6–19   The power to prevent obstruction to view at corners is similar in some ways to the powers of highway authorities to prescribe improvement and building lines. The procedure comes into operation where the highway authority deems it necessary, in order to prevent danger arising from obstruction to the view of persons using the highway, to impose restrictions with respect to any land at or near any corner or bend in the highway, or any junction of the highway with a road to which the public has access.[54] The power may, therefore, be used in respect of land at any corner or junction in the highway, including junctions with roads which are not themselves highways. There is no restriction on how "near" to the corner, bend or junction the obstruction to the view of highway users should be for the power to arise; however, the obstruction must be such as to present sufficient danger to justify action under the section.

---

[48] See Highways Act 1980, s.308 and para. 14–49, below, for the determination of compensation.

[49] See *Wedmore* v. *Bristol Corpn.* (1862) 7 L.T. (N.S.) 459; *Atherton* v. *Cheshire C.C.* (1895) 60 J.P. 6; *Boulton* v. *Crowther* (1824) 2 B. & C. 703; *Bold* v. *Williams* (1857) 28 L.T. (O.S.) 269; and see the cases discussed at para. 6–05, above.

[50] *Rochford* v. *Essex C.C.* (1916) 14 L.G.R. 33.

[51] See Highways Act 1980, s.286(1).

[52] *Ibid.* s.154.

[53] *Ibid.* s.141.

[54] As to the meaning of "road to which the public has access," see n. 68 to para. 2–28, above.

A notice must then be served[55] on the owner or occupier of the land in   **6–20**
question, directing him to alter any wall (other than a wall forming part
of the structure of a permanent edifice), fence, hoarding, paling, tree,
shrub, or other vegetation on the land, so as to cause it to conform with
any requirements specified in the notice. "Building" and "wall" are
both given extended definitions in section 79(17). "Building" is defined
as including "any erection however, and with whatever material, it is
constructed, and any part of a building." "Wall" is defined as including
"any partition, with whatever material it is constructed, and any bank."
It seems that the notice must be directed to removing the obstruction
which is alleged to create the danger, and, insofar as it may purport to
require any other action on the part of the person on whom it is served,
it may be open to challenge. A notice may also be served on every
owner, lessee and occupier of the land, restraining them, either absolutely or subject to such conditions as may be specified in the notice,
from causing or permitting any building, wall, fence, hoarding, paling,
tree, shrub or other vegetation to be erected or planted on the land.

Notices under section 79 may not be served by the highway authority   **6–21**
unless the district council consents.[56] Where the notice requiring alteration of any object is served on the owner of the land, a copy must be
served on the occupier and vice versa. The recipient of any notice has 14
days, from the date of receipt by him of the notice, to object, stating his
reasons, to any requirement in it.[57] If the objection or the original notice
is not withdrawn, the question is referred to an arbitrator agreed
between the parties or, in default of agreement, determined by the
county court.[58]

A notice restraining the erection of any structure does not prevent   **6–22**
any works of reconstruction or repair of any existing building, provided
such works do not create a new obstruction to the view of persons using
adjacent highways.[59] All notices come into force immediately they are
served, and thereafter remain binding on the successor in title to every
owner and on every lessee and every occupier of the land to which they
relate.[60] Contravention of a notice is a criminal offence and continuation of the offence after conviction is subject to a daily penalty.[61] A person served with a notice may do all things required by the notice,
notwithstanding any restrictions which may usually be placed on such
acts by his conveyance, lease or any other agreement.[62] Compensation

---

[55] Together with a plan showing the land to which the notice relates: see Highways Act
1980, s.79(1). The notice must also comply with the provisions of ss.320–322.
[56] Or, in London, the consent of the London borough council or of the Common Council.
[57] Highways Act 1980, s.79(7).
[58] See *ibid.* s.79(8).
[59] *Ibid.* s.79(5).
[60] *Ibid.* s.79(6).
[61] *Ibid.* s.79(10).
[62] *Ibid.* s.79(9).

is payable to any person whose land is injuriously affected by the service of the notice.[63] The recipient of a notice is, in any event, entitled to recover from the authority the expenses reasonably incurred by him in complying with the notice.[64]

Fencing and boundaries

6–23   A highway authority may, for the purpose of preventing access to a highway maintainable by itself, or to land on which a highway maintainable at the public expense is being constructed, or on which such highway is intended to be constructed,[65] erect and maintain fences or posts.[66] Any such fences or posts may, thereafter, be altered or removed by the authority. In areas of countryside where the local walls are of a particular type of construction,[67] the authority must, instead of fencing, construct walls of a similar construction.[68] There are a number of important restrictions on the exercise of this power.[69] The power may not be used so as to interfere with a fence or gate required for the purpose of agriculture, to interfere with a public right of way, to obstruct any means of access for which planning permission has been granted under Part III of the Town and Country Planning Act 1971, including permission granted by the General Development Order 1977,[70] or to obstruct any means of access which was lawfully constructed, formed, or laid out, before July 1, 1948.[71]

6–24   The power under section 80 is expressed to be for the purpose of preventing persons from having access to the highway, rather than to prevent persons from leaving the highway. In an old case it was held that there is no duty to construct fences to prevent persons from straying off the highway[72]; however, highway authorities have been held liable to highway users injured when straying off unfenced roads onto dangers adjoining the highway.[73] Certainly, where a highway authority has constructed a fence and has then taken it down, thereby creating a danger which was not present before, or where it has raised the highway,

---

[63] Claims must be made within 6 months of the date of service of the notice.
[64] Disputes are determined by an agreed arbitrator or by the county court: Highways Act 1980, s.79(13). See para. 14–49, below.
[65] See Highways Act 1980, ss.14, 16 and 18.
[66] *Ibid.* s.80(1).
[67] *e.g.* dry stone walls.
[68] Wildlife and Countryside Act 1981, s.72(12).
[69] Otherwise it would negate the principle that a landowner has access to a highway from any part of his land: as to which, see paras. 3–32 *et seq.*, above. It does, however, limit the application of that principle.
[70] The operation of this section may also be excluded or modified by a development order: see Town and Country Planning Act 1971, ss.24 and 287.
[71] *i.e.* not in contravention of Restriction of Ribbon Development Act 1935.
[72] See *R.* v. *Llandilo Roads Commissioners* (1788) 2 Term. Rep. 232.
[73] *Evans* v. *Rhymney Local Board* (1887) 4 T.L.R. 72; *Whyler* v. *Bingham R.C.* [1901] 1 K.B. 45; *Nicholson* v. *Southern Ry. Co. and Sutton and Cheam U.D.C.* [1935] 1 K.B. 558.

creating a dangerous drop, liability may arise.[74] A local highway authority may also require landowners to fence dangerous land adjoining the highway.[75]

Ascertaining the true width of the public right of way has, in the past,   6–25
created problems generally in respect of unmade highways and, in particular, footpaths and bridleways. In order to mark the width of the highway over which the public have the right to pass and repass, highway authorities have power to erect and maintain, and thereafter to alter and remove, highway boundary posts. The limits of this power have been noted by the courts in the past; boundary posts are not intended to prevent trespass,[76] nor to indicate the route over which the highway passes.[77] It seems, therefore, that relatively infrequent posts, indicating the width of the public right of way, are contemplated by the section.

Cattle grids

The public right of passage along a carriageway highway usually   6–26
includes the right of driftway—the right to drive cattle.[78] However, in certain circumstances, it will be necessary for highways to contain cattle grids to restrict the movement of cattle or other livestock along the highway. This will usually be the case in agricultural areas where livestock are not generally fenced off the highway and where the route of the highway creates a gap in the landowner's own walls or fences through which his cattle might stray. In some moorland areas, highways may have become dedicated subject to the landowners' rights to gate the highway. A cattle grid may be a much more effective way of permitting free passage for highway users while safeguarding the position of local farmers. Sections 82 to 89 of the Highways Act 1980 contain a procedural code whereby such cattle grids may be installed.

Section 82 permits a highway authority,[79] where it considers it expedi-   6–27
ent for controlling the passage of animals along the highway, to instal and maintain a cattle grid in any carriageway highway or partly in that highway and partly in adjoining land.[80] A cattle grid is defined[81] as "a device designed to prevent the passage of animals, or animals of a particular description, but to allow the passage of all or some other traffic, and includes any fence or other works necessary for securing the efficient operation of the said device." The highway authority may act in

---

[74] *Whyler* v. *Bingham R.C.* [1901] 1 K.B. 45; *Nicholson* v. *Southern Ry. Co. and Sutton and Cheam U.D.C.* [1935] 1 K.B. 558.
[75] See Highways Act 1980, s.165 and para. 8–47, below.
[76] *Ellis* v. *Woodbridge* (1860) 8 C.B. (N.S.) 290.
[77] See *Radcliffe* v. *Marsden U.D.C.* (1908) 72 J.P. 475.
[78] See Co. Lit. 56a; *cf. Ballard* v. *Dyson* (1808) 1 Taunt. 279; and see, generally, para. 1–13, above.
[79] As to trunk roads, see Highways Act 1980, s.6(1)–(4) and s.89.
[80] Where the grid is to be placed in or near to bridges or tunnels, it may be necessary to obtain certain consents: see *ibid.* s.90.
[81] *Ibid.* s.82(6).

response to representations from local farmers, or may act on its own initiative after consultation[82] with such owners or occupiers of agricultural land as it considers requisite. Where a cattle grid is provided, it must be accompanied by a gate or bypass or some other means for permitting animals under proper control, and all other traffic unable to cross the cattle grid, to pass along the highway. The grid, gate or bypass may only be placed in highway land (which could, of course, be acquired for the purpose)[83] or on adjoining land, either by agreement[84] with the landowner or, where this land is common or waste land, after complying with the requirements of Schedule 10.[85] No bypass may be installed unless the authority considers it expedient after complying with the requirements of Schedule 10.[86] A "bypass" is defined as meaning "a way, over land not comprised within the limits of the highway, for the traffic for which the bypass is provided." The provision of a bypass creates a new right of way but one which may be subject to the provision of a gate and which is only open to the kind of traffic which is prevented from travelling along the highway by the provision of a cattle grid.[87] Unlike other improvement powers there is no requirement here that the highway should already be maintainable at the public expense. Once provided, however, the grid, bypass and the associated works will themselves be maintainable by the highway authority and any bypass will be fact become a highway maintainable at the public expense.[88] After installation, the cattle grid, bypass and associated works may be improved or altered by the highway authority, provided that the alteration or improvement does not prevent any kind of traffic from passing along the highway which could previously so pass.[89]

6–28   Where the purposes for which a landowner has the right to gate a highway will be adequately achieved by the provision of a cattle grid, the highway authority may require the installation of a cattle grid.[90] Whether a right to gate genuinely exists may itself be a difficult question to determine.[91] The authority is bound, on demand, to refund to the landowner the expenses reasonably incurred in removing a gate in compliance with such a requirement, and may elect to remove the gate itself. On removal of the cattle grid, the landowner has the right to re-instal his

---

[82] As to the meaning of consultation, see *Rollo* v. *Minister of Town and Country Planning* [1948] 1 All E.R. 13; *Re Union of Benefices of Whippingham and East Cowes, St. James* [1954] A.C. 245; *Agricultural, Horticultural and Forestry Industry Training Board* v. *Kent* [1970] 2 Q.B. 19.
[83] See Highways Act 1980, s.243.
[84] *Ibid.* s.87.
[85] *Ibid.* s.82(3).
[86] *Ibid.* s.82(5).
[87] *Ibid.* s.82(6).
[88] *Ibid.* s.84.
[89] *Ibid.* s.82(7), (8).
[90] *Ibid.* s.86, Sched. 10.
[91] See para. 2–42, above; *Barraclough* v. *Johnson* (1838) 8 A. & E. 99; *Davies* v. *Stephens* (1836) 7 C. & P. 570. See also Highways Act 1980, s.86(4).

gate and may recover the expenses of so doing from the highway authority.[92]

A cattle grid and bypass may be removed by the highway authority   **6–29**
after consultation with farmers when it is no longer required. The authority
is then under a duty to make good the highway and to remove all
the works connected with the grid or the bypass. The public will have
acquired a right of way through the bypass and this can be discontinued
by a direction that the bypass is to be discontinued.[93]

The placing of a cattle grid, bypass or associated works on land   **6–30**
adjoining the highway can be achieved by an agreement with the landowner under section 87 of the Highways Act 1980. Such an agreement
may provide for the highway authority and the public to have rights over
the land in question and may provide for payment by one party to the
other in consideration for the use of the land or for entering into the
agreement.[94] This section primarily contemplates payments by the highway authority for the use of the land. Contributions to the cost of install-
ing and maintaining a cattle grid from persons who will especially
benefit from the provision of the grid are covered by section 88. The
authority is expressly directed to have regard to the extent to which persons who will derive special benefit from the provision of the cattle grid
are prepared to enter into such agreements under this section, in making
its decision whether or not to exercise its powers.[95]

An agreement under section 87 for the use of private land for the pur-   **6–31**
pose of providing grids and bypasses may be made with any person
interested in any land for the use of the land for that purpose. One of
the effects of the creation of a bypass is that a new public right (for
example, for horses) may be created over that bypass. It might have
been expected, therefore, that the person entering into the agreement
would have to have a sufficient interest in the land to dedicate it as a
highway.[96] However, the provisions of an agreement under section 87
bind the interest of any person who is a party to the agreement "notwithstanding any devolution of that interest" and also bind any interest
of any person which is created out of that interest. The terms of the
agreement appear, therefore, not to "run with the land" but only to run
with the interest which has been bound by the agreement.[97] The rights
of another landowner over the land which is the subject of the agreement (for example, a right of way) will not be affected. An assignee

---

[92] Provided that he replaces the gate within twelve months of the highway authority removing the grid.
[93] Rights of way which may have existed before the creation of the bypass are not affected and any part of the bypass which obstructs the former right of way must now be removed: Highways Act 1980, s.83(4)(a), (b).
[94] Ibid. s.87(2).
[95] Ibid. s.88(3).
[96] See Chap. 2.
[97] See also Highways Act 1980, s.87(3).

from a lessor who has entered into an agreement would be bound.[98] The agreement is registrable as a local land charge.

6–32   Schedule 10 to the Highways Act 1980 provides a procedural code which must be complied with wherever a bypass is to be constructed on land which is not highway land, wherever a cattle grid is to be constructed on waste or common land not belonging to the highway authority, and wherever the highway authority proposes to instal a cattle grid in place of a landowner's right to gate the highway under section 86. Notices must be published in two successive weeks in one or more local newspapers circulating in the area, and a notice must also be displayed in a prominent position at the proposed location. These notices must state the question for determination, indicate a place where a copy of all such plans, or other descriptive matter as appears to the highway authority to be requisite for enabling the question to be understood may be inspected and allow not less than 28 days from the date of first publication of the notice within which representations may be made to the local highway authority. Where no representations are made, the highway authority may proceed to determine the question itself. If representations are made and not withdrawn, then they must be referred to the Minister who must then hold a public inquiry, or otherwise grant the persons making the representations a hearing, (unless, because of the special circumstances of the case and where the representation does not come from another highway authority, he considers it unnecessary) before determining the question himself,[99] or consenting to the local highway authority proceeding with the proposal. The consent may be conditional.

Bridges

6–33   Bridges over flowing water have, historically, been treated separately from the highways which reach up to the banks of the waters which they bridge. Chapter 11 deals with the position of bridges and their relationship to general highway powers. However, highway authorities may, as part of their powers of improvement, construct or reconstruct bridges[1] to carry highways which are maintainable at the public expense.[2] A new bridge may be constructed within 200 yards of the old one. However, it may be necessary to divert the highway onto and over the new bridge where it is not reconstructed in the same location. Privately maintainable bridges may be dealt with in two ways: by order, or by agreement under the powers contained in sections 93 to 95 of the Highways Act 1980.

---

[98] As to other persons and bodies who have power to enter into such an agreement, see Highways Act 1980, s.87(4), (5), (6).
[99] Where he is the highway authority.
[1] "Bridges" do not include culverts: see Highways Act 1980, s.329(1). See also Chap. 11.
[2] Highways Act 1980, ss.91 and 92.

Power to lay out verges and to plant trees

A highway authority, or a local authority or parish or community **6–34** council with the consent of the highway authority,[3] may plant trees, shrubs, and plants of any description in a highway maintainable at the public expense. The same powers may be exercised in relation to land acquired in connection with the construction and improvement of highways, notwithstanding that such land may not be part of the highway.[4] These authorities may also lay out grass verges in such highways and land, and erect and maintain guards or fences, and do anything else expedient for the maintenance or protection of trees, shrubs and grass verges planted or laid out—whether or not by them—in such a highway. There is a similiar power to alter or remove grass verges and guards or fences, whether or not provided by them.[5] No trees, shrubs, grass verges, plants of any description, guards or fences may be planted, laid out or erected, so as to cause a hindrancc to the reasonable user of the highway by any person entitled to use it, or so as to be a nuisance or injurious to the owner or occupier of premises adjacent to the highway. Where trees, verges, etc., have been planted, laid out or erected under this section, they may not be allowed to remain so as to cause such a hindrance or nuisance.[6] Where damage is caused to the property of any person by the exercise of these powers, there is a right to compensation, unless the claimant's own negligence caused the damage, and the principles of contributory negligence will apply.[7]

Lighting

Until the passing of the Local Government Act 1966, highway auth- **6–35** orities had neither any duty nor any power to light highways. The lighting of highways was not considered to be part of the duty to maintain a highway.[8] Other local authorities, known as lighting authorities, had been given power under various statutes to light highways, along with other public areas.[9] Section 28 of the Local Government Act 1966 empowered highway authorities to provide lighting for the purposes of any highway or proposed highway for which they were or would become the highway authority. Under the same Act, the powers of existing lighting auhorities, in relation to highways for which they were not the highway authority, were made subject to the consent of the relevant highway authority. Existing lighting systems were transferred from lighting

---

[3] Highways Act 1980, s.96(1), (4), (5). Two or more highway authorities may exercise their powers jointly: see *ibid.* s.96(9).
[4] *Ibid.* s.96(1), (3), (10).
[5] *Ibid.* s.96(2).
[6] *Ibid.* s.96(6); for a discussion of the extent of this provision, see Chap. 3.
[7] Highways Act 1980, s.96(7), (8).
[8] *Richardson* v. *Tubbs* (1847) 4 C.B. 304; see also *Harris* v. *Baker* (1815) 4 M. & S. 27; *Cowley* v. *Newmarket Local Board* (1890) A.C. 345; *Sheppard* v. *Glossop Corpn.* [1921] 3 K.B. 132.
[9] See Public Health Act 1875, s.161; Parish Councils Act 1957, s.3.

authorities to highway authorities.[10] Lighting authorities were left with responsibility for "footway lighting systems."[11] Powers were given, however, to highway authorities to delegate their functions to, or to agree that certain works should be carried out by, lighting authorities.

6–36   Under the Highways Act 1980, all highway authorities may provide lighting for the purposes of any highway for which they are, or will become, the highway authority and may enter into contracts with any persons for the supply of (*inter alia*) electricity for that purpose. They may construct such lamps, posts and other works as they consider necessary.[12] Any works constructed by them may later be altered or removed. Compensation is payable to any person who sustains damage by reason of the exercise of works under these powers.[13] The authority may also rely upon the powers contained in the Public Health Act 1961[14] to attach street lamps to buildings and to recover summarily, as a civil debt, damages for negligent damage to any lamp or lamp post.

6–37   Street lighting authorities[15] may exercise powers to maintain lighting systems in certain highways with the consent of the highway authority.[16] This consent may be unconditional or conditional and may be given generally or in respect of any particular highway or length of highway.[17] A highway authority may, by agreement, delegate any of its functions relating to the lighting of highways to a lighting authority. The delegatee will then act as the agent for the highway authority in the discharge of its functions, subject to close control by the highway authority who must approve the works to be executed and the expenditure to be incurred, and who may make requirements as to the manner in which works are to be carried out and may give directions as to the terms of any contracts to be entered into for the purposes of the discharge of the delegated functions. Finally, all works are subject to highway authority approval.[18] During the currency of the delegation agreement the highway authority may, if it is satisfied that a lighting system which is the subject of the delegation is not in proper repair or condition, serve notice on the lighting authority requiring it to put the system in proper repair and, in default, may do anything itself which is necessary to put the lighting system into the proper condition. A delegation agreement may be determined by either side by notice given within the first nine months of the

---

[10] See Local Government Act 1966, s.31.
[11] Defined by their height above ground level and the distance between individual lamps: see *ibid.* s.32.
[12] Highways Act 1980, s.97(1).
[13] *Ibid.* s.97(3).
[14] ss.45 and 81.
[15] *i.e.* a district council or a parish or community council or meeting: Highways Act 1980, s.329(1); Public Health Act 1875, s.161; Parish Councils Act 1957, s.3; Local Government Act 1972, Sched. 14.
[16] Highways Act 1980, s.301.
[17] Except in respect of lighting systems not transferred to the highway authority: see *ibid.* s.301(2).
[18] *Ibid.* s.98(2).

calendar year to expire on April 1st in the following calendar year. Alternatively, the highway authority may agree with the lighting authority that individual works be carried out by it in its area in connection with a lighting system. Similar tight control continues to be exercised by the highway authority by the terms of such an agreement.[19]

Under the Local Government Act 1966, lighting systems for which   6–38
the highway authority was to become responsible were transferred to the highway authorities. "Footway lighting systems" were, however, left with the lighting authorities. "Footway lighting systems" are defined[20] as being systems which contain no lamp mounted more than 13 feet above the ground or, alternatively, systems where no lamp is more than 20 feet above ground level and there is at least one interval of more than 50 yards between adjacent lamps. Once a "footway lighting system" ceases to fall within the definition, it must be transferred to the highway authority.[21] Alternatively, the highway authority may itself convert a "footway lighting system" into a system for which they are responsible by giving appropriate notice.[22]

Local authorities have been held not to be liable for any accident aris-   6–39
ing out of the failure to exercise powers of lighting in respect of highways[23] but this would not be the case where an obstruction is placed by the authority in a highway and that obstruction is not adequately lit.

Safety provisions

Many of the powers of improvement contained in Part V of the High-   6–40
ways Act 1980 are concerned with safety. There are powers for the construction of footways, guard rails, refuges, subways, footbridges over highways and margins for horses and livestock.

Section 66 of the Highways Act 1980 imposes a duty on a highway   6–41
authority to provide in or by the side of a highway maintainable by it at the public expense, and which consists of or comprises a made-up carriageway, a proper and sufficient footway as part of the highway in any case where it considers the provision of a footway to be necessary or desirable for the safety or the accommodation of pedestrians. Having provided such a footway, the authority is empowered to light it. Although the section is expressed as a duty, it is a duty which only arises where the highway authority considers the provision of the footway to be necessary or desirable for the safety or accommodation of pedestrians. It is doubtful whether a private individual has a right of action to enforce this duty.[24]

---

[19] Highways Act 1980, s.98(4).
[20] *Ibid.* s.270(1).
[21] As to the terms of such transfers, see *ibid.* s.270(4)–(6).
[22] See also *ibid.* s.66.
[23] See *Sheppard* v. *Glossop Corpn.* [1921] 3 K.B. 132; *Fisher* v. *Ruislip-Northwood U.D.C. and Middlesex C.C.* [1945] K.B. 584.
[24] *cf. Read* v. *Croydon Corpn.* [1938] 4 All E.R. 631.

6-42   Under the same section,[25] a highway authority may provide and maintain in a highway maintainable at the public expense and which consists of or comprises a carriageway, such raised paving, pillars, walls, rails or fences as it may think necessary for the purpose of safeguarding persons who are using the highway. In *Ching Garage Ltd.* v. *Chingford Corporation*,[26] the House of Lords held that this power was wide enough to permit the construction of a structure described as a "street refuge," by raising the pavement and partially obstructing a means of access, although compensation was payable for any damage sustained. There is a similar power to provide and maintain in highways consisting of a footpath, such barriers, rails and fences as the authority thinks necessary for the purpose of safeguarding persons who are using the highway.

6-43   All these powers include a power to alter or remove any works already provided.[27] However, the power to erect barriers, rails or fences in footpaths, and the power to alter or remove any works must not be exercised so as to obstruct any private access to premises or interfere with agricultural operations. Implicitly, therefore, the other powers could be used in such a way that they obstruct private accesses,[28] although the exercise of the power will be subject to the overall test of reasonableness.[29] The powers of highway authorities in relation to roads for which the Minister is the highway authority may, in certain circumstances, be exercised by other highway authorities.[30] Compensation is payable to any person who sustains damage by reason of the exercise by a highway authority of works under the permissive powers to provide raised pavings, pillars, walls, rails or fences in carriageways, and barriers, rails or fences in footpaths. However, there is no power to obtain compensation in respect of the provision of a footway under section 67(1). Disputes as to the amount of compensation which should be awarded will be referred to the county court for determination.[31]

6-44   Local authorities may provide and maintain pillars, rails and fences as they may think necessary for the purpose of safeguarding persons in streets which are not highways maintainable at the public expense, but which consist of, or comprise, carriageways.[32] They may subsequently alter or remove such works. Schedule 8 to the Highways Act 1980 provides that certain consents must be obtained before such works are carried out. These consents would include those of any other highway authority for the street, statutory undertakers (where the street belongs to them), persons in whom any bridges comprised in the street are vested, and owners and occupiers of land or premises whose existing

---

[25] Highways Act 1980, s.66(2).
[26] [1961] W.L.R. 470.
[27] Highways Act 1980, s.66(4).
[28] See *Ching Garage Ltd.* v. *Chingford Corpn.* [1961] W.L.R. 470.
[29] See para. 6–05, above.
[30] Highways Act 1980, s.66(6), (7).
[31] *Ibid.* s.308. See also para. 14–49, below.
[32] Highways Act 1980, s.67(1).

access has been interfered with or obstructed. Such consents may not be unreasonably withheld, but may be given subject to any reasonable conditions.[33] Compensation is payable to any person who sustains damage by reason of the execution by the local authority of works carried out under these provisions.[34]

Highway authorities may also (in relation to a highway maintainable **6–45** at the public expense which consist of or comprise a made-up carriageway) construct and maintain works in that carriageway for providing places of refuge for the protection of pedestrians crossing the carriageway. Such refuges may be lit, paved, grassed or otherwise covered. Pillars, walls, rails or fences may be erected and trees, shrubs or other vegetation may be planted.[35] The works, once constructed, may be removed. The refuge must be constructed in the carriageway, and this power cannot be used outside the carriageway.[36] There are powers to provide ancillary works, including lighting and paving,[37] and Part II of the Public Utilities Street Works Act 1950[38] applies to works executed under the powers contained in section 68. The installation within the carriageway of a potential obstacle to highway users, such as a refuge, may place on the highway authority a continuing obligation to light that obstruction.[39]

Powers to construct subways under, footbridges over and margins by **6–46** the side of highways are given by sections 69 to 71 of the Highways Act 1980.

Drainage of highways

At common law, it remains the responsibility of the owner or occupier **6–47** of land adjoining the highway to scour and cleanse his ditches for the purpose of preventing the highway from being flooded and obstructed to the nuisance of passers by.[40] The Highway Act 1835 gave a power to the surveyor to cleanse, scour and keep open ditches, drains and watercourses necessary to drain the highway for which he was responsible, and the present provisions for draining highways are now contained in sections 100 to 101 of the 1980 Act.

By section 100, the highway authority is given powers to drain its **6–48** highways and to prevent surface water from flowing on to them. It may construct or lay such drains as it considers necessary in the highway or in

---

[33] Including a condition that the authority shall remove the works either at any time, or after the expiration of a period, if reasonably required to do so by the person giving the consent.

[34] Disputes over compensation will be determined by arbitration in the county court under section 308 of the Highways Act 1980: see para. 14–49, below.

[35] Highways Act 1980, ss.68(2) and 64(2)–(5).

[36] See *Ching Garage Ltd.* v. *Chingford Corpn.* [1961] 1 W.L.R. 470 (above).

[37] Highways Act 1980, ss.68(2) and 64(2)–(3).

[38] See Chap. 13.

[39] See *Polkinghorn* v. *Lambeth B.C.* [1938] 1 All E.R. 339.

[40] *Att.-Gen.* v. *Waring* (1899) 63 J.P. 789. See also *Repair of Bridges, etc. Case* (1609) 13 Co. Rep. 33.

land adjoining[41] or lying near to the highway. The highway authority has a similar power to erect barriers to divert surface water into or through any existing drain, and furthermore, all existing drains situated in the highway or land adjoining or lying near to the highway may be scoured, cleansed and kept open. "Drains" includes ditches, gutters, water-courses, soak-aways, bridges, culverts, tunnels and pipes.[42] The water so drained or diverted may then be discharged into any inland waters (whether natural or artificial) or into tidal waters.[43] However, the consent of the drainage authority or the water authority will be required where the exercise of these powers interferes with a watercourse vested in such an authority.[44] Compensation is payable to the owner[45] or occupier of any land who suffers damage by reason of the exercise by the authority of its powers.[46] All of these powers are also given (subject to the same responsibility to pay compensation) to any person liable to maintain a highway by reason of tenure, inclosure or prescription.[47] Similiar rights to discharge water from a highway, proposed highway, maintenance compound, trunk road, picnic area, lorry area or service area to any inland waters is given by the Highways Act 1980, section 299, in relation to drains or other works constructed or laid in land, or in the exercise of rights acquired by the highway authority in the exercise of highway land acquisition powers.

6–49   The powers granted by section 100 clearly permit some interference with the adjoining landowner's land. Drains, etc., may be constructed on his land, and officers of the highway authority may enter onto his land for the purposes of construction. Although compensation will be payable, there is no need for the highway authority to acquire any easement to drain onto or across the adjoining land. It has been held that the powers conferred by the similarly-worded section 67 of the Highway Act 1835 did not extend simply to the discharge of water onto adjoining land otherwise than through the types of channels mentioned in the section.[48] The discharge of water from the highway onto adjoining land otherwise than into a drain or ditch, etc., can only be justified by the finding of some prescriptive easement.[49]

6–50   It is an offence to alter, obstruct or interfere with a drain or barrier which has been constructed, laid or erected by the authority under these powers (or which is under the control of the highway authority) without

---

[41] As to the meaning of "adjoining," see Highways Act 1980, s.329(1) and the cases discussed at para. 10–28, below.
[42] Highways Act 1980, s.100(9).
[43] Although this power is expressed to be without prejudice to any enactment whose purpose is to protect water against pollution: *ibid.* s.100(8).
[44] *Ibid.* s.339(3).
[45] As to the definition of which, see *ibid.* s.100(9).
[46] *Ibid.* s.100(3).
[47] *Ibid.* s.100(7).
[48] *Croft* v. *Rickmansworth Highway Board* (1888) 39 Ch.D. 272; *Croysdale* v. *Sunbury-on-Thames U.D.C.* [1898] 2 Ch. 515; *Thomas* v. *Gower R.C.* [1922] 2 K.B. 76.
[49] See *Att.-Gen.* v. *Copeland* [1902] 1 K.B. 690; *King's C.C.* v. *Kennedy* [1910] 2 I.R. 544.

the authority's consent and the authority may also recover from such a person its expenses of repair or reinstatement necessitated by his action.[50] The fine is expressed to be "not exceeding three times the amount of those expenses," and it would seem to follow that an offence is only committed if the authority is actually put to a quantifiable expense. It is not an offence under this section to obstruct a private culvert, even if that obstruction interferes with the proper working of the highway authority's drains to which that culvert is connected.[51]

The highway authority may also exercise certain of the powers of a   **6–51** water authority under the Public Health Act 1936, for the purpose of draining highways (actual and proposed) within the water authority's area.[52] A county council may also enter into agreements with a local authority as to the use of highway drains for sanitary purposes under the Public Health Act 1936, section 21.

Where it appears to the highway authority for any highway that a   **6–52** ditch on land adjoining or lying near to the highway constitutes a danger to highway users, that authority may then, if it considers the ditch unnecessary for drainage purposes and any occupier of the land known to the authority agrees in writing that it is unnecessary for those purposes, fill it in, or alternatively, the authority may place in the ditch or in any land adjoining or lying near to it, such pipes as it considers necessary in substitution to the ditch and may thereafter fill it in. These powers are subject to a duty to pay compensation to the owner or occupier of any land which suffers damage by reason of the exercise of these powers.[53] Where these powers have been exercised, any person who, without the highway authority's consent, opens up or keeps open the ditch which has been filled in will commit an offence, and the authority may additionally recover from him expenses of the repair or reinstatement.[54] "Ditch," for the purposes of this section, includes a watercourse and any part of a ditch or watercourse and also includes pipes, including culverts, tunnels and other works.[55] The highway authority's powers may not be used in such a manner as to be likely to cause damage to or so as to affect the drainage of any land or works used for the purposes of a railway or canal undertaking, unless notice is given of the nature of the works and the highway authority then complies with any reasonable requirements of the undertakers.

---

[50] Highways Act 1980, s.100(4).
[51] *Johnston* v. *Essex C.C.* (1971) 69 L.G.R. 498. See, however, Public Health Act 1936, s.264.
[52] Subject, in the case of a county council, to the giving of notice to the district council and the water authority: see Highways Act 1980, s.100(5), (6). See also Public Health Act 1936, Part II.
[53] "Owner" is not specifically defined and, therefore, the definition in s.329(1) will apply: see para. 15–22, below.
[54] See n. 50 above.
[55] Highways Act 1980, s.101(6).

Protection of the highway from various hazards of nature

6-53   The highway authority may also provide and maintain barriers and other works as it considers necessary for the purpose of protecting the highway against snow, flood, landslide or other hazards of nature. These works may be provided on the highway or on land which has been acquired or over which rights have been acquired by the highway authority in the exercise of highway land acquisition powers for that purpose.[56] Once provided, the works may be altered or removed. Compensation is payable to any person who suffers damage by reason of the execution of works on a highway under this section.

6-54   It is also the duty of the highway authority to provide, in connection with any highway for which it is the highway authority, and which is subject to flooding to any considerable depth, graduated posts or stones in any case where it considers the provision of these to be necessary or desirable for the purpose of indicating the depth of water covering the highway. Such posts or stones may be altered or removed, once provided.[57]

6-55   Under section 104, a highway authority may, in relation to a highway maintainable by itself at the public expense, treat the highway for mitigating the nuisance of dust.[58]

Dual carriageway, roundabouts and cycle tracks

6-56   The power to construct and maintain dual carriageways in a highway, and to construct roundabouts at crossroads may be exercised by the authority liable to maintain that highway at the public expense.[59] The highway authority may also light dual carriageways or roundabouts, pave, grass or cover them, erect pillars, walls, rails or fences on or around or across them or any part of them, and plant trees, shrubs or any other vegetation on them either for ornament or for safety reasons.[60] Works constructed under this provision may be altered or removed. The code contained in the Public Utilities Street Works Act 1950 will apply to works carried out under this provision.[61]

6-57   Highway authorities may, in or by the side of any highway maintainable at the public expense and which consists of or comprises a made-up carriageway, construct and light a cycle track as part of that highway. Once constructed, such a cycle track may be altered or removed.[62] This

---

[56] Highways Act 1980, s.102(1). For highway land acquisition powers, see Chap. 14.

[57] Highways Act 1980, s.103(1), (2).

[58] *Ibid.* s.104.

[59] *Ibid.* s.64. See also *Birmingham & Midland Motor Omnibus Co. Ltd.* v. *Worcestershire C.C.* [1967] 1 W.L.R. 409; *Hambledon R.D.C.* v. *Hinde* (1968) 66 L.G.R. 495.

[60] Highways Act 1980, s.64(2).

[61] *Ibid.* s.63(5) and Public Utilities Street Works Act 1950, s.21(1)(*a*).

[62] Highways Act 1980, s.65. This power is necessary here, as otherwise it could be argued that the cycle track created new highway rights which could only be extinguished by stopping up.

power has recently been amplified by the Cycle Tracks Act 1984 and regulations made under that Act.

A cycle track is defined[63] as: **6–58**

> "a way constituting or comprised in a highway being a way over which the public have the following, but no other, rights of way, that is to say, a right of way on pedal cycles (other than pedal cycles which are motor vehicles within the meaning of the Road Traffic Act 1972)[64] with or without a right of way on foot."

Footpaths may be converted to cycle tracks by an order made by the local highway authority and either confirmed by them unopposed, or confirmed by the Minister in other cases.[65] Barriers may be provided in and maintained by the highway authority for the purpose of safeguarding persons using the cycle track. Where the cycle track is adjacent to a footway or to a footpath maintainable at the public expense, works may be provided which separate the two ways, in the interests of safety.[66] Compensation is payable where damage is caused to any person through the exercise of works converting a footpath to a cycle track or separating a cycle track from a footpath or footway.[67]

Miscellaneous powers

The Minister may construct as part of a trunk road a highway for the   **6–59**
purpose of relieving a main carriageway of the trunk road from local traffic, so long as the new highway is not separated from the remainder of the trunk road by intervening land.[68] A non-metalled highway may be converted into a metalled highway under section 99. The provision of road ferries is permitted by section 24. Section 105 empowers a highway authority to improve any road ferry so provided.

Traffic signs

The general power of improvement includes the power to erect and   **6–60**
maintain traffic signs. "Traffic signs" are defined in the Road Traffic Regulation Act 1984[69] as:

> "any object or device (whether fixed or portable) for conveying, to traffic on roads or any specified class of traffic, warnings, information, requirements, restrictions or prohibitions of any description—

---

[63] Highways Act 1980, s.329(1) as amended.
[64] As to which pedal cycles will be regarded as motor vehicles for the purposes of the 1972 Act, see Road Traffic Act 1972, s.190(1). See also *Floyd* v. *Bush* [1953] 1 W.L.R. 242; *Lawrence* v. *Howlett* [1952] 2 All E.R. 74.
[65] The procedure for the making of such an order is set out in Cycle Tracks Act 1984, s.3 and in the Cycle Tracks Regulations 1984 (S.I. 1984 No. 1431).
[66] Cycle Tracks Act 1984, s.4.
[67] *Ibid.* s.5. In certain circumstances, compensation may also be payable in respect of depreciation: see Chap. 14.
[68] Highways Act 1980, s.63.
[69] s.64; and see Highways Act 1980, s.329(1).

(a) specified by regulations made by the Ministers jointly or
(b) authorised by the Secretary of State
and any line or mark on a road for so conveying such warnings, information, requirements restrictions or prohibitions."

Specific power is given to highway authorities to place traffic signs in roads by section 65 of the Road Traffic Regulation Act 1984.[70] Traffic signs must be of the size, colour and type prescribed by regulations,[71] unless specifically authorised by the Secretary of State. A specific power of entry onto land for the purpose of placing, maintaining, etc., traffic signs is given by section 71.

Provision of highway facilities

6–61   Although not strictly powers of improvement, Part VII of the Highways Act 1980 contains several powers for the provision of special facilities in highways, including picnic sites for users of trunk roads,[72] public conveniences for highway users,[73] and heavy goods vehicle parking areas (lorry areas).[74] Part VIIA of the Act allows for the provision of special facilities in pedestrian areas.[75] Other facilities may be provided in streets under other legislation, including seats and drinking fountains,[76] bus shelters,[77] cabman's shelters,[78] statues and public monuments.[79]

---

[70] And to other bodies, in particular circumstances, by ss.66–72.
[71] See the Traffic Signs (Speed Limits) Regulations and General Directions 1969 (S.I. 1969 No. 1487) as amended; the "Zebra" Pedestrian Crossings Regulations 1971 (S.I. 1971 No. 1524); the Traffic Signs Regulations and General Directions 1981 (S.I. 1981 No. 859) as amended; the Traffic Signs (Temporary Obstructions) Regulations 1985 (S.I. 1985 No. 463); the "Pelican" Pedestrian Crossings Regulations and General Directions 1987 (S.I. 1987 No. 16).
[72] Highways Act 1980, s.112.
[73] *Ibid.* ss.112, 114.
[74] *Ibid.* s.115.
[75] See paras. 12–41 *et seq.*, below.
[76] Public Health Act 1925, s.14.
[77] Local Government (Miscellaneous Provisions) Act 1953, s.4.
[78] Public Health Acts (Amendment) Act 1890, s.40.
[79] *Ibid.* s.42.

CHAPTER 7

PROTECTION OF THE HIGHWAY AND OF HIGHWAY USERS: (1) PUBLIC NUISANCE AND ITS REMEDIES

INTRODUCTION

The balance between the rights of highway users to the free and unin-   **7–01**
terrupted user of the highway and the rights of adjoining occupiers to
the full and beneficial use of their land requires a discussion both of the
nature of the respective legal interests and rights of the public, the highway authority and adjoining landowners, and also of the powers which
are available to such persons and bodies in order to enforce their rights
and protect their interests. Chapter 3 has considered the nature of these
rights and interests and the extent of the rights of adjoining landowners.
This chapter and the following chapter are concerned with the powers
which are available, principally to highway authorities, but also to other
local authorities, to secure free, safe and uninterrupted passage for the
public along the highway. Inevitably, the powers available to highway
and local authorities to protect user of the highway place corresponding
restrictions on the activities of other persons, particularly those of
adjoining landowners. However, there are also a substantial number of
powers available to authorities to permit and control acts and works,
necessary for the beneficial use of adjoining land, which would otherwise create potential nuisances and obstructions to the highway.

DUTY OF THE HIGHWAY AUTHORITY TO ASSERT AND PROTECT HIGHWAY RIGHTS

At common law
At common law the highway authority had the right and duty to abate   **7–02**
a nuisance and to remove any obstruction interfering with the free passage along the highway.[1] The authority performed that duty either by
taking action to remove the obstruction or to abate the nuisance, or by
bringing criminal proceedings against the wrongdoer by way of indictment. Any member of the public could institute civil proceedings for
obstruction where he had suffered special damage or, where no special
damage had been suffered, the Attorney-General might be persuaded
to bring proceedings on behalf of the public.[2]

---

[1] *Bagshaw* v. *Buxton Local Board of Health* (1875) 1 Ch.D. 220; *Reynolds* v. *Presteign U.D.C.* [1896] 1 Q.B. 604.
[2] As to these remedies, see paras. 7–36, *et seq.*, below.

141

Duty under statute

7–03   By section 130(1) of the Highways Act 1980, a general duty is imposed on all highway authorities to assert and protect the rights of the public to the use and enjoyment of any highway for which they are the highway authority, including any roadside waste which forms part of such a highway. A specific duty, which in no way detracts from that general duty, is placed on the highway authority by section 130(3) to prevent as far as possible the stopping up or obstruction, both of highways for which it is responsible, and of highways for which it is not responsible, but where, in its opinion, the stopping up or obstruction would be prejudicial to the interests of its area. Where a parish or community council or a parish or community meeting represents to a local highway authority that such a highway has been unlawfully stopped up or obstructed, then the highway authority is under a duty to commence proceedings in its own name to deal with the obstruction, unless it is satisfied that those representations are incorrect.[3] The highway authority has a further duty to prevent any unlawful encroachment on any roadside waste comprised in the highway for which it is the highway authority.[4] All other councils[5] have a power to assert and protect the rights of the public to the use and enjoyment of any highway within their areas.[6] It is specifically provided that where proceedings or steps are taken by a council in relation to an alleged right of way, those proceedings will not be taken to be unauthorised simply because the alleged right of way is found not to exist.[7]

7–04   Two matters which are left unexplained by the wording of section 130 are the nature of the action which a highway authority is required to pursue in order to fulfil its obligations, and the extent to which the authority may be required to take up, on behalf of the public, cases of disputed public highway rights. The extent to which highway authorities are bound to resort to legal action to perform their obligations under section 130 has been considered in two reported cases.

7–05   In *R.* v. *Surrey County Council, ex parte Send Parish Council*,[8] a path had been blocked by the actions of frontagers in extending their gardens. The path was not on the definitive map, although the county council had resolved to include it in the next revision. The county council served notices under what was then section 124 of the Highways Act 1959[9] requiring the removal of the structures obstructing the path. No further action followed until the parish council made representations under what is now section 130(6). The highway authority then resolved

---

[3] Highways Act 1980, s.130(6).

[4] *Ibid.* s.130(4); s.130(6) applies also to this duty.

[5] *i.e.* the councils of counties, non-metropolitan districts, metropolitan districts, London boroughs and the Common Council; see Highways Act 1980, s.329(1).

[6] *Ibid.* s.130(3); including any roadside waste which forms part of it: s.130(3).

[7] *Ibid.* s.130(7).

[8] (1979) 40 P. & C.R. 390.

[9] Now Highways Act 1980, s.143.

to enforce the notices. At this point, the frontagers commenced legal proceedings seeking a declaration that the path was not a public footpath and claiming injunctions restraining the highway authority from enforcing their notices. These proceedings appeared to have been issued at the instigation of the county council itself, which took no steps to contest them. The parish council applied for and obtained an order of mandamus requiring the highway authority to take action to perform its obligations under what is now section 130. The court accepted that the highway authority had a discretion not only as to the form of any proceedings which it might instigate but also as to the way in which and the extent to which those proceedings ought to be prosecuted. However, the court determined, applying the principles set out in *Padfield* v. *Minister of Agriculture*,[10] that there were limits to this discretion and that the authority was required at all times to act within and to promote the objectives of the Highways Acts. Those objectives were to protect the interests of those who had rights over highways. Equally, the discretion should be exercised in such a way as to operate against the interests of those who sought to interrupt the public enjoyment of highways. The county council had not acted so as to forward the purposes of the Act and the court granted the order of mandamus. One interesting aspect of this case is that the county council had sought to argue that where there was any doubt over the status of the highway then the council's duty under the section disappeared. The court rejected this argument. However, on the facts of the case, the evidence that the way was a highway appears to have been very strong. This aspect was considered in greater depth by the Court of Appeal in a later case.

In *R.* v. *Lancashire County Council, ex parte Guyer*,[11] the Court of **7–06** Appeal declined to grant an order of mandamus against a highway authority where the authority, after an investigation (including a public inquiry), was not satisfied of the existence of public rights over a disputed path, but where there was some evidence to support the claims that the way was a highway. Here, the applicant for judicial review was a private individual; the parish council having taken the view that the path was private. The Court of Appeal held that on a true construction of the statutory provisions the highway authority was under a duty to assert and protect the rights of the public to the use and enjoyment of a highway only if it was beyond serious dispute that the particular way was indeed a highway. The court considered the meaning of the words "to assert and protect." Stephenson L.J. said[12]:

> "It is not easy to see why Parliament added "assertion" to "protection." We are told there is no decision of the court which can explain the addition, but in my judgment Parliament cannot have

[10] [1968] A.C. 997; see also *Meade* v. *Haringey L.B.C.* [1979] 1 W.L.R. 637.
[11] *Sub nom. Re Guyer's Application* [1980] 1 W.L.R. 1024.
[12] *Ibid.* at 1033.

meant the addition of those words to require an authority to assert claims in which they have no faith. It may be that the words stress the importance of authorities regarding their duty as not merely passive or defensive to action taken by others, but as requiring them at times to initiate action; something which might be held not to be clearly expressed or implicit in a duty merely to protect rights of the public for the use and enjoyment of a highway."

Ackner L.J. considered that the word "assert" in the context of the sub-section meant "in essence to claim that there exists."[13] However, the words must be seen in the context of what it is that the highway authority must assert and protect. "The subject matter is a highway for which the highway authority is responsible." Ackner L.J. also pointed to the distinction between the obligation in subsection (1) and that in subsection (6) which had been the subject of the *Surrey* decision[14]:

> "The parish council, or such other body referred to in that subsec-tion, is put in a privileged position, presumably because it is assumed that it can be relied on to act responsibly. Its represen-tation must be acted on unless a highway authority is satisfied that it is incorrect."

7–07   There is no doubt that the highway authority has a discretion regard-ing the manner in which it acts in the assertion and protection of the public right in the case of undisputed highways and also that this dis-cretion must be exercised in accordance with the overall purposes of the Highways Act 1980.[15] Where a right of way is in dispute (and this will almost always be the case where serious issues of obstruction or encroachment are involved) it seems that the authority is not under a duty unless the way is not "seriously" in dispute. This clearly requires the authority to investigate the evidence for and against the existence of the highway. However, where the evidence is fairly evenly balanced, it appears that the authority has no obligation to commence proceedings or to take any steps in the assertion of the public right, unless the parish council makes representations under subsection (6), in which case, the emphasis changes and the authority becomes under an obligation to take action *unless satisfied that the representations are incorrect.* Whether Parliament really intended the role of the parish council to be so signifi-cant in imposing an enforceable obligation on the highway authority is unclear. It seems, however, that where an individual wishes to assert the existence of public rights over a particular way he would be well advised to seek the support of the parish or community council or meeting. Other-wise, the rights of the individual depend upon his own ability to bring proceedings in his own name (where he has suffered special damage) or

---

[13] *Sub nom. Re Guyer's Application* [1980] 1 W.L.R 1024 at 1034.
[14] *Ibid.* at 1035.
[15] *R. v. Surrey C.C., ex p. Send Parish Council* (1979) 40 P. & C.R. 390.

where he is able to persuade the Attorney-General to add his *fiat* in the commencement of *relator* proceedings.[16]

Following the logic of the Court of Appeal's reasoning in the *Guyer* case,[17] it would seem to be arguable that the *power* to assert and protect the rights of the public to the use and enjoyment of any highway within its area also can only arise where there is no serious dispute as to the existence of the highway. However, there is specific protection given to any highway authority which commences proceedings or takes any steps in relation to an alleged right of way and where it is found that the right of way does not exist.[18] The authority which takes up doubtful disputed cases may therefore be protected from challenge.

Power to institute proceedings in their own name, to defend any such proceedings and generally to take such steps as they may deem expedient, is given to all councils which are subject to duties or granted powers by section 130.[19] Section 333 of the Highways Act 1980 makes it clear that neither the general nor the specific provisions contained in the Act concerned with the removal of obstructions from the highway are to be taken as affecting any right of a highway authority or other person, whether under any other enactment or under any rule of the common law, to remove an obstruction from a highway or to abate a nuisance or other interference with the highway. Nor will these provisions affect the civil or criminal liability of any person for causing such an obstruction or nuisance.

Public nuisance

A public nuisance is a nuisance which materially affects the reasonable comfort and convenience of life of a class of Her Majesty's subjects who come within its sphere of influence.[20] In the case of a highway, a public nuisance involves some act or omission which "prevents the convenient use of the way by passengers."[21] A public nuisance to a highway can be committed in two ways. First, an obstruction of the highway which is unreasonable in extent or duration will be a public nuisance. Secondly, an act which does not physically obstruct the highway but which renders the highway dangerous or less convenient for public passage may be a public nuisance, whether it arises on the highway or on adjoining land.[22] Different principles may apply to these two categories of nuisance, but there are many elements common to both and it may not always be possible to draw clear lines of distinction between the two

7–08

7–09

7–10

[16] See para. 7–37, below.
[17] [1980] 1 W.L.R. 1024.
[18] Highways Act 1980, s.130(7).
[19] *Ibid.* s.130(5); see also Local Government Act 1972, s.222 and *Stoke-on-Trent City Council* v. *B. & Q. (Retail)* [1984] A.C. 754.
[20] *Att.-Gen.* v. *P.Y.A. Quarries Ltd.* [1957] 2 Q.B. 169 at 184; *Att.-Gen.* v. *Keymer Brick and Tile Co. Ltd.* (1903) 67 J.P. 434.
[21] *per* Byles J. in *R.* v. *Mathias* (1861) 2 F. & F. 570.
[22] *R.* v. *Train* (1862) 3 F. & F. 22; *Trevett* v. *Lee* [1955] 1 W.L.R. 113; *Morton* v. *Wheeler, The Times,* February 1, 1956; *Dymond* v. *Pearce* [1972] 1 Q.B. 496.

categories. Edmund Davies L.J. pointed out the difficulties in categorisation, in *Dymond* v. *Pearce*[23]:

> " . . . it is by no means always possible to allocate the facts of a particular case to only one or other of these two categories. It is notorious that what obstructs a highway may also create great danger to those who travel along it, while, on the other hand, danger unaccompanied by obstruction or obstruction giving rise to no danger may occur."

To some extent, the principles which have evolved have been governed by the kind of loss alleged to have been occasioned by the nuisance. On the one hand, the classic case of obstruction might involve the unusual expense to which a member of the public has been put in overcoming the obstruction. On the other hand, the claim may arise from an injury suffered by a member of the public passing along the highway. In the latter situation, the issues which the courts have had to resolve have been whether, in the case of an obstruction, it is necessary to establish that the obstruction also constituted a danger, whether an element of negligence is required or, at least, whether the possibility of injury or damage must be reasonably foreseeable.

Element of unreasonableness in public nuisance

7–11   The law of nuisance depends upon the balancing of competing interests and upon the assessment of whether one of those interests is unreasonably interfering with another. In highway nuisance, the issue is whether there is an unreasonable interference with the rights of the public to pass and re-pass along, and to have access to, the highway. Such interference may arise from the acts or omissions of the adjoining landowners or from other users of the highway. It is essentially a matter of degree—whether the act or user complained of is unreasonable in nature, or by reason of its effects. The courts may have regard to the manner of creation of the interference, the status of its creator, the degree of fault, if any, attributable to its creation or continuance, and the physical or temporal extent of the interference.

Negligence and fault, foreseeability and causation in public nuisance

7–12   It has often been stated that it is not necessary, in order to establish that a public nuisance relating to a highway has taken place, to prove negligence.[24] However, the degree of fault, if any, in the creation or continuance of the nuisance will be one factor in assessing the reasonableness of the action which is alleged to constitute the nuisance. Lord Greene M.R., in *Maitland* v. *Raisbeck & R.T. & J. Hewitt Ltd.*,[25]

---

[23] *Dymond* v. *Pearce* [1972] 1 Q.B. 496 at 505.
[24] See Lord Reid in *The Wagon Mound (No. 2)* [1967] 1 A.C. 617; *Farrell* v. *John Mowlem & Co. Ltd.* [1954] 1 Lloyd's Rep. 437 at 440; *Morton* v. *Wheeler, The Times*, February 1, 1956; *Dymond* v. *Pearce* [1972] 1 Q.B. 496.
[25] [1944] K.B. 689.

expressed the view that an obstruction becomes a nuisance *only* if there is fault on the part of the person responsible. He said[26]:

> "Every person who uses the highway must exercise due care but he has a right to use the highway and, if something happens to him which, in fact, causes an obstruction to the highway, but is in no way referable to his fault, it is wrong to suppose that *ipso facto* and immediately a nuisance is created. A nuisance will obviously be created if he allows the obstruction to continue for an unreasonable time or in unreasonable circumstances, but the mere fact that an obstruction has come into existence cannot turn it into a nuisance. It must depend upon the facts of each case whether or not a nuisance is created."

It may be that this proposition is too wide to cover every example of public nuisance on a highway, but it appears likely that it will be the basis upon which liability for accidents arising out of obstructions on the highway is assessed. The liability of occupiers of land adjoining the highway appears to vary according to the nature of the nuisance, but again fault, often bearing a strong similarity to negligence, appears to be a prime factor in determining liability. Whilst there seems to have been a tendency in one line of cases to equate liability in negligence and in nuisance[27]—at least where accidental damage is caused—it seems that there may be an element of strict liability for certain other categories of nuisance.[28] Related to fault is the need for foreseeability as an element of public nuisance.

The classic discussion of the necessity for foreseeability as an element **7–13** in the tort of public nuisance appears in *The Wagon Mound (No. 2)*.[29] In concluding that negligence in the narrow sense was not necessary for the tort of nuisance, Lord Reid suggested that[30] fault of some kind was almost always necessary and that fault generally involved foreseeability. The Court of Appeal in *Dymond* v. *Pearce*[31] discussed the question of causation and the need for foreseeability in different types of highway nuisance. The case concerned a lorry parked on a highway overnight. It stood under a street lamp and it had its lights on. There was nothing to obstruct the lorry from view for at least 200 yards, but a motorcyclist hit it. The evidence suggested that the attention of the motorcyclist had been distracted by pedestrians. The court found that there was obstruction such as to be a nuisance but the obstruction was not the cause of the

---

[26] [1944] K.B. 689 at 691. See also *Hudson* v. *Bray* [1917] 1 K.B. 520; *Parish* v. *Judd* [1960] 1 W.L.R. 867.
[27] See, *e.g.* Lord Parker C.J. in *British Road Services* v. *Slater* [1964] 1 W.L.R. 498.
[28] *Wringe* v. *Cohen* [1940] 1 K.B. 229. See below, at para. 7–31, and see also the discussion in *Winfield and Jolowicz on Tort* (11th ed.) pp. 357–362.
[29] [1967] 1 A.C. 617.
[30] *Ibid.* at 639.
[31] [1972] 1 Q.B. 496.

accident. The plaintiff's case failed. Sachs L.J.[32] felt that it would be rare for a plaintiff to succeed in a claim for damages based upon nuisance, where a claim for negligence would not succeed, for:

" . . . only rarely will that which was found not to be a foreseeable cause of an accident also be found to have been in law the actual cause of it."

Questions of causation and foreseeability relate to the damage which has been suffered by reason of the wrongful act. They will, therefore, only need to be limiting factors in the law of public nuisance where special damage is alleged. It is perfectly possible for the tort of public nuisance to be committed and for the Attorney-General or the local authority[33] successfully to bring proceedings in cases where no such damage is alleged.

Obstruction of the highway

7–14   An obstruction of the highway has been defined as "something which permanently or temporarily removes the whole or part of a highway from the public use altogether."[34] However, use of the highway may itself involve occasional halts by one traveller, which obstruct the highway for another traveller. Whether or not a particular use of the highway is an obstruction ultimately merges with the question as to what is a reasonable use. In *Harper* v. *Haden & Sons Ltd.*,[35] Romer L.J. indicated that a common-sense approach should be adopted to what is or is not a reasonable use of the highway:

"The law relating to the user of highways is in truth the law of give and take. Those who use them must in doing so have reasonable regard to the convenience and comfort of others, and must not themselves expect a degree of convenience and comfort only obtainable by disregarding that of other people. They must expect to be obstructed occasionally. It is the price they pay for the privilege of obstructing others."

An obstruction which is *de minimis* will not be actionable.[36] It is not, however, a defence to proceedings brought alleging a public nuisance that the obstruction, although substantial, itself confers a benefit upon the public.[37] Nor, in the absence of express statutory authority, may the

---

[32] At 503.
[33] See Highways Act 1980, s.130(5).
[34] *per* Lord Evershed in *Trevett* v. *Lee* [1955] 1 W.L.R. 113 at 117.
[35] [1932] 1 Ch. 298 at 320.
[36] *R.* v. *Russell* (1854) 3 E. & B. 942; *R.* v. *Train* (1862) 2 B. & S. 640; *R.* v. *Lepine* (1866) 30 J.P. 723; *R.* v. *Bartholomew* [1908] 1 K.B. 554.
[37] See *R.* v. *Morris* (1830) 1 B. & Ad. 441; *R.* v. *Train* (1862) 2 B. & S. 640; *Att.-Gen.* v. *Barker* (1900) 83 L.T. 245.

highway authority itself licence the obstruction by granting its consent to the obstructing acts.[38]

Temporary obstructions

In *Harper* v. *Haden & Sons*,[39] the plaintiff's business as a fruiterer **7–15** depended to some extent upon passing trade. His next-door neighbour, in the course of alterations, erected scaffolding, a hoarding and a gangway around that hoarding, on the highway. It was found as a fact that the obstruction caused to the highway was not greater than was reasonably necessary for the purpose of carrying out the defendant's operations and that it did not continue for any period longer than was reasonably required to carry out those operations. The plaintiff, however, was able to show that he had in fact suffered financial loss, in that his weekly takings were reduced by reason of the fact that his premises were rendered less obvious to passers by. The Court of Appeal held that an actionable public nuisance had not been shown to exist. The Court considered the authorities. Lord Hanworth M.R.[40] said:

> "These cases establish the following propositions:
> (i) A temporary obstruction to the use of the highway or to the enjoyment of adjoining premises does not give rise to a legal remedy where such obstruction is reasonable in quantum and in duration.
> (ii) If either of those limitations is exceeded so that a nuisance to the public is created the obstruction is wrongful and an indictment to abate it will lie.
> (iii) If an individual can establish:
> (a) a particular injury to himself beyond that which is suffered by the rest of the public;
> (b) that the injury is directly and immediately the consequence of the wrongful act;
> (c) that the injury is of a substantial character, not fleeting or evanescent, he can bring his action and recover damages for the injury he has suffered: . . . "
>
> These conditions mean that there must be a wrongful act in the sense that the user complained of was unreasonably exercised . . . something 'exceptive and unreasonable' . . . ; and an injury thereby directly caused to the plaintiff."

The same principles apply to works carried out on the land adjoining the highway and to the use of the adjoining land and to the use of its access to the highway generally.[41] It is difficult to classify obstructions in any

---

[38] *Att.-Gen.* v. *Barker* n.37 above; *R.* v. *Sheffield Gas Consumers' Co.* (1853) 1 C.L.R. 916; *Preston Corpn.* v. *Fullwood Local Board* (1885) 53 L.T. 718; *Harvey* v. *Truro R.C.* [1903] 2 Ch. 638.
[39] [1932] 1 Ch. 298.
[40] [1932] 1 Ch. 298 at 304.
[41] See *R.* v. *Jones* (1812) 3 Camp. 230; *cf. Almeroth* v. *Chivers* [1948] 1 All E.R. 53.

meaningful way, other than by giving examples. In each case, however, the reasonableness of the act complained of in relation to the reasonable user of the highway will have to be balanced. Many of the judicial decisions involving obstruction of the highway arise out of criminal proceedings, where the burden of proof is different and where there is no need to prove special damage. These decisions have to be dealt with cautiously and, to some extent, separately.[42]

Obstructions caused by highway users

7–16　It is accepted that highway users may stop to rest whilst using the highway.[43] A vehicle which comes to a halt on the highway because of mechanical failure is not itself an obstruction, although the abandonment or parking of the vehicle on the highway for an overly long period may then render it an obstruction.[44] In *Dymond* v. *Pearce*,[45] Sachs L.J. approached the matter in this way:

> "Leaving on one side those in somewhat special positions, such as frontagers, the common law rights of users of highways are normally confined to use for passage and repassage and for incidents usually associated with such use, such as temporary halts and those emergency stops which often give rise to difficulties, and have had to be considered in a number of authorities. The leaving of a large vehicle on a highway for any other purpose for a considerable period (it is always a matter of degree) otherwise than in a layby prima facie results in a nuisance being created, for it narrows the highway."

Parking on the highway verge does not necessarily prevent the creation of an obstruction.[46] The courts will also have regard to the purpose for which the vehicle is parked on the highway.[47]

7–17　The relationship of public nuisance and negligence in these situations is not always clear from the cases. The creation of the initial obstruction may not be negligent but the leaving of the vehicle on the highway in such a way that it is a danger to passing traffic may well be evidence of negligence.[48] In *Dymond* v. *Pearce*,[49] the court took the view that it would be rare for liability in public nuisance for an injury accident on the highway to result from an obstruction where it was not reasonably

---

[42] See paras. 8–13, *et seq.*, below.

[43] *Hadwell* v. *Righton* [1907] 2 K.B. 345.

[44] See *Maitland* v. *Raisbeck and R.T. & J. Hewitt Ltd.* [1944] 1 K.B. 689; *Ware* v. *Garston Haulage Co. Ltd.* [1944] 1 K.B. 30.

[45] [1972] 1 Q.B. 496 at 502.

[46] See *Harris* v. *Mobbs* (1878) 3 Ex. D. 268; *Wilkins* v. *Day* (1883) 12 Q.B.D. 110.

[47] *Nagy* v. *Weston* [1965] 1 W.L.R 280; *Pitcher* v. *Lockett* (1966) 64 L.G.R. 477; *Nelmes* v. *Rhys Howells Transport Ltd.* [1977] R.T.R. 266; *Waltham Forest L.B.C.* v. *Mills* (1978) 78 L.G.R. 248.

[48] See *Hill-Venning* v. *Beszant* [1950] 2 All E.R. 1151; *Parish* v. *Judd* [1960] 1 W.L.R. 867.

[49] [1972] 1 Q.B. 496, *per* Sachs L.J. at 503.

foreseeable that the obstruction would cause such injury. The court found that the accident had not been caused in fact by the obstruction, but rather by the plaintiff's own negligence.[50]

Meetings, processions and picketing

The public right over a highway is that of passage and re-passage, 7–18 together with purposes incidental to those rights.[51] The gathering of people on the highway for other purposes is, therefore prima facie an obstruction. In *Hubbard* v. *Pitt*,[52] Forbes J. emphasised the importance of looking at the purpose of the gathering:

> "Because the highway is used also as a means of access to places abutting on the highway, it is permissible to queue for tickets at a theatre or other place of entertainment, or for a bus. But wherever a person is using a highway other than purely as a means of passage, he is only entitled to use it for a purpose which is reasonably incidental to the right of passage. . . . Now, even then, such user must be reasonable in extent. The tired pedestrian or the motorist with the breakdown can only rest for a reasonable while. Those who queue for theatre tickets or stop to watch window displays must do so reasonably and in such a way as not unduly to obstruct other users."

On the other hand, a procession is simply a number of users of the highway who have chosen to travel together. On the face of it they are only using the highway for the legitimate purpose of passing along it. A procession will not normally be an obstruction of the highway unless its manner of proceeding is such that it unreasonably restricts the user of the highway for other road users. Whilst any user of the highway is entitled to use the full width, he should not do so in such a way as to render the highway impassable for other highway users.[53]

A stationary meeting on the highway will normally be sufficient to 7–19 constitute an obstruction, because the purpose for which the people have gathered has nothing to do with the accepted purposes for which highways are used. The law does not recognise any right of public meeting on a highway,[54] although it may be that the law is not always strictly enforced in this regard. In such a case it does not matter that sufficient room has been allowed for the public to pass,[55] although an obstruction which is *de minimis* will be ignored.

[50] See also *Wills* v. *Martin* (*T.F.*) (*Roof Contractors*) *Ltd.* [1972] R.T.R. 368.
[51] *Hickman* v. *Maisey* [1900] 1 Q.B. 752 at 757–758. See also *Hadwell* v. *Righton* [1907] 2 K.B. 345.
[52] [1976] 1 Q.B. 142 at 149–150.
[53] *Lowdens* v. *Keaveney* [1903] 2 I.R. 82; see also *R.* v. *Clark* (*No. 2*) [1964] 2 Q.B. 315.
[54] *R.* v. *Cunninghame Graham & Burns* (1888) 4 T.L.R. 212; *Ex parte Lewis* (1888) 21 Q.B.D. 191.
[55] See *Homer* v. *Cadman* (1886) 54 L.T. 421; *cf. Burden* v. *Rigler* [1911] 1 K.B. 337.

7–20   Picketing has created some problems in relation to the assessment whether or not the highway has been unreasonably obstructed. Pickets may be static or moving, in large numbers or small, and their purpose usually has little to do with the normal user of the highway. Indeed, their purpose may well be to deter the use of the highway or, at any rate, the use of the access to premises from the highway. In *Hubbard* v. *Pitt*,[56] Forbes J. held that the stationing of pickets on a public highway was "a use not responsive to the purposes for which the highway was dedicated," a use which was designed to interfere with the rights of an adjoining owner to have free and unimpeded access from the highway and which would, therefore, usually be an obstruction, unless it was "so fleeting and so insubstantial" as to fall under the *de minimis* rule. In *Tynan* v. *Balmer*,[57] pickets were held to be causing an obstruction, notwithstanding the fact that they kept on the move by walking in a circling manoeuvre over the highway. The purpose of the manoeuvre was to seal off the access to premises fronting onto the highway, and this purpose rendered the activity unreasonable.

7–21   The collection of crowds outside premises adjoining the highway has created difficulties in reconciling the entitlement of the landowner to use his land lawfully and beneficially, and the rights of the public to free and unimpeded passage along the highway. In accordance with the principles set out in *Harper* v. *Haden & Sons Ltd.*,[58] an actionable obstruction will only arise where the obstruction is unreasonable in extent or duration.[59] The landowner does not himself actually obstruct the highway in these instances. It is the individual members of the crowd or queue who cause the obstruction. The courts have been prepared to find an actionable obstruction caused by the landowner where he has chosen to carry on his trade in such a way or has chosen to create an attraction on his land such that a crowd develops obstructing the highway.[60] The same approach is likely to be taken where the actions of the landowner have caused traffic to build up on the highway by encouraging such traffic to enter his land.[61] Where the landowner carries on business in an ordinary way, resulting in the collection of queues or crowds outside his shop, the courts have been reluctant to intervene, unless the obstruction is very extensive in physical or temporal terms.[62] Where the collection of such crowds is inevitable or is beyond the shopkeeper's control, he cannot be said to have caused the obstruction.[63]

---

[56] [1976] Q.B. 142; see also *Hunt* v. *Broome* [1973] Q.B. 691; *News Group Newspapers* v. *Society of Graphical and Allied Trades 1982 (No. 2)* [1987] I.C.R. 181.

[57] [1967] 1 Q.B. 91.

[58] [1933] 1 Ch. 298; para. 7–15, above.

[59] See *Lyons Sons & Co.* v. *Gulliver* [1914] 1 Ch. 631.

[60] *R.* v. *Moore* (1832) 3 B. & Ad. 184; *R.* v. *Carlile* (1834) 6 C. & P. 636; *Walker* v. *Brewster* (1867) L.R. 5 Eq. 25; *Bellamy* v. *Wells* (1890) 60 L.J. Ch. 156; *Fabbri* v. *Morris* [1947] 1 All E.R. 315.

[61] See *e.g. Lewis* v. *Dickson* [1976] R.T.R. 431.

[62] *Barber* v. *Penley* [1893] 2 Ch. 447; *Lyons* v. *Gulliver* [1914] 1 Ch. 631.

[63] *Dwyer* v. *Mansfield* [1946] K.B. 437.

Encroachment on the highway by adjoining landowners

It will always be a defence to proceedings for public nuisance to estab- 7–22
lish that the alleged obstruction of the highway is an obstacle pre-dating
the dedication of the highway, and subject to which the highway has
been dedicated.[64] Similarly, a highway may be dedicated subject to the
right of the landowner to deposit or display his goods on part of it,[65] to
plough up the footpath,[66] or to retain a gate or low bridge across the
highway.[67] Where the evidence of dedication subject to the right to
obstruct is unclear, the courts have been reluctant to infer the reservation simply from long exercise of an alleged right to obstruct.[68] Where
the obstructed way is an admitted highway, it seems that the burden of
proving the limitation on the dedication will be on the person asserting
it.[69] Apart from cases of limited dedication, any permanent erection
which substantially encroaches on a highway will undoubtedly be an
obstruction to the highway.[70]

Claims to market rights over highways have often led to problems in 7–23
resolving conflicting evidence as to the limitations to be assumed on the
extent of dedication.[71] Where market rights can be established as having
been reserved on dedication of the highway, or as having been created
contemporaneously with the dedication of the highway, then there will
be no obstruction of the highway by the exercise of those rights.[72]

Obstructions caused during operations carried out on neighbouring land

The courts have recognised that in order to carry out lawful oper- 7–24
ations on or to their own land, landowners may require entry onto the
highway and to some extent may need to obstruct the passage along the
highway. The landowner is, in all probability, the sub-soil owner, and
the courts have tended to take the view that when the highway was dedicated, the landowner would not have wished to deprive himself of his
full rights of access to his land. The balance of reasonableness is again in
issue. In *Harper* v. *Haden & Sons Ltd.*,[73] it was held that the temporary
obstruction of the highway by the erection of a wooden hoarding, par-

---

[64] *Fisher* v. *Prowse, Cooper* v. *Walker* (1862) 2 B. & S. 770. See also *Robbins* v. *Jones*
(1863) 15 C.B. (N.S.) 221; *Le Neve* v. *Mile End Old Vestry* (1858) 8 E. & B. 1054.
[65] See *Morant* v. *Chamberlin* (1861) 6 H. & N. 541; *Spice* v. *Peacock* (1875) 39 J.P. 581.
[66] See *Mercer* v. *Woodgate* (1869) L.R. 5 Q.B. 26; *Harrison* v. *Danby* (1870) 34 J.P. 759;
Arnold v. *Blaker* (1871) L.R. 6 Q.B. 433.
[67] *Att.-Gen.* v. *Meyrick & Jones* (1915) 79 J.P. 515; *Warner* v. *Wandsworth Board of
Works* (1889) 53 J.P. 471.
[68] *Spice* v. *Peacock* (1875) 39 J.P. 581; *Brackenborough* v. *Thorsby* (1869) 19 L.T. 692;
Whittaker v. *Rhodes* (1881) 46 J.P. 182; *Openshaw* v. *Pickering* (1912) 77 J.P. 27; *cf.*
Jones v. *Matthews* (1885) 1 T.L.R. 482.
[69] See *Leicester Urban Sanitary Authority* v. *Holland* (1888) 57 L.J.M.C. 75.
[70] See *Seekings* v. *Clarke* (1961) 59 L.G.R. 268; *Wolverton U.D.C.* v. *Willis* [1962] 1
W.L.R. 205; *Hinchon* v. *Briggs* (1963) 61 L.G.R. 315.
[71] See *Lawrence* v. *Hitch* (1868) L.R. 3 Q.B. 521; *Att.-Gen.* v. *Horner* (1885) 11 App.Cas.
66; *Stepney Corpn.* v. *Gingell Son & Foskett Ltd.* [1909] A.C. 245.
[72] *R.* v. *Starkey* (1837) 7 Ad. & El. 95; *Elwood* v. *Bullock* (1844) 6 Q.B. 383.
[73] [1933] 1 Ch. 298.

tially obstructing the footway, was not an actionable nuisance, since it was reasonable in duration and extent.[74] In *Herring* v. *Metropolitan Board of Works*,[75] an obstruction consisting of a hoarding, occupying the whole width of the street and erected for the purpose of enabling the defendants to construct a sewer running under the street, was held not to be an unlawful obstruction. This decision was explained by Vaughan Williams L.J. in *Lingke* v. *Christchurch Corporation*[76]:

> "All that was held there as not an obstruction was the hoarding, which I have already pointed out, I think, in the course of the discussion, when a house is being pulled down, is essential for the protection of the public, for the protection of the King's subjects who are using the King's highway; and you should put up such a hoarding as will prevent the stones and other things, which often result in the course of road repairing or building a house, falling on those who are using the King's highway."

Obstructions caused by straying animals

7–25   At common law there was no duty on the landowner of land adjoining the highway to fence his land. In *Searle* v. *Wallbank*,[77] Viscount Maugham explained the reasons for this as being founded in the historical development of highways over uninclosed land, and pointed to the absence, save in Inclosure Acts, of statutory provisions dealing with any requirement of landowners to fence their land. Since there was no duty to fence, there was no duty (at common law) to keep existing fences or hedges in repair. The fact that road traffic had changed in its nature and extent could not impose a duty on landowners which had not existed previously. In the absence of any duty to fence or to keep fences in repair, a landowner could not be found liable by virtue only of the fact that his animals had strayed onto the highway.[78] Liability in respect of straying animals was, therefore, a question of establishing whether the animal had exhibited special characteristics known to the owner or keeper of the animal so as to impose a duty of care in negligence rather than an application of the law of public nuisance. Furthermore, in *Allison* v. *Corby District Council*,[79] it was held that the presence of five dogs crossing a road could not be regarded as an obstruction of the highway which it was the duty of the highway authority to prevent. The transience of such events would be unlikely, in any event, to give rise to liability as obstruction *per se*.

---

[74] See para. 7–15, above.
[75] (1865) 19 C.B. (N.S.) 510.
[76] [1912] 3 K.B. 595 at 604; *cf. Almeroth* v. *Chivers* [1948] 1 All E.R. 53.
[77] [1947] A.C. 341. See also *Higgins* v. *Searle* (1909) 100 L.T. 280; *Jones* v. *Lee* (1911) 106 L.T. 123; *Heath's Garage Ltd.* v. *Hodges* [1916] 2 K.B. 370; *Hughes* v. *Williams* [1943] K.B. 574.
[78] *Hughes* v. *Williams* [1943] K.B. 574; *Gomberg* v. *Smith* [1963] 1 Q.B. 25.
[79] [1980] 78 L.G.R. 197.

Section 8 of the Animals Act 1971 has abolished this rule of the com- **7–26** mon law insofar as it excludes or restricts the duty which a person may owe to others to take such care as is reasonable to see that damage is not caused by animals straying onto the highway. The standard will now be whether reasonable steps have been taken by the animal's owner or keeper to prevent foreseeable harm from being occasioned to persons falling within the "neighbour" principle. The Act, however, draws a distinction in some situations between a failure to fence and a failure to keep fencing in repair. In areas of common land, towns or village greens, and in areas where fencing is not customary, an owner or keeper of animals who has the right to place animals on the land will not be liable, simply by reason of his placing the animals there, for damage caused by them straying onto the highway from the unfenced land. Where, therefore, the land in question has traditionally been fenced and is not common land or a town or village green, the landowner may be liable where the fence has negligently been allowed to fall into disrepair. Where the land is unfenced and falls within the categories described in the section, liability may still attach where there has been negligence unrelated to any failure to fence. Thus, where activities in which animals are under human control are being conducted on land adjoining the highway there may be liability if an animal escapes onto the highway where this is a foreseeable result of the activity concerned.[80] Section 2 of the Animals Act 1971 sets out the circumstances generally where liability will arise from damage caused by domestic animals.[81] Where damage, which would fall within section 2, is caused on a highway by an animal placed on common land, it would appear that liability under section 2 would not be excluded by section 8.[82]

Dangers to the user of the highway

A highway nuisance may also be created where there is a danger **7–27** caused to highway users from the condition of adjoining land or from an activity on that land. As has already been noted,[83] there often is a very large overlap between dangers to the highway which constitute a nuisance and obstructions to the highway which constitute a nuisance. An excavation in the highway, for example, is both an obstruction and a danger to highway users and many other forms of obstruction will carry with them an element of danger from collision. Whereas the courts have principally been concerned in obstruction cases with the extent of the obstruction and the purpose for which the obstructing article or event was on the highway, the judicial approach to the question of highway nuisance caused by the creation of a danger to highway users has tended

---

[80] *Bativala* v. *West* [1970] 1 Q.B. 716.
[81] For a consideration of these provisions of the Animals Act 1971, reference should be made to standard works of authority on the law of torts.
[82] See, under the common law, *Fitzgerald* v. *Cooke (E.D. & A.D.) Bourne (Farms)* [1964] 1 Q.B. 249; and see the offence created by Highways Act 1980, s.155.
[83] At para. 7–10, above.

to concentrate on the source of the danger and the reasonableness of the use of land which creates the danger. The standard of liability may differ depending upon the source of the danger which causes the nuisance.

7–28 Liability for private nuisance generally falls upon the occupier of land only where he has caused the nuisance, or where he may be said to have continued it. To be liable for continuing a nuisance it is established that the occupier should be actually aware of the nuisance or should reasonably have become aware of the existence of the nuisance and have failed to take reasonable steps to abate it.[84] In *Leakey* v. *National Trust for Places of Historic Interest or Natural Beauty*,[85] the Court of Appeal confirmed that liability for nuisance caused by hazards of natural origin is also dependant upon whether the defendant knew or ought reasonably to have known of the risk of the hazard. It is not entirely clear whether these principles apply to every kind of highway nuisance, since a distinction has appeared in the earlier cases between nuisances caused by natural objects, such as trees and vegetation, and nuisances caused by structures erected alongside highways and by operations carried on near to highways, causing danger to highway users.

Dangers arising from natural causes or natural vegetation on land adjoining the highway

7–29 Trees or other vegetation may grow in such a way as to cause a nuisance to highway users by the encroachment of their roots undermining the highway or by overhanging branches interfering with free passage along the highway. In *Hale* v. *Hants. and Dorset Motor Services Ltd. and Another*,[86] it was established that the overhanging branch of a tree could constitute an actionable nuisance. In that case the tree in question had been planted in the highway by the highway authority under statutory powers which expressly required that the authority should not allow such trees to hinder the reasonable use of the highway[87] but the same principle will apply to the situation where the tree is growing on adjoining land and a common law nuisance arises. The liability of the occupier of the adjoining land for such a nuisance will only arise when he is aware of the existence of the nuisance, or ought reasonably to have become aware of it. Thus, in *British Road Services* v. *Slater*,[88] a bough which had protruded over a highway for many years without causing an accident was held to be a nuisance when a lorry carrying a high load caught it and part of the load became dislodged. However, although the bough was in plain view, the landowners were not aware that it constituted a nuisance, and the court appears to have been satisfied they should not reasonably have been aware of the potential of the branch as a nuisance.

[84] *Sedleigh Denfield* v. *O'Callaghan* [1940] A.C. 880.
[85] [1980] Q.B. 485.
[86] [1947] 2 All E.R. 628.
[87] Roads Improvement Act 1925, s.1(1), (2), now repealed.
[88] [1964] 1 W.L.R. 498.

Lord Parker C.J., therefore, held, applying the principles of *Sedleigh Denfield* v. *O'Callaghan*,[89] that this lack of knowledge, actual or presumed, relieved the defendants from liability for nuisance, commenting that the tendency of the law was "more and more to assimilate nuisance and negligence."

It would appear that the same principles apply, howsoever the tree or **7–30** vegetation actually causes the nuisance. Thus, the encroachment of the roots of a tree onto adjoining land causing damage, has been held to constitute a private nuisance, and there seems to be no reason why the same principle should not apply to highway nuisance.[90] Where danger has been caused to the highway by decaying and dangerous trees, there will be liability if the defect in the tree is known to, or is discoverable on reasonable inspection by, the landowner, but he will not be absolutely liable for latent defects of which he was neither aware nor should have been aware.[91] Similarly, where a danger has arisen by other natural means, liability depends upon actual or constructive knowledge. Thus, where snow had accumulated on the roof of property adjoining the highway and had not been cleared for four days, it was found that the occupier ought reasonably to have been aware that it constituted a danger to users of the highway, and he was therefore liable in nuisance.[92]

Dangerous structures causing a hazard to users of the highway

In *Mint* v. *Good*,[93] the strict attitude of the courts towards dangerous **7–31** structures adjoining the highway was explained by Denning L.J.[94]:

> "The law of England has always taken particular care to protect those who use a highway. It puts on the occupier of adjoining premises a special responsibility for the structures which he keeps beside the highway. So long as those structures are safe, all well and good; but if they fall into disrepair, so as to be a potential danger to passers by, then they are a nuisance, and, what is more, a public nuisance; and the occupier is liable to anyone using the highway who is injured by reason of the disrepair. It is no answer for him to say that he and his servants took reasonable care; for, even if he has employed a competent independent contractor to repair the structure, and has every reason for supposing it to be safe, the occupier is still liable if the independent contractor did the work badly: see *Tarry* v. *Ashton* (1876) 1 Q.B.D. 314.
>
> The occupier's duty to passers-by is to see that the structure is as

---

[89] [1940] A.C. 880.
[90] See *Butler* v. *Standard Telephones and Cables Ltd.* [1940] 1 K.B. 399; *Bridges* v. *Harrow L.B.C.* (1981) 160 E.G. 284; *Solloway* v. *Hampshire C.C.* (1981) 79 L.G.R. 449; *Russell* v. *Barnet L.B.C.* (1985) 83 L.G.R. 152.
[91] See *Noble* v. *Harrison* [1926] 2 K.B. 332; *Caminer* v. *Northern and London Investment Trust* [1951] A.C. 88; *Quinn* v. *Scott* [1965] 1 W.L.R. 1004.
[92] *Slater* v. *Worthington's Cash Stores (1930) Ltd.* [1941] 1 K.B. 488.
[93] [1951] 1 K.B. 517.
[94] At 526–527.

safe as reasonable care can make it; a duty which is as high as the duty which an occupier owes to people who pay to come on to his premises. He is not liable for latent defects, which could not be discovered by reasonable care on the part of anyone, nor for acts of trespassers of which he neither knew, nor ought to have known: see *Barker* v. *Herbert* [1911] 2 K.B. 633, 634; but he is liable when structures fall into dangerous disrepair, because there must be some fault on the part of someone or other for that to happen; and he is responsible for it to persons using the highway, even though he is not actually at fault himself. That principle was laid down in this court in *Wringe* v. *Cohen* [1940] 1 K.B. 233, where it is to be noted that the principle is confined to 'premises on a highway,' and is I think, clearly correct in regard to the responsibility of an occupier to passers-by."

This statement appears to be an attempt to reconcile different lines of authority which have stressed, on the one hand, the need for fault and foreseeability in this kind of nuisance, and on the other hand, an element of strict liability for certain kinds of highway nuisance. It is by no means a complete reconciliation. Where a structure has been allowed to fall into decay, thereby causing a danger to users of the highway, it may be a reasonable supposition that the occupier knows or ought to have known of the danger which has in fact been brought about by his own or his predecessor's neglect, but this is not inevitably so. In *Tarry* v. *Ashton*,[95] it was held that the employment of an independent contractor did not absolve the occupier of land adjoining a highway from his duty to repair all known defects in his property which might cause a danger to users of the highway. The occupier was held to be liable for a public nuisance caused when a gas lamp overhanging the highway fell onto the highway. Whilst Blackburn J. appears to have founded the liability on the basis of the occupier's knowledge that the lamp was out of repair[96] Lush and Quain JJ. did not expressly do so. In *Wringe* v. *Cohen*,[97] the Court of Appeal went further and found that where an injury is caused to the user of a highway through the disrepair of premises adjoining the highway, the occupier (or in some cases, the owner) would be liable whether or not he knew of the danger. From this wide proposition the Court of Appeal then withdrew situations where the danger was caused by a latent defect or where it was caused by the act of a trespasser or by a secret or unobservable process of nature, unless the occupier or owner had allowed the danger to continue. It may be that in practical terms there is little difference between this approach and one which requires the landowner to have actual or constructive knowledge of the danger.

[95] (1876) 1 Q.B.D. 314.
[96] Although this interpretation of his judgment was expressly refuted by Atkinson J. in *Wringe* v. *Cohen* [1940] 1 K.B. 229.
[97] [1940] 1 K.B. 229.

In subsequent cases involving natural objects, the courts have declined to apply the form of strict liability which *Wringe* v. *Cohen* implies.[98]

Generally, it is the occupier having control over land who is liable for nuisances arising on that land, except where the nuisance is caused by a third party and is not adopted by him. However, the owner of land, rather than the occupier, may be liable for the disrepair if a structure causes danger to the highway where the owner is liable on a covenant for repair, or where he has reserved a right to enter.[99] Whilst, in the absence of a covenant of repair, the courts were prepared to imply a right of entry where the landlord had in practice carried out repairs, in *Mint* v. *Good*, Denning L.J. indicated that even where the landlord had taken an express repairing covenant from his tenant, the courts might still look critically at the landlord's position.[1] **7–32**

Dangerous excavations on land adjoining the highway

The liability of adjoining landowners for highway nuisance extends to situations where the danger does not actually impinge upon the highway but where users of the highway may accidentally be caused to deviate from the highway into, for example, a dangerous excavation. Although generally there is no duty on the landowner to fence the land adjoining the highway (unless he has received a statutory notice to do so)[2] he may, nonetheless, be liable where injury is caused to a highway user who accidentally falls from the highway or steps from the highway to his injury.[3] Liability will only attach where the dangerous excavation or object is on land adjoining or near to the highway and depends upon the risk of accident to a highway user being reasonably foreseeable.[4] This liability only relates to persons who accidentally leave the highway and not to those who deliberately choose to leave the way for some other purpose.[5] Although the liability of the landowner towards trespassers generally is now governed by the Occupiers Liability Act 1984, that Act neither imposes any duty in respect of persons using the highway nor does it affect any duty already owed to such persons.[6] It would appear, therefore, that the common law rules relating to the liability towards highway users who stray from the highway are unchanged. **7–33**

---

[98] See para. 7–29, above.
[99] See *Mint* v. *Good* [1951] 1 K.B. 517; *Wilchick* v. *Marks and Silverstone* [1934] 2 K.B. 56; *Heap* v. *Ind Coope & Allsopp Ltd.* [1940] 2 K.B. 476.
[1] [1951] 1 K.B. 517 at 528.
[2] See Highways Act 1980, s.165.
[3] *Barnes* v. *Ward* (1850) 9 C.B. 392; *Harrold* v. *Watney* [1898] 2 Q.B. 320; *Barker* v. *Herbert* [1911] 2 K.B. 633.
[4] See *Hardcastle* v. *South Yorkshire Ry. Co.* (1859) 4 H. & N. 67 at 74; *Caseley* v. *Bristol Corpn.* [1944] 1 All E.R. 14; *Binks* v. *South Yorkshire Ry. and River Dun Co.* (1862) 3 B. & S. 244.
[5] *Bromley* v. *Mercer* [1922] 2 K.B. 126; *Mumford* v. *Naylor* [1951] W.N. 579; *Jacobs* v. *L.C.C.* [1950] A.C. 361; *Creed* v. *McGeoch & Sons Ltd.* [1955] 1 W.L.R. 1005.
[6] Occupiers Liability Act 1984, s.1(7).

7–34   There will be no liability in the landowner for any failure to fence a natural danger, such as a stream or valley,[7] but where there is a fence in existence defining the line of the highway adjacent to a dangerous area of land, it may be negligent for the highway authority or for the adjoining landowner to remove it.[8] Where a dangerous difference in the levels of the highway and the adjoining land is caused by the highway authority raising the level of the highway, then any liability for danger thereby resulting will fall on the highway authority rather than the landowner.[9] The occupier of land may still be required to rebuild a fence protecting the public from the danger, even where the dangerous excavation has been created by a previous occupier of the land.[10]

Activities on land adjoining the highway

7–35   Liability may attach to dangerous activities and operations on land adjoining the highway, as well as to dangerous land or structures.[11] A golf course or cricket pitch adjoining a highway may be a highway nuisance depending on the likelihood and seriousness of the risk of danger.[12]

Remedies for highway nuisance

Indictment

7–36   At common law the highway authority had the right to abate a nuisance and to remove any obstruction interfering with the free passage along the highway.[13] The remedy for a nuisance lay in criminal proceedings by way of indictment.[14] Although this procedure has fallen into disuse, it is still possible to bring criminal proceedings for a public nuisance, and such an offence is triable either on indictment or summarily.[15] The principles applicable to proceedings brought by way of indictment are essentially similar to those relating to a civil action in nuisance.[16] Under the old law, the court had power to order the defend-

---

[7] *Morrison* v. *London Midland & Scottish Ry. Co.* [1929] S.C. 1.

[8] *Whyler* v. *Bingham R.C.* [1901] 1 K.B. 45.

[9] See *Nicholson* v. *Southern Ry.* [1935] 1 K.B. 558; *Myers* v. *Harrow Corpn.* [1962] 2 Q.B. 442.

[10] *Att.-Gen.* v. *Roe* [1915] 1 Ch. 235.

[11] See *Holling* v. *Yorkshire Traction Co.* [1948] 2 All E.R. 662; *Dollman* v. *Hillman* [1941] 1 All E.R. 355.

[12] *Castle* v. *St. Augustine's Links Ltd.* (1922) 38 T.L.R. 615; *cf. Bolton* v. *Stone* [1951] A.C. 850.

[13] *Bagshaw* v. *Buxton Local Board of Health* (1875) 1 Ch.D. 220; *Reynolds* v. *Presteign U.D.C.* [1896] 1 Q.B. 604.

[14] See *R.* v. *Clark (No. 2)* [1964] 2 Q.B. 315.

[15] Criminal Law Act 1977, s.16(1) and Sched. 2; see also *R.* v. *Andrews, Ex p. Cheshunt U.D.C.* (1962) 60 L.G.R. 211, where the standard of proof was considered.

[16] See *R.* v. *Bartholomew* [1908] 1 K.B. 554; *R.* v. *Clark (No. 2)* [1964] 2 Q.B. 315; *cf.* the position under Highways Act 1980, s.121.

ant to abate a continuing nuisance.[17] The reported cases show a greater concern in the court for the exercise of this power than for the imposition of punishment. Thus, where the nuisance had been abated before trial, the courts tended to impose nominal penalties.[18]

Role of the Attorney-General

A highway nuisance is a wrong to the public at large and the **7–37** Attorney-General has power to bring proceedings, on behalf of the public, for a declaration or an injunction to restrain the commission, or to require the removal of a highway nuisance. This power applies whether or not any special damage has occurred.[19] These proceedings are generally brought on the relation of a private individual or of a local authority, and the Attorney-General is joined to the proceedings. The decision of the Attorney-General as to whether or not to grant his *fiat* for the institution of proceedings in his name is not susceptible to challenge in the courts.[20]

Proceedings brought by local authorities in their own name

Local authorities now have the right to bring proceedings in their own **7–38** name by virtue of the Local Government Act 1972, section 222. They may do this where they consider it expedient for the promotion or protection of the interests of the inhabitants of their area. The councils of counties, non-metropolitan districts, metropolitan districts and London boroughs, and the Common Council also have power to bring proceedings in their own name in order to perform their functions in protecting and asserting highway rights under the Highways Act 1980, section 130.[21] It is now established that the insertion of the words "in their own name," in section 222 of the Local Government Act 1972, empowers local authorities to commence proceedings without the necessity of joining the Attorney-General in a relator action.[22] The same reasoning is equally applicable to proceedings justified by section 130(5) of the Highways Act 1980.[23]

---

[17] *R.* v. *Stead* (1799) 8 Term.Rep. 142; *R.* v. *Incledon* (1810) 13 East 164; *R.* v. *Pappineau* (1726) 2 Stra. 686.

[18] *R.* v. *Dunraven (Earl)* (1837) Will. Woll. & Dav. 577; *R.* v. *Paget* (1862) 3 F. & F. 29; *R.* v. *Lewes Corpn.* (1886) 2 T.L.R. 399.

[19] *Ware* v. *Regent's Canal Co.* (1858) 3 De G. & J. 212; *Att.-Gen.* v. *Shrewsbury (Kingsland) Bridge Co.* (1882) 21 Ch.D. 752; *Att.-Gen.* v. *Roe* [1915] 1 Ch. 235; *Att.-Gen.* v. *Wilcox* [1938] Ch. 934.

[20] See *Gouriet* v. *Union of Post Office Workers* [1978] A.C. 435; see also the discussion of this procedure in De Smith, *Judicial Review of Administrative Action* (4th ed.) at 449.

[21] Highways Act 1980, s.130(5).

[22] See *Stoke-on-Trent Council* v. *B. & Q. (Retail) Ltd.* [1984] 2 W.L.R. 929; *Solihull Metropolitan Council* v. *Maxfern* [1977] 1 W.L.R. 127.

[23] See, *per* Lord Templeman in *Stoke-on-Trent Council* v. *B. & Q. (Retail) Ltd.* [1984] 2 W.L.R. 929 at 937.

Actions by a private individual

7–39   A private individual has the right to bring proceedings for damages, and for an injunction to restrain or to require the removal of a highway nuisance, where he has suffered special damage.[24] It is not sufficient that a person has been interrupted in his user of the highway (even if he incurs expense in removing the obstruction[25]) because the public at large suffers the same inconvenience. There has to have been some damage particular to the highway user himself, or to his trade or calling.[26] The damage does not have to have been special in the sense of being precisely quantifiable, but it has to have been special to the individual himself, that is, loss over and above that which has necessarily been suffered by the public at large in consequence of the nuisance.[27] The rationale of this restriction is apparently to avoid multiplicity of actions, bearing in mind that the perpetrator of the nuisance may be liable, in any event, in criminal penalties, and also that the Attorney-General has the power to bring proceedings on behalf of the public. It is difficult to see exactly where the line is to be drawn in cases where a person is delayed, in his use of the highway, by an obstruction. In *Miles* v. *Rose*,[28] a barge owner successfully brought an action for public nuisance in relation to the obstruction of a navigable waterway, which had obliged him to unload his merchandise and convey it over land, thereby incurring expense. Lord Ellenborough distinguished between the situation of this plaintiff, who had actually suffered loss by reason of the obstruction, and that of the public at large who might only have had in contemplation passage along the waterway. If this was a general proposition, then it would seem that any person who has actually been obstructed in his use of a highway is capable of mounting an action for public nuisance—at least where he has suffered some pecuniary loss.[29] However, in *Winterbottom* v. *Lord Derby*,[30] evidence that the plaintiff, in common with other members of the public, had to turn back and take a more circuitous route without incurring identifiable pecuniary loss was held to be insufficient damage to support an action. The special damage must be substantial and directly attributable to the obstruction, or other public nuisance, which is the subject of complaint. The fact that users of the highway have trespassed on the plaintiff's land in order to overcome an obstruction placed on the highway by the defendant has been held to

---

[24] *Fritz* v. *Hobson* (1880) 14 Ch.D. 542; *Winterbottom* v. *Derby* (*Lord*) (1867) L.R. 2 Ex 316; *Wallasey Local Board* v. *Gracey* (1887) 36 Ch.D. 593; *Boyce* v. *Paddington Corpn.* [1903] 1 Ch. 109.

[25] *Winterbottom* v. *Lord Derby* (1867) L.R. 2 Ex. 316.

[26] *Ibid.*

[27] *Rose* v. *Groves* (1843) 5 Man. & G. 613.

[28] (1815) 4 M. & S. 101. See also *Hart* v. *Basset* (1681) T. Jo. 156; *Chichester* v. *Lethbridge* (1738) Willes 71; *Greasly* v. *Codling* (1824) 2 Bing. 263.

[29] *Blagrave* v. *Bristol Waterworks Co.* (1856) 1 H. & N. 369.

[30] (1867) L.R. 2 Exch. 316. See also *Paine* v. *Partrich* (1691) Carth. 191.

be insufficient.[31] Loss in the value of land by reason of the obstruction,[32] loss of trade,[33] or the occasioning of extra expense,[34] would all be sufficient. Loss of enjoyment of property and loss of light have also been held to be capable of constituting special damage.[35]

Abatement of the nuisance

A highway authority may take action to abate a nuisance once a court   **7–40** has determined that the nuisance exists.[36] The highway authority may also abate a nuisance without instituting legal proceedings.[37] This right or power should be exercised cautiously and, in practice, the highway authority will be able, in the great majority of cases, to use one of the specific statutory powers contained in Part IX of the Highways Act 1980. These powers are not, however, exclusive. A council which has general powers under section 130(2)[38] may also exercise this power of abatement.[39]

Private individuals using the highway are entitled to abate a nuisance   **7–41** in the highway.[40] The right only arises where they have suffered some special damage and may be exercised only to the extent necessary for the reasonable enjoyment of their right of passage along the highway.[41] The right of an adjoining landowner who owns the subsoil of the highway may be somewhat greater. He may take action to remove from the highway anything which is not justified by the nature of the public rights over the highway.[42] Wherever a right to abate is exercised it must be done with care, for the person exercising the right will be liable for any damage done which goes beyond the mere abatement of the nuisance.[43]

Compensation under the Public Health Act 1936, section 278

Where acts, which would otherwise constitute a public nuisance in the   **7–42** highway, are carried out by a public authority under statutory powers, an action in damages will not lie against the public authority provided that it acts within those powers, and is not negligent. There is provision,

---

[31] *Blagrave* v. *Bristol Waterworks Co.* (1856) 1 H. & N. 369.
[32] But only where the obstruction is sufficiently permanent; see *Baker* v. *Moore*, cited in (1696) 1 Ld. Raym. at 491; *Mott* v. *Shoolbred* (1875) L.R. 20 Eq. 22; *Cooper* v. *Crabtree* (1882) 20 Ch.D. 589.
[33] *Wilkes* v. *Hungerford Market Co.* (1835) 2 Bing. N.C. 281; *Fritz* v. *Hobson* (1880) 14 Ch.D. 542; *Campbell* v. *Paddington Corpn.* [1911] 1 K.B. 869.
[34] See *News Group Newspapers* v. *Society of Graphical and Allied Trades '82 (No. 2)* [1987] I.C.R. 181.
[35] *Benjamin* v. *Storr* (1874) L.R. 9 C.P. 400. For examples of other cases of special damage, see *Iveson* v. *Moore* (1699) 1 Ld. Raym. 486; *Medcalf* v. *Strawbridge Ltd.* [1937] 2 K.B. 102; *Spencer* v. *London & Birmingham Ry. Co.* (1836) 8 Sim. 193.
[36] *Bagshaw* v. *Buxton Board of Health* (1875) 1 Ch.D. 220.
[37] *Reynolds* v. *Presteign U.D.C.* [1896] 1 Q.B. 604.
[38] See para. 7–03, above.
[39] *Reynolds* v. *Presteign U.D.C.* [1896] 1 Q.B. 604.
[40] *James* v. *Hayward* (1630) Cro. Car. 184; *Anon.* 3 Salk. 182.
[41] *Dimes* v. *Petley* (1850) 15 Q.B. 276; *Bateman* v. *Bluck* (1852) 18 Q.B. 870.
[42] *R.* v. *Mathias* (1861) 2 F. & F. 570.
[43] *Dimes* v. *Petley* (1850) 15 Q.B. 276.

however, in the Public Health Act 1936, section 278 for the payment of compensation to persons who have suffered damage by reason of the exercise of the statutory powers to which the section applies.[44] The right to compensation depends upon the commission by the authority of acts which, but for the existence of statutory powers, would have been unlawful.[45] The principles upon which liability to pay compensation is assessed are broadly similar to those used in establishing a claim in damages.[46]

[44] *i.e.* powers contained within the Public Health Act 1936 itself, or in other legislation which is to be construed in accordance with that Act.
[45] *Ricket* v. *Metropolitan Ry.* (1867) L.R. 2 H.L. 175.
[46] See *Lingke* v. *Christchurch Corpn.* [1912] 3 K.B. 595; *Herring* v. *Metropolitan Board of Works* (1865) 34 L.J.M.C. 224; *Harrison* v. *Southwark and Vauxhall Water Co.* [1891] 2 Ch. 409; *Leonidis* v. *Thames Water Authority* (1979) 77 L.G.R. 722.

CHAPTER 8

PROTECTION OF THE HIGHWAY AND HIGHWAY USERS: (2) STATUTORY POWERS RELATING TO AUTHORISED AND UNAUTHORISED INTERFERENCES WITH THE HIGHWAY

HIGHWAYS ACT 1980, PART IX

Part IX of the Highways Act 1980 provides local authorities with a large **8–01** number of specific powers to authorise certain limited obstructions in the highway, and to take action to prevent or remove unauthorised obstructions. This miscellany of powers derives from various earlier statutory sources and there has only been a limited attempt at rationalisation. Authorities are often faced with difficulties in deciding which powers are the most suitable to govern particular situations. Choice of the wrong provision can cause delays and may possibly prejudice an authority's ability to deal with potential dangers on the highway.

Without lawful authority or excuse

Many of the powers contained in Part IX of the Highways Act 1980 **8–02** create criminal liability where persons damage, obstruct or interfere with the user of the highway. In most cases, the offence is only committed if the defendant has acted without lawful authority or excuse. Highways may be dedicated to the public subject to existing obstructions and subject to the rights of the landowner to interrupt the highway from time to time and the exercise of reserved rights of this sort will constitute lawful authority. A statutory power to break open the surface would clearly be lawful authority, but strict compliance with the terms of that authority is required.[1] In some cases the highway authority has express statutory authority to grant permission to a landowner to break into the highway, for example, to remove a tree placed in the highway by licence of the authority.[2] A contractor carrying out works under the terms of a contract with a highway authority will have lawful authority or excuse to interfere with the highway if the authority itself has power to carry out those works.[3] Apart from these situations, the local authority may not license acts which create an unlawful obstruction.[4] Lawful authority to obstruct a highway cannot be acquired by prescription, nor can the acquiescence of the highway authority authorise an obstruction.[5]

---

[1] *Hawkins v. Robinson* (1873) 37 J.P. 662; *Beaumont v. Wilson* (1942) 40 L.G.R. 171.
[2] See Highways Act 1980, s.142.
[3] *King (Contractors) Ltd. v. Page* (1970) 114 S.J. 335.
[4] *Redbridge L.B.C. v. Jaques* [1970] 1 W.L.R. 1604.
[5] *Pugh v. Pigden* (1987) 151 J.P. 644.

8–03   It is more difficult to understand what might constitute lawful excuse. A minor interference with the user of the highway may be justifiable where a landowner seeks to abate a nuisance caused to his own land,[6] or where the interference arises out of the reasonable use of his own land. The reasonableness of the activity which interferes with user of the highway goes to the question whether or not an obstruction has been committed, but it may also be relevant to the question of lawful excuse— particularly where the landowner is charged under a statutory provision other than obstruction.[7]

8–04   In *St. Mary, Newington, Vestry* v. *Jacobs*,[8] a landowner used a warehouse for the purpose of storing heavy machinery. After the highway surveyors refused his application to construct a proper crossing from the highway to the warehouse, the landowner caused the machinery to be carried from the highway across a footway to his warehouse, thereby causing damage to the footway. He was prosecuted under section 72 of the Highway Act 1835 for causing injury or damage to be done to the highway. The Divisional Court held that unless the landowner were permitted to exercise access to his premises in this manner, he could not beneficially use his land. Whilst accepting that the landowner may not derogate from his grant (that is, the dedication of the highway in the first place) by doing anything which would "really and substantially" interfere with the public's right of passage, the court also felt that dedication could not be intended to deprive a landowner of the beneficial use of his adjoining land. Two findings were crucial to this decision. The first was that the property could not be reasonably enjoyed without access being gained across the existing footway. The second was that the rights of ownership and those of the general public could be exercised consistently with the general welfare.[9] The reasonableness of a landowner's desire to protect his land cannot justify a permanent obstruction to the highway.[10]

8–05   Commercial expediency or practicability is not a lawful excuse[11]; nor may an employee rely upon the instructions of an employer who himself has no lawful authority or excuse to interfere with highway user.[12] In *Cambridgeshire and Isle of Ely County Council* v. *Rust*,[13] it was held that an honest belief in the existence of facts which, if true, would have provided lawful authority or excuse, can establish a defence in criminal

---

[6] This remedy must be exercised cautiously; see *Reynolds* v. *Presteign U.D.C.* [1896] 1 Q.B. 604.

[7] See *Hirst and Agu* v. *Chief Constable of West Yorkshire* [1987] Crim. L.R. 330.

[8] (1871) L.R. 7 Q.B. 47; *cf. R.* v. *Longton Gas Co.* (1860) 2 E.& E. 651.

[9] *cf. Curtis* v. *Geeves* (1929) 94 J.P. 71 (a case on the City Police Act 1839); *Goodson* v. *Richardson* (1874) 9 Ch. App. 221; *Att.-Gen.* v. *Ashby* (1908) 72 J.P. 449.

[10] *Campodonic* v. *Evans* (1966) 200 E.G. 857; *Dixon* v. *Atfield* [1975] 1 W.L.R. 1171; *Putnam* v. *Colvin* [1984] R.T.R. 150.

[11] *Gatland* v. *Commissioner of Police of the Metropolis* [1968] 2 Q.B. 279.

[12] *Lewis* v. *Dickson* [1976] R.T.R. 431; *cf. Gabriel (G.)* v. *Enfield B.C.* (1971) 115 S.J. 364.

[13] [1972] 2 Q.B. 426.

proceedings based upon "lawful excuse," as long as the belief is formed on reasonable grounds. However, lack of knowledge of the legal requirement that permission to make an excavation in the highway is required from the highway authority is not a defence.[14] Furthermore, the belief that a permission has been granted by the highway authority which that authority has no power to authorise will not establish the defence.[15]

Statutory powers to prevent damage to the highway

Sections 131 to 136 of the Highways Act 1980 are concerned with the **8–06** protection of the physical structure of the highway. Section 131 creates a number of criminal offences.[16] Similar offences under the Highway Act 1835 were held not to be continuing offences, and a prosecution must, therefore, be brought within six months from the completion of the act complained of.[17] Liability depends upon the act having been done without lawful authority or excuse.[18]

Section 131(1)(a) prohibits the making of a ditch or excavation in a **8–07** highway which consists of or comprises a carriageway. Opening up a highway under statutory powers without giving the required notice may result in an offence being committed.[19] This provision is not appropriate where subsidence caused by mining operations beneath the highway has resulted in a hole being opened up in the highway.[20] Section 131(1)(b) prohibits the removal of soil or turf from a highway, except for the purpose of improving the highway with the consent of the highway authority. This provision covers both unmade carriageways, and verges running alongside made-up carriageways.[21] If a landowner wishes to improve the standard of an unadopted highway, for example, to make it up to adoption standard, then he will require the consent of the highway authority to avoid committing an offence under this section. A landowner who is liable to maintain a highway by reason of tenure, prescription or inclosure would implicitly have lawful authority to remove soil and turf in the carrying out of necessary acts of repair. A landowner who wishes to construct an access over the verge may commit an offence under this section but he may be entitled to rely on "lawful authority or excuse" where the access is essential for the beneficial use of his land.[22]

---

[14] *Greenwich B.C.* v. *Millcroft Construction Ltd.* (1987) 85 L.G.R. 66 ; see also *Brook* v. *Ashton* [1974] Crim. L.R. 105.
[15] *Cambridgeshire and Isle of Ely* v. *Rust* [1972] 2 Q.B. 426.; *Redbridge L.B.C.* v. *Jaques* [1970] 1 W.L.R. 1604; see also *Pugh* v. *Pigden* (1987) 151 J.P. 644.
[16] Punishable by a fine not exceeding level 3 on the standard scale.
[17] *Coggins* v. *Bennett* (1877) 2 C.P.D. 568; *Ranking* v. *Forbes* (1869) 34 J.P. 486; *Hyde* v. *Entwistle* (1884) 52 L.T. 760.
[18] See para. 8–02, above.
[19] *Beaumont* v. *Wilson* (1942) 40 L.G.R. 171.
[20] *Pease* v. *Paver* (1875) 39 J.P. Jo. 407; see also Highways Act 1980, s.133.
[21] See *Easton* v. *Richmond Highway Board* (1871) L.R. 7 Q.B. 69.
[22] *St. Mary, Newington, Vestry* v. *Jacobs* (1871) L.R. 7 Q.B. 47; *cf. Curtis* v. *Geeves* (1929) 94 J.P. 71; *R.* v. *Longton Gas Co.* (1860) 2 E. & E. 651.

In any event, powers are available to a local planning authority to deal with accesses opening onto highways without planning consent.[23] Section 131(1) (c) deals with damage caused by the deposit of anything on the highway; it would apply, for example, where a corrosive substance was left on the highway, damaging the surface.[24] There is a separate offence committed, under section 148, where certain materials are deposited on a highway so as to interrupt user of the highway. Section 131(1) (d) prohibits the lighting of fires and the discharging of firearms or fireworks on the highway, or within 50 feet of any highway[25] where damage is caused to the highway.[26] The offence only applies to carriageway highways. Where a fire is accidently started through no fault of the defendant, it appears that no offence will be committed. This was certainly so under the Highway Act 1835, which required the offence to have been committed wilfully.[27] It seems that the prosecution have to prove that the defendant was guilty of *lighting* the fire, which suggests an intentional act of creating a fire.

8–08   Section 131(2) makes it an offence to pull down or obliterate traffic signs, milestones and direction posts. This offence applies to all highways and to all signs lawfully placed on or over the highway. Authority is given to highway authorities and local authorities to place signs in highways under Part V of the Road Traffic Regulation Act 1984. A traffic sign is defined [28] as:

> "any object or device (whether fixed or portable) for conveying, to traffic on roads or any specified class of traffic, warnings, information, requirements, restrictions or prohibitions of any description—(a) specified by regulations made by the Ministers acting jointly, or (b) authorised by the Secretary of State, and any line or mark on a road for so conveying such warnings, information, requirements, restrictions or prohibitions."

Under the 1984 Act, the definition of a "road" includes "any length of highway."[29] Highway authorities are empowered to place traffic signs on or near any road in their area. Police constables have power to place traffic signs for the purpose of giving effect to local traffic regulations and in order to deal with emergencies and temporary obstructions.[30] Local authorities, having power to make certain road traffic regulation orders under the 1984 Act,[31] may erect traffic signs in order to give effect to those orders. Since orders are immune from judicial challenge

---

[23] See also Highways Act 1980, s.184, below.
[24] See generally Circular No. Roads 1/82: *Spillages of Hazardous Substances on the Highway*.
[25] See *Hunton* v. *Last* (1965) 109 S.J. 391.
[26] *Stinson* v. *Browning* (1866) L.R. 1 C.P. 321; *Hill* v. *Somerset* (1887) 51 J.P. 742.
[27] *Tunnicliffe* v. *Pickup* [1939] 3 All E.R. 297.
[28] See Road Traffic Regulation Act 1984, s.64.
[29] *Ibid.* s.142.
[30] *Ibid.* ss.66, 67.
[31] See *ibid.* s.68(1).

after the expiry of six weeks from the date on which they are made,[32] the placing of a traffic sign giving effect to such an order cannot thereafter be challenged on the ground that the original order is invalid. Where the order-making authority is not the highway authority there are provisions for consultation with the highway authority.[33] For a traffic sign to have been lawfully placed on the highway, the sign must conform to the prescribed description and must be placed in accordance with directions given by the Secretary of State.[34]

Section 132 of the Highways Act 1980 creates a criminal offence[35] of **8–09** making unauthorised marks on the highway, and authorises the highway authority to remove such marks, whether or not any criminal proceedings are instituted.

Where the footway of a street which is also a highway maintainable at **8–10** the public expense is damaged by, or in consequence of, any excavation or other work on or adjoining[36] the street, the highway authority for the highway may make good the damage and recover the expenses reasonably incurred by it in so doing, from the owner of the land in question, or from the person causing or responsible for the damage.[37] The existence of this power does not prevent the highway authority from pursuing its remedies at common law to sue in nuisance.[38] The authority is only entitled to make good the damage. In *Lodge Holes Colliery* v. *Wednesbury Corporation*,[39] subsidence had occurred due to mining operations. Passage along the highway was not, however, impaired. It was held that the authority could recover from the mine owners only what it would have cost to have made the road equally commodious, and not what it would have cost to raise the highway to the old level.[40]

Sections 134 and 135 deal with the ploughing of paths and the tempor- **8–11** ary diversions of paths or ways. These are considered in Chapter 12.

If a highway consisting of or comprising a carriageway is being **8–12** damaged, by reason of the exclusion from it of the sun and wind by a hedge or tree (other than a tree planted for ornament or for shelter to a building, courtyard or hop ground) a magistrates' court, on a complaint made by the highway authority, may order the owner or occupier of the land on which the hedge or tree is growing so to cut, prune or plash the hedge or prune or lop the tree as to remove the cause of damage. Failure to comply with the order of the magistrates' court is an offence.[41] The highway authority then has default powers to carry out the order

---

[32] Road Traffic Regulation Act 1984, Sched. 9, paras. 35–37.
[33] *Ibid.* s.68(2).
[34] See the Traffic Signs Regulations and General Directions 1981 (S.I. 1981 No. 859) (as amended).
[35] Punishable with a fine not exceeding level 4 on the standard scale.
[36] As to the meaning of which, see para. 10–28, below.
[37] Highways Act 1980, s.133.
[38] *Ibid.* s.333.
[39] [1908] A.C. 323.
[40] See Sched. 22 for other statutory provisions affecting the operation of this section.
[41] Punishable with a fine not exceeding level 1 on the standard scale.

and recover the expense from the person in default. No order made under this section may require or permit any person to cut or prune a hedge at any time, except between the last day of September and the first day of April. The word "lop" is a technical expression meaning "to cut laterally."[42]

Obstructions in highways

Prosecution for wilful obstruction

8–13   By section 137 of the Highways Act 1980, it is an offence for any person, without lawful authority or excuse,[43] wilfully to obstruct the free passage along a highway. The question as to what may or may not be an obstruction in law, and as to what may constitute lawful authority or excuse, has been discussed above.[44] It appears that the rules relating to what is or is not capable of amounting to an obstruction are substantially similar whether civil or criminal proceedings are concerned. The obstructing act must be an unreasonable use of the highway,[45] and this question is to be judged by the duration and extent of the obstruction, its cause and purpose.[46] In *Seekings* v. *Clarke*,[47] it was made clear that anything which substantially prevented the public from having free access over the whole of the highway was an unlawful obstruction. The *de minimis* rule would apply, but in that case, where the obstruction consisted of a projection two and a half feet in depth at maximum, over a sixteen foot wide pavement, the court held that there was no room for the application of the *de minimis* principle.[48] The court indicated, however, that it hoped that the enforcement of these statutory provisions would be done reasonably. Unlike the civil action for damages, it is not a necessary element of the criminal offence of obstruction that any person should actually be obstructed.[49] Evidence of actual obstruction will, however, be indicative that the act or obstacle is an unreasonable use of the highway.[50]

8–14   The question as to whether or not an obstruction is sufficiently permanent to amount to a criminal offence has sometimes arisen under the defence of "lawful excuse." Thus, in *Scarfe* v. *Wood*,[51] it was held that proof that the defendants had been standing on a pavement, and had

---

[42] See *Unwin* v. *Hanson* [1891] 2 Q.B. 115.
[43] See para. 8–02, above.
[44] See paras. 7–14, *et seq.* and para. 8–02, above.
[45] *Gill* v. *Carson & Nield* [1917] 2 K.B. 674; *Nagy* v. *Weston* [1965] 1 W.L.R. 280; *Pitcher* v. *Lockett* (1966) 64 L.G.R. 477; *Waltham Forest L.B.C.* v. *Mills* (1978) 78 L.G.R. 248.
[46] See e.g. *Nelmes* v. Rhys Howells Transport Ltd. [1977] R.T.R. 266; *Cooper* v. *Metropolitan Police Commissioner* (1986) 82 Cr. App. R. 238; *Dunn* v. *Holt* (1904) 73 L.J.K.B. 341.
[47] (1961) 59 L.G.R. 268.
[48] See also *Hertfordshire C.C.* v. *Bolden* (1987) 151 J.P. 252; *Wolverton U.D.C.* v. *Willis* [1962] 1 W.L.R. 205; *Hinchon* v. *Briggs* (1963) 61 L.G.R. 315.
[49] *Hinde* v. *Evans* (1906) 96 L.T. 20; *Absalom* v. *Martin* [1974] R.T.R. 145.
[50] See *Dunn* v. *Holt* (1904) 73 L.J.K.B. 341.
[51] (1969) 113 S.J. 143; See also *Waite* v. *Taylor* (1985) 82 L.S. Gaz. 1092.

refused to move when requested to do so by a constable was sufficient to call for an answer from the defendant. Standing on the pavement was *pro tanto* an obstruction of the highway and the issue was whether the defendant had a lawful excuse. This approach is misleading. Whilst a temporary act of obstruction may call for an answer from the defendant as to its purpose, in order to establish the reasonableness or otherwise of the act, this point goes to the main issue that the prosecution must prove—that there has been an obstruction. Only when there is shown to have been an act which is an obstruction of the highway in law does the burden of proof shift to the defendant to establish that he had a lawful excuse for that obstruction.[52]

The criminal offence has, however, to be committed "wilfully." In **8–15** *Arrowsmith* v. *Jenkins*,[53] it was held that this did not require any intention or knowledge in the defendant that his acts would cause what was, in law, an obstruction. So long as the defendant by the exercise of free will did something which caused an obstruction, the offence was committed. This may apply to the doing of an act off the highway which causes a crowd to gather and obstruct the highway.[54] The owner of a skip which has been wrongfully deposited on a highway may be liable, even where the driver (not the owner) has deposited the skip in accordance with the customer's instructions.[55] However, in *Eaton* v. *Cobb*,[56] it was held that the intentional opening of a car door, which accidentally caused an injury to a passing cyclist, was not a wilful obstruction of the highway for the purposes of the similar provision in the Highway Act 1835. Although the court appears to have based its decision on the fact that the obstruction was not wilful, it is probably better explained by recognising that such a temporary act as the opening of a car door is not an unlawful obstruction, but rather one of the inevitable consequence of the use of vehicles on the highway. Allowing a tree to grow across a footway will not be a *wilful* obstruction,[57] and the same should apply to incursions of tree roots.

Section 28 of the Town Police Clauses Act 1847

The Town Police Clauses Act 1847 contains a number of measures **8–16** which deal with the routing of public processions. Section 28 makes it an offence to carry out any of a number of activities, which are specified in the section, "to the obstruction, annoyance, or danger of the residents or passengers." The offences under section 28 go further than obstruction of the highway, and cover dangers to highway users, as well as acts

---

[52] See also *Hirst and Agu* v. *Chief Constable of West Yorkshire* [1987] Crim. L.R. 330.
[53] [1963] 2 Q.B. 561; see also *Homer* v. *Cadman* (1886) 54 L.T. 421; *R.* v. *Senior* [1899] 1 Q.B. 283; *Tunnicliffe* v. *Pickup* [1939] 3 All E.R. 297.
[54] See *Fabbri* v. *Morris* [1947] 1 All E.R. 315; *cf. Dwyer* v. *Mansfield* [1946] 1 K.B. 437; and see para. 7–21, above.
[55] *Gabriel (G.)* v. *Enfield B.C.* (1971) 115 S.J. 364
[56] [1950] 1 All E.R. 1016.
[57] *Walker* v. *Horner* (1875) 1 Q.B.D. 4.

which are not highway nuisances. There is no requirement that the obstruction should be committed "wilfully," and there is no defence of lawful authority or excuse. It is still necessary, however, for the prosecution to establish that an obstruction has occurred, and it appears that similiar principles apply here to those discussed above.[58] The activities described in the section range from exposing horses for sale to hanging a clothes line across the highway.

Other offences relating to obstructions

8–17   By section 138 of the Highways Act 1980, the erection of a building or fence, or the planting of a hedge in any carriageway highway, without lawful authority or excuse, is an offence.[59] There are also a number of specific offences relating to particular types of obstruction.[60] These are considered, together with the highway authority's other powers relating to that type of obstruction, below. Unless the particular offence in question is expressly made a continuing offence, it seems likely from decisions on similiar provisions in earlier legislation that time begins to run from the time the obstruction or encroachment on the highway first occurred.[61]

Powers to remove unlawful obstructions and deposits

8–18   A highway authority has power under section 149 of the Highways Act 1980 to serve a notice on any person who has deposited on a highway anything which constitutes a nuisance[62] requiring him to remove it forthwith. Failure to comply with the notice entitles the authority to make a complaint to a magistrates' court for a removal and disposal order.[63] Where the highway authority has reasonable grounds for considering that anything unlawfully deposited on the highway constitutes a danger (including a danger caused by an obstruction of the view) to users of the highway, and that the object in question ought to be removed without the delay involved in giving notice or obtaining a removal and disposal order from a magistrates' court, the authority may remove the object forthwith and recover the expenses of so doing from the person who has deposited the object on the highway. The authority may then make a complaint to a magistrates' court for a disposal order.[64] Under earlier legislation, it was held that the justices have juris-

---

[58] *Gill* v. *Carson & Nield* [1917] 2 K.B. 674; *Ball* v. *Ward* (1875) 33 L.T. 170.
[59] Punishable by a fine not exceeding level 3 on the standard scale.
[60] See Highways Act 1980, ss. 139(3), (4), 140(3), 141(3), 144(5), 145(2), 147A(2), 148(*a*), (*b*), (*c*), (*d*), 151, 152(4), 153(5), 155(1), (2), 155(4), 171(6).
[61] See *Ranking* v. *Forbes* (1869) 34 J.P. 486; *Hyde* v. *Entwistle* (1884) 52 L.T. 760; *cf. Coggins* v. *Bennett* (1877) 2 C.P.D. 568.
[62] As to nuisances, see paras. 7–10, *et seq.*, above.
[63] See Highways Act 1980, s.149(4)–(5).
[64] *Ibid.* s.149(2), (3).

diction to determine whether or not the way on which materials have been deposited is a highway.[65]

By section 150 of the Highways Act 1980, the highway authority is   **8–19** under a specific duty to remove obstructions to a highway which result from the accumulation of snow, or from the falling down of banks on the side of the highway, or from any other cause. The words "from any other cause" are to be construed *ejusdem generis* with the foregoing words and are, therefore, confined to sudden and substantial obstructions attributable to natural causes occuring without warning and requiring urgent removal. Gradual incursions from a natural object such as a tree or an overgrown hawthorn hedge will not fall within this section.[66] If the authority fails to remove such an obstruction, a magistrates' court may, on the complaint of any person, by order require the highway authority to remove the obstruction within such period from the making of the order (not being less than 24 hours) as the court thinks reasonable, having regard to all the circumstances of the case. The court is required, in particular, to have regard to the character of the highway to which the complaint relates, the nature and amount of traffic by which it is ordinarily used, the nature and extent of the obstruction, the resources of manpower, vehicles and equipment for the time being available to the highway authority for work on highways, and the extent to which those resources are being, or need to be, employed elsewhere by that authority on such work.[67] The highway authority may, in relation to any obstruction which it is under a duty to remove under this section, take any reasonable steps for warning highway users of the presence of the obstruction, sell anything removed in carrying out the duty (unless the object is claimed by its owner before the expiration of seven days from the date of its removal) and recover its reasonable expenses from the owner of anything which caused or contributed to the obstruction. It is a defence to proceedings for recovery of such expenses that the person concerned took reasonable care to secure that the object in question did not cause or contribute to the obstruction. It has been held that this defence is made out if the landowner establishes that he had taken reasonable steps to ensure that the obstruction did not arise in the first place, and that it is not required of him to prove further that he had taken reasonable steps to secure the removal of the obstruction once it had arisen.[68] After deductions for the costs of removal and of warning highway users, the proceeds must be handed back to the owner. The duty imposed by this section is unlikely to form the basis of an

---

[65] See *Williams* v. *Adams* (1862) 2 B.& S. 312; *Mould* v. *Williams* (1844) 5 Q.B. 469; *R.* v. *Gaisford* [1892] 1 Q.B. 381.

[66] *Worcestershire C.C.* v. *Newman* [1974] 1 W.L.R. 938 (reversed in part on other grounds at [1975] 1 W.L.R. 901).

[67] As to factors which may be relevant to this consideration, see the discussion of Highways Act 1980, s.58(2) at para. 5–28, above.

[68] *Williams* v. *Devon C.C.* (1967) 65 L.G.R. 119; *cf. Hudson* v. *Bray* [1917] 1 K.B. 520.

action for breach of statutory duty,[69] but the negligent failure of a highway authority to remove an obstruction or to give due warning of the obstruction may give rise to liability for failure to maintain under section 41 of the Highways Act 1980.[70]

8–20   In a number of instances highway authorities and local authorities have power to remove obstructions in the event of the owner having failed to do so after service upon him of a notice requiring removal of the obstruction.[71] Highway authorities also have power to licence the placing on highways of articles which amount to obstructions.

Builders' skips

8–21   Sections 139 and 140 of the Highways Act 1980 are concerned with controlling the placing of builders' skips on highways. It is an offence for a builders' skip to be deposited on a highway without a permission granted by the highway authority.[72] The highway authority may grant permission either conditionally or unconditionally. The conditions may specifically relate to the siting of the skip, its dimensions, the manner in which it is to be coated with paint and other material for the purpose of making it immediately visible to oncoming traffic, the care and disposal of its contents, the manner in which it is to be lit or guarded, and its removal at the end of the period of the permission. "Deposited" has been held to refer to the state of the skip, and is not restricted to the act of placing it on the highway in the first instance. The offence will, therefore, be committed if the skip is left on the highway for longer than the permitted period.[73]

8–22   The owner of the skip is required to ensure that it is properly lit during the hours of darkness, and regulations made by the Secretary of State[74] prescribe reflecting and fluorescent material which must be used to mark the skip. The owner must ensure that the skip is clearly and indelibly marked with his name and telephone number or address. He is also required to ensure the removal of the skip as soon as is practicable after it has been filled and to secure compliance with each of the conditions subject to which the permission was granted. Failure to comply with any of these requirements is an offence.[75] Where the commission of an offence is due to the act or default of some other person,[76] then there is provision for that person to be charged with and convicted of the

---

[69] See, *per* Lord Denning M.R. in *Haydon* v. *Kent C.C.* [1978] 2 W.L.R. 485 at 493; *cf.* *Saunders* v. *Holborn District Board of Works* [1895] 1 Q.B. 64.

[70] See Chap. 5.

[71] See *e.g.* Highways Act 1980, ss.140 and 152.

[72] Punishable by a fine not exceeding level 3 on the standard scale; Highways Act 1980, s.139(1), (3).

[73] *Craddock* v. *Green* [1983] R.T.R. 479.

[74] See the Builders' Skip (Markings) Regulations 1984 (S.I. 1984 No. 1983).

[75] Punishable with a fine not exceeding level 3 on the standard scale; Highways Act 1980, s.139(4).

[76] As to "act or default," see *Lambeth L.B.C.* v. *Saunders Transport* [1974] R.T.R. 319; *York D.C.* v. *Poller* (1975) 73 L.G.R. 522; see also *Nathan* v. *Rouse* [1905] 1 K.B. 527.

offence in substitution to or in addition to the owner of the skip. Where any person charged under section 139 proves that the commission of the offence was due to the act or default of another person, and that he himself had taken all reasonable precautions and exercised all due diligence[77] to avoid the commission of the offence by himself or by any person under his control, he will have a defence to the proceedings brought against him.[78] This defence is also available where the defendant is charged with an offence of failing to ensure that the skip is properly lit.[79] Where a permission has been granted and complied with, then the owner will have a defence to any criminal proceedings brought against him for obstruction or interruption of the user of the highway. The "act or default" defence is also available.[80] Where the skip has been vandalised, and its lights stolen or destroyed, it is not necessary for the owner to be able to name the culprits in order to rely upon the defence.[81]

The grant of permission under these provisions provides no defence   **8–23** to any action in civil law for nuisance.[82] Nor is any liability imposed on the highway authority who grants permission under this section for any injury or damage or loss resulting from the presence of the skip on the highway. Where an accident occurs on the highway due to the presence of a skip it is unlikely that an action in public nuisance would succeed simply because of the presence of the skip, since this is unlikely to be of such an extent or of such a duration so as to give rise to an actionable obstruction.[83] However, the skip must be lit so as to be instantly visible[84] and must be so positioned as to encroach upon the highway no more than is reasonably necessary.[85]

The highway authority or a constable in uniform may require the   **8–24** owner of any skip placed (lawfully or not) on the highway to remove or reposition it.[86] The skip may be removed or repositioned in default. If the owner cannot be traced or if, after a reasonable period of time, he has not recovered the skip, it may be disposed of and the proceeds from its sale may be used to defray the removal and storage charges. These expenses may alternatively be recovered from the owner of the skip in any court of competent jurisdiction, or summarily as a civil debt.

---

[77] As to what must be shown in relation to "due diligence" with respect to a limited company, see *Tesco Supermarkets Ltd.* v. *Nattrass* [1972] A.C.153.
[78] Notice of intention to rely upon this defence must be served on the prosecutor seven clear days before the hearing: s.139(7). As to the contents of such a notice, see *Barnet L.B.C.* v. *S.& W. Transport* [1975] R.T.R. 211.
[79] *e.g.* under Highways Act 1980, s.171.
[80] *Ibid.* s.139(9).
[81] *P.G.M. Building Co. Ltd.* v. *Kensington L.B.C.* [1982] R.T.R. 107.
[82] Highways Act 1980, s.139(10).
[83] See para.7–14, above.
[84] See *Saper* v. *Hungate Builders* [1972] R.T.R. 380; *Drury* v. *Camden L.B.C.* [1972] R.T.R. 319.
[85] See *Wills* v. *Martin (T.F.) (Roof Contractors) Ltd.* [1972] R.T.R. 368.
[86] Highways Act 1980, s.140(1), (2). Failure to comply is an offence punishable by a fine not exceeding level 3 on the standard scale; subs.(3).

Planting of trees in the carriageway

8–25   Sections 141 and 142 of the Highways Act 1980 are concerned with trees and shrubs positioned in or near highways. Section 141 prohibits the planting of any tree or shrub in a made-up carriageway, or within 15 feet from the centre of a made up carriageway, unless in accordance with a licence granted by the highway authority under section 142 or by a highway authority under its powers under section 64 or 96 of the Highways Act 1980. Where a tree or shrub has been planted in contravention of this section, the highway authority may give the owner or occupier of the land on which the tree or shrub is planted notice requiring him to remove it within 21 days, and failure to do so renders the person liable to an offence.[87]

8–26   A highway authority may, by licence, permit the occupier or owner of any premises adjoining a highway to plant, or retain, and thereafter to maintain, trees, shrubs, plants or grass in such part of the highway as may be specified in the licence. The licence may be for a limited period and may be granted to an occupier of premises with a prohibition against assignment, or may be granted to the owner of premises and his successors in title and may run with the land.[88] The authority may charge a reasonable sum in respect of legal or other expenses in connection with the grant of the licence, and an annual charge for administering the licence.[89] It is a condition of any licence that within one month after any change in the ownership of the premises, the former licensee informs the highway authority of that change.[90] The highway authority may attach to any licence such conditions as it may consider necessary to ensure the safety and convenience of passengers on the highway, to prevent traffic from being delayed, to prevent any nuisance or annoyance being caused to the owners or occupiers of any other premises adjoining the highway, and to protect the apparatus of statutory undertakers, sewerage authorities and the operators of telecommunications code systems.[91] Planting a tree or shrub other than in accordance with the conditions will result in an offence under section 141 being committed.[92]

8–27   Licences may be withdrawn by the highway authority on seven days' notice where any condition of the licence is contravened or, in any case where the highway authority considers that the withdrawal of the licence is necessary for the exercise of its functions as highway authority, on three months' notice. Where a licence granted under section 142 expires or is withdrawn or surrendered, the highway authority by whom it is granted may remove, or authorise the last licensee to remove at his own

---

[87] Punishable with a fine not exceeding level 1 on the standard scale, and at a fine of 50p for each day, after conviction, for which the offence is continued: Highways Act 1980, s.141(3).

[88] *Ibid.* s.142(2).

[89] *Ibid.* s.142(3).

[90] *Ibid.* s.142(4).

[91] *Ibid.* s.142(5).

[92] See para. 8–25, above.

expense, all or any of the trees, shrubs or grass to which the licence relates, and may reinstate the highway. Where the authority carries out the work itself, it may recover the expenses reasonably incurred by itself in so doing, from the last licensee.[93] The highway authority's rights as owner of the subsoil of the highway, where this is the case, are not affected by these provisions.[94]

Licensees (and any person who immediately before the expiration, **8–28** withdrawal or surrender of a licence was the licensee, or his personal representatives) must indemnify the highway authority[95] in respect of any claim in respect of injury, damage or loss, arising out of the planting or presence in the highway of trees, shrubs, plants or grass to which the licence relates, or out of the execution by any person of any works authorised by the licence, or by the highway authority, in removing the tree and re-instating the highway, or the execution by or on behalf of the highway authority of any such works. The grant of a licence to plant a tree will not afford a defence to an action for public nuisance should the tree become a danger to highway users. Under section 96 of the Highways Act 1980, a highway authority may not exercise its own powers to plant or maintain trees or shrubs in highways so as to hinder the reasonable use of the highway, or so as to be a nuisance to or injurious to the owner or occupier of premises adjacent to the highway. It is well established that in the absence of express statutory authority, the "licence" of a highway authority will not be a defence to an action for public nuisance.[96] If the authority in the exercise of its own powers to plant trees may not commit a nuisance, it would be surprising if, in the absence of explicit statutory authority, it could permit another person to do so. Indeed, the indemnity provision suggests the contrary. Equally, the grant of a licence will not exempt the licensee from any liability in private nuisance for the incursion of roots onto private property, although whether the licensee or the authority will be primarily liable in such a case depends to some extent on the terms of the licence. The test will be: who has sufficient control over the tree in order to abate the nuisance?[97]

Structures, gates and stiles

There are a number of provisions in Part IX of the Highways Act 1980 **8–29** concerning the prevention of the erection of buildings and other structures in a highway. Under section 143, where a structure has been erected or set up on a highway otherwise than under a provision in the

---

[93] Highways Act 1980, s.142(6), (7).
[94] *Ibid.* s.142(10).
[95] Except in relation to the authority's own negligence: *ibid.* s.142(8).
[96] See *Harvey* v. *Truro R.C.* [1903] 2 Ch. 638.
[97] See *Russell* v. *Barnet L.B.C.* (1985) 83 L.G.R. 152; *Solloway* v. *Hampshire C.C.* (1981) 79 L.G.R. 449.

1980 Act or some other enactment, a highway authority, or a district council exercising powers under the Highways Act 1980, sections 42 or 50,[98] may, by one month's notice, require the person having control or possession of the structure to remove it. The authority may, in default, remove the structure and recover the expenses reasonably incurred by it in so doing.[99] The word "structure" includes "any machine, pump, post or other object of similar nature as to be capable of causing an obstruction," notwithstanding that it has wheels.[1] In *R. v. Welwyn Hatfield District Council, ex parte Brinkley*,[2] it was held that a caravan was capable of being a structure within the meaning of this section. The question as to whether a caravan could be "erected" depended on the degree of permanence involved.

8–30   Section 144 of the Highways Act 1980 empowers a local authority, with the consent of the highway authority, and subject to certain safeguards, to erect flagpoles, pylons and other structures on any highway in its area for the purpose of displaying decorations, to make slots in the highway for the purpose of erecting those structures, and to remove such slots and structures.[3]

8–31   A gate is prima facie an obstruction to a highway; however, the highway may have been dedicated with the gate already in existence. By section 145 of the Highways Act 1980, where there is a gate across so much of a highway as consists of a carriageway or a bridleway, the highway authority may, by notice, require the owner of the gate to enlarge or remove it. It is a criminal offence to fail to comply with a notice.[4] Highway authorities also have power to step in to maintain stiles, gates, and other structures lawfully in the highway, which are out of repair, in order to prevent unreasonable interference with the right of persons using the footpath or bridleway.[5] The owner, lessee, or occupier of agricultural land may make representations to the relevant authority that, to secure that the use or a particular use of the land for agriculture be efficiently carried on, it is expedient that stiles, gates and other works for preventing the ingress or egress of animals be erected on the path or way. In these circumstances, the authority may authorise the erection of the stiles, gates or other works, subject to conditions, including conditions as to maintenance. Thereafter, the public right of way is subject to the stile, gate or other works, as long as the conditions of the authorisation have been complied with.[6]

---

[98] See Chap. 4.
[99] Highways Act 1980, s.143(2), (3).
[1] *Ibid.* s.143(4).
[2] (1982) 80 L.G.R. 727.
[3] Highways Act 1980, s.144.
[4] Punishable with a fine not exceeding 50p for each day of non-compliance: *ibid.* s.145(1), (2).
[5] *Ibid.* s.146.
[6] *Ibid.* s.147(3).

Roadside sales and itinerant traders

It is an offence[7] for any person to use any stall or similar structure or   **8-32**
any container or vehicle, kept or placed on the verge of a principal or
trunk road, or on a layby on any such road or on uninclosed land within
15 metres of any part of any such road, where its presence or its use for
the purpose causes, or is likely to cause, danger on the road, or inter-
rupts, or is likely to interrupt, any user of the road. There are various
exceptions to the operation of this section,[8] and there is a defence open
to a person charged, namely, for him to show that he took all reasonable
precautions and exercised all due diligence to avoid commission of the
offence.

Section 148 creates a number of offences concerned with the deposit   **8-33**
of items on the highway.[9] It is also an offence under section 148(*d*)
where, without lawful authority or excuse,[10] a hawker or other itinerant
trader pitches a booth, stall or stand or encamps[11] on a highway. The
stopping of an ice cream van on the highway or in a layby to make a sale
has been held not to constitute the pitching of a booth or stall under this
section,[12] but may, on certain roads, be an offence under section 147A.
The lawful exercise of market rights will constitute lawful authority or
excuse in relation to proceedings under this section. However, there is
no prescriptive right to obstruct the highway.[13]

Obstructions derived from the adjoining land

Highway authorities and district councils may, by notice to the owner   **8-34**
or occupier of any land adjoining a street which is also a highway maintainable at the public expense, require him, within 28 days from the date
of service of a notice upon him, to execute such works as will prevent
soil or refuse from that land from falling or being washed or carried on
to the street or into any sewer or gully in such quantities as to obstruct
the street or choke the sewer or gully.[14] Any person aggrieved by the
service of such a notice has a right of appeal to the magistrates' court.
Failure to comply with such a notice renders the recipient liable to a
criminal penalty.[15]

The local authority for the area in which any street is situated, and the   **8-35**
highway authority for any highway, have power under section 152 of the

---

[7] Punishable with a fine not exceeding level 3 on the standard scale; Highways Act 1980,
s.147A(2).
[8] *e.g.* sale of newspapers, street trading under licence, markets, etc.: *ibid.* s.147A(4).
[9] Punishable with a fine not exceeding level 3 on the standard scale.
[10] See *Cambridgeshire and Isle of Ely C.C.* v. *Rust* [1972] 2 Q.B. 426 and the discussion at
para. 8-02, above.
[11] See *Smith* v. *Wood* (1971) 115 S.J. 187.
[12] See *Divito* v. *Stickings* [1948] 1 All E.R. 207; *Waltham Forest L.B.C.* v. *Mills* (1978) 78
L.G.R. 248.
[13] *Elwood* v. *Bullock* (1844) 6 Q.B. 383; *Simpson* v. *Wells* (1872) L.R. 7 Q.B. 214.
[14] Highways Act 1980, s.151.
[15] Punishable with a fine not exceeding level 3 on the standard scale and not exceeding £1
for each day the offence is continued after conviction: *ibid.* s.151(3).

Highways Act 1980 to require, by notice to the owner and/or the occupier of any building, the removal or alteration of any porch, shed, projecting window, step, cellar, cellar door, cellar window, sign,[16] signpost, sign iron, showboard, window shutter, wall, gate, fence or other obstruction or projection which has been erected or placed against or in front of the building, and which is an obstruction to safe or convenient passage along a street. Any person aggrieved by the service of such a notice has a right of appeal to the magistrates' court. Failure to comply with such a notice renders the recipient liable to a fine.[17] It will not be sufficient for the object forming the projection or obstruction to extend over an area which has never become part of the street.[18]

8–36   The authority has power in default to remove the obstruction in any case and to recover the expenses of so doing from the person on whom the notice was served. Where the obstruction to which the notice relates was not erected or placed by the occupier of the relevant building, then he may recover any sum paid in connection with complying with a notice or with reimbursing the authority, from his landlord by way of deduction from rent.[19] These provisions were originally contained in section 69 of the Towns Improvement Clauses Act 1847, and cannot be used in respect of obstructions pre-dating the application of that section in the area in question. In such a case, the authority may still remove such obstructions which are against or in front of a building in a street, after giving notice of its intention so to do and, where the obstruction was lawfully so placed, on payment of compensation to any person who suffers damage by reason of removal or alteration of the obstruction.[20]

8–37   By section 153 of the Highways Act 1980, doors, gates or bars shall not be put up on any premises opening onto a street so as to open outwards, unless the building is a public building, and the local authority (and where the street is a highway, the highway authority) consents. Notice may be served on the owner or the occupier of the building, requiring him to alter the door, gate or bar. A person aggrieved by such a notice may appeal to the magistrates' court. Failure to comply with a notice is a criminal offence.[21] The authority may execute the required works in default and recover the expenses of so doing. Where the person who put up the door, etc., is not the occupier, then the occupier may recover the expense to which he has been put from his landlord.[22]

---

[16] A pole carrying a flag advertisement can be a "sign": see *Goldstraw* v. *Jones* (1906) 96 L.T. 30.

[17] Not exceeding level 1 on the standard scale: Highways Act 1980, s.152(4).

[18] See *Piggott* v. *Goldstraw* (1901) 84 L.T. 94; *Le Neve* v. *Mile End Old Town Vestry* (1858) 8 E.& B. 1054; *Hoare* v. *Lewisham Corpn.* (1901) 85 L.T. 281.

[19] Highways Act 1980, Sched. 13.

[20] See *ibid.* s.152(8).

[21] Punishable with a fine not exceeding level 1 on the standard scale: *ibid.* s.153(4).

[22] See *ibid.* Sched. 13.

Where a hedge, tree, shrub or vegetation of any description over-   **8–38**
hangs a highway, or any other road or footpath to which the public has
access, and endangers or obstructs the passage of vehicles or pedestrians, or obstructs or interferes with the view of drivers of vehicles or
the light from a public lamp, the district council or the highway authority may serve a notice on the owner of the tree, shrub or hedge, or on
the occupier of the land on which it is growing, requiring him, within 14
days from the date of service of the notice, so to lop[23] or cut it as to
remove the cause of the danger, obstruction or interference.[24] Any person aggrieved by a requirement of such a notice has a right of appeal to
the magistrates' court. Where the works are not carried out in accordance with the notice, the authority may itself carry out the works in
default and recover the expenses of so doing from the person in
default.

Except for where a highway crosses[25] common land, waste land or   **8–39**
uninclosed land,[26] or where there are rights of pasture at the side of the
highway, any horses, cattle, sheep, goats or swine found straying on or
lying[27] on, or at the side of, the highway will cause their keeper to be
guilty of a criminal offence.[28] The reasonable expenses of removing any
such animals to the premises of their keeper, or to the common pound
or to such other place as may have been provided for the purpose, will
be recoverable summarily as a civil debt. Animals will not be straying if
they are under the control of a person driving them on the highway.[29]
However, where the control of the animals is deficient, or where the
animals are, in any event, "lying" in the highway, then an offence may
be committed.[30] The section imposes no duty enforceable in the civil
law.[31]

Works in highways

Section 156 of the Highways Act 1980 imposes restrictions on the   **8–40**
exercise by statutory undertakers of powers to break up or open a highway maintainable at the public expense which consists of or comprises a
carriageway. These powers are considered in Chapter 13.

---

[23] "Lop" means to cut laterally: see *Unwin* v. *Hanson* [1891] 2 Q.B. 115.

[24] Highways Act 1980, s.154(1), (2). See also paras.7–29, *et seq.*, above, for a discussion of the circumstances in which overhanging trees may constitute a nuisance.

[25] See *Davies* v. *Davies* [1974] 3 All E.R. 817, where Lord Denning M.R. expressed the view that this proviso applied also where the highway abutted a common.

[26] See *Bothamley* v. *Danby* (1871) 24 L.T. 656; *Plumbley* v. *Lock* (1902) 67 J.P. 237.

[27] See *Lawrence* v. *King* (1868) L.R. 3 Q.B. 345.

[28] "Keeper" means any person in whose possession they are: Highways Act 1980, s.155(1). The offence is punishable with a fine not exceeding level 3 on the standard scale: *ibid.* s.155(2).

[29] See *Morris* v. *Jeffries* (1866) L.R. 1 Q.B. 261.

[30] See *Lawrence* v. *King* (1868) L.R. 3 Q.B. 345; *Golding* v. *Stocking* (1869) L.R. 4 Q.B. 516; *Horwood* v. *Goodall, Horwood* v. *Hill* (1872) 36 J.P. 486.

[31] See *Heath's Garages Ltd.* v. *Hodges* [1916–17] All E.R. 358.

Danger or annoyance to users of the highway

8–41   Sections 161 and 161A of the Highways Act 1980[32] provide penalties
for causing certain kinds of danger or annoyance to highway users. It is
an offence for any person, without lawful authority or excuse, to deposit
anything whatsoever on a highway, in consequence of which, user of the
highway is injured or endangered.[33] It is an offence[34] to light any fire on
or over a highway which consists of or comprises a carriageway, or to
discharge a firearm or firework within 50 feet of the centre of such a
highway, causing injury, interruption or danger to any user of the highway.[35] In *Crane* v. *South Suburban Gas Co.*,[36] a gas company was held
liable for a nuisance where its workmen had, for the purpose of carrying
out repairs to a gas main in the highway, placed on it a fire pail on which
was a ladle containing molten lead. A young child knocked over the fire
pail, and suffered injury when the molten lead spilled onto her. It was
held that what the defendants had done was a nuisance, in that it was
dangerous unless precautions were taken to protect persons using the
highway from the danger.

8–42   It is an offence to play football, or any other game, on the highway to
the annoyance of a user of the highway, or to allow any filth, dirt, lime
or offensive matter or thing to run or flow onto a highway from the
adjoining premises.[37]

8–43   A new section 161A now deals separately with fires near to highways.
It is an offence[38] to light a fire on any land off a highway, or to direct or
permit a fire to be lit on any such land if, in consequence, a user of a
highway is injured, interrupted or endangered by smoke from that fire,
or from any fire caused by that fire.[39] The new offence is much wider
than that formerly contained in section 161 which was restricted to fires
within 50 feet of the highway. Section 161A also clarifies the question of
causation. If a fire causes other fires which eventually lead to an offence
being committed, the person responsible for the original fire may be
liable.[40] A specific defence is created where the accused can prove that,
at the time when the fire was lit, he was satisfied on reasonable grounds
that it was unlikely that the circumstances giving rise to an offence
would occur, and that, after the fire was lit, he took reasonable steps to
prevent those circumstances from occurring, or that he had a reasonable
excuse for not doing so.

---

[32] Substituted and inserted by Highways Amendment Act 1986, s.1(3).
[33] Highways Act 1980, s.161(1).
[34] Punishable by a fine not exceeding level 3 on the standard scale: *ibid.* s.161(1), (2).
[35] *Hill* v. *Somerset* (1887) 51 J.P. 742.
[36] [1916] 1 K.B. 33.
[37] Highways Act 1980, s.161(3), (4); both offences being punishable by a fine not exceeding level 1 on the standard scale.
[38] Punishable by a fine not exceeding level 5 on the standard scale.
[39] See *Stinson* v. *Browning* (1866) L.R. 1 C.P. 321 for a case where a nuisance at common
law was similarly caused; *cf.* Highways Act 1980, s.131(1)(*d*)
[40] *cf. Hunton* v. *Last* (1965) 109 S.J. 391.

By section 162 it is an offence for any person to place any rope, wire   **8-44**
or other apparatus across a highway in such a manner as to be likely to
cause danger to persons using the highway, unless he proves that he has
employed all necessary means to give adequate warning of the danger.
Curiously, this does not require the person placing the rope, etc., across
the highway to have lawful authority or excuse, but only to establish that
he had given adequate warning.

By section 163, the highway authority or the non-metropolitan district   **8-45**
council may give 28 days' notice to the occupier of premises adjoining
the highway, requiring him to construct or erect and thereafter maintain
such channels, gutters or downpipes as may be necessary to prevent
water from the roof or from any other part of the premises from falling
on persons using the highway or, so far as is reasonably practicable, to
prevent surface water from the premises flowing onto or over the footway of the highway. The notice may be served on either the owner of
the premises, or the occupier, or on both. A person aggrieved by a
requirement of the notice may appeal to a magistrates' court. Failure to
comply is a criminal offence.[41] There is no express default power in this
section, but a highway authority has powers in any event to abate a nuisance in the highway.[42]

Where, on adjoining land, there is a barbed wire fence causing a nuis-   **8-46**
ance to the highway, the highway authority or the non-metropolitan district council may serve an abatement notice on the occupier of the
land.[43] Upon failure to comply with the notice, a magistrates' court
may, on a complaint made by the authority, and if satisfied that the wire
is a nuisance, order the occupier to abate the nuisance. Failure to comply with this order within a reasonable time entitles the authority to act
in default, and to recover the expenses incurred by it in so doing.
Barbed wire is defined as being wire with spikes or jagged projections,
and it is deemed to be nuisance to a highway if it is likely to be injurious
to persons or animals lawfully using the highway.[44] Where it is the local
authority who owns the land in question, proceedings may be brought
by any ratepayer in the same way as by a local authority.

Power to serve notices requiring works of repair, protection, removal,   **8-47**
or inclosure of unfenced or inadequately fenced sources of dangers to
persons using any street is given to local authorities[45] by section 165 of
the Highways Act 1980. There is an appeal to a magistrates' court and
failure to comply with the notice entitles the authority to act in default
and recover the expenses. Problems have arisen under this section and
its predecessors in relation to the circumstances in which the powers

---

[41] Punishable with a fine not exceeding level 3 on the standard scale.
[42] See para. 7–40, above.
[43] Highways Act 1980, s.164.
[44] See *Stewart* v. *Wright* (1893) 9 T.L.R. 480.
[45] As to which, see Highways Act 1980, s.329(1); and as to the responsibility of the highway authority, see s.165(4), (5).

under the section arise where the danger arises from factors outside the control of the landowner. Thus, where a footpath had become dangerous because of natural causes affecting the adjoining land, it was held that the power could not be invoked.[46] Equally, where the danger has been caused by the raising of the level of the highway rather than by anything done in the adjoining land, the courts have refused to sanction use of such powers under similar statutory provisions.[47]

8–48   Section 166 of the Highways Act 1980 empowers a highway authority or a local authority[48] to deal with danger, obstruction or inconvenience arising from the forecourt of any premises abutting on a street, or any steps or projection, or any goods placed in such a forecourt. The authority may, by notice, require the owner or occupier of the forecourt to fence the forecourt from the street or, at his election, to take such other steps as may be specified in the notice to obviate the danger of obstruction or inconvenience to the public. Similarly, if it appears that a stall or other erection on a forecourt of premises abutting on a street is, by reason of its character, injurious to the amenities of the street, the authority may, by notice, require the owner or occupier of the forecourt to make such necessary alterations in the stall or other erection or, at his election, to remove it.[49] The appeal provisions of Part XII of the Public Health Act 1936 apply with respect to appeals against, and the enforcement of notices under, this section. By section 190(6) of the 1936 Act, the authority may, at its election, take either of the courses which were open to the person on whom the notice was served in order to comply with it.

8–49   Section 167 of the Highways Act 1980 places a prohibition on retaining walls being erected except in accordance with plans, sections and specifications approved by the local authority.[50] The prohibition applies where any cross section of the wall is wholly or partly within four yards of a street and is at a greater height than four feet six inches above the level of the ground, at the boundary of the street, nearest to that point. The prohibition does not apply to any retaining wall erected on land belonging to any transport undertakers and used by them primarily for the purpose of their undertaking, nor does it apply to any length of retaining wall for whose maintenance the highway authority is responsible. Any person aggrieved by the refusal of a highway authority to approve plans may appeal to the magistrates' court. Contravention of the prohibition renders the person liable to a criminal offence.[51] The

---

[46] *Cheshire Lines Committee* v. *Heaton Norris U.D.C.* [1913] 1 K.B. 325; *cf. Carshalton U.D.C.* v. *Burrage* [1911] 2 Ch. 133.

[47] *Nicholson* v. *Southern Ry. Co. and Sutton and Cheam U.D.C.* [1935] 1 K.B. 558; *Myers* v. *Harrow Corpn.* [1962] 2 Q.B. 442.

[48] As to which, see Highways Act 1980, s.166(5).

[49] For exceptions to the application of this power, see s.166(2), (3).

[50] The highway authority must be consulted on approvals.

[51] Punishable with a fine not exceeding level 3 on the standard scale: Highways Act 1980, s.167(4).

local authority, by notice, may require the owner or occupier of land on which any length of retaining wall is situated and which is in such a condition as to be liable to endanger persons using the street, to execute such works as will obviate the danger. The appeal provisions of section 290 of the Public Health Act 1936 again apply.[52] A retaining wall is defined as meaning "a wall not forming part of a permanent building which serves, or is intended to serve as a support for earth or other material on one side only."[53]

Precautions to be taken in doing certain works in or near streets or highways

Section 168 of the Highways Act 1980 creates a criminal offence **8–50** where building operations have endangered public safety.[54] Where the commission of the offence is due to the act or default of some other person, then that other person may be charged. It is a defence for any person to show that he had taken all reasonable precautions to secure that the building operation was carried out so as to avoid causing danger to persons in the street, or that the commission of the offence was due to the act or default of another person and that he had taken all reasonable precautions and exercised all due diligence to avoid the commission of such an offence by himself or any person under his control. Seven days' notice of reliance on such a defence must be given to the prosecutor in writing. "Building operation" means the construction, structural alteration, repair or maintenance of a building (including re-pointing, external redecoration and external cleaning), the demolition of a building, the preparation for, and the laying of the foundations of, an intended building, and the erection or dismantling of cranes or scaffolding.[55]

By section 169 of the Highways Act 1980 the highway authority may **8–51** control, by the grant of licences, the erection of scaffolding on highways.[56] The licence may contain such terms as the highway authority thinks fit. The highway authority must issue a licence when requested to do so and when provided with all relevant information, unless it considers that the structure would cause unreasonable obstruction to the highway or that a different structure, causing less obstruction to the highway, could conveniently be used for the work in question. There is an appeal to the magistrates' court against the refusal of a licence, or against the conditions imposed by it. The magistrates may allow the appeal and direct the highway authority to issue a licence, or they may alter the conditions. A person who has been granted a licence is under a

---

[52] As do ss.300–302 of Public Health Act 1936.
[53] Highways Act 1980, s.167(9).
[54] Punishable with a fine not exceeding level 5 on the standard scale.
[55] Highways Act 1980, s.168(5).
[56] See s.169(6) for certain exceptions.

duty to ensure that the structure is adequately lit during the hours of darkness, to comply with any directions given to him in writing by the authority with respect to the erection and maintenance of traffic signs in connection with the structure, and to comply with the reasonable requests of statutory undertakers relating to the protection of or access to their apparatus.[57] Contravention of the terms of these provisions is a criminal offence.[58] As long as the structure is erected and maintained in the highway in accordance with the terms of the licence, no civil or criminal proceedings will lie in respect of any obstruction to the highway which is caused by it. Equally, the highway authority by whom the licence is issued does not incur any liability by reason of the issue of the licence.[59]

8–52   Any person who mixes or deposits on a highway any mortar, cement or any other substance which is likely to stick to the surface of the highway, or which if it enters the drains or sewers of the highway is likely to solidify, is guilty of an offence.[60]

8–53   By section 171 of the Highways Act 1980, a person may, with the consent of the highway authority for a street which is a highway maintainable at the public expense, temporarily deposit building materials, rubbish or other things in the street, or make a temporary excavation in it. The consent may be conditional. A person aggrieved by a refusal of consent or by the conditions imposed on such a consent may appeal to the magistrates' court. Where a person makes such a deposit or excavation, he is obliged to comply with any directions given to him in writing by the highway authority with respect to the erection and maintenance of traffic signs, and furthermore, he must cause the obstruction or excavation to be properly fenced and, during the hours of darkness, properly lit and must, if required to do so by the relevant authority,[61] remove the obstruction or fill in the excavation. In any event, he may not allow the obstruction to remain in the street longer than is necessary. Contravention of these provisions without reasonable excuse is an offence.[62] The highway authority may remove the obstruction or fill in the excavation and recover the expenses of so doing from the person convicted of the offence.

8–54   A person proposing to erect or take down a building, or to alter or repair the outside of a building in a street or court must, before beginning the work, erect a close-boarded hoarding or fence separating the building from the street or court, to the satisfaction of the appropriate

---

[57] As to the meaning of statutory undertakers, see Highways Act 1980, s.169(4).

[58] *Ibid.* s.169(5); punishable with a fine not exceeding level 5 on the standard scale.

[59] *Ibid.* s.169(7).

[60] Punishable by a fine not exceeding level 4 on the standard scale. As to exceptions to these provisions, see *ibid.* s.170(2).

[61] See *ibid.* s.171(7).

[62] Punishable by a fine not exceeding £10 in respect of each day on which the contravention or failure occurs.

authority,[63] unless that authority has dispensed with the requirement. The authority may require the construction of a convenient covered platform and handrail to serve as a footway for pedestrians outside the hoarding or fence. The hoarding, fence, platform and handrail must be maintained in good condition to the satisfaction of the authority, must be lit during the hours of darkness, and must be removed when required by the authority. Any person aggrieved by the refusal of a consent may appeal to a magistrates' court. Contravention of this section is an offence.[64] Hoardings or similar structures in or adjoining any street must be securely fixed, to the satisfaction of the appropriate authority. Contravention of this provision renders a person liable to a fine.[65]

Any person executing works in a street is required to erect barriers **8–55** and traffic signs preventing danger to traffic, for regulating traffic and for warning traffic of danger as may be necessary and is required to remove them as soon as they cease to be needed for those purposes. There is also a requirement to keep the works properly guarded and lit during the hours of darkness and, where the nature of the works so requires, to cause any building adjoining the street to be shored up or otherwise protected. Failure to satisfy any of these obligations renders the person liable to an offence.[66] Any person who, without lawful authority or excuse, interferes with any such traffic sign, support, or light or any other fence, barrier, traffic sign, or light lawfully placed so as to warn users of a street of any obstruction or to protect them from danger arising out of such obstruction is guilty of an offence.[67]

Officers or servants of a highway authority,[68] who leave any heap of **8–56** materials or any other object on the highway at night to the danger of traffic without taking all reasonable precautions for the prevention of accidents, will be guilty of an offence.[69] By section 175A, persons exercising statutory powers in relation to a highway are required to have regard to the needs of disabled and blind people, where their works may impede the mobility of such persons. Similar regard must be had when permanent obstructions are placed in highways and streets, and when the desirability of ramps is being considered.

---

[63] *i.e.* the council of the county, metropolitan district, London Borough, or the Common Council.

[64] Highways Act 1980, s. 172(5); punishable by a fine not exceeding level 3 on the standard scale and £2 for each day on which the offence is continued after conviction.

[65] Not exceeding level 1 on the standard scale, with a continuing penalty of £1 for each day during which the offence is continued after conviction.

[66] Punishable by a fine not exceeding £10 in respect of each day of failure; Highways Act. 1980, s.174(2).

[67] Punishable by a fine not exceeding level 3 on the standard scale. See also *ibid.* s.174(5); British Telecommunications Act 1981, s.187, Sched. 3, Part 2, para. 74(2).

[68] Or of a non-metropolitan district council or of any person liable to maintain a highway by reason of tenure, inclosure or prescription exercising powers to maintain a highway.

[69] Punishable by a fine not exceeding level 1 on the standard scale: Highways Act 1980, s.175.

The construction of structures over and under highways

8–57   Sections 176 to 180 of the Highways Act 1980 are concerned with situations where licences or consents may be granted to persons wishing to construct various structures over or under highways. In each of these cases, it is an offence to construct the structure without the licence or consent required or to construct it in breach of the terms or conditions of that licence or consent.[70] There are provisions protecting the position of statutory undertakers and telecommunications code operators.[71]

8–58   Section 176 requires a licence for the construction of a bridge[72] over a highway. Such a licence may be conditional and *must* include a condition requiring the removal or alteration of the bridge, where the highway authority considers such removal or alteration necessary or desirable in connection with the carrying out of improvements to the highway. This condition runs with the land. The authority's decision on the need for removal is final and may not be the subject of any appeal.[73] Apart from this last condition, and certain conditions imposed by the Minister (where he is the highway authority) there is a right of appeal to the Crown Court against the refusal of the highway authority to grant a licence under this section, or against conditions imposed on the grant of the licence. Contravention of these provisions is a criminal offence.[74]

8–59   By section 177 of the Highways Act 1980, there is a similar prohibition on the construction of buildings (other than bridges) over highways maintainable at the public expense, or on the alteration of buildings so constructed without, in either case, a licence from the highway authority. Licences may again be conditional and, once granted, will run with the land. There is an appeal against the refusal of a licence or against a term of that licence, but this right of appeal does not arise where the land on which the highway is situated is owned by the highway authority, nor does it lie against any term or condition which the highway authority declares to be necessary for the purpose of securing the safety of persons using the highway, or for the purpose of preventing interference with traffic thereon.[75] Where a building has been constructed or altered otherwise than in accordance with the terms of a licence granted by the highway authority, that authority may serve a notice requiring the demolition or alteration of the building. Similarly, where the conditions of a licence are not being complied with, the authority may serve a notice requiring compliance. Default powers in the event of non-compliance with the notice exist in both cases. The grant of a licence under this section does not permit the commission of what

---

[70] See Highways Act 1980, ss.176(7), 177(1), 178(4), 179(3), 180(4).

[71] See *ibid.* ss.176(3), 177(4), (12), 178(5), 179(5), (7).

[72] *i.e.* a structure, the sole purpose of which is to provide a way over the highway: *ibid.* s.176(8).

[73] *Ibid.* s.176(4).

[74] Punishable by a fine not exceeding level 2 on the standard scale and £5 per day for each day the offence is continued after conviction: *ibid.* s.176(7).

[75] *Ibid.* s.177(6).

would otherwise be a public nuisance, as the licence may not permit any interference with the convenience of persons using the way; nor may it affect the rights of owners of premises adjoining the highway, nor the rights of statutory undertakers or the operator of a telecommunications code system.

Section 178 prohibits the fixing or placing of overhead beams, rails, **8-60** pipes, cables, wires or other similar apparatus over, along or across a highway without consent. Such consent may be subject to such reasonable terms and conditions as the authority thinks fit. An appeal lies to the magistrates' court.[76] By section 179 of the Highways Act 1980, the construction of any part of a building, or a vault, arch or cellar under any part of a street, without the consent of the appropriate authority,[77] is prohibited. Any works carried out in contravention of this section may lead to a notice requiring or restricting their removal or alteration. A person aggrieved by a refusal of consent or by the terms of a notice may appeal to a magistrates' court. Openings in the footway of a street as entrances to cellars or vaults thereunder are prohibited by section 180 unless the consent of the appropriate authority[78] is obtained. By section 180(2), no person may carry out works in a street to provide means for the admission of air or light to premises situated under or abutting on a street without the consent of the local authority for that street. The authority may also make requirements as to the manner of construction. There is an appeal to the magistrates' court against the refusal of a consent or the making of a requirement. Every vault, arch, and cellar under a street and every opening into them, every door or covering to such opening, every cellar head, grating, light and coal hole in the surface of a street and all landings, flags or stones of the street supporting any of the above must be kept in good condition or repair by the owner or occupier of the premises to which they belong. The local authority has default powers of maintenance.

Provisions relating to the placing of apparatus in or under a highway

Section 181(1) places a general prohibition on the placing, without **8-61** lawful authority or excuse, of apparatus in or under a highway and the breaking open of the highway for the purpose of placing, maintaining, repairing or reinstating any apparatus in or under it. Contravention of the prohibition is punishable by a fine.[79] The highway authority may grant a licence to break open the highway and to place, and thereafter maintain, apparatus in or under the highway. Such a licence may be subject to conditions, including conditions concerning the transferability of the licence, and it must contain a condition[80] safeguarding the apparatus

[76] Except for certain conditions imposed by the Minister as highway authority for the highway.
[77] See s.179(1).
[78] See n. 63 above.
[79] Not exceeding level 3 on the standard scale; Highways Act 1980, s.181(1).
[80] The full requirements of which are set out in Highways Act 1980, s.182(1).

of statutory undertakers, telecommunications code operators and sewerage authorities. The section does not affect the rights of statutory undertakers to place apparatus in or under highways. Whilst highway authorities are not permitted to make charges in respect of the grant of licences, except to cover their administrative costs, they may, where they are the owners of the sub-soil, charge for an easement.[81] Licences may be withdrawn, where the highway authority considers it necessary for the exercise of its functions as highway authority, or in accordance with the terms of the licence itself.[82] The holder of a licence is bound to idemnify the highway authority against any injury, damage or loss arising out of the placing, or presence in or under a highway of apparatus to which the licence relates, or the execution of works authorised by the licence.[83] The only appeal against refusal to grant a licence or against conditions imposed in the licence (other than compulsory ones) is to the Minister, and is only available where the application relates to the placing of apparatus *across* the highway.[84]

Vehicle crossings over footways and verges

8–62   At common law every landowner whose land adjoined the highway was presumed to have the right of access from any point on his land to the highway. This could give rise to problems of damage where landowners habitually exercised rights of access to the highway other than over properly constructed vehicular accesses. By section 184(1),[85] the highway authority may serve a notice on the occupier of land, stating that it proposes to execute works for the construction of a vehicle crossing, or alternatively, imposing reasonable conditions on the use of the existing crossing.[86] In determining whether a vehicular crossing is required, the authority should have regard to the need to prevent damage to the footway or verge and to the need to ensure, so far as is practicable, safe access to and from premises and the need to facilitate the passage of vehicular traffic in highways.[87] Where development or proposed development, in accordance with planning permission, leads to a need for a crossing over a kerbed footway, or a verge in a highway maintainable at the public expense, so as to provide an access for mechanically propelled vehicles between the highway and the land, or for the improvement of an existing access, the authority may serve a notice on the owner and occupier of the premises stating that it proposes to execute these works. The landowner may object to the notice,[88] and

---

[81] Highways Act 1980, s.181(4), (10).
[82] *Ibid.* s.182(3).
[83] *Ibid.* s.182(6).
[84] *Ibid.* s.183.
[85] See *ibid.* s.184(2) for the exceptions to this power.
[86] Once conditions have come into effect it is an offence to fail to comply with them: *ibid.* s.184(17).
[87] *Ibid.* s.184(5).
[88] The notice must itself inform the recipient of his right of objection: *ibid.* s.184(8).

there is then an appeal procedure to the Minister, on somewhat narrow grounds.[89] Where the developer has offered to carry out the works, he may be authorised by the highway authority to do them, and the provisions of Part II of the Public Utilities Street Works Act 1950, relating to works carried out for road purposes, will be deemed to apply to him for this purpose.[90] The authority may carry out the work at his expense in the event of default.

Power to instal refuse or storage bins in street

The highway authority for a street, or the local authority for a street **8–63** which is not a highway, may provide and maintain in a street, orderly bins or receptacles of such dimensions and in such positions as the authority may determine, for the collection and temporary deposit of street refuse and waste paper and the temporary deposit of sand, grit and other materials.[91] There are some restrictions placed on the exact location of such bins near to railway bridges, and accesses to various undertakers' land. The bins must not be placed so as to cause a nuisance.

Road humps

A highway authority may construct road humps in roads which carry a **8–64** statutory speed limit of 30 miles per hour, and in other roads, as authorised by the Secretary of State, under its powers of improvement.[92] Such road humps might otherwise be regarded as potential obstructions or as causing a potential danger to road users. Sections 90A to 90F of the Highways Act 1980, therefore, contain a series of consultations and a publication process leading to a possible public inquiry where an authority proposes to instal road humps in a highway. Regulations prescribe the nature, dimensions, location and spacing of road humps and the circumstances in which they may be placed in certain kinds of highways.[93] Once installed, the road humps will become a part of the highway rather than as an obstruction to the highway and is maintainable together with the highway.

Charges for permissions and licences

The various statutory provisions deal in different ways with the ques- **8–65** tion of whether a charge may be made for the grant of a licence. Sections 142, 176, 177 and 181 expressly prohibit the making of a charge for the granting of a licence except in connection with legal or other expenses. Sections 142, 177 and 181 make it clear that these expenses are to relate to the grant of the licence and to the continuing administra-

---

[89] See Highways Act 1980, Sched. 14.
[90] See Public Utilities Street Works Act 1950, s.21(1)(*a*).
[91] Highways Act 1980, s.185.
[92] *Ibid.* s.90A.
[93] See the Highways (Road Humps) Regulations 1983 (S.I. 1983 No. 1087).

tion of the licence.[94] Sections 139, 171 and 178 give power to the high-way authority to grant licences and consents, but neither prohibit nor empower the authority to make any charge at all. It is a fundamental principle of English constitutional law that public bodies may not impose charges as a means of deriving revenue, without express statutory power being given to them for this purpose.[95] The existence of specific powers to make charges for administration costs may be taken as an indication that no similar power is to be implied into those sections which do not have any such power written into the enabling section.

Level crossings

8–66   The private legislation empowering railway companies to cross public highways always contemplated that, instead of being carried over or under the road, railways could be constructed so as to carry the track across the highway on the level. This immediately created safety problems and questions of priority. Initially, a distinction was drawn between carriage and turnpike roads (the major highways) and other roads. Crossing a public carriageway might be expressly permitted in the Special Act; in the case of other ways, it could be authorised by obtaining the consent of two or more justices.[96]

8–67   From the start, the railway companies were required to take steps to safeguard the safety of highway users. Where a company's railway crossed any public carriage road on a level, it was under a duty to erect, and at all times maintain, good and sufficient gates across the road on each side of the railway.[97] It was also bound to employ proper persons to open and shut the gates. The duty on the person operating the gates was to keep them closed to road traffic until traffic wished to cross and then immediately to close them again. The Board of Trade could, however, order that, in the interests of public safety, the gates would be kept open to road traffic and would only be closed when necessary to allow a train to pass.[98] The latter procedure has, of course, become the norm. Penalties were available to be imposed on any person defaulting in their duty to close and open the gates.

8–68   The Railway Clauses Act 1863 also imposed a number of safety requirements on the railway companies. Shunting was not to be permitted over level crossings, and trains were not to stand across level crossings.[99] Lodges were to be erected and permanently maintained at the point where the railway crossed the road, so that the crossing could be

---

[94] Highways Act 1980, ss.142(3), 171(3) and 181(4).
[95] See *Att.-Gen.* v. *Wilts. United Dairies* (1921) 37 T.L.R. 884, affirmed by the House of Lords at (1922) 91 L.J.K.B. 897; *Liverpool Corpn.* v. *Arthur Maiden Ltd.* [1938] 4 All E.R.220.
[96] See Railways Clauses Consolidation Act 1845, ss.46, 59, 60; *Dartford R.D.C* v. *Bexley Heath Rail Co.* [1898] A.C. 210.
[97] Highway (Railway Crossings) Act 1839, s.1; Railway Regulation Act 1842, s.9; Railways Clauses Consolidation Act 1845, s.47.
[98] Railway Regulation Act 1842, s.9; Railways Clauses Consolidation Act 1845, s.47.
[99] Railway Clauses Act 1863, s.5.

adequately supervised. The Board of Trade[1] had power to regulate the operation of these crossings and, where necessary, to require the road to be carried either over or under the railway instead of crossing on the level.[2] The Road and Rail Traffic Act 1933 gave a wider power to the Minister to direct that the gates of level crossings in public roads should be kept closed against trains rather than against road traffic and opened only to allow trains to pass,[3] overriding anything to the contrary in any Special Act.

On other types of highway, the railway company was not, at first, **8–69** required to construct gates. However, on these accommodation crossings it was required to make convenient approaches for highway users, to erect fences and stiles and to provide handrails.[4] In default the company could be ordered by the justices to provide these facilities. By the Transport Act 1968, greater control over accommodation crossing was given to the Minister, by empowering him, by order, to direct that lifting or other barriers be provided and that lights, signals and other safety and warning devices be installed. The Transport Act 1968 also gave power to local authorities to contribute to the expense of providing lifting or other barriers, lights, signals and other safety equipment generally—in order to encourage the provision by the Railways Board of speedier and safer methods of operating crossings.[5]

The Level Crossings Act 1983 has now provided a wide and general **8–70** power for the Secretary of State for Transport, at the request of the crossing operator, to require that provision be made for the protection of persons using any level crossing. The Secretary of State is now empowered to specify the kind of barriers and other protective equipment which is to be provided and maintained at or near to the level crossing. Orders made under this Act will replace any order previously made under the earlier legislation, but that legislation is not repealed. Notice that such an order is being requested must be sent to various local authorities for the area, who may then make representations to the Secretary of State.

---

[1] Now the Secretary of State for Transport: see the Transfer of Functions (Transport) Order 1981 (S.I. 1981 No. 238).
[2] Railway Clauses Act 1863, ss.6, 7.
[3] Road and Rail Traffic Act 1933, s.42.
[4] Railway Clauses Consolidation Act 1845, ss.61–62.
[5] Transport Act 1968, s.123.

CHAPTER 9

EXTINGUISHMENT AND DIVERSION OF HIGHWAYS

INTRODUCTION

9–01 Little public benefit can be gained from the continuance of a public right of way which has long since fallen into disuse. Equally, as circumstances change, the burden of the public right of way over a particular piece of land may become oppressive. As populations move and their settlements are relocated, the convenience of old highways may become greatly reduced—particularly with changing traffic needs. It may, therefore, become important for a highway authority to have power to review the question as to whether a particular right of way is still necessary, or whether its line might more suitably be diverted so as, for example, to allow to a landowner the better use of his land, to enable development to take place or to provide a more convenient route for the public. The common law did not recognise a concept of abandonment of a public right of way.[1] In order to extinguish a public right of way, or to cause its diversion, some positive judicial or administrative intervention has always been required, except possibly in the peculiar situation where the highway has been physically destroyed.

9–02 From a relatively early stage, however, it was recognised that a change in circumstances might warrant the alteration of the line of a highway or its official closure. By the writ *ad quod damnum*, addressed to the Sheriff, an inquiry by a local jury of twelve might be held, in order to ascertain whether the proposed stopping up would be injurious to the public interest.[2] Similarly, a highway could be diverted by this process. Apart from this formal procedure, the common law recognised a limited right in the public to deviate onto adjoining land where the owner of the subsoil had illegally obstructed the highway land or allowed it to become foundrous.[3]

Destruction of the highway

9–03 Although a public right of way cannot be lost through abandonment, it is, by its very nature, attached to land and can, therefore, be destroyed along with the land itself.[4] The relatively few cases which have

---

[1] See *Gwyn* v. *Hardwicke* (1856) 25 L.J.(M.C.) 97; *Dawes* v. *Hawkins* (1860) 8 C.B. (N.S.) 848; *Turner* v. *Ringwood Highway Board* (1870) L.R. 9 Eq. 418; *R.* v. *Burney* (1875) 31 L.T. 828; *Harvey* v. *Truro R.C.* [1903] 2 Ch. 638; *cf. Bailey* v. *Jamieson* (1876) 1 C.P.D. 329.

[2] See *R.* v. *Warde & Lyme* (1632) Cro. Car. 266; *Ex p. Vennor* (1754) 3 Ak. 766; *R.* v. *Russell* (1827) 6 B. & C. 566; *Esher and Dittons U.D.C.* v. *Marks* (1902) 86 L.T. 222.

[3] See *Dawes* v. *Hawkins* (1860) 8 C.B. (N.S.) 848.

[4] See *R.* v. *Paul* (*Inhabitants*) (1840) 2 Mood. & R. 307.

considered such an extreme change in circumstances have been concerned with the effect of the destruction of the highway on the liability of the parish to repair. These cases indicate that, where the line of the road has been totally obliterated by the destruction of the underlying land, the highway ceases to exist, but where the land remains intact (even if the line of the highway is no longer visible) the duty to repair (and therefore to re-establish the line) remains.[5] In *R.* v. *Greenhow* (*Inhabitants*),[6] Blackburn J. took commercial common sense into account when deciding whether a road was economically worth repairing. It is suggested that one approach is to ask whether the land to which the right of way attaches can still be said to exist. Thus, a path which is regularly flooded by a river, but which can still be walked over at other times of the year, might still be regarded as being a highway even though the line of the path is often washed away. A cliff path which falls into the sea through erosion will obviously cease to exist.

A more difficult point is whether a highway, which becomes isolated **9–04** through the physical destruction or legal stopping up of all its connecting highways, remains a public right of way even though the public no longer have any access to it. In *Bailey* v. *Jamieson*[7] it was held that a highway, connected at both ends to a highway which was then stopped up, itself ceased to be a highway. In that case there was no question of any other land being served by the highway which had become isolated, and the decision seems to emphasise the maxim that a highway needs a *terminus a quo* and a *terminus ad quem*. However, that maxim is most commonly applied to the need for evidence of public utility in order to establish public user, and is not an essential attribute of a highway. The extent of the principle in *Bailey* v. *Jamieson* must be uncertain.

Statutory intervention

From the eighteenth century onwards, the need for a more flexible **9–05** procedure to allow stopping up and diversion of highways became recognised. The inclosure movement also led to the need to stop up and divert public rights of way. The construction of canals and railways across the lines of highways led to statutory sanction for interference with highways on a large scale. The growth of compulsory purchase powers during the nineteenth century became matched by the multiplicity of powers to stop up and divert highways. Thus, there still exist many such powers in the different statutory codes concerned with the acquisition and development of land.

The Highway Act 1835, and its predecessors,[8–9] gave powers to the **9–06** parish, on the application by its surveyor to two justices of the peace

---

[5] Compare *R.* v. *Bamber* (1843) 5 Q.B. 279; *R.* v. *Hornsea* (*Inhabitants*) (1854) 23 L.J.(M.C.) 59; *R.* v. *Greenhow* (*Inhabitants*) (1876) 1 Q.B.D. 703.
[6] (1876) 1 Q.B.D. 703.
[7] (1876) 1 C.P.D. 329.
[8–9] See Highways Act 1773, Highways Act 1815.

(subject to confirmation at quarter sessions), to initiate the stopping up or diversion of highways. The procedure in the 1835 Act remains of some interest today, since its basic form is retained by sections 116 and 117 of the Highways Act 1980, which contain the only "judicial" process currently available for highway extinguishment and diversion.

Effect of stopping up

9–07   A stopping up order only extinguishes the public right to pass and repass over the land in question. This necessarily means that the limited interest of the highway authority in the "top two spits" ceases.[10] The surface of the highway, therefore, re-vests in the original landowner, who is then entitled to re-enter.[11] In some cases, the highway authority itself may be the owner of the subsoil, having acquired all the land for the purpose of constructing the highway. In such an event the authority will remain the owner of the land after stopping up. It must be emphasised that the extinguishment of the public right of way will not affect any private rights of way which existed over the land prior to its dedication to the public.[12] The dedication would necessarily have been subject to these existing rights of way; for example, where there has been dedication of a footpath subject to a private right of way by carriage. This situation will be particularly common where public rights have grown up over pre-existing private roads. A more difficult issue is whether a private landowner may have acquired rights in excess of the public right of way over an existing highway. It is likely that, where the public right encompasses a vehicular right of way, a further private right of way can only be acquired by express grant, since any use of the highway would otherwise be presumed to be in exercise of the public right.

9–08   Whether a stopping up order is intended to or does have the effect of existinguishing all the public rights of way, rather than, for example, only the vehicular right of way, depends on the wording both of the order itself and of the statutory powers under which the order is being made.[13] Many statutory provisions permit the combination of a stopping up order with the creation of some new right of way—which could, of course, be a lesser right of way over the same ground.[14] In every case of ambiguity, the order should be strictly construed, so as to interfere with the public right of way as little as possible.

9–09   The greatest practical problems to the practitioner are likely to come from the effect of the stopping up order on the rights of statutory undertakers, British Telecommunications and other licensed telecommunica-

---

[10] per Lord Herschell in *Tunbridge Wells Corpn.* v. *Baird* [1896] A.C. 434; see also paras. 3–08 *et seq.*, below.
[11] *Rolls* v. *St. George the Martyr, Southwark, Vestry* (1880) 14 Ch.D. 785.
[12] *Allen* v. *Ormond* (1806) 8 East. 4; *Walsh* v. *Oates* [1953] 2 Q.B. 578.
[13] See *e.g.* Highways Act 1980, s.116(4).
[14] See *ibid.* s.118(5); Acquisition of Land Act 1981, s.32; Town and Country Planning Act 1971, ss.210, 214.

tions operators.[15] Each code of legislation contains its own series of provisions dealing with the notification of the statutory undertakers, etc., for relocating (where necessary) their apparatus, and for meeting the expenses arising out of such relocation. These are often extremely complex.

Effect of diversion

Generally, a diversion will also encompass a stopping up of the old highway from the point where the diversion leaves the line of the old way,[16] and the creation of a new right of way over the length of the diversion. However, one question which occasionally arises is whether the diversion *must* consist of newly created rights of way, or whether it may utilise other existing highways.

9–10

The case law on earlier statutory provisions contained differing views as to whether a diversion could incorporate within its length part of an existing highway. In *Welch* v. *Nash*,[17] a highway was to be diverted in such a way that the new route would consist principally of another existing highway. This other highway was to be widened so as to take traffic from the old road. Lord Ellenborough C.J. drew a clear distinction between powers to widen highways and powers of diversion[18]:

9–11

> "The magistrates . . . may divert an old road, so as to make it nearer or more commodious to the public; that is by making a new road. The whole section comtemplates that a new highway is to be made in lieu of the old one, which is to be stopped up, and the magistrates can only order the old highway to be stopped up on the condition that a new highway has been made and put in a proper state. But what diverting or turning of the old road has there been in this case? . . . Increasing the width of one old highway is neither diverting another old highway, nor making a new one."

Welch v. *Nash* was decided under the Highway Act 1773, section 19. The decision has not been followed in later cases concerned with similar statutory powers.

In *De Ponthieu* v. *Pennyfeather*,[19] Gibbs C.J. had to interpret the same section. He came to the view that, so long as the diversion carried the subject into a public highway, which would lead him to the same point as the old would have taken him, then this was a sufficient diversion.[20] However, in this case it seems that there was, at least, some newly created road. In *R.* v. *Phillips*,[21] however, the contemplated diversion involved the throwing of extra land into an old narrow highway,

9–12

---

[15] See Telecommunications Act 1984, ss.5–11 for the licensing of other operators.
[16] *cf.* Highways Act 1980, s.116(4).
[17] (1807) 8 East. 394.
[18] *Ibid.* at 402–3.
[19] (1814) 5 Taunt. 634.
[20] See also Highways Act 1980, s.119(2).
[21] (1866) L.R. 1 Q.B. 648.

thereby widening it and making the improved way nearer and more commodious to the public than was the old way. The Queen's Bench held that this was a sufficient diversion and *Welch* v. *Nash* was disapproved. Blackburn J.[22] saw no difference between the situation where a new right of way was created over entirely new land and the situation where the diversion encompassed a newly-widened existing highway: " . . . in either case there is a substitution offered to the public for the old right of way which they had before." Mellor J. was influenced by the overall benefit to the public of the proposed scheme, and felt that Lord Ellenborough had fallen into uncharacteristic error[23]:

> "Now, I think that the mistake, as I venture to suggest, that Lord Ellenborough fell into, was in reading "new highway" as if it meant an actually different highway, something different in its position and situation, and so on. I think, when you couple it with the preceding part of the section, the meaning is, that the highway proposed to be diverted by making it nearer or by making it more commodious, when diverted is the "new" highway contemplated by this section."

9–13   Under the modern legislation it will be seen that whereas some of the statutory provisions expressly or implicitly make allowance for the possibility of diversion onto an existing highway (with or without the improvement of that highway), others do not. Section 116 of the Highways Act 1980 is silent on the point but, since it is in many ways the successor to those statutory provisions on which *R.* v. *Phillips*, and *De Ponthieu* v. *Pennyfeather* were decided, it might be supposed that the decisions in those cases are still applicable. A different result, however, has been reached in the interpretation of the diversion procedures under the Highways Act 1980, section 119.[24] Section 210 of the Town and Country Planning Act 1971 expressly provides, at subsection (2)(*a*), that a diversion may provide for the improvement of an existing highway to replace the one which is being ordered to be stopped up or diverted.[25] Except for the fact that section 119 of the 1980 Act is a provision solely for the benefit of the landower over whose land the existing highway passes, it is not obvious why these distinctions should exist.

EXTINGUISHMENT AND DIVERSION BY JUDICIAL PROCESS

Highways Act 1980, section 116
9–14   The origins of section 116 of the Highways Act 1980 are to be found in the code set out in sections 84 to 92 of the Highway Act 1835. That code was modified and simplified in a number of respects in the model

---

[22] (1866) L.R. 1 Q.B. 648 at 660–1.
[23] *Ibid.* at 665.
[24] *R.* v. *Lake District Special Planning Board, ex p. Bernstein, The Times,* February 3, 1982. See para. 9–46, below.
[25] See also Civil Aviation Act 1982, s.48.

clauses, prepared, and from time to time revised, by a committee appointed by the Chairman of Ways and Means in the House of Commons and adopted by many local authorities in local acts. It was on one of these model clauses[26] that the immediate predecessor to section 116 was based.[27] Under section 116 an application may be made by a highway authority to a magistrates' court[28] to stop up any type of highway, other than a trunk road or a special road, on the grounds that it is unnecessary. Similarly, an application may be made to divert a highway on the ground that it may be made nearer or more commodious to the public.

Circumstances in which section 116 is appropriate

In many respects, section 116 provides a versatile and comprehensive **9–15** procedure for stopping up and diverting highways where the highway itself or its line no longer serves its original function. The section applies to all types of highways (other than trunk roads and special roads) whereas many of the statutory procedures found elsewhere are restricted in their operation to footpaths and bridleways. In relation to some roads and paths there are, however, stringent requirements regarding the obtaining of the consent of the parish and district councils in whose area the highway lies. This procedure is, therefore, not appropriate where there is substantial public opposition supported by one or other of those councils. In such cases the administrative procedures whereby the final decision is taken by the Secretary of State (or his Inspector) are more suitable.

Section 116 expressly provides for a situation where a footpath may **9–16** be stopped up or diverted subject to the reservation of a footpath or bridleway along the line of the old highway. It is the only statutory procedure expressly to make this provision.[29] However, a similiar result may be achieved by the combination of a stopping up order and a public path creation order or agreement.[30] Since the word "highway" is defined in section 328(1) of the 1980 Act as meaning the whole or any part of a highway, it follows that section 116 could be used to reduce the width of a highway,[31] although this would usually only be done where a footway or bridleway was being reserved.[32]

---

[26] No. 43.

[27] *i.e.* Highways Act 1959, s.108.

[28] By way of a complaint for an order, see ss.116(1) and 316(1).

[29] See also *R. v. Winter* (1828) 8 B. & C. 785.

[30] See Highways Act 1980, ss.25 and 26. See also the powers under other legislation to create new highways, *e.g.* Civil Aviation Act 1982, s.48.

[31] See, however, under earlier legislation, *R. v. Milverton (Inhabitants)* (1836) 5 Ald. & El. 841.

[32] See also Highways Act 1980, s.256 (power to alter the boundaries of a highway by agreement with an adjoining landowner).

Procedure

9–17   An application for an order under section 116 is made by means of a complaint to the magistrates' court for the commission area in which the highway lies.[33] The application may involve two or more highways, as long as they are connected with one another.[34] A number of consents to the making of the order must be obtained well in advance of the application. Where the road is not a classified road and is, therefore, more likely to be of local importance, notice must be given to the district and parish councils[35] of the intention to apply for the order. If these bodies, within the following two months, send a written notice[36] refusing their consent, the application cannot be made. There is no express provision that these consents may not be unreasonably withheld, so that these councils effectively have a power of veto over the application. Where a diversion order is proposed, the written consent of every person having a legal interest in the land over which the highway is to be diverted must be obtained and produced to the court.[37]

9–18   Further notices of intention to apply for an order must be given at least 28 days prior to making the application. These notices must specify the time and place at which the application is to be made, the terms of the proposed order and must also include a plan showing the effect of the order.[38] The recipients of these notices will be the owners or occupiers of all the lands which adjoin the highway, together with any statutory undertakers having apparatus in, over, along or across the highway. Where the highway is a classified road, the notices must also be served on the Minister and, (since in this case no prior notices will have been served on them) on the district, parish and community councils.[39] Further notices must be displayed in prominent positions at the ends of the highway. The expression "ends of the highway" appears to mean the ends of that part of the highway which is to be stopped up. Where several interconnecting highways are to be stopped up, the notices should be sufficient, where one order is involved, if they are placed at the extreme ends of the relevant sections; thus, if the section is Y-shaped then the notices should be placed at the end of each stroke of the Y. If, on the other hand, interconnecting highways are to be the subject of different orders, then the notices must be displayed at each end of the section to be stopped up.[40]

9–19   Problems may arise as to who is to be treated as being the owners or occupiers of land *adjoining* the highway to be stopped up or diverted.

---

[33] Highways Act 1980, s.316; Magistrates' Courts Act 1980, s.52.
[34] Highways Act 1980, s.116(5).
[35] Or, where appropriate, to the chairman of the parish meeting, or in Wales, to the community council.
[36] As to form and authentication, see Highways Act 1980, ss.316–8.
[37] *Ibid.* s.116(8).
[38] *Ibid.* Sched. 12, para. 1.
[39] See para. 9–17, above.
[40] See *R.* v. *Surrey J.J.* (1870) L.R. 5 Q.B. 466.

"Adjoining" is defined in section 329(1) of the 1980 Act as including "abutting on," but it also appears to encompass land which is not immediately contiguous to the highway; for example, where a stream, ditch or wall separates the land from the highway.[41] There may also be circumstances in which owners or occupiers of land adjoining the same highway at a point which is not being stopped up or diverted will be entitled to notice.[42]

There are elaborate provisions for the protection of statutory under- **9–20** takers. Their rights and powers, in respect of apparatus in the highway to be stopped up or diverted, are retained.[43] However, they may, and if reasonably requested to do so by the authority which is applying for the order, must, remove that apparatus and replace it (or place new apparatus) elsewhere. The statutory undertakers will recover their reasonable costs in carrying out these works, together with their incidental expenses from the order-making authority.[44] In the event of a dispute between the undertakers and the authority as to the amount of these costs, the matter is to be determined by arbitration in the county court.[45]

At the hearing of the application for an order, all the recipients of the **9–21** notices served under Schedule 12, any person who uses the highway, and any person aggrieved[46] by the making of the order, have a right to be heard. The justices may view the highway.[47] Before the justices may make an order, they must be satisfied that the required notices have been given, and that the written consent of every person having a legal interest in any land over which the highway is to be diverted has been deposited with the court.[48] The order, when made, must be accompanied by a plan signed by the chairman of the court and must be transmitted to the proper officer of the applicant authority. Where the order contemplates the diversion of the highway, it should not authorise the stopping up of any part of the highway until the new part to be substituted has been completed to the satisfaction of two justices of the peace acting for the same petty sessional area as the court by which the order was made.[49] A certificate to this effect, signed by those justices, is then to be transmitted to the clerk of the applicant authority. Where a diversion falls to be carried out under orders made by two different courts, the justices of each court must certify their satisfaction that the diversion

---

[41] See *Wakefield Local Board of Health* v. *Lee* (1876) 1 Ex. D. 336. See also the cases cited at para. 10–28, below; *cf. Lightbound* v. *Higher Bebington Local Board* (1885) 16 Q.B.D. 577; *Buckinghamshire C.C.* v. *Trigg* [1963] 1 W.L.R. 155.

[42] See *Linton* v. *Newcastle upon Tyne Corpn.* (1929) 142 L.T. 49.

[43] Highways Act 1980, Sched. 12, para. 4.

[44] Subject to any element of betterment; see *ibid.* Sched. 12, paras. 7–9.

[45] *Ibid.* s.308; as to the position of British Telecommunications and other telecommunications operators, see *ibid.* s.334 and Telecommunications Act 1984, Sched. 2.

[46] See paras. 15–34 *et seq.*, below.

[47] Highways Act 1980, s.116(1); see *R.* v. *Cambridgeshire JJ.* (1835) 4 Ad. & El. 111.

[48] Highways Act 1980, s.116(6), (8).

[49] *Ibid.* s.116(8)(*a*).

(including that part outside their jurisdiction) has been completed.[50] Failure to obtain a certificate of satisfaction from the justices will prevent the diversion order becoming effective.[51] Issue of a certificate of satisfaction when the road was not in fact completed may give rise to an application for judicial review and an order of certiorari quashing the certificate. There is an appeal to the Crown Court against the decision of the magistrates' court by the applicant or by any person who was entitled to be heard at first instance.[52]

Substantive conditions

Stopping up

9–22   A highway may be stopped up under section 116 if it appears to the magistrates that the way is unnecessary. This will be a question of fact. Evidence of lack of current public use will be important, but is not essential. The issue before the magistrates is not whether the way is being used, but rather whether it is needed for public use. Generally, these two aspects will be inter-related. However, the fact that two points linked by the highway are also served by an equally convenient route would be evidence on which the justices could conclude that the highway was unnecessary.

9–23   A point which arises from time to time under this section relates to the kind of public use to which the highway is being put and the relevance of this kind of use to the question of need. It may be that the highway no longer serves its original purpose of linking two places of public resort or of giving access to land, and that a new use (for example, parking) has developed. This user should not be taken into account in assessing the need for the highway; parking is not to be considered a relevant use of the highway. Indeed parking which is not of a short duration, or which is excessive in its extent, may constitute a public nuisance[53] and, in some cases, a trespass to the owner of the subsoil.[54] Whether the highway is or is not necessary must be decided with regard to the circumstances existing at the time of the making of the order. It is not sufficient that the construction of a *new* highway will at some future time, render the road unnecessary.[55]

Diversion

9–24   A highway may be diverted if, as a consequence of that diversion, it can be made nearer or more commodious to the public. It is immediately obvious, therefore, that the onus on the landowner who seeks to

---

[50] Highways Act 1980, s.116(8)(*b*).
[51] See *Stockwell* v. *Southgate Corpn.* [1936] 2 All E.R. 1343 at 1352.
[52] Highways Act 1980, s.317.
[53] See *Dymond* v. *Pearce* [1972] 1 Q.B. 496.
[54] See *Harris* v. *Rutland* (*Duke*) [1893] 1 Q.B. 142; *Hickman* v. *Maisey* [1900] 1 Q.B. 752; *R.* v. *Pratt* (1855) 4 E. & B. 860; *Mayhew* v. *Wardley* (1863) 14 C.B. (N.S.) 550.
[55] *R.* v. *Midgley* (1864) 5 B. & S. 621.

obtain the order is not to show the benefit to his land of the diversion,[56] but rather to show the added benefit to the public of a more convenient road. It is, therefore, less likely to prove an attractive provision for the private landowner when compared with other statutory powers of diversion.

9–25   The "or" in the phrase "nearer or more commodious" has been interpreted under earlier legislation in a disjunctive sense.[57] It will be sufficient, therefore, if either of the conditions is satisfied. When considering whether the proposed diversion is "nearer," the justices must have regard to all the places served by the highway.[58] Similar regard should be had to all the places served by the highway, and to all the known types of highway user of the way, when considering the words "more commodious." "Commodious" is, it has been held, an ordinary English word, having a flavour of convenience, roominess and spaciousness.[59] Case law supports, on balance, the proposition that a diversion under this section may encompass an existing highway.[60] If, however, reliance for the public passage is to be placed entirely on an existing highway, then it is suggested that the proper procedure is to stop up under section 116 on the ground that the highway is unnecessary, rather than to divert onto that highway. The diversion must give the public the same permanent rights to pass and re-pass along the carriageway as did the old road.[61] If, therefore, the carriageway is to be discontinued but the footpath or bridleway rights are to be diverted, then the carriageway must be formally stopped up independently of the act of diversion.

Section 117

9–26   A private person may request the authority to make the application on his behalf. In such a case, the authority may require that person to make provision for the reasonable costs incurred in making the application. It appears that these costs may include only the costs of actually applying for the order and not any further cost or expense which will be incurred by the authority as a consequence of making the order.[62] The local authority has a discretion as to whether or not to apply for the order in this situation.

EXTINGUISHMENT AND DIVERSION BY ADMINISTRATIVE PROCESS

General

9–27   Over the years, a multiplicity of statutory powers to stop up and divert highways have developed as part of other legislative codes affecting highways. Thus, in the exercise of compulsory acquisition, planning

---

[56] cf. s.118, below.
[57] See *R. v. Phillips* (1866) L.R. 1 Q.B. 648; *Wright v. Frant Overseers* (1863) 4 B. & S. 118; *R. v. Surrey J.J.* (1872) 26 L.T. 22; cf. *R. v. Shiles* (1841) 1 Q.B. 919.
[58] See *R. v. Shiles* (1841) 1 Q.B. 919.
[59] See *Gravesham B.C. v. Wilson and Straight, The Times*, March 3, 1983, per Woolf J.
[60] See the cases cited at paras. 9–11 *et seq.*, above.
[61] *R. v. Winter* (1828) 8 B. & C. 785.
[62] See *United Land Co. v. Tottenham Local Board of Health* (1884) 13 Q.B.D. 640.

and housing powers, it is sometimes necessary for a local authority to
deal with a public highway which is affected by those powers. There are,
additionally, extinguishment and diversion powers, now contained in
the Highways Act 1980 and which have arrived there by consolidation
from earlier legislation, which invoke an administrative process. The
typical procedure adopted in most of these cases involves the making of
an order by the local authority or the publication of a draft order by the
appropriate Minister. Various publication requirements are imposed on
the local authority and a period is then allowed for objections. If there
are no objections then the order may be confirmed or made without any
further steps being required. Where objections are received, they must
be taken into consideration, and in some cases a public local inquiry
may be held into those objections. Whilst very many of the procedural
codes for extinguishment and diversion powers follow this broad pat-
tern, there are many different codes containing slightly differing
elements.[63]

Highways Act 1980, sections 118 and 119

Circumstances in which orders under sections 118 and 119 are
appropriate

9–28   The first important limitation on the use of these sections is that they
are confined to footpaths and bridleways. Whilst the application for the
order must be made by a local authority, it is envisaged in the legislation
that a diversion order will be made at the request of a landowner. The
substantive condition which must be satisfied before an extinguishment
order is made is similar to that contained in section 116.[64] However, in
considering the need for the path, the Secretary of State is expressly
directed to look at the likely use of the path by the public if the order
were not made. Further, in considering the effect on land served by the
path, account may be taken of the compensation provisions.[65] The existence of compensation provisions for those affected by extinguishment
and diversion orders is an important aspect of these two sections.[66] Any
landowner seeking to persuade a council to make a diversion order in
respect of a path crossing his land should be aware that he may be
required to contribute not only towards the cost of making the order,
but also to the cost of paying compensation.[67] The apparatus of statutory undertakers is protected, not by a series of complex provisions, but
by making it a condition that their consent to the order must be obtained
whenever their equipment is affected.[68]

---

[63] *e.g.* there are often differences in the identification of those persons who must be served
with notice of the making of the order.
[64] See para. 9–22, above.
[65] Highways Act 1980, s.118(2).
[66] See *ibid.* s.28.
[67] See *ibid.* ss.119(5), 120(5).
[68] *Ibid.* s.121(4).

A diversion order under section 119 must not alter the point of termi-   **9–29**
nation of the path which is being stopped up, unless it ends in a highway
which itself connects with the point to which the original path had led.
Whilst this indicates that an existing highway may link the end points of
the old and the newly-created ways, there is some doubt as to whether
an existing way may carry any other part of the diversion.[69] These
restrictions on the scope of the diversion order are, however, by far out
weighed by the terms on which a diversion can be obtained under section 119. Essentially, this is a power whereby the landowner may put the
interests of his own land, if not above that of highway users, then certainly on an equal footing with their interests.

Procedure

A stopping up order made under section 118 is known as a "public   **9–30**
path extinguishment order" and a diversion order made under section
119 is known as a "public path diversion order." The procedure governing both types of order is contained in sections 118 to 121 of and Schedule 6 to the Highways Act 1980 and in the Public Path Orders and
Extinguishment of Public Right of Way Orders Regulations 1983.[70] Both
types of order may be made concurrently with each other and/or with a
"public path creation order," made under section 26 of the 1980 Act.[71]

The order-making authority may either be a "council" or the Sec-   **9–31**
retary of State. "Council" includes both county and district councils, a
joint planning board, the London borough councils and the Common
Council.[72] Where a path lies partly within and partly outside the area of
one council, provision is made for that body to make an order, with the
consent of any other councils in whose area the path also lies, in respect
of the whole path.[73] Where a path lies in the area of a national park, the
consent of the Countryside Commission must also be obtained. The Secretary of State may himself make public path extinguishment and diversion orders in certain circumstances. The legislation contemplates that
diversion orders will be made on the representations of a landowner,
and provision is made for such a landowner to defray the costs of making a diversion order.[74]

The form of the order is prescribed by the regulations.[75] It must be   **9–32**
accompanied by a map, although, in the case of any differences between
the written schedule to the order and the map, the written schedule will
prevail.[76] In the case of diversion orders, the map must contain both the

[69] See *R.* v. *Lake District Special Planning Board, ex p. Bernstein, The Times,* February 3,
1982.
[70] S.I. 1983 No. 23.
[71] *Ibid.* reg. 11; Highways Act 1980, Sched. 6, para. 3 and see para. 2–13, above.
[72] Highways Act 1980, s.329(1): notice must be given to the relevant highway authority.
[73] *Ibid.* s.120(1), (2).
[74] *Ibid.* ss.119(5), 120(5).
[75] S.I. 1983 No. 23, regs. 4–6.
[76] *Ibid.* reg. 6.

existing site of the path to be diverted, and the new site onto which it is to be diverted.[77] The map must also indicate whether the new line encompasses any existing footpaths or bridleways or whether new rights of way will be created.

9–33   Once the order is made, it will either be submitted to the Secretary of State for confirmation, or it may be confirmed as an unopposed order by the council. Prior to submission or confirmation, however, various notices must be served or published. These notices must state the general effect of the order and should indicate that the order has been made and is about to be submitted for confirmation, or is to be confirmed as unopposed order. A place where the order may be inspected must be specified, and a period of at least 28 days allowed for the making of objections or representations.[78] Similar notices must be published and served when the Secretary of State proposes to make the order.[79] These notices must be published in at least one local newspaper circulating in the area in which the land to which the order relates is situated.[80] Every owner, occupier and lessee[81] of the land to which the order relates and the councils in whose area the land lies must be served with a notice.[82] Various specified interest groups must also be served.[83] Provision is made for any person or group, on payment of a reasonable charge, to require that they be given notice of orders within a given area.[84] Finally, notices must be displayed at the ends of so much of the path which is to be stopped up or diverted, at council offices in the locality and at such other places as may be specified by the Secretary of State.[85] All these notices must be accompanied both by a copy of the order and of the plan.[86] Failure to serve, display or publish notices may cause the order to be open to judicial challenge, on the grounds that there has been a failure to comply with the requirements of the Act.[87] However, such a failure will not automatically mean that the order is void, and it will be necessary for an appellant to establish that he was prejudiced by the failure.[88]

9–34   If, after the expiry of the 28 day period (or whatever longer period has been specified), no objections or representations have been made in respect of the order or, if any such objections or representations are

---

[77] Highways Act 1980, s.119(7).
[78] *Ibid.* Sched. 6, para. 1(1).
[79] *Ibid.* para. 1(2).
[80] *Ibid.* para. 1(3).
[81] Except very short and some statutory tenancies; *ibid.* Sched. 6. para. 1(3)(*b*)(i). Where the owners are not known, see *ibid.* para. 1(3C).
[82] Including parish and community councils and parish meetings: *ibid.* s.329(1).
[83] S.I. 1983 No. 23 at Sched. 3.
[84] Highways Act 1980, Sched. 6, para. 1(3A) (3B).
[85] *Ibid.* para. 1(3)(C)(i) and (ii).
[86] *Ibid.* para. 1(4B) and (4C).
[87] See *ibid.* Sched. 2.
[88] See *Allen* v. *Bagshot R.D.C.* (1971) 69 L.G.R. 33.

subsequently withdrawn, then the order may be confirmed unopposed. If the order has been modified (for example, to meet objections which are then withdrawn) this confirmation must in any event be by the Secretary of State. In other cases, the order-making authority may confirm the unopposed order itself. Where the order is opposed, then the Secretary of State must either cause a local inquiry to be held, or must afford to any objector an opportunity of being heard by a person appointed. The latter procedure is less formal than a public local inquiry and is not governed by the same procedural rules. After such an inquiry or hearing, the Secretary of State[89] may confirm or make the order, as the case may be, with or without modifications.

A similar process of publication, inquiry or hearing must be repeated   **9–35** if the Secretary of State proposes to modify the order in such a way as to affect land not originally affected.[90] Further notices must be served on the relevant parties once the order is confirmed. Where the order is not confirmed, a copy of the decision letter must be sent to those parties.[91] Finally, if the order is to come into operation at some future unspecified date, a notice of its coming into operation must be published in a local newspaper at the relevant time.[92] There is provision for judicial challenge to the confirmation of an order, or to the refusal to confirm it within six weeks of notice of confirmation, or refusal to confirm having been given.[93]

The position of statutory undertakers is protected by section 121(4).   **9–36** Their consent is necessary where a right of way over land carrying their apparatus is extinguished by the order.[94] This consent may not be unreasonably withheld, but may be given subject to reasonable conditions for the protection of their apparatus.[95] British Telecommunications are to be treated as statutory undertakers for the purposes of Schedule 6[96] but not for the purposes of section 121. However, the position of British Telecommunications is protected by section 334 (as amended)[97] whereby the corporation is left in the same position regarding its apparatus as if the order had not been made, unless the owner of the stopped up highway land requires alteration of the line.[98]

[89] Or his inspector: Highways Act 1980, Sched. 2, para. 2A.
[90] *Ibid.* para. 2(3).
[91] *Ibid.* para. 4(2).
[92] *Ibid.* para. 4A.
[93] *Ibid.* Sched. 2. See para. 15–32, below.
[94] In other cases an objection by statutory undertakers will render the order subject to special parliamentary procedure.
[95] Any dispute over the reasonableness of refusal or of conditions is to be decided by the Secretary of State: Highways Act 1980, s.121(5).
[96] *Ibid.* Sched. 6, para. 2.
[97] See *ibid.* at para. 3(2): British Telecommunications Act 1981, s.87, Sched. 3, Pt. II, paras. 10(5) and 74.
[98] Highways Act 1980, s.334(3); Telegraph Act 1878, s.7. In which case the landowner may have to meet the costs of this alteration.

Substantive Conditions

9–37   **Section 118.** The first test to be applied in deciding whether a public path extinguishment order should be made is whether there is a continuing need for the path. The order-making authority may only make the order if it appears to it to be expedient that the path or way should be stopped up on the ground that it is not needed for public use.[99] The authority is expressly directed to consider the effect of the making of any other public path creation or diversion order when considering the question of need,[1] and to disregard any temporary circumstances preventing or diminishing the use of the path by the public.[2]

9–38   Prior to confirmation, however, there is another test by which the expediency of the order is to be judged. Whether the order is to be confirmed unopposed by the order-making authority or, after the statutory procedures have been completed, by the Minister, the confirming authority must be satisfied as to the expediency of confirmation, having regard both to the extent to which it appears that the path would be likely to be used apart from the order, and the effect of the extinguishment on land served by the path.[3] In its consideration of the former matter, the confirming authority may again take into account the effect of the provision of an alternative path by means of a concurrent diversion or creation order.[4] Temporary circumstances preventing or diminishing use of the path are again to be disregarded.[5] In considering the effect on land served by the path, the compensation provisions in section 28 must be taken into account.[6]

9–39   Whilst it need only "appear" to the order-maker that it is expedient to make the order on the grounds of lack of need, the confirming body must be "satisfied" of expediency (on the grounds set out in subsection (2)) before the order is confirmed. The difference in wording here seems primarily designed to take into account the pure administrative (or quasi-legislative) act of making the order, as distinct from the quasi-judicial process of considering the objections which may have been raised before the order is confirmed. In both cases, there must be evidence before the relevant authorities to support their action. However, an affirmative case in favour of the order must be made out before it is confirmed. Lack of any objection may well be a factor influencing and satisfying the authority that the order should be confirmed. In both cases, the expediency of the action to be taken must be considered. This suggests that considerations other than the matters expressly referred to may be taken into account. However, the only *ground* on which the

---

[99] Highways Act 1980, s.118(1).

[1] *Ibid.* s.118(5).

[2] *Ibid.* subs. (6).

[3] *Ibid.* subs. (2).

[4] *Ibid.* subs. (5).

[5] *Ibid.* subs. (6).

[6] *Ibid.* ss.118(5), 121(2).

order can be made under subsection (1) is where it appears to the council that the path is not needed for public use. Only when the evidence supports that precondition, may the overall expediency be taken into account. Expediency in subsection (1), therefore, can only operate as a restriction on the use of the power to extinguish; it cannot extend it. Under subsection (2), the confirming authority must be satisfied of the expediency of confirmation having regard to the other matters thereafter set out. This wording does not suggest that these other matters are to be conclusive. The expediency of confirmation must, therefore, to some extent, require a reference back to subsection (1) to consider whether there is still sufficient evidence of lack of need. Where, however, the Secretary of State, in confirming an order, appeared to be applying the test of 'need' rather than having regard to the matters set out in subsection (2), the confirmation of the order has been successfully challenged. In *R. v. Secretary of State for the Environment, ex parte Stewart*,[7] Phillips J. felt that the choice of language in the two subsections must be presumed to be deliberate, and pointed to the similar distinction in what is now section 119(6). He took the view that there were some cases where the distinction could be a matter of importance and where the use of what was the wrong test would undoubtedly falsify the conclusion thus reached:

> "One could see that under the proper test confirmation would not necessarily be ruled out by the fact that the path was, or was going to be, used to something more than a minimal extent. Whereas the test which he (the Minister) had in fact applied, which was that he should not confirm unless he was satisfied that the path was not needed for public use, precluded confirmation if there was any more than minimal public need: "need" as distinct from "use." But there were cases and to some extent this case was one of them, where the test adopted by the Minister favoured the would-be stopper-up because it meant that he could confirm, although the path was likely to be used, if he thought that despite the fact it was likely to be used, it was not needed: as for example, because there was another path."

It would appear that the converse is not true and that the Secretary of State must still have lack of need in mind (in considering expediency) as well as the degree of use. It seems, therefore, that both need *and* use are important factors, and that substantial evidence of either would be likely to prevent the confirmation of the order.

A further matter which arises quite frequently in considering both   **9–40**
need and use is the extent, if any, to which physical obstruction to the path or the obscurity of the line of the path may be considered. These situations may occur where the motive for applying for the order stems

---

[7] [1980] J.P.L. 175.

from the erection of some physical obstruction such as a house, or where the line of the path has become so obscured by vegetation that it is not used. In *Wood* v. *Secretary of State for the Environment*,[8] planning permission for a garage had been granted. However, the garage was completed before an order for the diversion of a footpath which the garage obstructed had been successfully made and confirmed. The council, being unable to proceed under the Town and Country Planning Act 1971,[9] made an order under section 110 of the Highways Act 1959[10] and, after a public inquiry, the Secretary of State confirmed the order. An application to quash the order was rejected. Phillips J. held that there was no principle that the section would not be used in such a way as, in effect, to legalise what had been in the first instance unlawful. He also held that where an order under the Town and Country Planning Act 1971 could no longer be made,[11] the inspector should put the obstruction out of his mind in weighing up the likely attractions of the old path. This approach should be treated with caution. Subsection (6) requires that any temporary circumstances preventing or diminishing the use of a path by the public must be disregarded in considering both the degree of use, and the need for the path. Unlawful obstructions (for example, a house) may be lawfully required to be removed. Encroachments on the line of a path by hedges and trees may also be cleared in order to protect the public right of way. Whether an obstruction is temporary or not is a question of degree. In the *Stewart* case,[12] Phillips J. doubted whether he had been correct in the *Wood* case[13] to take the view that in deciding whether an obstruction could be a temporary circumstance it was irrelevant to consider whether it could, or was likely to be, removed. The primary question has to be whether the obstruction is likely to endure. Even an obstruction which seemed permanent might be regarded as temporary if provisions exist which empower its removal and it appears likely to be removed. The court indicated, in both the *Wood* and the *Stewart*[14] cases, that only rarely could it be right to make an order stopping up a highway on the ground that as a result of an unlawful obstruction, or as a result of doubt as to the line of the highway, it was difficult to use it. Any other view would mean that the easiest way to get a footpath stopped up would be to obstruct it unlawfully.

9–41   It remains difficult, in the light of the reasoning in these two cases and in view of the facts on which this reasoning was based, to say when, if ever, an obstruction which could be legally and physically removed may properly be taken into account. The proper approach must always be to look at what evidence there is as to need and use before the obstruction

---

[8] [1977] J.P.L. 307.
[9] See para. 9–55, below.
[10] Now s.118 of Highways Act 1980.
[11] *i.e.* because development was complete.
[12] [1980] J.P.L. 175.
[13] [1977] J.P.L. 307.
[14] [1977] J.P.L. 307; [1980] J.P.L. 175.

had developed. If there is evidence of lack of need or use, the order may be made and confirmed. If there is evidence of need or use having been curtailed by the obstruction, then the order should not be made or confirmed unless the obstruction has existed for so long that there can be no real suggestion of continuing need, or (if the path was reinstated) substantial continuing use.

So far as any consideration of the effect of extinguishment on land is concerned, two factors stand out. First, the existence of co-existent private rights of way may be taken into account in deciding whether it is expedient to stop up the public right. Secondly, any harm that may be suffered by the landowner which can be measured in finite monetary terms must play very little part in the consideration of the confirming authority, since compensation will be available and should provide an adequate remedy.   **9–42**

Section 119.   A council may make a public path diversion order where it appears to it to be expedient, either in the interests of the owner, lessee or occupier of land crossed by the path, or in the interests of the public, that it should be diverted. Section 119 was introduced in its present form by an amendment contained in the Wildlife and Countryside Act 1981.[15] The former provision was much narrower in scope, requiring that the council be satisfied by the landowner (or lessee or occupier) that the diversion was expedient for securing the more *efficient* use of the land crossed by the path, or other land held with it, or for providing a shorter or more commodious path or way. The present section permits the council to act of its own initiative, allows broader issues to be considered, and allows consideration of the interests of the landowner or, in the alternative, those of the public as a whole. It is likely that the interests of the public can best be promoted by a diversion which does render the path nearer or more commodious,[16] but wider issues may be considered at this stage. It is the public interest which determines whether the order may be confirmed.[17]   **9–43**

Under the section, as previously worded, a relatively flexible approach was adopted in assessing wether a diversion would allow the more efficient use of the land. In *Roberton* v. *Secretary of State for the Environment*,[18] it was held that in considering the land "crossed by" the path, the court was entitled to look not just at the soil over which the path ran but at the whole hereditament. In that case, an application was made to divert a footpath which crossed the Chequers Estate at a point approximately 450 yards from the official country residence of the Prime Minister. The grounds on which the order was made were that there was   **9–44**

---

[15] s.63 and Sched. 16 which came into force on February 28, 1983 (S.I. 1983 No. 20).
[16] As to what is meant by "nearer and more commodious" see para. 9–25, above and *Gravesham B.C.* v. *Wilson and Straight, The Times,* March 3, 1983.
[17] Highways Act 1980, s.119(6).
[18] [1976] 1 W.L.R. 371.

a security risk to the occupants of the residence from potential terrorist attack. In dismissing an application to quash the confirmed order, Phillips J. held that the question for the court was whether the diversion was necessary in order to enable the land (including the house) to be used to its best advantage according to the purpose for which it was occupied.[19] One of the attributes of a dwelling house is peace and quiet, and if the diversion would reduce to a sensible degree the risk of disturbance to the occupation of the residence then the diversion could be said to be helping to secure that the dwelling house was being put to the best possible and most advantageous use. Under the present section an even wider approach could be adopted, since the order-making authority is entitled to look at the landowner and to consider his interests. This appears to allow the identity of the landowner to become relevant, although his interests should properly only be considered *qua* landowner. However, the *Roberton* case and the amended section do give rise to important issues regarding the extent to which a landowner's desire for privacy should permit interference with an established public right of way. Subject to further judicial interpretation, it appears that the present law allows this to be a justification for making a diversion order subject to the order-making body's view of expediency, and subject to confirmation. The broader definition of the public interest in section 119 (as amended) would probably enable a similar application to that in the *Roberton* case to be made on this ground alone.

9–45   The confirming authority must be satisfied that the diversion is expedient, and that the path will not be substantially less convenient to the public as a consequence of the order. Particular regard must be had to the effect on public enjoyment of the path as a whole, the effect on other land served by the existing path, and the effect of the new diversion on the land, and other land held with it, to be crossed by the diversion. In deciding whether the diverted path is substantially less convenient than the original, similar issues to those raised in the consideration of whether the diverted path is nearer and more commodious for the public are likely to be relevant. It will be difficult to justify a diversion which makes a path substantially longer than the original, unless there are compensating advantages in terms of size or ease of use. Regard must be had to the effect on the public enjoyment of the path as a whole. Scenic considerations may be relevant here, and the relationship of the path to the network of paths in the area will be important. In considering the effect of the order, any financial consequences which can be adequately offset by compensation must be ignored by the confirming authority.[20]

9–46   The Act places specific limitations on the route of diversions made under this section. A diversion order may not alter a point of termina-

---

[19] *Ibid.* at 379.
[20] Highways Act 1980, s.119(6).

tion of the path or way, unless that point is on a highway and the diversion takes the path to another point on the same public highway or onto a highway connected with it which is substantially as convenient to the public.[21] Clearly, therefore, where such a diversion is made, the connecting highway must be one which will give the public similar rights along it. These provisions[22] suggest that the diversion can indeed encompass, at least at either end, an existing highway.[23] However, it has been held that the section as a whole contemplates a new path and not a diversion along an existing right of way.[24] Where a diversion entails the entire use of another existing highway, the proper approach would be to extinguish rather than to divert. The diversion may create a right of way subject to limitations and conditions—whether or not the previous right of way was so subject.[25] However, these proposed limitations and conditions would, no doubt, be a factor in deciding whether the proposed diversion would be substantially less convenient.

Compensation for extinguishment or diversion

By section 121(2), the compensation provisions of section 28 of the **9–47** Highways Act 1980 are applied to extinguishment and diversion orders. Thus, compensation will be payable if it can be shown that the value of an interest in land is depreciated, or that disturbance in the enjoyment of land, by virtue of the making and confirming of an order, will occur. The persons entitled to compensation are those over whose land the right of way affected or created by the order passes—who may claim in respect of that land and in respect of any land held therewith—and those persons who would have had a right of action if the acts which caused the diversion or extinguishment had occurred otherwise than through the exercise of statutory powers. Any claimant must have an interest[26] in the relevant land.

An application for compensation should be made in writing and **9–48** should be served on the authority by whom the order was made, or on the local authority nominated by the Secretary of State (where he himself has made the order), within six months of the coming into operation of the order.[27] Any dispute over the amount of compensation payable is to be determined by the Lands Tribunal.[28] There is provision for the voluntary contribution by one local authority towards the expenses of another where compensation has been paid under section 28.[29] This

[21] Highways Act 1980, s.119(2).
[22] See also *ibid.* s.119(7)(*b*), (*c*).
[23] Compare the discussion at paras. 9–11 *et seq.*, above.
[24] See *R. v. Lake District Special Planning Board, ex p. Bernstein, The Times,* February 3, 1982.
[25] Highways Act 1980, s.119(4).
[26] See *ibid.* s.28(5).
[27] Public Path Orders and Extinguishment of Public Right Of Way Orders Regulations 1983 (S.I. 1983 No. 23), reg. 16.
[28] Highways Act 1980, ss.307, 309.
[29] *Ibid.* s.275(*a*).

might be applicable where the diversion was carried out by one authority at the request of another.

Walkways

9–49   Walkways cannot be stopped up or diverted under Part VIII of the Highways Act 1980, even though they are a type of footpath.[30] However, the walkway agreement itself may provide for the termination of the public rights.[31]

Extinguishment or diversion incidental to road construction and improvement

9–50   The Secretary of State and local highway authorities have power to construct new highways under section 24 of the Highways Act 1980. All highway authorities have power to improve highways under section 62 of that Act. In the course of road construction and improvement, it is frequently desirable to limit the number of highways which cross or join the route of the new or improved road. This may involve stopping up some existing roads and paths and re-routing others around, over or under the new or improved road. In the case of trunk and classified roads which are being constructed or improved, the extinguishment and diversion powers are contained in section 14 of the Highways Act 1980. In the case of special roads, similar powers are given by section 18. Both sets of provisions are governed by the procedural provisions of Schedule 1 to the Act of 1980.

9–51   An order under section 14 may authorise a highway authority to stop up, divert, improve, raise, lower or otherwise alter a highway which crosses or enters the route of, or is otherwise affected by, the construction of a trunk or classified road.[32] Temporary diversions may also be created during the construction or improvement of the trunk or classified road, and these themselves may later be closed.[33] Provision may be made in the order for the preservation of the rights of statutory undertakers and sewerage authorities. In the case of a classified road, the order is made by the local highway authority and must be submitted to the Minister for confirmation. The Minister must neither make nor confirm an order authorising the stopping up of a highway unless he is satisfied that another reasonably convenient route is available or will be provided before the road is actually stopped up.[34] The order will come into operation on the same day as the principal order under section 10. The order may provide for the transfer to another highway authority, at some future time, of any roads constructed pursuant to the order, and may provide for the payment of contributions from one highway auth-

---

[30] See the Walkways Regulations 1973 (S.I. 1973 No. 686), Sched. 1.
[31] Highways Act 1980, s.35(3).
[32] *Ibid.* s.14(1)(*a*)(i).
[33] *Ibid.* s.14(1)(*a*)(ii).
[34] *Ibid.* s.14(6).

ority to another in respect of any additional liabilities imposed on that other authority in consequence of the order.[35]

An order under section 18 may authorise the special road authority to stop up, divert, improve, raise or otherwise alter a highway which crosses or enters the route of the special road, or is or will otherwise be affected by the construction or improvement of the special road. Temporary highways may be constructed in connection with the alteration, and these may themselves be closed at a future date.[36] As with the provisions in section 14, protection is given to the rights of statutory undertakers and sewerage authorities, and provision is made for the transfer of any new highways constructed under the section to another highway authority and for the payment of contributions by one highway authority to another.[37] The order under this section is made either by the Minister or by the local highway authority (depending upon which authority is providing the special road) but, in the latter case, the order must be submitted to the Minister for confirmation. The Minister must neither make nor confirm an order unless he is satisfied that some other reasonably convenient route is available or will be provided for traffic (other than traffic of the class authorised by the scheme) or that no such other route is reasonably required for any such traffic.[38]

Extinguishment and Diversion Powers under the Town and Country Planning Act 1971

Orders made by the Secretary of State: section 209

Section 209 of the Town and Country Planning Act 1971 empowers the Secretary of State for the Environment to authorise, by order, the stopping up or diversion of any highway, if he is satisfied that it is necessary so to do in order to enable development to be carried out in accordance with certain planning permissions or by a government department. The power to make an order under this section includes power to provide for the improvement of any other highway as appears to the Secretary of State to be expedient or necessary. The order may provide that any such highway created or improved by virtue of the order becomes a highway maintainable at the public expense.[39] Provision may also be made for the payment of contributions to the cost of carrying out any of the works made necessary in consequence of the order by another authority or by a specified person. Similar provision may be made for the repayment of any compensation which has been required to be paid under sections 1 or 2 of the Restriction of Ribbon

9–52

9–53

---

[35] Highways Act 1980, s.14(1)(*b*) and (7). Provision is made for the determination of disputes by arbitration.

[36] *Ibid.* s.18(1)(*c*).

[37] *Ibid.* s.18(1)(*d*), (2) and (7). Provision is made for the determination of any disputes by arbitration.

[38] *Ibid.* s.18(6).

[39] Town and Country Planning Act 1971, s.209(2).

Development Act 1935, in relation to any highway stopped up under the order.[40] Thus, the person who seeks to persuade the Secretary of State to use his powers under this section may be required to meet certain of the expenses to which the Secretary of State or the highway authority have been put. Protection is given to the apparatus of statutory undertakers and this may also be incorporated into the order.[41]

9–54   An order under section 209 may be made in relation to any highway however created and no matter of what type.[42] The first precondition is the existence of a planning permission[43] under the provisions of Part III of the 1971 Act or under Schedule 32 to the Local Government, Planning and Land Act 1980.[44] The second precondition is that the extinguishment or diversion should be necessary to enable development *to be carried out*. "Development" is defined in section 22 of the 1971 Act as meaning:

> "the carrying out of building, engineering, mining or other operations in, on, or over or under land, or the making of any material change in the use of any buildings or other land."

The first point to note is, therefore, that the development need not actually involve the construction of any physical object over the highway. A change of use of existing premises fronting a highway would, in theory, be sufficient to empower the Secretary of State to make an order, although convincing arguments as to the overall desirability of interfering with an established highway might be required by the Secretary of State before his agreeing to make an order.

9–55   It has been held by the Court of Appeal, in *Ashby* v. *Secretary of State for the Environment*,[45] that it is essential that the development for which permission has been granted should not have been substantially completed before the order is made, or in the case of section 210, confirmed. It does not, however, matter that development has already begun before the order is authorised (whether or not the development was, at that stage, permitted by virtue of a relevant planning permission) nor that the development has already obstructed the highway. In the *Ashby* case,[46] the argument was accepted that if the work on a house, which actually obstructed the highway, was incomplete, then the diversion of the highway was "necessary" in order to enable the development to be carried out. Goff L.J. said[47]:

---

[40] Town and Country Planning Act 1971, s.109(3).
[41] *Ibid.* s.209(3)(*b*).
[42] See *Harlow* v. *Minister of Transport* (1951) 2 K.B. 98: including a highway governed by an Inclosure Act.
[43] But see the procedure under s.216 for publication of notices of draft orders in advance of planning permission.
[44] Orders designating enterprise zones.
[45] [1980] 1 W.L.R. 673.
[46] *Ashby* v. *Secretary of State for the Environment* [1980] 1 W.L.R. 673.
[47] *Ibid.* at 681.

"If necessary I would say that any further building on the site of the highway, even though it is physically stopped up by what has already been done already, is itself a further obstruction which cannot be carried out without an order."

Stephenson L.J. does not appear to have gone so far. He said[48]:

"I am, however, in agreement with the view that, on the facts of the case, development was still being carried out which necessitated the authorisation of a diversion order at the time when the diversion order was authorised and confirmed. I agree with the deputy judge that on the inspector's findings of fact it was then still necessary to enable a by no means minimal part of the permitted development to be carried out. . . . In my judgment, development which consists of building operations, and it may be development which consists of a change of use, as to which I express no concluded opinion, is a process with a beginning and an end; once it is begun, it continues to be carried out until it is completed or substantially completed."

It may be, therefore, that the leaving of a nominal amount of work to be completed will not be sufficient to permit the use of this section.

9–56 It is important to distinguish between the matters relevant to the application for permission which will ultimately bring about the need for the diversion of the highway, and the factors which will be relevant to the extinguishment or diversion of the highway itself. The arguments against the loss of open land will have been decided at the planning permission stage. Once the decision has been taken in favour of a development, then the highway considerations, including convenience, degree and kind of user, safety, and the effect of traffic on public amenity, must be balanced against the need to extinguish or divert the highway in order to permit the development to take place. An inquiry into an order made under sections 209 and 210 of the 1971 Act may not necessarily be an appropriate forum for objection to the grant of the planning permission itself.[49]

9–57 In practice, orders under this section are frequently made by the Secretary of State not on his own initiative, but on the application of a local authority or of some private person.[50]

9–58 In certain circumstances, notice of a draft order to be made under section 209 may be published by the Secretary of State in advance of a grant of planning permission. Section 216(2) permits the use of this procedure where an application for permission has been made by a local authority or by the National Coal Board, where the application has been "called

[48] [1980] 1 W.L.R. 673 at 683.
[49] See Goff L.J. in the *Ashby* case: [1980] 1 W.L.R. 673 at 682.
[50] See Town and Country Planning Act 1971, s.209(3)(*a*) and Local Government Act 1972, s.250(4), (5), empowering the Secretary of State to require some other person to meet the expenses incurred in using the procedure.

in" under section 35 of the 1971 Act, or where the applicant has appealed either against the refusal of permission or against a condition imposed by the grant of a permission. Subsection (3) allows advance publication where certain kinds of development requiring the authorisation of a government department are to be carried out by a local authority, a statutory undertaker or the National Coal Board and where the developers have applied for that authorisation and have requested a direction that planning permission be deemed to be granted for that development.[51] Subsection (4) deals with situations where certain local authorities have certified that they have followed the "deemed permission" procedure prescribed by section 270 of the 1971 Act and the Town and Country Planning General Regulations 1976.[52] The order itself cannot be made, however, until the required permission has been granted.[53]

9–59   The procedure to be followed in making an order under section 209 is entirely contained within section 215 of the 1971 Act.[54] This procedure entails the publication in a local newspaper circulating within the relevant area, and in the London Gazette, of a notice describing the effect of the proposed order, the serving on various local authorities and statutory undertakers of copy notices together with a copy of the draft order and of any relevant plans or maps, and the display, at a prominent position at the ends of the highway to be stopped up or diverted, of a copy of the notice, draft order and relevant plans and maps. The published notice must specify facilities for inspection of the draft order and must give notice of the period within which objections to the order may be made. Where there are unresolved objections, the Secretary of State must hold a local inquiry unless no relevant local authority or statutory undertaker has objected and he is satisfied that in the special circumstances of the case an inquiry is unnecessary.[55]

Orders made by local planning authorities: section 210

9–60   Footpaths and bridleways may be stopped or diverted by local planning authorities under the Town and Country Planning Act 1971, section 210. Save for its limitation to footpaths and bridleways, this section mirrors the powers of the Secretary of State under section 209. Thus, the power can only be exercised where the local planning authority is satisfied that the stopping up or diversion of the highway is necessary in order to enable development to be carried out in accordance with a planning permission granted under Part III of the 1971 Act, or under

---

[51] *e.g.* under Town and Country Planning Act 1971, s.40.
[52] S.I. 1976 No. 1419.
[53] Town and Country Planning Act 1971, s.216(5).
[54] Contrast the procedure under section 210 which is contained in Sched. 20.
[55] *e.g.* where a previous inquiry has been held into a proposed order and which was not confirmed because of a technicality and where the circumstances on the substantial issues have not changed.

Schedule 32 to the Local Government, Planning and Land Act 1980. The substantive conditions for the use of the power are the same as with section 209.[56] The order may be made in respect of a highway which is temporarily stopped up or diverted under any other enactment[57]; however, the procedure for making the order and the content of the order are slightly different.

The order may contain provisions for the creation of an alternative 9–61 highway for use as a replacement for the one authorised to be stopped up or diverted by the order, or for the improvement of an existing highway for use as such a replacement.[58] Works may be authorised to be carried out on the highway which is to be stopped up or diverted by the order.[59] The rights of statutory undertakers may be preserved under the order.[60] Provision may be made in the order for the payment by, or contribution from, any person named in the order, towards the cost of carrying out "any such works." It seems likely that this relates to the whole of section 210(2), rather than to section 210(2)(b), which is the only other part of that section to refer to any "works" to be carried out. There is no procedure for publication of notice of a draft order, in advance of the grant of planning permission, as there is in the case of an order under section 209.

The order under section 210 is made by the local planning authority 9–62 which has either granted the planning permission, or which would have been the local planning authority with power to grant the permission where the permission has been granted by the Secretary of State or where development is to be carried out by a government department.[61] Before it can be effective, the order must be confirmed by the authority as an unopposed under or, if there are unresolved objections, by the Secretary of State. Where the Secretary of State confirms the order, he must be satisfied as to every matter of which the order-making authority is required to be satisfied.[62] The order cannot take effect until it is confirmed.[63]

The procedure for the making of orders under section 210 is governed 9–63 by Schedule 20 to the Town and Country Planning Act 1971, and by the Town and Country Planning (Public Path Orders) Regulations 1983.[64] This procedure, in summary, involves an order being made by the local planning authority subject to confirmation either as an unopposed order by the authority itself, or by the Secretary of State after the local inquiry procedure has been followed. Before the order is confirmed by the

[56] See paras. 9–53 et seq., above.
[57] Town and Country Planning Act 1971, s.210(3).
[58] Ibid. s.210(2)(a).
[59] Ibid. s.210(2)(b).
[60] Ibid. s.210(2)(c).
[61] Ibid. s.210(4).
[62] See para. 9–53, above.
[63] Town and Country Planning Act, s.217.
[64] S.I. 1983 No. 22.

authority or submitted to the Secretary of State, notice must be given stating the general effect of the order, and specifying a time and place where the order may be inspected. A period of 28 days from first publication of the notice is allowed for objections.[65] The required notice must be published in at least one local newspaper circulating in the area where the land to which the order relates is situated. It must be served on every owner, occupier or lessee,[66] and on every council[67] in whose area the relevant land lies. Statutory undertakers owning or using apparatus under, in, on or over, along or across the land must also be served with a notice. A number of other bodies are also entitled to be served with notice. These bodies are either listed in the Town and Country Planning (Public Path Orders) Regulations 1983[68] or, alternatively, may have required the relevant authority, on payment of a reasonable charge, to give them notice of all orders made under the section within a specified area and during a specified period.[69] Where no objections are received within the prescribed time limit (or those that are received have been withdrawn) and where the authority does not wish to make any modifications, the order may be confirmed by the authority itself. In all other situations, the order must be submitted to the Secretary of State, who must, where there are any outstanding objections, either hold a public local inquiry or who may, where the outstanding objector is not a local authority, afford any objector a "hearing" before a person appointed.[70] After the holding of such a public local inquiry or hearing, the Secretary of State may confirm the order, with or without modifications.[71] However, he must be satisfied as to every matter which the local planning authority was required to be satisfied of before he makes the order. Further protection is given to the rights of statutory undertakers, and publicity must again be given to the confirmed order. The path must not be stopped up or diverted until the order has been properly confirmed.

Orders in relation to roads crossing or entering the route of a proposed highway: section 211

9–64   Where planning permission is granted for the construction or improvement of a highway, the Secretary of State may make an order stopping up or diverting any highway which crosses or enters the route of, or is otherwise affected by, that highway. Before making any such order, the Secretary of State must be satisfied that it is expedient to

---

[65] Town and Country Planning Act 1971, Sched. 20, para. 1.
[66] Apart from tenants for a period of less than one month, or statutory tenants within the meaning of the Rent Acts: see para. 1(2).
[67] Including, for this purpose, parish councils and parish meetings.
[68] S.I. 1983 No. 22.
[69] Town and Country Planning Act 1971, Sched. 20, para. 1(2A).
[70] *Ibid.* Sched. 20, para. 3.
[71] As to the delegation of the decision to the "person appointed," see *ibid.* Sched. 20, para. 3A.

make the order in the interests of road safety or traffic movement.[72] An order under this section then takes effect subject to the same procedure as and in the same way as an order under section 209.[73]

Orders extinguishing the right to use vehicles on a highway: section 212

9–65 Where a local planning authority resolves to adopt a proposal for improving the amenity of its area which involves the conversion of a carriageway highway (other than a trunk or principal road) to a footpath or bridleway, that authority may apply to the Secretary of State for an order extinguishing the right to use vehicles on that highway.[74] The order may provide for the continued use of the highway, in specified circumstances, by certain classes of vehicle, or by vehicles belonging to certain people. In such cases, the restrictions contained elsewhere on the use of footpaths and bridleways will not apply to a highway which is subject to an order made under this section.[75] The order may contain provisions for the creation or improvement of any other highway, may direct that any such highway so improved or created should become a highway maintainable at the public expense and may direct who is to be the highway authority for the highway.[76] As with section 209, the order may require payment or contributions in respect of the cost of carrying out work necessitated by the order and the repayment of compensation previously paid by the highway authority under the Restriction of Ribbon Development Act 1935, and may contain provision for the preservation of the right of statutory undertakers.[77]

9–66 Anyone losing their lawful right of access to the highway by virtue of an order under this section is entitled to compensation based on any depreciation in the value of his land and any other consequential damage which is directly attributable to the making of the order.[78] Lawful access is defined as meaning any access granted by virtue of planning permission under the 1971 Act or its predecessors, or any access in respect of which no such planning permission is necessary. A claim for compensation under this section must be made to the local planning authority within prescribed time limits.[79] The claim will be governed by the rules set out in the Land Compensation Act 1961, section 5 and, in

---

[72] Town and Country Planning Act 1971, s.211. Compare the procedures contained in Highways Act 1980, ss.14 and 18.

[73] See paras. 9–53 *et seq.*, above.

[74] A local authority other than a local planning authority may also make orders under this section in respect of highways within its General Improvement Areas: see Housing Act 1985, s.256.

[75] Town and Country Planning Act 1971, s.212(4). The vehicles of the emergency services and statutory undertakers will usually be excluded from the order: see Circulars Nos. Roads 13/71 and 36/74.

[76] Town and Country Planning Act 1971, ss.219(9), 209(2).

[77] *Ibid.* ss.219(9) and 209(3).

[78] *Ibid.* s.212(5).

[79] See the Town and Country General Regulations 1976 (S.I. 1976 No. 1419), reg. 14: presently 6 months from the date of the decision giving rise to the claim.

the case of any dispute, may be referred to the Lands Tribunal.[80] Orders made under this section may be revoked by the Secretary of State, after consulting the local highway and planning authorities, by a further order reinstating the right of vehicles to use the highway.[81]

9–67 It appears that the Secretary of State will take into account the general planning considerations in the area immediately surrounding the road, together with the traffic implications of making the order, including the suitability of alternative routes for any displaced traffic. The availability of other means of access to any premises served by the road, and the walking distance from the nearest parking place are also likely to be considered. Difficulties which might be caused by the exclusion of all traffic from the path may be overcome by permitting continued access to restricted categories of vehicles.[82]

9–68 A further power to extinguish public rights of way over land is contained within the Town and Country Planning Act 1971, section 214. This empowers the Secretary of State, in respect of all kinds of highways, and the local planning authority, in respect of footpaths and bridleways, to extinguish public rights of way across land which has been acquired or appropriated by a local authority for planning purposes under Part VI of the 1971 Act. Local authorities may acquire land within their area, either by agreement or compulsorily, for various planning purposes.[83] The effect of such an order is the same as under section 209.[84] Where the order is made by the local planning authority, the procedure is governed by Schedule 20.[85]

Powers under other statutes

Housing Act 1985, section 294

9–69 This section empowers a local authority to extinguish any right of way over land purchased by itself for clearance. The order has to be approved by the Secretary of State after (where it is opposed) a public inquiry. There are provisions for compensating any statutory undertakers whose equipment is affected by the order.

Acquisition of Land Act 1981, section 31

9–70 An acquiring authority, acting either under compulsory powers or by agreement, is empowered by section 31 of the Acquisition of Land Act 1981 to extinguish footpaths and bridleways by order, where it is satisfied that a suitable alternative right of way has been or will be provided, or that the provision of such an alternative is not required. An order

---

[80] Town and Country Planning Act 1971, ss.178–179.
[81] *Ibid.* s.212(8).
[82] See, for guidance hereof, Circulars Nos. Roads 13/71 and 36/74.
[83] See Town and Country Planning Act 1971, ss.114 and 119.
[84] See paras. 9–59 *et seq.*, above.
[85] See also the Town and Country Planning (Public Path Orders) Regulations 1983 (S.I. 1983 No. 22).

under this section may be made before the land is actually acquired, but if the acquisition plans are abandoned, then the local authority must direct that the right of way revives.

Civil Aviation Act 1982, section 48

This section empowers the Secretary of State to stop up or divert any **9–71** highway if he is satisfied that it is necessary so to do in order to secure the safe and efficient use for civil aviation purposes of any land which he or the Civil Aviation Authority proposes to acquire. Such an order may provide for the provision or improvement of an existing highway if the Secretary of State thinks it necessary or desirable in consequence of the stopping up or diversion.[86] The order may also declare that any highway thereby provided or improved shall become a highway maintainable at the public expense, and may identify the highway authority which is thereafter to be responsible for it. Safeguards are provided for the apparatus of statutory undertakers. There are similar provisions for the recovery of the cost of works necessitated by the extinguishment of diversion, and for the repayment of any compensation previously paid under the Restriction of Ribbon Development Act 1935, as are contained in the Town and Country Planning Act 1971, section 209.[87] The making of the order under this Act is subject to special parliamentary procedure. Schedule 1 to the Statutory Orders (Special Procedure) Act 1945 applies generally to the procedure of publication of the order. The making of the order must be published in much the same way as is required by Schedule 20 to the Town and Country Planning Act 1971.[88] Where there are unresolved objections, a public local inquiry must be held unless the Secretary of State is satisfied that, in the special circumstances of the case, the holding of such an inquiry is unnecessary. Provision is made for the apparatus of statutory undertakers.

New Towns Act 1981, section 23

The Secretary of State or the local highway authority may, by order, **9–72** extinguish any public right of way over land which has been acquired by a New Town Development Corporation.

[86] Civil Aviation Act 1982, s.48(3)(*a*).
[87] See para. 9–53, above.
[88] See para. 9–63, above.

CHAPTER 10

STREETS, NEW STREETS AND PRIVATE STREETS

STREETS

10–01 Many of the powers of a highway authority relate not to highways at all but to streets. A street may be a highway but it need not be. In section 329(1) of the Highways Act 1980, a street is defined as including:

> "any highway and any road, lane, footpath, square, court, alley or passage whether a thoroughfare or not and includes any part of a street."

Whilst this definition does not define the essential characteristics of a street, it does make it clear that the street may or may not be a thoroughfare,[1] and that where there is a public right of way, that right need not be a right of carriageway.[2] The inclusion of squares and courts indicates that the linear shape normally associated with a street is not essential. The width of the street is unimportant, since alleyways, passages and footpaths fall within the definition. The definition implies that not all highways or roads are automatically streets. The statutory definition derives from section 4 of the Public Health Act 1875 which was not an attempt to rationalise any common law notion of the word "street," but rather was an attempt to provide a working definition for the statutory powers and responsibilities which were created in that Act. Since then the definition has received a considerable amount of judicial interpretation. It may be, however, that close attention has to be given to the context of the use of the word "street" in the different legislation.[3]

10–02 In the subsequent judicial decisions there have been two schools of thought. In one line of cases, the courts have decided that the word "street" should carry its ordinary, popular meaning and that roads, lanes, alleys or passages should fall within the defined meaning only if they also possess the essential attributes of a street as commonly understood.[4] The second school of thought is that the definition section is intended to indicate that the word "street" is to have a wider meaning than the ordinary meaning of the word. It might appear that the word

---

[1] See *R.* v. *Goole Local Board* [1891] 2 Q.B. 212; *Hill* v. *Wallasey Local Board* [1894] 1 Ch. 133; *Midland Ry.* v. *Watton* (1886) 17 Q.B.D. 30; *Taylor* v. *Oldham Corpn.* (1876) 4 Ch. D. 395.

[2] *Fenwick* v. *Croydon Rural Sanitary Authority* [1891] 2 Q.B. 216.

[3] *cf. Marks* v. *Ford* (1880) 45 J.P. 157; *R.* v. *Goole Local Board* [1891] 2 Q.B. 212.

[4] See *Galloway* v. *London Corpn.* (1866) L.R. 1 H.L. 34; *R.* v. *Burnup* (1886) 50 J.P. 598; *Allen* v. *Fulham Vestry* [1899] 1 Q.B. 681; *Arter* v. *Hammersmith Vestry* [1897] 1 Q.B. 646.

"street" must mean something different from the words "highway" and "road" and that it is implicit in the definition that there should be some houses fronting onto the way. It appears from the decided cases, however, that there need not be any particular regularity in the positioning of those houses, and that where the "street" falls within one or other of the ways expressly mentioned in section 329(1) of the 1980 Act it may not be necessary for there to be any existing houses at all. In every case, the question as to whether something is or is not a street within the meaning of the 1980 Act is a matter of fact and degree.[5]

In *Robinson* v. *Barton-Eccles Local Board*,[6] the court took the view **10–03** that the interpretation clause in section 4 of the Public Health Act 1875 could not prevent the word "street" from having its ordinary, popular and natural meaning, whenever that could properly be applied. The definition clause was to enable something not ordinarily within the popular sense of the term to be brought in where the context so required, or where there was nothing in the context to the contrary. This decision was followed in *Attorney-General* v. *Laird*[7] where it was held that for a road to fall within the definition, there must be a succession of houses or dwellings in reasonable contiguity and proximity on at least one side of the road. Only in such a case could a court hold as a question of fact that what had originally been a mere road or highway had become a street.

In *Attorney-General* v. *Gibb*,[8] the view was taken that, in relation to **10–04** new street by-laws, the intention of the legislature must have been that the power to make by-laws should not be confined to new streets in the broad, popular sense—meaning ways with houses on either side. The court was influenced by the fact that under the provisions concerned with new streets, there might well be no houses in existence at the time the by-laws were to be made. In *Warwickshire County Council* v. *Atherstone Common Right Proprietors*,[9] the Divisional Court had to consider the meaning of the word "street" in the context of the private street works code. The Justices who had heard objections to street works had concluded that a road which did not have a reasonable number of buildings on both sides, or at least on one side, could not properly be regarded as being a "street" so as to bring into operation the street works code. The Divisional Court allowed an appeal, holding that the Justices had erred in law and had unnecessarily confined the definition contained in the Highways Act 1959. This view has also been confimed by the Privy Council in *Attorney-General of Hong Kong* v. *Mighty Stream Ltd.*,[10] where a similar definition (but also including the word

[5] *R.* v. *Fullford* (1864) 10 L.T. 346; *Maude* v. *Baildon Local Board* (1883) 10 Q.B.D. 394.
[6] (1883) 8 App. Cas. 798.
[7] [1925] 1 Ch. 318; see also *R.* v. *Fullford* (1864) 10 L.T. 346; *R.* v. *Platts* (1880) 43 L.T. 159; *Simmonds Bros.* v. *Fulham Vestry* [1900] 2 Q.B. 188.
[8] [1909] 2 Ch. 265; *cf. St Mary, Battersea, Vestry* v. *Palmer* [1897] 1 Q.B. 220.
[9] (1964) 65 L.G.R. 439.
[10] [1983] 1 W.L.R. 980.

"roadbridge") was involved. The Privy Council had no difficulty in including a bridge as part of a street and rejecting the Attorney-General's arguments, based on the *Robinson* and *Laird* cases, that the bridge had to possess the ordinary qualities of a street in order to fall within the definition.[11]

NEW STREETS

10–05   In order to secure that new streets[12] constructed by developers are of proper width and construction, and to make adequate provision for sewerage, the councils of every county, metropolitan district and London borough and the Common Council may make, and if required by the Secretary of State, shall make, by-laws for regulating these matters.[13] By-laws may require that any person constructing a new street must provide separate sewers for foul water drainage and for surface water drainage respectively, but cannot regulate the level, width, or construction of a new street in so far as it is to be carried by a bridge or is to form the approaches to a bridge. Furthermore, where it appears to the relevant council that an existing highway in its area will be converted into a new street as a consequence of building operations which have been, or are likely to be, undertaken in the vicinity, the council may, by order, prescribe the centre line of the new street and the outer lines defining the minimum width of the new street. This is to be the same minimum width as is required by the relevant by-law provisions. New street by-laws may be relaxed, with the consent of the Secretary of State, where the authority considers that the operation of those by-laws would be unreasonable in relation to a particular street.[14]

10–06   New street by-laws may include provisions for the giving of notices and the deposit of plans, the inspection of work, the testing of sewers and the taking of samples of the various materials to be used in the execution of works. The by-laws may require that plans be deposited in duplicate.[15] Where plans of any proposed works are deposited with the relevant council then that council must pass those plans, unless they are either defective or show that the proposed work would contravene the relevant by-laws. In that case the council must reject the plans. In any event, notice of rejection or notice that the plans have been passed must be given within one month[16] from their deposit. In cases of dispute, an application may be made to the magistrates' court for determination of

---

[11] See also *Jowett* v. *Idle Local Board* (1883) 36 W.R. 530; *Taylor* v. *Oldham Corpn.* (1876) 4 Ch. D. 395.
[12] Including a continuation of an existing street: Highways Act 1980, s.187.
[13] *Ibid.* s. 186(1): subject to a default power in the Secretary of State; s. 186(3).
[14] *Ibid.* s.190(1).
[15] *Ibid.* s. 186(5), (6); see also s.201.
[16] 5 weeks in some cases: see *ibid.* s.202.

the question[17] However, under section 191, work must not be commenced before such an application has been determined. Unless work is commenced within three years of the deposit of plans then the deposit may be declared by the relevant council to be without effect and, if so, the situation will be the same as if no plans had ever been deposited.[18]

An existing highway may, by order, be declared to be a new street **10–07** under section 188. A notice of the proposal must be displayed at least one month before the order is made in a conspicuous position in each street to which the proposal relates, and shall include a statement indicating that the order may be made on or at any time after the date specified in the notice.[19] These orders continue until revoked or amended.

Otherwise, whether a new street is being created is a question of fact and degree.[20] Generally, it appears that the building works must cause a change in character giving the place the attributes of a street.[21] The erection of a single house adjoining a road,[22] or of a group of houses which do not directly front onto a road,[23] or the opening of an access onto a road[24] are insufficient by themselves to involve the laying out of a new street.

Where plans are deposited indicating that a new street will become a **10–08** main thoroughfare, a continuation of a main thoroughfare, a means of communication between main thoroughfares, a continuation of a main approach, or a means of communication between main approaches, the relevant council may, as a condition of passing the plans, require that the new street be of a certain width and may determine the relative arrangement between the footway and the carriageway. Where the width required under these provisions exceeds the normal maximum width by an amount greater than 20 feet, compensation is payable for any loss or injury which may be sustained by reason of the requirement. The "normal maximum width" is defined as the maximum width of which, apart from the operation of these particular provisions, the street could have been required to be formed under by-law or enactment with respect to the width of new streets which is in force in the relevant area. The cost incurred by the extra width will be met by the relevant council.[25]

---

[17] It is questionable whether this precludes any other remedy by way of judicial review; see *R.* v. *Tynemouth Corpn., ex p. Cowper* [1911] 2 K.B. 361; *R.* v. *Preston R.D.C.* (1911) 106 L.T. 37.

[18] Highways Act 1980, s.192.

[19] *Ibid.* s.189.

[20] *R.* v. *Dayman* (1857) 7 E. & B. 672; *R.* v. *Sheil* (1884) 50 L.T. 590; *St Mary, Battersea, Vestry* v. *Palmer* [1897] 1 Q.B. 220; *Allen* v. *Fulham Vestry* [1899] 1 Q.B. 681.

[21] *Crosse* v. *Wandsworth Board of Works* (1898) 79 L.T. 351; *Dryden* v. *Putney Overseers* (1876) 1 Ex. D. 223; *Att.-Gen.* v. *Dorin* [1912] 1 Ch. 369.

[22] *St Georges Local Board* v. *Ballard* [1895] 1 Q.B. 702.

[23] *Gozzett* v. *Maldon Sanitary Authority* [1894] 1 Q.B. 327.

[24] *Devonport Corpn.* v. *Tozer* [1903] 1 Ch. 759.

[25] Highways Act 1980, s.193(3).

10–09   On receipt of deposited plans, the relevant council may, by order, vary the intended position, direction, termination or level of the new street in order to secure more direct, easier or more convenient means of communication with any other street or intended street, or to achieve an adequate opening at one end or at each of the ends of the new street, or to obtain compliance with any by-law in force within its area for the regulation of streets or buildings.[26] The points at which the new street is to be deemed to begin or end may be fixed, so defining the limits of the street for the purposes of the Highways Act 1980. Any person aggrieved by an order under this provision has a direct right of appeal to the Crown Court.[27] Laying out a street in contravention of such an order is a criminal offence. Compensation is payable to anyone who has suffered loss by the operation of these provisions. An order cannot require the developer to acquire land beyond his own membership, nor can it require the execution of works other than on the area intended for the new street.[28] There are similar requirements for the approval of plans where the construction of a new street involves the construction of a bridge.[29]

10–10   Where it is proposed to lay out a street along the line of an existing highway, but buildings are intended only on one side of that street, the authority may, instead of requiring the owner to widen the existing highway so as to comply with the by-laws, make an order permitting the highway to be widened, on the side proposed, to such width as would make the street not less than one half of the required width.[30] Notice of intention to make such an order must be sent to the landowners on both sides of the street. The order will have the effect of requiring the widening of the highway to comply with the by-laws on the opposite side of the street if any building occurs on that side. These provisions apply only to new buildings. Non-compliance with these provisions is a criminal offence. A right of appeal is given to the Crown Court.

Remedies for breach of the by-law provisions

10–11   If any work contravenes the by-laws, the relevant council may, by notice, require any person by or on whose behalf the work was executed either to remove the work or, if he so elects, to effect such necessary alterations to make it comply with the by-laws.[31] Where works have been commenced which will form a new thoroughfare[32] the council may, by notice, require works to be removed if they have already been started or alternatively may permit the works to continue subject to conditions which could legitimately have been imposed on the passing of plans. In

---

[26] Highways Act 1980, s.194(1).
[27] *Ibid.* s.194(3).
[28] *Ibid.* s.194(6).
[29] *Ibid.* s.195(1).
[30] *Ibid.* s.196.
[31] *Ibid.* s.197(1).
[32] Or otherwise fall within the provisions of Highways Act 1980, s.193(1)(*a*),(*b*).

this case only, if plans have not been rejected within the relevant period then they are deemed to have been passed. There are similar powers to require removal of works or to prohibit the continuance of works subject to conditions where work has been carried out in breach of conditions imposed on the passing of plans in respect of new streets which form parts of main thoroughfares.[33] In this case the right of appeal is to the magistrates' court.

Where notices have been served on any person requiring works to be removed or carried out subject to conditions, the council may remove the works in question or effect such alterations as it deems necessary after the expiration of 28 days (or any such other period as the magistrates' court may allow). The expenses of carrying out such works may be recovered by the council. These enforcement powers do not preclude any application for an injunction.[34] However, if such an application is made where plans have been deposited and passed, or where notice of rejection was not given within the appropriate period and the developer has executed works in accordance with those plans then, on granting an injunction, the council involved may be ordered to pay to the owner of the works such compensation as the court considers just. Contravention of conditions on the passing of plans is also a criminal offence. The conditions may, in any event, be enforced at any time by the council, against the owner for the time being of any land which the conditions relate. In other words, the conditions run with the land.[35] **10–12**

MAKING UP OF PRIVATE STREETS

Introduction

Part XI of the Highways Act 1980 is concerned with the making up of private streets. Basically, this covers the situation where a street which is not maintainable at the public expense is considered by the relevant local authority to be deficient in one or more respects and to require making up to highway standard. The authority may, by resolution, decide to make up the street. Initially, at least, this may be at the frontagers' expense. Before April 1, 1974 there were two procedures by which private streets could be made up. The first derived from the Public Health Act 1875. This was abolished by the Local Government Act 1972, Schedule 30. The other code was originally contained in the Private Street Works Act 1892 and is now contained in Part XI of the 1980 Act, and referred to as the "street works code". It must be noted, however, that authorities may still have powers to make up private streets under local Acts of Parliament. Also contained in Part XI of the 1980 Act is the "advance payments code," which is designed to ensure that when streets are constructed, but are not immediately to be adopted by **10–13**

---

[33] Or which otherwise fall within the provisions of Highways Act 1980, s. 193(1)(*a*).
[34] *Ibid.* s.197(7).
[35] *Ibid.* s.199.

way of an agreement under section 38 of the 1980 Act, these streets may subsequently be made up with the developer contributing some part of the expense of making up. This procedure has very largely fallen into disuse. Part XI is also concerned with emergency street works in private streets.

Private streets

10–14   The provisions of Part XI of the Highways Act 1980 apply only to private streets. A private street[36] is defined in three ways. First, it is a street which is not a highway maintainable at the public expense. Secondly, it is to include any land which is deemed to be a private street by virtue of section 232 of the Highways Act 1980.[37] Thirdly, for the application of the advance payments code or for the purposes of section 229,[38] the term includes any land shown as a proposed street on building regulation plans or on an application for planning permission under the Town and Country Planning Act 1971, together with any land which would have become part of the highway by virtue of section 188(6),[39] if work for the erection of the building had been commenced.

Outline of the code

10–15   The basic outline of the private street works code is as follows. The street works' authority[40] passes a resolution to execute street works within the street or within some part of the street. A specification of the street works required, an estimate of the probable expenses and a provisional apportionment of the expenses amongst the frontagers are then drawn up. Notices concerning the proposed street works are served, *inter alia*, on the frontagers. Owners of premises shown in the provisional apportionment as liable to be charged with part of the expenses of executing the works then have the opportunity to object on a specified, and somewhat limited, number of grounds. These objections may eventually be determined by a magistrates' court. Subsequently, after the street works have actually been executed, a final apportionment of the expense is served upon the frontagers who have a further limited right to object; the objection is again heard and determined by the magistrates' court. The relevant authority may then have power to recover, from the occupiers of the affected premises, the sums which are due in respect of the street works, and these sums may eventually become a charge against the property. There is a further opportunity to appeal to the Minister at the time when the relevant authority seeks to

---

[36] Highways Act 1980, s.203(2); as to the meaning of "street", see paras. 10–01 *et seq.*, above.

[37] Where land is defined in a development plan as the site of a proposed road.

[38] The section which enables a majority of frontagers to require adoption where advance payments have been made.

[39] *i.e.* by an order declaring an existing highway to be a new street; see para. 10–07, above.

[40] The council of a county, a metropolitan district, or a London borough or the Common Council of the City of London: Highways Act 1980, s.203(3), as amended by the Local Government Act 1985, s.8 and Sched. 4.

recover the expenses. This appeal must cover grounds other than those which could have been the subject of objections to the magistrates' court. Subsequently, the street in which the works have been carried out may become a highway maintainable at the public expense. The procedure is quite complex and will be discussed in more detail below.

Resolution of dissatisfaction

The street works' authority may, from time to time, resolve to **10–16** execute street works in a private street where that street is not sewered, levelled, paved, metalled, flagged, channelled, made good or lit to the satisfaction of the authority.[40a] Having so resolved, the authority must then instruct its proper officer to prepare specifications, plans, sections and a provisional apportionment, amongst all the relevant frontagers, of the expenses of the works. These are then submitted back to the authority for approval ("the resolution of approval") with or without modification. This approval must relate to the works with which the authority has expressed itself dissatisfied in the first resolution, and the modifications must therefore relate to such works, and may not include the addition of further areas of work.[41]

Extent and content of the resolution

Since the authority may express its dissatisfaction from time to time **10–17** about the state of the street, it may, therefore, find the street deficient in one respect at one time, and in another respect at another time, so long as the street remains a private street.[42] Difficult questions have, however, arisen as to whether the authority may express dissatisfaction in relation to any parts of the street in which it or its predecessors have previously carried out works, or for which it has been responsible for maintenance. These questions have, in the past, arisen in relation to sewers and lighting. Three situations may be identified. The first is where the street works' authority has become liable to maintain sewers in a street. The second is where there has been some act of the authority which is taken to be a past indication of satisfaction with the state of the street. The third is where the resolution expresses dissatisfaction with the extent of works previously carried out in the street, rather than with the condition of those works.

It seems clear that where the authority has carried out works for the **10–18** maintenance of which it thereafter became responsible, no further expression of dissatisfaction may be given in relation to the condition of those works.[43] Neither may the authority express dissatisfaction with a

---

[40a] Highways Act 1980, s.205(1).
[41] *Ibid*. s.205(2). See also *Ware U.D.C.* v. *Gaunt* [1960] 1 W.L.R. 1364.
[42] *Barry and Cadoxton Local Board* v. *Parry* [1895] 2 Q.B. 110.
[43] *Poole Corpn.* v. *Blake* [1956] 1 Q.B. 206; *East Barnet U.D.C.* v. *Stacey* [1939] 2 K.B. 861.

street which it has itself laid out.[44] Liability to maintain the street or sewer has fallen upon the ratepayers at large, and should not be thrown upon the frontagers by reason of the failure of the public body to perform its duty. Since 1974, the functions of the street works' authority and of the sewerage authority have been separated, in that the sewerage functions are now the responsibility of regional water authorities.[45] The principle that the frontagers cannot have imposed upon them a financial burden arising out of the default of the sewerage authority should not have been altered.

10–19 Questions have arisen on the law prior to the passing of the Public Health Act 1936, as to whether sewers in a street had already become maintainable at the public expense. To some extent this has become intertwined with the question of whether the previous acceptance of the condition of a street can preclude an authority from subsequently declaring its dissatisfaction with that condition. It is a well-established principle of administrative law that a public authority may not bind itself not to exercise a discretion, if to do so would be to defeat the purposes for which that discretion has been granted.[46] In the specific context of street works, it has been held that the action of a local authority, as part of a private contract in the making up of roads outside its area to the satisfaction of the Ecclesiastical Commissioners, did not estop that authority, when later the roads came within its area, from resolving that street works were required.[47] A promise by an authority not to charge certain premises with private street works will not prevent the authority from applying the code at a later date.[48] Acts of maintenance by a local authority in the street do not, of themselves, involve any acceptance or adoption of the street by that authority, but may be relevant evidence on the general question of whether the street is already an adopted highway.[49] The court may consider whether the authority has, at some earlier time, adopted the street or the sewer in the street. This is particularly relevant in relation to sewers constructed in streets prior to 1936—which generally will have become vested in the sewerage authority under the law then prevailing. Thus, under the provisions of the Public Health Act 1875,[50] a failure to express dissatisfaction with the state of a sewer at, or within a reasonable time of, its construction has been held to be evidence of the satisfaction of the authority with the construction of the sewer, resulting in the adoption of the sewer.[51] This has been held to be the case even though the sewer never became a working sewer,

---

[44] *Kingston on Hull Local Board* v. *Jones* (1856) 26 L.J. Ex 26.
[45] Although local authorities may still be the agents of the water authority.
[46] *Ayr Habour Trustees* v. *Oswald* (1883) 8 App. Cas.623.
[47] *Sunderland Corpn.* v. *Priestman* [1927] 2 Ch. 107. See also *Smith* v. *Croydon Local Board* (1868) 32 J.P. 709.
[48] *Dodworth U.D.C.* v. *Ibbotson* (1903) 67 J.P. 132.
[49] *Doncaster R.D.C.* v. *Freeman* (1973) 229 E.G. 263.
[50] ss.13 and 150 (now repealed).
[51] *Bonella* v. *Twickenham Local Board of Health* (1887) 20 Q.B.D. 63.

because it had no outfall.[52] Where a sewer had existed in a private street for many years prior to 1936, during which time no objection had been made by the local authority to its adequacy as a sewer, it was held that the street must have been sewered to the satisfaction of the local authority, thereby precluding a further resolution to carry out works to improve that sewer.[53]

The question as to whether the authority has expressed satisfaction **10–20** with the street is always a question of fact.[54] It may be necessary to consider whether the earlier expression of satisfaction actually covered the part of the street or the works which are the subject of the present resolution. Thus, an expression of satisfaction with the foul sewering of a street may not preclude a subsequent resolution dealing with the separate surface water drainage of the street.[55] It is less clear whether the authority may express dissatisfaction with the *extent* of works already carried out by itself or its predecessors, and require that further works be carried out. As indicated in the preceding paragraph, where a system of foul drainage has previously been installed, this would not preclude the authority from finding that it was not satisfied with the surface water drainage of the street and vice versa. Where, however, a public sewer has become overloaded because of the additional numbers of houses constructed in the street, the burden of the improvement cannot be placed on the frontagers.

The authority may resolve to execute street works in part only of the **10–21** street.[56] The resolution, therefore, may relate to a section of the street across its full width or to a longitudinal strip. Where an authority has resolved to carry out only some of the works which the section empowers, it may be critical to assess whether the works fall within the description in the resolution. Thus, parts of the drainage systems may more properly be regarded as part of the sewerage system than as part of the making up of the carriageway.[57]

Fences and walls

These cannot be included in the works even though their removal or **10–22** renovation may be necessary to make the street up to a satisfactory standard. They will not form part of the street and cannot, therefore, be the

---

[52] *Hornsey Local Board* v. *Davis* [1893] 1 Q.B. 756.
[53] *Re Jesty's Avenue, Broadway, Weymouth* [1940] 2 K.B. 65; *Wilmslow U.D.C.* v. *Sidebottom* (1906) 70 J.P. 537; *East Barnet U.D.C.* v. *Stacey* [1939] 2 K.B. 861.
[54] *Bloor* v. *Beckenham U.D.C.* [1908] 2 K.B. 671; *Handsworth D.C.* v. *Derrington* [1897] 2 Ch. 438.
[55] *Poole Corpn.* v. *Blake* [1956] 1 Q.B. 206; *cf. East Barnet U.D.C.* v. *Stacey* [1939] 2 K.B. 861.
[56] Highways Act 1980, ss.205(2), 329(1).
[57] *Wandsworth B.C.* v. *Golds* [1911] 1 K.B. 60; *East Barnet U.D.C.* v. *Stacey* [1939] 2 K.B. 861.; *Bloor* v. *Beckenham U.D.C.* [1908] 2 K.B. 671; *Ware U.D.C.* v. *Gaunt* [1960] 1 W.L.R. 1364.

subject of the street works. Retaining walls may, however, form part of the street itself.[58]

Footpaths

10–23   Public footpaths in existence before the coming into force of the National Parks and Access to the Countryside Act 1949 will, prima facie, have been repairable at the public expense.[59] Thus, such footpaths cannot be included in the works.[60] The reason for this is that footpaths were excluded from the provisions of section 23 of the Highway Act 1835. That section did apply to roads laid out as occupation ways after the passing of the Act. Where public rights on foot have grown up over such roads, however, then they still remain caught by section 23, and neither the roads nor the footpaths will have become maintainable.[61] Where, therefore, a public footpath runs along the line of a street, it is necessary to know whether the public right pre-dated the laying out of the street. If it did, then unless the line of the footpath can be distinguished from the remainder of the street, the public right of way will be taken to extend over the full width of the street.[62]

Other necessary works

10–24   Section 206 of the Highways Act 1980 provides that a street works' authority may include in street works to be executed under the street works code, any works which it believes to be necessary for bringing the street, as regards sewage, drainage, level or other matters, into conformity with other streets (whether or not maintainable at the public expense) including the provision of separate sewers for the reception of sewerage and of surface water respectively.[63] The works within the street may, therefore, include a sewer, a footway, and provision for drainage or lighting where there were no such works previously. The authority may also include a variation of the respective widths of the footway and carriageway in a street,[64] but otherwise the highway authority must take the street as it is found.[65] The power to carry out these works will not otherwise, however, justify the carrying out of more extensive works than are necessary for the street, and which benefit other areas, unless the authority itself bears the extra costs involved.[66]

---

[58] See Chap.4.
[59] See para. 12–12, below.
[60] See *Richmond Corpn.* v. *Robinson* [1955] 1 All E.R. 321.
[61] *Margate Corpn.* v. *Roach* [1960] 1 W.L.R. 1380; *Ware U.D.C.* v. *Gaunt* [1960] 1 W.L.R. 1364.
[62] See also on a similiar point. *Kingston upon Thames Corpn.* v. *Baverstock* (1909) 100 L.T. 935.
[63] The extent of this provision was considered in *Poole Corpn.* v. *Blake* [1956] 1 Q.B. 206.
[64] Highways Act 1980, s.226(1).
[65] *Robertson* v. *Bristol Corpn.* [1900] 2 Q.B. 198.
[66] *cf. Acton U.D.C.* v. *Watts* (1903) 1 L.G.R. 594; see also Public Health Act 1936, s.19.

Abandonment

The resolution may be expressly rescinded. The passage of a sub-**10–25**
sequent resolution or inaction on the initial resolution over a period of
time may lead to the resolution being treated as having been abandoned.[67]

Procedure

When preparing the specification, a county council must, if the works**10–26**
include the sewering of the street, consult the council of the district in
which the works are to be carried out.[68] After the resolution of approval
has been passed, a notice must be published in each of two successive
weeks in a local newspaper circulating in the area of the authority.[69]
This notice must contain a statement to the effect that the authority has
resolved to execute street works in the private street, and must contain
information as to where and at what times the resolution and other
documents may be inspected. The notice must also contain a statement
to the effect that an owner of premises liable to be charged with any part
of the expenses of executing the street works may object to the proposal
to execute works, and it must give the period during which such objection may be made.[70] Similiar notices must be posted in a prominent position, in or near to the street to which the resolution relates, at least
once in each of three successive weeks. Within seven days from the date
of first publication of the newspaper notice, a further notice containing
the same particulars must be served on the owners of premises shown in
the provisional apportionment as liable to be charged, together with a
statement of the sum apportioned on those premises by the provisional
apportionment.[71] Failure to serve an owner will prevent the recovery of
expenses from him.[72] For a period of one month from the date of the
first newspaper notice, a copy of the resolution and copies of the
approved documents must be kept on deposit and available for inspection at the offices of the street works' authority and, where relevant, at
the offices of the non-metropolitan district council. There is power to
amend the specification, apportionment, etc., from time to time.[73]
When this is done, a similiar procedure applies.

Provisional apportionment

The decision to apportion the expenses of making up the street**10–27**
amongst the premises fronting the street will have been taken at the
time of the resolution of dissatisfaction. The provisional apportionment

[67] *Southampton Corpn.* v. *Lord* (1903) 67 J.P. 189; *Glynn Evans* v. *Liverpool Corpn.*
[1959] 2 Q.B. 249; *Wilson* v. *Wrexham Corpn.* [1960] 1 W.L.R. 319.
[68] Highways Act 1980, s.205(4).
[69] See *Aberdeen (City)* v. *Watt* (1901) 3 F. (Ct. of Sess.) 787.
[70] Highways Act 1980, s.205(5) and Sched. 16.
[71] Highways Act 1980, s.205(5), (6).
[72] *Maguire* v. *Leigh on Sea U.D.C.* (1906) 70 J.P. 479; *Wirral R.D.C.* v. *Carter* [1903] 1
K.B. 646. See also Highways Act 1980, s.297.
[73] *Ibid.* s.210; see also *Wilson* v. *Wrexham Corpn.* [1960] 1 W.L.R. 319.

will then apportion the expenses according to length of frontage. The authority may, however, resolve that in settling the apportionment, regard should be had to the greater or lesser degree of benefit to be derived by any premises from the street works, and/or to the amount and value of any work already done by the owners or occupiers of any premises.[74] The authority may also resolve to include premises which do not front the street but which have access to it, and which, in the opinion of the authority, will be benefited by the works. It may then fix the amount to be apportioned to those premises according to the degree of benefit to be derived by those premises.[75] Frontage, however, remains the overriding consideration,[76] and cannot be disregarded by the authority. The apportionment will have to be adjusted amongst the other properties according to frontage. The provisional apportionment must state the amounts charged on the respective premises, the names of the respective owners, or reputed owners, whether the apportionment is made according to the frontage of the respective premises or not, the measurements of the frontages and the other considerations (if any) on which the apportionment is based.[77] The adoption of any of the modifications to frontage basis of apportionment should be expressly referred to in one of the resolutions, although the approval of the provisional apportionment, which itself states the other considerations taken into account, may be sufficient.[78]

Apportionment according to frontage

10–28   The word "fronting" includes "adjoining" and "adjoining" includes "abutting."[79] This extended definition seems to indicate that there should be some physical contact between the premises and the street. Thus, an upstairs maisonette which was separated from the street by the garden over the ground floor property was held not to have a frontage to the street in *Buckinghamshire County Council* v. *Trigg*[80] In that case, however, the property was separated from the street by the frontage of other premises. A mere difference in level between the premises and the street would not prevent those premises from fronting onto the street.[81] In the *Buckinghamshire* case, Salmon J., in his concurring judgment, appears to have used a test of "close proximity."[82] In one early case, the presence of a stream, separating the premises from the street, was ignored in deciding whether the premises fronted the street.[83] On the

---

[74] Highways Act 1980, s.207(2).
[75] *Ibid.* s.207(3).
[76] *Parkstone Primrose Laundry Ltd.* v. *Poole Corpn.* (1950) 48 L.G.R. 637.
[77] Highways Act 1980, Sched. 16.
[78] *Oakley* v. *Merthyr Tydfil Corpn.* [1922] 1 K.B. 409; *Hornchurch U.D.C.* v. *Webber* [1938] 1 All E.R. 309; *cf. Bridgewater Corpn.* v. *Stone* (1908) 72 J.P. 487.
[79] Highways Act 1980, ss.203 and 329(1).
[80] [1963] 1 W.L.R. 155.
[81] *Newport Urban Sanitary Authority* v. *Graham* (1882) 9 Q.B.D. 183.
[82] [1963] 1 W.L.R. 155 at 163.
[83] See *Wakefield Local Board of Health* v. *Lee* (1876) 1 Ex. D. 336.

other hand, in *Lightbound* v. *Higher Bebington Local Board*,[84] it was held that the presence of a public footpath running between the premises and the street prevented those premises from fronting the street. The court, however, had regard not only to the fact that there was no physical contact between the premises and the street, but also to the fact that there was no advantage to the premises from the street.

In some cases, it is alleged that a strip of land has been left between **10–29** the properties apparently fronting the street and the street itself. The question here will be whether the strip has been "thrown into" the street or, where the remainder of the street is itself a highway, whether it has become dedicated to the public. Such a conclusion may be difficult where there is evidence that the strip was deliberately retained in order to prevent the properties behind it from becoming liable to road charges. In *Warwickshire County Council* v. *Adkins*,[85] a developer had left a strip of land some 12 feet wide between the properties alongside the street and the street itself. The original purpose of the strip was to comply with a planning condition that room be left for the widening of the street, and thereafter the strip had been left uncultivated and used only for car parking and for access to the houses. It was held that the only conclusion that could be drawn with respect to this strip was that it had become part of the street.[86]

Exemptions from the charges

The charge for street works falls upon the owner of property; where **10–30** there is no such owner, therefore, the charge cannot fall. Such property is described as land *extra commercium*. This is complicated by the somewhat obscure definition of "owner" in the Highways Act 1980 and other similiar statutes.[87] In calculating the apportionment, all the premises in the street must be taken into account including those which are *extra commercium* or otherwise exempt.[88]

In order to be classed as land which is *extra commercium*[89]: **10–31**

> "it must be shown that the premises have not got an owner because of some statute, or by the common law, or by some irrevocable disposition which is to endure forever, the land in question is struck with sterility."

This is not always an easy test to apply. Trustees of a school have been

---

[84] (1885) 16 Q.B.D. 577.
[85] (1967) 66 L.G.R. 486.
[86] See also *West End Lawn Tennis Club (Pinner) Ltd.* v. *Harrow Corpn.* (1965) 64 L.G.R. 35.
[87] Highways Act 1980, s.329(1); see also para. 15–22, below.
[88] *Herne Bay U.C.* v. *Payne and Wood* [1907] 2 K.B. 130.
[89] *Ibid. per* Lord Alverstone C.J. at 140; see also *Wright* v. *Ingle* (1885) 16 Q.B.D. 379.

held to be owners, even though the School Sites Act 1841 restricted the use of the land.[90] A common held by a local authority and dedicated in perpetuity to the public as a recreation ground has been held to be *extra commercium*,[91] but not land acquired and held by an authority to be used as public walks or pleasure grounds under section 164 of the Public Health Act 1875[92]—apparently because the court took the view that the land could be alienated in certain circumstances. A cemetery company which could not alienate its land but which was empowered to sell the right of burial within individual plots was held to be the owner of the cemetery.[93] Statutory undertakers have been held to be the owners of land essential for the operation of their undertaking,[94] and the Lord of the Manor the owner in respect of the soil of a common.[95] The owner of the sub-soil of a highway entering the private street is not chargeable in respect of street works, and this land is *extra commercium*, since it could not be let at a rack rent.[96] Street ends should also be treated in the same way as cross streets. Their presence should be taken into account in the apportionment, but the sum relating to that frontage will be charged to the authority.[97]

10–32 Land held by the Crown is excluded from the provisions as to apportionment[98] unless these provisions are applied by agreement.[99] The incumbent or Minister or trustee of a place of public religious worship is not liable for the expenses of street works as the owner of that place or of a churchyard or burial ground attached to it. In this case, the proportion of the expenses which would otherwise be borne by this property expressly falls upon the street works' authority.[1] Under the earlier law, this exemption was restricted to buildings exclusively used for public worship.[2] Under the present law, all the land in the curtilage of the church could fall within the definition, although the reference to a churchyard or burial ground "attached to it"[3] might suggest that apart

---

[90] *Bowditch* v. *Wakefield Local Board* (1871) L.R. 6 Q.B. 567; *Hornsey D.C.* v. *Smith* [1897] 1 Ch. 843.

[91] *London C.C.* v. *Wandsworth B.C.* [1903] 1 Q.B. 797; *Plumstead Board of Works* v. *British Land Company* (1874) L.R. 10 Q.B. 203.

[92] *Herne Bay U.C.* v. *Payne & Wood* [1907] 2 K.B. 130; see also *St. Mary Islington, Vestry* v. *Cobbett* [1895] 1 Q.B. 369; *Fulham Vestry* v. *Minter* [1901] 1 K.B. 501.

[93] *St. Giles, Camberwell, Vestry* v. *London Cemetery Co.* [1894] 1 Q.B. 699.

[94] *Hackney Corpn.* v. *Lee Conservancy* [1904] 2 K.B. 541; *Hampstead Corpn.* v. *Midland Ry. Co.* [1905] 1 K.B. 539.

[95] *Re Christchurch Inclosure Act, Meyrick* v. *Att.-Gen.* [1894] 3 Ch. 209.

[96] *Plumstead Board of Works* v. *British Land Co.* (1874) L.R. 10 Q.B. 203; *Stretford U.D.C.* v. *Manchester South Junction and Altrincham Ry. Co.* (1903) 68 J.P. 59.

[97] See the discussion of this point at para. 2–341 of the *Encyclopedia of Highway Law and Practice*, Vol.1.

[98] *Hornsey U.C.* v. *Hennell* [1902] 2 K.B. 73.

[99] Highways Act 1980, s.327.

[1] *Ibid.* s.215.

[2] *North Manchester Overseers* v. *Winstanley* [1908] 1 K.B. 835; *Walton le Dale U.D.C.* v. *Greenwood* (1911) 105 L.T. 547; *Ilford Corpn.* v. *Mallinson* (1932) 30 L.G.R. 201.

[3] See *Holy Law South Broughton Burial Board* v. *Failsworth U.D.C.* [1928] 1 K.B. 231.

from this extension, the exemption still applies to the building alone. Equally, it is not obvious that there is still the necessity for the premises to be exclusively used for worship, provided that they are used for church purposes.

Railway and canal undertakers are not to be deemed to be owners or **10–33** occupiers of land upon which a street wholly or partly fronts, if the land has no direct communication with the street, and at the time of the laying out of the street was used solely as part of the line of the railway, canal, siding, station, towing path or works, by those or other undertakers.[4] In this case, the burden of the apportioned expenses relating to this property falls on the other frontagers; it is subject to repayment by the undertakers if subsequently connected to the street.[5] If the undertakers' land is mistakenly included in the apportionment, then they must lodge an objection to avoid being bound by it.[6]

Apportionment according to benefit

Where the benefit test is adopted, the authority must direct its mind **10–34** to the question of whether any property benefits more than any other. No guidance is given as to what factors may be taken into consideration in coming to these conclusions, but the particular demands or needs of certain types of properties calling for a higher specification than would otherwise be required, or the fact that some properties have flank or rear frontages to the street, will be relevant. The authority's decision to apportion on a frontage rather than on the benefit basis cannot be challenged in the magistrates' court,[7] but the inequity thereby caused may be raised in the appeal to the Minister.[8]

Inclusion of properties having access to the street

Whether or not access is gained to the street through a court or pas- **10–35** sage or otherwise is principally a question of fact. However, access in this context has been interpreted as meaning "something in the nature of a feeder of the street."[9] Premises fronting a part of the street which is not to be made up cannot be charged for having access to that part which is to be made up.[10] Whether access from another private street may be considered has been subject to different views,[11] but it seems

---

[4] Highways Act 1980, s.216. See also *R.* v. *Jones and Barry U.D.C.*, *ex p. Mein* (1907) 71 J.P. 326; *Re Carlisle Corpn. and Saul's Executors* (1907) 71 J.P. 502.
[5] Highways Act 1980, s.216(2), (3).
[6] *Watford Corpn.* v. *London Passenger Transport Board* [1945] K.B. 129.
[7] *Bridgewater Corpn.* v. *Stone* (1908) 72 J.P. 487; *Chester Corpn.* v. *Briggs* [1924] 1 K.B. 239; *Allen* v. *Hornchurch U.D.C.* [1938] 2 K.B. 654.
[8] See para. 10–49, below.
[9] *Oakley* v. *Merthyr Tydfil Corpn.* [1922] 1 K.B. 409.
[10] *Chadderton* v. *Glanford R.D.C.* [1915] 3 K.B. 707.
[11] *cf. Chadderton* v. *Glanford R.D.C.* [1915] 3 K.B. 707 and *Newquay U.C.* v. *Rickeard* [1911] 2 K.B. 846.

clear that access over streets which are adopted or which are laid out as public streets must be disregarded.[12]

Specification, plans, sections and estimate

10–36 The specification must describe generally the works and what is to be done, and in the case of structural works must specify, as far as practicable, the foundation, form, material and dimensions thereof. The plans and section must show the constructional character of the works, the connections (if any) with existing streets, sewers or other works, and the line and levels of the works (subject to any indicated limits of deviation).[13] The estimate must show the probable costs of all the works including any additional charge for surveys, superintendence and notices.[14] The estimate may also include an item for contingencies.[15]

Objections to proposed works

10–37 An owner of premises liable to be charged in respect of street works in a provisional apportionment has one month from the date of the first publication of the newspaper notice to object to the provisional apportionment on specified grounds. The objection, if not withdrawn, will then be determined by a magistrates' court. The grounds, which are set out below, are limited and exclusive.[16] They may be raised only by objection at this stage, and not in any other proceeding[17]; however, there is a further right of appeal to the Minister at a later stage and on different and somewhat wider grounds of appeal.[18] It may also be possible to challenge the validity of the resolutions of the authority by way of judicial review, on the basis that they are a nullity.[19] However, certain procedural or formal defects may be the subject of an objection under section 208(1)(*b*), and judicial review in relation to these matters is unlikely to be available. An objection is made by serving a notice on the local authority, specifying the grounds of objection. The objection must be made on the correct grounds and must be made in time. In *Brighton Borough Council* v. *Peachy (Investments)*,[20] it was held that since the justices had no power to amend an objection, choice of the incorrect ground of was fatal. The safest course is, therefore, where there is uncertainty as to the correct ground of objection, to object on several grounds initially and withdraw those which are inappropriate later.

---

[12] *Newquay U.C.* v. *Rickeard* [1911] 2 K.B. 846.
[13] Highways Act 1980, Sched. 16.
[14] *Ibid.*
[15] *Standring* v. *Bexhill Corpn.* (1909) 73 J.P. 241.
[16] *Southampton Corpn.* v. *Lord* (1903) 67 J.P. 189.
[17] Highways Act 1980, s.217.
[18] *Ibid.* s.233; para. 10–49, below. See also *R.* v. *Minister of Health, ex p. Aldridge* [1925] 2 K.B. 363.
[19] See *Wilson* v. *Wrexham Corpn.* [1960] 1 W.L.R. 319.
[20] [1957] J.P.L. 585.

Since the time limit for registering an objection is a statutory time limit, it is not capable of being extended.[21]

Subject matter of the resolution is not a private street

This objection is, of course, fundamental to the whole proceedings. **10–38**
Objection can be made on the ground that all or part of the area to be made up is not a "street," or that it is not a "private street" (that is, that the street is an adopted highway). It is under this ground that the extent of the works may be examined, to establish that, included within the works, is land which is not part of a street; for example, a fence, wall or bank.[22] It may also be alleged that the road in question is not a street as defined in the Act.[23] Principally, this ground will raise the question of whether or not the road has been adopted by the highway authority in the past, or whether it is an "ancient highway." It may be, especially with respect to footpaths, that part of the street has been adopted and that part has not.[24] If the street is a highway, the burden of proof in establishing that it is not maintainable at the public expense is on the local highway authority.[25]

Material informality, defect or error in, or in respect of, the resolution, notice, plans, sections or estimate

An example of challenge on this ground would be where the pro- **10–39**
visional apportionment includes works which were not within the terms of the resolution of dissatisfaction.[26] Otherwise, if the notices have not been properly published or served, or if the particulars contained in the estimate, etc., are incorrect, there may be a ground of challenge under this head. The value of this ground of objection in relation to purely procedural errors is principally one of delay, since the authority may simply re-start the whole process. The magistrates have power to adjourn the hearing to enable further notices to be given.[27]

Proposed works are insufficient or unreasonable

This ground relates only to the sufficiency or reasonableness of the **10–40**
works with regard to the intended scheme of the authority. Matters cannot be raised under this head to suggest that the works should be carried out in conjunction with other works relating to other streets.[28] It may, on the other hand, be argued that the works are to a higher standard than is necessary for the road[29] or that the works are not sufficient to

[21] See also Highways Act 1980, s.209(1).
[22] See para. 10–22, above.
[23] See paras. 10–01 *et seq.*, above.
[24] See Highways Act 1980, Sched. 23, para. 12.
[25] *Huyton with Roby U.D.C.* v. *Hunter* [1955] 1 W.L.R. 603.
[26] See *Ware U.D.C.* v. *Gaunt* [1960] 1 W.L.R. 1364, and para. 10–16, above.
[27] Highways Act 1980, s.209(2).
[28] *Mansfield* v. *Butterworth* [1898] 2 Q.B. 274; *Bognor Regis U.D.C.* v. *Boldero* [1962] 2 Q.B. 448.
[29] But see Highways Act 1980, s.206 and para. 10–24, above.

achieve the objective of sewering, etc., the street, to the satisfaction of the council. The justices have no power to impose any part of the financial burden on the authority.[30] In *Southgate Borough Council v. Park Estates (Southgate) Ltd.*,[31] it was held that the justices were entitled to take account of the fact that the works were premature, since utility services which would require the breaking up of the road were likely, within a short space of time, to be laid in the street. The adoption by the authority of the frontage or any other basis of assessment cannot be challenged under this ground, nor can the inclusion of any particular frontager in the apportionment.[32]

Estimated expenses of the proposed works are excessive

10–41   This ground is very limited and, in practice, of very little use. It is restricted to argument that the charges for the specified works are too great. This will generally be met by the response that the authority has been out to tender. It cannot be used to argue that particular works should not be included in the apportionment.

Premises ought to be excluded from or inserted in provisional apportionment

10–42   Again this ground is limited. The objectors may not argue that regard should have been had to the degree of benefit enjoyed by the properties if the authority has not resolved to take this into consideration under section 207, or vice versa.[33] It can argue that its property does not front the street[34] or, where appropriate, that its property does not have access to the street.[35] These matters can only be raised at this stage.[36] It is important, therefore, that a person served as an owner with notice of the provisional apportionment should carry out a close inspection both of the title deeds and on the ground to ascertain that the property is properly included. An indemnity given by the authority to landowners in the past to the effect that they would not be liable to road charges has been held not to be a valid ground of objection under this head[37]

Incorrect provisional apportionment

10–43   Here it can be alleged that the provisional apportionment is incorrect in respect of some matter of fact to be specified in the objection or, where the provisional apportionment is made with regard to consider-

---

[30] *Coulsdon and Purley U.D.C. v. Cherry* (1965) 63 L.G.R. 283; *Chester Corpn. v. Briggs* [1924] 1 K.B. 239; *Chatham Corpn. v. Wright* (1929) 94 J.P. 43; *Allen v. Hornchurch U.D.C.* [1938] 2 K.B. 654.
[31] [1954] 1 Q.B. 359.
[32] *Chatham Corpn. v. Wright and Le Mesurier* (1929) 94 J.P. 43; *Allen v. Hornchurch U.D.C* [1938] 2 K.B. 65.
[33] *Hornchurch U.D.C. v. Webber* [1938] 1 All E.R. 309; see also para. 10–27, above.
[34] See para. 10–28, above.
[35] See para. 10–35, above.
[36] *Wallasey U.D.C. v. Walker (W.H.) & Co.* (1906) 70 J.P. 199; *Porthcawl U.D.C. v. Brogden* [1917] 1 Ch. 534.
[37] *Dodworth U.D.C. v. Ibbotson* (1903) 67 J.P. 132.

ations other than frontage, in respect of the degree of benefit to be derived by any premises, or of the amount or value of any works already carried out by the owner or occupier of premises. Matters which may be raised under other grounds of objection would also appear to fall within this objection, and it may be desirable to include both grounds. Specifically, this is the place to argue that the authority has made a factual mistake in the apportionment (for example, a wrongly measured frontage). It may also be the place to argue that land is *extra commercium* or is otherwise exempt, if the error is one of fact.[38]

Hearing and determination of objections

At the end of the 28 day period for lodging an objection, the street **10-44** works' authority may apply to a magistrates' court to appoint a time for the hearing and determination of all objections which have been made within the required time limit, and have not been withdrawn. Notice of the time and place must then be served on the objectors.[39] The application to the court must be made by way of a complaint for an order.[40] The authority need not make the application to the court if it abandons the scheme. Where the authority amends the scheme,[41] a similar process of objection and reference to the court follows.

The function of the justices is to hear and determine the objection in **10-45** the same manner, as far as possible, as if the authority were proceeding summarily against the objectors to enforce payment of a sum of money summarily recoverable. This means that the authority opens the proceedings, and that the burden of proof is upon the authority to establish the matters required to justify its apportionment. The justices may then quash in whole or in part or amend the resolution of approval, the specification, plans, sections, estimate and provisional apportionment, or any of these. The court may also adjourn to enable further notices to be given. The court may not adopt a different basis of assessment from that adopted by the authority notwithstanding its power to amend the resolution of the authority,[42] but, where frontage has been miscalculated or where benefit has been taken into account, the court may re-adjust the apportionment between premises. In so doing, the court may not reduce the apportionment of certain properties without compensating for this adjustment in relation to other properties or giving the authority time to resolve whether or not to contribute to the expenses.[43] In *Twickenham Urban Council* v. *Munton*,[44] a decision by magistrates to amend the

---

[38] It may also fall under the ground discussed in para. 10–42, above.
[39] Highways Act 1980, s.209(1).
[40] *Ibid.* s.316.
[41] Under *ibid.* s.210.
[42] See para. 10–27, above.
[43] *Chatham Corpn.* v. *Wright* (1929) 28 L.G.R. 4.
[44] [1892] 2 Ch. 603.

scheme to exclude a part of the street which was found to be maintainable at the public expense was upheld. However, where major alterations are required, it may be desirable to adjourn to enable fresh notices to be served or, in some cases, to quash the whole scheme. The court is limited to determining the objections raised before it and has no power of its own initiative to amend the scheme.[45] Costs are in the discretion of the court, but where an objector is ordered to pay the costs it may be ordered that the local authority pay the costs in the first instance, and that they be added to the expenses of the street works, to be recovered as a charge on that property or on the property of the different objectors, as appears to be just.

Final apportionment

10–46   When the street works have been completed and their expenses ascertained, the proper officer of the council makes the final apportionment, by dividing the expenses in the same proportions as those in which the estimated expenses were divided in the original or amended provisional apportionment. Notice of this final apportionment is then served on the owners of the premises affected. These owners then have 28 days to make further objection.[46] The grounds of objection on this occasion are that:

(a) there has been an unreasonable departure from the specification, plans, and sections;

(b) the actual expenses have without sufficient reason exceeded the estimated expenses by more than 15 per cent.;

(c) the apportionment has not been made in accordance with the requirements of section 211.

There is then an identical procedure for reference to the magistrates' court and determination of the objections as there was for the provisional apportionment. In this case the magistrates' court will have power to quash or amend the final apportionment.[47] The stated grounds are the only matters which can be raised before the magistrates. In *Hayles* v. *Sandown Urban District Council*,[48] it was held that the failure of the authority to complete the works could not be raised. However, it would seem that since the jurisdiction of the officer to prepare the final apportionment depends upon such completion, judicial review might be available to quash the apportionment on this ground. There is little authority on these grounds of appeal. It seems likely that the inclusion

---

[45] *R.* v. *West Kent Quarter Sessions Appeal Committee, ex p. Jarvis* (1955) 119 J.P. 302; but see *Hall* v. *Bolsover U.D.C.* (1909) 73 J.P. 140.
[46] Highways Act 1980, s.211.
[47] See para. 10–45, above.
[48] [1903] 1 K.B. 169.

in the final apportionment of the legal costs of determining objections would be found to be properly included.

Recovery of expenses

The street works' authority may, from time to time, recover expenses **10–47** from the owner for the time being of any premises in respect of which the whole of or any part of the expenses of the street works are due.[49] Interest is recoverable from the date of the final apportionment at such reasonable rates as the authority may determine. The apportioned sum is a charge on the premises registrable in Part II of the local land charges register.[50] The charges may be recovered against the owner for the time being and there is nothing to prevent a fresh demand being served on each new owner.[51] Until it is registered, the street works' authority has the same powers and remedies in respect of the charge as if it were a mortgage by deed having powers of sale and lease and the power to appoint a receiver.[52] The authority may also declare that the expenses under the final apportionment, together with interest, be payable by annual instalments within a period not exceeding 30 years. Any instalment may then be recovered from the owner *or occupier* of the premises for the time being.[53] Whilst this procedure has the advantage of enabling recovery against the occupier (who may be more visible than the owner), it carries with it accompanying disadvantages. The decision to seek repayment by instalments may not be rescinded without the consent of the landowner.[54] Failure to meet one payment does not render the whole due.[55]

The expenses of making up the street, together with interest from the **10–48** date of service of a demand, may be recovered either summarily or in a court of competent jurisidiction.[56] Time for recovery of expenses runs from the date of service of the demand or from the date on which the Minister's decision on appeal is notified to the appellant or from the date on which the appeal is withdrawn.[57] Provision is made for recovery in the case of transfers designed to evade road charges.[58] Where some other person satisfies the authority that money has been paid or advanced for street works' expenses, the authority may grant that person an order charging the premises with payment of an annuity[59] to

---

[49] Highways Act 1980, s.212(1).
[50] Local Land Charges Act 1975; Local Land Charges Rules 1977 (S.I. 1977 No. 985).
[51] *Dennerly* v. *Prestwich U.D.C.* [1930] 1 K.B. 334.
[52] Highways Act 1980, s.212(3); Law of Property Act 1925, s.101.
[53] Highways Act 1980, s.305(2). Subject to the right of the occupier to recover from the owner by deduction from rent: see *ibid.* Sched. 13.
[54] *Tottenham Local Board of Health* v. *Rowell* (1880) 15 Ch.D. 378.
[55] *Payne* v. *Cardiff R.D.C.* [1932] 1 K.B. 241.
[56] Highways Act 1980, s.305.
[57] *Ibid.* s.306.
[58] *Ibid.* s.235.
[59] *Ibid.* ss.237(2), s.237(4) and Sched. 13.

repay the sum so expended or advanced. There is an appeal to the magistrates's court against the making or refusal to make such an order.

Appeal to the Minister

10–49   A person aggrieved by the decision of a street works' authority, in a case where the authority is empowered to recover the expenses of making up a private street under the street works code, may appeal to the Minister who may then make such order as appears to him to be equitable. His decision is final and binding on the parties.[60] The appeal must be brought within 21 days from the date on which the demand for payment of the expenses or any part of them was first served on the person wishing to appeal. The appeal must state the grounds on which it is made, and a copy must be served on the street works' authority. Any proceedings for recovery of the expenses are thereupon stayed. The Minister may, if he thinks fit, as part of his decision order the authority to pay compensation to the appellant for loss and damage sustained by reason of the proceedings.[61] An appeal cannot be made, however, on any ground which could have been the subject of an objection to the magistrates' court.[62]

10–50   The powers of the Minister on appeal are very wide and include his determination on any relevant question of law.[63] An analysis of appeal decisions appears in the *Encyclopedia of Highway Law and Practice*.[64]

Contribution by street works' authority

10–51   A street works' authority may at any time resolve to bear the whole or a portion of the expenses of any street works in its area under the private street works code, and the effect of such a resolution is to discharge or reduce proportionately the liabilities of the owners of all the premises in the street.[65] An authority may not select deserving cases from a particular street. The authority is expressly empowered, however, to resolve to bear, in whole or in part, the costs of the owners of rear or flank frontagers, but again this resolution must benefit all such frontagers affected by the relevant street works.[66] There is no express remedy for a failure to make these resolutions, although such a failure is one of the matters which could be raised on an appeal to the Minister.[67] A magistrates' court dealing with an appeal under section 209(2)[68] cannot

---

[60] Highways Act 1980, s.233, although an application for judicial review against this decision may still lie in appropriate circumstances; *R. v. Medical Appeal Tribunal, ex p. Gilmore* [1957] 1 Q.B. 574.

[61] Highways Act 1980, s.233(4).

[62] *Ibid.* ss.233(1) and 217; *R. v. Minister of Health ex p. Aldridge* [1925] 2 K.B. 363.

[63] *R. v. Minister of Housing and Local Government, ex p. Finchley B.C.* [1955] 1 W.L.R. 29.

[64] Vol. 1, paras. 2–395 *et seq.*

[65] Highways Act 1980, s.236(1).

[66] *Ibid.* s.236(2).

[67] *Chatham Corpn. v. Wright* (1929) 142 L.T. 431.

[68] See para. 10–44, above.

vary the proportion which the authority has resolved to contribute and cannot reduce a provisional apportionment so as to have this effect.[69]

ADVANCE PAYMENTS CODE

In order to ensure that when new buildings are constructed the roads **10–52** which serve those streets may be adopted by local highway authorities without placing a financial burden either on the highway authority or on the owners of the premises then fronting onto the street, a procedure exists for ensuring that a payment is made, or security[70] provided, by the developer to cover the future need to make up the street and to enable frontagers to require the carrying out of streets works and the adoption of the street when development has reached a certain stage.[71] A payment made and security given will be registrable as a local land charge.[72] This procedure, known as the advance payments code, is much less used than hitherto, and in most cases a developer will construct roads to highway authority standards and dedicate the roads as highways pursuant to section 38 of the Highways Act 1980. The advance payments code applies in all outer London boroughs, in all areas in counties in which the code was in force before April 1974,[73] and in any parish or community in which the advance payments code has since been adopted by resolution of the county council in accordance with Schedule 15.[74] The procedure applies where it is proposed to erect a building for which plans are required to be deposited with the local authority in accordance with building regulations[75] and which will have a frontage onto a private street which could be subject to the street works code. It is sufficient that the authority has power to pass a resolution under section 205,[76] and it is not necessary that it should actually have passed such a resolution.[77] Until the payment is made or security is given, no work may be done in erecting the building. Work carried out in contravention of these provisions renders the landowner and the builder liable to a criminal offence.[78]

There are a number of exceptions to the provisions of section 205. It **10–53** does not apply to those owners who would be exempt from apportionment

---

[69] *Purley U.D.C.* v. *Cherry* (1965) 63 L.G.R. 283.
[70] As to security by means of a charge on land, see Building Societies Act 1986, ss.11, 12 and Sched 4.
[71] Highways Act 1980, s.219(1).
[72] Local Land Charges Act 1975.
[73] Under the provisions of Highways Act 1959.
[74] Or *ibid.* Sched. 14.
[75] See Public Health Act 1936, s.64; Building Act 1984, Part I; see also Housing and Building Control Act 1984, ss. 39, 40(2), (3), 46 and Sched. 8. There is an exemption where the plans were deposited before a certain date: Highways Act 1980, s.219(4)(c).
[76] See paras. 10–16 *et seq.*, above.
[77] See *Ramsden* v. *Bowercastle* (1982) 80 L.G.R. 182.
[78] Highways Act 1980, s.219(2); as to a defence available to a builder who is not the owner of the property, see subs.(3).

under the street works code,[79] nor to buildings to be erected within the curtilage[80] of and appurtenant to an existing building.[81] Buildings having a frontage to part of a street which is the subject of an enforceable section 38 agreement are exempted.[82] The street works' authority may, by notice, exempt a building from the operation of section 219 in a number of situations. These are: where the authority is satisified that the whole or the relevant part of the street is not, and is not likely within a reasonable time to be, substantially built up or in so unsatisfactory a condition as to justify the use of powers under the private street works code; where it is satisfied that the street is not, and is not likely within a reasonable time to become, joined to a highway maintainable at the public expense; or where it is satisfied that the whole of the street was, on the material date,[83] substantially built up.[84] The street works' authority may also resolve to exempt the street or the relevant part of it where it is satisfied that more than three-quarters of the aggregate length of all the frontages on both sides of the street (or a part of the street not less than 100 yards in length and comprising the whole or part on which the frontage of the building will be) consists, or will at some future time consist, of the frontages of industrial premises, and that its powers in relation to private street works are not likely to be exercised within a reasonable time.[85] Where a notice or resolution under the above-mentioned provisions is served or made, after a payment has already been made or security has already been given by a building owner, the authority must refund that payment to the owner for the time being of the land and must release any security.[86] Certain streets which were already largely built up at the date on which the New Streets Act 1951 came into force in the authority's area are exempted,[87] as are buildings proposed to be erected on land belonging to or in the possession of certain transport authorities,[88] county, district or London borough councils, or the Common Council, or the Commission for New Towns, or a new town development corporation.[89] Where the building is to be erected by a company whose objects include the provision of industrial premises for use by other persons, and whose constitution prohibits the distribution of the profits of the company to its members, and where the cost of the building is to be defrayed wholly or mainly by a government department, the building will be exempt.[90]

---

[79] Highways Act 1980, s.219(4)(*a*); see also para. 10–30, above.
[80] See *Sinclair-Lockhart's Trustees* v. *Central Land Board* (1951) 1 P. & C.R. 320.
[81] Highways Act 1980, s.219(4)(*b*).
[82] *Ibid.* s.219(4)(*d*).
[83] *Ibid.* s.219(6).
[84] *Ibid.* s.219.(4)(*e*), (*f*), (*h*).
[85] *Ibid.* s.219(4)(*k*).
[86] *Ibid.* s.219(5); there is provision for apportionment where the land has become divided.
[87] *Ibid.* s.219(4)(*g*); as to the relevant dates, see subs (6).
[88] See *ibid.* s.219(4)(*i*).
[89] *Ibid.* s.219.(4)(*i*).
[90] *Ibid.* s.219(4)(*j*).

The procedure to be followed is set out in section 220. Where the   **10–54**
advance payments code is applicable, the street works' authority must,
within six weeks from the passing of any building regulation plans for
the building, serve a notice[91] on the person by or on whose behalf the
plans were deposited, requiring that payment or the securing of the
specified sum.[92] The notice is registrable as a local land charge.[93] The
sum so required is that which, in the opinion of the street works' authority, would be recoverable under the street works code, in respect of
the frontage of the proposed building, if the authority were then to carry
out the required street works[94] in the street in order to bring the highway up to maintainable standard.[95] An appeal lies to the Minister, and
the appellant must then be given the opportunity of being heard before
a person appointed by the Minister.[96] Provision is made for reducing the
sum so required,[97] for refunding sums paid or for releasing security
given[98] in appropriate circumstances. There are similar provisions
where the works are, subsequently, carried out otherwise than at the
authority's expense or where a section 38 agreement is entered into with
some person in respect of the frontage.[99] The sums so paid or secured
are registrable as a local land charge,[1] and discharge the liability of the
owner for street works up to the amount of the specified figure. The
sums paid bear simple interest at the rate determined by the Treasury in
respect of local loans for periods of ten years on the security of local
rates.[2] If, however, when the works are carried out under the street
works code, the cost is greater or less than the amount paid or secured,
the balance is recoverable by the street works' authority (in the normal
way) or is refundable.[3]

Urgent repairs to private streets

Where repairs are needed in a private street, in order to obviate   **10–55**
danger to traffic, the street works' authority may, by notice, require the
owners of the premises fronting the street (or the relevant part of that
street) to execute specified repairs within a stated period of time.[4] An

---

[91] See Highways Act 1980, s.322; *Whitstable U.D.C.* v. *Campbell* [1959] J.P.L. 46: service
on the respondent's architect held to be sufficient.
[92] Non-metropolitan district councils must notify the street works' authority of the passing
of plans: Highways Act 1980, s.220(2).
[93] *Ibid.* s.224(2)(*a*); as is a refund or release, s.224(2)(*f*).
[94] *Ibid.* s.220. See also s.220(5).
[95] *Ibid.* s.220(3). "Street," here, does not include part of a street, unless the authority
treats that part on which the relevant building is proposed as a separate street.
[96] *Ibid.* s.219(6).
[97] *Ibid.* s.219(4).
[98] *Ibid.* ss.219(7), (8), (9): with provision for apportionment where necessary. See also
s.223.
[99] *Ibid.* s.221.
[1] *Ibid.* s.224(*c*).
[2] *Ibid.* s.225.
[3] *Ibid.* s.222: provision is made for apportionment where the land has been split up. See
also *Henshall* v. *Fogg* [1964] 1 W.L.R. 1127.
[4] Highways Act 1980, s.230(1), (2).

appeal against such a notice lies to the magistrates' court. The authority has power to carry out the works in default and to recover the expenses[5] from the owners—apportioned as to the length of their frontage. If, within the specified time limit, the majority, by number or rateable value, of the frontagers of premises in the part of the street to which the repairs are to be carried out, by notice require the street works' authority to proceed in relation to the street under the street works code, the authority must then proceed under the code and on completion of the necessary works must forthwith declare the street to be a highway maintainable at the public expense.[6] The street works' authority[7] has a general power to carry out urgent repairs in private streets in order to prevent or remove danger to persons or vehicles in the street.

Adoption of street after private street works

10–56   After executing private street works in a street, the authority may,[8] or shall (if required to do so by the application of a majority in rateable value of the owners of premises in the street) by means of a notice displayed in a prominent position in the street, declare the street to be a highway maintainable at the public expense.[9] The authority's own power to declare the street a highway maintainable at the public expense arises where "any" street works have been carried out—including urgent repairs. The power of frontagers to require the declaration of the street as a maintainable highway arises only when "all street works (whether or not including lighting)" have been executed in the street to the satisfaction of the authority.[10] "Street," for the purposes of this subsection, means the whole of the street[11] and not part of it. A bridge may form part of a street for this purpose.[12] The authority may also be required to adopt the street by notice from a majority in number of the owners of a built-up street, or from as many of those owners as have, between them, more than half of the aggregate length of all the frontages on both sides of the street, where a payment under the advance payments code has been made.[13]

---

[5] See Highways Act 1980, s.305, Sched. 13; *Shoeburyness U.D.C.* v. *Burgess* (1924) 22 L.G.R. 684; *Nash* v. *Giles* (1926) 96 L.J.K.B. 216.

[6] Highways Act 1980, s.230 (5).

[7] And in some cases the district council; see *ibid.* ss.42(2)(*c*), 230(7) and Sched. 7.

[8] Subject to a determination in the magistrates' court where objections are lodged by a majority in number of owners: see *ibid.* s.228(2).

[9] See paras. 2–14 *et seq.*, above, for a description of the procedures to be followed. As to cases where the street lies in the area of two or more authorities, see Highways Act 1980, s.234 and *Newton* v. *Lambton Hetton and Joicey Collieries Ltd.* (1937) 35 L.G.R. 607.

[10] Highways Act 1980, s.228(7).

[11] See *Urban Housing Company Ltd.* v. *Oxford Corpn.* [1940] 1 Ch. 70.

[12] *Att.-Gen.* v. *Hornsey B.C.* [1927] 1 Ch. 331; *Regent's Canal and Docks Co.* v. *Gibbons* [1925] 1 K.B. 81; *Att.-Gen. of Hong Kong* v. *Mighty Stream Ltd.* [1983] 1 W.L.R. 980.

[13] Highways Act 1980, s.229; para. 2–17, above.

Compensation

Where damage is caused to any person by reason of the execution of   **10–57**
street works under the street works code, compensation is recoverable
from the authority and disputes over compensation are determinable
either by arbitration or by the county court.[14]

---

[14] Highways Act 1980, s.308. See para. 14–49 and Appendix 3, below.

CHAPTER 11

BRIDGES

INTRODUCTION

11–01 Historically, bridges in highways have been treated somewhat differently from the highways leading to them. The primary responsibility for repair of bridges fell upon the inhabitants of the county as a whole, rather than on the parish in which the bridge was situated. By the Highways Act 1959, the county council was made the highway authority for all "county bridges" within a county.[1] "County bridges" were defined[2] as being:

(a) bridges which the county council were liable to maintain immediately prior to the commencement of the 1959 Act[3];

(b) bridges constructed by the county council after the commencement of the 1959 Act;

(c) bridges adopted in accordance with the provisions of the 1959 Act[4];

(d) bridges whose maintenance was undertaken by the county council under the provisions of the 1959 Act[5]; and

(e) bridges which were transferred to the county council under the provisions of the 1959 Act[6] or of the Bridges Act 1929.[7]

Under the Local Government Act 1972, section 187, the county councils became the local highway authorities outside Greater London, and the distinction between the authority liable for the maintenance of the bridge, and that responsible for the highway, effectively disappeared.[8]

11–02 The Highways Act 1980 contains a number of specific provisions dealing with the construction and repair of bridges in highways. The majority of the statutory provisions applicable to highways will, because of the way in which the terms "highway" and "bridge" are defined, apply equally to bridges. Section 328(2) of the Highways Act 1980 states that:

---

[1] Highways Act 1959, s.1(3) (now repealed).
[2] *Ibid.* s.23 (now repealed).
[3] Except for those bridges maintained by the county simply because they carried county roads under Local Government Act 1929, s.29(4).
[4] *i.e.* under s.23(2) (now repealed).
[5] *i.e.* by agreement under Highways Act 1959, s.40 (now replaced by Highways Act 1980, s.38: see Chap. 4.)
[6] Highways Act 1959, Parts V and X (now replaced by Highways Act 1980, Parts V and XII: see paras. 11–39 and 11–43, below.)
[7] Now repealed.
[8] ss.23–25 of Highways Act 1959 were repealed by Local Government Act 1972, s.272 and Sched. 30. See also para. 11–04, below.

"Where a highway passes over a bridge or through a tunnel, that bridge or tunnel is to be taken for the purposes of this Act to be part of the highway."

Correspondingly, section 329(1) of the Highways Act 1980 defines the word "bridge" as meaning:

"a bridge or viaduct which is part of a highway and includes the abutments and any other part of a bridge but not the highway carried thereby."

It follows, therefore, that when the Act refers to a "bridge," it means only the structure of a bridge situated in a highway, but that where it refers to "highway" this will, unless the context indicates otherwise, include any bridge which lies in the highway.

The highway authority has never been liable to maintain all bridges in **11–03** highways, nor even all bridges in highways maintainable at the public expense. The Highways Act 1980 itself recognises that there may continue to be bridges in highways which are maintainable by persons other than the highway authority.[9] Different persons or bodies might be responsible for the maintenance of the way carried by the bridge, and for the structure itself. This may be the case, for example, in respect of railway and canal bridges after the commencement of the Transport Act 1968.[10] The major concerns for modern highway law, in respect of bridges, have been to determine those other persons or bodies who are liable to repair bridges, to apportion the financial responsibility for the repair of bridges between bridge owners and the relevant highway authority, and to provide for the transfer of responsibility of repair. However, in order to determine whether a bridge is maintainable by some person or body other than the highway authority and, if so, by whom, it is often necessary to investigate the history of the bridge and the common law liabilities in respect of the repair of bridges. In relation to bridges, however, the common law of England and Wales is a minefield of misunderstanding and compromise.

HIGHWAY AUTHORITIES FOR BRIDGES

County councils and metropolitan district councils are the local highway **11–04** authorities for bridges outside London. London borough councils and the Common Council are the highway authorities for bridges within Greater London.[11] The Minister is the highway authority for bridges in roads for which he is responsible.[12] Rivers, however, frequently define county boundaries; thus, section 3 of the 1980 Act provides that, where

---

[9] See, in particular, ss.55, 56, 93, 94.
[10] See Transport Act 1968, s.116, and para. 11–46, below.
[11] Highways Act 1980, s.1, as amended by Local Government Act 1985, ss.8, 102 and Scheds. 4 and 17.
[12] See Chap. 1 and para. 11–41, below.

a bridge carrying a highway for which the Minister is not the highway authority is situated partly in the area of one county, and partly in the area of another, those authorities are to agree which of them is to be the highway authority for the whole bridge.[13] Where the county boundary falls across the approaches to the bridge, the highway authority for the approaches will be the authority for the bridge as a whole.[14]

CONSTRUCTION OF BRIDGES

At common law

11–05   At common law there was no duty placed on any person to construct bridges. River crossings were frequently achieved by the use of fords and ferries. Indeed, Magna Carta itself protected subjects from being compelled to construct bridges where none had existed before, and sought to limit the liability to repair bridges to persons who had of old been under an obligation to maintain bridges.[15] Thus, no doctrine arose in the common law that a bridge might be required as a necessary incident to the crossing of rivers by highways.[16] It was not until the Local Government Act 1888 that statute gave the new county councils a general power to construct new bridges. However, over the years, many bridges had been constructed by private persons and by communities, and the common law recognised, in certain circumstances, a responsibility to keep such bridges in repair.

Statutory powers to construct bridges

11–06   A highway authority is given express power by section 91 of the Highways Act 1980 to construct bridges to carry highways maintainable at the public expense.[17] Highway authorities may also reconstruct bridges which are highways maintainable at the public expense either on the same site or on a new site within 200 yards of the old one.[18] Bridges may be constructed by private persons to carry new streets, provided that the width of the approaches and the gradients are approved by the local highway authority.[19] The construction of bridges under and over railways is governed by the Railways Clauses Consolidation Act 1845,[20] the

---

[13] In default of agreement, see Highways Act 1980, s.3(1) and the Boundary Bridges (Appointed Day) Order 1973 (S.I. 1973 No. 2147). See also Local Government Act 1985, Sched. 4, para. 54, in relation to metropolitan district councils.

[14] The approaches consist of 100 yards of the highway at either end of the bridge: Highways Act 1980, s.3(4).

[15] See 2 Co. Inst. 29.

[16] See *R.* v. *Devon (Inhabitants)* (1825) 4 B. & C. 670 at 679.

[17] Subject to Treasury approval in the case of the Minister.

[18] Highways Act 1980, s.92.

[19] *Ibid.* s.195(1).

[20] ss.46–51.

Transport Act 1968,[21] and the Railway Bridges (Load-Bearing Standards) (England and Wales) Order 1972.[22]

Part VI of the Highways Act 1980 provides statutory authority for the **11–07** construction of bridges over navigable waters. By section 106 it is provided that the Minister may make an order for the construction of a bridge over, or a tunnel under, any specified navigable waters,[23] as part of a trunk road. Such an order may also be incorporated in an order, made under section 10 of the Highways Act 1980, directing that a road is to become a trunk road,[24] or as part of a special road scheme made by a highway authority under section 16 of the Act.[25] Local highway authorities may undertake schemes for the construction of bridges or tunnels over and under navigable waters, as part of a highway or proposed highway, other than a special road, which is or is to be a highway maintainable at the public expense by the authority.[26] Such schemes may be submitted jointly by two or more local highway authorities, and may provide for the financial responsibility for the maintenance of the bridge when constructed and for the carrying out of highway functions by one authority in relation to the bridge.[27] Similarly, bridges and tunnels may be constructed over navigable waters as part of an order under sections 14 and 18.[28] Bridges may also be provided as the means of access to any premises from a highway authorised under an order made under those sections.[29]

The reason for these specific powers relating to navigable waters is **11–08** that express authority is needed for the potential interruption and disturbance of any rights of navigation along the river or waterway. The need to protect navigation rights along navigable highways is recognised in section 107. The Minister is required to take into consideration the requirements of navigation before he makes or confirms an order or scheme which involves the construction of a bridge or tunnel. The order or scheme itself must include plans and specifications indicating the position and dimensions of any proposed bridge and, in the case of a swing bridge, must contain such provisions as the Minister considers expedient for its operation. Similarly, proposals for a tunnel must include details of its position and depth. The order may become subject to special parliamentary procedure where certain objections to the order or scheme are made and maintained by a navigation authority or water authority.

---

[21] s.117.

[22] S.I. 1972 No. 1705.

[23] *i.e.* waters or a watercourse over which a public right of navigation exists, together with certain watercourses specified in Part I and II of Sched. 12 to Transport Act 1968: see Highways Act 1980, s.111.

[24] As to the procedure for making orders, see *ibid.* s.106(5) and Sched. 1, Parts I and III.

[25] *Ibid.* s.106(2). As to the procedure for such schemes, see *ibid.* s.106(5) and Sched. 1, Parts II and III.

[26] *Ibid.* s.106(3): such schemes are subject to confirmation by the Minister.

[27] *Ibid.* s.106(6).

[28] See Chap. 1.

[29] Highways Act 1980, s.106(4).

REPAIR AND MAINTENANCE OF BRIDGES PRIOR TO THE PASSING OF THE
HIGHWAYS ACT 1959

History

11–09   The responsibility for the repair of bridges was, at one time, part of
the feudal obligations—the *trinoda necessitas*—imposed on all holders
of land,[30] but by 1215 the responsibility to repair existing bridges had
become more specifically attached to certain lands and bodies *ratione
tenurae* or by prescription. Magna Carta recognised that some bridges
were repairable by persons who "from of old were legally bound to do
so." Bridges continued, however, to be constructed, for a variety of
reasons, in highways and in roads which later became highways. They
were constructed both out of the benevolence of individuals and by
townships and other communities for the public welfare. The common
law recognised the desirability of those bridges, once constructed, being
maintained, and placed the responsibility for their repair on the community. In some cases, small streams were culverted under the highway
by the parish, as part of the maintenance of the highway, in order to prevent erosion. The structure forming this kind of crossing of a stream was
thereafter regarded as part of the highway itself, and was subject to the
same principles as the remainder of the highway. More substantial
bridges, which were repairable publicly, became the responsibility of
the county—apparently because of the greater importance of bridges to
the inhabitants of the county as a whole.[31] By the middle of the six-
teenth century, however, many bridges were falling into dilapidation,
and disputes were arising as to the responsibility for their maintenance.

The Statute of Bridges 1530

11–10   The Statute of Bridges 1530, section 1, gave the justices of the peace
power and authority to enquire, hear and determine in the general
sessions:

> "all manner of annoyances of bridges broken in the highe wayes to
> the damage of the Kynges liege people"

and to take steps for the repair of these bridges. By section 2, the Act
provided that where it could not be known or proved what hundred,
riding, wapentake, city, borough, town or parish, nor what person certain or body politic:

> "ought of right to make suche bridges decayed, by reasone whereof
> suche decayed bridges for lacke of knowledge of such as owen to
> make them for the mooste parte lyen long without any amende-
> ment, to the great anoyaunce of the Kynges subjectes"

---

[30] See Stephen's *Blackstone* (15th ed.) Vol.3, p.92; Bacon's *Abridgement* (17th ed.) Vol 1,
p.784. See also Sidney and Beatrice Webb, *The Story of the King's Highway* (2nd ed.,
1963) p. 86.
[31] 2 Co. Inst. 700–701.

then, in the case of bridges outside incorporated towns and cities, the liability for repair was to fall on the inhabitants of the shire or riding in which the bridge happened to be. Within incorporated towns and cities the inhabitants of that town or city were, similarly, liable for repair.[32] With the responsibility for repair of the bridge went the responsibility for the repair of 300 feet of the highway at either end.[33]

The Statute of Bridges 1530 was said to be declaratory of the common **11–11** law with respect to the identification of the county's responsibility to repair bridges.[34] The Act did, however, create a local and more efficient administration for the repairing of bridges, by giving powers to the local justices of the peace at quarter sessions. Subsequent legislation refined and extended the powers of quarter sessions to enforce the liability to repair bridges, and to raise the necessary finance.[35]

Growth in bridge building

The rules as to public liability for repair of bridges appear confused **11–12** during the eighteenth century. The available authorities were sparse. In his *Abridgement*, Lord Rolle had stated the proposition that[36]:

> "If a man erect a mill for his own profit, and make a new cut for the water to come to it, and make a new bridge over it, and the subjects use to go over this as over a common bridge, this bridge ought to be repaired by him who has the mill, and not by the county, because he erected it for his own benefit."

This implied that some bridges built for private purposes would be repairable by the landowner and not by the county. For many years the extent of this proposition was to be subject to scrutiny, explanation, misunderstanding and challenge.[37] Lord Coke, in his *Institutes*, had, however, described the common law thus[38]:

> "If a man make a Bridge, for the common good of all the subjects, he is not bound to repair it; for no particular man is bound to reparation of bridges by the common law, but ratione tenurae, or praescriptionis."

In the *Langforth Bridge Case*,[39] it was successfully argued before the court that the county ought to repair a bridge erected by the King for the

---

[32] See, however, *R. v. New Sarum (Inhabitants)* (1845) 7 Q.B. 941.

[33] Statute of Bridges 1530, s.7; *R. v. West Riding of Yorkshire (Inhabitants)* (1806) 7 East 588.

[34] 2 Co. Inst. 701; *R. v. St. Peter's, York, J.J.* (1706) 2 L. Raym. 1249 at 324; *R. v. West Riding of Yorkshire (Inhabitants)* (1806) 7 East 588.

[35] See Bridges Acts 1670, 1702, 1740, 1803 and 1812, County Rates Act 1738 and Highway Act 1773.

[36] 1 *Rolle's Abridgment*, 368, tit. Bridges, pl. 2. The translation is taken from *R. v. Kent (Inhabitants)* (1814) 2 M.&S. 513.

[37] See *e.g. R. v. Kent (Inhabitants)* (1814) 2 M.&S. 513; *R. v. Isle of Ely (Inhabitants)* (1850) 15 Q.B. 827.

[38] 2 Co. Inst. 701. See also the *Repair of Bridges Case* (1609) 13 Co. Rep. 33.

[39] (1634) Cro. Car. 366.

benefit of his mills, because bridges were "for the ease and benefit of the people." In *R. v. Wiltshire (Inhabitants)*,[40] the court firmly stated the law to be that "if a private person builds a private bridge which after-wards becomes of public convenience, the whole county is bound to repair it." However, apparently under the belief that the common law and the Statute of Bridges only imposed liability on the county in the case of ancient bridges whose origins were unknown, the justices in some counties began to make allowances out of the county rates for the construction of "gratuity" bridges. In many cases these contributions were made expressly on condition that no responsibility for the future repair of the bridge was being assumed by the county by virtue of such contribution.[41] The number of new bridges which were constructed by voluntary subscription, by turnpike trustees and by private landowners appears to have mushroomed, and by 1770, it was clear that law required some clarification.

The Glusburne Bridge Case, 1770

11–13   In *R. v. West Riding of Yorkshire (Inhabitants)*,[42] it was held that where a bridge had been privately constructed but had subsequently become of public utility, having been used by the public over a number of years, it became repairable by the county under the terms of the Stat-ute of Bridges and at common law, unless the county could prove the liability of any other person to maintain it by prescription or tenure. This decision was consistently followed in a number of subsequent cases which established public utility as the test for identifying public respon-sibility for repair.[43] The effect of these decisions was, therefore, that large numbers of bridges, which had not previously been assumed to be publicly repairable, were identified as being the liability of the county. Furthermore, the obligation of the county to keep bridges in repair became an expanding and potentially onerous duty.

Bridges Act 1803

11–14   In order to place some limits on the liability of the county, both to ensure that the number of bridges for which the county would become liable was not unnecessarily increased, and to ensure that those bridges which were to be constructed by other persons or bodies should be prop-erly and soundly built, Lord Ellenborough's Act, the Bridges Act 1803, was passed. Section 5 of that Act provided that:

> "for the more clearly ascertaining the description of bridges here-after to be erected, which inhabitants of counties shall and may be bound or liable to repair and maintain, be it further enacted, that

---

[40] (1704) 6 Mod. 307.

[41] See *R. v. West Riding of Yorkshire (Inhabitants)* (1770) 5 Burr. 2594; see also Sidney and Beatrice Webb, *The Story of the King's Highway*, pp. 94–96.

[42] *Glusburne Bridge Case* (1770) 5 Burr. 2594.

[43] See *R. v. West Riding of Yorkshire (Inhabitants)* (1802) 2 East 342.

no bridge hereafter to be erected or built in any county by or at the expense of any individual or private person or persons, body politick or corporate, shall be deemed or taken to be a county bridge, or a bridge which the inhabitants of any county shall be compellable or liable to maintain or repair, unless such bridge shall be erected in a substantial and commodious manner under the direction or to the satisfaction of the county surveyor, or person appointed by the justices of the peace at their general quarter sessions assembled . . . "

The surveyor was commanded to inspect the erection of bridges if requested to do so, and in the case of dispute the matter was to be determined at quarter sessions.[44] The Act did not apply to any bridges or roads which "any person or persons or body politick is, are, or shall be liable to maintain or repair by reason of tenure or by prescription."[45]

The present position

The result of this mixture of judicial decision and statutory intervention has been that, in order to establish who, if anyone, is liable to repair a bridge, it is necessary to consider a series of issues. The first is whether the structure in question is of sufficient substance, and of such a nature, to be regarded as a "county bridge" to which the law of bridges applies, rather than as part of the highway. Secondly, only bridges which are of sufficient utility to the public will have become maintainable at the public expense in the absence of a formal adoption by, or transfer to, the highway authority. There may need to be some evidence of public acceptance of, or acquiescence in, the existence of the bridge in order to establish public utility. In some cases this has been described as a need to show adoption by the public of the bridge. The existence of a bridge in a pre-existing highway will generally demonstrate sufficient utility. The next question is whether the bridge was first constructed before or after the passing of the Bridges Act 1803.[46] If it was constructed after that date, then it will be maintainable at the public expense only: **11–15**

(a) where it was constructed to the satisfaction of the county surveyor in accordance with the provisions of the Bridges Act 1803;

(b) where it was constructed as part of a highway maintainable at the public expense by a relevant highway authority; or

(c) where it has subsequently been formally adopted by or transferred to the highway authority.

If the bridge was originally constructed prior to 1803, the question will be whether it carried public rights at that date. This also revolves around the question of whether the bridge had become of sufficient "public utility" to impose the liability to repair on the public. If so, then the bridge

---

[44] See, however, *R. v. Southampton County (Inhabitants)* (1887) 19 Q.B.D. 590.
[45] Bridges Act 1803, s.7.
[46] June 24, 1803.

will be maintainable at the public expense, unless the highway authority can prove that some other person or body is liable to repair by statute, prescription or tenure or, possibly, that a person or body is liable to repair by reason of their interference in the route of an existing highway. It will still be necessary to consider whether there has been some later, formal act of adoption by, or transfer to, the highway authority.

Structures which could become county bridges

11–16   A county bridge was understood to involve the crossing of running water, rather than of a ravine or another road,[47] although in *R. v. Derbyshire (Inhabitants)*,[48] it was held that a constant stream or course of water need not necessarily flow at all times through the arches of the "bridge". A bridge over a canal was held to satisfy the general requirement of flowing water.[49]

11–17   Other structures which would have fallen within the general description of bridges were excluded from the responsibility of the county, because they were not regarded as being structures independent of the highway. Thus, in *R. v. Southampton County (Inhabitants), Black Bridge, Sandown Bridge & Tinkers Bridge Cases*,[50] a footbridge formed of three planks only nine feet in length, and including a hand rail, which carried a public footpath across a small stream was held not to be repairable as a county bridge, despite evidence that it had been repaired by commissioners under statutory authority relating to public bridges. Footbridges could, however, be county bridges, since the liability of the county attached to all bridges in highways, without distinction as to the nature and extent of the public right which they carried.[51] Whether a structure should be regarded as being a bridge independent of the highway was a matter of fact and degree; a question of "magnitude and construction."[52]

11–18   Very often the dispute is whether a structure should properly be regarded as a bridge rather than a culvert. In *R. v. Lancaster County (Inhabitants)*,[53] an artificial cutting made in a moss, in order to drain off water, had been crossed by a highway, and the water had been carried under the highway in a structure originally made of wood and subsequently made of stone. This structure had been enlarged and widened on more than one occasion. Although the parish, from time to time, had repaired the structure together with the highway it was subsequently

---

[47] See *R. v. Oxfordshire (Inhabitants)* (1830) 1 B. & Ad. 289; *R. v. Derbyshire (Inhabitants)* (1842) 2 Q.B. 745.

[48] (1842) 2 Q.B.745.

[49] *North Staffordshire Ry. Co. v. Hanley Corpn.* (1909) 73 J.P. 477.

[50] (1852) 18 Q.B. 841.

[51] *R. v. Salop County (Inhabitants)* (1810) 13 East 95.

[52] *per* Blackburn J. in *R. v. Lancaster County (Inhabitants)* (1868) 32 J.P. 711; see also *R. v. Whitney (Inhabitants)* (1835) 3 A. & E. 69; *R. v. Gloucester (Inhabitants)* (1842) Car. & M. 506.

[53] (1868) 32 J.P. 711.

sought to make the county liable for its repair. It was held that this structure was not a county bridge but was part of the highway.

Requirement of public utility

In the *Glusburne Bridge Case*,[54] the court affirmed that where a pri-   **11–19**
vate person or persons erected a bridge of public utility in a highway, the public, in the form of the county or riding, became liable for its repair. In that particular case, the bridge had been erected partly with the aid of money provided by the justices of the West Riding, but the principle was subsequently applied to cases where the bridge was constructed by parishes and townships, turnpike trustees and by other persons.[55]

The requirement that a bridge should be of public utility was necess-   **11–20**
ary to prevent landowners imposing on the public the liability to repair bridges constructed for their own benefit.[56] Where a bridge was originally constructed in a highway for the private benefit of the landowner, but became well used by the public, the probability would be that the bridge had become of public utility in improving passage over the highway; perhaps having replaced a ferry or a ford. Such a bridge would become repairable by the inhabitants of the county with the passage of time.[57]

Need for some act of adoption

In 1886, in *R. v. Southampton County (Inhabitants)*,[58] it was held that   **11–21**
public liability depended upon proof of the county's acquiescence in the construction of a bridge, or upon proof of the adoption of the bridge. Utility to the public and user by the public were only matters of evidence upon which a jury might find that the necessary preconditions for public liability to repair were established. In this case, a developer had acquired building land on the left bank of the River Itchen; Southampton was on the other bank. In order to make the land more attractive to potential purchasers, the developer constructed an access road and bridge which linked with a public highway on the other bank of the river, thereby providing easy access from his land to and from Southampton. He then dedicated the road and the bridge to the public at a

---

[54] *R. v. West Riding of Yorkshire (Inhabitants)* (1770) 5 Burr. 2594.
[55] *R. v. West Riding of Yorkshire (Inhabitants)* (1802) 2 East 342; including the Crown, see *R. v. Buckinghamshire (Inhabitants)* (1810) 12 East 192.
[56] See *R. v. West Riding of Yorkshire (Inhabitants)* (1802) 2 East 342; *R. v. Glamorgan (Inhabitants)* (1788) 2 East 356n.; *R. v. Southampton (Inhabitants)* (1887) 19 Q.B.D. 590.
[57] See *R. v. Buckinghamshire (Inhabitants)* (1810) 12 East 192; *R. v. West Riding of Yorkshire (Inhabitants)* (1802) 2 East 342; *R. v. Devon (Inhabitants)* (1811) 14 East 477; *R. v. Kent (Inhabitants)* (1814) 2 M.&S. 513; *R. v. Northampton(Inhabitants)* (1814) 2 M. & S. 262; *Robbins v. Jones* (1863) 15 C.B. (N.S.) 221.
[58] (1887) 19 Q.B.D. 590.

11–22

11–23

formal opening ceremony. The bridge was much used, and there appears to have been no doubt as to its usefulness.

The case came before the Divisional Court on two occasions. On the first occasion, Wills J.[59] attempted to bring together the earlier authorities. He placed considerable reliance on earlier remarks made by Lord Ellenborough C.J. in *R. v. West Riding of Yorkshire*,[60] to the effect that use of a bridge by the public, rather than the indictment of the bridge builder for nuisance, indicated that the bridge was not to be treated as a nuisance to the highway.[61] In the case of bridges constructed other than in existing highways and where, therefore, the absence of an indictment for nuisance could not be relied upon as the necessary evidence of acquiescence, some indication of the county's acquiescence, or some act of adoption, was required in order to make the bridge a public bridge. Wills J., however, declined to say what acts of acquiescence or adoption might be sufficient or required. On the second occasion,[62] Lord Coleridge C.J. attempted to take a middle course between two possible points of view. On the one hand, he rejected the proposition that public user and public utility was, of itself, sufficient to establish the county's liability to repair. On the other hand, he accepted that there was no need for proof of an overt act amounting to formal adoption by a body capable of representing the county. However, having rejected these two extremes, Lord Coleridge did not then go on to provide any clear principle upon which public liability would depend. Rather, he indicated that the public liability depended upon the evidence, that it was a question of fact for the jury, rather than of law, and that public utility and public user were, together with any other evidence, matters which might, but need not necessarily, lead a jury to conclude that the county was liable.

It is doubtful how much weight can be given to any absence of indictment for nuisance. In many cases, the bridge which replaced the ford or ferry was not constructed in the line of the highway itself but rather on private land adjoining the highway and, in some cases, some distance away.[63] Unless, therefore, the approaches of the bridge interfered with the user of the highway, it is difficult to see how a nuisance would have arisen. The decision in the *Southampton* case[63a] probably had little practical effect on the law, in so far as it dealt with bridges constructed in existing highways, although the legal theory behind public liability for bridges was left confused. Of greater practical importance is the effect

---

[59] (1886) 17 Q.B.D. 424.
[60] (1802) 2 East. 342 at 348.
[61] See also the first instance judgment of Bayley J. in *R. v. St. Benedict, Cambridge* (1821) 4 B.& Ald. 447.
[62] (1887) 19 Q.B.D. 590.
[63] In *R. v. West Riding of Yorkshire* (*Inhabitants*) (1770) 5 Burr. 2594, the replacement bridge was some 60 yards from the original bridge although still said to be in the same highway.
[63a] (1887) 19 Q.B.D. 590.

which the decision may have had on the assumption of public liability for bridges constructed in private roads which later became highways.

Bridges erected prior to the dedication of the highway
There is little judicial authority on the question as to whether the **11–24** growth of public rights of way over a pre-existing private bridge will cause the bridge to become maintainable at the public expense. The first principle ought to be whether there is sufficient evidence to give rise to the implication that the landowner intended to dedicate the structure of the bridge as well as the surface of the way over the bridge. In *R.* v. *Buckinghamshire* (*Inhabitants*),[64] Lord Ellenborough C.J. defined public bridges as:

> " . . . such bridges as all His Majesty's subjects had used freely and without interruption as of right, for a period of time competent to protect them and all who should thereafter use them from being considered as wrong-doers in respect of such use, in any mode of proceeding, civil or criminal, in which the legality of such use might be questioned."

The *Southampton* case,[64a] however, has stressed that evidence of adoption is necessary before the liability of the public is established. Furthermore, public user generally proves only the dedication of the surface of a highway and not the liability of the highway authority to repair. Where the private bridge is erected after 1803 it is unlikely that it will have been constructed to the satisfaction of the county surveyor—although this had apparently been achieved in the *Southampton* case. Where the bridge was in existence in 1803 and highway rights over it have been acquired since that date, it would seem that the *Southampton* case is some authority for the bridge not being publicly repairable. If so, it would appear that the bridge might be repairable by no-one, and that the user by the public of the path or road leading to the bridge will ultimately be frustrated when the bridge collapses. It is also unclear as to whether the highway authority might incur any civil liability for not taking any action to safeguard the public passage over a bridge which is in a dangerous state of repair. However, except for taking steps to adopt the bridge and to acquire the land necessary in order to reconstruct the bridge, it is not easy to see what powers the highway authority may have to make the bridge safe. This point was raised but not decided in *Campbell Davys* v. *Lloyd*,[65] where it was held that a member of the public had no power to construct a bridge to replace one which had fallen into disrepair, in order to abate the alleged nuisance.[65a]

---

[64] (1810) 12 East 192 at 203.
[64a] (1887) 19 Q.B.D. 590.
[65] [1901] 2 Ch. 518.
[65a] See, however, *Sandgate U.D.C.* v. *Kent C.C.* (1898) 79 L.T. 425, *per* Lord Halsbury L.C. at 427.

Post 1803 bridges

11–25   The Bridges Act 1803 contained a number of provisions which were designed to improve the administration of bridges and their repair. Section 5, however, provided an important attempt to restrict the liability of the county to those bridges which were either already in existence or which were built, subsequently, to the satisfaction of the county surveyor.[66] Unlike the position with highways under the Highway Act 1835, no procedure was created whereby the county could decide whether or not to accept liability to repair bridges. It might have been thought that once the county surveyor had declared his satisfaction with the bridge, then the county became liable to repair. However, it was held in *R. v. Southampton (Inhabitants)*[66a] that this was not the case.

11–26   The substantial repair and improvement of an old bridge after 1803, at the expense of the parish and not under the direction of the county surveyor, did not render the repaired bridge a new bridge "erected or built" after the passing of the Bridges Act 1803 so as to exempt the county from liability to repair.[67] Whether or not a new bridge has been created or whether the new bridge is substantially the same as the old one is a matter of fact and degree, to be determined not so much from the identity of the materials from which it is composed, but from the identity of the public right of passage over a bridge at that place.[67a] Bridges erected by turnpike trustees were treated as bridges erected by private persons so as not to be publicly repairable by the county after 1803 unless approved by the county surveyor.[68]

BRIDGES REPAIRABLE BY PERSONS, BODIES OR AREAS OTHER
THAN THE COUNTY

11–27   Bridges may be maintainable by persons or bodies other than the county by virtue of statute, prescription or by tenure and, in some circumstances, because the bridge was originally made necessary by the bridge builder's interference with the highway. All these types of bridges are still regarded as public bridges, in the sense that the public has the entitlement to their maintenance and repair. In *R. v. Chart and Longbridge Inhabitants*,[69] Bovill C.J. explained that, at common law, the expression "county bridge" is not an expression known to law, but is, rather, a compendious way of speaking of a public bridge which the county is liable to repair:

"All public bridges are county bridges, although they may be

---

[66] For the wording of Bridges Act 1803, s. 5, see para. 11–14, above.
[66a] (1887) 19 Q.B.D. 590; see para. 11–21, above.
[67] *R. v. Lancashire (Inhabitants)* (1831) 2 B. & Ad. 813; *R. v. Devon (Inhabitants)* (1833) 5 B. & Ad. 383.
[67a] *Ibid., per* Lord Denman C.J. at 387.
[68] *R. v. Derby County (Inhabitants)* (1832) 3 & Ad. 147; *North Staffordshire Ry. Co. v. Hanley Corpn.* (1909) 73 J.P. 477 at 480.
[69] (1870) L.R. 1 C.C.R. 237 at 239.

repairable by the hundred, or borough, or division, or by individuals instead of by the county."

Hundreds, towns, parishes, etc.

Corporations may be liable to repair by reason of tenure[70] or prescription.[71] Where the county was divided into ridings or divisions, then the riding or division would be liable in the same way as the county.[72] A hundred might, by immemorial custom, have repaired bridges, even though its boundaries had changed over the years.[73] Parishes, however, were not regarded as divisions of the county and they could not be liable by reason of tenure.[74] The Statute of Bridges clearly recognised that parishes and unincorporated townships might be liable to repair bridges. In *R. v. Hendon (Inhabitants),*[75] the liability of parishes and townships was regarded as being prescriptive. All bridges which were repairable by the inhabitants at large of any area will now be repairable by the highway authority. **11–28**

Liability arising out of tenure or prescription

Liability to repair a bridge by reason of tenure can only fall upon a body capable of holding land. The liability can be proved by evidence that the landowner had repaired immemorially.[76] Although the ultimate liability *ratione tenurae* falls upon the owner of the land, who is liable by reason of his tenure, it appears that the occupier is responsible to the public for non-repair, subject to a right of recovery from the owner.[77] This appears to be because the public are readily able to identify the occupier of the land. Where a private individual is liable to repair *ratione tenurae,* and the land which is subject to the burden of repair is divided, the liability may attach to both parts of the land so divided.[78] A prescriptive liability can attach to corporate bodies and individuals. In the case of the latter, however, the liability must be supported by proof of some consideration, such as the taking of toll or arising out of the tenure of land.[79] **11–29**

---

[70] *R. v. Ecclesfield (Inhabitants)* (1818) 1 B.& Ald. 348; *R. v. Machynlleth and Pennegoes (Inhabitants)* (1823) 2 B.& C. 348.
[71] *R. v. Stratford-upon-Avon Corpn.* (1811) 14 East 348.
[72] See *R. v. Isle of Ely (Inhabitants)* (1850) 15 Q.B. 827.
[73] *R. v. Oswestry (Inhabitants)* (1817) 6 M.& S. 361.
[74] *R. v. Machynlleth and Pennegoes (Inhabitants)* (1823) 2 B.& C. 348.
[75] (1833) 4 B. & Ad. 628; *R. v. West Riding of Yorkshire (Inhabitants)* 2 East 342; *R. v. Ecclesfield (Inhabitants)* (1818) 1 B.& Ald. 348; *R. v. West Riding of Yorkshire (Inhabitants)* (1821) 4 B. & Ald. 623.
[76] *R. v. Middlesex (Inhabitants)* (1832) 3 B. & Ad. 201, *per* Taunton J. at 210.
[77] *R. v. Sutton* (1835) 3 A. & E. 597; *Baker v. Greenhill* (1842) 3 Q.B. 463; *R. v. Bucknall* (1702) 7 Mod. 54; *R. v. Stoughton* (1670) 2 Wms. Saund. 157 at 158; *R. v. Kerrison (Inhabitants)* (1815) 3 M.& S. 526; *R. v. Barker* (1890) 25 Q.B.D. 213.
[78] *R. v. Bucklugh (Duchess)* (1704) 6 Mod. Rep. 150; *R. v. Oxfordshire (Inhabitants)* (1812) 16 East 223.
[79] *Repair of Bridges* 13 Co. Rep. 33; see also para. 4–11, above.

Bridges constructed for private benefit to mitigate interference with an existing highway

11–30   It has often been stated that where a person widens or deepens a river for his own benefit, thereby rendering the passage of the highway across it less convenient or impassable, he may be under a continuing duty to repair the bridge thereby constructed. It seems that this was originally a rule of the common law.[80] The basis for the rule is said to be that where a person commits a nuisance, by making a new cut across the highway, which might have been the subject of an indictment, then any bridge constructed by him to mitigate his interference with the highway must be regarded as continuing to be for his own benefit, and is therefore repairable by him.[81] However, the lack of any indictment against a bridge builder had led the court, in *R. v. Southampton (Inhabitants)*[82] to find evidence of adoption by the county. The principle has also been explained in a slightly different way, in some cases, as being based upon some express or implied authority to interfere with the highway, conditional upon the bridge being maintained. Failure to maintain would mean that the original nuisance was revived, leading to a possible indictment.[83] The existence of any such general principle was doubted by Lord Ellenborough, in the light of the *Glusburne Bridge* case,[84] in *R. v. Kent (Inhabitants) (Footscray Bridge)*.[85] In *R. v. Kerrison*,[86] a court, which included Lord Ellenborough, distinguished the *Footscray Bridge* case on the grounds that there had been a benefit to the public arising from the erection of a bridge in place of a ford. Where, however, the highway was opened up to make a cut for a navigation or canal, then no such benefit could accrue, and the person who so interfered with the highway became liable to maintain the bridge.

11–31   In the great majority of cases, the interference has been carried out by a body empowered by statute to carry on certain operations and the decision in each case has depended upon the construction of that statute. Thus, in *R. v. Kent (Inhabitants)*, *St. Helens Bridge*,[87] the Medway Navigation Company had been given statutory power to widen, deepen and make navigable the river Medway in Kent and Sussex. It was held on a construction of the company's statutory powers that it only had power to alter the old highway on condition that it left as convenient a passage in the highway's place. This was a continuing condition, and the company was bound to give another passage over the

---

[80] See 1 *Rolle's Abridgement* 368 pl. 2; *cf.* 2 Co. Inst. 701.
[81] See, *per* Lord Ellenborough C.J., in *R. v. West Riding of Yorkshire (Inhabitants)* (1802) 2 East at 342.
[82] (1887) 19 Q.B.D. 590; *R. v. West Riding of Yorkshire (Inhabitants) (Pace Gate Bridge)* (1802) 2 East 342; see also para. 11–21, above.
[83] *R. v. Isle of Ely (Inhabitants)* (1850) 15 Q.B. 827.
[84] *R. v. West Riding of Yorkshire (Inhabitants)* (1770) 5 Burr. 2594.
[85] (1814) 2 M. & S. 513. This decision was, in turn, doubted in *R. v. Isle of Ely (Inhabitants)* (1850) 15 Q.B. 827.
[86] (1815) 3 M. & S. 526.
[87] (1811) 13 East 220.

bridge and to keep it for the public. Similar decisions followed in *R. v. Lindsey (Inhabitants)*,[88] and *R. v. Kerrison*.[89]

THE EXTENT OF REPAIR

Bridges maintainable by the highway authority

As with highways, bridges which are maintainable by the highway **11–32** authority must be maintained to such a standard that they meet the needs of the ordinary traffic of the day which may reasonably be expected to use the highway.[90] The duty does not extend to widening the bridge.[91] This rule was adopted, by analogy, from the similiar rule relating to highways, and was partly based upon the same reasoning[92]— that the county had no power at common law to purchase the land or rights which would be necessary in order for the ends of the bridges to be placed in private land.[93] However, where a bridge maintainable by the county had fallen into disrepair and been destroyed or demolished, the liability of the county would extend to rebuilding the bridge,[94] and this might involve raising the height of the bridge, if this was necessary to prevent the reconstructed bridge from being a nuisance to navigation.[95]

Privately maintainable bridges

A person or body liable to repair by prescription is not required to put **11–33** a highway or bridge in a better condition than it has been time out of mind.[96] The extent of the liability of persons or bodies whose liability arises out of statute depends very much on the interpretation of the special enactment relating to them. In *Attorney-General for Ireland v. Lagan*,[97] it was held that the bridge owner's responsibility extended only to keeping the bridge in an adequate state of repair for ordinary traffic at the date of the passing of the special Act.[98] Similarly, bridges constructed under the Railways Clauses Consolidation Act 1845[99] were to be maintained only to the extent which was, at the date of their

---

[88] (1811) 14 East 317.
[89] (1815) 3 M. & S. 526.
[90] See Chap. 4
[91] *R. v. Devon (Inhabitants)* (1825) 4 B. & C. 670; *R. v. Middlesex (Inhabitants)* (1832) 3 B. & Ad. 201, *per* Lord Tenterden C.J. at 208.
[92] See *ibid., per* Abbott C.J., Bayley J. at 677–8 and Littledale J. at 680; see also *R. v. Stretford (Inhabitants)* (1705) 2 Ld. Raym. 1169.
[93] Statutory power to purchase land for widening bridges had existed since the Bridges Act 1740; see also *Re Newport Bridge* (1859) 2 El. & El. 377.
[94] *R. v. Buckinghamshire (Inhabitants)* (1810) 12 East 192.
[95] *North Staffordshire Ry. Co. v. Hanley Corpn.* (1909) 73 J.P. 477.
[96] *R. v. Cluworth (Inhabitants)* (1704) 6 Mod. *Rep.* 163. *R. v. Lincoln Corpn.* (1838) 8 A. & E. 65.
[97] [1924] A.C. 877.
[98] See also *R. v. East & West India Dock Co.* (1889) 53 J.P. 277.
[99] s.46.

completion, sufficient for traffic.[1] In *Sharpness New Docks and Glouces-ter and Birmingham Navigation Company* v. *Attorney-General*,[2] the House of Lords held that a statute which required the canal company to construct bridges "of such dimensions and in such manner" as com-missioners appointed by the Act considered proper, and "from time to time" to support, maintain and keep in sufficient repair those bridges, should be considered with reference to the class of traffic on the high-ways when the bridges were built. No obligation was imposed on the company to maintain and keep up such bridges in a condition to carry the increased volume of traffic of the modern day. Where, however, the bridge was constructed to cross a cut made in a highway for which there was no statutory authority, or where the statute was silent[3] on the ques-tion of repair, the liability to maintain was very much closer to the com-mon law rules in relation to the highway itself. That responsibility of repair was to keep the roads in a reasonably fit state to bear the ordinary traffic of the district which might reasonably be expected to use the roads.[4]

Liability for the approaches to and the way carried by the bridge

11-34   The common law always seems to have accepted that the liability to repair a bridge must carry with it a responsibility to repair the approaches to the bridge.[5] The approaches might have to be altered in height or position whenever the bridge itself was repaired or rebuilt,[6] and the extra user attributable to the existence of the bridge—attracting travellers from a wide area wishing to cross the river conveniently—would otherwise place an unfair burden on the parish which was liable to repair the highways leading to the bridge. The precise extent of the county's liability, prior to the passing of the Statute of Bridges 1530, is uncertain, but that Act certainly crystallised the liability for the approaches to 300 feet on either side of the bridge proper.[7] After the passing of the Highway Act 1835, liability for the repair of the highway adjoining a bridge built after that date fell to the person or body liable to repair the highway leading to the bridge.[8] The distinction between the approaches to the bridge, and the bridge itself, is still retained in the

---

[1] *Att.-Gen.* v. *Great Northern Ry.* [1916] 2 A.C. 356; *West Lancashire R.C.* v. *Lancashire and Yorkshire Ry. Co.* [1903] 2 K.B. 394.
[2] [1915] A.C. 654.
[3] *R.* v. *Kerrison (Inhabitants)* (1815) 1 M.& S. 526; *Hertfordshire C.C.* v. *Great Eastern Ry. Co.* [1909] 2 K.B. 403.
[4] *Sharpness New Docks and Gloucester and Birmingham Navigation Co.* v. *Att.-Gen.* [1915] A.C. 654, *per* Lord Atkinson at 665 and Lord Parmoor at 688; *Manley* v. *St Helens Canal and Ry. Co.* (1858) 2 H. & N. 840.
[5] *Combe (Abbot) Case* (1369) 43 Lib. Ass. fo. 275, pl. 37, cited in *R.* v. *Staffordshire and Worcestershire Canal Co.* (1901) 65 J.P. 505.
[6] *R.* v. *West Riding of Yorkshire (Inhabitants)* (1806) 7 East 588; affirmed (5 Taunt 284).
[7] Statute of Bridges 1530, s.7; *R.* v. *West Riding of Yorkshire (Inhabitants)* (1806) 7 East 588; affirmed (1813 2 Dow. 1).
[8] Highway Act 1835, s.21; but the county was still responsible for walls, banks, fences, raised causeways and raised approaches.

Highways Act 1980 for some purposes.[9] Persons liable to repair by tenure or prescription are also liable to maintain the full approaches to the bridge.[10]

The extent of the liability of railway and canal undertakers for the maintenance of the approaches to the bridge has been open to some doubt. In *Hertfordshire County Council* v. *Great Eastern Railway Company*,[11] it was held that the liability did not necessarily extend to the 300 feet usually associated with the approaches to a bridge. Essentially, liability appears to have depended upon the construction of the statute.[12] So far as most railway and canal bridges are concerned, the respective responsibilities of the highway authority and the bridge owner are now governed by the Transport Act 1968.[13] **11–35**

Normally, responsibility for maintaining a bridge will also carry with it the liability for maintaining the road carried by the bridge.[14] The judicial decisions dealing with statutory interference with highways have, in some cases, drawn a distinction between the approaches to a bridge and the highway carried by the bridge. In *Lancashire and Yorkshire Railway Company* v. *Bury Corporation*,[15] it was held that the Railways Clauses Consolidation Act 1845 imposed an obligation on railway companies to maintain the roadway carried by the bridge, as well as the bridge structure. In *London & North Eastern Railway Company* v. *North Riding of Yorkshire County Council*,[16] a similiar construction was placed upon a special Act empowering the erection of a bridge carrying a road over the railway.[17] These cases must be taken to have settled that, where a statute empowers undertakers to interrupt the highway and to carry the highway over their railway or canal, then, unless there are clear words to the contrary, the liability of the undertaker will extend not only to the fabric of the bridge, but also to maintaining the way which crosses it. It seems, therefore, that the same principle will apply where the bridge has been made necessary by an unauthorised interference with the highway, since the obligation to maintain the bridge, in those circumstances, is effectively to restore and maintain the public right of passage which was initially interrupted.[18] **11–36**

---

[9] See Highways Act 1980, ss.3 and 49.
[10] *R.* v. *Lincoln* (1838) 8 Ad. & E. 65.
[11] [1909] 2 K.B. 403.
[12] *Nottingham C.C.* v. *Manchester, Sheffield and Lincolnshire Ry. Co.* (1894) 71 L.T. 430; *R.* v. *Staffordshire and Worcestershire Canal Co.* (1901) 65 J.P. 505; *Hertfordshire C.C.* v. *Great Eastern Ry. Co.* [1909] 2 K.B. 403.
[13] See para. 11–46, below.
[14] See, *per* Swinfen Eady J. in *Herfordshire C.C.* v. *New River Co.* [1904] 2 Ch. 513 at 521.
[15] (1889) 14 App. Cas. 417.
[16] [1936] 1 All E.R. 692; see also *Att.-Gen.* v. *Midland Ry. Co.* (1909) 100 L.T. 866.
[17] See also *Macclesfield Corpn.* v. *Great Central Ry. Co.* [1911] 2 K.B. 528.
[18] *R.* v. *Kerrison* (1815) 2 M.& S. 526; *Hertfordshire C.C.* v. *Great Eastern Ry. Co.* [1909] 2 K.B. 403; see also the dissenting judgment of Viscount Haldane in *Att.-Gen.* v. *Great Northern Ry. Co.* [1916] 2 A.C. 356.

STATUTORY POWERS GOVERNING THE RELATIONSHIP BETWEEN THE
OWNERS OF PRIVATELY MAINTAINABLE BRIDGES AND HIGHWAY
AUTHORITIES

11–37 Where a bridge is maintainable as part of a highway, the general powers given to highway authorities will also apply to the bridge. However, it may happen that the liability to repair the bridge is placed upon a body other than the highway authority. The legislation, therefore, contains a number of provisions which govern the relationship between the highway authorities and the bridge owners.

Enforcement of liability to repair bridges

11–38 Section 56 of the Highways Act 1980, which provides a procedure for compelling the maintenance of highways maintainable at the public expense, may be used in respect of either a "way" or a "bridge." The notice served under section 56(1) may be served on "the highway authority or other person alleged to be liable to maintain the way or bridge." An order under this section for the repair of a bridge may, therefore, relate to the way carried by the bridge or to the structure, or to both. The procedure for compelling maintenance of the bridge may also be used in respect of privately maintainable bridges, against those persons who are liable to repair. Where that liability arises out of tenure, proceedings should be brought against the occupier of the land burdened with the responsibility and, where the land originally burdened has been split up into more than one ownership, the occupiers for each of those parts will be liable.[19]

Order for reconstruction or transfer of privately maintainable bridges

11–39 Where a bridge is maintainable by some person or body other than a highway authority, that person, or the highway authority for the highway carried by the bridge, may make an application to the Minister for an order to provide for the reconstruction, improvement or maintenance of the bridge, or of the highway carried by the bridge, or of the approaches to the bridge. The section applies to bridges which are not themselves part of a highway maintainable at the public expense, and which carry a carriageway across a railway, canal, river, creek, watercourse, marsh or other place where water flows or is collected, or over a ravine or other depression.[20] A highway authority may only make such an application itself where it considers either that the bridge, by reason of its construction, position, or state of repair, is, or may be, dangerous or unsuitable for the requirements of existing or expected road traffic or, alternatively, that for some other reason, responsibility for the

---

[19] See, generally, Chap. 4
[20] Thus, the range of "bridges" covered by the section is wider than the meaning of "bridge" at common law: see para. 11–16, above.

maintenance and improvement of the bridge should be transferred from the owners to a highway authority.[21]

Before making an order, the Minister must consult the owners of the **11–40** bridge and every relevant local highway authority and, if requested to do so by these parties, he must hold a local inquiry. The order may contain provisions requiring the execution, either by the owners of the bridge or by the highway authority, of any such works of reconstruction or improvement as may be specified in the order. The Minister may determine and direct by whom the bridge and its approaches are to be maintained. He may provide for the transfer to and vesting in a highway authority of the property in the bridge, or of the highway carried by the bridge, or of the approaches to the bridge, or of all or any of the rights and obligations attaching to the bridge, highway or approaches. The consent of railway and dock or harbour undertakers and of the British Waterways Board may be required to the inclusion, within the order, of certain of the above provisions.[22] Statutory provisions relating to the bridge may also be modified by the order, unless they are concerned with the precedence of traffic in relation to a swing bridge.[23] The order cannot direct that a swing bridge over a canal is to be operated other than by the owners of the canal, unless the Minister is satisfied (after hearing representations from the owners of the canal) that facilities for traffic on the canal will not be prejudiced thereby.[24] The procedure for the making of an order under section 93 is contained within Schedule 11, and involves the preparation of a draft order subject to confirmation with or without modification. There are complex publication and notice requirements.[25] Where there are unresolved objections, a local inquiry must be held or a hearing afforded to the objector (together with the bridge owner and the highway authority). The order may be made with or without modifications, or the Minister may decide not to make the order. The order, when made, must be published and served in a similiar way to the draft order.

Highway authorities may acquire land, and the Minister may author- **11–41** ise the owners of a bridge to acquire land, to enable them to comply with a requirement or direction contained in an order made under section 93.[26] The powers exercisable under section 93 and 94 of the Highways Act 1980 may not be exercised in such a way as to stop traffic on any canal without the consent of the canal owners,[27] and must be exercised generally so as to prevent, so far as is practicable, interference with traffic on a canal.

---

[21] Highways Act 1980, s.93(1).
[22] See *ibid.* Sched.11, para.4.
[23] *Ibid.* s.93(3)(*e*) and Sched. 11, para.2.
[24] *Ibid.* Sched. 11, para.1.
[25] *Ibid.* Sched. 11, para.8. Protection is given to the apparatus of statutory undertakers: *ibid.* paras. 13–14.
[26] *Ibid.* s.242(1), (2).
[27] Which consent must not be unreasonably witheld: see *ibid.* s.95(7).

Agreements between highway authorities and bridge owners

11–42 Power is also given to highway authorities to enter into agreements with the owners of bridges[28] which carry carriageway highways not maintainable at the public expense, for the payment of contributions by the highway authority to the cost of reconstruction, improvement or maintenance of the bridge, or of the highway carried by the bridge, or of the approaches to the bridge.[29] Agreements may also provide for the transfer to the highway authority of responsibility for maintaining the bridge or its approaches, or of the property in the bridge, its approaches and the highway carried by it, or of any rights or obligations relating to the bridge.[30]

Bridges carrying trunk roads and special roads

11–43 Where a highway comprising a privately-maintainable bridge becomes a trunk road, the bridge[31] is automatically transferred, by virtue of the Highways Act 1980, section 266, to the Minister on the date on which the whole of that highway becomes a trunk road. The whole of the estate or interest of the bridge owner in the bridge and the highway carried by it will vest in the Minister,[32] and any statutory provisions relating to the protection of statutory undertakers will thereafter apply to the Minister as they had formerly applied to the bridge owner. The Minister must pay compensation to the bridge owner[33] based upon the value of the bridge as an asset productive of revenue. The bridge will only be treated as such an asset where the owners have a contractual right to payments in respect of use of the bridge or where the bridge includes a building constructed or adapted for use by the owners in connection with their undertaking.[34] Protection is given to any undertaking of the bridge owner which may be crossed by the bridge by maintaining the headway or span of the bridge and by requiring notice to be given before the Minister enters onto the bridge owners' land in order to carry out works of maintenance on the bridge.[35] Disputes between the Minister and the bridge owner are to be settled by arbitration.[36] Similiar provisions apply where a highway carried by a privately-maintainable bridge is included in the route of a special road.[37]

---

[28] As to railways undertakers' bridges, see Highways Act 1980, s.95(5) and the Transport Act 1968, Part VII.

[29] Highways Act 1980, s.94(1).

[30] *Ibid.* s.94(1).

[31] Including so much of the approaches thereto as supports or protects the surface of the trunk road: *ibid.* s.266(9). As to the bridges covered by these provisions, see *ibid.* 266(9).

[32] Unless otherwise agreed between the bridge owner and the Minister: *ibid.* s.166(4).

[33] Including anyone who immediately before the transfer was discharging the responsibility of maintenance on behalf of the person liable to repair: *ibid.* s.266(10).

[34] *Ibid.* s.226(5).

[35] See *ibid.* s.266(6), (7).

[36] *Ibid.* s.266(5), (8).

[37] *Ibid.* s.267.

The liability of the bridge owner to maintain or improve[38] a bridge **11–44** will be extinguished on the road becoming a trunk road or special road, and the bridge owner may be liable to make payments to the Minister in respect of the value of that extinguishment of liability.[39] In the case of bridges belonging to the Railways Board, London Regional Transport or the Waterways Board, the bridge owners will neither be required to make any payment in respect of the extinguishment of their liability, nor be entitled to compensation for the value of the bridge as a revenue producing asset, unless, and insofar as, the entitlement to compensation exceeds the liability to make payments.[40]

Where a trunk road carried by a bridge vested in a Minister under section 266 ceases to be trunk road, the Minister may contribute towards **11–45** the expenses to be incurred in the maintenance of the bridge[41] by the council which becomes the highway authority for the road.

Canal and railway bridges

Respective responsibilities of highway authorities and railway or canal undertakers

The Transport Act 1968, Part VIII, contains a number of provisions **11–46** for regulating the responsibilities of highway authorities and the Railways Board, London Regional Transport and the Waterways Board,[42] in respect of bridges[43] carrying highways over railways[44] or inland waterways. Where one of the Boards or London Regional Transport[45] was responsible for maintaining the highway carried by the bridge and where the highway at each end of the bridge was a highway maintainable at the public expense, then the highway carried by the bridge became a highway maintainable at the public expense on *the appointed day*.[46] Bridges to be constructed by the Boards or by London Regional Transport, which fulfill the same conditions, will also become maintainable at the public expense.[47] Where one of the Boards or London Regional Transport is also responsible for maintaining the highway giving access to the bridge, then that highway will become maintainable at the public expense in similiar circumstances.[48] These provisions

---

[38] *e.g.* under statute a liability to improve the bridge may be imposed.
[39] Highways Act 1980, s.55.
[40] Transport Act 1968, s.119.
[41] Including the highway carried by the bridge and so much of the approaches as supports or protects the surface of the trunk road: Highways Act 1980, s.277.
[42] As to bridges owned by other bodies which are covered by these provisions, see Transport Act 1968, s.121.
[43] Tunnels carrying railways and canals under highways are to be treated as if the structure of the tunnel was a bridge: *ibid.* s.122.
[44] Including railways which have ceased to carry traffic and the sites of railways from which the track has been removed : see *ibid.* s.122.
[45] Or its predecessors.
[46] See Transport Act 1968, s.166(2)
[47] *Ibid.* s.116(4).
[48] *Ibid.* s.116(1).

override any agreement, between the highway authority and the Boards or London Regional Transport, for the maintenance of the bridge beyond the appointed day.[49] The provisions affect only the surface of the highway and do not affect the liability to maintain the bridge itself. Furthermore, the highway authority will not be under any duty to make good, nor to incur any liability by reason of, any defect in the surface of the highway, where the defect is due to the failure of the Boards or London Regional Transport to maintain the structure and fabric of the bridge itself.[50] The highway authority will not be liable for any defect in the highway arising out of any act or omission which had occurred before it became responsible for the maintenance of the highway. This immunity will, presumably, not last forever, and a failure to deal with a pre-existing defect in the surface of the highway, known to the highway authority, may eventually become a present failure of the highway authority to maintain the highway. The highway authority must permit the Boards or London Regional Transport to carry out works in the surface of the highway in order to fulfil their responsibility to maintain the bridge and to obtain access to their apparatus. The highway authority may not, without the Boards' or London Regional Transport's consent, increase to a significant extent the weight of the materials constituting the surface of the highway.[51]

Duties of railway and canal undertakers

11–47   Where a bridge belonging to the Waterways Board, the British Railways Board or the London Regional Transport Executive[52] carries a highway over their railway[53] or inland waterway or over any installation or land used in connection with their railway or inland waterway, the Boards and London Regional Transport come under various duties with respect to the construction and maintenance of those bridges regarding the preservation of their load-bearing capacity.[54] The Boards must maintain bridges belonging to them which carry highways and, where necessary, improve or strengthen them so that they have the required load-bearing capacity. Where it is not reasonably practicable to improve or strengthen a bridge, they will be required to reconstruct the bridge or to replace it with a new bridge.[55]

---

[49] Transport Act 1968, s.116(2), (3).

[50] *Ibid.* s.116(6); civil liability for failure to maintain would, therefore, not fall on the highway authority.

[51] *Ibid.* s.116(6).

[52] As to bridges owned by other bodies which are covered by these provisions, see *ibid.* s.121.

[53] See *ibid.* s.122.

[54] As to the "required load bearing capacity" see *ibid.* s.117(2), (3) and the Railway Bridges (Load Bearing Standards) (England and Wales) Order 1972 (S.I. 1972 No. 1705) and Circular No. Roads 63/72.

[55] As to the relationship of these provisions to Railways Clauses Consolidation Act 1845, ss.46, 50, 51, 52, 66, or under any similar enactment, see Transport Act 1968, s.117(6).

Duty of highway authorities and bridge owners

Where a bridge is owned by a highway authority or by some person, **11–48** other than the Waterways Board, the British Railways Board or London Regional Transport,[56] whose canal or railway is crossed by the bridge, the bridge owner is placed under certain duties with respect to the maintenance of the bridge, over and above his duty to maintain the bridge for the purposes of the highway. By section 118 of the Transport Act 1968, the bridge owner is required to maintain the bridge in such a condition that it is not a source of danger to, and does not interfere with, or require any restriction to be placed upon, the traffic from time using the inland waterway or railway crossed by the bridge.[57] In order to carry out the responsibilities of maintenance, the bridge owner must be afforded access to the land occupied by the relevant Board or London Regional Transport, except where to do so would involve danger to, or interference with, or would require any restriction to be placed upon, the traffic using the waterway or railway. In these cases, the bridge owner is not under any further duty of maintenance in respect of those works which it is prevented from carrying out, but the Boards or London Regional Transport may themselves carry out the works and recover the reasonable expenses of so doing from the bridge owner.[58]

The Boards or London Regional Transport are themselves entitled to **11–49** inspect and survey the bridge and may serve a notice requiring the bridge owner to bring the bridge up to the necessary standard. They may, themselves, carry out the works in default or in cases of urgency.[59] However, these powers in themselves do not authorise any interference with traffic using the highway which crosses the bridge, and the provisions of the Public Utilities Street Works Act 1950 will apply to works carried out in the highway.[60] The right of entry into the bridge is only exercisable after service of seven days' notice stating the purpose of the proposed entry, except in cases of urgency. The bridge owner will be entitled to compensation if his bridge is damaged by the Boards or London Regional Transport.[61] Disputes between the bridge owner and the Boards or London Regional Transport are to be referred to arbitration, except where the dispute concerns one of those matters which is to be determined by the opinion of the Boards or London Regional Transport. However, the reference to arbitration is not to preclude the carrying out of the works.[62] The duties imposed by section 118 of the Transport Act 1968 are in addition to those imposed on the highway authority or bridge owner by virtue of any other enactment, or by

[56] As to bridges owned by other bodies which are covered by these provisions, see Transport Act 1968 s.121.
[57] *Ibid.* s.118(2).
[58] *Ibid.* s.118(4).
[59] *Ibid.* s.118(3).
[60] *Ibid.* s.118(12); see Chap. 13.
[61] Transport Act 1968, s.118(7).
[62] *Ibid.* s.118(9).

agreement.[63] Arrangements between the Boards or Executive and the bridge owner, arising out of agreements, may themselves be modified or abrogated by agreement or by arbitration.[64] Protection is provided for the apparatus of the bridge owner or of the other persons, which is incorporated in, or attached to, the bridge.

11–50   In many cases, railway companies and canal companies had, in the past, entered into agreements with highway authorities for the payment of contributions by them to the upkeep of highway bridges crossing railways, whilst the highway authority was actually to maintain them. These agreements have, to some extent, been supplanted by the provisions of sections 116 to 118. However, for some purposes, those agreements will still have effect.

[63] Transport Act 1968, s.118(8).
[64] *Ibid.* s.118(8).

CHAPTER 12

FOOTPATHS AND BRIDLEWAYS

INTRODUCTION

Footpaths and bridleways, by the nature of the public rights which they **12–01** carry, have been less obviously visible on the ground than have carriageway highways. They are generally much narrower than carriageway highways and are seldom made up. Although the inhabitants at large were liable at common law to repair footpaths and bridleways in the same way as they were required to maintain carriageway highways, the degree of repair was, in practice, never as great. The duty to repair was always related to the kinds of traffic which a highway might carry, and there was, therefore, not the same need to undertake extensive maintenance work in those paths which carried no heavy traffic. The major problem with footpaths and bridleways has always been one of identification.

Footpaths and bridleways have attained further significance over the **12–02** last century, by providing access into the countryside for the increasing number of ramblers and leisure horse riders. A number of active pressure groups have become established whose aims include the preservation and improvement of the footpath and bridleway network. It was thus out of legislation aimed at improving the access of the city dweller to the countryside, that the first attempt came to provide a comprehensive basis for the identification and mapping of the footpaths across the countryside.

MAPPING OF PUBLIC PATHS

National Parks and Access to the Countryside Act 1949

The National Parks and Access to the Countryside Act 1949 required **12–03** the councils of counties[1] to undertake a survey of the public paths within their area and to prepare a map, to be known as the "definitive map and statement," of these public paths. The procedure for preparation of these maps was long and complex.

First, the authority were required, in consultation with the councils of **12–04** county districts and parishes, to prepare a *draft* map indicating all footpaths, bridleways and roads used as public paths which, in the authority's opinion, subsisted or were reasonably alleged to have subsisted at

---

[1] s.27. The councils of county boroughs were given power to adopt these provisions: *ibid.* s.36.

a specified date.[2] Notice of the preparation of the draft map was to be published. Provision was made for the lodging of objections. There then followed a hearing by a person appointed by the authority to determine those objections. Where, in response to objections, a modification was made to the draft map by the addition or the deletion of a path, a further publication, objection and hearing process was necessary in relation to each such modification. A person aggrieved by a decision taken after this stage of the process, involving the omission or deletion of an alleged path from the map, then had a further right of appeal to the Minister.

12–05   Once the objection and appeal procedures belonging to this stage were completed, the authority was required to prepare a *provisional* map and statement,[3] containing the particulars making up the draft map, together with any modifications made to it. A publication process was again prescribed. A right of appeal to quarter sessions and subsequently to the Crown Court[4] was available to a landowner who disputed the existence, extent or route of a path crossing his land.[5] Only after the expiry of the time for an appeal, or the determination of such an appeal, could the authority finally prepare its *definitive* map and statement. A final right of challenge to the High Court, on the grounds that the map or statement was not within the powers of the Act, or that some procedural irregularity had occured, was granted by Part III of Schedule 1 to the Act.[6]

12–06   The 1949 Act also required the authority to keep its definitive map under periodic revision, having regard to events which had occurred at any time between the date on which the definitive map was based and the date of the review.[7] The only events which justified such a review, however, were the creation or extinguishment of rights of way in the intervening period, and the discovery of new evidence which would have required the authority, had it then been preparing a draft map, to show on that map, as a highway of a particular description, a way not in fact shown on the definitive map. The Act, therefore, allowed for the alteration of the map by the addition of paths mistakenly omitted from the original draft map but not for the removal of paths wrongly recorded, unless the statutory process for stopping up had been carried out. A similiar process of hearing and determining objections was then

---

[2] National Parks and Access to the Countryside Act 1949, ss. 27 and 28. See also the National Parks and Access to the Countryside Regulations 1950 (S.I. 1950 No. 1066).

[3] As to the status of a provisional map, see *Armstrong* v. *Whitfield* [1974] Q.B. 16.

[4] National Parks and Access to the Countryside Act 1949, s.31 and the Public Rights of Way (Applications to Quarter Sessions) Regulations 1952 (S.I. 1952 No. 559) (as amended).

[5] See *Armstrong* v. *Whitfield*, n. 3, above; *Walwin* v. *West Sussex C.C.* [1975] 3 All E.R. 604.

[6] Challenge to the validity of the map after the six-week period was thereafter precluded: National Parks and Access to the Countryside Act 1949, Sched. 1, Part III, para.10. See also *Chivers & Sons Ltd.* v. *Cambridge C.C.* [1957] 2 Q.B. 68.

[7] National Parks and Access to the Countryside Act 1949, s.33.

applicable in the same way as when the original map was being prepared.[8]

Countryside Act 1968

The Countryside Act 1968 modified the procedure for the preparation   12–07
and revision of definitive maps in a number of ways.[9] The procedure for
the revision of a map was amended to allow for a definitive map to be
revised, on the discovery by an authority of new evidence, or of
evidence *not previously considered* by the authority, that there was *no*
public right of way of the sort shown on the definitive map or that any of
the particulars shown in the map or statement were not within the
powers of the 1949 Act. This extension of the power to revise could,
however only apply to revisions carried out after the commencement of
the 1968 Act,[10] and was subject to the proviso that no account should be
taken of any evidence which the surveying authority was satisfied could
have been produced by the person prejudiced at the time of the original
preparation process, in the absence of any reasonable excuse for his failing to do so. The process of review was also simplified to avoid the three
stages of draft, provisional and definitive map preparation, and the procedure for dealing with objections was itself streamlined.[11] The 1968
Act also required a special review of all "roads used as public paths," to
be carried out, with a view to re-classifying them as footpaths, bridleways or "byways open to all traffic."

Local Government Act 1972

Schedule 17 to the Local Government Act 1972 extended the duty to   12–08
prepare definitive maps to the councils of the new administrative counties. It followed, therefore, that these new councils inherited, within the
new county boundaries, areas which might be in different stages of preparation or review of the definitive map. A chaotic situation, therefore,
could potentially have arisen, especially within the new metropolitan
counties. The 1972 Act attempted to deal with this situation. Whilst the
county councils were permitted to retain the adoptive nature of the 1949
Act in those parts of the county which formerly consisted of a county
borough and which had not adopted the provisions of the 1949 Act, the
county council was placed under a duty to concentrate on the preparation of the first definitive map or maps before continuing with any
reviews which might already have been commenced within the county.[12]
Once the council's area was covered by a definitive map or maps, a
review of the whole of the county was to be carried out. The county
council was also permitted to abandon surveys which were in the earlier

---

[8] National Parks and Access to the Countryside Act 1949, ss.33–34.
[9] Countryside Act 1968, s.31 and Sched. 3.
[10] August 3, 1968.
[11] Countryside Act 1968, Sched. 3, Part II.
[12] Local Government Act 1972, Sched. 17, Part II, paras. 27 and 29.

stages of preparation and to start again.[13] Schedule 17, therefore, provided a recipe for limiting the confusion faced by county councils which had inherited maps in varying stages of preparation. However, the process of bringing the whole of a county up to the same level remained cumbersome and time-consuming. The duty to prepare maps was still not universal, in that the areas of some of the former county boroughs could still be excluded.

Wildlife and Countryside Act 1981

12–09   Although the 1968 Act simplified the process by which a revision of the definitive map could be undertaken, the procedure for the preparation of draft, provisional and definitive maps was retained insofar as preparation had been commenced before the 1968 Act came into force. The preparation of reviews of the definitive map and, in some cases, the preparation of the map itself, still, in some areas, progressed very slowly. The response of the government was to incorporate in the Wildlife and Countryside Act 1981 provisions to eliminate the need for formal "across the board" reviews, and to establish a more flexible incremental system, whereby the definitive map was to be kept under continuous review with necessary changes being carried out on a piecemeal basis. The Wildlife and Countryside Act 1981, therefore, repealed those parts of the National Parks and Access to the Countryside Act 1949 which were concerned with the preparation of definitive maps, and replaced them with a much simpler procedure, involving continuous review of the definitive map.

The definitive map and statement

12–10   The definitive map and statement for any area may fall into one of three possible categories. Where there is a revised map prepared under the provisions of section 33 of the 1949 Act,[14] then this will be the definitive map and statement. Where there is no such map, the original definitive map prepared under section 32 of the 1949 Act will remain the definitive map. Otherwise, a map and statement is to be prepared under the provisions of the Wildlife and Countryside Act 1981, and this will then become the definitive map and statement. Thus, the definitive map for any area may have been prepared under the onerous provisions of the 1949 Act in its original form, or under the much shorter procedure contained in the 1981 Act. The safeguards against error have been much reduced by the procedure contained in the 1981 Act but, on the other hand, the procedure for correcting mistakes has been made correspondingly easier.

---

[13] Local Government Act 1972, Sched. 17, Part II, paras. 24–26.
[14] As amended and modified by Countryside Act 1968.

Where, at the date of the commencement of the 1981 Act,[15] no defini- **12–11**
tive map had been completed by an authority for any part of its area[16] or
where a review of the definitive map was still in preparation, the Secretary of State may, after consultation with the surveying authority,[17]
direct the authority to complete the survey or to review or abandon it,
either wholly or partially.[18] Where the authority is directed to abandon
a survey or review, it is obliged to prepare a map and statement which is
then to become the definitive map and statement for the area, by means
of a modification order made under the Act. The authority is required to
incorporate into that map and statement such work as had been completed prior to the commencement of the the the 1981 Act and which had
not been objected to within the prescribed period, together with any
determinations by the authority or the Secretary of State which had
become final.[19]

The definitive map is required to be at a scale of not less than two and **12–12**
a half inches to one mile (1/25,000) but it may contain inset maps for
particular areas at a larger scale. The notation to be used for indicating
different classes of paths is prescribed by regulations.[20] The statement
which accompanies the map is required to record the "relevant date,"
for the purposes of the map, together with particulars as to the position
and width of the path and any limitations or conditions affecting the
public right of way. The "relevant date" is the base date of the survey
from which the map has been prepared or modified. This date must have
been no earlier than six months before the date on which notice of the
preparation of the draft map or review was published in the case of maps
prepared under the 1949 Act provisions, and not earlier than six months
before the preparation of the map in those cases where the map is prepared under the provisions of the 1981 Act.[21] Where the map is modified by an order under section 53(4), the order itself must prescribe the
"relevant date," which must not be earlier than six months prior to the
making of the order.[22] So far as the other details are concerned, there
have been wide discrepancies between different authorities as to the
amount of detail which is included in the statement. Little statutory
guidance is provided on this matter. Where there is a conflict between
the statement and the map itself, then the usual principle would be that
the statement is to prevail, but, again, there is no confirmation in the
statute that this is to be the case.

---

[15] February 28, 1983 (S.I. 1983 No.20).
[16] *e.g.* in the area of a former county borough.
[17] As to which, see n. 23 below.
[18] Wildlife and Countryside Act 1981, s.55.
[19] *i.e.* under s.29(3), (4) and (6) of the 1949 Act, and para. 4(4) of Part II of Schedule 3 to the 1968 Act.
[20] Wildlife and Countryside Act 1981, s.57(2); Wildlife and Countryside (Definitive Maps and Statements) Regulations 1983 (S.I.1983 No. 21).
[21] National Parks and Access to the Countryside Act 1949, ss.27(3) and 34.
[22] Wildlife and Countryside Act 1981, s.56(3).

Duty of the surveying authority

12–13   The duty to prepare and review the definitive map falls upon the "surveying authority."[23] Where there is no definitive map for any part of its area, the surveying authority is under a duty to prepare a definitive map and statement. Where there is a definitive map and statement for its area, the surveying authority is to modify it as soon as practicable after the commencement date of the Act, and is thereafter to keep the definitive map and statement under continuous review. Any review of the definitive map is, however, only to be carried out on the occurrence of any one of five specified events.[24] These are:

(a) the stopping up, diversion, widening or extension of any highway under statutory powers;

(b) the alteration of the status of any highway under statutory powers;

(c) the creation of a public path, for example, under a public path creation order or agreement, by dedication and acceptance;

(d) the expiration of the 20 year period under section 31 of the Highways Act 1980, giving rise to a presumption that a way has been dedicated as a highway;

(e) the discovery by the authority of evidence which, when considered with all other evidence available to it, shows that a right of way not shown on the map subsists or is reasonably alleged to subsist, or that a highway of a particular description on the map should be shown as a highway of a different description, or that there is no public right of way over land shown as being a highway, or that any particulars contained in the map require modification.

12–14   Where the object of a review is to remove a path from the map or to downgrade a bridleway to a footpath, a number of problems may arise. Section 53(2)(c) requires "the discovery by the authority of evidence . . . . . . that there *is* no public right of way . . . " The Countryside Act 1968[25] had specifically required that the evidence required to justify a removal of a path should be "new evidence, or . . . evidence not previously considered by the authority concerned showing that there *was* no public right of way . . . ." It remains unlikely that, in the absence of any *new* evidence, the surveying authority is permitted under the Wildlife and Countryside 1981 Act to regard the original survey work and procedures as having been mistaken. This approach would run

---

[23] The "county council, metropolitan district council or London borough council": see Wildlife and Countryside Act 1981, s.66(1) as amended by Local Government Act 1985, s.7 and Sched. 3.

[24] Wildlife and Countryside Act 1981, s.53(2), (3).

[25] Sched. 3, Part I; see also para. 12–07, above.

counter to the conclusive nature of the definitive map.[26] Indeed, it has been held, in *Rubinstein* v. *Secretary of State for the Environment*,[27] that, in view of the conclusive evidence provisions of section 56 and the apparent need to look at the situation as at the date of the review, the review procedure cannot be used to remove a path from the map unless the evidence which is discovered affects the status of the way *after* the original inclusion of the path in the map. If so, then, in view of the principle "once a highway always a highway," it is difficult to envisage in what circumstances, other than the physical destruction of the land over which the highway passes, the review mechanism could operate to remove a path. It seems highly unlikely that this rare situation was in the mind of the parliamentary draftsman, and the consequent alteration in the law involved appears to have been entirely unanticipated by the Department of Environment which promoted the legislation.[28] The decision in *Rubinstein* emphasises the use of the word "is" in section 53, compared with the use of "was" in the 1968 Act—the latter provision, but not the former, permitting a consideration of the situation at the time when the original maps came into being. The decision does not cover the downgrading of paths, which only requires evidence to show "that a highway shown in the map and statement as a highway of a particular description ought to be there shown as a highway of a different description." A downgrading would, however, operate to deny the existence of rights of which the map is also conclusive evidence. The *Rubinstein* decision has made it far more difficult to remove a path from the map than had been the case under the 1968 Act. This approach is at odds with the remainder of the provisions of the 1981 Act, which are designed to make the procedures (certainly insofar as they may involve the addition of paths) more flexible.[29]

The Wildlife and Countryside Act 1981 requires that surveying auth- **12-15** orities carry out a review to reclassify those rights of way which were shown on the definitive map as "roads used as a public path" (RUPPS). It was the Countryside Act 1968 which had first required that this reclassification be carried out. The purpose of reclassification was to have these RUPPS described in the definitive map as footpaths, bridleways or byways open to all traffic.[30] The definition of "road used as a public path" in the National Parks and Access to the Countryside Act 1949 defined these ways as being:

---

[26] *Morgan* v. *Hertfordshire C.C.* (1965) 63 L.G.R. 456; *Armstrong* v. *Whitfield* [1974] Q.B. 16; *R.* v. *Secretary of State for the Environment, ex p. Hood* [1975] 1 Q.B. 891; *Walwin* v. *West Sussex C.C.* [1975] 3 All E.R. 604.
[27] [1988] J.P.L. 485.
[28] See Circular 1/83, para. 16.
[29] See also under the former law, *R.* v. *Secretary of State for the Environment, ex p. Stewart* (1978) 77 L.G.R. 431.
[30] Countryside Act 1968, Sched. 3, paras. 7 and 8; Wildlife and Countryside Act 1981, s.54(2).

> "a highway, other than a public path, used by the public mainly for the purposes for which footpaths or bridleways are so used."

The effect of this definition appeared to indicate that the road in question, being a *highway* other than a public path, must be a cartway (carriageway), since this was the only other kind of highway (other than footpaths and bridleways) which was known to the law. Section 32(4)(*b*) of the 1949 Act, however, went on to say that the inclusion within the definitive map of a RUPP was to be conclusive proof:

> "that there was at the said date a highway as shown on the map, and that the public had thereover at that date a right of way on foot and a right of way on horseback or leading a horse, so however that this paragraph shall be without prejudice to any question whether the public had at that date any right of way other than the rights as aforesaid . . ."

The only other public right which could have existed would have been the public right of cart or carriageway. It seems, therefore, that whilst a surveying authority would have had to have believed that the RUPP was a public carriageway highway in order to put it on the map in the first place, the map was not conclusive as to the existence of any greater rights over it, other than those of foot and bridleway. At the date of any re-classification, however, horse riders would have been permitted to use the way as a bridleway for many years. To confuse matters further, some local authorities had included, as RUPPs, in their definitive maps, roads which were not public cartways or carriageways, but which were private roads carrying public rights of way by foot or on horse. In *R. v. Secretary of State for the Environment, ex parte Hood*,[31] a RUPP was, as the result of a special review, downgraded to a footpath. This was challenged by the Horse Society, who alleged that it should have been reclassified as a bridleway. The Court of Appeal held that since a RUPP would have been conclusively presumed to have carried rights of bridleway as well as footway under the National Parks and Access to the Countryside Act 1949, it was necessary, on a special review, for there to be positive new evidence to the effect that there was *no* public right of bridleway, before the path could be reclassified as footpath. Where the evidence was inconclusive as to the extent of the public right of way, the reclassification had to be as a bridleway. The 1968 Act could be construed as permitting the downgrading of a RUPP by the extinguishment of vehicular rights (in relation to which the map had never been conclusive) but not as involving the loss of the right of bridleway.

12–16   The 1981 Act also requires that RUPPs be reclassified but, in the light of the *Hood* decision, it specifies more precisely how the road is to be treated on such a reclassification. Section 54(3) states that a road used as a public path shall be shown on the definitive map after such a review:

[31] [1975] 1 Q.B. 891.

"(a) if a public right of way for vehicular traffic has been shown to exist, as a byway open to all traffic;

(b) if paragraph (a) does not apply and public bridleway rights have not been shown not to exist, as a bridleway; and

(c) if neither paragraph (a) nor paragraph (b) applies, as a foot-path."

The effect of paragraph (*b*), therefore, is to incorporate the decision in *Hood*, thereby requiring the authority to be convinced that the way is not a bridleway whilst the burden is otherwise on the person asserting the vehicular right to convince the authority that there are vehicular rights of way. It seems likely that wherever a path is to be downgraded, the *Hood* approach is likely to be followed by a court.

Procedure

Any person may apply to the surveying authority for an order modify- **12–17** ing the definitive map, but the discretion as to whether or not to make the order remains with the authority, who must decide whether one of the necessary "events" justifying and requiring a review has occurred. The form of an application is prescribed by regulations.[32] The application must be accompanied by a map and by any documentary evidence, including the statements of any witnesses, which the applicant wishes to adduce in support of his application.[33] The applicant must serve notice of the application on the owners and occupiers of any land to which the application relates, and must supply a certificate to the authority to the effect that he has complied with this requirement.[34] In certain cases, the authority may authorise the service of the notice by addressing it to "the owner or occupier" and affixing it to some conspicuous object on the land. After receipt of the certificate, the authority must, as soon as is practicable, investigate the matters stated in the application and must, after consulting with every local authority[35] whose area includes land affected by the application, decide whether to make the order. Where the authority fails to determine the application within 12 months of receipt of a certificate, the applicant may make representations to the Secretary of State, who may direct the authority to determine it within a specified time. There is no further sanction provided against a dilatory authority, and the Secretary of State is not *required* to make a direction. Where an authority fails to determine an application, after a direction from the Secretary of State, the direction ought to be capable of enforcement by him by an application of judicial review seeking an order of mandamus. It is less clear whether a similar remedy

[32] See the Wildlife and Countryside (Definitive Maps and Statements) Regulations 1983 (S.I. 1983 No.21).
[33] Wildlife and Countryside Act 1981, Sched. 14, para.1.
[34] The form of the notice and of the certificate is prescribed in the regulations.
[35] *i.e.* any non-metropolitan district council, parish or community council, or the parish meeting where there is no parish council.

would be available to the applicant. Where, after considering the application, the authority decides not to make an order, the applicant may appeal to the Secretary of State within 28 days of the service on him of notice of the decision. The decision as to whether the modification order should be made then lies with the Secretary of State, who may issue directions to the authority concerned.

12–18   Once the authority has decided to make an order, the procedure for modifying the definitive map by way of a review and the procedure for the preparation of any first definitive map are contained in the Wildlife and Countryside Act 1981, sections 53 to 57 and Schedules 14 and 15. Before making such an order, the surveying authority must consult with every local authority whose area includes the land to which the order relates. On making the order, the authority must give notice, in the form prescribed by regulations,[36] to the owners and occupiers of the land affected,[37] to local authorities whose area includes the land, to any person who, on payment of a reasonable charge to the authority, has required the authority to give him notice of such orders, and to a number of organisations which are prescribed in the regulations. The notice must also be advertised in local papers and must be displayed at the ends of so much of any way as is affected by the order,[38] in council offices in the locality of the affected land and at such other places as the authority considers appropriate. The notices must indicate the general effect of the order, that it has been made, and that it requires confirmation. The notices must name a place where the order may be inspected free of charge, and must specify both the time (being not less than 42 days from date of first publication of the notice) and the manner in which representations may be made with respect to the order. The notices given to landowners and occupiers and to local authorities must include a copy of the order itself, insofar as it relates to their land or area.[39]

12–19   During the 42 day period for the making of representations, any person may require the authority to permit him to inspect and take copies of any documentary evidence which was taken into account by the authority in making the order. Where no representations are received within the prescribed period, or where all representations have been withdrawn, the authority may then confirm the order itself, without modification.[40] Otherwise, where the authority wishes to modify the order, or

---

[36] See the Wildlife and Countryside (Definitive Maps and Statements) Regulations 1983 (S.I. 1983 No.21).

[37] Where these are not known or cannot be found, the Secretary of State may direct that the notice be addressed to "The owners and any occupiers" of the land and the notice affixed to some conspicuous object on the land: Sched. 15, para.3(3).

[38] Together with a plan: Wildlife and Countryside Act 1981, Sched. 15, para.3 (7).

[39] Wildlife and Countryside Act 1981, Sched. 15, para.3.

[40] Provision is made for treating certain representations made to a draft map, where the survey has been abandoned by virtue of a direction under s.55, as having been made to the order: see *ibid.* Sched.15, para.4.

where there are unresolved representations or objections, the order must be submitted to the Secretary of State for confirmation. In the latter case, the Secretary of State must either cause a local inquiry to be held or must afford the person making the representation or objection the opportunity of being heard before a person appointed by the Secretary of State and who may be authorised to make the decision.[41] Thereafter, the Secretary of State, after considering the representations and the report of his inspector, may confirm the order with or without modifications. In any case where the order is confirmed with modifications which involve land not affected by the order or where the modifications add or delete a highway or alter its status, the Secretary of State is first required to give at least 28 days' notice of his proposal to modify the order, permitting representations or objections to the modification. Where representations or objections are made and are not withdrawn, a further local inquiry must be held or a hearing afforded before the order is confirmed. In order to prevent all the modifications from being delayed by this lengthy process, the authority is permitted to give notice to the Secretary of State that it is severing the opposed modifications from those which are unopposed, so as to create two separate orders. The unopposed order could then be confirmed by the authority itself.

Notice of a final decision on the confirmation of an order must be **12–20** given by the authority.[42] There is then a 42 day period within which a challenge on *ultra vires* grounds may be made to the High Court. Thereafter, the order may not be questioned in any legal proceedings whatsoever.[43]

The situation in London

The National Parks and Access to the Countryside Act 1949 did not **12–21** require the then London County Council to prepare definitive maps, but permitted the Council, by resolution, to adopt the survey provisions for any part of the county. The London Government Act 1963 abolished the London County Council and established the new London boroughs. The outer London boroughs were comprised of areas which had, formerly, been part of other counties within which the general survey provisions of the 1949 Act applied. The Local Government Act 1985 has amended the definition of "surveying authority" in the Wildlife and Countryside Act 1981, to include the councils of the London boroughs, so that all London boroughs are now under a duty to prepare a definitive map, if they have not already done so, and to keep the definitive map for their area under review.[43a]

---

[41] Wildlife and Countryside Act 1981, Sched. 15, para.10.
[42] In accordance with Sched. 15, para.11.
[43] Wildlife and Countryside Act 1981, Sched. 15, para.12. As to the effect of such a clause, see *R. v. Secretary of State, ex p. Ostler* [1977] Q.B. 122.
[43a] Wildlife and Countryside Act 1981, ss.53–54; Local Government Act 1985, s. 7 and Sched. 3.

Effect of the definitive map

12–22   The importance of the definitive map is not simply that it maps the footpath and bridleway rights which exist throughout the country, but that the marking on the map of a path is deemed to be conclusive evidence of the minimum status of the public right of way over that path at a particular date, and also of a number of other matters relating to the path.[44] The particular date is that specified in the statement to be the relevant date for this purpose or, where the way has been placed on the map by an order, the date specified in that order.[44a]

12–23   Where a footpath is shown, the map will be conclusive evidence that, at the relevant date, there was such a highway, as shown on the map, over which the public had a right of way on foot.[45] Where the map shows a bridleway, a byway open to all traffic, or a road used as a public path, then the map is conclusive evidence that there was, at the relevant date, a highway as shown on the map and that the public had over it the rights associated with that particular kind of highway; again this is expressed to be without prejudice to the question of whether the public had any greater rights of way over the path at that date.[45a] The right of way over a bridleway is a right of way on foot and on horseback or leading a horse. The right of way over a byway open to all traffic is a right of way for vehicular and all other kinds of traffic. The right of way over a road used as a public path (RUPP) is a right of way on foot and on horseback or leading a horse.[46]

12–24   The map does not, however, prevent the calling of evidence to establish that a path:

(a) carried greater rights of way at the relevant date than are shown on the map;

(b) now carries greater rights of way which have grown up since the relevant date;

(c) no longer carries a particular right of way by reason of the legal extinguishment or diversion of the right of way since the relevant date.

Where the map is conclusive evidence of any of the above matters, then it is also conclusive evidence of any particulars contained in the statement as to the position or width of the way at that date, and as to any conditions or limitations on the right of way. However, this is again expressed to be without prejudice as to whether the right of way was subject to any other conditions or limitations.[47] It seems to follow,

[44] Wildlife and Countryside Act 1981, s.56(1)(*a*).
[44a] *Ibid.* s.56(2).
[45] *Ibid.* s.56(1)(*a*); *Suffolk C.C.* v. *Mason* [1979] A.C. 705.
[45a] Although cyclists also are permitted to use bridleways, by virtue of the Countryside Act 1968, s.30(1), the definitive map is not conclusive as to any rights which may exist for cyclists over such ways: Wildlife and Countryside Act 1981, s.66(3).
[46] As to the re-classification of RUPPs, see para. 12–15, above.
[47] Wildlife and Countryside Act 1981, s.56(1)(*e*).

therefore, that neither the landowner, nor the user of the path, can dispute the particulars contained in the statement to the definitive map as to width and position, but that the landowner may claim that there are unrecorded limitations and restrictions which apply to the path.

CREATION, MAINTENANCE AND PROTECTION OF FOOTPATHS AND BRIDLEWAYS

Creation of footpaths and bridleways

The creation of footpaths by dedication and acceptance follows the **12–25** general rules applicable to all highways. The Highways Act 1980 does, however, specifically provide for the creation of footpaths and bridleways by agreement and by order. These are discussed in Chapter 2.[48] One other, unique way in which a footpath or bridleway can be created, occurs when vehicular rights are extinguished in a carriageway highway by virtue of an order under the Town and Country Planning Act 1971, section 212.[49]

Maintenance of footpaths and bridleways

Section 23 of the Highway Act 1835 did not apply to footpaths and **12–26** bridleways as such. It followed, therefore, that the duty to maintain paths continued after 1836, whether or not there had been any formal adoption. Whatever doubt there may have been about this was resolved by section 47 of the National Parks and Access to the Countryside Act 1949, which declared that all existing public paths were repairable by the inhabitants at large, but which also provided that section 23 was to apply to all paths dedicated after the commencement of the 1949 Act,[50] otherwise than in pursuance of a public path agreement. The present situation is that all paths dedicated prior to December 16, 1949, all paths created since that date by virtue of public path creation orders or agreements, and all paths which have otherwise been adopted by the highway authority by virtue of the adoption procedures in the Highways Act 1980 and its predecessors, will be highways maintainable at the public expense.[51] Footpaths and bridleways which are created as replacements for stopped up or diverted paths will also usually be maintainable at the public expense.[52] Roads used as public paths, and byways open to all traffic will be subject to the usual rules about maintenance.[53]

Non-metropolitan district councils may undertake the maintenance of **12–27** footpaths and bridleways which are maintainable at the public expense. These councils may be reimbursed by the county council for expenses

---

[48] See paras. 2–11 *et seq.*, above.
[49] See Chap. 9. A similar result can be achieved by an order under Road Traffic Regulation Act 1984, s.2.
[50] *i.e.* December 16, 1949.
[51] Highways Act 1980, s.36(2); see also Chap. 4.
[52] See *ibid.* s.36(2)(*d*) and Chap. 5.
[53] See Chap. 4.

incurred in maintaining such highways.[54] Schedule 7 to the Highways Act 1980 sets out a procedure whereby the district council must give notice to the county council of its intention to exercise these powers, specifying the highways concerned. Where the county council is of the view that any highway so specified does not fall within the district council's maintenance powers, it may serve a counter-notice to this effect. Where the dispute cannot be resolved, it must be referred to the Minister.[55] In exercising these powers, the district council stands in the shoes of the county council, and may sue and be sued in its own name. Indeed, an indemnity must be given to the county council in respect of any claim made against it, with regard to any failure to maintain a highway at a time when the district council was exercising its powers in respect of that highway, or any claim arising out of any maintenance works carried out by the district council pursuant to these powers.[56] Non-metropolitan district councils may also undertake the maintenance of footpaths and bridleways which are maintainable by some other person (without affecting the continuing liability of that person to maintain the way) or which are maintainable by no-one.[57] The provisions of Schedule 7, with respect to notices and indemnities, apply also here.

12–28   Parish and community councils may also undertake the maintenance of footpaths and bridleways, whether maintainable by the highway authority,[58] or whether maintainable by some other person, or by no-one at all.[59] These powers of the parish are exercisable, however, without affecting the liability of the highway authority or other person to maintain the path. The parish council is not entitled to automatic reimbursement of its expenses, and is subject to overall statutory limitations on its expenditure.[60] However, the highway authority or district council (where that council is itself exercising maintenance powers under section 42) may undertake to defer all or part of the parish or community council's expenses in maintaining publicly-maintainable paths.[61]

Extent of maintenance

12–29   The same basic test applies to the standard of maintenance of footpaths as it does to any other highway.[62] However, footpaths will not require a particularly high standard of maintenance and will not usually

---

[54] Highways Act 1980, s.42.
[55] Where it is decided against the district council, then no further notice may be served by that council in relation to that highway, unless there is a change in the character or status of the way: *ibid.* Sched. 7, para. 3.
[56] *Ibid.* Sched. 7, para. 7.
[57] *Ibid.* s.50.
[58] Under *ibid.* s.43.
[59] *Ibid.* s.50.
[60] See Local Government Act 1972, s.150.
[61] Highways Act 1980, s.43(2). Such expenses will not then form part of the expenditure of the parish or community council.
[62] See paras. 4–36 *et seq.*, above.

need to be metalled, although the surface must be kept clear and pass-able.[63] The highway authority will have separate responsibility to effect the removal of vegetation which obstructs the highway, pursuant to its duties to assert and protect the rights of highway users.[64]

Protection of highway rights over footpaths and bridleways

12–30   Footpaths and bridleways will generally cross open country, including farmland. They are less well defined on the ground than are carriageway highways and sometimes, perhaps for that reason, appear to be less well established and are less acceptable to landowners. In any event, it is regarding the footpaths and bridleways in country areas that most con-flict between the interests of ramblers and landowners has occurred. There are, therefore, a number of provisions which are designed to pro-tect the public right of way from encroachment by the landowner whilst attempting also to recognise and protect his interest in the proper hus-bandry of his land.

Signposts

12–31   It is an offence for any person to place or maintain, on or near any public path or road used as a public path (shown on a definitive map or on a revised map prepared in definitive form), any false or misleading statement, likely to deter the public from using the way.[65]

12–32   Highway authorities have power,[66] in consultation with the owner or occupier of the land concerned, to erect and maintain signposts along any footpath, bridleway or byway for which they are the highway auth-ority. They are under a duty to erect a signpost at every point at which a public path or byway leaves a metalled road, unless they are satisfied that a sign is not necessary and the parish council or chairman of the par-ish meeting (who must be consulted) agrees. Such a sign should indicate the nature of the path and, so far as the authority considers appropriate or convenient, where the path leads. The highway authority is also under a duty to erect such signposts as it considers to be necessary to assist persons unfamiliar with the locality to follow the course of a foot-path, bridleway or byway. Persons other than highway authorities may erect and maintain signposts along paths and byways, with the consent of the highway authority. It is an offence to pull down or obliterate any signpost erected or placed along a footpath, bridleway or byway, pur-suant to these provisions.[67]

---

[63] See, generally, *Worcestershire C.C.* v. *Newman* [1975] 1 W.L.R. 901; *Whiting* v. *Hill-ingdon L.B.C.* (1970) 68 L.G.R. 437.
[64] See Highways Act 1980, s.130 and Chaps. 8 and 9.
[65] National Parks and Access to the Countryside Act 1949, s.57.
[66] Countryside Act 1968, s.27.
[67] Highways Act 1980, s.131(2); Countryside Act 1968, s. 27(6).

Stiles and gates

12–33   A footpath or bridleway may be dedicated (either expressly or impliedly) subject to obstructions across the way, which are not inconsistent with its dedication as a public path. Stiles and gates are not inconsistent with dedication,[68] and may, in fact provide a means for the rambler or rider to circumvent fences, walls and hedges, which are necessary for the proper agricultural use of the land, but which otherwise would provide an obstacle to the exercise of the right of way. However, once dedicated free from such obstacles, the creation of a stile or gate in an otherwise unrestricted part of the path would constitute an obstruction.[69] In order to reconcile the potentially conflicting needs of the farmer and of the user of the path, the highway authority is empowered, on representations being made by the owner of agricultural land or of land which is being brought into use for agriculture,[70] to authorise the erection on the path of stiles, gates or other works for preventing the ingress or egress of animals.[71] The authorisation may be conditional as to the maintenance of the gate or stile, and unless the conditions are complied with, the gate or stile will cease to be an authorised structure in the highway and may be subject to removal under the provisions of section 143 of the Highways Act 1980. Where the path is being maintained by a district council under the provisions of sections 42 or 50 of the Highways Act 1980, then the authorisation may be given by that council.

12–34   All gates in carriageway highways and bridleways are required to be of a minimum width. In case of the bridleways, this width is feet, measured between the posts of the gate. Where, across such a highway, there is a gate of less than the minimum width, the highway authority may, by notice to the owner of the gate, require him to enlarge or remove it. Failure to comply with this notice is an offence.[72]

12–35   Stiles across footpaths and bridleways are required to be maintained by the owner of the land in a safe condition, and to the standard of repair required to prevent unreasonable interference with the rights of the persons using the footpath or bridleway. This duty of maintenance is subject to a contribution from the highway authority (or from the district council where the path is maintained by the district council).[73] The duty does not apply to any structure which is the subject of an agreement between the landowner and the highway authority or district council, and which agreement imposes the liability of maintenance on that authority. Nor does the duty apply if any conditions for the maintenance of the structure are in force under section 147 of the 1980 Act. The high-

---

[68] *Davies* v. *Stephens* (1836) 7 C. & P. 570; *Att.-Gen.* v. *Meyrick & Jones* (1915) 79 J. P. 515.
[69] See *James* v. *Hayward* (1630) Cro. Car. 184; *Bateman* v. *Burge* (1834) 6 C. & P. 391.
[70] "Agriculture" includes forestry for this purpose.
[71] Highways Act 1980, s.147.
[72] *Ibid.* s.145.
[73] *Ibid.* s.146(1),(4).

way authority (or district council) has default powers after giving the landowner not less than 14 days' notice and has power to recover all or part of its expenses reasonably incurred, from the landowner.[74] It seems, therefore, that it is in the financial interests of the landowner to maintain his stiles subject to the authority's contribution rather than to run the risk of that authority recovering all of its costs of exercising the default power.

Ploughing

The dedication of footpaths and bridleways subject to the right of the   **12–36** landowner to plough the land was recognised at common law.[75] Where such a limited dedication had occurred, it was not the case that the public had the right to deviate from the path around the ploughed area, nor that they lost the right to follow the line of the path over the ploughed area.[76]

Under the Highways Act 1980, section 134, a statutory right to plough   **12–37** up paths in the interests of good husbandry is given to any occupier of any agricultural land (or of land which is being brought into use for agriculture) and the public right of way is subject to this right to plough. The farmer is obliged, however, to make good the surface of the footpath or bridleway within two weeks or, in exceptional weather conditions, as soon as is practicable. It is an offence to plough up any footpath or bridleway other than in accordance with the provisions of this section.[77] Enforcement of these penal provisions is the duty of the highway authority, but the district and parish or community councils also have a power to enforce them. There is a default power for the highway authority[78] to reinstate the path and recover the expenses of so doing from the occupier of the land who has carried out unauthorised ploughing.

The legislation does not provide any guidance as to what is sufficient   **12–38** to "make good" the path. In may cases it may not be possible to replace the firm, defined track which formerly existed. The duty to "make good" should be satisfied if the path is reasonably convenient for the normal user of the path,[79] although the width and position must not be altered. Nor does the legislation indicate whether this permissive power may extend beyond the farming activity of ploughing, to other forms of cultivation which may be required at other times of the year (for example, discing, harrowing), or to the breaking up of the footpath whilst recovering the grown crop. Ploughing will usually occur once a year, but other methods of effectively working the land may involve disturbance of the highway surface at more frequent intervals. In such

---

[74] Highways Act 1980, s.146(2),(3).
[75] *Mercer* v. *Woodgate* (1869) L.R. 5 Q.B. 26; *Arnold* v. *Blaker* (1871) L.R. 6 Q.B. 433; *Denis* v. *Good* (1918) 88 L.J.K.B. 388.
[76] *Arnold* v. *Holbrook* (1873) L.R. 8 Q.B. 96.
[77] Highways Act 1980, s.134(5A).
[78] Or district council acting under *ibid.* ss. 42 or 50, above.
[79] See hereon, *Woodcock* v. *Solari* (1966) 203 E.G. 133.

cases, it may be more suitable for the landowner to apply to the highway authority for a temporary diversion under section 135 or a permanent diversion order under section 119 of the Highways Act 1980.

12–39   The permissive power in section 134 does not act as a diversion of the path, and the public may still cross the ploughed land during the period when the surface of the path is broken up. In practice, however, they are more likely to walk around the edge of the field. The practicalities of the situation, and a recognition that the working of land may take a longer period than is allowed in section 134, led to the creation of a power to divert a path temporarily, in order to permit ploughing to be carried out. This power is now contained within section 135 of the Highways Act 1980. The landowner may apply to the highway authority for a temporary diversion order, diverting the path for a period of up to three months from the time at which he first began to plough the path. The highway authority must be satisfied that it is expedient, in the interests of good farming, that the order should be made, and must also take into account the interests of the users of the way.[80] The order may require the provision of any necessary facilities for the convenient use of the diversion which is temporarily to replace the existing footpath, and which are to be provided at the expense of the applicant.[81] The diversion must be onto land which is occupied by the applicant, otherwise the written consent of the occupier (and any other person whose consent is required) must be obtained. The order, once made, must forwith be displayed in a prominent position at each end of the diversion.

12–40   The general provisions in the Highways Act 1980 concerning obstructions of the highway apply also to public paths. One or two provisions have particular relevance to public paths. By section 164 of the Highways Act 1980, a highway authority or district council may, by notice, require the removal of barbed wire, in any fence adjoining a highway, which constitutes a nuisance. Where the occupier of the land has failed to comply with the notice, the authority may apply to the magistrates' court for an order that the nuisance be abated and, where that order is not complied with within a reasonable period of time, the authority may take whatever steps are necessary to secure compliance, and may recover the expenses from the occupier of the land. Where the presence of the wire is likely to be injurious to persons or animals lawfully using the way, it will be deemed to be a nuisance.[82] Where the land in question is occupied by the highway authority or district council, any ratepayer may stand in the shoes of the authority for the purpose of these provisions.

12–41   There are specific provisions concerned with the prohibition of vehicular traffic on footpaths and bridleways. The Town Police Clauses Act 1847 makes it an offence to drive any cart or carriage upon any footway

---

[80] Highways Act 1980, s.135(1), (3).
[81] *Ibid.* s.135(4).
[82] *Ibid.* s.164. See *Stewart* v. *Wright* (1893) 9 T.L.R.

of any street.[83] This section is concerned with footways rather than foot-paths. Section 33 of the Road Traffic Act 1972, however, prohibits the driving of motor vehicles "onto any common land, moorland or other land of whatsoever description, not being land forming part of a road, or on any road being a footpath or bridleway." There is a defence in subsection (2) which is available where a person has driven his vehicle "on any land within fifteen yards of a road, being a road on which a motor vehicle may lawfully be driven, for the purpose only of parking the vehicle on that land." There appear to be two separate ways in which an offence may be committed under section 36(1)—the driving on land of whatsoever description (not being land forming part of a road) and the driving on those roads over which the only public rights are those on foot or of bridleway. The defence in subsection (2) appears to be concerned with the first way in which the offence under section 36(1) can be committed; it cannot have been contemplated by the legislators that they would, in effect, be permitting vehicular rights to be created over the first fifteen yards of every footpath or bridleway which leads off a carriageway highway. No driver may lawfully park his vehicle on a foot-path or bridleway, and yet the defence is only available to a person driving on land for the purpose of parking on that land. It appears, therefore, that this defence is not available to a driver who has driven his vehicle onto a footpath or bridleway, even if the vehicle is still within 15 yards of a carriageway highway. The holding of motor vehicle trials on footpaths may, however, be authorised by a local authority, where the owner and occupier of the land have consented in writing.[84] There are also powers under the Road Traffic Regulation Act 1984 which prohibit or restrict the use of footpaths and bridleways, including their use by pedestrians.[85] Local authorities may use mechanically propelled appliances or vehicles for cleansing, maintaining or improving foot-paths, footways or bridleways or their verges, or for maintaining structures or other works situated therein.[86]

PROVISION OF AMENITIES IN PEDESTRIAN WAYS

Part VIIA of the Highways Act 1980[87] empowers councils[88] to provide **12–42** special facilities in certain kinds of pedestrian ways. The highways in which these powers may be exercised are:

(a) footpaths and bridleways;

---

[83] s.28.

[84] Road Traffic Act 1972, s. 35.

[85] Road Traffic Regulaton Act 1984, ss. 2(3), 14, 127.

[86] Highways Act 1980, s.300 and the Vehicles (Conditions of Use on Footpaths) Regulations 1963 (S.I. 1963 No. 2126 as amended by S.I. 1966 No. 864).

[87] Inserted by Local Government (Miscellaneous Provisions) Act 1982.

[88] *i.e.* county councils, metropolitan district councils, non-metropolitan district councils, London borough councils and the Common Council of the City of London.

(b) highways which have been the subject of an order under the Town and Country Planning Act 1971, section 212 (2)[89];

(c) footways;

(d) subways and footbridges constructed under Highways Act 1980, sections 69 and 70;

(e) walkways (including those walkways and pedestrian ways which owe their existence to local Act powers);

(f) highways which are the subject of orders under the Road Traffic Regulation Act 1984, sections 1, 6 and 9—prohibiting vehicular traffic either wholly, or for certain periods of the day or year.

12–43   The powers contained in Part VIIA fall into two categories. The council is empowered to provide services and amenities in these highways—which may involve the carrying out of works in, on or over the highway, or the placing of structures in the highway. Secondly, the authority is empowered to grant permissions to other persons to provide facilities and place objects in the highways.

Provision of services and amenities by councils

12–44   A council may carry out works and place objects or structures on, in or over highways, for the purposes of giving effect to a pedestrian planning order,[90] of enhancing the amenity of the highway and its immediate surroundings, and of providing a service for the benefit of the public or a section of the public. The council may maintain the works, objects or structures which have been carried out or installed. The Act gives as examples of ways in which the amenity of the highway may be enhanced, the provision of lawns, trees, shrubs or flowers. Councils are also empowered to provide, maintain and operate facilities for recreation or refreshment on these kinds of highways.

12–45   It may well be the case that the exercise of these powers under Part VIIA of the Highways Act 1980 will obstruct the highway. Section 115D makes it clear that this is permissible, subject to some over-all restrictions. The council may not exercise its powers in such a way as to prevent traffic, other than vehicular traffic, from entering the highway, at any place where traffic could have entered it before the making of any pedestrian planning order or traffic order, nor from passing along the highway, nor from having normal access to any premises adjoining the highway. Furthermore, the exercise of these powers cannot be used to restrict any use of vehicles which is allowed under the terms of a pedestrian planning order, or which is not prohibited by the road traffic regulation order, nor to prevent statutory undertakers, sewerage authorities

---

[89] See Chap. 9. These are, in any event, footpaths or bridleways.
[90] *i.e.* an order under Town and Country Planning Act 1971, s.212.

or telecommunications operators from having access to their apparatus under, in, on, or over the highway.[91]

Grant of permissions by councils for the execution of works and use of objects or structures

The council may grant to a person permission to do anything which **12–46** the council may itself do under this Part of the Act, in relation to the placing of objects and structures in, on, or under highways, or in providing facilities for recreation or refreshment.[92] It may also permit the use, by other persons, of objects or structures in the highway, for a purpose which will result in the production of income, or for the purpose of providing a centre for advice and information, or for the purpose of advertising.[93] It follows that the council's permission can be granted to a third party to place objects or structures in the highway only for the same purposes as the council may itself place those objects or structures. However, if an object or structure has been lawfully placed in the highway by the council, either under the powers contained in this Part of the Act, or by virtue of any other powers, then that object or structure may be used for a further purpose of advertising. It seems unlikely that the powers in this part of the Act may be used simply to permit a shopkeeper to place an advertising board in the highway outside his shop, unless it could be argued that the board could have been placed there by the council itself to provide a service for the benefit of the public or of a section of the public. The cases in which permission can be justified in this way are likely to be extremely limited.

Permissions may be granted conditionally, including on requirement **12–47** to pay to the council its reasonable charges.[94] The council may require an indemnity to be given against any claim in respect of any injury, damage or loss arising out of the grant of permission, except in respect of the council's own negligence.[95] Where any person granted a permission is in breach of the terms of that permission, the council may serve a notice on him requiring him to take steps to remedy the breach. The council may itself take steps to remedy the breach in default of compliance with the notice, and may recover its expenses from the person on whom the notice was served.[96]

Procedure

Except where the council is exercising its powers under sections 115B **12–48** or 115C,[97] in relation to highways which are the subject of pedestrian

[91] Highways Act 1980, s.115D.
[92] *Ibid.* s.115E.
[93] *Ibid.* s.115E(1)(*b*).
[94] This will be standard charge except where the council owns the subsoil: *ibid.* s.115F(3).
[95] *Ibid.* s.115F(4).
[96] *Ibid.* s.115K.
[97] *i.e.* where the council is not granting any permissions to third parties.

planning orders or traffic orders, notices must be displayed at or near the position to which the proposal relates, and a copy must be served on the owner and occupier of any premises which appear to the council to be materially affected.[98]

12–49   A number of consents have to be obtained before the council may exercise its powers under this Part of the Act. "Walkway consent" must be obtained where the council itself carries out works or places any object or structure in, on, or over any walkway, or provides facilities for recreation or refreshment therein.[99] A "Walkway consent" involves the consent of occupiers of the building in which the walkway subsists and whom, in the opinion of the council, are likely to be affected by the exercise of the powers, and also the consent of the persons whose agreement would be needed to the creation of the walkway in the first place.[1] In the case of local Act walkways, the consent of any person who is the owner or occupier of premises adjoining the walkway and who is, in the opinion of the council, likely to be affected by the exercise the power, and of the consent of the owner of the land on, under, or over which the walkway subsists, must be obtained.

12–50   Where the council is using the power to place an object or structure in a footpath or bridleway or in a footway relating to which no pedestrian planning order is in force, and does so either for a purpose which will result in the production of income, or for the purpose of providing a centre for advice or information, it is necessary to obtain the consent of interested frontagers to the placing of the object in the highway for the purpose for which it is placed there. Where the council grants permission to a person to use an object or structure placed in *any* of the types of highway to which this Part of the Act applies, the consent of these frontagers must be obtained, not only to the placing of the object or structure and its purpose, but also to the grant of the permission.[2] Frontagers are regarded as having an interest if their land adjoins that part of the highway and the object or structure is to be placed between their land and the centre of the highway.[3]

12–51   Where the highway in question is maintained by the British Railways Board, London Regional Transport (or any subsidiary of London Regional Transport), then the consent of these bodies must also be obtained. All consents should be obtained in writing.

12–52   Consents may not be witheld unreasonably, but it is not unreasonable for a consent to be given for a specified period of time or subject to the payment of a reasonable sum. Where a council has served a notice requesting consent, and no reply is given within 28 days, then the con-

---

[98] Highways Act 1980, s.115G(1),(2).
[99] *i.e. ibid.* ss.115B, 115C.
[1] See Chap. 2.
[2] Highways Act 1980, s.115B(7).
[3] *Ibid.* s.115A(7).

sent will be deemed to have been refused unreasonably. Any question as to whether the consent has been reasonably refused is otherwise referrable to arbitration and the arbitrator has power to direct that the consent, though unreasonably witheld, should only be given subject to conditions. The council is also required to consult the highway authority and the local planning authority (where it is not itself those authorities).

CHAPTER 13

THE PUBLIC UTILITIES STREET WORKS ACT 1950

INTRODUCTION

History

13–01   A great variety of statutory powers have been granted to diverse bodies and individuals to carry out works on highways, the exercise of which will usually, if not invariably, interfere with the normal use of the highway. From the mid-nineteenth century, the public utilities were given powers to break open highways and streets in order to lay their apparatus under the highway and to gain access to it for subsequent maintenance.[1] These rights had to be balanced against the rights of users of the highway and, with respect to maintainable highways, the interests of the bodies or authorities whose responsibility it was to maintain them. The enabling legislation, therefore, contained provisions governing the breaking open of the highways and the placing of apparatus in, on, under, or over the highway. Subsequently, as the needs of the statutory undertakers became more complex and the use of the highways more intense, there came a need for more comprehensive provisions governing the relationship between the highway authority (and the users of the highway) and the public utilities. As early as 1925, the need for a standardised code was recognised when a joint negotiating committee, consisting of representatives of highway authorities and of the public utilities, was set up with the aim of agreeing a standard clause for insertion in future special Acts of Parliament promoted by the utilities. Although a large measure of agreement was achieved, it proved impossible to achieve a consensus. The principal areas of disagreement arose over the apportionment of financial responsibility for moving or altering statutory undertakers' apparatus consequent to highway works, and the liability for costs arising out of bursts, escapes or explosions from utility apparatus. After thirteen years of trying, the committee had to report that it was unable to reach agreement. In response to this stalemate, a joint committee of both Houses of Parliament was appointed. This committee, the Carnock Committee, which reported in 1939, built on the work of the joint negotiating committee and recommended that legislation should be introduced to provide a uniform code for all the utilities. The Public Utilities Street Works Act 1950 (hereafter referred

---

[1] See Gasworks Clauses Act 1847; Waterworks Clauses Act 1847; Electric Lighting Act 1882; Telegraph Act 1863 and Public Health Act 1875.

to as the P.U.S.W.A.) eventually emerged from these recommendations.

Aims of the Public Utilities Street Works Act

The aims of the P.U.S.W.A are threefold: 13–02

    (a) to regulate the exercise of powers of statutory undertakers for the protection of the authorities, bodies and persons having the control or management of highways, streets, bridges, sewers, drains, tunnels, and transport undertakings[2];

    (b) to enable those powers, insofar as they are powers exercisable in a street which is a maintainable highway, or is prospectively a maintainable highway, to be exercised, in accordance with the code, in land abutting the street ("controlled land") thereby reducing interference with the highway[3];

    (c) to protect undertakers whose apparatus may be affected by roadworks.

The three codes

The Act established three codes for regulating the relations between   13–03
the utilities and the highway and street authorities and between the various utilities themselves, arising from the placing, maintaining or removing of apparatus in, on, under, or over highways. The "street works code" which is to be found in Part I of and Schedules 1 to 3 to the P.U.S.W.A. is intended to provide a uniform code for the exercise by statutory undertakers of their powers to break up or open highways and streets. Part II and Schedule 4 provide a similar code governing the relationship between undertakers and highway authorities promoting roadworks. Part III deals with the relationship of undertakers amongst themselves.

Subsequent history

The codes contained in the P.U.S.W.A. are extremely complex,   13–04
although in some instances important issues are left unresolved. In particular, the responsibility for and the quality of reinstatement is imprecise and is not always easily enforceable. Although the Act was designed to establish a uniform system throughout the country, the possibility of particular highway authorities and undertakers entering into agreements with respect to reinstatement and making good was left open by section 16. The Act was supplemented, as early as 1952, 1953 and 1957, by codes of engineering practice. In 1974, the Department of the Environment published a Model Agreement and Specifications aimed at improving the standard of reinstatements carried out by the undertakers and reducing the time taken by highway authorities to carry out

---

[2] P.U.S.W.A., s.1(*a*).
[3] *Ibid.* s.1(*b*).

permanent reinstatements. In 1985, a survey indicated that 34 of the 95 highway authorities in Great Britain operated the Model Agreement and Specifications in a standard or modified form with all the utilities in their area.[4]

13–05 The operation of the Act has been monitored frequently. In 1966, the Lofthouse Report, *Efficiency in Road Construction,* published by the National Economic Development Office, expressed concern over aspects of the working of Part II of the Public Utilities Street Works Act 1950. This report was considered by a P.U.S.W.A. Technical Group, convened by the Minister in 1968,[5] and was followed by the setting up of the P.U.S.W.A. Conference and the establishment of a working party to consider solutions to the problems identified by the Technical Group. The working party produced a number of recommendations[6] on practice. In 1973, further improvements in procedure were suggested by the Minister[7] and a *Guide to the Public Utilities Street Works Act 1950* was published by the Department,[8] and in 1974, the Model Agreement and Specifications was published. In 1983, the House of Commons Transport Committee produced a report on road maintenance including the problems of utility works,[9] and in 1984 the Minister appointed Professor Horne O.B.E. to chair a committee to review all aspects of the P.U.S.W.A. The report of this committee[10] made 73 main recommendations for the improvement of the system and commented upon the confusion regarding responsibility for reinstatement of utility openings inherent in the present system, the undesirability of the many variations around the country in the specifications for reinstatements, the cumbersome and unsatisfactory nature of the P.U.S.W.A. notice system, the degree of supervision of reinstatements, the need for a "guarantee period" from the completion of permanent reinstatement by a utility, the need for a reorganisation of the sharing of costs involved in utility works in the highway, and the need for a standardised system for recording the location of underground plant. Even this latest report, however, found it impossible to achieve unanimity among committee members on the question of utility costs associated with highway improvement schemes. The Government has now published its response to the Horne Report, accepting most of its recommendations, and legislation is promised.[11]

---

[4] See *Roads and the Utilities: Review of the Public Utilities Street Works Act 1950* (H.M.S.O., 1985) Chap. 4.
[5] See Circular No. Roads 19/68.
[6] See Circular No. Roads 60/72.
[7] Circular No. Roads 23/73.
[8] H.M.S.O., 1973.
[9] Transport Committee First Report (1982–83) *Road Maintenance.*
[10] *Roads and the Utilities: Review of the Public Utilities Street Works Act 1950* (H.M.S.O., 1985).
[11] *The Government Response to the Horne Report on the Review of the Public Utilities Street Works Act 1950* (H.M.S.O., 1986).

THE STREET WORKS CODE

Application of the code

Outside Greater London, the street works code governs the exercise   **13–06** of all statutory powers[12] to execute the undertakers' works in, under, over, across, along, or upon a street. A "statutory power" means a power conferred by any enactment, including a provision of an order, scheme, regulations or other instrument made under, or confirmed by, any Act other than the P.U.S.W.A.[13] In Greater London various statutory powers are excluded from the operation of the P.U.S.W.A.[14]

Undertakers' works

"Undertakers' works" are defined[15] by reference first to apparatus   **13–07** and secondly to physical works in a street or controlled land required for, or incidental to, acts concerning apparatus. They consist of works, executed or to be executed (including works executed on behalf of the Crown) for any purposes other than road purposes,[16] of any of the following kinds:

(a) placing apparatus, inspecting, maintaining, adjusting, repairing, altering or renewing apparatus, and changing the position of apparatus or removing it; and

(b) the following acts if they are carried out for the purposes of works mentioned in head (a), namely breaking up or opening a street or controlled land, tunnelling or boring under a street or controlled land, breaking up or opening a sewer, drain, or tunnel and other works requisite for or incidental to the purposes mentioned in head (a).[17]

For the purposes of the P.U.S.W.A., "street" means any length of a   **13–08** highway (other than a waterway), any length of a road, lane, footway, alley or passage, any square or court, and any length of land laid out as a way, whether it is for the time being formed as a way or not, irrespective of whether the highway, road, etc., is a thoroughfare or not.[18] This wide definition of "street" includes not only unadopted highways over which public rights of way may exist, but also ways which are private. It has been held[19] that such a definition is wide enough to include a disused

---

[12] Except a power conferred for the purposes of a railway or tramway undertaking; P.U.S.W.A., ss.1(1), 37(2), 39(1).
[13] See *ibid*. s.39(1).
[14] See *ibid*. s.35(1), (2), Sched. 7, para. 1; London County Council (Subways) Act 1893; City of London (Various Powers) Act 1900, ss.29–50; London Government Act 1963, s.19.
[15] P.U.S.W.A., s.1(2).
[16] As to which, see *ibid*. s.39(1), as amended by Highways Act 1980, s.343(2), Sched. 24, para. 5.
[17] P.U.S.W.A., s.1(2).
[18] For a discussion on the similar definition in the Highways Act 1980, see Chap. 12; see also P.U.S.W.A., s.38(1)(*a*), (*b*), (*c*).
[19] *Strathclyde Regional Council* v. *British Railways Board* 1978 S.L.T. 8.

road running across a bridge. In Greater London, a walkway is deemed to be a "street," for the purpose of statutory undertakers' works.[20]

Maintainable and prospectively maintainable highways

13–09   In the P.U.S.W.A. there are references to streets which are "maintainable highways" or "prospectively maintainable highways." A "maintainable highway" is a highway maintainable at the public expense.[21] A street is a prospectively maintainable highway if, whether being a highway or not, it is declared likely to become a maintainable highway in a declaration made by the local highway authority under Schedule 2 to the Act, and is thereafter registered in the register of local land charges.[22] The significance of such a declaration is that the local highway authority, rather than the street managers, becomes entitled to notice under the street works code.

Code-regulated works

13–10   Undertakers' works executed or proposed to be executed in accordance with the street works code, and which are executed either in a street or in controlled land (together with an authorisation to do works in such land) in exercise of that power, are referred to as "code-regulated works" in the Act.

Controlled land

13–11   The objective of minimising the number of occasions on which works must be carried out on the the highway itself, is facilitated by allowing those works to be carried out, in accordance with the street works code, in "controlled land." "Controlled land" is defined[23] as land abutting on a street, which is also a maintainable highway or a prospectively maintainable highway, and which either:

(a) belongs to the street authority and is for the time being held by that authority, or is capable of being immediately appropriated by it for road purposes; or

(b) is the subject of a subsisting authorisation of compulsory acquisition by the street authority given with a view to its being held for road purposes; or

(c) lies between the boundary of the street and an improvement line prescribed under statutory powers.[24]

If land comes within this definition, its use for the time being is irrel-

---

[20] Greater London (General Powers) Act 1969, s.24.
[21] P.U.S.W.A., s.1(4)(*a*); Highways Act 1980, s.36; Chap. 4.
[22] P.U.S.W.A., s.1(4)(*b*), as amended by Local Government Act 1972, s.188(7)(*b*) and Sched. 21, and Sched. 2, para. 2, as substituted by Local Land Charges Act 1975, s.17(2) and Sched. 1. See also P.U.S.W.A., Sched. 2, para. 1.
[23] *Ibid.* Sched. 1, para. 1(1); see also s.38(1)(*c*).
[24] See Highways Act 1980, s.73; paras. 6–09, *et seq.*, above.

evant, but certain buildings and structures on the land will be excluded.[25]

Parties to proceedings under the street works code

Statutory undertakers

Statutory undertakers are defined[26] as the authority, body or person **13–12** by whom a statutory power to execute undertakers' works in the capacity in which that power is vested in them is exercisable. In practice, this includes the electricity and gas undertakers, the operators of telecommunications apparatus and the sewerage and water authorities.

Authorities and managers concerned

The street works code, generally, requires consultation with the rel- **13–13** evant persons or bodies concerned with the control and management of a street or controlled land (the "authority or managers concerned") before the more significant types of code-regulated works are carried out. These relevant persons or bodies are the street authority,[27] where the street is a maintainable or prospectively maintainable highway, or the street managers where it is not.[28] As regards works executed, or proposed to be executed in controlled land, the authority or managers concerned is the street authority for the street on which that land abuts.[29] The "street managers" are the authority, body or persons liable to the public to maintain or repair the street,[30] or, if there is no such person, any authority, body or person having the management or control of the street.[31] The highway authority will not be the person having management or control of an unadopted highway.[32] Where the presumption of ownership *usque ad medium filum* applies, the frontagers will, generally, be the relevant street managers.[33]

In some circumstances other persons or bodies, such as sewer and **13–14** transport authorities, and bridge authorities or managers, may be the authority or manager concerned.[34]

Settlement of plan and section to be a condition of execution of major works

Subject to three important exceptions, undertakers are prohibited **13–15** from executing code-regulated works until a plan and section of the works has been submitted to, and settled by agreement between, the

---

[25] P.U.S.W.A., Sched. 1, paras. 1(2), 13, 26.
[26] *Ibid*. s.39(1).
[27] *i.e.* the relevant highway authority: *ibid*. s.2(4).
[28] *Ibid*. s.2(1)(*a*)
[29] *Ibid*. s.2(2)(*a*)
[30] See Chap. 4.
[31] P.U.S.W.A., s.2(5)(*a*), (*b*).
[32] *Redhill Gas Co.* v. *Reigate R.C.* [1911] 2 K.B. 565.
[33] *Postmaster-General* v. *Hendon U.D.C.* [1914] 1 K.B. 564; see also Chap. 3.
[34] P.U.S.W.A., ss.2(1), 37(1), (2), 38(2) and 39(1).

undertakers and each of the authorities or managers concerned, or has been referred to, and settled by, arbitration.[35] The Act does not define what is meant by "a plan and section," nor does it set any standard for them. In the case of a similar plan submitted under section 31 of the Waterworks Clauses Act 1847, it was held that the plan should give information to the street authority as to the nature and character of the work proposed, not merely as to the breaking up and opening of the surface of the road, but also showing, and giving information as to, what is to be done underground.[36] The authority or managers concerned may accept as, or in lieu of, a plan and section, any description, whether in diagram form or not, which appears to them to be sufficient.[37] The requirement to settle and submit a plan can be waived completely by the authority or managers concerned, if the code-regulated works become necessary because of works to be executed by the authority or managers as a promoting authority.[38]

Minor works

13–16   The requirement to settle and submit plans and sections is only intended to cover major works, and minor works are excepted. The excepted minor works are grouped into four categories,[39] which are:

  (a) inspecting, maintaining, adjusting or repairing apparatus;
  (b) placing, altering, renewing, changing the position of, or moving, a service pipe or service line[40] or overhead telecommunications apparatus in or from a place other than in a trunk road or a classified road,[41] or in or from a place in such a road unless the works are to be executed elsewhere than in the carriageway of such a road, and so as not to affect substantially the traffic on the carriageway thereof;
  (c) placing elsewhere than in a maintainable highway, apparatus which is required only in connection with the doing of any building or other work on land adjacent to the street and is intended to be removed on completion of the building or other work;
  (d) any breaking up or opening (other than breaking up or opening any public sewer), tunnelling or boring, insofar as it is to be executed for the purpose of work falling within any of the pre-

---

[35] P.U.S.W.A., s.3(1). As to sevice of documents, see s.34(2)–(6).
[36] *East Molesey Local Board* v. *Lambeth Waterworks Co.* [1892] 3 Ch. 289.
[37] P.U.S.W.A., s.3(7).
[38] *Ibid.* s.22(3); see also paras. 13–57 *et seq.*, below.
[39] P.U.S.W.A., s.3(2)(*a*)–(*d*).
[40] As to which, see *ibid.* s.38(2), as amended by Telecommunications Act 1984, s.109 and Sched. 4.
[41] See para. 1–16, above.

ceding sections, and any other works so far as requisite for, or incidental to, works so falling.

Emergency works

The second exception concerns emergency works. "Emergency **13–17** works" are works whose execution, at the time when they are executed, is requisite in order to put an end to, or prevent the arising of, circumstances then existing or imminent, which are calculated to cause danger to persons or property, interruptions of a supply or service afforded by undertakers or by a transport authority, or substantial loss to undertakers or to such an authority, or in order to enable undertakers to satisfy an obligation created by an enactment.[42] Although undertakers may execute emergency works without submitting a plan and section, or before a plan or section has been settled, they must still furnish a plan and section to each of the authorities or managers concerned, as soon as is reasonably practicable after executing works.[43] The authorities and managers may, however, object to a work which has been carried out as emergency work, in the same way in which they may object to any other work which has been executed without the submission of a plan and section.[44]

Streets which are not maintainable highways

The third and final exception concerns streets which the street **13–18** managers have no liability to the public to maintain or repair.[45] Again, it is only a partial exception. A notice indicating the general nature of the works proposed or of the emergency works executed must be served on the street managers, who may, within 15 days from the date of this notice, give a counter notice to the undertakers requiring the submission of a plan and section to them.[46]

Where undertakers execute any works without a settled plan and sec- **13–19** tion (where these are required), or, in the case of emergency works, where they fail to furnish a plan and section after the works are executed, they are liable on summary conviction to a fine.[47] Where works are executed before a plan and section have been settled, and the authority or managers concerned object to the works executed, the authority or managers may, after giving the undertakers the opportunity to meet their objection, refer the matter to arbitration.[48] This procedure

---

[42] P.U.S.W.A., s.39(1). See also Drought Act 1976, s.2.
[43] P.U.S.W.A., s.3(3)(*a*), (*b*).
[44] See para. 13–20, below.
[45] P.U.S.W.A., s.3(4).
[46] *Ibid.* s.3(4).
[47] Not exceeding level 3 on the standard scale; *ibid.* s.3(5), as amended by Criminal Justice Act 1982, ss.38, 46.
[48] P.U.S.W.A., ss.3(6), 31(1).

applies to emergency work as well as to work which is carried out in contravention of the requirement to settle the plan and section.

Procedure on submission of plans and sections

13–20 An authority or managers concerned, to whom a plan and section of code-regulated works are submitted, are required to give notice to the undertakers approving the plan and section (with or without modification), objecting to them in form (as being on too small a scale or as giving insufficient particulars), approving them subject to specified modifications, or disapproving them.[49] The notice must be given without avoidable delay and, in any event, within certain specified time limits.[50] If the authority or managers fail to give notice within the relevant prescribed period, they will be deemed to have agreed the plan and section as submitted.

13–21 Where an authority or managers give a notice approving the plan and section with modifications, or disapproving the plan and section, they must state their grounds.[51] In some cases, these grounds are expressly limited or indicated by the statute. The grounds available to a sewer or bridge authority or to managers concerned, acting in that capacity alone, are confined to any alleged injurious effect of the proposed works on their sewer, or on the structure or stability of their bridge, as the case may be.[52] A special objection open to street authorities only, where works are proposed to be executed in a street which is a maintainable highway or prospectively maintainable highway, is that the works ought to be executed in controlled land.[53] Further restrictions are placed upon objections to pipelines, to government oil pipelines and works accessory to them,[54] by the Requisitioned Land and War Works Act 1948[55] and by the Requisitioned Land and War Works Act 1945.[56] Arbitrators settling plans and sections are also governed by these restrictions.

Reference to arbitration

13–22 Where notice is given objecting to the plan and section in form, or approving them subject to modifications to which the undertakers do not agree, or disapproving them, then, unless each such notice is withdrawn, the undertakers may refer the matter to arbitration.[57] Where the notice is withdrawn by each authority or managers concerned who have given it, it is deemed to have been settled by agreement.

---

[49] P.U.S.W.A., s.4(1).
[50] See *ibid.* ss.4(2)(*a*), (*b*), (as amended by Telecommunications Act 1984, s.109 and Sched. 4) and s.16(2)(*a*).
[51] P.U.S.W.A., s.4(3).
[52] *Ibid.* s.4(6).
[53] *Ibid.* s.5(1).
[54] Pipelines Act 1962, s.16(2)(*b*).
[55] s.12: relating to government oil pipelines; Land Powers (Defence) Act 1958 and the Defence (General) Regulations 1939, reg. 50.
[56] s.28(1), (3)(*a*); P.U.S.W.A., s.4(8)(*a*), (*b*).
[57] *Ibid.* s.4(4).

Procedure as to plans and sections for work in controlled land

There are special provisions governing the situation where a street **13–23** authority has disapproved the plan and section, or approved them with modifications, on the ground that the works, or some of them, ought to be executed in controlled land.[58] This right of objection does not apply to the exercise of the statutory power to place pipelines in streets under the Pipelines Act 1962, and it is subject to the special provisions protecting government oil pipelines.[59] The street authority may rely on this ground of objection only where it is satisfied that it has power to confer on the undertakers the necessary rights to execute the works in the controlled land and all the like rights in relation to their apparatus as the undertakers would have if it were placed in the street. These rights must be exercisable not later than the expiration of the period of 22 days from when the plan and section have been settled.[60] However, the fact that a street authority has consented to works being executed in the street does not prevent it from relying upon this ground of objection.[61]

The street authority may authorise the undertakers to execute rel- **13–24** evant works in controlled land, and such an authorisation may be given as to such works either generally, or as respects a particular class of such works, or as respects particular works.[62] Notice of intention to give such an authorisation must be published by the street authority, and notice must be given to every owner, lessee or occupier of the controlled land.[63] Once given, such authorisation is irrevocable, and it may not be questioned in any proceedings after one month has expired from the date of publication of the notice.[64] Where authorisation has been duly given, the undertakers have the like power to execute the works in the controlled land, and the like rights in relation to apparatus placed in exercise of that power as if the controlled land had been comprised in the street, and they have the power to enter upon the controlled land for the purpose of the execution of the works in it.

Undertakers can agree to the execution of any works in controlled **13–25** land after notification to them of disapproval or modification of a plan and section on those grounds[65] or, if they do not agree, they can refer the matter to arbitration.[66] Where either the arbitrator determines, or the undertakers agree, that any works ought to be executed in controlled land, those works are excluded from the power of the undertakers to execute works in the street.[67]

---

[58] P.U.S.W.A., s.5.
[59] See para. 13–21, above.
[60] P.U.S.W.A., s.5(1).
[61] *Ibid.* s.17(4).
[62] *Ibid.* s.5(1): subject to the provisions contained in Sched. 1.
[63] *Ibid.* s.5(1), Sched. 1, para. 4.
[64] *Ibid.* Sched. 1, para. 3.
[65] *Ibid.* s.5(3)(*b*).
[66] *Ibid.* s.5(2).
[67] *Ibid.* s.5(3).

13–26   A plan and section of the works to be executed in the controlled land is to be settled, in default of agreement, by arbitration.[68] If, at the expiration of 22 days from the date on which the plan and section of the works to be executed in controlled land are settled, any of the rights to execute works in controlled land have not been rendered exercisable by the undertakers, their right to execute the works in the street is revived. The street authority must then pay to the undertakers the amount of any cost reasonably incurred by the undertakers in executing any of the abortive works in controlled land, between the time the authority has purported to authorise their execution and the time when the failure to render exercisable the right or rights in question was ascertained, together with the costs of removal of apparatus rendered necessary thereby.[69] Disputes as to whether costs were incurred, their amount, or whether they are reasonable must be determined by arbitration.[70]

13–27   A street authority which authorises works to be done in controlled land must pay compensation to the owner of an interest in the controlled land in respect of any diminution in value of his interest in that land, or in land adjacent to it and held with it, caused by the giving of such authorisation. Compensation is also payable in respect of any damage caused by the lawful execution of works in it, or by entry upon it, pursuant to such an authorisation.[71] Any disputes as to whether compensation is payable, or as to the amount of any such compensation, are to be determined by the Lands Tribunal. There are provisions for the recoupment from the undertakers of compensation paid by the street authority and of any savings achieved by the undertakers in carrying out the works in controlled land rather than the street.[72] Conversely, where the cost of carrying out the works in controlled land is greater, the authority which objected to the works being carried out in the street must reimburse the undertakers their extra costs.[73] Any disputes between the street authority and the undertakers, concerning these provisions, are to be determined by arbitration.[74]

13–28   If the land, or any part of it, ceases to be controlled land, without having become part of the street, there are provisions for six months' notice to be given by the relevant owners, lessees or occupiers, terminating the powers and rights of the undertaker to maintain his apparatus in that land.[75] Where this occurs, the street authority has to pay to the undertakers the amount of any costs reasonably incurred by them in connection with the necessary removal of apparatus and in executing any other

---

[68] P.U.S.W.A., s.5(3).
[69] *Ibid.* s.5(4).
[70] *Ibid.* s.31(2).
[71] *Ibid.* s.5(1), Sched. 1, para. 6(1).
[72] *Ibid.* Sched. 1, paras. 6(2)(*a*), 7(1).
[73] *Ibid.* Sched. 1, para. 7(2).
[74] *Ibid.* Sched. 1, para. 7(3) and s.31.
[75] *Ibid.* Sched. 1, para. 8(1); but see also Sched. 1, para. 1(2), proviso.

undertakers' works or in taking any other necessary measures for the purpose of supply or service for which the apparatus removed was used.[76]

Requirement of notice of commencement of works

Except for minor surface works and emergency works,[77] undertakers **13–29** proposing to begin the execution of any code-regulated works in a street are required to give to each of the relevant authorities or managers a notice stating the undertakers' intention to execute the works and giving the date on which, and the place at which, they intend to begin the works.[78] The undertakers must not, without consent, commence the works until after a fixed period has elapsed from the date on which the notice was given.[79]

The minor works which do not require the service of a notice of inten- **13–30** tion to execute works are those set out in section 3(2)(a), (b) and (c) of the Act,[80] which do not involve either breaking up or opening of the street or any public sewer in the street, or tunnelling under the street.[81] In the case of emergency works[82] for which a notice of intention and time of execution of works would otherwise be required, the under-takers may commence these works before the time when they could otherwise lawfully begin them. As soon as is reasonably practicable thereafter, they must give to each of the authorities, bodies or persons to whom notice is required to be given, a notice stating the reasons for having begun the works before they were entitled to do so.[83] In addition to these exceptions, where the undertakers' works are necessary because of work to be carried out by the authority or managers as pro-moting authority, the authority or managers may waive observance by the undertakers of these requirements as far as notice to them is con-cerned.[84]

If the execution of the works has not been substantially begun at the **13–31** expiration of two months from the date on which a notice of intention and time of execution of works was given, or at the expiration of any extension of that period which the authority or person concerned may allow, the notice is invalid for the purposes of excuting the works, and a new notice must be given.[85] If the undertakers begin the execution of any works before they may lawfully do so, or fail to give a notice as

---

[76] P.U.S.W.A., Sched. 1, para. 8(2).
[77] See para. 13–17, above.
[78] As to the full requirements of the notice, see P.U.S.W.A., s.6(1), (2).
[79] *Ibid.*
[80] See paras. 13–16 and 13–17, above.
[81] P.U.S.W.A., s.6(4); but see the position regarding works at level crossings and see s.11(2).
[82] See *ibid.* s.39(1) and para. 13–17, above.
[83] See *ibid.* s.6(5).
[84] *Ibid.* s.22(3); and see paras. 13–57 *et seq.*, below.
[85] P.U.S.W.A., s.6(3).

required after beginning emergency works, they commit an offence.[86] There would also appear to be a potential liability under the provisions of section 131 of the Highways Act 1980, since the undertakers would not have the requisite lawful authority.[87]

13-32 There are special provisions as to notice of execution of works in controlled land. Undertakers proposing to begin code-regulated works in controlled land must give to the street authority and, in the case of land occupied by a person other than the street authority, to that person, a notice stating the general nature of the works and their intention to execute them.[88] The undertakers may not begin the execution of such works except with the consent of the street authority and of any other person in occupation, until after a fixed period has elapsed since the notice was given.[89] However, the undertakers may begin the execution of any *emergency* works before the time when they could otherwise lawfully begin works.[90] Execution of any works otherwise than in accordance with these provisions may render the undertakers liable to a fine.[91]

Requirements as to mode of executing works, and as to reinstatement

13-33 Undertakers executing works for which the prior settling of a plan and section is required must execute the work in accordance with the plan and section, and any incidental works must be executed to the reasonable satisfaction of the authorities or managers concerned.[92] Where a street or controlled land is broken up or opened, or where there is tunnelling or boring under a street or controlled land, the works must be carried out with all such dispatch as is reasonably practicable.[93]

13-34 The undertakers must reinstate and made good the street or controlled land as soon as is reasonably practicable after the completion of the works.[94] The obligation to reinstate is an obligation to restore the *status quo ante*.[95] The duty to make good the road is not performed unless the works have an element of stability,[96] and under earlier legislation it was held that there was a continuing duty to see that the ground is properly filled in.[97] In the case of works which involve the actual breaking up or opening of the street or controlled land, the undertakers must reinstate it and make it up to the previous surface level, subject to the right of the street authority or street managers to elect to do the

---

[86] Punishable on summary conviction by a fine not exceeding level 3 on the standard scale: P.U.S.W.A., s.6(6), as amended by Criminal Justice Act 1982, ss.38, 46.
[87] See *Beaumont* v. *Wilson* (1942) 40 L.G.R. 169.
[88] P.U.S.W.A., s.5(1), proviso; Sched. 1, para. 5.
[89] *Ibid.* s.5 (1) proviso; Sched. 1, para. 5 (1)(*a*).
[90] *Ibid.* s.5(1), proviso; Sched. 1, para. 5(1), proviso.
[91] *Ibid.* as amended by Criminal Justice Act 1982, ss.38, 46.
[92] P.U.S.W.A., s.7(1)(*a*), (*b*), (*c*).
[93] *Ibid.* s.7(2).
[94] *Ibid.* s.7(2)(*a*).
[95] *Schweder* v. *Worthing Gas Light and Coke Co.* [1912] 1 Ch. 83.
[96] *Withington* v. *Bolton B.C.* [1937] 3 All E.R. 108.
[97] *Huyton and Roby Gas Co.* v. *Liverpool Corpn.* [1926] 1 K.B. 146.

reinstatement and making good at upper levels themselves.[98] Reasonable facilities must be afforded to each of the authorities or managers concerned, for supervising the execution of the reinstatement and making good, and the undertakers must comply with any reasonable requirements of these authorities or bodies. Failure to carry out reinstatement and making good in accordance with these obligations renders the undertakers liable upon summary conviction to a fine.[99] If the undertakers are negligent in carrying out the reinstatement, so that the street is left in such a state as to constitute a public nuisance, the undertakers will also be liable in damages to persons injured as a consequence.[1]

Supervision and inspection of undertakers' works

13–35   Undertakers executing any code-regulated works are required to reimburse the reasonable supervision costs of each of the authorities or managers concerned.[2] They must also pay, to any transport authority concerned, an amount equal to any cost reasonably incurred in signalling or otherwise controlling traffic or for securing the safety of persons employed in connection with the works or the carrying out of reinstatement and making good thereafter.[3] Where proper facilities for inspection have not been accorded by the undertakers, the authority or managers concerned may execute such works as may be needed for enabling them to inspect the works, or reinstatement and making good, executed by the undertakers, and the undertakers will have to reimburse their costs of executing such works.[4]

Failure to comply with plan and section

13–36   Where it is claimed, by the authority or managers concerned, that the undertakers have executed works or reinstatement and making good otherwise than in accordance with the plan and section and the statutory requirements, or the works have not been executed to their reasonable satisfaction, the authority or managers may give notice to the undertakers to this effect.[5] Any works required to remedy such a defect must be carried out by the undertakers.[6] In certain circumstances, the undertakers will be liable for the cost of remedying subsidence or deterioration of the street or controlled land which occurs within six months after reinstatement and making good,[7] unless that subsidence or

---

[98] P.U.S.W.A., s.7(2)(c) and Sched. 3. See para. 13–41, below. For exceptions for sewers, drains or tunnels see paras. 13–46, et seq., below.
[99] P.U.S.W.A., s.7(2).
[1] *Goodman* v. *Sunbury Gas Consumers' Co. Ltd.* (1986) 75 L.T. 251; see also *Withington* v. *Bolton B.C.* [1937] 3 All E.R. 108.
[2] P.U.S.W.A., s.7(3)(a).
[3] *Ibid.* s.7(3)(b).
[4] *Ibid.* s.7(5).
[5] *Ibid.* s.7(4).
[6] *Ibid.* s.7(4).
[7] *Ibid.* s.7(6).

deterioration is attributable to the defective workmanship of, or the use of defective materials in the making good or reinstatment by the street authority or managers pursuant to their election under Schedule 3.[8] Notice must be given to the undertakers in respect of these claimed defects, so as to allow the examination by them of the area in question.[9] The mere fact that the street authority or street managers have omitted to rectify subsidence occasioned by the undertakers' neglect in making good the street will not exonerate the undertakers from liability for an injury caused by the subsidence.[10]

Requirements as to safety and obstructions which must be observed in the execution of works

Undertakers who are executing or who have executed any code-regulated works are obliged, at their own expense, to secure that requirements as to safety and obstruction are observed during and in connection with the execution of the works and of reinstatement and making good thereafter.[11] So long as the street or controlled land is open or broken up (except in any place where the public have no right to access and are not permitted to have access), it must be fenced, guarded and lit in such a manner as to give proper warning to the public during the hours of darkness.[12] Traffic signs[13] must be placed and operated in accordance with any directions of the relevant authority.[14] Any spoil or other material not required for the execution of works or for the reinstatement and making good must be carried away as soon as is reasonably practicable.[15] If the undertakers fail to satisfy any of the preceding obligations, the street authority or managers may do anything necessary for securing observance of the requirement in question, and the undertakers must then pay to the authority or managers an amount equal to any cost reasonably incurred by them in so doing.[16] No greater width or length of any street or controlled land than is reasonably necessary must be open or broken up at any one time, and there must not occur any greater obstruction of traffic on any street, or interference with the normal use of controlled land, than is reasonably necessary.[17] Failure to satisfy any of these provisions renders the undertakers liable to a fine in respect of each day of failure,[18] but will not give rise to liab-

13–37

---

[8] See para. 13–41, below.
[9] P.U.S.W.A., s.7(6).
[10] *Hartley* v. *Rochdale Corpn.* [1908] 2 K.B. 594.
[11] See P.U.S.W.A., s.8(1).
[12] See Road Traffic Act 1972, s.82.
[13] Within the meaning of Road Traffic Regulation Act 1984, ss.64–80.
[14] See P.U.S.W.A., s.8(1)(*b*) (as amended).
[15] *Ibid.* s.8(1)(*e*).
[16] *Ibid.* s.8(4).
[17] *Ibid.* s.8(1)(*d*).
[18] *Ibid.* s.8(3). See also Highways Act 1980, s.174.

ility for breach of statutory duty to an individual injured as a result of this failure.[19]

Greater London

Further provisions apply in Greater London. Undertakers must not, **13–38** in the execution of any code-regulated works, other than emergency works, or works relating to a service pipeline or service line or overhead telecommunication apparatus, break up or open a highway in the Metropolitan or City of London Police District which is part of a special road, trunk road or classified road, so as to reduce the width of the carriageway available for vehicular traffic to less than two-thirds of its width, unless they have given the required notice to the police, stating the place of the intended breaking up or opening and the date intended for commencement of the work.[20] Failure to comply is a criminal offence.[21] Where a transport authority elects to carry out the initial breaking up or opening of the highway then the same requirement applies to that authority.[22]

Protection for street managers of a street which is prospectively maintainable

Where code-regulated works are executed in a street which is a **13–39** prospectively maintainable highway, the street authority is under an obligation to the street managers to secure the performance, by the undertakers, of their duties in relation to mode of execution, reinstatement, prevention of obstructions and safety precautions and to exercise the powers vested in the authority in such manner as may be reasonably required for the protection of the street managers.[23] In particular, the street authority must comply with any reasonable request, as to the performance of those duties or the exercise of those powers, which may be made by the street managers to the authority.[24]

Reinstatement and making good by street authority or street managers after execution of undertakers' works

In any case in which undertakers are obliged to reinstate and make **13–40** good a street or controlled land after the completion of any code-regulated works involving breaking up or opening, other than certain minor works relating to a service-pipe or service line or overhead telecommunications apparatus,[25] the street authority or street managers

---

[19] *Keating* v. *Elvan Reinforced Concrete Co. Ltd.* [1968] 1 W.L.R. 722.
[20] P.U.S.W.A., s.35(1), (2), Sched. 7, para. 8(1); London Government Act 1963, s.19(1), (3); Telecommunications Act 1984, s.109 and Sched. 4.
[21] P.U.S.W.A., Sched. 7, para. 8(2), as amended by Criminal Justice Act 1982, ss.38, 46.
[22] P.U.S.W.A., Sched. 7, para. 8(3).
[23] *Ibid.* s.9(*a*).
[24] *Ibid.* s.9(*b*).
[25] As for the situation in London, see *ibid.* s.35(1), Sched. 7, para. 6, as amended by London Government Act 1963, s.19(1)(6) and Telecommunications Act 1984, s.109 and Sched. 4.

may, by notice given to the undertakers, elect themselves to do the permanent reinstatement and making good of the street or controlled land, or of any part of it at upper levels.[26] None of these powers of election apply to a street which is a highway which no person is liable to maintain or repair.[27]

Notice of election

13–41   The authority or managers may give notice to undertakers that they desire to exercise their power of election in the case of *all* code-regulated works, or all such works of a specified class, executed by the undertakers in particular streets or controlled land.[28] In this case, individual notices on each separate occasion when works are executed are not required. Otherwise, an individual notice of election must be given without any avoidable delay, and in any event within eight days of settlement of plan and section. Where a plan and section have not been settled, notice of election given after the undertakers have begun reinstatement or making good of any part of the street or controlled land will be ineffective as to that part.[29] If a notice of election is given both by the street authority and by the street managers, in relation to the reinstatment of a street which is a prospectively maintainable highway, the election of the authority has effect to the exclusion of that of the street managers. If two or more bodies or persons are street managers for the street, and notice of election is given by two or more of them, the election of such of them as the local highway authority may determine has effect to the exclusion of that of any of the others.[30]

Undertakers' obligations

13–42   Where the street authority or street managers elect to do works of reinstatement and making good, the only obligations, as to reinstatement, which remain with the undertakers are:

(a) to carry out interim restoration during the period between the time when their obligations to begin reinstatement and making good arises and the time when they are given notice that the electing authority or managers are about to begin their permanent reinstatement and making good; and

(b) to carry out such of the permanent reinstatement and making good as is not within the obligation of the electing authority or managers.[31]

"Interim restoration" means all such works as are requisite for securing

---

[26] P.U.S.W.A., s.7(2)(c), Sched. 3, para. 1(1), as amended by Telecommunications Act 1984, s.104 and Sched. 4.
[27] P.U.S.W.A., Sched. 3, para. 1(1).
[28] *Ibid.* Sched. 3, para. 1(2).
[29] *Ibid.* Sched. 3, para. 1(2).
[30] *Ibid.* Sched. 3, para. 1(3).
[31] *Ibid.* Sched. 3, para. 3.

that the street or controlled land does not remain open or broken up for any longer than is reasonably necessary, and that its state, during the period before it is permanently reinstated or made good at surface level, is not such as is likely to cause danger.

The undertakers must begin such restoration as they are obliged to **13–43** carry out as soon after completion of any part of their works as is reasonably practicable, must afford facilities for reasonable supervision, and must carry out the work to the satisfaction of the street authority or street managers.[32] The duty to secure observance of the requirements as to safety precautions, obstructions, and other matters, in section 8(1)(*a*) to (*e*) of the 1950 Act[33] remains with the undertakers until the electing authority has given them notice that it is about to begin its permanent reinstatement and making good—at which time the duty devolves upon the electing authority or managers.[34] After election, the street authority or managers are under an obligation to execute the permanent reinstatement and making good at surface level, and at such lower levels as may be requisite for securing that the street or controlled land is permanently reinstated and made good at the surface level. However, the street authority or street managers are not obliged to and have no power to execute any of the permanent reinstatement and making good within 12 inches (or within such other measure as may be agreed with the undertakers) above the undertakers' apparatus.[35]

A detailed procedure for determining when the undertakers have **13–44** completed their works is laid down in Schedule 3.[36] Notice of completion must be given to each of the relevant authorities. The works are then to be treated as having been completed together with such reinstatement and making good as the undertakers are obliged to carry out, if either of two conditions are fulfilled. These are:

(a) that no notice requiring the remedying of any defect is given[37]; or

(b) that any notice requiring the remedying of a defect is withdrawn or is determined in the undertakers' favour by arbitration.[38]

Permanent restoration

Notice must be given to the undertakers by the electing authority or **13–45** managers when works of permanent reinstatement and making good are about to be begun. During the period between the time when the notice

---

[32] P.U.S.W.A., s.7(2) is applied to the carrying out of these works by Sched. 3, para. 3; see para. 13–34, above.
[33] See para. 13–37, above.
[34] P.U.S.W.A., Sched. 3, para. 6(1).
[35] *Ibid.* Sched. 3, para. 4(1).
[36] *Ibid.* Sched. 3, para. 5(2).
[37] Within 8 days in the case of a Minister of the Crown, a county council or a transport authority, and 4 days in any other case: *ibid.* Sched. 3, para. 5(2)(i).
[38] *Ibid.* Sched. 3, para. 5(2)(ii).

is given and the time of completion of the works, the electing authority or managers are obliged to execute interim restoration at the site.[39] The costs reasonably incurred by the electing authority or managers in carrying out their obligation of permanent and interim restoration must be paid to them by the undertakers.[40] Where extra work is necessary to obviate a subsequent subsidence, the undertakers will also be liable to the electing authority or managers for the cost of that extra work,[41] unless the subsidence is attributable to defective workmanship or defective materials used in the reinstatement by the electing authority or managers.[42] The undertakers are not liable for any damage caused by negligent reinstatement by the electing authority or managers.[43] The electing authority or managers are entitled, if and so far as it may be required for the discharge of their obligation as to permanent reinstatement and making good, to undo and do again reinstatement and making good previously executed by the undertakers; the cost of this will be included in the amount payable by the undertakers for permanent reinstatement and interim restoration.[44] Furthermore, although the duty to secure observance as to safety precautions, obstructions and other matters passes to the electing authority upon their giving notice of permanent reinstatement and making good, the undertakers must reimburse to the electing authority or managers an amount equal to the cost reasonably incurred by them in respect of that duty.[45]

Special protection for transport authorities

13-46   A transport authority is an authority, body or person having the control or management of a transport undertaking. A transport undertaking is a railway, dock, harbour, pier, canal, or inland navigation undertaking, all or some of the activities of which are carried on under statutory authorisation.[46] Special protection is given to the operations and property of transport authorities where works requiring the settlement of a plan and section (other than emergency works) are to be executed in a street which is carried by, or goes under, a bridge vested in a transport authority, or in a street which crosses, or is crossed by, any other property which is held or used for the purposes of a transport undertaking. Where the works involve breaking up or opening the street, or tunnelling or boring under it, the transport authority may, within defined time limits, give notice of its election to execute all or any of certain specified works itself, insofar as they are to be executed in that

---

[39] P.U.S.W.A., Sched. 3, para. 4(2).
[40] *Ibid.* Sched. 3, para. 4(3).
[41] *Commercial Gas Co.* v. *Poplar B.C.* (1906) 94 L.T. 222.
[42] P.U.S.W.A., s.7(6)(*a*).
[43] *Cressy* v. *South Metropolitan Gas Co.* (1906) 94 L.T. 790.
[44] P.U.S.W.A., Sched. 3, para. 4(4).
[45] *Ibid.* Sched. 3, para. 6(2).
[46] *Ibid.* s.39(1).

street.[47] The undertakers may not then execute any of the works or reinstatement and making good specified in the notice, but must reimburse the transport authority their costs.[48]

There are also special provisions applying to works in a street which is **13–47** carried by or goes under a bridge vested in a transport authority, or which crosses or is crossed by any other property held or used for the purpose of a transport undertaking.[49] If it appears to the transport authority that an undertaker's works render certain other works[50] necessary, the authority may, within 29 days from the date on which the plan and section were submitted to the authority, give notice specifying these works. If the plan and section fell to be settled by arbitration, the transport authority must claim in the arbitration proceedings that the works are rendered necessary. If the undertakers agree, or if it is so determined by arbitration, that any works are rendered necessary, the undertakers must pay to the authority an amount equal to the costs reasonably incurred by the authority in executing those works and must not act so as to interfere with the execution of those works. In such a case, the transport authority must execute the works (so far as they are to be executed on the occasion of the execution of the undertaker's works) as soon as is reasonably practicable after the agreement or determination has been made. Failure by a transport authority to execute works of reinstatement and making good in accordance with the above provisions is a summary offence.[51]

If undertakers execute any works of reinstatement and making good **13–48** in contravention of any of these provisions, the transport authority may, where necessary, undo such of those works in relation to which it had the right of election and do any of them again; and the undertakers must reimburse the authority its reasonable costs.[52] The authority is then under similar obligations to those to which the undertakers would have been subject in carrying out those works.[53] Any cost reasonably incurred by the authority in action necessary for the discharge of these obligations and liabilities must be treated as part of the cost of the works or reinstatement and making good in question, payable by the undertakers, except in the case of a liability arising by reason of a default on the authority's part.

Undertakers executing any code-regulated works in a street crossing, **13–49** crossed by, or in the vicinity of, a railway, dock, harbour, pier, canal or inland navigation, must comply with any reasonable requirements made to them, by the relevant authority, relating to the display of lights. This

---

[47] P.U.S.W.A., s.10.

[48] *Ibid.* s.10(1); these provisions may be varied by agreement.

[49] *Ibid.* s.10(2).

[50] See *ibid.* s.10(2).

[51] Punishable by a fine not exceeding £10 in respect of each day of failure; *ibid.* s.10(4).

[52] *Ibid.* s.10(3).

[53] See *ibid.* s.10(5) for the differences in that liability.

is to avoid the risk of their being mistaken for any signal light or other light used for controlling, directing or securing the safety of traffic, or being a hindrance to the ready interpretation of any such signal or other light.[54] Similarly, undertakers executing any code-regulated works at a crossing of a railway on the level must comply with any reasonable requirements, as to the arrangements for executing the works, which are made of them by the relevant authority for reducing, so far as is practicable, interference with railway traffic. In the case of any such works requiring notice to the authority under section 6 of the Act,[55] but where submission of a plan and section is not required, the undertakers must defer beginning the works for such further period as the authority may reasonably request to enable it to formulate its requirements or make its traffic arrangements.[56]

Protection for sewer authorities

13–50   A sewer authority may, within 29 days from the date on which a plan and section were submitted or furnished to it, give to the undertakers a notice[57] specifying works which it claims to be necessary in order to make proper provision for drainage for which a public sewer of the authority is then used.[58] If the undertakers agree, or if it is determined by arbitration, that the works are necessary, the undertakers must execute those works at such time, and in such manner, as may be needed to secure the purposes of the works rendered necessary.[59] Failure to do so is an offence.[60]

13–51   Undertakers executing any code-regulated works which include breaking up or opening a public sewer, or any other works rendered necessary for proper drainage must afford to the sewer authority reasonable facilities for supervision.[61] The undertakers must reimburse the sewer authority for the reasonable costs of such supervision.[62] Undertakers executing any code-regulated works which include the breaking up or opening of a public sewer are obliged to reinstate it and make it good.[63] However, this obligation is subject to the sewer authority's power to elect to do this work itself. The undertakers are obliged to begin these works as soon as is reasonably practicable and to complete them with all reasonable dispatch.[64] If the undertakers fail to carry out their obligations to reinstate and make good, the sewer authority may itself do the work and may then recover from the undertakers an

---

[54] P.U.S.W.A., s.11(1).
[55] See para. 13–31, above.
[56] P.U.S.W.A., s.11(1). Failure is an offence subject to a fine not exceeding level 3.
[57] Or claim in the arbitration; *ibid.* s.12(1)(*a*).
[58] *Ibid.* s.12(1).
[59] *Ibid.* s.12(1)(*b*).
[60] Punishable by a fine not exceeding level 3 on the standard scale.
[61] *Ibid.* s.12(2).
[62] *Ibid.* s.12(5).
[63] *Ibid.* s.12(3).
[64] *Ibid.* s.30(4).

amount equal to the costs reasonably incurred in so doing. These provisions are unaffected by the right of the street authority or managers to elect to carry out the permanent reinstatement of the street.[65]

Alternatively, the sewer authority may itself elect to execute works **13–52** involving the breaking up or opening of the sewer, the reinstatement and making good of the sewer, and works rendered necessary for proper drainage.[66] Notice of election may be general, or may be particular to the works in question, and an individual notice must be given not later than 29 days from the date on which the plan and section are submitted to the authority, or 15 days from the date of any arbitration award. Notice of the extra works must be given at the time when the sewer authority claims them to be rendered necessary, or in the proceedings for the settlement of the plan and section.[67] Where notice of election is duly given, the undertakers must not execute any of the works or reinstatement and making good specified in the notice. The sewer authority is then entitled to reimbursement of its reasonable costs in executing the works.[68] Matters to which the notice refers may be varied by agreement between the sewer authority and the undertakers.

Protection for managers of sewers, drains or tunnels which are not public

Undertakers executing any code-regulated works which include **13–53** breaking up or opening a sewer, drain or tunnel, which is not a public sewer, are obliged to reinstate it and make it good.[69] They must begin and complete the reinstatement and making good as soon as is reasonably practicable. If they fail to do so, the authority, body or person having the management or control of the sewer, drain or tunnel may itself carry out the work, and the undertakers must then pay the costs reasonably incurred. These provisions are unaffected by the right of the street authority or managers to elect to carry out the permanent reinstatement of the street.[70]

Conflicting statutory provisions and inconsistent agreements

The street works code is intended as complete guidance to the regula- **13–54** tion of matters coming within its ambit. Therefore, from the date on which the code came into effect,[71] no enactment passed or made before the passing of the P.U.S.W.A. nor, unless the contrary intention appears, any enactment passed thereafter (whether it be a general or

---

[65] P.U.S.W.A., Sched. 3, para. 7.
[66] *Ibid.* s.12(4).
[67] *Ibid.* s.12 (4)(i), (ii).
[68] *Ibid.* s.12(5).
[69] *Ibid.* s.13(19).
[70] *Ibid.* Sched. 3, para. 7.
[71] April 26, 1951 where the power to execute street works was governed by general legislation, and October 26, 1951 in other cases.

special enactment) is to extend to the regulation of the exercise of a power to which the code applies.[72]

13–55   Any agreement which makes provision for regulating, in any respect, the exercise of a statutory power, which is subject to the street works code, regarding the relationship between the undertakers and any authority, body or person concerned, is of no effect in relation to code-regulated works to the extent that its effect is inconsistent with any of the provisions of the street works code.[73] However, any agreement will be effective insofar as it relates to reinstatement or making good,[74] and any agreement for the waiver or variation of a right conferred on any authority, body or person by any of the provisions of the code is effective if the agreement is made after the right has accrued, and if it is not inconsistent with the future operation of any of those provisions.[75] This power to enter into agreements to vary the code has been exercised frequently, and has resulted in different arrangements operating in different parts of the country. Attempts have been made to standardise these agreements to achieve consistency, but without complete success.[76]

13–56   The need to obtain extra consents from highway authorities or transport and bridge authorities, contained in earlier legislation, was removed by the 1950 Act, and no subsequent Act is to be construed as requiring the obtaining of any such consent unless the contrary intention appears in the Act. There are, however, certain exceptions where special consent may still be required.[77] Conditions imposed on a consent for the execution of code-regulated works are also of no effect unless they would have been saved by the proviso to section 16,[78] had they been contained in an agreement, or unless they are expressly saved by Order.[79] The giving of a consent by a street authority does not prejudice its right to disapprove or modify a plan on the ground that the works should be executed in controlled land.

SPECIAL CODE WHERE APPARATUS IS AFFECTED BY ROAD, BRIDGE OR TRANSPORT WORKS

Application of the code

13–57   The second code contained in the 1950 Act aims to establish uniform provisions for regulating the relations between highway authorities and undertakers, where the undertakers' apparatus is affected by roadworks. This has always been one of the most contentious areas of dispute between statutory undertakers and local authorities.

---

[72] P.U.S.W.A., s.15(3); see also s.15(6).
[73] *Ibid.* s.16.
[74] *Ibid.* s.16, proviso (*a*).
[75] *Ibid.* s.16, proviso (*b*).
[76] See para. 13–04, above.
[77] P.U.S.W.A., s.17 and Sched. 6, para. 4.
[78] See para. 13–55, above.
[79] P.U.S.W.A., s.17(3).

Terms and definitions

The "authority's works," which are the subject of this code, consist of **13–58** "road alterations," "bridge alterations" and "transport works."[80] "Road alterations" are works executed for road purposes by, or on behalf of, the highway authority,[81] consisting of:

(a) reconstruction or widening of the street;

(b) substantial alteration to the level of the street;

(c) the provision, alteration of the position or width, or substantial alteration to the level, of a carriageway, footpath or cycle track in the street;

(d) the provision of a cattle grid in the street or works ancillary thereto;

(e) tunnelling or boring under the street[82];

(f) the construction of dual carriageways and roundabouts[83];

(g) the construction of street refuges[84]; and

(h) the construction or alteration of a crossing over a kerbed footway or verge to provide access for mechanically-propelled vehicles in accordance with planning permission.[85]

"Bridge alterations" consist of the replacement, reconstruction or **13–59** substantial alteration of bridges which carry or cross a street repairable by the highway authority or under the control or management of a transport authority.[86] "Transport works" consist of substantial works (other than the replacement, reconstruction or substantial alteration of a bridge) required for the purposes of a transport undertaking and executed in property held or used for the purposes of the undertaking which is crossed by or crosses a street repairable by a highway authority or controlled or managed by the transport authority.[87] The code also applies, with modifications, to the placing of pipelines in streets[88] and to the execution of works on delineated lands under the Thames Barrier and Flood Prevention Act 1972.[89]

"Undertaker's apparatus" is defined as apparatus placed in a street **13–60** under a power to which section 1 of the Act applies[90] or over which such a power is exercisable, and to apparatus in controlled land which was placed in the exercise of such a power, together with an authorisation

[80] P.U.S.W.A., s.21(3).
[81] Including works carried out by a district council under Highways Act 1980, ss.42(1), (2), 230(7); P.U.S.W.A., s.21(4) (as amended).
[82] *Ibid.* s.21(1)(*a*), (3), as amended by Local Government Act 1972, s.188 and Sched. 21, para. 98(3)(*a*).
[83] Highways Act 1980, s.64(5).
[84] *Ibid.* s.68(2).
[85] *Ibid.* s.184(9)
[86] P.U.S.W.A., s.21(1)(*b*), (3), (as amended).
[87] *Ibid.* s.21(1)(*c*), (3); see also s.37(1), (2).
[88] Pipelines Act 1962, s.17.
[89] But not Coastal Flooding (Emergency Provisions) Act 1953; see P.U.S.W.A., s.2(5).
[90] See para. 13–07, above.

under Schedule 1 to the Act.[91] For the purposes of this code, the "promoting authority" is the highway authority executing the road alteration, the bridge authority or managers (in the case of a bridge alteration), and the transport authority (in the case of transport works).

Procedure where two or more promoting authorities

13–61   Where two or more operations, each consisting of authority's works, are executed in connection with each other at the same time, but by different authorities, those operations are treated as together comprising the authority's works.[92] In such a case, the rights and obligations of a promoting authority under the code are vested in only one of the authorities executing the works in question ("the negotiating authority").[93] The authorities may agree amongst themselves as to the discharge and exercise of the obligations and rights which are vested in the negotiating authority, and as to how expenses and receipts arising from that discharge and exercise are ultimately to be allocated between them. In default of agreement as to any of these matters, the issue must be determined by arbitration on a reference by one of the authorities. Nothing in any such agreement or determination will affect the right of the undertakers to deal only with the negotiating authority.[94]

Operation of the code

Requirement to give notice

13–62   The promoting authority must give to the undertakers notice of its intention to execute works affecting undertakers' apparatus in a street, or in controlled land abutting on a street, which will render necessary[95] works or any other measures to protect their apparatus or supply.[96] The notice must be given to all the undertakers whom the authority knows to have relevant apparatus,[97] and to any other undertakers having relevant apparatus who give notice, not later than the expiration of 15 days from the date on which the authority's works are begun, that they have such apparatus.[98]

13–63   Where it is claimed that a plan and section of the authority's works or any part of them ought to be furnished to the undertakers, they must give notice[99] to the authority, requiring it to furnish a plan and section of the works.[1] Where it is claimed that any undertakers' work or any

[91] P.U.S.W.A., s.21(2).
[92] *Ibid.* s.21(3) proviso, Sched. 4, para. 8(1).
[93] *Ibid.* Sched. 4, para. 8(2). See also *ibid.* para. 9(1), (2).
[94] *Ibid.* Sched. 4, para. 10.
[95] See *Paisley Magistrates* v. *South of Scotland Electricity Board* 1956 S.C. 502, where the moving of electricity apparatus to lie under the footway rather than under a widened carriageway was held to be necessary to maintain the efficiency of the system.
[96] P.U.S.W.A., s.22 and Sched. 4, paras 1, 2(1); see also Sched. 4, para. 8(2).
[97] But see *ibid.* s.37(1).
[98] *Ibid.* Sched. 4, paras.2(1)(*b*), 2(2), (road alterations).
[99] As early as is practicable and within the required time limits.
[1] *Ibid.* Sched. 4, para. 2(2).

measures are necessary to protect apparatus for the purposes of the supply or service for which the apparatus is used, the undertaker must give notice[2] to the authority specifying the necessary works and measures.[3] When such a notice has been duly given by the undertakers, the authority must give notice to the undertakers without avoidable delay, either accepting the notice as a specification of works and measures to be treated as being necessary, or objecting to it.[4] If the authority gives no notice objecting to the undertakers' notice, a specification may be settled by agreement between the authority and the undertakers, or, in default of agreement, by arbitration.[5] Where any necessary works come within the street works code, the authority may waive observance by the undertakers of section 3 (submission of plans and sections) or section 6 (notice of the beginning of undertakers' works) so far as they concern that authority.[6]

Commencement of authority's works and reimbursement of costs

Works commenced by an authority, except for emergency works, **13–64** may not be begun until either the time for giving a notice claiming that works or measures are rendered necessary has expired or, where such notice has been given, until a specification of those works has been settled or it has been agreed or determined that none of the works or measures claimed ought to be treated as necessary.[7] Where such works have been begun, and undertakers having relevant apparatus but who have had no notice of the authority's works then give notice of the existence of their apparatus, the authority must reimburse those undertakers any loss sustained by them by reason of the authority's failure to give notice.[8] The promoting authority must reimburse the undertakers for their reasonable costs in executing works or other measures rendered necessary by the authority's works.[9] In the case of dispute, the amount is referred to arbitration.[10] Where an authority's works comprise the making up of a street under the private street works code, the costs payable to undertakers for the removal of their apparatus may not be recovered from frontagers by inclusion of those works in the specification of works.[11]

There are three situations in which undertakers may not be entitled **13–65** to payment in respect of their works or measures. The first is where the authority's works consist only of works executed, after subsidence, for reinstating and making good the area of subsidence to its level

---

[2] As early as is practicable and within the required time limits.
[3] P.U.S.W.A., Sched. 4, para. 3.
[4] *Ibid.* para. 4.
[5] *Ibid.* para. 4(*a*); as to arbitration, see s.31.
[6] *Ibid.* s.22(3); see also Sched. 4, para. 9(2).
[7] *Ibid.* Sched. 4, para. 5.
[8] *Ibid.* Sched. 4, para. 6.
[9] *Ibid.* s.22(1).
[10] *Ibid.* s.31. As to pipelines, see Pipelines Act 1962, s.17(1).
[11] *Re Jesty's Avenue, Broadway, Weymouth* [1940] 2 All E.R. 632.

immediately before the subsidence occurred, unless the undertakers' prove that the subsidence was attributable to matters for which the promoting authority was to blame.[12] The second is where the placing of the apparatus was a code-regulated work and due notice of intention to carry out the authority's works was given. In such a case, the undertaker's entitlement to payment is only excluded if the authority's works are substantially begun within two years, or within such longer period as the Minister of Transport may, by order, subsititute, from the date on which notice was given, and if they are executed without any material departure from the plan and section.[13] Lastly, where the placing of the apparatus is not a code-regulated work, but notice of the authority's intended works and particulars thereof have been given in accordance with the provisions corresponding to the street works code contained in any corresponding enactment,[14] the conditions as to commencement and execution of the works are the same as in the situation where the works were code-regulated.

13–66 Undertakers' payments may be subject to reductions where there has been an element of betterment.[15] Indeed, if the placing of apparatus of a better type, greater dimensions or greater capacity involves extra costs, the undertakers must reimburse the promoting authority those extra costs.[16] Where agreement cannot be reached on these issues, the matter may be referred to arbitration.[17]

Execution of undertakers' works

13–67 Where authority's works are to be executed by the promoting authority, it may require the execution of any undertakers' works necessary for the purposes of the carrying out with reasonable facility of the authority's works, and which the undertakers have power to execute. Upon the making of such a request, the undertakers are obliged to execute any such works as soon as is reasonably practicable. Failure to do so renders them liable upon summary conviction to a fine.[18] The requirement to carry out works is subject to limitations. The permanent removal of any apparatus in a street or controlled land may not be required, nor may the temporary removal[19] of apparatus from a street or controlled land be required unless this can be achieved consistently with the maintenance of the supply or service for which the apparatus is used without

---

[12] P.U.S.W.A., s.23(1).
[13] *Ibid.* s.23(2).
[14] *Ibid.* s.23(2)(*b*), 24(1).
[15] *Ibid.* s.23(3)(i), (4); Thames Barrier and Flood Prevention Act 1972, s.51(3).
[16] P.U.S.W.A., s.23(3)(*a*), (*b*).
[17] *Ibid.* ss.23(5), 31.
[18] Not exceeding £10 in respect of each day of failure: *ibid.* s.30(4). This is without prejudice to any civil liability for such failure: *ibid.* s.30(1).
[19] To adjacent land in which the undertakers have power to place it or to another part of the bridge where the bridge authority or managers consent: *ibid.* s.22(2).

undue interruption or restriction.[20] The promoting authority must pay to the undertakers an amount equal to the cost of complying with their requirements.[21]

Conflicting statutory provisions and inconsistent agreements

This code operates to the exclusion of earlier general acts which were **13–68** accordingly amended by Schedule 5 to the 1950 Act. Unless the contrary is expressed in any Act passed after the 1950 Act, the code will automatically apply to any new statutory powers to execute authority's works.[22] An agreement concerning authority's works, whenever made, is of no effect in so far as it appears inconsistent with any provision of the code. However, an agreement, waiving or varying a right conferred on any authority, body or person by the code, made after the right has accrued is valid if it is not inconsistent with the future operation of the code.[23]

UNDERTAKERS' WORKS AFFECTING OTHER UNDERTAKERS' APPARATUS

Application of the code

The third code contained in the P.U.S.W.A. sets out special pro- **13–69** visions where the execution of works by undertakers ("operating undertakers") may affect apparatus of other undertakers ("owning undertakers").[24] These provisions apply to any undertakers' works[25] (other than works for the purposes of a railway undertaking) executed in a street or in controlled land, in exercise of a statutory power, or of such a power together with an authorisation, given under Schedule 1 to the Act, to do the works in controlled land.[26]

Requirement to give notice

Operating undertakers must not begin any works which are governed **13–70** by these provisions and which are likely to affect apparatus protected by the provisions (other than "excepted works")[27] until three days after they have given notice to the owning undertakers, indicating the nature and location of the works.[28] Emergency works may be executed without prior notice but as soon as is reasonably practicable after commencement,

---

[20] As to special provisions relating to pipelines, see Requisitioned Land and War Works Act 1948, s.12; P.U.S.W.A., s.22(2); Pipelines Act 1962, s.17(2).

[21] P.U.S.W.A., s.22(2)(*b*): subject to the same restrictions and limitations as are set out above.

[22] *Ibid.* s.24.

[23] *Ibid.* s.25.

[24] *Ibid.* s.26(1).

[25] And certain other works; see Highways Act 1980, s.290(8); Local Government (Miscellaneous Provisions) Act 1976, s.15(4); Thames Barrier and Flood Prevention Act 1972, s.51(7), (8).

[26] See para. 13–11, above.

[27] *i.e.* works relating only to a service pipe or service line or overhead telecommunication apparatus; P.U.S.W.A., s.26(2), as amended by Telecommunications Act 1984, s.109 and Sched. 4.

[28] P.U.S.W.A., s.26(2).

notice must be given to the undertakers stating the reasons for so doing. Failure to comply with these provisions renders the operating undertakers liable to a fine,[29] unless they can prove that the failure was attributable to their ignorance of the existence or position of the apparatus of the owning undertakers in question, and that their lack of knowledge was not due to any lack of diligence on their part or to any failure to make some inquiry which they ought reasonably to have made.

Supervision of works

13–71   During the execution of any works which are likely to affect apparatus protected by these provisions, the operating undertakers must give to the owning undertakers reasonable facilities for supervising the execution of the works.[30] In addition, apart from excepted works, the operating undertakers must comply with any requirement as to the nature or execution of the works which is reasonably necessary for the protection of apparatus or for the securing of access to such apparatus, and which is reasonably practicable at the time when the requirement is made.[31] Where the works include tunnelling or boring under apparatus, the operating undertakers must secure that there is proper temporary support for the apparatus during the execution of the works and that a proper permanent foundation is provided.[32] Where works include the laying of an electric line crossing or near to protected apparatus, the operating undertakers must secure that it is effectively insulated, is not capable of touching such apparatus and is not used as a conductor for electric current transmitted by the line laid.[33] Failure to comply with the requirements to provide reasonable facilities for supervision, or as to the execution of the works, renders the operating undertakers liable to a fine.[34] Compensation is payable to the owning undertakers in respect of damage to their apparatus caused by the lawful execution of works, or by the failure of the operating undertakers to comply with any provision as to the execution of the works, unless such damage is caused by misconduct or negligence on the part of the owning operators or their contractors or any employee thereof.[35] In the case of emergency works, the duty of operating undertakers as to the supervision and execution of the works is to take all such steps as are reasonably practicable consistent with meeting the circumstances for which the works are required.[36]

13–72   These provisions are intended only as a "minimum code to operate where little or no provision is made under existing enactments"[37] and,

---

[29] Not exceeding level 3 on the standard scale: P.U.S.W.A., s.26(8), as amended by the Criminal Justice Act 1982, ss.38, 46.
[30] P.U.S.W.A, s.26(3).
[31] *Ibid.* s.26(4)(*a*)
[32] *Ibid.* s.26(4)(*b*).
[33] *Ibid.* s.26(4)(*c*).
[34] *Ibid.* s.26(8), and see n. 29, above.
[35] *Ibid.* s.26(6).
[36] *Ibid.* s.26(5).
[37] Ministry of Transport Memorandum No. 665, para. 115.

unlike the two codes set out earlier in this chapter, they operate in addition to, and not in substitution for, any other obligations or liabilities to which the parties are subject, except that a similiar restriction on double recovery applies.[38]

CIVIL LIABILITY ARISING OUT OF WORKS CARRIED OUT IN THE HIGHWAY

In the absence of statutory authority, the breaking open of a highway, **13-73** the placing of apparatus upon it, or the carrying out of works upon it may give rise to liability at common law for nuisance, and may also constitute an offence under section 181(1) of the Highways Act 1980. However, even where the works are authorised by statute, the person executing them may be liable to others for the manner in which those works are carried out. The Public Utilities Street Works Act 1950 regulates the respective liabilities of authorities and undertakers towards each other but the position of third parties is generally left to the general principles of the common law.

Specific provisions of the Public Utilities Street Works Act

Where the lawful execution of code-regulated works in a street causes **13-74** damage to the property of the street authority or managers or, in the case of a street carried by or going under a bridge, to the bridge, the undertakers must pay compensation to the street authority or managers, or to the bridge authority or managers, equal to the expenses reasonably incurred in making good the damage to that property or to the bridge, unless the damage in question would not have been sustained but for misconduct or negligence on the part of the authority or managers or their contractors or of any person employed by them.[39] Civil liability to these bodies remains where any nuisance is caused by the execution of code-regulated works, or by explosion, ignition or discharge, or any other event arising out of, the escape of gas, electricity, water or any other substance from apparatus, the placing or maintenance of which was or is a code-regulated work and required for the purposes of a supply or service afforded by undertakers.[40] The effect of section 18 is to make uniform provision for the liability of statutory undertakers where a nuisance is caused by the carrying out of street works in the exercise of a statutory power, but it does not affect the ordinary common law rules that an undertaker, in the absence of negligence, is not liable for a nuisance inevitably attributable to the performance of its statutory duty.[41] Nor do these provisions affect the undertakers' liability

---

[38] P.U.S.W.A., s.26(7).
[39] *Ibid.* s.18(1).
[40] *Ibid.* s.18(2).
[41] *Department of Transport* v. *North West Water Authority* [1984] A.C. 336.

to street authorities, managers or other persons, arising otherwise under any statutory provision or at common law.[42]

Liabilities of undertakers to transport authorities

13–75   The rights of transport authorities are dealt with separately under section 19 of the 1950 Act. Where damage or obstruction is caused, either by the execution of code-regulated works, or by an explosion or other escape from apparatus in a street carried by, or going under, a bridge vested in a transport authority, or which crosses or is crossed by other property held or used for the purposes of a transport undertaking, the undertakers must indemnify the transport authority against the reasonable costs of remedying the damage or removing the obstruction and any directly resulting losses occasioned by interference to traffic.[43] Where undertakers are required to indemnify a transport authority in these circumstances in respect of the tortious act of some other party against whom the authority would have had a right of action, but in respect of which the undertakers are not tortiously liable, then the undertakers have the like right to recover contribution from that other person under the Civil Liability (Contribution) Act 1978.[44] The undertakers are not, however, liable for any damage or obstruction caused by misconduct or negligence on the part of the authority, their contractors or employees.[45]

13–76   Undertakers carrying out code-regulated works of maintaining apparatus in a street carried by or going under a bridge vested in a transport authority, or which crosses or is crossed by other property held or used for the purposes of a transport undertaking, must secure that the apparatus is maintained to the reasonable satisfaction of the transport authority and must afford reasonable inspection facilities to the authority.[46] Otherwise, the authority may execute any works required to enable it to inspect the apparatus, including any necessary breaking up or opening of the street. If the undertakers fail to secure that the apparatus is maintained in accordance with these provisions, the authority may execute any emergency works rendered necessary by the failure, including any necessary breaking up or opening of the street, and the undertakers must reimburse the authority's reasonable costs of executing such works.[47] Notice stating the general nature of the works must be given to each of the relevant authorities or managers concerned, as soon as is reasonably practicable after the commencement of any such works.[48] The undertakers are not exempted by any of these special provisions for

[42] P.U.S.W.A., s.18(4); see *e.g. Longhurst* v. *Metropolitan Water Board* [1948] 2 All E.R. 834.
[43] P.U.S.W.A., s.19(1).
[44] *Ibid.* s.19(4), as amended by Civil Liability (Contribution) Act 1978, s.9(1).
[45] P.U.S.W.A., s.19(1).
[46] *Ibid.* s.19(2).
[47] See also *ibid.* s.19(2)(*a*).
[48] *Ibid.* s.19(2)(*b*).

recovery from any other liability which they may have to a transport authority or to any other person.[49] These provisions are not subject to the arbitration procedure.[50]

Double compensation

Provision is made in section 32 to prevent recovery of double compen- **13–77** sation where a right to compensation arises under two or more provisions of the 1950 Act, or under both the 1950 Act and an earlier provision.[51] For the purposes of this section, any provision of the Highways Act 1980 derived from the Highways Act 1959, is to be deemed to have been passed on the date of the enactment from which the relevant provision of the 1959 Act was derived (whether or not modified by the 1959 Act).

Exemption from liability for damage caused by the storage of materials at the side of the road

A street authority is not liable for any damage to undertakers' appara- **13–78** tus caused by storage by the authority, in connection with the execution of works for road purposes, of any plant, equipment, or materials, on any part of the street other than a carriageway, cycle track or footpath or on the controlled land. The exemption only applies where the apparatus is placed in a street which is a maintainable highway, or is a prospectively maintainable highway, in exercise of a power to which section 1 of the Public Utilities Street Works Act 1950 applies, or over which such a power is exercisable, or where apparatus is placed in controlled land in exercise of such a power together with an authorisation[52] under Schedule 1 to the Act. The street authority and the undertakers may alter these provisions by agreement.[53]

Liability at common law

In the absence of negligence, no action will lie for nuisance or damage **13–79** which is the inevitable result of carrying out works in the exercise of statutory powers, provided that the injury incurred is one contemplated by the statute.[54] Although this common law rule provides a very wide protection for those exercising statutory powers, it does not apply to every exercise of a statutory power; it can only apply if the terms of the statute and the nature of the actions empowered by the statute are such that Parliament must be taken to have contemplated the probability, if

---

[49] *Ibid.* s.19(3).
[50] *Ibid.* s.31(2).
[51] *Ibid.* s.32(1), (2); see also Highways Act 1980, Sched. 23, para. 21.
[52] See para. 13–11, above.
[53] P.U.S.W.A., s.29.
[54] See *Allen* v. *Gulf Oil Refining Ltd.* [1981] A.C. 1001; see also the discussion and cases cited at paras. 6–07—6–08.

not the certainty, that the interference complained of would occur. In that situation, the statute will impliedly have authorised the interference, even though it has not provided for any compensation.[55] Thus, where there is a power to erect an obstruction in the highway, the nuisance created by that obstruction is contemplated and impliedly authorised. However, where the place at which an act is to be done is not specified there is no implied power or authorisation to do it in a place where it will cause a nuisance.[56] Similarly it is insufficient that Parliament should have contemplated some injury but not the injury which actually incurred.[57]

An empowering statute may sometimes contain an express provision **13–80** preserving the rights of third parties to recover damages for nuisance if caused by the undertakers' exercise of statutory powers. Such a clause does not prevent the carrying out of an act prescribed in the statute by plans and specifications, or an act where the nature of the power must cause some obstruction to the public or to adjoining owners, or to both.[58]

A statutory power to carry out works in a highway may provide for **13–81** the payment of compensation to any person sustaining damage from the execution of those works. In the absence of such a provision, there is no remedy for the damage caused by the execution of such works, unless the statutory power has been exceeded or is exercised in bad faith or negligently, or where the works themselves have been executed negligently. Parliament is not to be taken to have impliedly authorised the negligent exercise of a power, and reasonable care and diligence must, therefore, be applied in exercising such a power.[59] The duty to to take reasonable care applies to the choice of place and manner of executing a statutory power[60] and to subsequent maintenance,[61] use and improvement,[62] as well as to the acts of original construction.[63] The onus of proving negligance is on the person injured.[64]

[55] *Edgington* v. *Swindon Corpn.* [1939] 1 K.B. 86; *Chaplin (W. H.) & Co. Ltd.* v. *Westminster Corpn.* [1901] 2 Ch. 329; *Goldberg & Son Ltd.* v. *Liverpool Corpn.* (1900) 82 L.T. 362.
[56] *Vernon* v. *St. James, Westminster, Vestry* (1881) 16 Ch.D. 449.
[57] See *Fisher* v. *Ruislip-Northwood U.D.C. and Middlesex C.C.* [1945] K.B. 584; *Marriage* v. *East Suffolk Rivers Catchment Board* [1950] 1 K.B. 284; *R.* v. *Bradford Navigation Co.* (1865) 34 L.J.Q.B. 191; *Nicholson* v. *Southern Ry. Co. and Sutton and East Cheam U.D.C.* [1935] 1 K.B. 558; *Lewys* v. *Burnett and Dunbar* [1945] 2 All E.R. 555.
[58] *Att.-Gen.* v. *Gas Light & Coke Co.* (1877) 7 Ch.D. 217; *Jordeson* v. *Sutton Southcoates and Drypool Gas Co.* [1899] 2 Ch. 217; *Smeaton* v. *Ilford Corpn.* [1954] Ch. 450.
[59] See *Howard-Flanders* v. *Maldon Corpn.* (1926) 90 J.P. 97 and Chap. 6, para. 6–07.
[60] *Chaplin (W. H.) & Co. Ltd.* v. *Westminster Corpn.* [1901] 2 Ch. 329; *Goldberg & Son Ltd.* v. *Liverpool Corpn.* (1900) 82 L.T. 362.
[61] *Baldwin's Ltd.* v. *Halifax Corpn.* (1916) 85 L.J.K.B. 1769.
[62] *Manchester Corpn.* v. *Farnworth* [1930] A.C. 171.
[63] *McClelland* v. *Manchester Corpn.* [1912] 1 K.B. 118; *Baxter* v. *Stockton-on-Tees Corpn.* [1959] 1 Q.B. 441.
[64] *Marriage* v. *East Suffolk Rivers Catchment Board* [1950] 1 K.B. 284.

A person interfering with a highway under a statutory power must **13–82** exercise due care to see that the works are carried out in a manner which will not injure the public[65] or cause unreasonable obstruction.[66] Where compensation for injury is provided by the empowering statute, defective or careless work may come within the statutory compensation, if it is part of the product of the authorised act, or if it aggravates an injury which is the product of the authorised act and which is contemplated by the statute,[67] but the remedy for any other carelessness is in nuisance or negligence, or both.[68] Any person, irrespective of his authority, who interferes with the ordinary structure and condition of the highway, is responsible until it is restored to its proper and normal condition such that it can be properly traversed by the public without undue risk.[69]

A person's duties in respect of statutory works do not cease upon **13–83** completion of the installation of the works and the restoration of the highway. Reasonable care must be exercised in using or operating statutory works in the highway,[70] and they must be kept in repair and maintained in a safe condition by the person erecting them, unless he is absolved from so doing by the statute authorising the works.[71] Where the statutory works are rendered dangerous by the acts of third parties, an authority will not be liable unless and until it knew, or ought to have known, of the danger.[72] Where a manhole placed level with the highway is found to be projecting above the highway because the highway has

---

[65] See *e.g. Holliday* v. *National Telephone Co.* [1899] 2 Q.B. 392; *Scott* v. *Manchester Corpn.* (1857) 2 H.& N. 204; *Maxwell* v. *British Thomson Houston Co. Ltd.* (1902) 18 T.L.R. 278; *Crane* v. *South Surburban Gas Co. Ltd.* [1916] 1 K.B. 33.

[66] *R.* v. *Burt* (1870) 11 Cox C.C. 399; *Martin* v. *L.C.C.* (1899) 80 L.T. 866.

[67] *Uttley* v. *Todmorden Local Board of Health* (1874) 44 L.J.C.P. 19; *Hornby* v. *Liverpool United Gas Co.* (1883) 47 J.P. 231; *St. James and Pall Mall Electric Light Co. Ltd.* v. *R.* (1904) L.J.K.B. 518.

[68] See *Marriage* v. *East Suffolk Rivers Catchment Board* [1950] 1 K.B. 284.

[69] *Shoreditch Corpn.* v. *Bull* (1904) 68 J.P. 415; see also *Drew* v. *New River Co.* (1834) 6 C. & P. 754; *Ellis* v. *Sheffield Gas Consumers' Co.* (1896) 60 J.P. 585; *James Smith & Co.* v. *West Derby Local Board* (1878) 3 C.P.D. 423; *Cox* v. *Paddington Vestry* (1891) 64 L.T. 566; *Goodson* v. *Sunbury Gas Consumers' Co. Ltd.* (1896) 75 L.T. 251; *Hartley* v. *Rochdale Corpn.* [1908] 2 K.B. 594; *Newsome* v. *Darton U.D.C.* [1938] 3 All E.R. 93.

[70] *Wiggins* v. *Boddington* (1828) 3 C.& P. 544; see also *Manley* v. *St Helens Canal and Ry. Co.* (1858) 2 H.& N. 840; *Great Western Ry. Co.* v. *Bishop* (1872) L.R. 7 Q.B. 550; *Boyd* v. *Great Northern Ry. Co. Ltd.* [1895] 2 I.R. 555.

[71] *Great Central Ry. Co.* v. *Hewlett* [1916] 2 A.C. 511; *Bayley* v. *Wolverhampton Waterworks Co.* (1860) 6 H. & N. 241; *Mersey Docks Trustees* v. *Gibbs* (1866) L.R. 1 H.L. 93; *Oliver* v. *North Eastern Ry. Co.* (1874) L.R. 9 Q.B. 409; *White* v. *Hindley Local Board* (1875) L.R. 10 Q.B. 219; *Bathurst Borough* v. *Macpherson* (1879) 4 App.Cas. 256; *Blackmore* v. *Mile End Old Town Vestry* (1882) 9 Q.B.D. 451; *Alldred* v. *West Metropolitan Tramways Co.* [1891] 2 Q.B. 398; *Barnett* v. *Poplar Corpn.* [1901] 2 K.B. 319; *West Lancashire R.D.C.* v. *Lancashire and Yorkshire Ry. Co.* [1903] 2 K.B. 394; *Hertfordshire* v. *New River Co.* [1904] 2 Ch. 513; *Winslowe* v. *Bushey U.D.C.* (1908) 72 J.P. 259; *McLoughlin* v. *Warrington Corpn.* (1910) 75 J.Pl 57; *Skilton* v. *Epsom and Ewell U.D.C.* [1937] 1 K.B. 112; *Simon* v. *Islington B.C.* [1943] K.B. 188; *Railway Executive* v. *West Riding of York C.C.* [1949] Ch. 423.

[72] *Fisher* v. *Ruislip-Northwood U.D.C. and Middlesex C.C.* [1945] K.B. 584; *Hill* v. *New River Co.* (1868) 9 B.& S. 303; *Price* v. *South Metropolitan Gas Co.* (1895) 65 L.J.Q.B. 126; *Wringe* v. *Cohen* [1940] 1 K.B. 229.

worn away, the authority is likewise not liable.[73] In addition to carrying out statutory works with care, a person carrying out these works owes a duty to warn users of the highway of obstructions erected or works carried out in the highway.[74] The duty requires the exercise of reasonable skill and care, having regard to the protection which the public is entitled to expect.[75] To fulfil this duty may require lighting the obstruction, displaying warnings of it, stationing guard rails around it, or other measures or combinations of measures, depending upon the circumstances. In some cases, the nature of the duty of care is prescribed by the statute authorising the works.[76] Where a change of circumstances renders dangerous an obstruction or works which were previously safe, a fresh duty to warn and protect arises, but the person exercising the statutory power will not be liable for breach of it, until he knows, or ought to have known, of the danger and has had a reasonable opportunity to take necessary steps to remedy it.[77]

13–84   A problem which sometimes arises in respect of accidents involving the condition of statutory works is the question of whether the statutory undertakers or the highway authority, or both, should be liable for any damage resulting. Clearly, if the injury occurs directly as a result of the manner in which works are being carried out, the party carrying out the works will be responsible. More difficult problems arise if the highway is left in a dangerous condition after works have been completed, or where the highway subsequently becomes dangerous because the restoration was carried out inadequately. Under the Highways Act 1980, section 41, the highway authority is under a duty to maintain highways at the public expense.[78] In appropriate circumstances, the condition of statutory works in or on the highway may be such as to render the highway authority in breach of this duty, in which case it will be liable for any damage caused by the condition of the statutory works, as will be the statutory undertakers whose apparatus is involved.[79] However, where the highway authority elects to carry out permanent restoration of the highway under the Public Utilities Street Works Act, section 7(2)(c) and Schedule 3, it is not liable for the condition of the affected part of the highway until it gives notice of its intention to begin permanent reinstatement under Schedule 3, paragraph 5,[80] although it is unclear what the position is if the highway authority unreasonably delays in giving its notice of permanent restoration.

---

[73] *Thompson* v. *Brighton Corpn.* [1894] 1 Q.B. 332; *Moore* v. *Lambeth Waterworks Co.* (1886) 17 Q.B.D. 462.

[74] *Fisher* v. *Ruislip-Northwood U.D.C. and Middlesex C.C.* [1945] K.B. 584.

[75] *Morrison* v. *Sheffield Corpn.* [1917] 2 K.B. 866; *Greenwood* v. *Central Service Co. Ltd.* [1940] 2 K.B. 447.

[76] See *e.g. Great Central Ry. Co.* v. *Hewlett* [1916] 2 A.C. 511.

[77] *Fisher* v. *Ruislip-Northwood U.D.C. and Middlesex C.C.* [1945] K.B. 584.

[78] See Chap. 4.

[79] *Nolan* v. *Merseyside and North West Water Authority* (1982) (unreported).

[80] See *McKevitt* v. *Post Office, Kidd & Loftus and Merseyside C.C.* (1980) Boreham J., (unreported).

Compensation under the Public Health Act, section 278

13–85 In some cases, works carried out by undertakers (particularly sewerage works) may be subject to the compensation provisions contained in section 278 of the Public Health Act 1936. These allow for the payment of "full compensation" to any person who has sustained damage by reason of the exercise by an authority of any of its powers under the 1936 Act. The liability to pay compensation is limited to situations where the claimant himself has not been in default, where the actions of the authority would, but for the statute, have been unlawful,[81] and where there is a right of action at common law. Where a power is exercised negligently, the proper remedy is by way of an ordinary civil action. Section 278 applies where the power has been exercised lawfully. It does not apply to any action of the authority which it had a duty to undertake, but it will apply to the exercise of powers in performance of that duty. Compensation is assessed along similiar lines to those applicable in tort.[82] Disputes as to quantum of compensation are decided by arbitration.[83]

ADDITIONAL STATUTORY PROVISIONS

Restrictions on breaking up recently opened streets

13–86 A statutory power in undertakers to break up or open the carriageway of a highway maintainable at the public expense, other than a power conferred for road purposes, or for the purposes of a railway or tramway undertaking,[84] is not exercisable for a period following other road works in the same highway. This restriction applies during the 12 months following either:

(a) the end of any period during which the use by vehicles of the carriageway has been prohibited, or the width of the carriageway available for vehicular traffic has been reduced to less than two-thirds of its width, for the purposes of the execution of works for road purposes or of such works and other works; or

(b) the completion of a resurfacing extending to one-third or more of the width of the carriageway.[85]

For this restriction to apply, two conditions must be satisfied. The first is that, more than three months before the date on which the works for road purposes, or the resurfacing works, as the case may be, are substantially begun, the authority responsible for maintaining the highway[86] must give notice to the undertakers that the works are in prospect

---

[81] *Hall* v. *Bristol Corpn.* (1867) L.R. 2 C.P. 322.

[82] See *Lingke* v. *Christchurch Corpn.* [1912] K.B. 595; *Herring* v. *Metropolitan Board of Works* (1865) 19 C.B. (N.S.) 510; *Leonidis* v. *Thames Water Authority* (1979) 77 L.G.R. 722.

[83] *Lingke* v. *Christchurch Corpn.*, n. 82, above.

[84] See Highways Act 1980, s.156(10)(*a*), (*b*).

[85] *Ibid.* s.156(1).

[86] *Ibid.* s.156(2).

and must specify an intended date for their commencement. The second is that the works must be substantially begun on, or within one month from, the specified date or, in certain cases, a longer period.[87] There are also a number of exceptions to the operation of these restrictions.[88] The highway authority may consent to the breaking up or opening of the highway within the period.[89] The breaking up or opening of highways in Greater London is covered by separate statutory provisions.[90]

13–87 If undertakers break up or open a highway in contravention of the above provisions, they must pay to the highway authority the costs reasonably incurred in reinstating and making good the highway, and they will also be guilty of an offence.[91] Any question arising in relation to a claim made for payment for reinstating and making good the highway is to be determined by arbitration.[92]

Public Health Act 1875

13–88 Under the Public Health Act 1875, section 153, an urban authority[93] has power to require the alteration of gas and water pipes.[94] The procedure is by way of notice with default powers.[95] The expenses of, or connected with, any such alteration must be paid by the authority, except where under any local Act those expenses are directed to be borne by the owner, in which case the owner must bear those expenses. No alteration may be required or made which will permanently injure any such pipes, etc., or which will prevent the water or gas from flowing as freely and conveniently as usual.[96] The authority must pay compensation to any person who sustains damage by reason of the execution by it of works under these provisions.[97]

Statutory control under the Pipelines Act 1962

13–89 Pipelines may be placed in a street with the consent of the appropriate authority[98] for that street, which street may be broken open for the purpose of inspecting, maintaining, adjusting, repairing, altering or renewing a pipeline already placed there, or for changing the position of a pipeline so placed, or for removing it.[99] Where it is proposed that, in exercise of this power in relation to a street, a pipeline is to be placed

---

[87] See also Highways Act 1980, s.165(2).
[88] *Ibid.* s.156(3): emergency works; see also s.156(4).
[89] Consent must not to be unreasonably withheld: *ibid.* s.156(5).
[90] *Ibid.* ss.156(6), 157.
[91] Punishable by a fine not exceeding level 3 on the standard scale: *ibid.* s.156(4)(*b*).
[92] *Ibid.* s.156(7).
[93] See Local Government Act 1972, s.180(1) and Sched. 14, para. 29.
[94] For restrictions on the exercise of this power, see Highways Act 1980, s.188(1).
[95] Public Health Act 1875, ss.4, 153, 266, 267 (which has otherwise been repealed, see Public Health Act 1936, s.346(1), Sched. 3, Part I).
[96] Public Health Act 1875, s.153(9).
[97] Highways Act 1980, s.288(2).
[98] See Pipelines Act 1962, s.15(10).
[99] *Ibid.* s.15(1).

along a line crossing the street, the appropriate authority for that street may not withhold its consent unless there are special reasons for doing so.[1] Where it is proposed that a pipeline is to be placed otherwise than along a line crossing the street, the consent of the appropriate authority for the street may not be unreasonably withheld, and for this purpose the withholding of consent is to be treated as reasonable if the owner of the pipeline fails to show that there is no reasonably practicable alternative to the placing of the pipeline in accordance with the proposals.[2] The consent of an appropriate authority may be given subject to reasonable conditions.[3]

---

[1] Pipelines Act 1962, s.15(2).
[2] *Ibid.* s.15(3).
[3] For specific conditions which may be included, see *ibid.* s.15(4). As to determination of disputes, see s.15(6), (7).

CHAPTER 14

ACQUISITION OF LAND, INQUIRIES AND COMPENSATION

ACQUISITION OF LAND

Introduction

14–01   It is not intended in this section to deal exhaustively with the powers of acquisition of land for highway purposes; for a more detailed discussion, reference should be made to the specialist books on compulsory purchase. Highway authorities have powers to acquire land for the creation of highways, for the improvement of highways, for the erection of buildings required for the discharge of their functions, and for mitigating the adverse effects of constructing or improving highways. These powers of acquisition, which are contained in Part XII of the Highways Act 1980, may be exercised compulsorily or by agreement.[1] A highway authority cannot be compelled by mandamus to exercise its powers under this part of the Act.[2]

14–02   Section 249 of and Schedule 18 to the Highways Act 1980 place restrictions on the land which may be acquired for the construction or improvement of a highway or for highway purposes.[3] Basically, Schedule 18 prescribes distance limits from the highway or proposed highway beyond which the power of compulsory acquisition will not run. Section 249 does not apply, however, to acquisition of land required for highway drainage, for the diversion of a watercourse or for providing protection for a highway or proposed highway against snow, flood, landslide or other hazards of nature.[4] Nor do the restrictions apply to land acquired for the purposes of exchange, where land forming part of a common, open space or fuel or field garden allotment is acquired for highway purposes.[5]

14–03   Compulsory purchase order proceedings for special, trunk or classified roads may be taken concurrently with the proceedings for confirmation of the schemes and orders for those roads.[6] Similarly, proceedings relating to orders for the acquisition of land for the provision of a substitute access to replace a stopped up access may be taken concurrently with the proceedings under section 124.[7] Proceedings for orders required to give effect to directions under section 93 (reconstruction,

---

[1] Highways Act 1980, s.238.
[2] *Perry* v. *Stanborough (Developments)* [1978] J.P.L. 36.
[3] This applies to ss.239(1), (2), (3), (4) and 240.
[4] Highways Act 1980, ss.100, 102 and 110.
[5] *Ibid.* s.239(5).
[6] *Ibid.* s.257 and Sched. 1.
[7] *Ibid.* s.257(2).

etc., of privately maintainable bridges) and to determinations in relation to the provision of cattle grids under sections 82 to 90, may be taken concurrently with the proceedings leading to those directions or determinations.[8] Schedule 20 to the 1980 Act provides for certain related orders to come into effect on the same day.

Orders are subject to the procedure set out in the Acquisition of Land **14–04** Act 1981[9] and, where made by a local highway authority, will require to be confirmed by the Minister. The Minister may make or confirm part only of an order, and, where he has not decided whether or not the remainder ought to be made or confirmed, he may direct that consideration of the remainder be postponed.[10] Land already acquired by agreement may be included in the compulsory purchase order,[11] and some of the consequences following on from a compulsory acquisition will then apply to that land.[12] Land acquired for a service area by a special road authority, or land acquired for a trunk road picnic area by the Minister, or by a highway authority for a lorry area may, in any event, be used for those purposes, notwithstanding the existence of restrictive convenants to the contrary.[13]

General power of acquisition

The general power of acquisition is given by section 239 of the High- **14–05** ways Act 1980. The Minister is given power to acquire land required for the construction of a trunk road and for the carrying out of works authorised by an order relating to a trunk road, or for the provision of buildings or facilities to be used in connection with the construction or maintenance of a trunk road other than a special road.[14] Any highway authority may acquire land required for the construction of a highway, other than a trunk road, which is to become maintainable at the public expense.[15] A highway authority may acquire land required for the improvement of a highway, as long as the improvement is authorised by the 1980 Act.[16] A special road authority may acquire land for the improvement of a highway which is to be included in the route of a special road, but which has not been transferred to the authority by means of an order under section 18, for the purposes of any order made in relation to the special road under section 18, or for the provision of service stations or other buildings or facilities to be used in connection with the construction of the special road, or with the use or maintenance

---

[8] Highways Act 1980, s.27(4).
[9] In some cases subject to modifications. See also *ibid.* s.247(5), (6).
[10] *Ibid.* s.259.
[11] *Ibid.* s.260.
[12] *e.g.* the overriding of restrictive covenants; see also Local Government Act 1972, s.120(3).
[13] Highways Act 1980, s.260(3), (4).
[14] Subject to *ibid.* s.249; para. 14–02, above.
[15] *Ibid.* s.239(1).
[16] *Ibid.* ss.239(3), 249.

of it.[17] Land which is required for the purpose of exchange for the acquisition of land forming part of a common, open space or fuel or field garden allotment may be acquired by a highway authority as if it were land required for the construction or improvement of the highway.[18] A highway authority may acquire land required for the improvement or development of frontages to a highway for which it is the highway authority or for the improvement or development of the land adjoining or adjacent to that highway.[19] The procedure for compulsory acquisition is governed by the Acquisition of Land Act 1981.[20] Acquisition by agreement is governed by certain provisions in the Compulsory Purchase Act 1965.[21] Acquisition may, for the most part, occur in advance of requirements.[22] Subject to the provisions of section 248(3) and Schedule 17, land may be acquired in stages.

Specific powers of acquisition

Provision of new accesses

14-06 By section 240 of the Highways Act 1980, a highway authority may acquire land, which is required in connection with the carrying out of works, to provide a new access where an existing access has been stopped up, by order, by agreement[23]; or by an order relating to a classified road made under section 4 of the Highways Act 1980.[24] A highway authority may acquire land required by itself in connection with the construction or improvement of a highway, or with the carrying out of works authorised by an order under section 18 in connection with a special road.[25]

Construction of highway facilities

14-07 The Minister[26] may acquire land under section 112(5) for the construction of a trunk road picnic area or for the provision of public sanitary conveniences. A local highway authority may acquire land for providing public sanitary conveniences under section 114. Any highway authority may acquire land for the purposes of providing a lorry park under section 115. Land may also be acquired for use as exchange land where land forming part of a common, open space or fuel or field garden allotment is acquired for highway purposes.[27] Under section 143, land

---

[17] Highways Act 1980, ss.239(4), 249.
[18] *Ibid.* s.239(5).
[19] *Ibid.* s.239(6).
[20] Where acquisition is of rights pursuant to *ibid.* s.242(3); see s.247(5).
[21] See *ibid.* s.247(6).
[22] *Ibid.* s.248. But not in respect of the powers under ss.240 and 246: see below.
[23] See *ibid.* s.129.
[24] *i.e.* agreements as to the exercise of functions between the Minister and a local highway authority in relation to highways crossing or entering the route of a trunk road.
[25] *Ibid.* s.240(2)(*a*).
[26] Subject to *ibid.* s.249; para. 14-02, above.
[27] *Ibid.* s.240(3)-(6).

may be acquired for the purpose of providing a cattle grid or a bypass. A general power is given to a highway authority, by section 245, to acquire land required for the provision of any buildings or facilities needed for the purposes of its functions as a highway authority.

Diversion of watercourses

By section 240(2)(*a*) of the Highways Act 1980, land may be acquired **14-08** for the carrying out of any works in connection with the diversion of a navigable watercourse authorised by an order under section 108(1) of the Act.[28] Any power to acquire land for a purpose which involves the diversion of a navigable watercourse, or the carrying out of works in connection with the diversion of a non-navigable watercourse under section 110 of the 1980 Act, includes power to acquire land which is required for the carrying out of the diversion of works themselves.[29]

Acquisition of land between an improvement line and the boundary of the street

Where a highway authority has prescribed an improvement line[30] in **14-09** relation to any street, it may acquire any land not occupied by buildings, lying between the improvement line and the boundary of the street.[31] Land acquired under this provision is to be added to and made good as part of the street at such time or times as the highway authority may determine. Until such time, the occupier of the land severed from the highway is entitled to rights of reasonable access from his land to the highway over the land acquired, together with the same rights regarding the laying of pipes and drains, etc., as if the land acquired were already part of the street.[32]

Bridges and road ferries

A highway authority may acquire land to enable it to comply with a **14-10** requirement or direction under section 93 relating to the reconstruction or improvement of a privately-maintainable bridge, and the Minister may authorise the owner of a bridge to acquire land in order to comply with such an order or direction. Where the land which is required is in the ownership of a council or of transport undertakers,[33] only rights over the land to carry out the necessary works may be acquired. A highway authority may acquire land required for the purpose of providing or improving a road ferry.[34]

---

[28] See also s.140(6).
[29] Highways Act 1980, s.240(2)(*b*); see also s.240(6).
[30] Under *ibid.* s.73.
[31] *Ibid.* s.241; the power may be subject to the obtaining of certain consents, ss.241(3) and 73(11).
[32] *Ibid.* s.241.
[33] *i.e.* railway, canal, inland navigation, dock, harbour or pier undertakers: *ibid.* s.329(1).
[34] *Ibid.* s.144.

Acquisition of land for the purpose of mitigating the adverse effects of construction or improvement of a highway

14–11   Section 246 of the Highways Act 1980 enables a highway authority to acquire land to mitigate the adverse effects of the construction or improvement of highways, including construction or improvement pursuant to orders under sections 14 and 18 of the Act.[35] Compensation will be assessed as if the land was actually acquired for the construction or improvement.[36] A highway authority may acquire compulsorily, or by agreement, land which is required for the purpose of mitigating any adverse effect which the existence or use of a highway constructed or improved by it, or proposed to be constructed or improved by it, has or will have on the surroundings of the highway.[37] A highway authority may acquire by agreement, but not compulsorily, land, the enjoyment of which is seriously affected by the carrying out of works by the authority for the construction or improvement of the highway, or by the use of a highway which the authority has constructed or improved.[38] This power may only be exercised if the interest of the vendor is one which falls within section 192(3) to (5) of the Town and Country Planning Act 1971.[39] Time restrictions are imposed for the acquisition of land under these provisions.[40]

Acquisition of rights over land

14–12   By the Highways Act 1980, section 250, a compulsory purchase order made in the exercise of highway land acquisition powers[41] may provide for the acquisition of rights over land, both by acquisition of those already in existence, and by creating new rights. The statutory provisions governing the form and procedure relating to compulsory acquisition of land apply equally to the acquisition of rights under this section.[42] The acquisition of rights over land will include the right to do, or to place and maintain, anything in, on or under land, or in the airspace above its surface.[43] Rights acquired under these provisions[44] will be binding upon the successors in title of the original grantee, and the benefit of the rights may be transferred from one highway authority to another. The landowner may, however, compel the highway authority to acquire the whole interest in the land, rather than simply the rights in it, under a procedure set out in the Highways Act 1980, section 252.

---

[35] Highways Act 1980, s.247(7).
[36] *Ibid.* s.246(6).
[37] *Ibid.* s.246(1).
[38] *Ibid.* s.246(2).
[39] *i.e.* an interest entitling the vendor to serve a blight notice.
[40] *Ibid.* s.246(3), (4).
[41] *i.e. ibid.* ss.239, 240, 242–246 and 250(2); see s.250(1).
[42] *e.g.* Highways Act 1980, s.247(1)–(2); Acquisition of Land Act 1981, Sched. 3; Compulsory Purchase Act 1965 (subject to the modifications contained in Part II of Sched. 19 of Highways Act 1980); see Highways Act 1980, s.250(3)–(6).
[43] *Ibid.* s.150(8).
[44] See also *ibid.* s.251(2).

In order to mitigate the adverse effects on the surroundings of a high- **14–13**
way of construction, improvement or the existence or use of a highway,
highway authorities may enter into agreements with persons interested
in land adjoining or in the vicinity of the highway, restricting or regulating the use of that land, either permanently, or for a specified period.[45]
In particular, such agreements may make provision for the planting and
maintenance of trees, shrubs or plants on the land and for restricting the
lopping or removal of trees, shrubs or other plants from the land.
Agreements are binding on the successors in title of the landowner and
take effect as local land charges.

Acquisition of rights in land belonging to local authorities
Subject to the qualifications and procedural provisions set out in the **14–14**
Highways Act 1980, section 254, a highway authority may, in some circumstances, acquire rights over the land of other local authorities[46] or
over the operational land of statutory undertakers.[47] Such rights may be
acquired only for certain specified purposes, relating to the construction, maintenance, improvement or alteration of bridges and bridge
approaches, and for the purposes of a system of road drainage. The
authorising order may be subject to such conditions as the Minister,
after consultation with the authority or the statutory undertakers concerned, considers necessary for the purpose of securing that unreasonable interference with their functions is avoided.[48] Conditions may also
be imposed to ensure that no highway is drained into any watercourse
under the control of an internal drainage board or water authority without the consent of that board or authority, or drained into any reservoir,
river, canal, dock, harbour, basin, culvert, syphon or other work which
belongs to, or is under the jurisdiction of, a local authority or statutory
undertaker, without their consent. There are further restrictions on the
making of an order in relation to the acquisition of rights for the creation of a bridge over the Manchester Ship Canal.[49]

Provisions may be included in an order under section 254(1)(*a*) and **14–15**
(*b*), requiring that a bridge, the approaches to a bridge, or drainage
works, shall be constructed and maintained by the highway authority.[50]
Where a bridge is to be constructed to replace a level crossing, the
expenses are to be defrayed either by the highway authority alone or by
that authority and the railway owners, in proportions which take
account both of the benefit and of any additional expense accruing to
the railway owners. These proportions are to be agreed, failing which

[45] Highways Act 1980, s.253(1).
[46] See Acquisition of Land Act 1981, s.7.
[47] Including, for this purpose, the Civil Aviation Authority and the Post Office.
[48] Highways Act 1980, s.254(3).
[49] *Ibid.* s.254(5).
[50] *Ibid.* s.255(1), (7).

they are subject to determination after arbitration.[51] Once an order is made, the expense of widening or altering any railway, canal, inland navigation, dock, harbour, works or apparatus is to be defrayed by the highway authority.[52]

Exchange of land

14–16   Land may be acquired for the purposes of exchange where land which forms part of a common, open space or fuel or field garden allotment is being acquired for highway purposes. A highway authority may also, by agreement, exchange land within the highway boundary with land adjoining the highway, in order to straighten out or otherwise adjust the boundaries of the highway. This power operates to transfer to the owner of the exchanged land, the fee simple in the highway land free from the public right of way. Significantly, the power operates whether or not the highway authority owns the subsoil and, therefore, the interest of the subsoil owner may be divested and transferred to another party. A procedure for publication of proposals for such an exchange is prescribed which enables objections to be lodged and determined by a magistrates' court. The court must consider any representations made to it on behalf of any party to the appeal, and must consider the desirability in the public interest of the proposed agreement. The court can either dismiss the appeal or order the highway authority not to enter into the proposed agreement.[53] Compensation[54] is payable for any damage suffered by any person by reason of being deprived of his interest. It is unlikely, however, that this compensation will be substantial where the only loss is the value of the subsoil over which there is a public right of way.[55] Protection is given to the rights of statutory undertakers.[56]

Powers of land acquisition in other statutes

14–17   Specific powers of acquisition are given in other statutes, dealing with particular highway issues, for example, powers to enable the diversion of highways.[57]

Concurrent proceedings

14–18   Where orders made by a local authority or a highway authority, in connection with highways, also require the acquisition of land or the making of other orders relating to that land, there is usually provision

---

[51] Highways Act 1980, s.255(2), (3); as to method of payment of expenses by the undertaker, see *ibid.* subs. (4).
[52] *Ibid.* s.255(5); to be determined by arbitration in default of agreement, *ibid.* subs.(6).
[53] *Ibid.* s.256(2)–(3).
[54] See paras. 14–35 *et seq.*, below.
[55] Mineral rights are unaffected by the exchange: Highways Act 1980, s.256(7).
[56] *Ibid.* s.256(6); Sched. 7, Part II.
[57] See Town and Country Planning Act 1971, s.218; Civil Aviation Act 1982, s.49; Road Traffic Regulation Act 1984, s.40 (provision of parking spaces).

for the taking of the two sets of proceedings concurrently,[58] including, where appropriate, the holding of concurrent inquiries.[59]

INQUIRIES

The Minister and the Secretary of State for the Environment have a **14-19** general power to hold inquiries, where these are considered necessary or desirable in order to carry out their functions under the 1980 Act.[60] Specific powers and duties to hold inquiries are given under a number of other provisions in the 1980 Act (for example, concerning special road schemes, trunk road and classified road orders, the making of public path creation orders and public path extinguishment or diversion orders[61]) and in other related legislation (for example, the Town and Country Planning Act 1971 and the Wildlife and Countryside Act 1981[62]). Costs may be awarded at these inquiries, and witnesses may be compelled to give evidence.[63]

Joint inquiries may be held into certain road orders and schemes and **14-20** the compulsory purchase orders which give effect to them.[64] In other cases, any objections received, in relation to a compulsory purchase order, which are, in substance, objections to a confirmed scheme or order, may be disregarded by the Secretary of State.[65]

Road orders and schemes

Inquiries into road orders or schemes made under the Highways Act **14-21** 1980,[66] are governed by the Highway Inquiries Procedure Rules 1976.[67] The rules differ slightly, depending upon whether the order or scheme is made by the Secretary of State or by a local highway authority.

Rules 4 and 9 prescribe similar requirements regarding the giving of **14-22** notice of the inquiry. A pre-inquiry statement, containing the reasons

---

[58] See Town and Country Planning Act 1971, s.219; the Stopping Up of Highways (Concurrent Proceedings) Regulations 1948 (S.R. & O. 1948 No. 1348); Highways Act 1980, Sched. 1, para. 20; *ibid.* Sched. 6, para. 3(2).

[59] See the Public Path Orders and Extinguishment of Public Right of Way Orders Regulations 1983 (S.I. 1983 No. 23).

[60] Highways Act 1980, s.302.

[61] See *ibid.* ss.10, 14, 16, 18, 28, 118, 119 and Sched. 1. See also ss.82, 86, 93 and Scheds. 10 and 11.

[62] See Town and Country Planning Act, ss.209, 210; Wildlife and Countryside Act 1981, Sched. 15, para. 8.

[63] Local Government Act 1972, s.250; except for inquiries relating to the reconstruction of privately-maintainable bridges. See Highways Act 1980 s.302(2).

[64] See *ibid.* s.258(1) and Sched. 20 for the orders to which this provision applies.

[65] See generally the Compulsory Purchase of Land Regulations 1982 (S.I. 1982 No. 6), the Compulsory Purchase by Ministers (Inquiries Procedure) Rules 1967 (S.I. 1967 No. 720) and the Compulsory Purchase by Local Authorities (Inquiries Procedure) Rules 1976 (S.I. 1976 No. 746).

[66] Highways Act 1980, ss.10, 14, 16, 18, 106 and 108.

[67] S.I. 1976 No. 721.

for making the order or scheme, must be served on each statutory objector[68] not less than 28 days before the date of the inquiry. This statement should contain sufficient information to enable objectors to challenge the accuracy of any facts and the validity of any arguments relied upon by the promoting authority,[69] together with a list of documents intended to be referred to at the inquiry, and any expression of view in support of the order or scheme from any government department and upon which reliance will be placed at the inquiry.[70] Facilities for inspection of the documents must be made available to objectors. The promoting authority must make witnesses available at the inquiry to give evidence in elucidation of the pre-inquiry statement and these witnesses are subject to cross-examination. No representative of a government department may, however, be questioned on the merits of government policy.[71] Statutory objectors have the right to appear and to be heard at the inquiry. Other persons may be heard at the discretion of the Inspector. Where the inquiry concerns orders made under the Highways Act 1980, sections 10, 14, 16, 18, 106 or 108, objectors proposing an alternative route may be required to submit sufficient information about that route to enable it to be identified.[72] Failure to do so may result in the objection being disregarded.

14–23   Procedure at the inquiry is at the discretion of the Inspector, subject to his overriding duties to act fairly and honestly,[73] and not to frustrate the purpose of the inquiry.[74] However, the promoting authority has the right to begin and the right of final reply. The promoting authority and the statutory objectors have the right to call evidence and to cross-examine, but other parties may do so only at the discretion of the Inspector. A refusal to allow cross-examination in these cases is not, *per se*, unfair. The nature of the evidence, the qualifications and competence of witnesses to deal with it, the forensic competence of the proposed cross-examiner, and the Inspector's own views on the assistance likely to be gained by him through that cross-examination, measured against the possible unnecessary prolongation of the inquiry, are all relevant factors to be considered in deciding whether to permit cross-examination. Fairness normally requires that other objectors and supporters of the order or scheme should be given some opportunity to express their views.[75] The Inspector may also take into account written representations received by him before the inquiry, where he considers

---

[68] See *ibid.* r. 3 for definition of "statutory objector."
[69] See *Bushell* v. *Secretary of State for the Environment* [1981] A.C. 75 at 96.
[70] In which case a representative from that department must be made available at the inquiry; rr. 5(2), 7 and 11.
[71] rr. 6 and 11(2). See also paras. 14–28, *et seq.*, below.
[72] See also Highways Act 1980, s.258.
[73] *Bushell* v. *Secretary of State for the Environment* [1981] A.C. 75 at 95.
[74] *R.* v. *Secretary of State for Transport, ex p. Gwent C.C.* [1987] 2 W.L.R. 961.
[75] *Bushell* v. *Secretary of State for the Environment*, n. 73 above.

them to be relevant and proper, and provided that he discloses them.[76] Site inspections may be carried out.[77]

The inquiry procedure is not to be regarded as subject to the same **14–24** formal rules which apply in litigation between parties in court.[78] Hearsay evidence will be admitted, provided that the other parties are given a fair opportunity to comment on it and to contradict it.[79] Procedural unfairness at the inquiry stage may be capable of remedy by the Secretary of State when he makes his decision.[80]

After the inquiry has closed, the Inspector makes a report to the Sec- **14–25** retary of State containing his findings of fact, conclusions and recommendations about whether the order or scheme should be made or confirmed as proposed, with modifications, or not at all. Failure to make a material recommendation will not invalidate the decision-making process if sufficient facts have been found to enable the Secretary of State to come to his own decision.[81] Where the Secretary of State differs from his Inspector on any finding of fact, or where he takes into consideration any new evidence (including expert opinion on a matter of fact) or any new fact (not being a matter of government policy) which was not raised at the inquiry, and is disposed to disagree with his Inspector's recommendations, he must first notify all statutory objectors who appeared at the inquiry of his disagreement, and of his reasons for it, and must afford them an opportunity of making representations in writing. Where new evidence is taken into account, the objectors must be given the opportunity of asking for the reopening of the inquiry.[82]

These rules, whilst limiting the consideration by the Secretary of State **14–26** of new evidence or new facts, do not prevent him from accepting his Inspector's findings of fact but disagreeing with his recommendations. In such a case, there is no duty to invite further representations or to reopen the inquiry. The Secretary of State is also permitted to have regard to expressions of government policy[83] received after the inquiry. The inquiry is not intended to be an opportunity to challenge that policy.

Significant distinctions have been drawn between inquiries held by the **14–27** Secretary of State into his own schemes and those held into schemes of another promoting authority. Whilst the Secretary of State is required to act as an impartial adjudicator between a promoting local authority and objectors, he cannot be expected to remain impartial as to the

---

[76] Highway Inquiries Procedure Rules 1976, r. 13.
[77] *Ibid.* r. 14.
[78] *Lovelock* v. *Secretary of State for Transport* [1979] J.P.L. 456. See also *Johnson* v. *Minister of Health* [1947] 2 All E.R. 395 at 399–400; *Ridge* v. *Baldwin* [1964] A.C. 40 at 72.
[79] *Bushell* v. *Secretary of State for the Environment*, n. 73 above.
[80] *R.* v. *Secretary of State for Transport, ex p. Gwent C.C.* [1987] 2 W.L.R. 961.
[81] See *R.* v. *Secretary of State for Transport, ex p. Gwent C.C.* [1987] 2 W.L.R. 961.
[82] Highway Inquiries Procedure Rules 1976, r. 16.
[83] See paras. 14–28 *et seq.*, below.

merits of his own schemes.[84] In *Bushell* v. *Secretary of State for the Environment*,[85] Lord Diplock described the functions of this type of inquiry in the following way:

> "The purpose of the inquiry is to provide the minister with as much information about those objections as will ensure that in reaching his decision he will have weighed the harm to local interests and private persons who may be adversely affected by the scheme against the public benefit which the scheme is likely to achieve and will not have failed to take into consideration any matters which he ought to have taken into consideration."

14–28   Confusion has often arisen over the distinction between government policy and other evidence. This distinction arises at several stages. Objectors may not cross-examine on the merits of government policy.[86] The Secretary of State may take into consideration any new issue of fact which is a matter of government policy after the close of the inquiry, without giving objectors any opportunity to make representations on that issue.

14–29   The decision to construct and improve a national road network is clearly a matter of government policy for which the Minister is answerable only to Parliament. The precise route of a particular road may be said to be part of government policy once the final route has been adopted. However, one of the functions of the inquiry is to assist the Secretary of State in determining which route to adopt. Other factors are more difficult to categorise.[87] The traffic need for a road and the cost benefit analysis justifying construction of the road are two factors which commonly dominate road inquiries. In a sense, they are policy issues. The government's declared policy objectives for building roads have included[88]:

> "(i) to assist economic growth by reducing transport costs;
> (ii) to improve the environment by removing through traffic (especially lorries) from unsuitable roads in towns and villages; and
> (iii) to enhance road safety."

The desirability of applying these objectives cannot be the subject of cross-examination at the inquiry. However, evidence which goes to whether or not these objectives are being achieved by the road scheme

---

[84] See *Re Trunk Roads Act 1936* [1939] 2 K.B. 515; *Franklin* v. *Minister of Town and Country Planning* [1947] 1 All E.R. 612.

[85] [1981] A.C. 75 at 95.

[86] rr. 6, 7, 11.

[87] See, in another context, *Luke (Lord) of Pavenham* v. *Minister of Housing and Local Government* [1968] 1 Q.B. 172.

[88] *Policy for Roads in England*, Cmnd. 125 (1987, H.M.S.O.).

in issue, would appear at first sight to be a proper subject for debate at the inquiry and for cross-examination.[89]

In *Bushell* v. *Secretary of State for the Environment*,[90] the House of Lords adopted a pragmatic approach in deciding between policy and other issues of fact. One of the issues considered by the House of Lords was the status of the "Red Book"—the *Advisory Manual on Traffic Prediction for Rural Roads*—which described the government's then approved methodology for predicting traffic growth. The House of Lords decided that, regardless of whether the methods of traffic forecasting were strictly a matter of government policy, they were an essential element in applying the policy for the construction of future motorways, and were to be regarded as policy, in the sense that the merits or otherwise of such methods were not appropriate for investigation by individual inspectors on whatever material happened to be put before them at local inquiries held throughout the country. The Inspector had, however, allowed objectors to present evidence criticising the methodology, but had refused to permit the cross-examination of the Department's witnesses on this issue.[91] Lord Diplock confirmed the Inspector's decision that the use of the assessment of traffic needs by a particular method as the yardstick for judging the priorities of road construction was a matter of government policy "in the relevant sense of being a topic unsuitable for investigation" at local inquiries.[92] Lord Lane may have taken a wider view, in saying[93] that "the question of need is a matter of policy or so akin to a matter of policy that it was not for the Inspector to make any recommendation." This latter view would seem too wide,[94] although, where the need for the road has been considered and determined at earlier inquiries, the courts will not require the issue to be reopened.[95] *Bushell* leaves the boundary between policy and other issues obscure, to be tested against whether or not the issue is a proper subject for debate at individual inquiries. The application of government policy to the need for a particular road should, on this basis, always be regarded as a proper issue for the inquiry.

14–30

This approach does not, however, deal with the related problem of the extent to which the Secretary of State is entitled to consider revised road traffic forecasts available after the close of an inquiry. These forecasts are used at inquiries to justify the new road in capacity, safety and economic terms. Any radical alteration in the methodology, subsequent to an inquiry, could potentially make a nonsense of the bulk of evidence produced by the Department to justify the scheme. The difficulty

14–31

[89] See also *R.* v. *Secretary of State for Transport, ex p. Gwent C.C.* [1987] 2 W.L.R. 961.
[90] [1981] A.C. 75.
[91] The 1976 Rules were not, at that time, in operation.
[92] At 616.
[93] At 633.
[94] See *R.* v. *Secretary of State for Transport, ex p. Gwent C.C.* [1987] 2 W.L.R. 961 at 968.
[95] *Lovelock* v. *Minister of Transport* [1979] J.P.L. 456; *Mayes* v. *Minister of Transport* [1982] L.S.Gaz. Rep. 448.

is that the inquiry is only one stage of the administrative process involved in deciding whether to build a road, and the Minister must be entitled to have (and in reality will have) contact with, and the advice of, his officials, together with the research and methodology available to those officials. The collective expertise of the department is to be regarded as the Minister's own. In *Bushell*, the House of Lords decided that the Secretary of State was not required to reopen the inquiry after considering new traffic forecasts. In fact he had indicated that fresh representations could be made to him "as part of the continuous consideration of any of the Department's proposals." Lord Diplock stressed that road schemes cannot be held up indefinitely, simply because the current methods of estimating and predicting future traffic needs are imperfect and likely to be improved as further experience is gained.

14–32   The extent to which the Secretary of State is required to invite representations or to reopen an inquiry or even to disclose to objectors new evidence available to him, where he is agreeing with his Inspector's recommendation, depends upon the common law rules of fairness and reasonableness. Where the Secretary of State is considering a proposal put forward by another promoting authority, he remains under a duty to act impartially as between the parties, although he is entitled to consider new issues of policy.[96] Where he is considering his own proposal, it appears that he will only come under a duty to disclose new factual information where that information alters the whole basis of his proposal or demonstrates that some material consideration has not been taken into account at the inquiry stage.[97]

14–33   The final decision, following an inquiry, is that of the Secretary of State. Whilst he is not bound to follow his Inspector's recommendations, he is, at least, bound to consider them and to give reasons for his disagreement.[98] Where it can be shown that he has not considered material parts of his Inspector's report, it may be possible to challenge the decision by way of appeal.[99]

Other inquiries

14–34   Inquiries held into footpath creation, diversion or extinguishment orders are not subject to the Highways Inquiries Procedure Rules 1976. The general procedures leading to these inquiries have been described in Chapters 2 and 9. The common law rules described in the previous paragraphs will, however, also apply to these inquiries. Compulsory

[96] *Errington* v. *Minister of Health* [1935] 1 K.B. 249; *Darlassis* v. *Minister of Education* (1954) 4 P. & C.R. 281.
[97] See *Rea* v. *Minister of Transport* [1984] J.P.L. 876; *cf. Prest* v. *Secretary of State for Wales* [1983] J.P.L. 112.
[98] Highways Inquiries Procedure Rules 1976, r. 15(2).
[99] See, generally, *Associated Provincial Picture Houses* v. *Wednesbury Corpn.* [1948] 1 K.B. 223; *Coleen Properties* v. *Minister of Housing and Local Government* [1971] 1 W.L.R. 433; *Ashbridge Investment Ltd.* v. *Minister of Housing and Local Government* [1965] 1 W.L.R. 1320.

purchase inquiries will be governed by the rules applicable to these types of inquiry.[1] The Tribunals and Inquiries Act 1971, section 12, which requires the giving of reasons for decisions, applies to other inquiries held under the Highways Act 1980,[2] and special provision is made by regulations for inquiries concerned with the provision of road humps.[3]

Compensation for the acquisition of land

Compensation generally is governed by Part II of the Land Compensation Act 1961, and the Land Compensation Act 1973.[4] For a consideration of the principles of compensation for land taken, injurious affection, severance and disturbance, reference should be made to the specialist books on compulsory purchase compensation. Section 261 of the Highways Act 1980 provides, however, that in assessing compensation in relation to land acquired for highway purposes under sections 239,[5] 240, 246 and 250(2), the Lands Tribunal is to have regard to a number of specified factors. The first of these is the extent to which the remaining contiguous lands belonging to the same person may benefit from the purpose for which the land is authorised to be acquired. Secondly, where land is to be acquired for widening, the increased value of other land in the same ownership, caused by the creation of a frontage to the highway as widened, must be set off against the value of the land acquired. Thirdly, the Lands Tribunal is to take account of, and to embody into its award, any undertaking given by the highway authority as to the use to which the land or any part of it will be put. **14–35**

Where acquisition occurs by virtue of section 252(3)(a),[6] account must be taken of (and this must be embodied within the award) any undertaking given by the acquiring authority regarding retention of rights of user, or occupation of or the exercise of other rights over the land.[7] Where rights are acquired over land under sections 239,[8] 240 or 246, the extent to which the land over which the right in question is, or is to be, acquired, or the extent to which any contiguous land belonging to the same person may be benefited by the purpose for which the right may be authorised to be acquired must be taken into account. Where **14–36**

[1] See the Compulsory Purchase by Ministers (Inquiries Procedure) Rules 1967 (S.I. 1967 No. 720) and the Compulsory Purchase by Local Authorities (Inquiries Procedure) Rules 1976 (S.I. 1976 No. 746).
[2] ss.90C and 302; see also the Tribunals and Inquiries (Discretionary Inquiries) Order 1975 (S.I. 1975 No. 1379).
[3] See the Road Humps (Secretary of State) Inquiries Procedure Rules 1986 (S.I. 1986 No. 1859).
[4] See hereon, Circular No. Roads 45/71.
[5] Except subs. (6).
[6] *i.e.* where the landowner over whose land the authority are acquiring rights compels the acquisition of the land itself.
[7] Highways Act 1980, s.261(2).
[8] Except subs. (6).

the right is acquired in connection with the widening of a road, account must be taken of the extent to which any increase in the value of the land, or any other land belonging to the same person, will accrue by reason of the creation of a frontage to the highway as widened. Any undertaking given by the highway authority, as to the manner in which the right will be exercised, must also be taken into account. Where the compulsory purchase order empowers the acquisition of two or more rights of a landowner, or adjoining land in the same ownership, the Lands Tribunal is to consider together the claims of the landowner to compensation.[9] Where compensation is to be assessed in relation to the acquisition of land between the improvement line and the boundary of a street, the benefit accruing to the claimant from the improvement of the street, except insofar as this may already have been taken into account in assessing compensation payable on the prescribing of the improvement line, must be considered.[10]

14–37   Where land is compulsorily acquired for the purposes of a service station or a lorry park to be used in connection with a special road, further assumptions may apply.[11] So far as the value of the relevant interest is attributable to any relevant planning permission, the assumption is that traffic carried by the special road will not have direct[12] or indirect access[13] to the relevant land. In so far as the value is not attributable to any such planning permission, the assumption is that traffic carried by the special road will not have direct access to the relevant land.

Compensation for depreciation caused by the use of new or improved highways

14–38   The Land Compensation Act 1973 provides compensation for the depreciation of the value of interests in land from physical factors caused by the use, as distinct from the construction,[14] of public works including highways. The physical factors which will give rise to compensation are noise, vibration, smell, fumes, smoke, artificial lighting and the discharge onto land of any solid or liquid substance.[15] Physical factors caused by accidents on highways involving vehicles are specifically excluded from the compensation provisions.[16] Claims for compensation can only be made in respect of highways which were first opened to public traffic on or after October 17, 1969.[17] Depreciation caused,

---

[9] Highways Act 1980, s.261(4).
[10] Under *ibid.* s.73(9). See also Land Compensation Act 1961, s.5.
[11] See Highways Act, s.262(1), (2).
[12] *i.e.* access otherwise than by means of a highway which is not a special road; *ibid.* s.262(4).
[13] *i.e.* access by means of a highway which is not a special road; *ibid.* s.262(4).
[14] As to compensation payable in respect of the construction of highways, see para. 14–44, below.
[15] Land Compensation Act 1973, s.1(2).
[16] *Ibid.* s.1(7).
[17] *Ibid.* s.1(8), (9).

indirectly, by an increase in traffic on side roads which are not the subject of works will not give a right to compensation.[18]

Interests qualifying for compensation are, in respect of dwellings, **14-39** those of fee simple owners, and tenants for a term of years certain of which at least three years remain unexpired.[19] Where the interest carries with it the right to occupy the dwelling, then the claimant must occupy the dwelling as his residence. In the case of other land, the qualifying interests are those of owner occupiers[20] of land forming part of an agricultural unit or of a hereditament, the annual value of which does not exceed the amount prescribed for the purposes of section 192(4)(*a*) of the Town and Country Planning Act 1971.[21] All interests must have been acquired[22] before the date on which the highway was first opened to traffic (the "relevant date") in order to qualify for compensation. The information which must be included in a claim is set out in the Land Compensation Act 1973, section 3. Claims must be made no earlier than one year after the highway was first opened to traffic and within two years of that date.[23] A landowner who wishes to dispose of his land between the date on which the road is first opened, but before the commencement of the claim period, may claim within that period, where he has entered into a contract for the sale of the land but has not actually disposed of his interest.[24]

The assessment of compensation involves reference not to prices current on the first day of the claim period, but to the nature of the interest **14-40** and the condition of the land as at the date of the claim.[25] Account is taken of the use of the highway as it exists on the first day of the claim period and of any intensification which may then be expected in the use of the works. Account must be taken of the benefit of any works of mitigation actually carried out by the highway authority, or which it has undertaken to carry out.[26] Any increase in the value of the claimant's interest in the land, or in land adjacent to that which is the subject of the claim,[27] which is attributable to the use or prospective use of the highway, must be offset against the compensation claimed.[28] The normal rules for assessment of compensation, contained in section 5 of the Land Compensation Act 1961, apply. The assumptions which are to be made

---

[18] Land Compensation Act 1973, s.1(5).

[19] As to mortgagees, tenants for life, interests acquired by inheritance, and tenants entitled to enfranchisement or extension under the Leasehold Reform Act 1967, see Land Compensation Act 1973, ss.10, 11, 12.

[20] See *ibid.* s.2(5).

[21] Interests qualifying for compensation under the planning blight provisions.

[22] See *ibid.* s.19(2).

[23] See, however, ss.12 and 14 which contain limited exceptions to this limitation.

[24] *Ibid.* s.3(3).

[25] *Ibid.* s.4(1), (4).

[26] *i.e.* under *ibid.* ss.23 and 27.

[27] See, however, *ibid.* subs. (5).

[28] *Ibid.* s.6.

as to the grant of planning permission are restricted by section 5 of the 1973 Act. Mortgages or contracts for sale made after the relevant date are ignored. New or improved buildings occupied after and changes of use of land made after the relevant date are also ignored.[29] Provision is made to prevent compensation from becoming payable more than once.[30]

14–41   The above provisions also apply[31] to situations where the carriageway of a highway has been altered after the highway has been opened to public traffic, and physical factors attributable to the use of the altered highway cause a depreciation of the value of an interest in land. Qualifying alterations are those where the location, width or level of the carriageway has been altered, other than by resurfacing, or where an additional carriageway is provided for the highway beside, above or below an existing one. The relevant date for the assessment of compensation then becomes the date on which the highway was first open to public traffic after completion of the works to the carriageway.

14–42   Highway authorities are required to keep records and to provide statements on demand as to the date on which the highway was first opened to traffic or was first opened after the completion of alterations to the carriageway. Disputes over compensation go to the Lands Tribunal. No compensation may be paid, nor may any reference be made to the Lands Tribunal, until the beginning of the claim period.[32] Interest is payable on compensation, from the date of service of notice of the claim or from the beginning of the claim period, whichever is the later, until payment.[33]

14–43   The expenses of people who are forced to move out of their homes temporarily, be reason of the construction or improvement of a highway, may be met by the highway authority.[34] Compensation may also be payable in respect of land which is blighted by the proposed construction or improvement of a highway, or by the acquisition of land or rights over land, by a highway authority.[35]

Mitigation of the injurious effect of public works

14–44   By section 20 of the Land Compensation Act 1973, the Secretary of State is empowered to make regulations imposing a duty or conferring a power upon responsible authorities to insulate buildings against noise caused, or expected to be caused, by the construction or use of public works, or to make grants in respect of such insulation. The Noise Insula-

---

[29] Land Compensation Act 1973, s.4(4), (5).
[30] *Ibid.* s.8.
[31] *Ibid.* s.9.
[32] *Ibid.* ss.3(3), 16(2).
[33] *Ibid.* s.18.
[34] *Ibid.* s.28.
[35] Town and Country Planning Act 1971, s.192; Land Compensation Act 1973, ss.69–76.

tion Regulations 1975[36] have been made under this provision. These regulations impose a duty upon highway authorities to carry out noise insulation works or to make a grant in respect of such works, where the use of certain highways[37] causes, or is expected to cause, noise at a certain level. There are three requirements which must be satisfied before the duty to pay compensation arises. The increase in noise level from the expected traffic on the new or altered highway must be at least one decibel on the A weighted scale (1dB(A))[38] higher than the existing noise level experienced at the claimant's property. Secondly, the expected noise level must be not less than an L 10 (18 hour) level of 68dB(A). Thirdly, the noise caused or expected to be caused by traffic using the new or altered highway must make an effective contribution to the relevant noise level of at least 1dB(A).[39]

A *power* to carry out noise insulation work or to make grants is given **14–45** where a similar increase in the noise level is expected to result from highways or additional carriageways to highways first opened to traffic between October 16, 1969 and October 16, 1972, where highways are altered,[40] and in cases covered by regulation 3, before the duty therein contained has actually arisen.[41] A similar power arises where a highway becomes maintainable at the public expense within three years after it is first opened, or an additional carriageway or relevant alteration has been carried out.[42] Where the highway authority is under a duty or has a power to carry out or make a grant towards insulation works in or to an eligible building, it may also carry out or make a grant towards the cost of carrying out insulation works to other eligible buildings if the facades of those buildings are contiguous or form part of a series of continuous facades.[43]

There is also power to provide insulation works or to make a grant **14–46** towards those works, where construction noise will seriously affect the enjoyment of an eligible building adjacent to a site where works are being, or are to be, carried out. There is no objectively assessed noise level which must be attained before this power is available. The construction noise must, however, be such that, in the opinion of the highway authority, the enjoyment of the eligible building will be seriously affected for a substantial period by construction works adjacent to it. Once a highway authority has made an offer to exercise this power, it

---

[36] S.I. 1975 No. 1763.
[37] *i.e.* highways or additional carriageways to highways which are first open to traffic after October 16, 1972.
[38] See Noise Insulation Regulations 1975, reg. 2 for the meaning of this.
[39] *Ibid.* regs. 2 and 3.
[40] *i.e.* highways of which the location, width or level of the carriageway has been altered otherwise than by resurfacing after October 16, 1969.
[41] Noise Insulation Regulations 1975 (S.I. 1975 No. 1763) reg. 4(1), (2).
[42] *Ibid.* reg. 4(3).
[43] *Ibid.* reg. 4(4).

must be accepted within two months of the offer being made, or within such longer period as the highway authority may allow.[44]

14–47   Calculation of the relevant noise levels and of the effective contribution of traffic using or expected to use a highway is achieved by reference to a technical memorandum.[45]

14–48   Eligible buildings are dwellings and other buildings, used for residential purposes, which will be not more than 300 metres from the nearest point on the carriageway of the highway after the works have been carried out. There are a number of types of dwellings which are excluded from the definition.[46] Highway authorities are under a duty[47] to deposit a map showing those buildings in respect of which a duty to insulate or to make a grant has arisen, or will arise. The authority must then make an offer to carry out insulation work or to make a grant in respect thereof, with regard to every building identified on the list, to the occupier or to the landlord or licensor of that person (if any). There are time limits for the acceptance of the offer, and if more than one person would be entitled to receive an offer, then after three months, if the original offer has not been accepted, it may be accepted by that other person.[48] Insulation work completed before the offer has been made may be the subject of a grant. The regulations specify the insulation works which may be the subject of grant or which may be carried out, and the rooms to which the duty to insulate arises.

Compensation in respect of other acts and decisions of a highway authority under the Highway Act 1980

14–49   Some disputes over compensation, arising under the Highways Act 1980, are determined by reference to the Lands Tribunal.[49] Other disputes, if the parties so agree, go to arbitration, and in default of such agreement, are determined by the county court.[50] The normal jurisdictional limits of the county court do not apply in determining these disputes. Where the dispute is dealt with by the Lands Tribunal, the calculation of any depreciation in the value of land follows rules 2 to 4 in section 5 of the Land Compensation Act 1961.[51] The Lands Tribunal is, in certain circumstances, required to have regard to benefits accruing to the claimant by reason of the exercise of the powers which give rise to the claim for compensation,[52] to new rights of access provided[53] and to

---

[44] S.I. 1975 No. 1763, reg. 5.
[45] Calculation of Road Traffic Noise 1988, H.M.S.O.; see also S.I. 1975 No. 1763, reg. 6.
[46] See *ibid.* reg. 7(2).
[47] *Ibid.* reg. 6(2), (3).
[48] *Ibid.* reg. 8(3), (4), (7).
[49] *i.e.* those arising under Highways Act 1980, ss.21, 22, 28, 73, 74, 109, 110, 121(2), 126, 193, 200(2) and 292. See also Appendix 3, below.
[50] *Ibid.* ss.307, 308. For a summary, see Appendix 3, below.
[51] *i.e.* basically, assessment by market value subject to certain other factors.
[52] *e.g.* under ss.73(9), 74(8), (9), 193 and 200.
[53] *Ibid.* ss.109, 110 and 126.

undertakings given[54] by the highway authority.[55] There are special provisions applicable where land is subject to a mortgage.[56]

Unless specifically restricted, where compensation is payable in **14–50** respect of acts which, but for the statutory authorisation under which they are carried out, would constitute a tort, the assessment of compensation broadly follows the tortious measure of damages.[57] Claims for loss of profits which are the reasonably foreseeable result of the authority's actions should, therefore, be recoverable.[58] Where, on the other hand, the compensation provision is limited to the depreciation in value of land, claims for loss of profits will not be recoverable, except insofar as they reflect in that value.[59]

POWER TO EXECUTE WORKS FOR MITIGATING THE ADVERSE EFFECTS OF THE CONSTRUCTION OR IMPROVEMENT OF A HIGHWAY

A highway authority may carry out works for mitigating any adverse **14–51** effects which the construction, improvement, existence or use of a highway has, or will have, on the surroundings of the highway.[60] Such works may be carried out on land acquired by the authority for that purpose,[61] on land otherwise belonging to the authority, on any highway for which it is the highway authority, and on any highway which it has been authorised to improve or construct under section 14 or 18 of the 1980 Act. The works may include the planting of trees, shrubs or plants and the laying out of grassland.[62] They may also include the construction of noise barriers. A further power to develop or redevelop land acquired for the purpose of mitigating the adverse effects of the construction or improvement of a highway, or of any other land belonging to the authority, for the general purpose of improving the surroundings of a highway in any manner which the authority considers desirable, by reason of the construction, improvement, existence or use of the highway, is given by section 282(3).

---

[54] Highways Act 1980, s.73.
[55] See para. 14–36, above.
[56] Highways Act 1980, s.309.
[57] *Ricket* v. *Metropolitan Ry.* (1867) L.R. 2 H.L. 17; *Lingke* v. *Christchurch Corpn.* [1912] 2 K.B. 595; *Herring* v. *Metropolitan Board of Works* (1865) 34 L.J.M.C. 224; *Harrison* v. *Southwark and Vauxhall Water Co.* [1891] 2 Ch. 409; *Leonidis* v. *Thames Water Authority* (1979) 77 L.G.R. 722.
[58] *Leonidis* v. *Thames Water Authority*, above.
[59] *Ricket* v. *Metropolitan Ry.* (1867) L.R. 2 H.L. 17; *Lingke* v. *Christchurch Corpn.* [1912] 3 K.B. 595; *Argyle Motors (Birkenhead) Ltd.* v. *Birkenhead Corpn.* [1975] A.C. 99.
[60] Highways Act 1980, s.282.
[61] Under *ibid.* s.246.
[62] *Ibid.* s.182(2).

CHAPTER 15

MISCELLANEOUS MATTERS

GENERAL PROVISIONS AS TO OWNERSHIP

Vesting of highways and highway drains

15–01   Every highway maintainable at the public expense, together with the materials and scrapings of it, vests in the highway authority by virtue of section 263 of the Highways Act 1980. This repeats provisions which go back to the Public Health Act 1848 and the Highway Act 1835.[1] The general rule does not apply to an existing highway which becomes a trunk road or special road, and for which special provision is made.[2] Where, in the case of joint special road schemes, provision is made in the scheme for one authority to be the special road authority, then the road vests in that authority.[3] The section does not operate where, in cases of transfer of responsibility for the maintenance of roads or bridges, the property in the road or bridge is not transferred to the highway authority.[4]

15–02   Highway drains vest in a highway authority under the general vesting provision in section 263—at least where they were constructed for the purpose of draining the highway. Public sewers are, however, vested in the water authority and neither they, nor private land drains, will lose their status by being used also for draining a highway.[5] The test which will generally be adopted is the purpose for which the drain was originally constructed.[6] Specific provision is made in section 264 of the Highways Act 1980 for the vesting of road drains in the highway authority for the area in which the road is situated. The right to use certain drains used at the material date[7] for the purpose of draining the road also passes to the highway authority. Special provision is made for highway drains constructed in former metropolitan roads after the passing of the Local Government Act 1985.[8] Disputes between district councils and highway authorities as to the vesting or use of drains, and between

---

[1] See para. 3–06, above.
[2] See para. 15–03, below.
[3] Highways Act 1980, s.263(3).
[4] See also *ibid.* ss.42, 50, 230(7).
[5] *Wilkinson* v. *Llandaff & Dinas Powis R.C.* [1903] 2 Ch. 695; *Att.-Gen* v. *St. Ives R.D.C.* [1961] 1 Q.B. 366
[6] See *White* v. *Hindley Local Board* (1875) L.R. 10 Q.B. 219; *Papworth* v. *Battersea Corpn. No. 2* [1916] 1 K.B. 583.
[7] *i.e.* the date on which the road first became maintainable at the public expense or April 1, 1974 (in those cases where the road became so maintainable before the passing of the 1980 Act but after April 1, 1974).
[8] Highways Act 1980, s.265(2), as substituted by Local Government Act 1985, ss.8, 102 and Scheds. 4 and 17.

358

highway authorities as to the use of public sewers, may be referred to and determined by the Secretary of State.[9] Agreements between highway authorities and water authorities may provide for the use of highway drains and sewers for sanitary purposes, and for the use of public sewers for the drainage of highways.[10]

Transfer of property and liabilities in certain situations

Sections 265 to 268 of the Highways Act 1980 are concerned with the transfer of property where a highway changes its status—for example from a local highway to a trunk road (and vice versa) or where a special road is created. Where a highway becomes a trunk road, the highway is transferred to the Minister together with certain property and liabilities.[11] All other property, previously vested in the local highway authority in respect of its highway functions, or in a council in respect of highway functions,[12] including the unexpended balances of any grants paid by the Minister to the former highway authority, but excluding materials to be used for the maintenance or improvement of the highway and the unexpended balance of any loans raised by the former highway authority or any council in respect of its functions in relation to the highway, will also vest in the Minister.[13] Rights and liabilities in respect of work done, services rendered, goods delivered, or money due, before the date on which the highway became a trunk road (the "operative date") are excepted from the transfer. The liability to pay damages and compensation for any act or omission which occurred before the operative date, and the liability for the price of, or compensation for, the purchase of land, where the contract of sale was concluded before the operative date, are also exluded from the transfer.[14] Apart from these liabilities, property which becomes vested in the Minister in accordance with these provisions is to be held by him, subject to all covenants, conditions and restrictions to which it was held by the former authority or council.[15] The Minister and the former highway authority may also agree as to the transfer of property and liabilities between each other.[16] Disputes between the Minister and any other person, as to the property or liabilities transferred by these provisions, are determined by arbitration.[17] Identical provisions apply where a road ceases to be a trunk road.[18] Transitional matters are dealt with in Schedule 21. Similar

15–03

---

[9] Highways Act 1980, s.264(3).
[10] Public Health Act 1936, s.21.
[11] Highways Act 1980, s.265.
[12] *i.e.* under *ibid.* ss. 42, 50, 230(7), 271; Road Traffic Regulation Act 1984, ss.1, 23, 85.
[13] Highways Act 1980, s.265(3).
[14] *Ibid.* s.265(2).
[15] *Ibid.* s.265(4).
[16] *Ibid.* s.265(5).
[17] *Ibid.* s.265(6).
[18] Except where the road becomes a special road: *ibid.* s.265(7).

provisions apply in respect of bridges which carry roads which are the subject of a special roads scheme.[19]

15–04   Where, by virtue of orders made under sections 14 or 18 of the Highways Act 1980,[20] provision is made for the transfer of a highway from one highway authority to another, or for enabling a highway authority to alter a highway vested in another, then the order may also transfer any property, rights or liabilities (other than loans or loan charges) vested in, or incurred by, the other authority in connection with the highway or the alteration. Similarly, where, in the case of an order made under section 18, the functions of a local authority are authorised, or required to be exercised, by a highway authority,[21] the order may transfer to the highway authority any property, rights or liabilities (other than loans or loan charges) vested in, or incurred by, that local authority for the purposes of those functions.[22] Bridges which are covered by the provisions of section 267[23] are excluded from these provisions.

Transfer of lighting systems

15–05   By sections 28 to 31 of the Local Government Act 1966, highway authorities were given, for the first time, the power to provide lighting systems for highways. Existing lighting systems (except for footway lighting systems,[24] which were left with the former lighting authorities) were transferred to highway authorities. On any transfer to the highway authority, all lamps, lamp–posts and other apparatus formerly vested in the lighting authority as part of the road lighting system, and all other property or rights which were vested in that authority for the purposes of the system, together with all liabilities incurred by that authority for the purposes of the system and not discharged before the agreed date, are vested in the highway authority.[25] The parties may agree between themselves what property is to be transferred, and such agreements may, in particular, deal with the situation whereby property, rights or liabilities are held for the purposes of two or more lighting systems or of a lighting system and for other purposes. The date of transfer is to be agreed between the two authorities or, in default of such agreement, may be determined by the Minister.[26] Disputes between the authorities are to be determined by the Minister or, where he is one of the parties, by arbitration.

---

[19] Highways Act 1980, s.267.
[20] Transfer of new highways constructed for the purposes of the alteration of a trunk or classified road and transfers to and from special road authority.
[21] Highways Act 1980, s.18(1)(e).
[22] See also ibid. s.265.
[23] See para. 15–03, above.
[24] For the circumstances in which such systems may become transferable to the highway authority, see para. 6–38, above.
[25] Highways Act 1980, s.270(3); certain rights and liabilities are excluded.
[26] Ibid. s.270(1).

Transfer of toll highways

Toll highways may be transferred to the highway authority[27] by agreement, or may be acquired compulsorily by the highway authority. The agreement or notice to treat may require that the right to toll, together with the property in the highway and other property, rights and obligations under the charter or special Act (being property, rights and obligations connected with the highway), be transferred to the highway authority.[28] On transfer, these rights and obligations vest in and are imposed upon the highway authority. There is no provision for any appeal against, or inquiry into, the compulsory acquisition. However, the consideration to be paid to any person for a compulsory transfer is determined, in default of agreement, by the Lands Tribunal.[29] Where the highway is situated in the area of more than one authority, then those authorities may agree that the power to acquire should be exercised by one authority on behalf of the others; such agreement will also determine into whose ownership the acquired rights will vest.[30] Toll highways vested in dock and harbour undertakers as such, and toll bridges vested in railway undertakers, are excluded from these powers of acquisition.

15–06

FINANCIAL PROVISIONS

Section 272 of the Highways Act 1980 confers a wide power on the Minister to advance funds to highway authorities and to local authorities for highway purposes. Treasury approval is required for all these advances, which may only be paid where it appears to the Minister that, notwithstanding the grants for which provision is made in Part I of the Local Government Act 1974, the whole, or any part, of any expenditure on highways should not fall on the authority in question. One of the factors to which the Minister is required to have regard, where the advance is requested for a purpose which will require the employment of labour on a considerable scale, is the general state of employment and the prospects for employment.[31] Councils may also raise finance for any of the purposes of the Act by borrowing.[32] Sums, paid to or recovered by a highway authority under various provisions[33] in the Act, which represent capital or which are paid as lump sums, are to be applied by the authority for purposes for which capital money is applicable by them.

15–07

---

[27] See Highways Act 1980, s.271(1).
[28] *Ibid.* On compulsory acquisition the actual transfer will be required on payment of the consideration.
[29] The provisions of Land Compensation Act 1961, s.5 will apply to the assessment of compensation: Highways Act 1980, s.271(3).
[30] *Ibid.* s.271(5),(6).
[31] *Ibid.* s.272(7).
[32] *Ibid.* s.279.
[33] ss.53(3),(4), 54(1), (2), 55(2)–(4), 255(4) and Sched 11, para. 19; see also s.280.

15–08   The prescribed purposes for which advances may be made are:

(a) the construction of highways which are to be maintainable at the public expense;

(b) the maintenance and improvement of highways;

(c) the provision, maintenance and improvement of road ferries;

(d) the acquisition of highway land;

(e) the provision of lorry areas, or public sanitary conveniences on, under, adjoining, or within the vacinity of, highways or proposed highways;

(f) the provision of a new means of access to a highway[34];

(g) the stopping up of private means of access[35];

(h) the acquisition of land, or rights over land, or the execution of works for mitigating the adverse effects of constructing or improving a highway; and

(i) the discharge of any duty or power imposed or conferred on the authority under the Land Compensation Act 1973, section 20.[36]

Surveys carried out in order to assess the need for the construction or improvement of highways and other incidental purposes may also be the subject of an advance.[37] Advances may also be payable in respect of the amount by which the annual expenditure, incurred by the authority in maintaining highway land during the period between its acquisition and the construction or improvement of the highway in question, together with the loan charges accruing due in that period in respect of any debt incurred by the authority for the purpose of acquiring the land, exceeds the annual income accruing to the authority from the land during the same period. Loan charges accruing due after the construction or improvement has occurred, in respect of money borrowed for the pur pose of acquiring highway land, may also be the subject of an advance. The advance may be paid to some other person in conjunction with the highway authority. There is a separate power to make advances to a district council in respect of any work done by the council in exercise of its powers to plant trees and shrubs and lay out verges in a highway.[38] Advances may be made either by way of grant, or by loan, or by both, and may be subject to such terms and conditions as the Minister thinks fit.[39]

---

[34] Under Highways Act 1980, s.129.

[35] Pursuant to *ibid.* ss.14, 18, 124, 127, or Town and Country Planning Act 1971, s.211.

[36] *i.e.* in relation to the soundproofing of buildings affected by public works; see the Noise Insulation Regulations 1975 (S.I. 1975 No. 1763).

[37] Highways Act 1980, s.272(2).

[38] *Ibid.* s.272(5).

[39] *Ibid.* s.272(6). For the grant procedures, see Local Government Act 1974, s.6 (as modified) and circulars Nos. 1/74, 2/84 and 3/84.

Sections 273 to 278 are concerned with the apportioning of contribu- **15–09** tions between different local authorities and between highway auth- orities and persons deriving special benefit from highway works. A county or district council, a London borough council or the Common Council may contribute towards any expenses incurred by a highway authority, if of the opinion that the expenditure will be of benefit to the council's area.[40] Local authorities or local planning authorities may con- tribute towards the expenses of other such authorities, incurred in con- nection with the provision, making up, diversion or closure of footpaths and bridleways.[41] The Minister may contribute to the expenses incurred by a water authority or internal drainage board, where drainage works are considered desirable for the protection or enjoyment of trunk roads.[42] Where a trunk road carried by a bridge ceases to be a trunk road, the Minister may make contributions to the local highway auth- ority towards the maintenance expenses of the bridge.[43]

A highway authority proposing to execute works in a highway may **15–10** enter into an agreement under section 278 with any other person who would derive a special benefit if those works incorporated particular modifications, additions, or features, or were to be executed at a par- ticular time or in a particular manner. The other party must agree to make a contribution towards the expense incurred by the authority in executing the works, and may provide for the making of payments to the highway authority in respect of the future maintenance of the works to which the agreement relates. Agreements may include such incidental and consequential provisions as appear to the highway authority to be necessary or expedient for the purposes of the agreement. Such agree- ments may only be entered into where the authority is satisfied that they will be of benefit to the public. The powers of the authority to acquire land compulsorily do not extend to the acquisition of land where that acquisition would not, save for the agreement, have been necessary.[44]

GENERAL POWERS

Powers of entry and powers to carry out works

A person duly authorised in writing by a highway authority may at any **15–11** reasonable time enter onto any land for the purpose of surveying that or any other land in connection with the exercise of highway functions.[45] Any person so entering must, if required to do so, produce evidence of his authority before or after entering onto that land. He may take with him such equipment and other persons as he considers necessary.

---

[40] Highways Act 1980, s.274.
[41] *Ibid.* s.275.
[42] *Ibid.* s.276.
[43] *Ibid.* s.277; see also *ibid.* s.55.
[44] *Ibid.* s.278(5).
[45] *Ibid.* s.289.

Apparatus may be placed and left on land for use in connection with any survey of that or other land (whether from the air or on the ground) and may later be removed.[46] There is power to search and bore, for the purpose of ascertaining the nature of the subsoil or the presence of minerals in it, or to ascertain whether any damage to a highway maintainable at the public expense is being caused, or is likely to be caused, by mining operations or other activities taking place under the highway or in or under land adjoining, or in the vicinity of the highway. Seven days' notice must be given to any occupier and, where it is intended to place apparatus in the land, also to the owner.[47] Notice of intention to search and bore must also be given, where their interests are affected, to the National Coal Board, the water authority or any statutory undertaker.[48] If these bodies object, then the works may not be carried out without the authority of the appropriate Minister.[49] No notice to the subsoil owner is required for the placing of apparatus in the highway by the highway authority, but other authorities must give notice to that highway authority.[50]

15–12 Where a highway authority has a power or a right to maintain, alter or remove any structure or work which is situated on, over or under non-highway land, then a person duly authorised in writing by that authority[51] may, where necessary, at any reasonable time after giving seven days' notice, enter onto land for the purpose of exercising that power or that right. "Structures" include bridges,[52] fences, barriers or posts, and "works" include tunnels, ditches, gutters, watercourses, culverts, drains,[53] soakaways or pipes.[54] The rights of the highway authority to enter onto land to maintain structures or to carry out works may also be the subject of agreements as to maintenance.[55] It is an offence to obstruct officers acting under these powers, or to remove or otherwise interfere with any apparatus placed or left on or in any land by the highway authority.[56] Compensation will be payable where damage is caused to land or to chattels upon the land, and in relation to any disturbance from the exercise of any power to enter for the above purposes. This right to compensation is similar to that contained in the Public Health Act 1936, section 278.[57] It does not provide a remedy for any unlawful act carried out by the officers of the authority—for which the ordinary

---

[46] See also Highways Act 1980, s.289(3) and Public Utilities Street Works Act 1950, s.26.
[47] Highways Act 1980, s.290(3), (4).
[48] See *ibid.* s.290(5),(9).
[49] *Ibid.* s.290(10).
[50] *Ibid.* s.290(6); see also Chap. 13.
[51] Together with vehicles, equipment and other persons; Highways Act 1980, s.291.
[52] But the power may be subject to Transport Act 1968, s.118; see Chap. 11.
[53] See also Highways Act 1980, s.100, which is not affected by these powers.
[54] *Ibid.* s.291(4).
[55] In which case the agreements are not affected by these powers; see *ibid.* s.291(6).
[56] *Ibid.* s.292(3).
[57] See para. 13–85, above.

tortious remedies will apply—but gives a right to compensation where damage is necessarily caused by the acts authorised.[58]

It is an offence for any officer, who is admitted to factory or workshop premises, to disclose to any person any information obtained by him, as to any manufacturing process or trade secret, unless such disclosure is made in the course of performing his duty in respect of the purposes for which he was authorised to enter the land.[59] **15-13**

Where a footpath creation or extinguishment order is proposed, then the officers of the authority making it, duly authorised in writing, may enter onto land for the purpose of surveying the land in connection with the making of that order.[60] Valuation officers or other authorised officers of the highway authority may also enter onto land for the purpose of survey, and in order to estimate the value of land in relation to a public path creation order or extinguishment order. These rights of entry are exercisable only upon notice, and written authority may be required to be produced. **15-14**

A further power of entry is contained in section 294. This applies where, in the discharge of functions conferred or imposed on a local authority or highway authority by specified statutory provisions, it becomes necessary for an authorised officer of the authority to enter, examine, or lay open, any premises for the purpose of surveying, making plans, executing or maintaining or examining works, ascertaining the course of sewers or drains, ascertaining or fixing of boundaries, or ascertaining whether any hedge, tree or shrub is dead, diseased, damaged or insecurely rooted. The authority may apply to a magistrates' court for an order of authorisation.[61] The sections to which this power applies are those listed in Schedule 22 to the 1980 Act and in sections 101 and 154(2)[62] of that Act. Compensation is payable for damage and disturbance. A magistrates' court can only make the order if no sufficient cause is shown against the making of the order by the landowner or occupier. This appears to require the justices to inquire into the necessity for an order, and to examine the purposes for which the order is sought.[63] **15-15**

A highway authority may, by agreement with any person, execute, at that person's expense, any work which it has required him to execute, or any work in connection with a highway which he is otherwise under an obligation or is entitled to execute, and for this purpose it has the same rights as he would have. This is not a default provision and it is dependant upon the other person's agreement. **15-16**

---

[58] Highways Act 1980, s.292; see also s.294(4).
[59] *Ibid.* s.292.
[60] *Ibid.* s.293(1).
[61] *Ibid.* s.294.
[62] *i.e.* ditches and trees which constitute a danger to users of the highway.
[63] *Robinson* v. *Sunderland Corpn.* [1899] 1 Q.B. 751.

Power to dispose of materials

15–17   A highway authority may, subject to the duty to pay the reasonable
value thereof to the owner, remove, appropriate, use or sell, or otherwise dispose of materials existing in a street other than a highway maintainable at the public expense at the time of the execution by the council
of any works in the street, unless those materials are removed by the
owners of premises in the street within three days from the date of service of a notice requiring them to do so.[64]

Ancillary powers

15–18   Highway authorities may require information as to the ownership of
land.[65] Other local authorities are also under a duty to furnish any information in their power which may reasonably be required by the highway
authority.[66]

15–19   Where drains, or other works for the drainage of highways, have been
constructed or laid in land in the exercise of highway land acquisition
powers by a highway authority, water may be discharged through those
drains into any inland waters, whether natural or artificial, or into any
tidal waters. Compensation may be payable for any damage caused by
the exercise of this right. Highway authorities are not, however,
exempted from the laws which seek to protect water from pollution.[67]

Obstruction of officers

15–20   It is an offence under section 303 of the Highways Act 1980 wilfully to
obstruct any person acting in the execution of the Act or any by-law or
order made under it. There are additional, specific offences relating to
obstruction of any person acting under the powers of entry.[68] The
obstruction need not be physical, and, in a different context, it has been
held that obstruction may occur where the accused has made it more difficult for the officer to carry out his duties.[69]

Default powers

15–21   A large number of provisions in the Highways Act 1980 provide for
the highway authority to require the owner or occupier of land to carry
out works or to do certain things, with a power in the authority to carry
out those works or to do those things in default and to recover the
expenses of so doing from the person in default. These powers are
sometimes directed at the occupier of premises, or the owner, or both.

---

[64] Highways Act 1980, s.295(1), (2); disputes as to compensation are determined by arbitration.
[65] *Ibid.* s.297.
[66] *Ibid.* s.298.
[67] *Ibid.* s.299.
[68] *Ibid.* ss.292(3), 293(4).
[69] *Hinchcliffe* v. *Sheldon* [1955] 1 W.L.R. 1207.

"Owner" is defined in the Act as a person, other than a mortgagee **15–22**
not in possession, who, whether in his own right or as a trustee for any
other person, is entitled to receive the rack rent of the premises or,
where the premises are not let at a rack rent, would be so entitled if the
premises were so let.[70] A mortgagee in possession is, therefore, an
owner,[71] as are trustees of settled estates, schools and churches,[72]
except where their land is not capable of being let at a rack rent and is
extra commercium.[73] An agent who collects rents of property comes
within the definition.[74]

"Rack rent" is defined as rent which is not less than two-thirds of the **15–23**
rent at which the premises might reasonably be expected to be let from
year to year, free from all the usual tenant's rates and taxes and tithe
rent charge, and after deduction of the probable average annual cost of
the repairs, insurance and other expenses necessary to maintain the
premises in a state to command such rent. What the rack rent for a given
property is, is a question of fact to be answered as at the date of the
lease reserving the rent.[75] Any covenants restricting the use to which the
premises may be put must be taken into account.[76]

In *Pollway Nominees* v. *Croydon London Borough Council*,[77] Lord **15–24**
Bridge described the rationale of making the rack rent owner responsible for the statutory liabilities arising from the property:

> "The owner of that interest in premises which carries with it the
> right, actual or potential, to receive the rack rent, as the measure of
> the value of the premises to an occupier, is the person who ought in
> justice to be responsible for the discharge of the liabilities to which
> the premises by reason of their situation or condition give rise."

Problems have sometimes arisen regarding identification of the rack
rent owner where property has been divided into several interests,
through sub-letting or division. The freeholder will be the "owner"
where he has let at a rack rent and where there is no sub-lease. The
lessee will be the rack rent owner if his own lease is granted at less than a

---

[70] Highways Act 1980, s.329(1).
[71] See *Tottenham Local Board* v. *Williamson* (1893) 60 L.T. 51; *Maguire* v. *Leigh-on-Sea U.D.C.* (1906) 70 J.P. 479.
[72] *Re Barney, Harrison* v. *Barney* [1894] 3 Ch. 562; *Bowditch* v. *Wakefield Local Board* (1871) L.R. 6 Q.B. 567; *London School Board* v. *St. Mary, Islington* (1875) 1 Q.B.D. 65; *Hornsey U.D.C.* v. *Smith* [1897] 1 Ch. 843; *Hornsey Local Board* v. *Brewis* (1890) 60 L.J.M.C. 48.
[73] *Plumstead District Board of Works* v. *Ecclesiastical Commissioners* [1891] 2 Q.B. 361; *Wright* v. *Ingle* (1886) 16 Q.B.D. 379.
[74] *Broadbent* v. *Shepherd* (1900) 65 J.P. 70: but not a receiver appointed by the court; see *Bacup Corpn.* v. *Smith* (1890) 44 Ch.D. 395.
[75] *London Corpn.* v. *Cusack-Smith* [1955] A.C. 337; *Borthwick-Norton* v. *Collier* [1950] 2 K.B. 594.
[76] *Borthwick-Norton* v. *Collier* [1950] 2 K.B. 594.
[77] [1986] 3 W.L.R. 277 at 282.

rack rent, since he is then the only person entitled to receive a rack rent in relation to the premises under the second limb of the definition.[78] Where the lessee has sub-let at a rack rent, he is the owner under the first limb of the definition.[79] If neither the head lease nor the sub-lease is at a rack rent, then it is the underlessee who is the only person entitled to let at a rack rent.[80] Where both leases are at a rack rent, but that of the underlease is the greater, then it may be the case that both lessors are the rack rent owner.[81] Where both leases are at the same rent, it has been held that the underlessor, who derives no real benefit from the land, drops out.[82] Where land has been let in parts to a number of tenants, such as in a block of flats, and the cumulative rents do not amount to a rack rent for the whole property, it may be the case that each tenant is a rack rent owner of the property. However, this depends upon the block of flats being treated as a single unit of property.[83]

15–25 Where an owner of premises is prevented by the occupier from carrying out work which he is required to execute under the Highways Act 1980, he may make a complaint to the magistrates' court, who may order the occupier to permit the execution of this work.[84]

Recovery of expenses

15–26 Any sum which a council or highway authority is entitled to recover under any provision of the Highways Act 1980, where no special provision is made, may be recovered either summarily as a civil debt,[85] or in any court of competent jurisdiction.[86] Certain expenses recoverable under specified sections of the Highways Act 1980, namely, sections 152, 153, 165, 167, 177, 180, 184 and 230 (except subsection (8)) may be recovered by the council or highway authority, together with interest from the owner for the time being of the premises to which they relate and take effect, and may be enforced as a local land charge[87] running with the land. A charge acquired by the Minister will also take effect as a local charge.[88] The council or highway authority may, by order, declare any expenses and interest to be payable by instalments within a period not exceeding 30 years, and any such instalments and interest

---

[78] *London Corpn.* v. *Cusack-Smith* [1955] A.C. 337.
[79] *London Corpn.* v. *Cusack-Smith*, above; *Truman, Hanbury, Buxton & Co.* v. *Kerslake* [1894] 2 Q.B. 774.
[80] *Truman, Hanbury, Buxton & Co.* v. *Kerslake*, above.
[81] *London Corpn.* v. *Cusack-Smith*, n. 78 above; *cf. Field and Sons* v. *Southwark B.C.* (1907) 96 L.T. 646; *Kensington B.C.* v. *Allen* [1926] 1 K.B. 576.
[82] *Walford* v. *Hackney Board of Works* (1894) 43 W.R. 110.
[83] See *Pollway Nominees* v. *Croydon L.B.C.* [1986] 3 W.L.R. 277: a "house."
[84] Highways Act 1980, s.304.
[85] See Magistrates' Courts Act 1980, s.58.
[86] Highways Act 1980, s.305(5).
[87] Appearing in Part II of the register: see Local Land Charges Act 1975 and the Local Land Charges Rules 1977 (S.I. 1977 No. 985).
[88] Highways Act 1980, s.305(6).

may be recoverable from the owner or occupier[89] for the time being of
the premises.

The local land charge binds the whole of the interest in the property.[90]   **15–27**
The charge cannot, however, override a restrictive covenant affecting the
use of the land for the benefit of an ajoining occupier.[91] The charge operates from the date of completion of the works, albeit the debt runs from
the date of service of the demand.[92] The charge may be enforced without
seeking an order from the court, but a declaration may be obtained from
the court if the authority so desires.[93] The remedies of the council or authority are set out in the Law of Property Act 1925, section 101.[94]

The various remedies are concurrent.[95] The council or authority may   **15–28**
choose whether to pursue the claim in the magistrates' court, or in the
county court,[96] or in the High Court. Proceedings in the magistrates' court
must be commenced within six months from the date of service of the
demand[97]; except in the case where an appeal has been made to the Minister under section 233, when time runs from the date on which notification
of the appeal is given or the appeal is withdrawn.[98] Otherwise, the normal
periods of limitation apply.[99] The charge may only be enforced within
twelve years from the date on which the right to recover the money
accrued; however, there is no limitation on the time for service of the
demand for payment, and it appears that a fresh demand may be served on
each new owner of the property and that the charge may be recovered
from that owner as a civil debt.[1] Time may also commence from an ack-
nowledgement of the debt, or in respect of a payment of part of it.[2]

A person aggrieved by an order of a council or authority to declare   **15–29**
the sum repayable by instalments, or by the failure of the council or
authority to make such an order, may appeal to a magistrates' court.[3]

---

[89] Provision is made in Highways Act 1980, Sched. 13 for deduction of a proportion of
these instalments from rent.
[90] See *Tottenham Local Board of Health* v. *Rowell* (1880) 15 Ch.D. 378; *Birmingham
Corpn.* v. *Baker* (1881) 17 Ch.D. 782; *Paddington B.C.* v. *Finucane* [1928] Ch. 567.
[91] *Guardians of Tendring Union* v. *Dowton* [1891] 3 Ch. 265.
[92] *Re Allen and Driscoll's Contract* [1904] 2 Ch. 226; *Stock* v. *Meakin* [1900] 1 Ch. 683;
Dennerley v. *Prestwich U.D.C.* [1930] 1 K.B. 334.
[93] *West Ham Corpn.* v. *Sharp* [1907] 1 K.B. 445; *cf. Friern Barnet U.D.C.* v. *Adams* [1927]
2 Ch. 25.
[94] See also *Paddington Council* v. *Finucane* [1928] Ch. 567; *Bristol Corpn.* v. *Virgin* [1928]
2 K.B. 622.
[95] *Sunderland Corpn.* v. *Priestman* [1927] 2 Ch. 107; *Tottenham Local Board of Health* v.
Rowell (1880) 15 Ch.D. 378.
[96] So long as the claim is within the jurisdictional limits of that court.
[97] Highways Act 1980, s.306(1); Magistrates' Courts Act 1980, s.127.
[98] Highways Act 1980, s.306(2).
[99] Limitation Act 1980, s.9.
[1] *Dennerley* v. *Prestwich U.D.C.* [1930] 1 K.B. 334; *Hampstead Corpn.* v. *Caunt* [1903] 2
K.B. 1; *Bermondsey Vestry* v. *Ramsey* (1871) L.R. 6 C.P. 247.
[2] Limitation Act 1980, s.29(5)
[3] Except under s.233 (appeal under the private street works code), where the appeal is to
the Minister.

PROSECUTIONS, NOTICES AND APPEALS

Prosecutions

15–30   All offences under the Highways Act 1980 and under by-laws made under it are summary offences, except for those under sections 292(4) and 297(3).[4] Informations must, therefore, be laid within six months of the offence occurring, except where the offence is a continuing offence.[5] Some offences, if repeated after conviction, give rise to a further offence, punishable by a daily penalty. In these cases, a court may fix a reasonable period for the defendant to comply with its directions; within which period the defendant will not be liable for the further offence.[6] Criminal proceedings may not be commenced without the written consent of the Attorney-General, except by any person aggrieved[7] by the offence, the highway authority or council which has an interest in the enforcement of the provision in question, and, in certain cases,[8] by a constable. Provision is made for the conviction of directors and other officers of corporate bodies who have consented to or connived in certain offences, or to whose neglect the offence is attributable.[9]

Notices and service of documents

15–31   All notices, consents, approvals, orders, demands, licences, certificates and other documents required to be given, made or issued by, or on behalf of, a highway authority or a council, under the Highways Act 1980, must be in writing, and must be signed by the proper or duly authorised officer of the authority or council.[10] The signature may be by way of facsimile. All such notices, etc., are deemed to have been duly given, made or issued, until the contrary is proved.[11] The provisions with respect to service of notices and other documents are set out in section 322.[12] Service of summonses is governed by the Magistrates' Courts Rules 1980.[13] Where the Highways Act 1980 prescribes any period to begin from or before a given date, that date is to be excluded from the period. Where any period of eight days or less is prescribed, then Sundays, Christmas Day, Good Friday and bank holidays[14] are to be excluded from the period. All notices, relating to matters from which there is a right of appeal to the magistrates' court or to the Crown

---

[4] Giving false information as to land and disclosing manufacturing processes or trade secrets.
[5] Magistrates' Courts Act 1980, s.127.
[6] Highways Act 1980, s.311.
[7] See para. 15–34, below.
[8] See Highways Act 1980, s.312(3).
[9] *Ibid.* s.314.
[10] As to the "proper officer," see Local Government Act 1972, Sched. 29, para. 4.
[11] Highways Act 1980, ss.320–1.
[12] See also Recorded Delivery Service Act 1962; Interpretation Act 1978; *Morecambe* v. *Warwick* (1958) 56 L.G.R. 283; *Whitstable U.D.C.* v. *Campbell* [1959] J.P.L. 46.
[13] S.I. 1980 No. 552.
[14] See Banking and Financial Dealings Act 1971, s.4.

Court, must state the right of appeal and the time within which it must be made.

Appeals and applications

A right of appeal to the High Court is given to any person aggrieved **15–32** by certain schemes or orders, on the ground that they are not within the powers of the Act, or that procedural rules have not been complied with.[15] This right of appeal, which is made by way of an originating notice of motion to the Divisional Court, under R.S.C. Order 90, must be exercised within six weeks from the date on which the required notice[16] of confirmation or making of the order is published.[17] The time limit is strict, and cannot be extended. Unless challenged by a timely appeal, the order or scheme cannot thereafter be questioned in any legal proceedings whatsoever.[18] The refusal of the Secretary of State to confirm an order or scheme is neither subject to the statutory right of appeal nor to the preclusive clause. Judicial review of such a decision will, therefore, be available.[19]

Appeals and applications to a magistrates' court are made by way of a **15–33** complaint for an order.[20] Where no other period is prescribed, any appeal must be brought within 21 days from the date on which notice of the decision of the highway authority is served on the person wishing to appeal. Since this is a statutory time limit, it cannot be extended. The highway authority may seek to recover, summarily, various expenses to which it is entitled under the provisions of the Highways Act 1980. Where two or more sums are claimed from any one person, a single complaint may include all of those sums.[21] There is a general right of appeal from the decisions and orders of a magistrates' court under the Highways Act 1980, to the Crown Court,[22] and such appeals are governed by the Crown Court Rules 1982.[23] An applicant for an order under section 116 of the 1980 Act,[24] and other persons heard by that court, may also appeal to the Crown Court. There may also be a right of appeal on a point of law by way of case stated to the Divisional Court against an order, determination or proceeding of the magistrates' court, or from the decision of the Crown Court.[25]

---

[15] Highways Act 1980, Sched. 2; see also Sched. 6, para. 5.
[16] See *ibid.* Sched. 2, para. 1(1); Sched. 4, para. 4.
[17] As to orders under *ibid.* s.124, see Sched. 2, para. 1(2).
[18] *Ibid.* para. 4. See *R* v. *Secretary of State for the Environment, ex p. Ostler* [1976] 3 W.L.R. 288; *Smith* v. *East Elloe R.D.C.* [1956] A.C. 736.
[19] See *London Borough of Islington* v. *Secretary of State for the Environment* [1980] J.P.L. 739; R.S.C. Ord. 53.
[20] Highways Act 1980, s.316; see also Magistrates' Courts Act 1980, ss.51 *et seq.*
[21] Highways Act 1980, s.313.
[22] *Ibid.* s.317; where no other right of appeal has been specifically granted.
[23] S.I. 1982 No. 1109.
[24] Applications to a magistrates' court for a stopping up or diversion order.
[25] Magistrates' Courts Act 1980, s.111; Courts Act 1971, s.10.

15-34   The general right of appeal to the Crown Court and, in some cases, the right to make the initial application to, or to be heard by, the magistrates' court is given to a "person aggrieved" by a decision. This expression has been the subject of some judicial consideration. However, it must be stressed that particular decisions under different statutes have to be treated with great caution, and the term "person aggrieved" may well mean different things in different statutes.[26] The starting point for judicial consideration has always been *Ex parte Sidebotham*,[27] where James L.J. drew a distinction between a person who is "disappointed of a benefit he might have received if some other order had been made," who would not generally be a person aggrieved, and someone who has suffered a legal grievance, who would. A person suffering a legal grievance was described as:

> "a man against whom a decision has been pronounced which has wrongfully deprived him of something, or wrongfully refused him something, or wrongfully affected his title to something."

This definition, however, is by no means exhaustive,[28] and does not direct itself to the nature of the "something" which has been refused. In a series of cases on the private street works code, the emphasis has been placed on decisions which impose a legal burden on one of the parties.

15-35   Many of the cases have concentrated upon the instances when a local authority may be a "person aggrieved" by successful appeals to the magistrates' against notices issued by the authority. By the Interpretation Act 1978, a council will be a "person" within the meaning of the section unless the contrary intention appears. No such intention is apparent.[29] However, it has not always been clear whether the authority, "frustrated in its legitimate purpose by an order of the justices,"[30] is necessarily aggrieved and therefore entitled to appeal.[31]

15-36   The award of costs against an authority will not necessarily make it a person aggrieved.[32] The courts have looked to whether the result of the decision appealed against has been to leave the authority with, or to impose upon the authority, a legal burden.[33] This approach has been specifically applied to the predecessor of section 317, in the same way as it applied to appeals from magistrates' decisions under the street works

---

[26] See *Sevenoaks U.D.C.* v. *Twynam* [1929] 2 K.B. 440 at 443.

[27] (1880) 14 Ch.D. 458 at 465.

[28] See *Ex p. Official Receiver, in Reed, Bowen and Co.* (1887) 19 Q.B.D. 174.

[29] See *Phillips* v. *Berkshire C.C.* [1967] 2 Q.B. 991. For such a contrary intention in a local Act, see *R.* v. *Surrey Quarter Sessions, ex p. Lilley* [1951] 2 K.B. 749.

[30] *per* Widgery J. in *Phillips* v. *Berkshire C.C.* [1967] 2 Q.B. 991 at 996.

[31] See *R.* v. *London Sessions, ex p. Westminster Corpn.* (1951) 49 L.G.R. 643; *R.* v. *London County Keepers of the Peace and JJ.* (1890) 25 Q.B.D. 357.

[32] *R.* v. *Dorset Sessions Appeals Committee, ex p. Weymouth Corpn.* [1960] 2 Q.B 230; *cf. Jennings* v. *Kelly* [1940] A.C. 206; *R.* v. *Surrey Quarter Sessions, ex p. Lilley* [1951] 2 K.B. 749.

[33] *R.* v. *Nottingham Quarter Sessions, ex p. Harlow* [1952] 2 Q.B. 601.

code.[34] In *Phillips v Berkshire County Council*,[35] the court adopted a similar approach and declined to distinguish between the burden cast upon the council as highway authority and as street works' authority. Under other statutes, where no such burden was involved, local authorities have been held not to be a person aggrieved.[36]

A very much wider approach, has, however, been adopted in relation to **15-37** *locus standi* to apply for judicial review; in some instances different tests have been applied depending upon which remedy is being sought.[37] This wider approach would apply to a consideration of whether a person is "aggrieved" by the making of a scheme or order so as to entitle him or her to appeal to the High Court under the Highways Act 1980, Schedule 2.[38]

---

[34] *R. v. Boldero, ex p. Bognor Regis U.D.C.* (1962) 60 L.G.R. 292.
[35] [1967] 2 Q.B. 991.
[36] *Ealing B.C. v. Jones* [1959] 1 Q.B. 384.
[37] *Att.-Gen. of the Gambia v. N'Jie* [1961] A.C. 617; see also de Smith, *Judicial Review of Administrative Action* (4th ed., 1980) pp. 411–421.
[38] See *Turner v. Secretary of State for the Environment* (1973) 28 P.& C.R. 123; *Bizony v. Secretary of State for the Environment* [1976] J.P.L. 306; *R. v. Secretary of State for the Environment, ex p. Hood* [1975] Q.B. 891; *Lovelock v. Secretary of State for Transport* [1979] J.P.L. 456.

APPENDIX 1

SUMMARY OF THE MAIN POWERS AVAILABLE FOR THE STOPPING UP OR DIVERSION OF HIGHWAYS

HIGHWAYS ACT 1980, s.14, SCHEDS. 1 AND 2

Order-making body:
Minister (trunk roads); local highway authority (classified roads), subject to confirmation by Minister.

Criteria:
Minister must be satisfied that another reasonably convenient route is available or will be provided before route is stopped up.

Types of highway to which power applies:
All types of highway crossing or entering route of a trunk road or classified road, or which will otherwise be affected by construction or improvement of such a road.

Protection of statutory undertakers, etc.:
Highways Act 1980, ss.14(2), 21, 22, 334(6), (7).

Publication of notices:
Local newspaper and London Gazette— stating general effect of proposed order, naming place for inspection of order and informing of right to object within specified time.

Service of notices:
Within 2 days of first publication of notices:
    (a) on council in whose area highway (or proposed highway) situated (trunk road schemes), or in whose area works authorised by the order are to be carried out (classified roads);
    (b) on navigation authority and water authority where bridge over or tunnel under navigable waters or where diversion of navigable waters is involved;
    (c) on parish council, parish meeting or (in Wales) council of community in which highway is situated;
    (d) on public utility undertakers having apparatus under, in, upon, over, along or across highway.

Display of notices:
No later than date of first publication of notice in prominent position at ends of highways to be stopped up or diverted.

Time for objections:	6 weeks or such longer period as specified in notice or any subsequent notice.
Operation of order:	Notice of making or confirmation must be published in London Gazette and order comes into operation on date of such notice or other later specified date.
Judicial challenge to validity of order:	Within 6 weeks of date of publication of notice of making or confirmation of order. Thereafter, order cannot be questioned in any legal proceedings whatsoever.

HIGHWAYS ACT 1980, S.18, SCHEDS. 1 AND 2

Order-making body:	Minister or local highway authority subject to Minister's confirmation.
Criteria:	Minister must be satisfied either that another reasonably convenient route is available for traffic other than traffic authorised by the scheme or that no such other route is reasonably required for such traffic.
Types of highway to which power applies:	All highways crossing or entering special road or otherwise affected by construction or improvement of such a road.
Protection of statutory undertakers, etc.:	Highways Act 1980, ss.18(2), 21, 22, 334(6), (7).
Publication of notices:	Local newspaper and London Gazette, stating general effect of proposed order, naming place for inspection of order and informing of right to object within specified time.
Service of notices:	Within 2 days of first publication of notices: (a) on council in whose area works authorised by the scheme are to be carried out; (b) on navigation authority and water authority where bridge over or tunnel under navigable waters or where diversion of navigable waters is involved; (c) on parish council, parish meeting or (in Wales) council of the community in which the highway is situated; public utility undertakers having apparatus under, in, upon, over, along or across highway.
Display of notices:	No later than date of first publication of notice in prominent position at ends of highways to be stopped up or diverted.

Time for objections:	6 weeks or such longer period as specified in notice or any subsequent notice.
Operation of order:	Notice of making or confirmation must be published in London Gazette. The order comes into operation on date of such notice or other later specified date.
Judicial challenge to validity of order:	Within 6 weeks of date of publication of notice of making or confirmation of order. Thereafter, order cannot be questioned in any legal proceedings whatsoever.

HIGHWAYS ACT 1980, s.116, SCHED. 12

Order-making body:	Magistrates' court on application by a highway authority.
Criteria:	The highway is unnecessary (stopping up) or can be diverted to make it nearer or more commodious to the public (diversion). Except in the case of classified roads, consent of the district and parish or community councils is required before application can be made.
Types of highway to which the power applies:	All highways except trunk and special roads.
Protection of statutory undertakers, etc.:	Highways Act 1980, s.334 (4), (5), Sched. 12, Part II.
Publication:	At least 28 days before application is made, in at least one local newspaper and London Gazette.
Service of notices:	At least 2 months prior to making application (except where highway is a classified road):

At least 2 months prior to making application (except where highway is a classified road):
  (a) on council of non-metropolitan district;
  (b) on parish council, chairman of parish meeting or (in Wales) council of community in which highway situated.
At least 28 days before application is made:
  (a) on owners and occupiers of all lands adjoining highway;
  (b) on statutory undertakers having apparatus in, upon, over, along or across highway;
  (c) on Minister (classified roads);
  (d) on non-metropolitan district council, parish or community council or chairman of parish meeting (classified roads).

Display of notices:	At least 28 days before application made, in prominent position at the ends of highway.
Time for objections:	Persons on whom notice of application is served, any person who uses highway and any other person aggrieved may appear and be heard at magistrates' court.
Operation of order:	Diversion order cannot take effect until substituted way is completed to justices' satisfaction.
Judicial challenge to validity of order:	By way of case stated or appeal to the Crown Court.

HIGHWAYS ACT 1980, SS.118, 119 AND SCHED. 6; PUBLIC PATH ORDERS AND EXTINGUISHMENT OF PUBLIC RIGHT OF WAY ORDERS REGULATIONS 1983 (S.I. 1983 No. 23)

Order-making body:	A council, subject, in the case of an opposed order, to confirmation by Secretary of State.
Criteria:	*Section 118*: That the way is not needed for public use (order making authority); that it is expedient to confirm the order having regard to the extent that the path would apart from the order be likely to be used by the public (disregarding temporary circumstances) and having regard to the effect which the extinguishment of the right of way would have on land served by the way (confirming body). *Section 119*: In the interests of the owner, lessee or occupier of land crossed by the path, or of the public, it is expedient that the line of the path or way or part of that line should be diverted (order-making authority); and, that the path or way will not be substantially less convenient to the public in consequence of the diversion and that it is expedient to confirm it having regard to the effect of the diversion on public enjoyment of the path or way as a whole, the effect of the order on land served by the existing right of way and the effect of any new right of way on the land over which it is created and any other land held with that land (confirming body).
Types of highway to which power applies:	Footpaths and bridleways only.
Protection of statutory undertakers, etc.:	Highways Act 1980, s.121 (4), (5).
Publication:	Local newspaper.

377

Service of notices: Not less than 28 days before time specified
                                       for objecting in notice:
                                         (a) on every owner, occupier and lessee
                                            of land to which order relates
                                            (subject to Sched. 6, para. 3C);
                                         (b) on every council;
                                         (c) on parish council, parish meeting or
                                            (in Wales) council of community in
                                            which highway situated;
                                         (d) on every person who has required
                                            that notice of this kind of order
                                            should be served on him in
                                            accordance with para. 3A or 3B of
                                            Sched. 6;
                                         (e) on Church Commissioners (where
                                            appropriate);
                                         (f) on other prescribed persons and
                                            such persons as Secretary of State
                                            may think fit.

Display of notices: In prominent position at ends of so much
                                       of footpath or bridleway as is stopped up
                                       or diverted by order; at council offices in
                                       locality and at other places as authority or
                                       Secretary of State deem appropriate.

Time for objections: 28 days from publication of notice, or
                                       longer if so specified.

Operation of order: Notice published in local paper and served
                                       and displayed as above.

Judicial challenge to validity of   Within 6 weeks of date of publication of
order: notice of making or confirmation of order.
                                       Thereafter, order cannot be questioned in
                                       any legal proceedings whatsoever.

TOWN AND COUNTRY PLANNING ACT 1971, ss.209, 215   *1990 ss 247, 252*

Order-making body: Secretary of State for the Environment.

Criteria: Stopping up or diversion is necessary in
                                       order to enable development to be carried
                                       out in accordance with planning
                                       permission granted under Part III of Town
                                       and Country Planning Act 1971 or to be
                                       carried out by a government department.

Types of highway to which the   Any highway.
power applies:

Protection of statutory   Town and Country Planning Act 1971,
undertakers, etc.:   s.209(3)(*b*).

Publication: Local newspaper and London Gazette.

Service of notices: Not later than date of first publication of
                                       notice:

	(a) on every local authority in whose area the highway or land is situated;
	(b) on relevant statutory undertakers.
Display of notices:	In prominent position at ends of so much of footpath or bridleway as is stopped up or diverted by order.
Time for objections:	28 days from date of publication of notice.
Operation of order:	Notice of making of order must be published and served as above.
Judicial challenge to validity of order:	Within 6 weeks of date of publication of notice of making of order. Thereafter, order cannot be questioned in any legal proceedings whatsoever; Town and Country Planning Act 1971, ss.242(1)(*b*), 244(3).

TOWN AND COUNTRY PLANNING ACT 1971, SS.210, 217
SCHED. 20; TOWN AND COUNTRY PLANNING (PUBLIC
PATHS ORDERS) REGULATIONS 1983 (S.I. 1983 NO. 22)

Order-making body:	Local planning authority, subject to confirmation by Secretary of State.
Criteria:	Stopping up or diversion is necessary in order to enable development to be carried out in accordance with planning permission granted under Part III of Town and Country Planning Act 1971 or to be carried out by a government department.
Types of highway to which power applies:	Footpaths and bridleways only.
Protection of statutory undertakers, etc.:	Town and Country Planning Act 1971, Sched. 20, paras. 3(1), 4.
Publication:	Local newspaper.
Service of notices:	Before submission of order for confirmation and not less than 28 days before objections are to be lodged:
	(a) on every owner, occupier and lessee of the land (subject to Sched. 20, para. 1(4));
	(b) on every council, rural parish council or meeting;
	(c) on relevant statutory undertakers;
	(d) other categories pursuant to Sched. 20, para. 1(2A).
Display of notices:	At ends of so much of footpath or bridleway as is stopped up or diverted by order (together with a plan).
Time for objections:	Not less than 28 days from publication of notice.

Operation of order: Publication and service of notice of confirmation as above.

Judicial challenge to validity of order: Within 6 weeks of date of publication of notice of making or confirmation of order. Thereafter, order cannot be questioned in any legal proceedings whatsoever; Town and Country Planning Act 1971, ss.242(1)(*b*), 244(3).

APPENDIX 2

SUMMARY OF MAXIMUM PENALTIES IMPOSED FOR OFFENCES CONTAINED IN THE PUBLIC UTILITIES STREET WORKS ACT 1950 AND THE HIGHWAYS ACT 1980

FINE NOT EXCEEDING LEVEL 1	SS.	SS.
Highways Act 1980	46(2)	161(4)
	46(3)	163(4)
	46(4)	173(2)
	73(6)	175
	74(5)	178(4)
	79(10)	179(3)
	136(3)	180(4)
	141(3)	194(4)
	152(4)	196(6)
	153(5)	287(5)
	161(3)	303

FINE NOT EXCEEDING LEVEL 2	SS.	SS.
Highways Act 1980	155(4)	195(3)
	176(7)	

FINE NOT EXCEEDING LEVEL 3	SS.	SS.
Public Utilities Street Works Act 1950	3(5)	11(3)
	6(6)	26(8)
Highways Act 1980	128	155(2)
	131(3)	161(1)
	134(5)	161(2)
	134(5A)	162
	137	167(4)
	138	172(5)
	139(3)	174(4)
	139(4)	181(1)
	140(3)	184(17)
	144(5)	219(2)
	147(2)	292(3)
	148	293(4)
	151(3)	297(2)

FINE NOT EXCEEDING LEVEL 4	SS.	SS.
Highways Act 1980	132(1)	170(1)

FINE NOT EXCEEDING LEVEL 5	SS.	SS.
Highways Act 1980	161A(1) 168(1)	169(5) 177(1)

SPECIFIC PENALTIES*	SS.	SS.
Highways Act 1980	291(4) 292(4)	297(3)

* "prescribed sum" or, on indictment, 2 years' imprisonment or a fine.

DAILY PENALTIES	SS.	£
Public Utilities Street Works Act 1950	3(6) 7(2) 7(4) 8(3) 10(4)	10.00 10.00 10.00 10.00 10.00
Highways Act 1980	73(6) 74(5) 79(10) 145(2) 151(3) 171(6) 172(5) 173(2) 174(2) 176(7) 177(1) 178(4) 179(3) 194(4) 196(6) 303	2.00 2.00 2.00 .50 1.00 10.00 2.00 1.00 10.00 5.00 50.00 1.00 2.00 2.00 2.00 5.00

SUMMARY OF THE MAIN DISPUTE AND COMPENSATION PROCEDURES UNDER THE HIGHWAYS ACT 1980

A: Compensation Disputes Determinable by the Lands Tribunal

The Highways Act 1980, section 307 provides for determination by the Lands Tribunal of disputes under the following sections:

ss.21 and 22	Compensation in respect of rights of statutory undertakers and sewerage authorities in relation to orders and schemes under ss.14, 16 and 18.
ss.28 and 121(2)	Compensation for loss caused by the making of public path creation orders and public path extinguishment orders.
ss.73 and 74	Compensation for injurious affection caused by the making of building and improvement lines.
ss.109 and 110	Compensation for damage caused by works for the diversion of navigable and non-navigable watercourses.
s.126	Compensation in respect of orders stopping up private accesses under ss.14, 18, 124 and 125, or under the Town and Country Planning Act 1971, s.211.
ss.193 and 200(2)	Compensation in respect of certain restrictions relating to new streets.
s.292	Compensation for damage resulting from, or offences connected with, certain powers of entry under ss.289 and 291.

B: Compensation Disputes Determinable by Arbitration (where the parties so agree) or by the County Court (in default of agreement)

The Highways Act 1980, s.308 provides for the determination of disputes by arbitration (where the parties so agree) or by the county court (in default of agreement). This provision applies where the relevant statutory provision provides for compensation but makes no express provision for its determination.

This provision applies to:

s.23	Compensation in respect of works executed in pursuance of orders under ss.14 and 18.

s.67	Compensation for damage caused by the execution of guard rails in streets.
s.70(6)	Compensation for damage caused by the execution of works relating to footbridges.
s.77(2)	Compensation for damage caused by alterations in levels of a highway.
s.79(11)	Compensation in respect of injurious affection through restrictions imposed by a notice under s.79 preventing obstruction of view at corners.
s.96(7)	Compensation for damage arising out of the exercise of powers of tree planting, etc.
s.97(3)	Compensation for damage caused by works in connection with the lighting of highways.
s.100(3)	Compensation for damage caused by drainage works.
s.101(2)	Compensation for damage caused by the exercise of powers to fill in roadside ditches.
s.102(3)	Compensation for damage caused by works to provide barriers and other works to protect highways against hazards of nature.
s.112(6)	Compensation for damage caused by works to provide picnic sites and public conveniences for users of trunk roads.
s.122(2)	Compensation for damage caused by the construction of a temporary highway diversion.
s.194(5)	Compensation in respect of loss caused by the exercise of powers to vary the position or direction, etc., of new streets.
s.231	Compensation in respect of works under the street works code.
s.283(4)	Compensation for damage caused by experiments conducted by the Minister.
s.294(4)	Compensation for damage in respect of the exercise of certain powers of entry.

C: OTHER DISPUTES DETERMINABLE BY ARBITRATION

A number of provisions in the Highways Act 1980 provide for certain disputes to be referred to arbitration. These include:

s.4(4)	Determination of disputes as to the payment of contributions between

	highway authorities in respect of additional liabilities arising out of orders made under ss.14 and 18.
s.20(5)	Disputes over consents for laying undertakers' apparatus in special roads.
s.53(3), (4), (5) and s.54(3)	Disputes as to sums payable to the highway authority on extinguishment and diversion of private liability to maintain a highway.
s.55(2)	Disputes as to sums payable to the Minister in respect of extinguishment of private liability to maintain bridges transferred to the Minister when a road carried by a bridge becomes a trunk road.
s.60(4)	Disputes as to extra costs claimed by highway authorities from statutory undertakers in respect of certain diversions caused by undertakers' works.
s.85(3)	Disputes between neighbouring highway authorities as to agreements relating to the exercise of powers relating to cattle grids.
s.115J(4)	Disputes over refusal of consents by highway local planning authorities to the exercise of powers for the provision of amenities in pedestrian ways.
s.156(7)	Compensation payable by statutory undertakers in relation to the unlawful breaking up of the highway surface.
s.265	Disputes between the Minister and any persons as to property or liabilities transferred upon a highway becoming or ceasing to be a trunk road.
s.266(7), (8)	Disputes over property and liabilities, and over the withholding of consents, in relation to the transfer to the Minister to privately-maintainable bridges carrying trunk roads.
s.270(6)	Disputes relating to the transfer of lighting systems where the Minister is one of the parties to the dispute.
s.295(2)	Disputes as to claims relating to recovery of the value of materials disposed of by the highway authority.

INDEX

metropolitan district council,
creation by declaration, 2–12
local highway authority, as, 1–31
metropolitan road,
status, removal of, 1–19
milestones,
damage, statutory powers to prevent,
8–08
mineral rights,
highway, under, interest in, 3–10
Minister—*see* **Secretary of State for Transport**
misfeasance,
non-feasance distinguished from, 5–02,
5–15
monuments—*see* **public monuments**
moped,
bridleway, exclusion from, 1–21
motor cycle,
bridleway, exclusion from, 1–21
motor vehicle,
bridleway, exclusion from, 1–21
meaning, 1–21

natural causes,
user of highway, danger to, 7–29—7–30
natural vegetation—*see* **vegetation**
negligence,
construction, 5–44
contributory, defence to action for
failure to maintain, 5–39
generally, 5–42
highway authority, liability of,
5–45—5–46
improvement, 5–44, 6–05
meaning, 6–05
public nuisance, 7–12
traffic signs, 5–43
non-carriageway highway,
bridleway, 1–21
byway open to all traffic, 1–25
categories, 1–20
cycle track, 1–26
footpath, 1–22
pedestrianised area, 1–28
public path,
meaning, 1–23
road used as, 1–24
walkway, 1–27
non-feasance,
misfeasance distinguished from, 5–02,
5–15
non-metropolitan district council,
bridleways, maintenance of, 12–27
footpaths, maintenance of, 12–27
highway authority, as, 1–32, 1–33
notices,
service of, 15–31
nuisance—*see* **public nuisance**

obstructions,
adjoining landowners, encroachment by,
7–22—7–23
bends, at, 6–18—6–22
corners, at, 6–18—6–22
crowds, collection of, 7–21
duty to repair distinguished from duty to
keep highway free from, 5–16
highway user, caused by, 7–16—7–17
meaning, 7–14
meetings, 7–19
neighbouring land, operations carried
out on, 7–24
offences,
adjoining land, obstruction derived
from, 8–34—8–39
builders' skips, 8–21—8–24
gates, 8–31
itinerant traders, 8–32—8–33
other, 8–17
planting of trees, 8–25—8–28
procession, 8–16
roadside sales, 8–32—8–33
stiles, 8–31
structures, 8–29—8–31
unlawful obstruction, removal of,
8–18—8–20
wilful obstruction, prosecution for,
8–13—8–15
works in highways, 8–40
picketing, 7–20
processions, 7–18
straying animals, caused by, 7–25—7–26
temporary, 7–15
unlawful, powers to remove, 8–18—8–20
wilful, prosecution for, 8–13—8–15
offences,
maximum penalties, App. 2
obstructions—*see* **obstructions**
prosecutions, 15–30
protection of rights—*see* **protection of rights**
officers,
obstruction of, 15–20
open space,
rights over, distinguished from highway
rights, 1–10
order,
creation of highway by, 2–13—2–16
extinguishment—*see* **extinguishment**
public path creation, 2–13—2–14
Ordnance Survey map,
dedication, evidence of, 2–53
ownership,
highway authority, of,
responsibilities, 3–16
rights, 3–15
highway drains, vesting of, 15–02
highways, vesting of, 15–01
liabilities, transfer of, 15–03
lighting systems, transfer of, 15–05